D1492590

First published 1980 by
British Aviation Research Group

ISBN 0 906339 03 0

BRITISH MILITARY AIRCRAFT SERIALS AND MARKINGS

Printed and bound in Great Britain by
Hollen Street Press Ltd
Slough, Berkshire

DEDICATION

This book is dedicated to the memory of STUART A. HICKS *who died suddenly, and tragically, on the 31st January 1980 following a short illness. Stuart was a well-respected person who had served on the BARG Committee for a number of years, mainly in the role of* GROUP LIBRARIAN.

Strangely enough, his interest was civil aviation with no more than a passing interest in military aircraft. However, as a historian in his own right, he always believed that any publication, whether civil or military orientated, should be "Well researched" and "Accurate".

We trust that this book complies with these two fine ideals.

PREFACE & ACKNOWLEDGEMENTS

To the best of our knowledge, this is only the third book ever to have been published on the subject of British military aircraft serial allocations. This in itself is quite remarkable bearing in mind the thousands of people in these Isles, and abroad, who are passionately interested in British military aircraft photographs, squadrons, unit markings and of course, serials.

In this one volume we have embraced all of the above aspects to a greater or lesser extent. We hope that the layout and content will appeal to the historian, aviation researcher and enthusiast alike.

The main emphasis of the book is on serial allocations together with a summarised history of each block of serials. We have also dealt almost exclusively with serial allocations from 1950 to date. There are three reasons for this. The first is very simple. It has never been tackled properly before now. Secondly, the last 30 years have seen a quite remarkable growth of interest in British and Foreign military aircraft, not only among 'enthusiasts' but even the general public. The vast numbers of people who turn up at Air Displays is witness to this fact. The third reason is that the 1950 - 1980 era covers the 'XA' to 'ZA' serial range. In effect, this represents a timescale in which the design, development and production (or non-production in some cases!) of military aircraft has been nothing short of remarkable, even from a purely British point of view.

One has only to look through the unique collection of over 300 photographs in this book to realise the incredible number of aircraft types and major sub-variants which have been allocated serials in the 'XA' to 'ZA' range.

A proper study of the serials, summarised histories and photographic coverage together with the Squadron and Unit markings is really an insight into British history over the last 30 years and the failures and fortunes of our military aircraft industry.

During 1950/51 when the 'XA' series was first introduced, Europe was still reeling from the effects of World War II and the subsequent blockade of Berlin. Elsewhere British military aircraft were involved in the Middle East, Malaya and Korea. Other significant events yet to come were Suez, Cyprus, Aden and a tightening situation in Eastern Europe.

These events directly affected procurement policy and accordingly serial allocations. Immediately apparent in the book are the allocations made under the 'Super-priority' programme. This programme was brought about by the need to modernise the Royal Air Force fighter force as quickly as possible. This is evidenced by the allocations for Hunters, Javelins and Swifts. The vulnerability of such projects is well highlighted by the vast ranges of cancelled Swift serials.

Other notable cancellations show the demise of many projects such as the SR.177, Gloster P.376 and the TSR-2. Changes of policy and restricted funding have also been key factors in programme cut-backs and premature termination of contracts such as the Lightning, Phantom and Buccaneer. All these events have also led to the demise or merger of companies. Look at the famous names in existence in 1950/51 and compare them with today.

Paradoxically, one of the most startling facts to emerge from this volume **is the** *extent of procurement of small, pilotless drones - over 1,000 examples are recorded in this book! Another interesting point is the number and types of hovercraft which have been allotted serials.*

A much more obvious fact which emerges is the gradual reduction over the years in the actual quantities of aircraft procured. Whereas in 1950 vast numbers of aeroplanes meant strength this is not exactly so in the 1980's. Today it is the quality of the aircraft as a weapons and avionics platform that counts, ie to a certain extent quality, not quantity.

In this book we have purposely avoided including details of write-offs; crashes; relating any particular aircraft to any given Squadron or Unit; any military aircraft equipment fits or modifications; which aircraft are in reserve storage or indeed the exact numbers of each aircraft on each Squadron or Unit. This book is about aircraft markings and serial numbers and in no way attempts to assess aircraft or Squadron capability.

We also hope that the 'Remarks' coloumn entries, pre 'XA' allocations, preserved aircraft and instructional airframe sections are of interest. To sum up, if the information in this book serves as an incentive for further research into British military aviation history, it has served its purpose. If the vacant columns are used to record aircraft sightings, then yet another elementary aspect of aviation research will have been established.

We trust that we have not made too many mistakes. Should any readers come across any, or can provide additional information, please contact the authors......

Martin H. Pettit (Research Co-ordinator) : Michael I. Draper (AAC Research)
Douglas A. Rough (FAA Research) : Trevor E. Stone (RAF Research)
......by writing to **M.H. Pettit** *at:-*
47, Yaverland Drive, Bagshot, Surrey, GU19 5DY, England.

The above persons have borne the brunt of the research and production of this book and deserve full credit for their efforts. Like everybody else involved in the project, they did it on a purely voluntary basis.

Especial thanks must also go to:- D.J. Allen (various roles including sales promotion); P. Hellier (Preserved Aircraft - Home & Abroad); I. Hunter (Cover design and advertising material); C.J. Howland (Photographic layout); C.H. Thomas (Photograph production); R.A. Walker (Photograph production); R.L. Ward (Artwork for Squadron & Unit Markings) and Merseyside Aviation Society for their co-operation in allowing us to use some of the artwork from their publication, "BRITISH AIR ARMS".

Aside of credits contained in the photo-captions, due thanks must go to:- I. MacFarlane; Philip Spencer; P.A. Tomlin; R.A. Walker and the various companies, organisations and museums for supplying us with a large selection of photographs.

Thanks for information used in the book goes to every aviation enthusiast over the last 30 years. Also, every non-official aviation journal and book issued over the same period. All the information is there, somewhere, if one looks for it. Thanks also to:- AAC Museum; P. Amos; R. Andrews; E. ap Rees; P. Beaver; P. Birtles; M. Burrows; P.H. Butler; W. Chorley; G. Cruikshank; D. Dorrell; W.J. Downing; J. Dyer; M.J. East; FAA Museum, R. Foster, P. Gosden; J. Gossling; A.W. Hall; P. Hewins; S. Hicks; M. Hockley; I. Huntley; P.A. Jackson; R.C. King; R. Lindsay; R. Lingwood; M.J. McEvoy; A. Merton-Jones; E. Morgan; E. Myall; L.G. Pain; A. Pearcy; P. Purdy; RAF Museum; D. Robinson; N. Rush; B. Russell; E. Shackleton; R. Simpson; C. Smith; R.C. Sturtivant; F.G. Tyler; C. Wills; D. Wilton and anybody that we've forgotten.

CONTENTS

PREFACE & ACKNOWLEDGEMENTS ______ *Pages 2-3*

BRITISH MILITARY IDENTIFICATION MARKS ______ *Pages 5-6*

BRITISH MILITARY DESIGNATIONS ______ *Page 7*

BRITISH MILITARY UNIT MARKINGS ______ *Page 8*

ROYAL AIR FORCE
SQUADRON & UNIT MARKINGS ______ *Pages 9-34*

FLEET AIR ARM
SQUADRON & UNIT MARKINGS ______ *Pages 35-46*

ARMY AIR CORPS
SQUADRON & UNIT MARKINGS ______ *Pages 47-54*

SERIAL ALLOCATIONS - XA100-ZA999 ______ *Pages 55-64, 81-208, 225-316*

plus supplement-ZB101-ZB999 ______ *Pages 316-333*

PHOTOGRAPHS ______ *Pages 65-80, 209-224, 337-352, 409-410*

plus supplement ______ *Pages 411-412*

THE PRE XA100 APPENDICES ______ *Page 334*

PRE XA100 SERIAL ALLOCATIONS
STILL IN CURRENT USE ______ *Pages 335-336, 353-366*

HISTORIC AIRCRAFT PRESERVED IN THE U.K. ______ *Pages 367-380*

HISTORIC AIRCRAFT PRESERVED ABROAD ______ *Pages 381-387*

INSTRUCTIONAL AIRFRAMES ______ *Page 388*

ROYAL AIR FORCE
INSTRUCTIONAL AIRFRAMES ______ *Pages 389-404*

ROYAL NAVY & ARMY
INSTRUCTIONAL AIRFRAMES ______ *Pages 405-408*

GLOSSARY ______ *Pages 413-419*

SALES ______ *Page 420*

BRITISH MILITARY IDENTIFICATION MARKS

British military aircraft carry a mixed array of markings; these include roundels, fin flashes, serials, codes and squadron insignia, whilst a few units also allocate individual names to their aircraft. This appendix is mainly concerned with the historical aspects of roundels and serials; squadron markings are covered in greater detail elsewhere.

ROUNDELS AND FIN FLASHES

The national roundel is the normal method of identifying aircraft belonging to one of the British armed forces, or to the MoD. There are however some airframes, such as unmanned targets and hovercraft, for which ownership can be recognised only by the allocated serial. The roundel originated at the end of 1914, as by then it had been realised that the St George's Cross at the centre of the Union Jack, used for identification, bore an uncomfortable resemblance to the German cross patee at a distance. It was decided that the Union Jack should be replaced by an emblem similar to that worn by our French allies, but with the common red white and blue colours reversed; a similar point of commonality coming in mid-1915, when the Royal Naval Air Service and Royal Flying Corps introduced rudder striping. With the introduction of camouflage the following year, a thin white or yellow ring often encircled the blue; and on night fighters and bombers, a red/blue roundel was frequently used. Both of these remained in general use in the Twenties and Thirties. With the onset of preparations for war in the late Thirties, and the more widespread introduction of camouflage, the red/white/blue and red/blue roundels were standardised and categorised as types 'A' and 'B' respectively. (Note: rudder striping appeared briefly on aircraft of the Advanced Air Striking Force during the early part of World War Two for the purpose of providing a common recognition point with our French allies). Fin flashes were introduced during 1940. These had acquired standard shapes and dimensions by the end of the year. Yellow outer rings were again used, particularly on fuselage roundels. The next major change was in 1942 when the 'C' roundel was introduced, with a thin white ring dividing red and blue, also with and without yellow outlining and with fin flashes similarly modified.

In 1947 the 'D' type roundel, being red/white/blue with the width of each colour being one-third of its radius, was introduced to replace the various versions still in service. The colours were initially matt, but by 1949 gloss bright red and blue were standard. The fin flash was 24" high, the width varying from type to type although the colours were always in three equal portions. A variation of this roundel was the 'anti-flash' version in very pale colours worn by white painted V-bombers, early Buccaneers, and TSR.2's. In the early seventies, a new tactical roundel made its appearance on front line aircraft, and at first sight it appeared to be a re-introduction of the red/blue 'B' type, but closer observation showed that both colour shades and proportions were different. The fin flash also lost its white at the same time. The 'D' type survived as the prime roundel only for a short while before it succumbed to the enthusiasm for low visibility markings. It is currently worn by second-line aircraft together with a few first-line types such as Nimrods and Sea Harriers, but these two could well change their plumage soon. Although instructions were of course issued for the application of all these different markings there are always errors and anomalies, as any modeller and enthusiast knows, which will always occur.

SERIALS

In order to identify individual airframes most governments allocate serials in some form. Some countries use a combination of letters commencing with the prefix applied to their civil registrations, with only the presence of fin flashes, roundels or camouflage indicating the military ownership (a prime example of this being Israeli transport aircraft). Other countries display a selection of numbers; some use consecutive figures, for instance in 1940 the United States Navy began at 00001 and has now exceeded 161000; some seem to pluck numbers from the air as no orderly system is discernible; while others make use of the number that manufacturers allocate each airframe, or alternatively the serial used by the previous owner. Current examples of this are Lynx helicopters which have been delivered to the French Navy complete with British serials. Some years ago Canadian and Greek Dakotas were common sights in the UK carrying RAF serials.

When the RFC was formed in May 1912, aircraft were identified by a letter/number combination, according to the manufacturer; but by the end of the year, the Air Committee had recommended a unified serial system for both Army and Navy aircraft, with different blocks allocated to each service. The first aircraft to be allocated a serial in this system was a Short S.34 of the RNAS. By 1916, when the number 10000 was issued to a Be.2c, it was decided to start an alpha-numeric series, A1 being Fe.2d. The last of the single letter airframes, Z9978 was followed by AA100 in 1940, both being Bristol 142L Blenheim IV's and this system has survived to this day. Not all letters are used in serials to avoid confusion with similar letters and numbers. Those currently excluded are, C (confusion with G); I (confusion with 1); O and Q (confusion with nought); U (confusion with V) and Y (confusion with X). From 1938 onwards, beginning in the 'P' series, 'blackout blocks' were introduced which were not allocated to aircraft to disguise the true number of machines ordered or available, and this practice also continues today.

The serial of each aircraft, which is allocated when a contract is placed with the manufacturer, is normally worn in four places: on either side of the aircraft on a vertical surface and on the undersides of both wings, one facing forward and one aft. The side number always used to be on the rear fuselage, but with the advent of aircraft like the Javelin and Vulcan with fuselages enclosed by wings, alternative positions had to be found. Serials were applied on intake nacelles and fin respectively. The Tornado prototypes have their serials painted under the tailplanes rather than the wings, as does the Hawk demonstrator ZA101/ G-HAWK. During the 1960's serials were removed from the wings of the V-bombers and have never been re-applied, not even when the Victors were converted to tankers. Serial presentation under the wings can be the normal letters next to numbers or letters above numbers. The number may also appear on nose wheel doors, fin tips and airbrakes, perhaps used as a code. Serials on helicopters only appear twice, ie on either side of the rear fuselage or tail boom.

The serial on the aircraft sides is generally one of two standard sizes, 8" high for the RAF and Army and 4" high for the Fleet Air Arm. Figures are of a standard design but some of the shapes can vary; the proportions are such that 8" characters are usually 5" wide and have 1" wide strokes. There are of course exceptions, eg the larger serials on Canberra rear fuselages or Vulcan fins, although the proportions remain the same.

Serial numbers stay with aircraft throughout their operational flying life, after which many machines remain in service for instructional purposes. At this stage a maintenance serial is issued, and details of the separate official systems operated by the RAF, FAA and AAC can be found in the appendix on Instructional Airframes. Occasionally ground units allocate their own serials, the best known example being the School of Aircraft Handling which applies SAH 1 etc to some of its aircraft.

What happens when ZZ999 is reached, is a matter for speculation but given the aircraft procurement policies of recent governments, the more pessimistic amongst us may wonder if ZZ999 will ever be reached?

BRITISH MILITARY DESIGNATIONS

Most British military aircraft are allocated a service name for reporting purposes and to this is added indicative letters denoting its function and a mark number of the type in Arabic numerals. This is sometimes followed by further individual letters which indicate modifications to the basic mark of aircraft. As time has evolved so these designations have changed, some being discontinued, and others being added. Below is a list, divided into two sections, of those used in this publication:

CURRENT DESIGNATIONS

AEW	Airborne Early Warning
AH	Army Helicopter
AL	Army Liaison
AS	Anti-Submarine
B	Bomber
B(I)	Bomber (Interdictor)
B(K)	Bomber (Tanker)
B(PR)	Bomber (Photographic Reconnaissance)
C	Transport
CC	Transport and Communications
D	Drone or Pilotless Aircraft
E	Electronic
F	Fighter
FG	Fighter Ground Attack
FGA	Fighter Ground Attack
FGR	Fighter Ground Attack Reconnaissance
FR	Fighter Reconnaissance
FRS	Fighter Reconnaissance Strike
GA	Ground Attack
GR	Ground Attack Reconnaissance
HAR	Helicopter Air Rescue
HAS	Helicopter Anti-Submarine
HC	Helicopter Cargo
HT	Helicopter Training
HU	Helicopter Utility
K	Tanker
MR	Maritime Reconnaissance
PR	Photographic Reconnaissance
R	Reconnaissance
S	Strike
SR	Strategic Reconnaissance
T	Training
TT	Target Tower
TX	Training Glider
W	Weather

DISCONTINUED DESIGNATIONS

AOP	Airborne Observation Post
COD	Courier (later Carrier) Onboard Delivery
ECM	Electronic Counter Measures
FAW	Fighter All Weather
FB	Fighter Bomber
HF	High Fighter
HR	Helicopter Rescue
LF	Low Fighter
NF	Night Fighter
TF	Torpedo Fighter
U	Drone or Pilotless Aircraft

BRITISH MILITARY UNIT MARKINGS

The Squadron has been the basic unit of British military aviation since the formation of the Royal Naval Air Service and the Royal Flying Corps. When the RFC decided in 1917 to add official unit identification to the national markings which were already carried, this was done on a Squadron basis taking the form of combinations of bars or geometric shapes. Some of these still survive today, as with 2 Squadron's triangle and 85 Squadron's hexagon, for example, and many of the markings illustrated on the following pages are rooted in the particular unit's own history and tradition. Soon after the First World War, more elaborate unofficial unit markings began to appear, although many of these were given official status in the Squadron insignia granted by the Chester Herald in 1936. A good example of this is the bomb-carrying eagle worn on the intakes of 216 Squadron's Buccaneers, first carried on their aircraft in the Middle East during the early Twenties. In the meantime, Fighter Squadrons in the UK had started to distinguish their aircraft by the addition of coloured bands down the length of the fuselage (and later on the upper wings). The red and blue squares and black and white checks painted on the tail and fuselage of Phantoms belonging to 23 and 43 Squadrons appeared on the Gamecocks and Siskins of these units as well.

Naval aircraft of the inter-war period, even though controlled and flown by the RAF, carried markings which took the form of coloured bands around the fuselage, and were related as much to the base or ship from which the aircraft flew as to the units to which they belonged. By 1938 the bright colours had submerged beneath the rising tide of drab camouflage, unit identity being worn only in the shape of code letters, and it was not until 1950 that colourful unit markings returned in force. Initially these took the form of coloured spinners or nacelles, but the Meteor and Vampire re-introduced the pre-war markings, usually painted on either side of the fuselage roundel and based wherever possible on those that had been over-painted on Gauntlets and Gladiators a dozen years before. With the arrival of the Canberra, Bomber Command evolved its own system of markings, sometimes taking the form of a base marking varied in colour to denote the Squadron, or an emblem either taken from the unit badge or showing some local affiliation.

Naval Squadron markings also began to re-appear in the Fifties, again led by the Fighter Squadrons. These were sometimes based on the unit's badge (as with 804's tiger's head) and in other cases were entirely new (as with 806's ace of diamonds and 830's "plum and custard" finlets). As, by their nature, Naval Sqdn's disbanded every two years or so, it was not unusual for new markings to be adopted on re-forming, often to show some new facet of the unit (examples include 800B's foaming tankard on its Scimitar tankers and 807's scimitar on its Scimitars). Today, Naval Squadron markings are just as varied and fall into less recognisable patterns than those of the RAF, as a glance at those emblems painted on Sea Kings alone will confirm.

Army aviation has never been as colourful as that of the other two services, one requirement of its role being easy concealment which would be compromised by vivid markings. Nevertheless, many of its aircraft carried small badges in the Sixties and Seventies, sometimes showing the unit's affiliation to a base or to a regiment. This has been much reduced recently, however, which is a pity bearing in mind the parent service's traditions of military heraldry.

This is what unit markings really are, a form of military heraldry. They are also a way for a unit to display its pride, history and tradition, and this is not limited to front-line units (the light and dark blue 'training' bands worn by aircraft of the RAF College, for example, have an honourable history). However, in the RAF at least, it has been rivalry between the Fighter Squadrons, each of whom believes that it is the best, that has led the way in British military aviation heraldry, and this will no doubt continue even though the service is once again embarking on a policy of toned-down insignia.

ROYAL AIR FORCE SQUADRON & UNIT MARKINGS

1 SQUADRON

BASE: UK Wittering
ROLE: Tactical strike, close support
AIRCRAFT: Harrier GR.3, T.4

CODE MARKINGS: Two digit fin-code in red commencing with '01'.

2 SQUADRON

BASE: W.Germany Laarbruch
ROLE: Tactical reconnaissance
AIRCRAFT: Jaguar GR.1, T.2

CODE MARKINGS: Single letter fin-code in black inside a white triangle.

3 SQUADRON

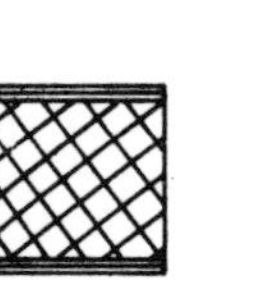

BASE: W.Germany Gutersloh
ROLE: Tactical strike, close support
AIRCRAFT: Harrier GR.3, T.4

CODE MARKINGS: Single letter fin-code in yellow commencing with 'A'.

4 SQUADRON

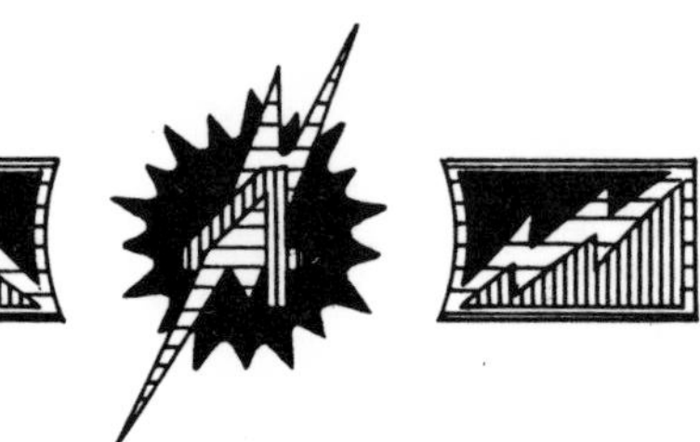

BASE: W.Germany Gutersloh
ROLE: Tactical strike, close support
AIRCRAFT: Harrier GR.3, T.4

CODE MARKINGS: Single letter fin-code in black commencing with 'A'.

5 SQUADRON

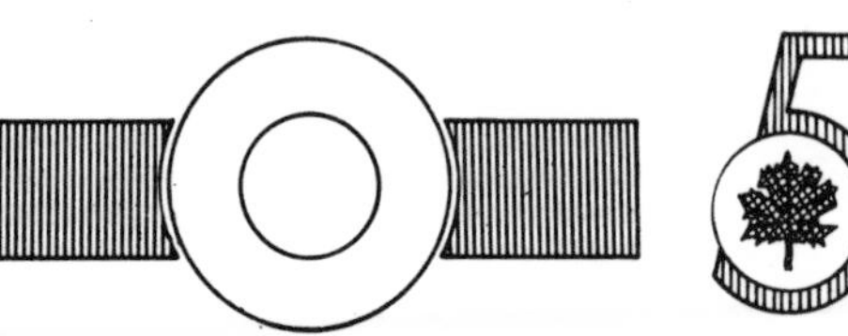

BASE: UK Binbrook
ROLE: Air defence
AIRCRAFT: Lightning F.3, F.6, T.5

CODE MARKINGS: Single letter fin-code in white commencing with 'A'.

6 SQUADRON

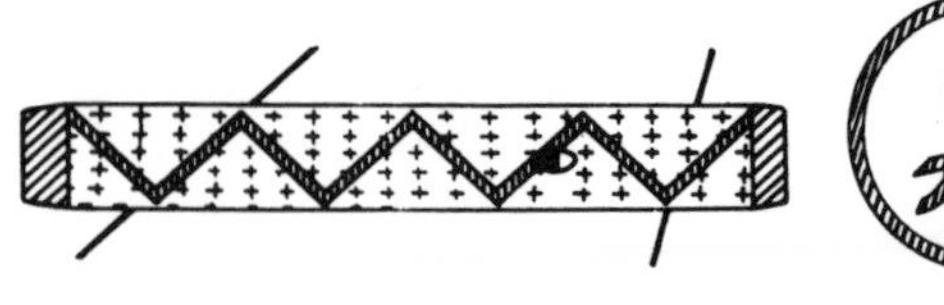

BASE: UK Coltishall
ROLE: Tactical strike
AIRCRAFT: Jaguar GR.1, T.2

CODE MARKINGS: None

RED

GOLD

YELLOW

DAY-GLO R/O

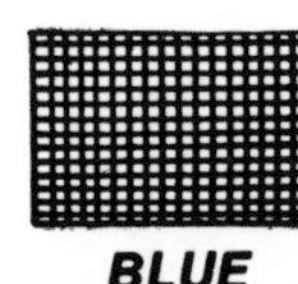
BLUE

PALE BLUE

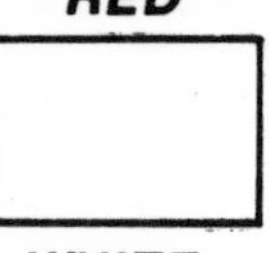
WHITE

BLACK

PURPLE

BROWN

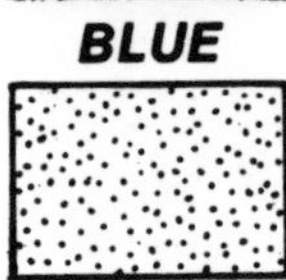
GREY

GREEN

7 SQUADRON

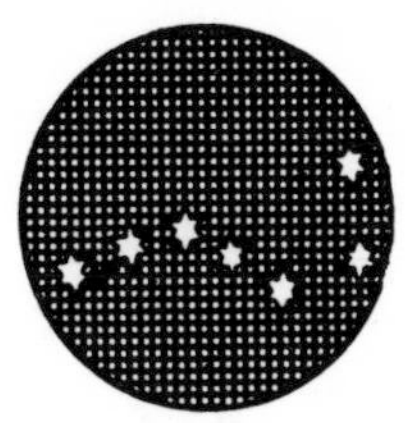

BASE: UK St.Mawgan
ROLE: Target facilities
AIRCRAFT: Canberra T.4, TT.18

CODE MARKINGS: Last two digits of serial on fin in red.

8 SQUADRON

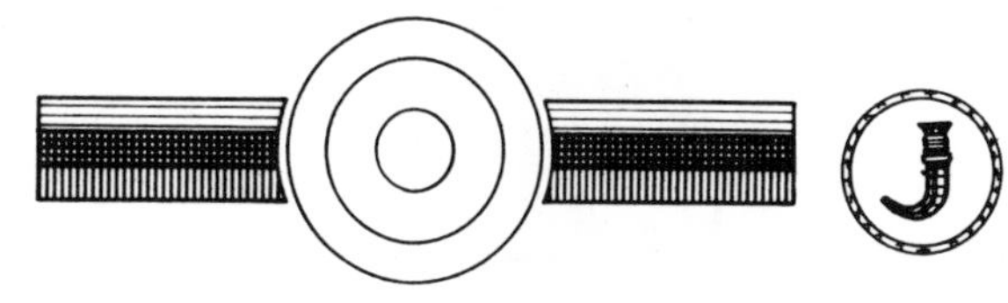

BASE: UK Lossiemouth
ROLE: Airborne early warning
AIRCRAFT: Shackleton AEW.2, MR.2/3

CODE MARKINGS: Last two digits of serial on fin in red.

9 SQUADRON

BASE: UK Waddington
ROLE: Strategic strike
AIRCRAFT: Vulcan B.2

CODE MARKINGS: None

10 SQUADRON

BASE: UK Brize Norton
ROLE: Strategic transport
AIRCRAFT: VC.10 C.1

CODE MARKINGS: None

11 SQUADRON

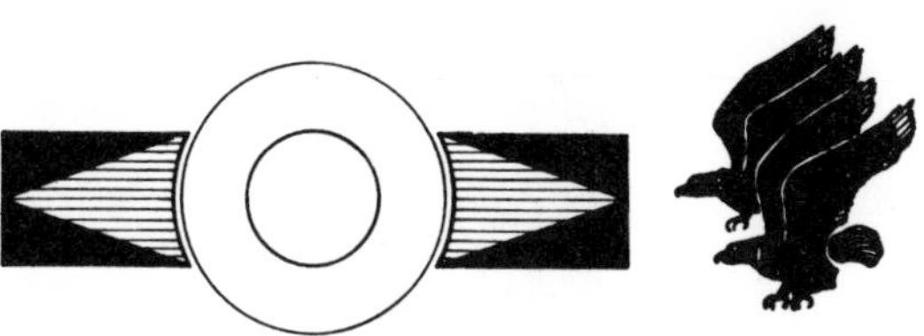

BASE: UK Binbrook
ROLE: Air defence
AIRCRAFT: Lightning F.3, F.6, T.5

CODE MARKINGS: Single letter fin-code in white commencing with 'A'.

12 SQUADRON

BASE: UK Honington
ROLE: Maritime strike
AIRCRAFT: Buccaneer S.2B

CODE MARKINGS: None

RED

GOLD

YELLOW

DAY-GLO R/O

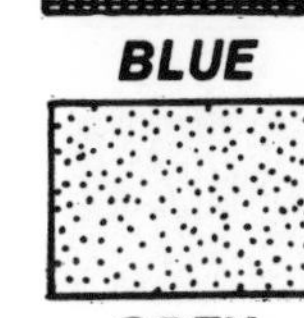
BLUE

PALE BLUE

WHITE

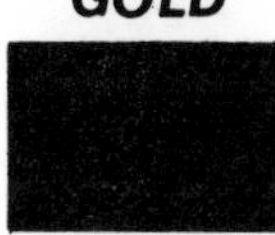
BLACK

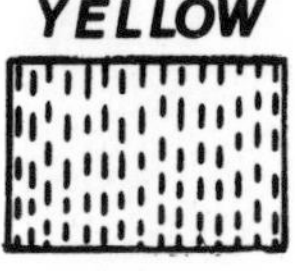
PURPLE

BROWN

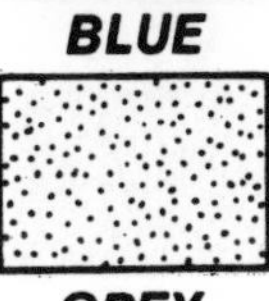
GREY

GREEN

13 SQUADRON

BASE: UK Wyton
ROLE: Photographic reconnaissance
AIRCRAFT: Canberra PR.7

CODE MARKINGS: None

14 SQUADRON

BASE: W.Germany Bruggen
ROLE: Tactical strike
AIRCRAFT: Jaguar GR.1, T.2

CODE MARKINGS: Two letter fin-code in black commencing with 'AA'.

15 SQUADRON

BASE: W.Germany Laarbruch
ROLE: Tactical strike
AIRCRAFT: Buccaneer S.2B

CODE MARKINGS: Single letter fin-code in black commencing with 'A'.

16 SQUADRON

BASE: W.Germany Laarbruch
ROLE: Tactical strike
AIRCRAFT: Buccaneer S.2B

CODE MARKINGS: Single letter fin-code in black commencing with 'P'.

17 SQUADRON

BASE: W.Germany Bruggen
ROLE: Tactical strike
AIRCRAFT: Jaguar GR.1, T.2

CODE MARKINGS: Two letter fin-code in black commencing with 'BA'.

18 SQUADRON

BASE: W.Germany Gutersloh
ROLE: Tactical support
AIRCRAFT: Wessex HC.2

CODE MARKINGS: Two letter code in black on rear fuselage commencing 'BA'.

RED
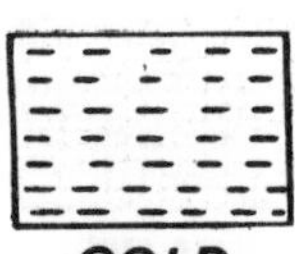
GOLD

YELLOW

DAY-GLO R/O
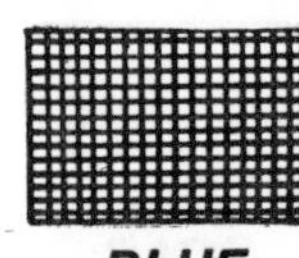
BLUE
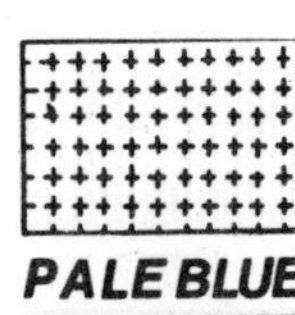
PALE BLUE

WHITE

BLACK
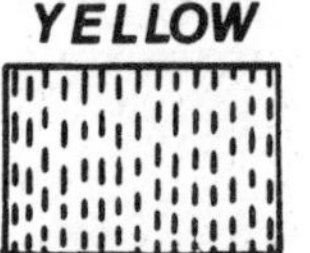
PURPLE

BROWN

GREY

GREEN

19 SQUADRON

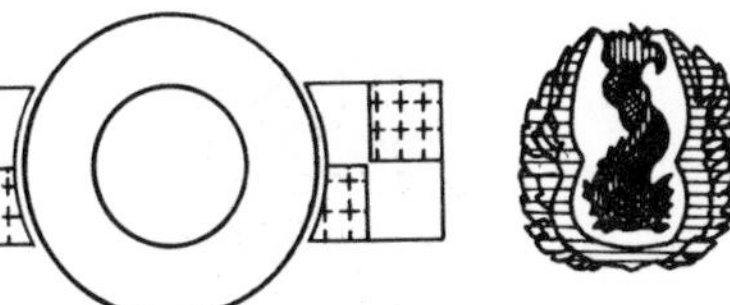

BASE: W.Germany Wildenrath
ROLE: Air defence
AIRCRAFT: Phantom FGR.2

CODE MARKINGS: Single letter fin-code in white commencing with 'A'.

20 SQUADRON

BASE: W.Germany Bruggen
ROLE: Tactical strike
AIRCRAFT: Jaguar GR.1, T.2

CODE MARKINGS: Two letter fin-code in black commencing with 'CA'.

22 SQUADRON

BASE: UK Finningley (& detachments)
ROLE: Search and rescue
AIRCRAFT: Wessex HC.2
Whirlwind HAR.10
CODE MARKINGS: None

23 SQUADRON

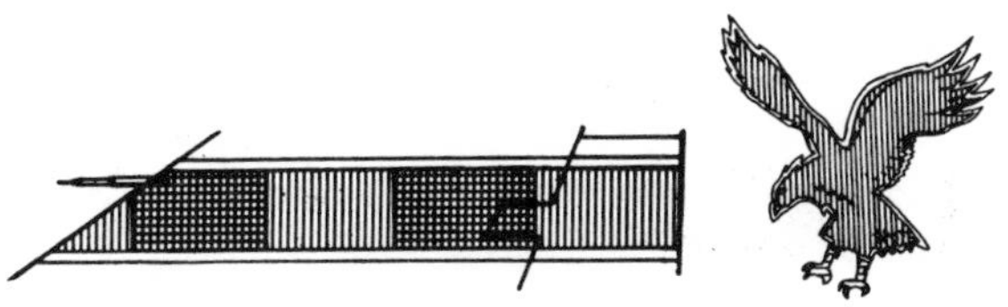

BASE: UK Wattisham
ROLE: Air defence
AIRCRAFT: Phantom FGR.2

CODE MARKINGS: Single letter fin-code in white commencing with 'A'.

24 SQUADRON

BASE: UK Lyneham
ROLE: Tactical transport
AIRCRAFT: Hercules C.1 (pooled with 30, 47 and 70 Sqdns plus 242 OCU under Lyneham Transport Wing)
CODE MARKINGS: None

25 SQUADRON

BASE: W.Germany (several locations)
ROLE: Air defence
AIRCRAFT: Bloodhound Mk.2 missiles

CODE MARKINGS: None

RED
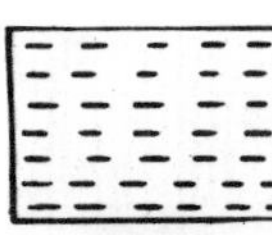
GOLD

YELLOW

DAY-GLO R/O
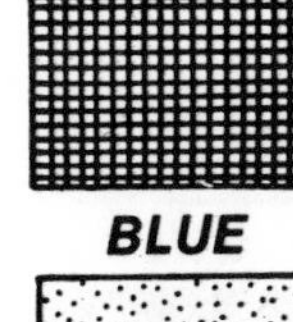
BLUE

PALE BLUE
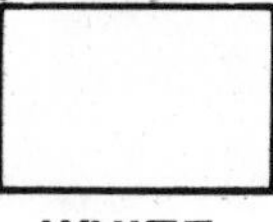
WHITE

BLACK
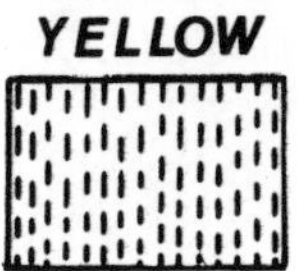
PURPLE

BROWN
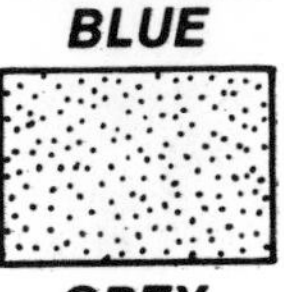
GREY

GREEN

27 SQUADRON

BASE: UK Scampton
ROLE: Strategic reconnaissance
AIRCRAFT: Vulcan B.2(MRR), B.2

CODE MARKINGS: None

28 SQUADRON

BASE: Hong Kong Sek Kong
ROLE: Tactical support
AIRCRAFT: Wessex HC.2

CODE MARKINGS: Single letter code in black on rear fuselage commencing 'A'.

29 SQUADRON

BASE: UK Coningsby
ROLE: Air defence
AIRCRAFT: Phantom FGR.2

CODE MARKINGS: Single letter fin-code in red commencing with 'A'.

30 SQUADRON

BASE: UK Lyneham
ROLE: Tactical transport
AIRCRAFT: Hercules C.1 (pooled with 24, 47 and 70 Sqdns plus 242 OCU under Lyneham Transport Wing)
CODE MARKINGS: None

31 SQUADRON

BASE: W.Germany Bruggen
ROLE: Tactical strike
AIRCRAFT: Jaguar GR.1, T.2

CODE MARKINGS: Two letter fin-code in black commencing with 'DA'.

32 SQUADRON

BASE: UK Northolt
ROLE: Communications & VIP transport
AIRCRAFT: Andover C.1, CC.2; HS.125 CC.1, CC.2; Gazelle HT.3; W'wind HAR.10, HCC.12
CODE MARKINGS: None

RED

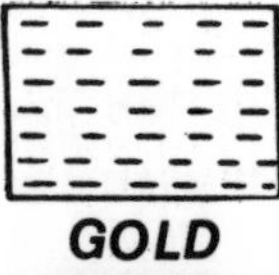
GOLD

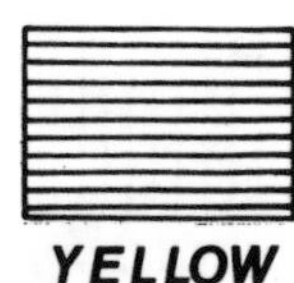
YELLOW

DAY-GLO R/O

BLUE

PALE BLUE

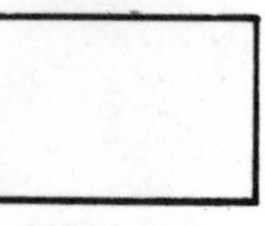
WHITE

BLACK

PURPLE

BROWN

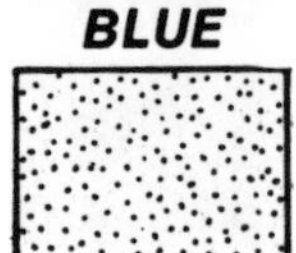
GREY

GREEN

33 SQUADRON

BASE: UK Odiham
ROLE: Tactical support
AIRCRAFT: Puma HC.1

CODE MARKINGS: Two letter code in black on boom commencing with 'CA'.

35 SQUADRON

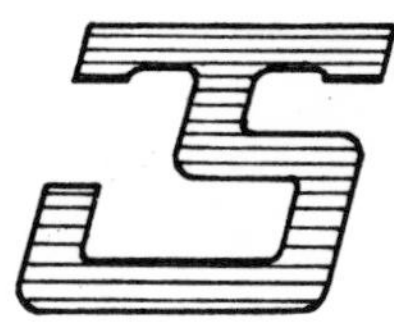

BASE: UK Scampton
ROLE: Strategic strike
AIRCRAFT: Vulcan B.2

CODE MARKINGS: None

38 SQUADRON

BASE: UK St.Mawgan
ROLE: Shadow squadron for 236 OCU
AIRCRAFT: Nimrod MR.1, MR.1A, MR.2 (pooled with 42 Sqdn)
CODE MARKINGS: None

39 SQUADRON

BASE: UK Wyton
ROLE: Photographic reconnaissance
AIRCRAFT: Canberra PR.9

CODE MARKINGS: None

41 SQUADRON

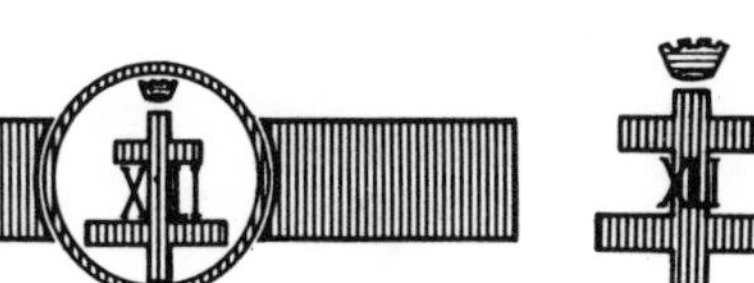

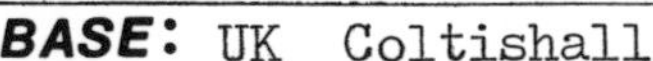

BASE: UK Coltishall
ROLE: Tactical reconnaissance
AIRCRAFT: Jaguar GR.1, T.2

CODE MARKINGS: Single letter fin-code in black commencing with 'A'.

42 SQUADRON

BASE: UK St.Mawgan
ROLE: Maritime reconnaissance
AIRCRAFT: Nimrod MR.1, MR.1A, MR.2 (pooled with 236 OCU)
CODE MARKINGS: None

RED

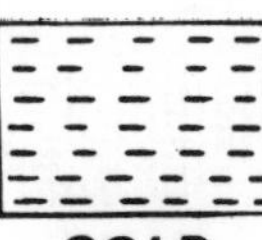
GOLD

YELLOW

DAY-GLO R/O

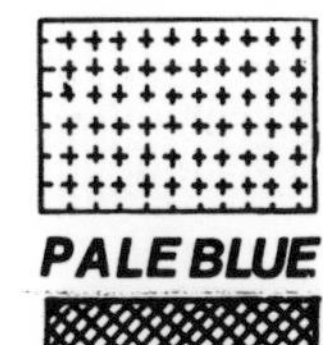
BLUE

PALE BLUE

WHITE

BLACK

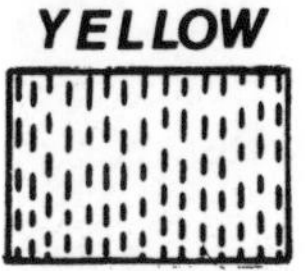
PURPLE

BROWN

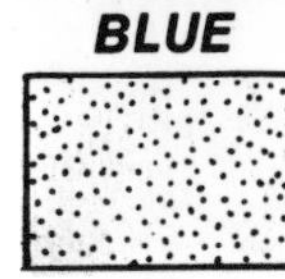
GREY

GREEN

43 SQUADRON

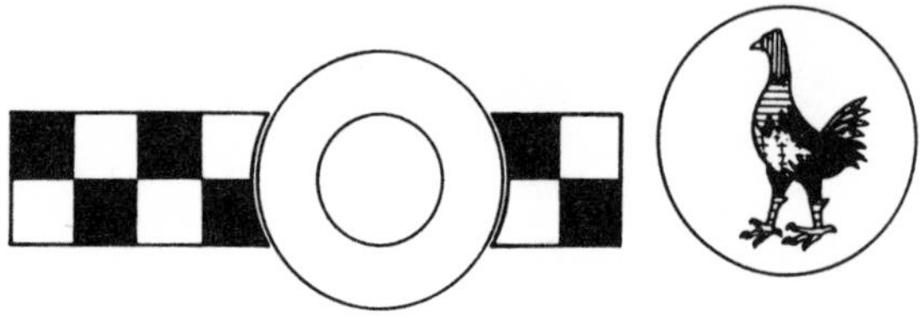

BASE: UK Leuchars
ROLE: Air defence
AIRCRAFT: Phantom FG.1

CODE MARKINGS: Single letter fin-code in white commencing with 'A'.

44 SQUADRON

BASE: UK Waddington
ROLE: Strategic strike
AIRCRAFT: Vulcan B.2

CODE MARKINGS: None

47 SQUADRON

BASE: UK Lyneham
ROLE: Tactical transport
AIRCRAFT: Hercules C.1 (pooled with 24, 30 and 70 Sqdns plus 242 OCU under Lyneham Transport Wing)
CODE MARKINGS: None

50 SQUADRON

BASE: UK Waddington
ROLE: Strategic strike
AIRCRAFT: Vulcan B.2

CODE MARKINGS: None

51 SQUADRON

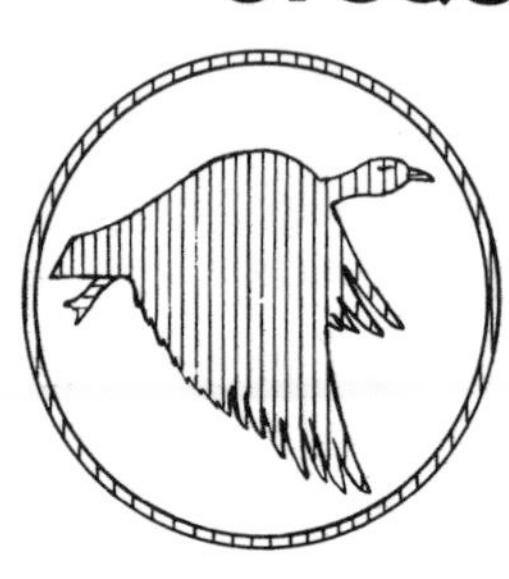

BASE: UK Wyton
ROLE: Electronic surveillance
AIRCRAFT: Nimrod R.1, Andover C.1(mod)

CODE MARKINGS: None

54 SQUADRON

BASE: UK Coltishall
ROLE: Tactical strike
AIRCRAFT: Jaguar GR.1, T.2

CODE MARKINGS: None

RED

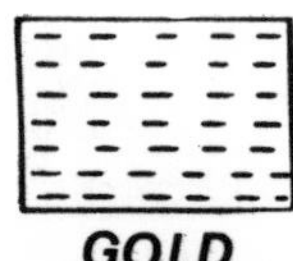
GOLD

YELLOW

DAY-GLO R/O

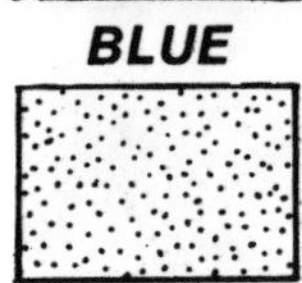
BLUE

PALE BLUE

WHITE

BLACK

PURPLE

BROWN

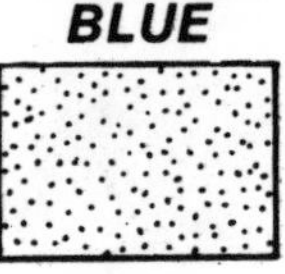
GREY

GREEN

55 SQUADRON

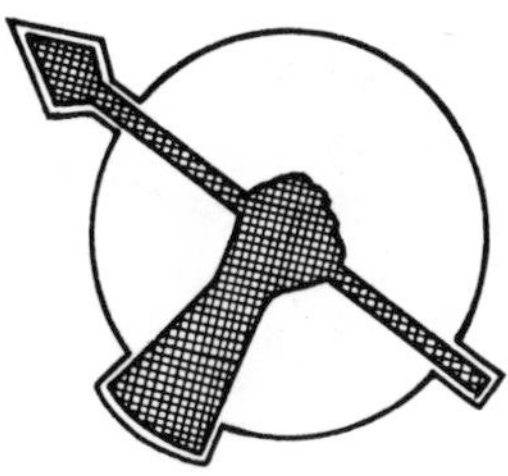

BASE: UK Marham
ROLE: In-flight refuelling
AIRCRAFT: Victor K.2

CODE MARKINGS: None

56 SQUADRON

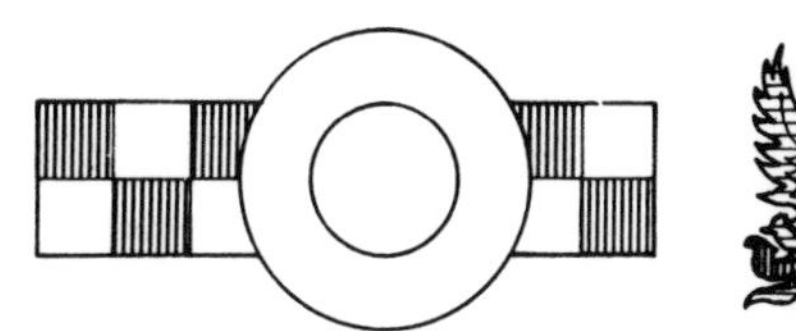

BASE: UK Wattisham
ROLE: Air defence
AIRCRAFT: Phantom FGR.2

CODE MARKINGS: Single letter code in yellow on rudder commencing with 'A'.

57 SQUADRON

BASE: UK Marham
ROLE: In-flight refuelling
AIRCRAFT: Victor K.2

CODE MARKINGS: None

60 SQUADRON

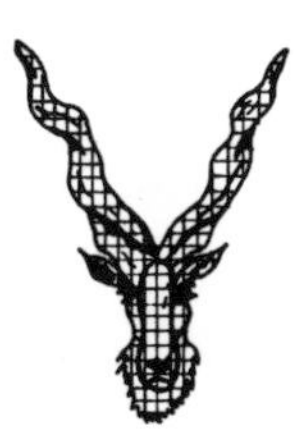

BASE: W.Germany Wildenrath
ROLE: Communications
AIRCRAFT: Pembroke C.1

CODE MARKINGS: None

63 SQUADRON

BASE: UK Brawdy
ROLE: Shadow squadron for No.1 TWU
AIRCRAFT: Hawk T.1

CODE MARKINGS: (see No.1 TWU)

64 SQUADRON

BASE: UK Coningsby
ROLE: Shadow squadron for 228 OCU
AIRCRAFT: Phantom FGR.2

CODE MARKINGS: (see 228 OCU)

RED
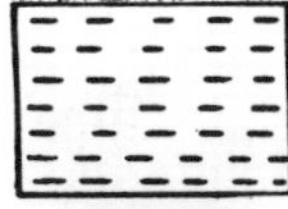
GOLD

YELLOW

DAY-GLO R/O
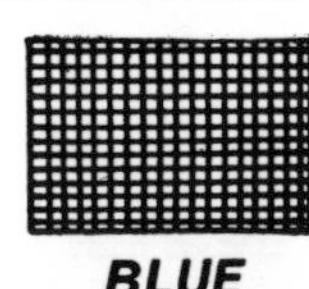
BLUE
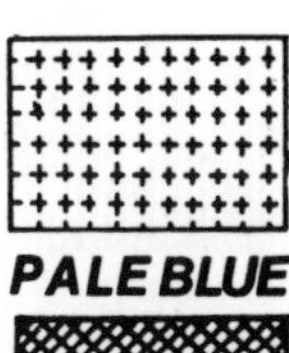
PALE BLUE

WHITE

BLACK
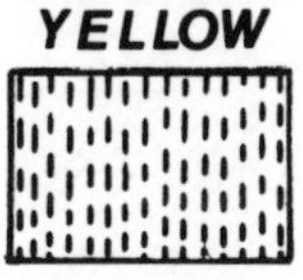
PURPLE

BROWN
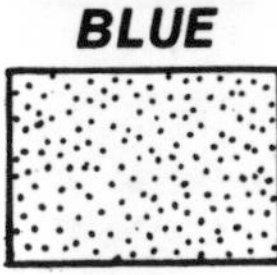
GREY

GREEN

70 SQUADRON

BASE: UK Lyneham
ROLE: Tactical transport
AIRCRAFT: Hercules C.1 (pooled with 24, 30 and 47 Sqdns plus 242 OCU under Lyneham Transport Wing)
CODE MARKINGS: None

72 SQUADRON

BASE: UK Odiham
ROLE: Tactical support
AIRCRAFT: Wessex HC.2

CODE MARKINGS: Two letter code in black on rear fuselage commencing 'AA'.

79 SQUADRON

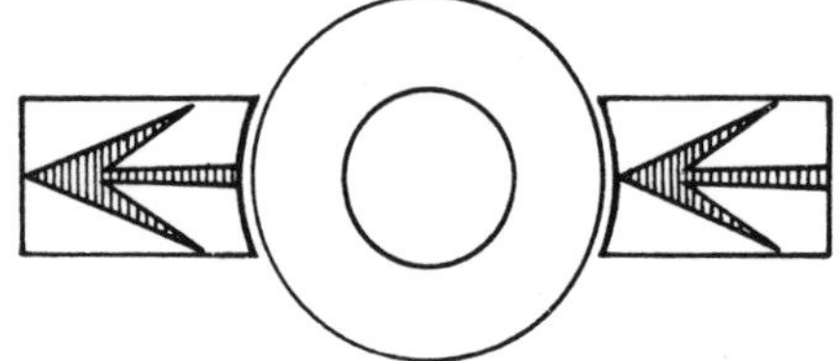

BASE: UK Brawdy
ROLE: Shadow squadron for No.1 TWU
AIRCRAFT: Hunter F.6A, FGA.9, Hawk T.1

CODE MARKINGS: (see No.1 TWU)

84 SQUADRON

BASE: Cyprus Akrotiri and Nicosia
ROLE: Search and rescue, UN support
AIRCRAFT: Whirlwind HAR.10

CODE MARKINGS: 'A' Flt (SAR) none; UN Flt single letter code on fuselage.

85 SQUADRON

BASE: UK West Raynham (& other sites)
ROLE: Air defence
AIRCRAFT: Bloodhound Mk.2 missiles

CODE MARKINGS: None

92 SQUADRON

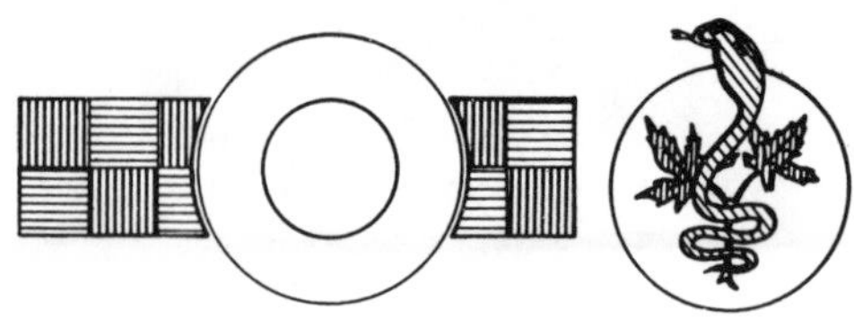

BASE: W.Germany Wildenrath
ROLE: Air defence
AIRCRAFT: Phantom FGR.2

CODE MARKINGS: Single letter fin-code in white commencing with 'N'.

RED

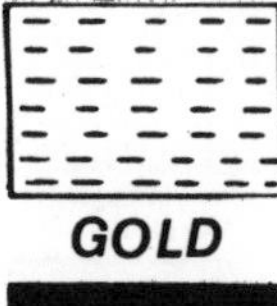
GOLD

YELLOW

DAY-GLO R/O

BLUE

PALE BLUE

WHITE

BLACK

PURPLE

BROWN

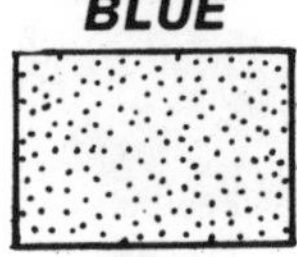
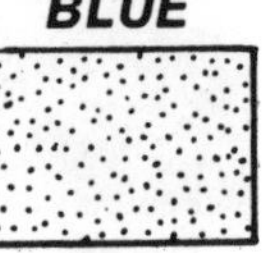
GREY

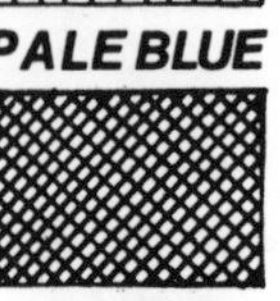
GREEN

100 SQUADRON

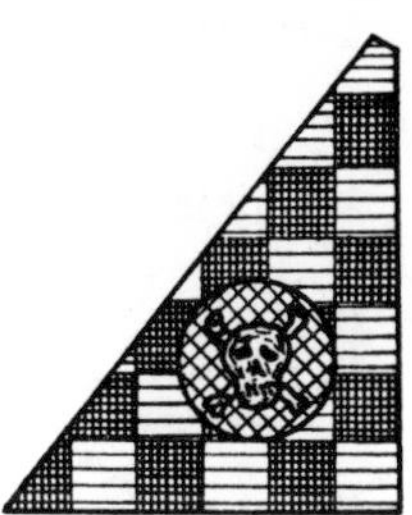

BASE: UK Marham
ROLE: Target facilities
AIRCRAFT: Canberra B.2, T.4, E.15

CODE MARKINGS: Single letter fin-code in black commencing with 'A'.

101 SQUADRON

BASE: UK Waddington
ROLE: Strategic strike
AIRCRAFT: Vulcan B.2

CODE MARKINGS: None

111 SQUADRON

BASE: UK Leuchars
ROLE: Air defence
AIRCRAFT: Phantom FG.1, FGR.2

CODE MARKINGS: Single letter fin-code in yellow commencing with 'A'.

115 SQUADRON

BASE: UK Brize Norton
ROLE: Navaid calibration
AIRCRAFT: Andover C.1, E.3, E.3A

CODE MARKINGS: None

120 SQUADRON

BASE: UK Kinloss
ROLE: Maritime reconnaissance
AIRCRAFT: Nimrod MR.1, MR.1A, MR.2 (pooled with 201 and 206 Sqdns under Kinloss Maritime Reconnaissance Wing)
CODE MARKINGS: None

201 SQUADRON

BASE: UK Kinloss
ROLE: Maritime reconnaissance
AIRCRAFT: Nimrod MR.1, MR.1A, MR.2 (pooled with 120 and 206 Sqdns under Kinloss Maritime Reconnaissance Wing)
CODE MARKINGS: None

RED

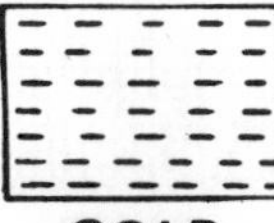
GOLD

YELLOW

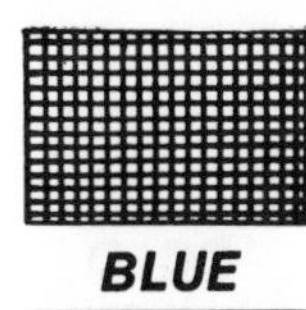
DAY-GLO R/O

BLUE

PALE BLUE

WHITE

BLACK

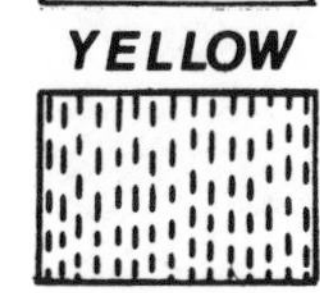
PURPLE

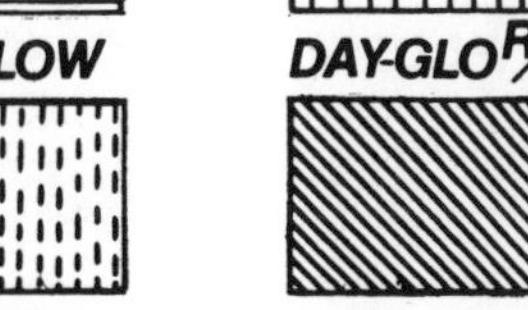
BROWN

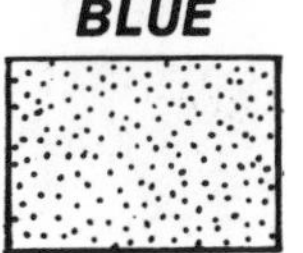
GREY

GREEN

202 SQUADRON

BASE: UK Finningley (& detachments)
ROLE: Search and rescue
AIRCRAFT: Sea King HAR.3

CODE MARKINGS: None

206 SQUADRON

BASE: UK Kinloss
ROLE: Maritime reconnaissance
AIRCRAFT: Nimrod MR.1, MR.1A, MR.2 (pooled with 120 and 201 Sqdns under Kinloss Maritime Reconnaissance Wing)
CODE MARKINGS: None

207 SQUADRON

BASE: UK Northolt (& detachments)
ROLE: Communications
AIRCRAFT: Devon C.2

CODE MARKINGS: None

208 SQUADRON

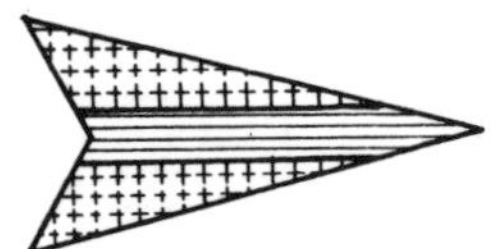

BASE: UK Honington
ROLE: Tactical strike
AIRCRAFT: Buccaneer S.2B
Hunter F.6A (temp)
CODE MARKINGS: None

216 SQUADRON

BASE: UK Honington
ROLE: Maritime strike
AIRCRAFT: Buccaneer S.2B
Hunter F.6A (temp)
CODE MARKINGS: None

230 SQUADRON

BASE: UK Odiham
ROLE: Tactical support
AIRCRAFT: Puma HC.1

CODE MARKINGS: Two letter code in black on boom commencing with 'DA'.

RED

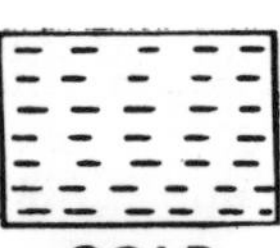
GOLD

YELLOW

DAY-GLO R/O

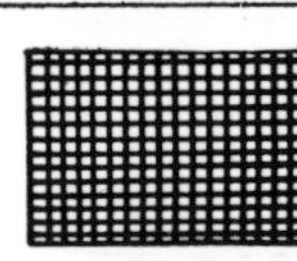
BLUE

PALE BLUE

WHITE

BLACK

PURPLE

BROWN

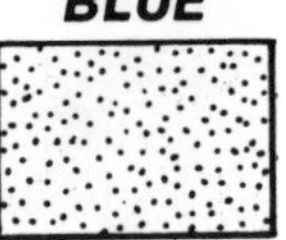
GREY

GREEN

234 SQUADRON

BASE: UK Brawdy
ROLE: Shadow squadron for No.1 TWU
AIRCRAFT: Hawk T.1

CODE MARKINGS: (see No.1 TWU)

360 SQUADRON

BASE: UK Wyton
ROLE: Electronic countermeasures
AIRCRAFT: Canberra T.17

CODE MARKINGS: Single letter fin-code in white commencing with 'A'.

617 SQUADRON

BASE: UK Scampton
ROLE: Strategic strike
AIRCRAFT: Vulcan B.2

CODE MARKINGS: None

SQUADRON

BASE:
ROLE:
AIRCRAFT:

CODE MARKINGS:

SQUADRON

BASE:
ROLE:
AIRCRAFT:

CODE MARKINGS:

SQUADRON

BASE:
ROLE:
AIRCRAFT:

CODE MARKINGS:

RED

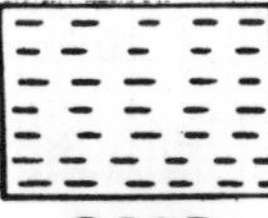
GOLD

YELLOW

DAY-GLO R/O

BLUE

PALE BLUE

WHITE

BLACK

PURPLE

BROWN

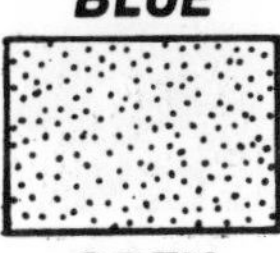
GREY

GREEN

226 OCU

BASE: UK Lossiemouth
ROLE: Operational Conversion Unit
AIRCRAFT: Jaguar GR.1, T.2
CODE MARKINGS: (GR.1) two digit black fin-code commencing '01'; (T.2) single letter black fin-code commencing 'A'.

228 OCU

BASE: UK Coningsby
ROLE: Operational Conversion Unit
AIRCRAFT: Phantom FGR.2 (shadow 64 Squadron)
CODE MARKINGS: Single letter fin-code in black commencing with 'A'.

230 OCU

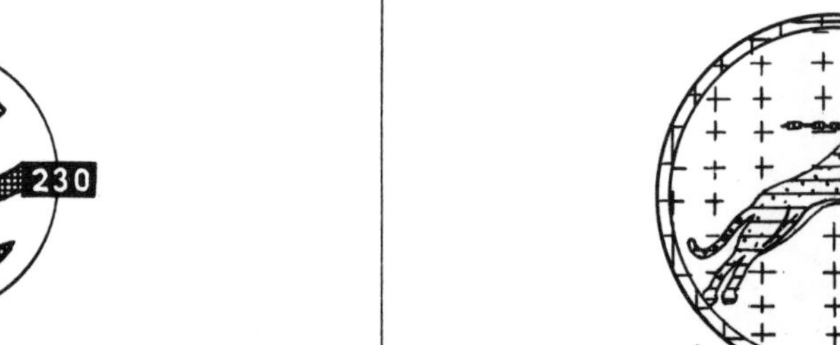

BASE: UK Scampton
ROLE: Operational Conversion Unit
AIRCRAFT: Vulcan B.2

CODE MARKINGS: None

231 OCU

BASE: UK Marham
ROLE: Operational Conversion Unit
AIRCRAFT: Canberra B.2, T.4

CODE MARKINGS: None

232 OCU

BASE: UK Marham
ROLE: Operational Conversion Unit
AIRCRAFT: Victor K.2 (borrowed as required from 55 and 57 Sqdns)
CODE MARKINGS:. None

233 OCU

BASE: UK Wittering
ROLE: Operational Conversion Unit
AIRCRAFT: Harrier GR.3, T.4
CODE MARKINGS: Single letter fin-code in blue commencing with 'A' (GR.3) and 'Q' (T.4).

RED

GOLD

YELLOW

DAY-GLO R/O

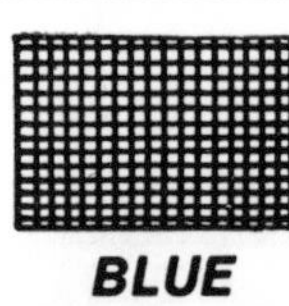
BLUE

PALE BLUE

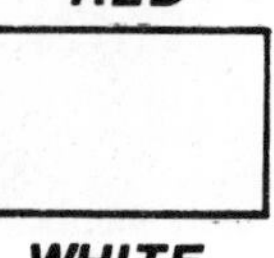
WHITE

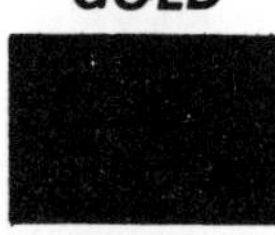
BLACK

PURPLE

BROWN

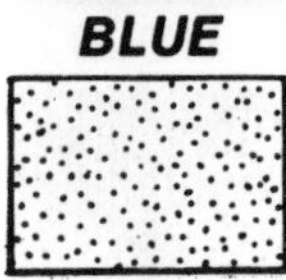
GREY

GREEN

236 OCU

BASE: UK St.Mawgan
ROLE: Operational conversion unit
AIRCRAFT: Nimrod MR.1, MR.1A, MR.2 (pooled with 42 Sqdn)
CODE MARKINGS: None

237 OCU

BASE: UK Honington
ROLE: Operational Conversion Unit
AIRCRAFT: Buccaneer S.2A, S.2B
Hunter F.6A, T.7, T.8B
CODE MARKINGS: None

240 OCU

BASE: UK Odiham
ROLE: Operational Conversion Unit
AIRCRAFT: Wessex HC.2, Puma HC.1
CODE MARKINGS: Two letter black code on rear fuselage (Wessex, commencing 'BU') or boom (Puma, commencing 'CU').

241 OCU

BASE: UK Brize Norton
ROLE: Operational Conversion Unit
AIRCRAFT: Andover C.1 (and VC.10 C.1 borrowed as required from 10 Sqdn)
CODE MARKINGS: None

242 OCU

BASE: UK Lyneham
ROLE: Operational Conversion Unit
AIRCRAFT: Hercules C.1 (pooled with 24, 30, 47 and 70 Sqdns under Lyneham Transport Wing)
CODE MARKINGS: None

BASE:
ROLE:
AIRCRAFT:

CODE MARKINGS:

RED	GOLD	YELLOW	DAY-GLO R/O	BLUE	PALE BLUE
WHITE	BLACK	PURPLE	BROWN	GREY	GREEN

LTF

BASE: UK Binbrook
ROLE: Lightning Training Flight
AIRCRAFT: Lightning F.3, F.6, T.5

CODE MARKINGS: Single letter fin-code in white commencing with 'A'.

TTTE

BASE: UK Cottesmore (forms in 1980)
ROLE: Tri-national Tornado Training Establishment
AIRCRAFT: Tornado GR.1 (with German and Italian aircraft)
CODE MARKINGS:

1 TWU

BASE: UK Brawdy
ROLE: Tactical Weapons Unit (shadow 63, 79 and 234 Squadrons)
AIRCRAFT: Hawk T.1; Hunter F.6A, FGA.9, T.7; Jet Provost T.4, Meteor T.7, F.8
CODE MARKINGS: (Hawk T.1) none; (Hunter F.6A) two digit white fin-codes from '12'; (Hunter FGA.9) single letter white fin-codes from 'A'; (Hunter T.7); two digit white fin-codes from '81'.

2 TWU

BASE: UK Lossiemouth
ROLE: Tactical Weapons Unit
AIRCRAFT: Hunter FGA.9, T.7 (to re-equip with Hawk T.1 in 1980/81 at Chivenor)

CODE MARKINGS: (FGA.9) single letter white fin-codes from'A'; (T.7) two digit white fin-codes from '01'.

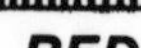

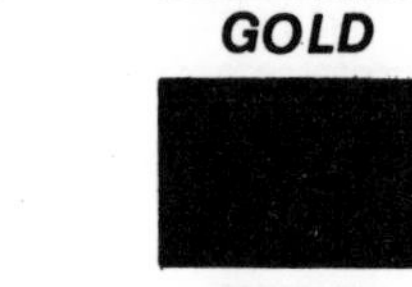
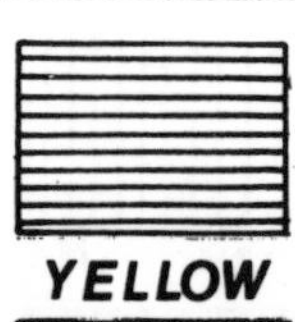

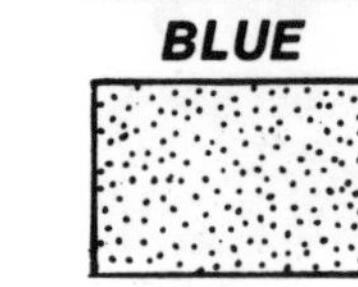
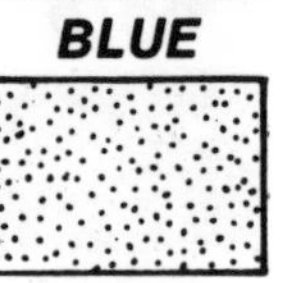

RED GOLD YELLOW DAY-GLO R/O BLUE PALE BLUE

WHITE BLACK PURPLE BROWN GREY GREEN

1 FTS

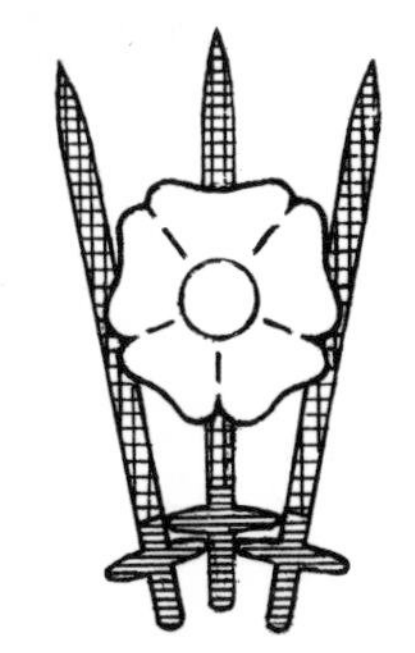

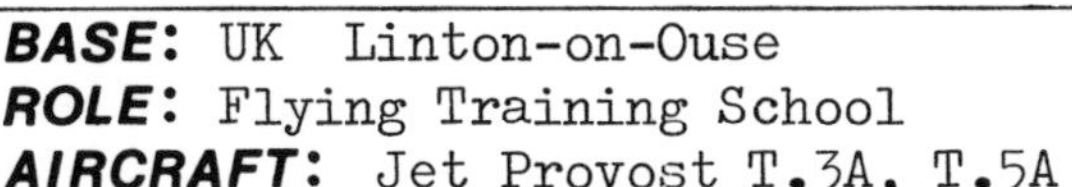

BASE: UK Linton-on-Ouse
ROLE: Flying Training School
AIRCRAFT: Jet Provost T.3A, T.5A

CODE MARKINGS: Two digit black fin-codes from '10' (T.3A) and '60' (T.5A).

2 FTS

BASE: UK Shawbury
ROLE: Flying Training School
AIRCRAFT: Whirlwind HAR.10
Wessex HU.5, Gazelle HT.3
CODE MARKINGS: Black letter/letters commencing with 'A' and 'AA'.

3 FTS

BASE: UK Leeming
ROLE: Flying Training School (incorporates the Refresher Flying Squadron and the Royal Naval Elementary Flying Training School)
AIRCRAFT: Jet Provost T.3A, T.5A; Bulldog T.1 (all aircraft pooled with the CFS)
CODE MARKINGS: Single letter fin-code in black commencing with 'H' (J.P. T.3A); 1/2 digit fin-code in black commencing with '1' (Bulldog) and '40' (J.P. T.5A).

4 FTS

BASE: UK Valley
ROLE: Flying Training School
AIRCRAFT: Hawk T.1

CODE MARKINGS: None

6 FTS

BASE: UK Finningley
ROLE: Flying Training School
AIRCRAFT: Jetstream T.1, Dominie T.1,
Jet Provost T.5B
CODE MARKINGS: Single letter white or black (JP's) fin codes from 'A'.

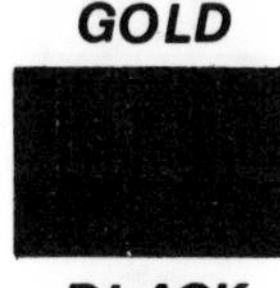
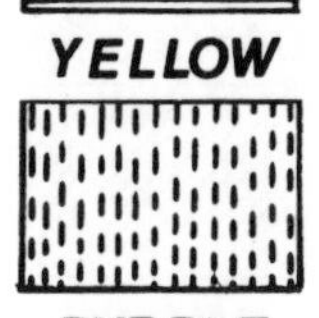
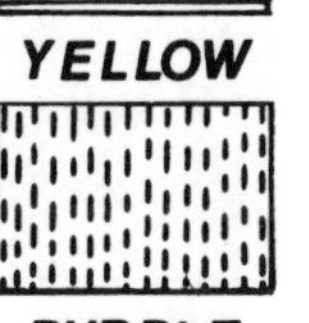

RED GOLD YELLOW DAY-GLO R/O BLUE PALE BLUE

WHITE BLACK PURPLE BROWN GREY GREEN

7 FTS

BASE: UK Church Fenton
ROLE: Flying Training School
AIRCRAFT: Jet Provost T.3A, T.5A

CODE MARKINGS: Two digit black fin-codes from '80' (T.3A) and '100' (T.5A).

CATCS

BASE: UK Shawbury
ROLE: Central Air Traffic Control School
AIRCRAFT: Jet Provost T.4

CODE MARKINGS: Single letter fin-code in black commencing with 'A'.

RAFC

BASE: UK Cranwell
ROLE: Royal Air Force College
AIRCRAFT: Jet Provost T.3A, T.5A

CODE MARKINGS: 1/2 digit black fin-codes from '1' (T.5A) and '50' (T.3A).

SARTS

BASE: UK Valley
ROLE: Search and rescue training
AIRCRAFT: Whirlwind HAR.10

CODE MARKINGS: None

CFS

BASE: UK Leeming (with detachments at Kemble, Shawbury and Valley)
ROLE: Instructor training
AIRCRAFT: Jet Provost T.3A, T.5A; Bulldog T.1 (Leeming, all pooled with 3 FTS); Chipmunk T.10; Meteor T.7 & Vampire T.11 'Vintage Pair' team (Leeming); Hawk T.1 'Red Arrows' team (Kemble); Gazelle HT.2, HT.3 (Shawbury); Hawk T.1 (Valley).
CODE MARKINGS: See 2 FTS (Gazelle), 3 FTS (Jet Provost, Bulldog), 4 FTS (Hawk).

RED

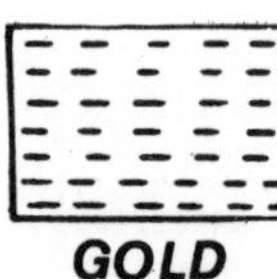
GOLD

YELLOW

DAY-GLO R/O

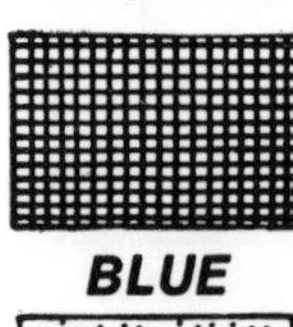
BLUE

PALE BLUE

WHITE

BLACK

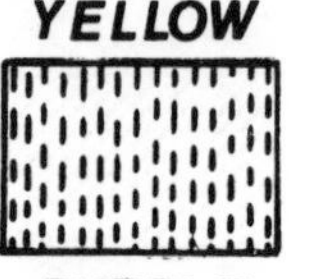
PURPLE

BROWN

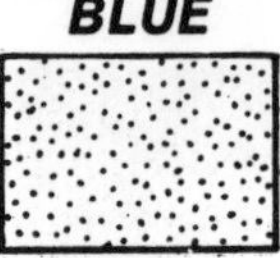
GREY

GREEN

FSS

BASE: UK Swinderby
ROLE: Pilot Aptitude Assessment
AIRCRAFT: Chipmunk T.10

CODE MARKINGS: Single letter black fin-codes from 'A'.

CSF

BASE: UK Wyton
ROLE: RAF Wyton Canberra Servicing Flt.
AIRCRAFT: Canberra T.4

CODE MARKINGS: None

BoBMF

BASE: UK Coningsby
ROLE: Battle of Britain Memorial Flight
AIRCRAFT: Spitfire IIA, VB, PR.19; Hurricane IIC; Lancaster B.I
CODE MARKINGS: World War II style codes, representing famous squadrons.

THE QUEEN'S FLIGHT

BASE: UK Benson
ROLE: The Queen's Flight
AIRCRAFT: Andover CC.2, Wessex HCC.4

CODE MARKINGS: None

BERLIN STN FLT

BASE: W.Germany Berlin-Gatow
ROLE: Station Flight
AIRCRAFT: Chipmunk T.10

CODE MARKINGS: None

CinC AFNE FLT

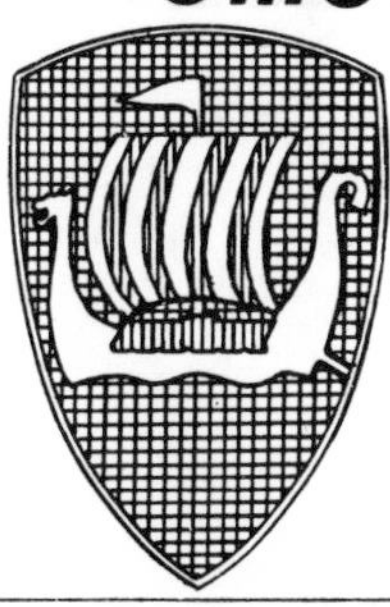

BASE: Norway Oslo-Fornebu
ROLE: Communications
AIRCRAFT: Andover C.1

CODE MARKINGS: None

RED

GOLD

YELLOW

DAY-GLO R/O

BLUE

PALE BLUE

WHITE

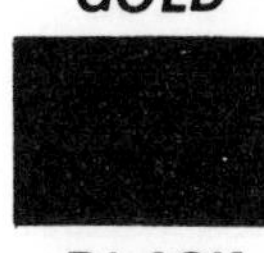
BLACK

PURPLE

BROWN

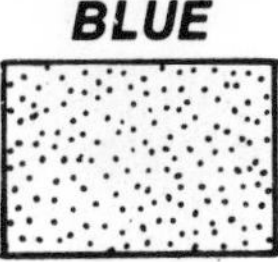
GREY

GREEN

ABERDEEN UAS

BASE: UK Aberdeen
ROLE: Basic flying training
AIRCRAFT: Bulldog T.1

CODE MARKINGS: Single letter black fin-codes from 'A'.

BIRMINGHAM UAS

BASE: UK Cosford
ROLE: Basic flying training
AIRCRAFT: Bulldog T.1

CODE MARKINGS: Single letter black fin-codes from 'A'.

BRISTOL UAS

BASE: UK Bristol-Filton
ROLE: Basic flying training
AIRCRAFT: Bulldog T.1

CODE MARKINGS: Single letter black fin-codes from 'A'.

CAMBRIDGE UAS

BASE: UK Cambridge
ROLE: Basic flying training
AIRCRAFT: Bulldog T.1

CODE MARKINGS: Single letter black fin codes 'C', 'U', 'A', 'S'.

EAST LOWLANDS UAS

BASE: UK Edinburgh
ROLE: Basic flying training
AIRCRAFT: Bulldog T.1

CODE MARKINGS: Two digit red fin-codes from '01'.

EAST MIDLANDS UAS

BASE: UK Newton
ROLE: Basic flying training
AIRCRAFT: Bulldog T.1

CODE MARKINGS: Single letter black fin-codes 'E', 'M', 'U', 'A', 'S'.

RED
GOLD
YELLOW

DAY-GLO R/O
BLUE
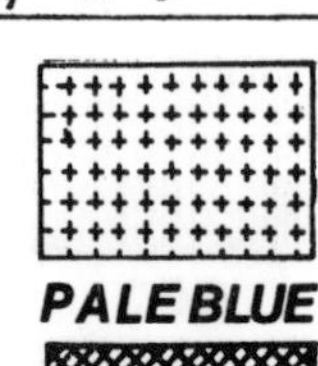
PALE BLUE

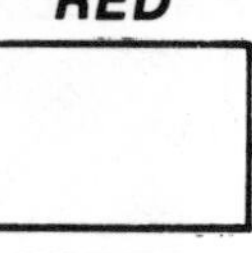
WHITE
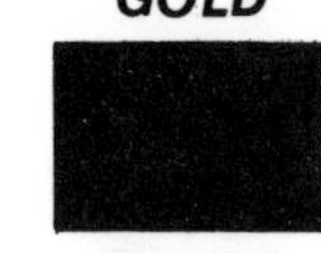
BLACK
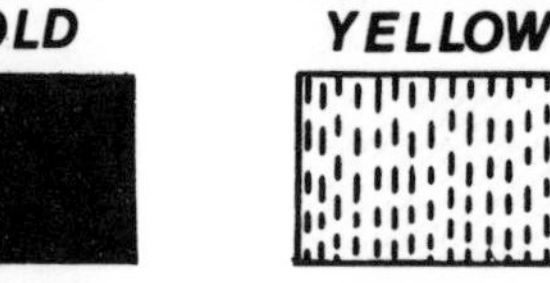
PURPLE

BROWN
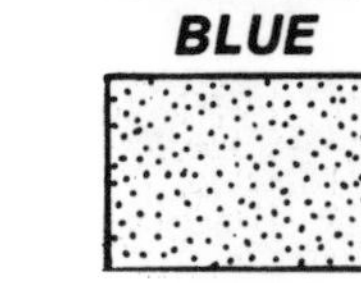
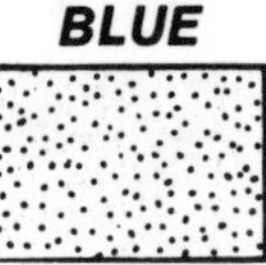
GREY

GREEN

GLASGOW&STRATHCLYDE UAS

BASE: UK Glasgow
ROLE: Basic flying training
AIRCRAFT: Bulldog T.1

CODE MARKINGS: Two digit black fin-codes from '01'.

LIVERPOOL UAS

BASE: UK Woodvale
ROLE: Basic flying training
AIRCRAFT: Bulldog T.1

CODE MARKINGS: Single letter black fin-codes 'L', 'U', 'A', 'S'.

LONDON UAS

BASE: UK Abingdon
ROLE: Basic flying training
AIRCRAFT: Bulldog T.1

CODE MARKINGS: Two digit black fin-codes from '01'.

MANCHESTER UAS

BASE: UK Woodvale
ROLE: Basic flying training
AIRCRAFT: Bulldog T.1

CODE MARKINGS: Single digit black fin-codes from '1'.

NORTHUMBRIAN UAS

BASE: UK Leeming
ROLE: Basic flying training
AIRCRAFT: Bulldog T.1

CODE MARKINGS: Single digit black fin-codes from 'V'.

OXFORD UAS

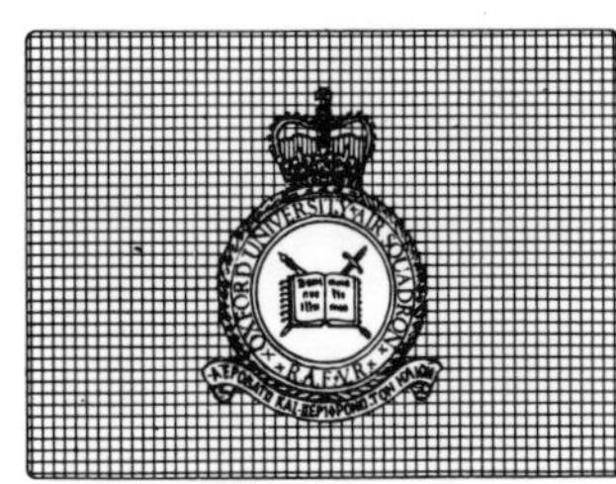

BASE: UK Abingdon
ROLE: Basic flying training
AIRCRAFT: Bulldog T.1

CODE MARKINGS: Single digit black fin-codes from 'A'.

RED

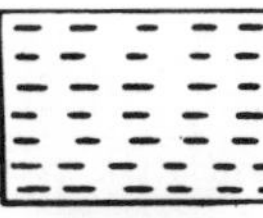
GOLD

YELLOW

DAY-GLO R/O

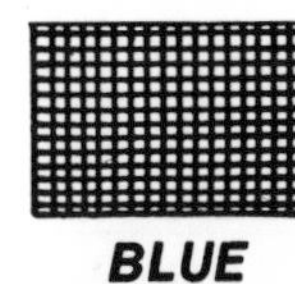
BLUE

PALE BLUE

WHITE

BLACK

PURPLE

BROWN

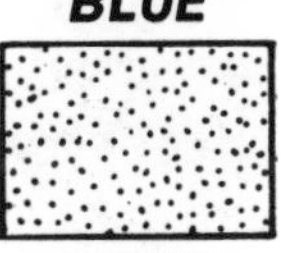
GREY

GREEN

QUEEN'S UAS

BASE: UK Belfast-Sydenham
ROLE: Basic flying training
AIRCRAFT: Bulldog T.1

CODE MARKINGS: Single letter black fin-codes 'Q', 'U', 'A', 'S'.

SOUTHAMPTON UAS

BASE: UK Bournemouth-Hurn
ROLE: Basic flying training
AIRCRAFT: Bulldog T.1

CODE MARKINGS: Two digit black fin-codes from '01'.

WALES UAS

BASE: UK St.Athan
ROLE: Basic flying training
AIRCRAFT: Bulldog T.1

CODE MARKINGS: Two digit black fin-codes from '45'.

YORKSHIRE UAS

BASE: UK Finningley
ROLE: Basic flying training
AIRCRAFT: Bulldog T.1

CODE MARKINGS: Single letter black fin-codes from 'A'.

1 AEF

BASE: UK Manston
ROLE: Air Experience Flight
AIRCRAFT: Chipmunk T.10

CODE MARKINGS: None

2 AEF

BASE: UK Bournemouth-Hurn
ROLE: Air Experience Flight
AIRCRAFT: Chipmunk T.10

CODE MARKINGS: Single digit black fin-codes from '9'.

RED

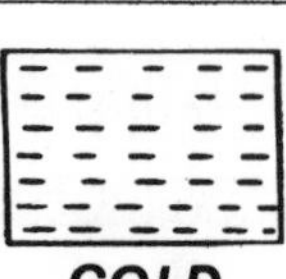
GOLD

YELLOW

DAY-GLO R/O

BLUE

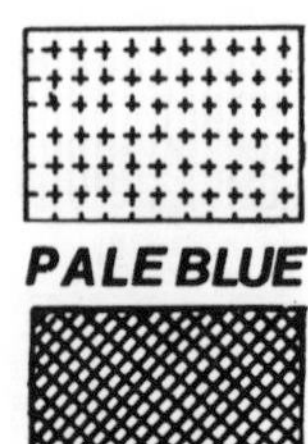
PALE BLUE

WHITE

BLACK

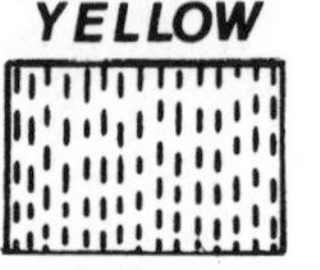
PURPLE

BROWN

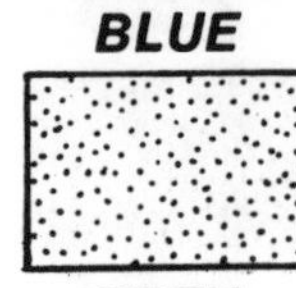
GREY

GREEN

3 AEF

BASE: UK Bristol-Filton
ROLE: Air Experience Flight
AIRCRAFT: Chipmunk T.10

CODE MARKINGS: Single letter black fin-code.

4 AEF

BASE: UK Exeter
ROLE: Air Experience Flight
AIRCRAFT: Chipmunk T.10

CODE MARKINGS: None

5 AEF

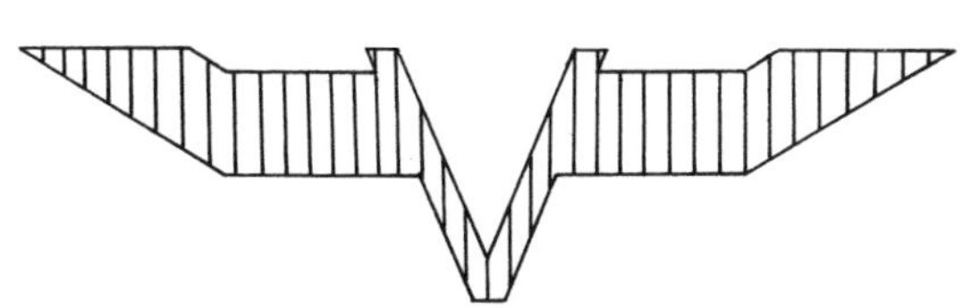

BASE: UK Cambridge
ROLE: Air Experience Flight
AIRCRAFT: Chipmunk T.10, Beagle Husky

CODE MARKINGS: Single letter white codes under cockpit (Chipmunk only).

6 AEF

BASE: UK Abingdon
ROLE: Air Experience Flight
AIRCRAFT: Chipmunk T.10

CODE MARKINGS: Single letter black fin-codes from 'A'.

7 AEF

BASE: UK Newton
ROLE: Air Experience Flight
AIRCRAFT: Chipmunk T.10

CODE MARKINGS: None

8 AEF

BASE: UK Cosford
ROLE: Air Experience Flight
AIRCRAFT: Chipmunk T.10

CODE MARKINGS: Single digit/letter black fin-codes '8', 'A', 'E', 'F'.

RED

GOLD

YELLOW

DAY-GLO R/O

BLUE

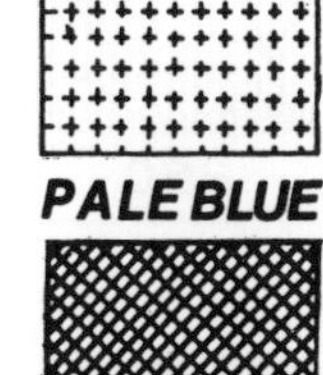
PALE BLUE

WHITE

BLACK

PURPLE

BROWN

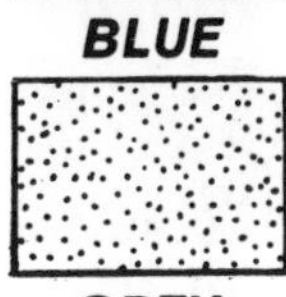
GREY

GREEN

9 AEF

BASE: UK Finningley
ROLE: Air Experience Flight
AIRCRAFT: Chipmunk T.10

CODE MARKINGS: Two digit white codes on the cowling from '80'.

10 AEF

BASE: UK Woodvale
ROLE: Air Experience Flight
AIRCRAFT: Chipmunk T.10

CODE MARKINGS: Two digit white codes on the cowling from '10'.

11 AEF

BASE: UK Leeming
ROLE: Air Experience Flight
AIRCRAFT: Chipmunk T.10

CODE MARKINGS: Two digit white codes on the cowling from '80'.

12 AEF

BASE: UK Edinburgh
ROLE: Air Experience Flight
AIRCRAFT: Chipmunk T.10

CODE MARKINGS: None

13 AEF

BASE: UK Belfast-Sydenham
ROLE: Air Experience Flight
AIRCRAFT: Bulldog T.1

CODE MARKINGS: Single aircraft; code 'E'

BASE:
ROLE:
AIRCRAFT:

CODE MARKINGS:

RED

GOLD

YELLOW

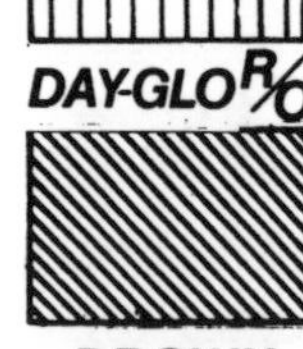
DAY-GLO R/O

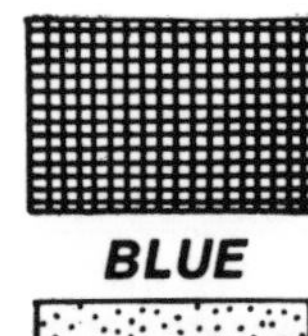
BLUE

PALE BLUE

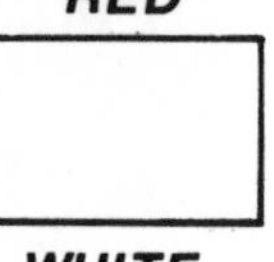
WHITE

BLACK

PURPLE

BROWN

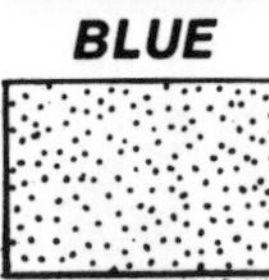
GREY

GREEN

CGS

BASE: Syerston
ROLE: Central Gliding School
AIRCRAFT: Venture T.1, T.2; Cadet TX.3; Grasshopper TX.1; Prefect TX.1; Swallow; Sedbergh TX.1; Sky.
CODE MARKINGS: Letter codes from 'A'.

BASE: Swanton Morley
ROLE: Central Gliding School det.
AIRCRAFT: Gliders detached from CGS

CODE MARKINGS: None

AIR CADETS GS

The Air Experience Flights and the Central Gliding School are controlled by H.Q. Air Cadets at RAF Newton, as are the following Gliding Schools:

611 GS	Swanton Morley
613 GS	Halton (det. at Benson)
614 GS	Debden
615 GS	Kenley
616 GS	Henlow
617 GS	Manston
618 GS	West Malling
621 GS	Weston-super-Mare
622 GS	Upavon
624 GS	Chivenor
625 GS	South Cerney
626 GS	Predannack
631 GS	Sealand
632 GS	Ternhill
633 GS	Cosford
634 GS	St.Athan
635 GS	Burtonwood
636 GS	Swansea
637 GS	Little Rissington
642 GS	Linton-on-Ouse
643 GS	Lindholme
644 GS	Syerston
645 GS	Catterick
661 GS	Kirknewton
662 GS	Arbroath
663 GS	Kinloss

A mixture of types is used by each school, usually consisting of Sedbergh TX.1's and Cadet TX.3's in varying quantities, although a few also use the Prefect TX.1, Grasshopper TX.1 and, in increasing numbers, the Venture T.2. The Grasshopper is also used by a number of Combined Cadet Forces, single examples being located at various public schools in the U.K.

CODE MARKINGS: Occasionally used by some units.

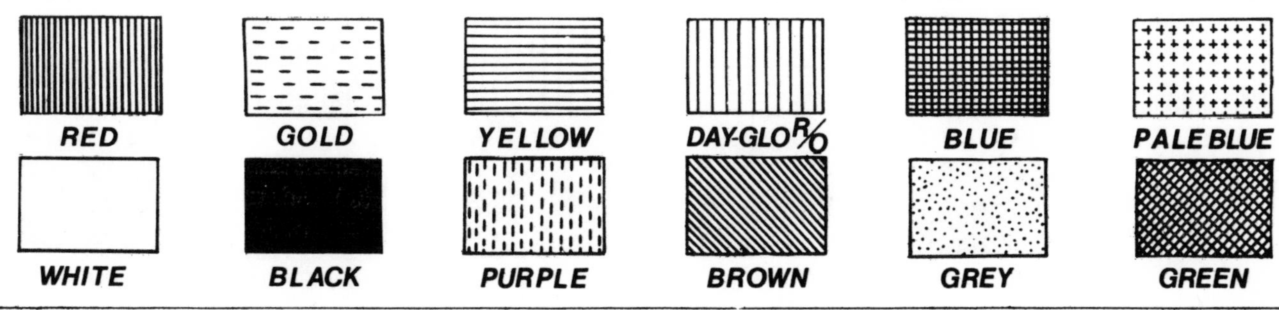

A & AEE

BASE: UK Boscombe Down
ROLE: Aeroplane and Armament Experimental Establishment
AIRCRAFT: Various, under 'A' Squadron (high-performance fighters/trainers), 'B' Squadron (bombers & maritime a/c), 'D' Squadron (helicopters) and 'E' Squadron (transport & communications a/c).
CODE MARKINGS: None

ETPS

BASE: UK Boscombe Down
ROLE: Empire Test Pilots School
AIRCRAFT: Various (fixed and rotary winged)
CODE MARKINGS: None

IAM

BASE: UK Farnborough
ROLE: Institute of Aviation Medicine
AIRCRAFT: Hunter T.7
CODE MARKINGS: None

RAE

BASE: UK Bedford, Farnborough (HQ), Larkhill, Llanbedr, West Freugh.
ROLE: Royal Aircraft Establishment
AIRCRAFT: Various. Farnborough research fleet operated by 'A' and 'C' Flights while Transport Flight operates comms. a/c and (autonomous) Met. Research Flight operates a Canberra PR.3 and Hercules W.2. The only permanent fin-codes are worn by the Transport Flight Devon C.2's ('J' to 'M', last letter of r/t c/s MPDXJ-M).

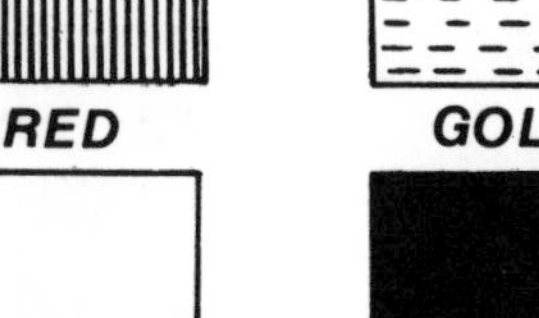
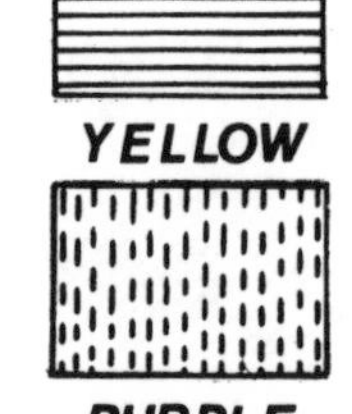

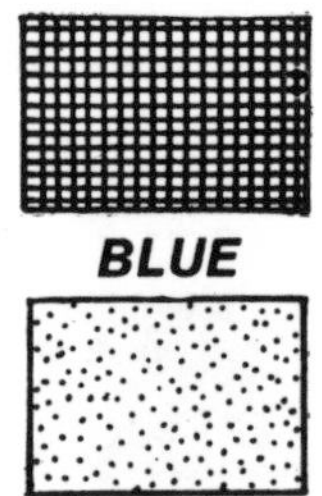

RED GOLD YELLOW DAY-GLO R/O BLUE PALE BLUE
WHITE BLACK PURPLE BROWN GREY GREEN

FLEET AIR ARM SQUADRON & UNIT MARKINGS

NOTES ON SHIP & AIRCRAFT MARKINGS

In addition to warships and auxiliaries etc, Fleet Air Arm air stations are also referred to as 'ships'. On ships, the deck letters are painted in large white characters on the flight deck or landing platform. By tradition, aircraft carriers have a single letter and all other 'ships' (ashore and afloat) have two.

Airfield deck letters are located in the Air Traffic Control Signals Square for daytime airfield identification. They are also flashed out in Morse Code on the airfield red pundit light for night-time airfield identification. Most Fleet Air Arm aircraft carry a deck letter (or letters) on the fin which denotes their operational base.

Aircraft code numbers are worn in a conspicuous position on the airframe. In addition, the 'last two' digits are carried in numerous other positions so that the aircraft can be identified from any angle. This is for a number of reasons, the main one being that each aircraft can be easily picked out in the crowded confines of a ship's hangar or flight deck. Easy identification is essential for parking or manoeuvring aircraft with folded wings or rotors especially in a restricted hangar area or a flight deck in bad weather.

Fleet Air Arm aircraft codes themselves have been a little confused over the last few years due to the overall reduction in numbers of operational aircraft. The current system was introduced in June/July 1965. The original main blocks were '000 - 399' for carriers; '400 - 499' for smaller ships and '500 - 999' for shore bases. Each of these bases has its own allocation within the main block which is further sub-divided for individual Squadron use. The system still holds good today although odd quirks sometimes arise.

Digits '8' and '9' are not used for aircraft operating at sea, being permanently restricted to shore-based aircraft. There have been, and still are, exceptions to this eg 824 Squadron's Sea Kings which make occasional sea deployments. 824 is however, essentially a shore-based Squadron and therefore in this case the rule can still be said to be applicable.

Commando units use letter codes to identify their aircraft.

As far as Fleet Air Arm Squadrons are concerned, 800-series squadron numbers indicate a front-line operational role: 700-series numbers signify a second-line training or support role. It should also be noted that some 700-series Squadrons also carry out a front-line task (eg 702 Naval Air Squadron with Lynx HAS.2's both shore-based (training) and ship-based (operational)). In addition to the 800 and 700 - series Squadrons, there are currently two RNR (Air Branch) Squadrons in the 1800 - series. Their role is to provide flying training for reserve aircrew officers so that they can augment the aircrews on rotary and fixed-wing Squadrons in time of war or periods of tension.

additional notes: *On the following pages, aircraft marked with an asterisk thus '*' represent proposed aircraft types.*

SHIPS CAPABLE OF OPERATING AIRCRAFT

SHIP	PENNANT NO.	DECK LETTER/S	A/C CODE/S	TYPE OF AIRCRAFT
ANTI-SUBMARINE/COMMANDO CARRIER : "HERMES" & "BULWARK" CLASSES				
HMS HERMES	R12	H	250 - 254	Sea King HAS.2/2A* Sea Harrier FRS.1* Wessex HU.5 *
HMS BULWARK	R08	B	140 - 143 264 - 274 VA - VS	Sea King HAS.2/2A Sea King HAS.2/2A Wessex HU.5/SK HC.4
ANTI-SUBMARINE CRUISER : "INVINCIBLE CLASS"				
HMS INVINCIBLE	R05	N		Sea Harrier FRS.1* Sea King HAS.2/2A* Wessex HU.5 *
HMS ILLUSTRIOUS	R06	L		Sea Harrier FRS.1* Sea King HAS.2/5 * Wessex HU.5 *
HMS ARK ROYAL	R07	R		Sea Harrier FRS.1* Sea King HAS.2/5 * Wessex HU.5 *
These vessels have a secondary role as Commando Carriers and can be expected to carry Wessex HU.5's and Sea King HC.4's when employed on these duties.				
HELICOPTER CRUISER : "TIGER CLASS"				
HMS TIGER	C20	TG		
HMS BLAKE	C99	BL		
ASSAULT SHIP : "FEARLESS CLASS"				
HMS FEARLESS	L10	FS		
HMS INTREPID	L11	ID		
DESTROYER : TYPE 82 "BRISTOL CLASS"				
HMS BRISTOL	D23	BS	334	
DESTROYER : "COUNTY CLASS"				
HMS GLAMORGAN	D19	GL	400	Wessex HAS.3
HMS KENT	D12	KE	401	Wessex HAS.3
HMS FIFE	D20	FF	404	Wessex HAS.3
HMS LONDON	D16	LO	405	Wessex HAS.3
HMS ANTRIM	D18	AN	406	Wessex HAS.3
HMS NORFOLK	D21	NF	407	Wessex HAS.3
DESTROYER : TYPE 42 "SHEFFIELD CLASS"				
HMS BIRMINGHAM	D86	BM	333	Lynx HAS.2
HMS CARDIFF	D108	CF	335	Lynx HAS.2
HMS COVENTRY	D118	CV	336	Lynx HAS.2
HMS SHEFFIELD	D80	SD	337	Lynx HAS.2
HMS GLASGOW	D88	GW	344	Lynx HAS.2
HMS NEWCASTLE	D87	NC	345	Lynx HAS.2
HMS YORK	D98			Lynx HAS.2 *

SHIP	PENNANT NO.	DECK LETTER/S	A/C CODE/S	TYPE OF AIRCRAFT
HMS EXETER	D89			Lynx HAS.2 *
HMS SOUTHAMPTON	D90			Lynx HAS.2 *
HMS NOTTINGHAM	D91			Lynx HAS.2 *
HMS LIVERPOOL	D92			Lynx HAS.2 *
HMS MANCHESTER	D95			Lynx HAS.2 *
HMS GLOUCESTER	D96			Lynx HAS.2 *
HMS EDINBURGH	D97			Lynx HAS.2 *
FRIGATE : TYPE 21 "AMAZON CLASS"				
HMS AMAZON	F169	AZ	320	Lynx HAS.2
HMS ANTELOPE	F170	AO	321	Lynx HAS.2
HMS ACTIVE	F171	AV	322	Wasp HAS.1
				Lynx HAS.2 *
HMS AMBUSCADE	F172	AB	323	Wasp HAS.1
				Lynx HAS.2 *
HMS ARROW	F173	AW	326	Lynx HAS.2
HMS ALACRITY	F174	AL	327	Lynx HAS.2
HMS ARDENT	F184	AD	340	Lynx HAS.2
HMS AVENGER	F185	AG	341	Lynx HAS.2
FRIGATE : TYPE 22 "BROADSWORD CLASS"				
HMS BROADSWORD	F88	BW	346	Lynx HAS.2
HMS BATTLEAXE	F89	BX	479	Lynx HAS.2 *
HMS BRILLIANT	F90			Lynx HAS.2 *
HMS BRAZEN	F91			Lynx HAS.2 *
HMS BOXER	F92			Lynx HAS.2 *
HMS BEAVER	F93			Lynx HAS.2 *
HMS				Lynx HAS.2 *
HMS				Lynx HAS.2 *
HMS				Lynx HAS.2 *
FRIGATE : "LEANDER CLASS" : (EXOCET Surface-to-Surface Missile conversion)				
HMS MINERVA	F45	MV	424	Lynx HAS.2
HMS SIRIUS	F40	SS	450	Lynx HAS.2
HMS PENELOPE	F127	PE	454	
HMS CLEOPATRA	F28	CP	463	Lynx HAS.2
HMS DANAE	F47	DN	464	Lynx HAS.2
HMS JUNO	F52	JO	465	Wasp HAS.1
				Lynx HAS.2 *
HMS ARGONAUT	F56	AT	466	Lynx HAS.2
HMS PHOEBE	F42	PB	471	Lynx HAS.2
FRIGATE : "LEANDER CLASS" : (Broad-beamed version)				
HMS DIOMEDE	F16	DM	423	Wasp HAS.1
				Lynx HAS.2 *
HMS BACCHANTE	F69	BC	425	Wasp HAS.1
				Lynx HAS.2 *
HMS ACHILLES	F12	AC	430	Wasp HAS.1
				Lynx HAS.2 *
HMS CHARYBDIS	F75	CS	431	Wasp HAS.1
				Lynx HAS.2 *
HMS SCYLLA	F71	SC	432	Wasp HAS.1
				Lynx HAS.2 *
HMS JUPITER	F60	JP	443	Wasp HAS.1
				Lynx HAS.2 *

SHIP	PENNANT NO.	DECK LETTER/S	A/C CODE/S	TYPE OF AIRCRAFT
HMS ARIADNE	F72	AE	455	Wasp HAS.1 Lynx HAS.2 *
HMS APOLLO	F70	AP	470	Wasp HAS.1 Lynx HAS.2 *
HMS ANDROMEDA	F57	AM	472	Wasp HAS.1 Lynx HAS.2 *
HMS HERMIONE	F58	HM	475	Wasp HAS.1 Lynx HAS.2 *
FRIGATE : "LEANDER CLASS" : (IKARA Anti-Submarine Missile conversion)				
HMS NAIAD	F39	NA	324	Wasp HAS.1 Lynx HAS.2 *
HMS AJAX	F114	AJ	421	Wasp HAS.1 Lynx HAS.2 *
HMS AURORA	F10	AU	422	Wasp HAS.1 Lynx HAS.2 *
HMS ARETHUSA	F38	AR	426	Wasp HAS.1 Lynx HAS.2 *
HMS EURYALUS	F15	EU	433	Wasp HAS.1 Lynx HAS.2 *
HMS GALATEA	F18	GA	461	Wasp HAS.1 Lynx HAS.2 *
HMS DIDO	F104	DO	473	Wasp HAS.1 Lynx HAS.2 *
HMS LEANDER	F109	LE	476	Wasp HAS.1 Lynx HAS.2 *
FRIGATE : TYPE 81 "TRIBAL CLASS"				
HMS ASHANTI	F117	AS	427	Wasp HAS.1
HMS ZULU	F124	ZU	442	
HMS GURKHA	F122	GU	444	
HMS ESKIMO	F119	ES	453	Wasp HAS.1
HMS NUBIAN	F131	NU	457	
HMS MOHAWK	F125	MO	474	
HMS TARTAR	F133	TA	477	Wasp HAS.1
FRIGATE : TYPE 12 "ROTHESAY CLASS"				
HMS BERWICK	F115	BK	440	Wasp HAS.1
HMS FALMOUTH	F113	FM	441	
HMS PLYMOUTH	F126	PL	445	Wasp HAS.1
HMS RHYL	F129	RL	446	Wasp HAS.1
HMS LONDONDERRY	F108	LD	447	
HMS LOWESTOFT	F103	LT	451	Wasp HAS.1
HMS BRIGHTON	F106	BR	452	Wasp HAS.1
HMS YARMOUTH	F101	YM	456	Wasp HAS.1
HMS ROTHESAY	F107	RO	462	Wasp HAS.1
SURVEY VESSEL : "HECLA CLASS"				
HMS HERALD	A138	HE	325	Wasp HAS.1
HMS HECATE	A137	HT	414	Wasp HAS.1
HMS HYDRA	A144	HD	415	Wasp HAS.1
HMS HECLA	A133	HL	416	Wasp HAS.1
ICE PATROL VESSEL				

SHIP	PENNANT NO.	DECK LETTER/S	A/C CODE/S	TYPE OF AIRCRAFT
HMS ENDURANCE	A171	ED	434 - 435	Wasp HAS.1
FLEET TANKER : "OL CLASS"				
RFA OLWEN RFA OLNA RFA OLMEDA	A122 A123 A124	OW ON OD	347 347 347	Wessex HU.5 and/or Wasp HAS.1
FLEET TANKER : "TIDE CLASS"				
RFA TIDEPOOL RFA TIDESPRING	A76 A75	TP TS	332 347	Wasp HAS.1 and/or Wessex HU.5
FLEET TANKER : "ROVER CLASS"				
RFA GREEN ROVER RFA GREY ROVER RFA BLUE ROVER RFA GOLD ROVER RFA BLACK ROVER	A268 A269 A270 A271 A273	GN GY BE GV BV		
STORES SUPPORT SHIP : "NESS CLASS"				
RFA LYNESS RFA STROMNESS RFA TARBATNESS	A339 A344 A345	LY ST TB		
STORES SUPPORT SHIP : "FORT CLASS"				
RFA FORT AUSTIN RFA FORT GRANGE	A386 A385	FA FG	342 not 343 used	Sea King HAS.2/2A Sea King HAS.2/2A
STORES SUPPORT SHIP : "REGENT CLASS"				
RFA REGENT RFA RESOURCE	A486 A480	RG RS	436 437	Wessex HU.5 Wessex HU.5
LOGISTIC LANDING SHIP : "SIR LANCELOT CLASS"				
RFA SIR BEDIVERE RFA SIR GALAHAD RFA SIR GERAINT RFA SIR LANCELOT RFA SIR PERCIVAL RFA SIR TRISTRAM	L3004 L3005 L3027 L3029 L3036 L3505	BD GD GR LN PV TM		
ROYAL NAVAL AIR STATIONS & AIR YARDS				
HMS GANNET (Prestwick Airport)		PW	301 - 307 310	Sea King HAS.2/2A Sea King HAS.2/2A
HMS OSPREY (RNAS Portland)		PO	500 - 507 510 - 517 614 - 617 634 - 636 650 - 657 660 - 666	Wasp HAS.1 Wessex HU.5 Wasp HAS.1 Wasp HAS.1 Wessex HAS.3 Wessex HAS.3

SHIP	PENNANT NO.	DECK LETTER/S	A/C CODE/S	TYPE OF AIRCRAFT
HMS SEAHAWK (RNAS Culdrose)		CU	520 - 530	Wessex HU.5
			531 - 538	Sea King HAS.2/2A
			540 - 559	Gazelle HT.2
			560 - 573	Jetstream T.2
			579	Chipmunk T.10
			580 - 598	Sea King HAS.2/2A
			599	Devon C.2
HMS HERON (RNAS Yeovilton)		VL	100 - 105	Sea Harrier FRS.1
				Harrier T.4 *
				Hunter T.8M *
			478, 480	Lynx HAS.2
			709	Heron C.4
			710	Sea Devon C.20
			738 - 739	Chipmunk T.10
			740 - 751	Lynx HAS.2
			830 - 838	Hunter GA.11
			840 - 848	Canberra TT.18
			850 - 856	Canberra T.22
			858 - 859	Canberra T.4
			860 - 868	Hunter GA.11
			870 - 879	Hunter T.8C
			RN	Wessex HU.5
			WM - WZ	Wessex HU.5
			YC - YU	Wessex HU.5
				Sea King HC.4 *
				Sea King HC.4 *
HMS DAEDALUS (RNAS Lee on Solent)		LS	810 - 813	Wessex HU.5
			814	Chipmunk T.10
			815 - 818	Wessex HU.5
			819 - 820	Sea Devon C.20
			821 - 823	Sea Heron C.1
			824	Sea Devon C.20
			825	Sea Heron C.1
			826 - 829	Sea Devon C.20
				Wasp HAS.1
	P236, P237		RF, RJ	Winchester Mk.2
	P238		EX	Winchester Mk.6
	P235		RW	Wellington
	P234			VT.2
BRNC DARTMOUTH (Britannia Royal) (Naval College) (Helicopter Flt.)		DM	895	Wasp HAS.1
(Britannia Royal) (Naval College) (Fixed Wing Flt.) (Roborough)			901 - 912	Chipmunk T.10
RNAY FLEETLANDS		FL		Gazelle HT.2
RNAY WROUGHTON		WU		

800 SQUADRON

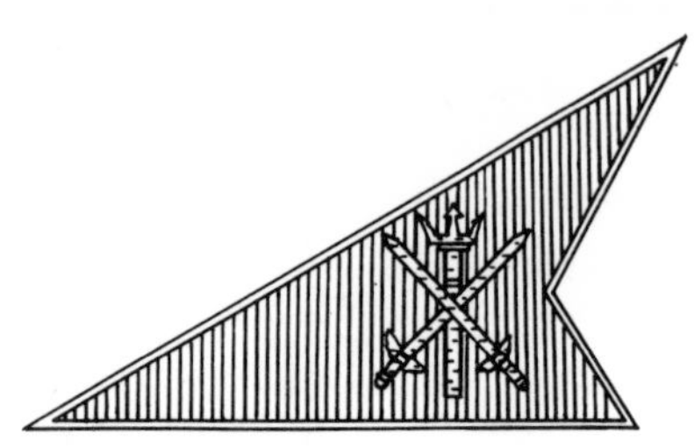

BASE: HMS Hermes
ROLE: Fighter Reconnaissance & Strike
AIRCRAFT: Sea Harrier FRS.1

CODE MARKINGS: In white: deck letter 'H' (on fin) & codes in range '250-254'.

801 SQUADRON

BASE: HMS Invincible
ROLE: Fighter Reconnaissance & Strike
AIRCRAFT: Sea Harrier FRS.1

CODE MARKINGS: In white: deck letter 'N' (on fin).

802 SQUADRON

BASE: HMS Illustrious
ROLE: Fighter Reconnaissance & Strike
AIRCRAFT: Sea Harrier FRS.1

CODE MARKINGS: In white: deck letter 'L' (on fin).

814 SQUADRON

BASE: HMS Bulwark
ROLE: Anti-Submarine Warfare
AIRCRAFT: Sea King HAS.2, HAS.2A

CODE MARKINGS: In white: deck letter 'B' (on fin) & codes in range '264-274'

819 SQUADRON

BASE: UK Prestwick (HMS Gannet)
ROLE: Anti-Submarine Warfare/SAR
AIRCRAFT: Sea King HAS.2, HAS.2A

CODE MARKINGS: In white: deck letters 'PW' (on fin) & codes in range '301-310'

820 SQUADRON

BASE: UK RNAS Culdrose/HMS Invincible
ROLE: Anti-Submarine Warfare
AIRCRAFT: Sea King HAS.2, HAS.2A

CODE MARKINGS: In white: deck letters 'N' (on fin) & codes in range '410-413'

RED
GOLD
YELLOW

DAY-GLO R/O
BLUE
PALE BLUE

WHITE

BLACK

PURPLE

BROWN
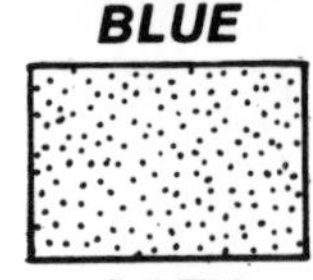
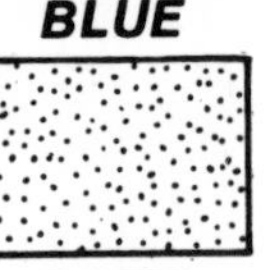
GREY

GREEN

824 SQUADRON

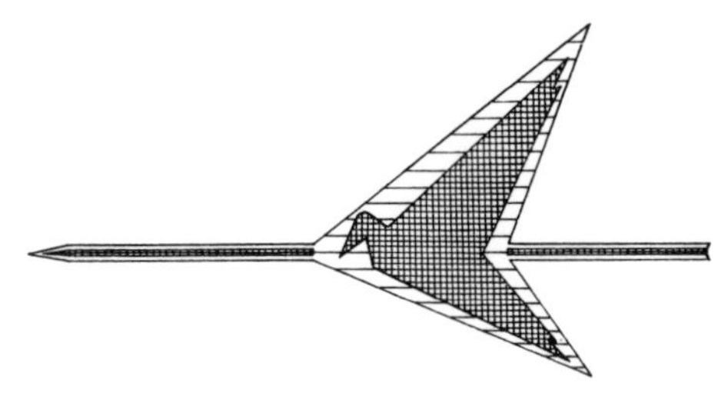

BASE: UK RNAS Culdrose (HMS Seahawk)
ROLE: ASW: RFA Flts & augment ASW Sqdns
AIRCRAFT: Sea King HAS.2, HAS.2A

CODE MARKINGS: In white: deck letters 'CU' (on fin) & codes in range '531-538'

826 SQUADRON

BASE: HMS Bulwark
ROLE: Anti-Submarine Warfare
AIRCRAFT: Sea King HAS.2, HAS.2A

CODE MARKINGS: In white: deck letter 'B' (on fin) & codes in range '140-143'

829 SQUADRON

BASE: UK Portland(HQ) & Ships' Flights
ROLE: ASW and Survey Ship Support
AIRCRAFT: Wasp HAS.1
CODE MARKINGS: In white: some Flights (not HQ) carry deck letters; code ranges '614-617'(HQ) & '322-325':'414-477'(Flts)

845 SQUADRON

BASE: UK RNAS Yeovilton (HMS Heron)
ROLE: Commando & Amphibious Forces Support
AIRCRAFT: Wessex HU.5
CODE MARKINGS: In black: deck letters 'VL' (on fin) & code letters in range '(Y)C-(Y)U'. Prefix (Y) not carried

846 SQUADRON

BASE: HMS Bulwark
ROLE: Commando & Amphibious Forces Support
AIRCRAFT: Wessex HU.5, Sea King HC.4
CODE MARKINGS: In white: deck letter 'B' (on fin) & code letters spell out 'THE POLAR CUBS'. Prefix 'V' is carried

899 SQUADRON

BASE: UK RNAS Yeovilton (HMS Heron)
ROLE: Fighter Reconnaissance & Strike
AIRCRAFT: Sea Harrier FRS.1, Harrier T.4, Hunter T.8M
CODE MARKINGS: In white: deck letters 'VL' (on fin) & codes in range '100-105'

RED

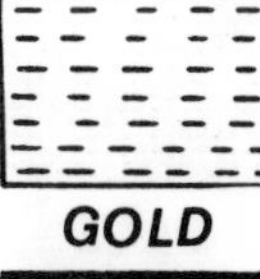
GOLD

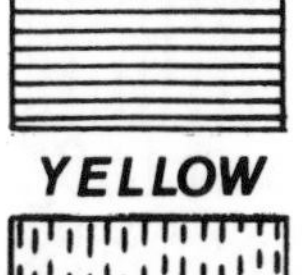
YELLOW

DAY-GLO R/O

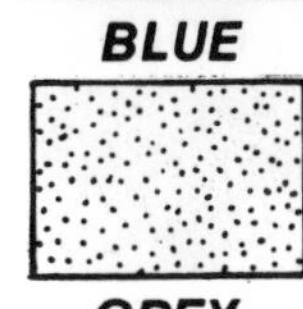
BLUE

PALE BLUE

WHITE

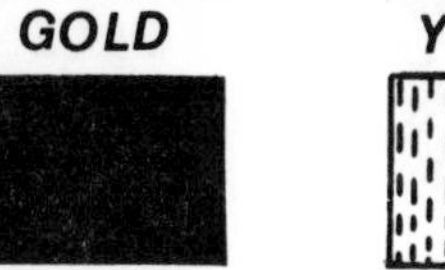
BLACK

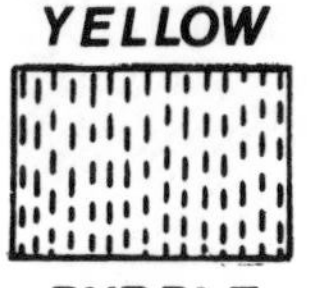
PURPLE

BROWN

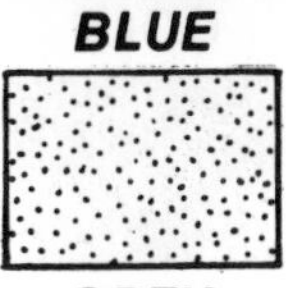
GREY

GREEN

702 SQUADRON

BASE: UK Yeovilton(HQ) & Ships' Flights
ROLE: Anti-Sub/Surface & HQ Training
AIRCRAFT: Lynx HAS.2
CODE MARKINGS: In white: deck letters eg 'VL' (on fin) & codes in ranges '740-751'(HQ); '320-346:424-480'(Ships' Flts)

703 SQUADRON

BASE: UK RNAS Portland (HMS Osprey)
ROLE: ASW Aircrew & Maintainer Training
AIRCRAFT: Wasp HAS.1

CODE MARKINGS: In white: no deck letters Codes in range '500-507:634-636'

705 SQUADRON

BASE: UK RNAS Culdrose (HMS Seahawk)
ROLE: Pilot Training/'SHARKS' Aero. Team
AIRCRAFT: Gazelle HT.2
CODE MARKINGS: In white: deck letters 'CU' (on fin). In black: codes in range '(5)40-(5)59'. Prefix (5) not carried

706 SQUADRON

BASE: UK RNAS Culdrose (HMS Seahawk)
ROLE: ASW Aircrew & Maintainer Training
AIRCRAFT: Sea King HAS.2, 2A (2 HAR.3 with Sqdn for RAF Continuation Training)
CODE MARKINGS: In white: deck letters 'CU' (on fin) & codes in range '580-598'

707 SQUADRON

BASE: UK RNAS Yeovilton (HMS Heron)
ROLE: Commando Helicopter A&OFT & RNPT
AIRCRAFT: Wessex HU.5
CODE MARKINGS: In white: deck letters 'VL' (on fin) & letter codes in range 'WM-WZ' plus RNPT code 'RN'

737 SQUADRON

BASE: UK Portland(HQ) & Ships' Flights
ROLE: ASW & A&OASW Obs/Aircrewman Trng.
AIRCRAFT: Wessex HAS.3
CODE MARKINGS: In white: deck letters eg 'PO' (on fin) & codes in ranges '650-666'(HQ); '400-407'(Ships' Flights)

RED

GOLD
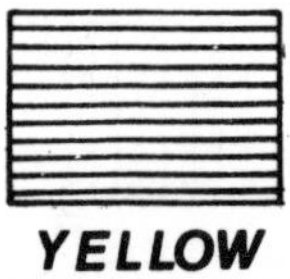
YELLOW

DAY-GLO R/O
BLUE
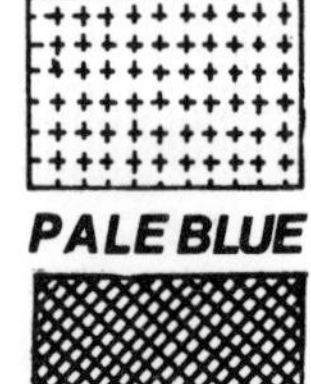
PALE BLUE

WHITE

BLACK
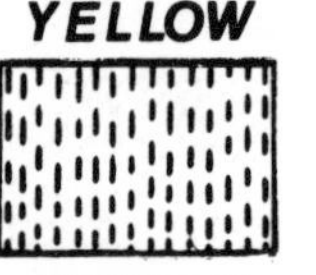
PURPLE

BROWN
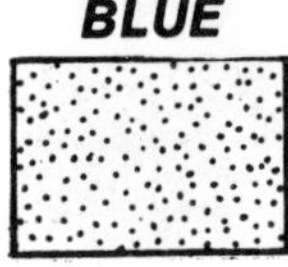
GREY
GREEN

750 SQUADRON

BASE: UK RNAS Culdrose (HMS Seahawk)
ROLE: Obs & Comms Aircrewman(FW) Trng.
AIRCRAFT: Jetstream T.2

CODE MARKINGS: In black: deck letters 'CU' (on fin) & codes in range '560-573'

771 SQUADRON

BASE: UK RNAS Culdrose (HMS Seahawk)
ROLE: SAR Aircrewman & OFT Training
AIRCRAFT: Wessex HU.5

CODE MARKINGS: In white: deck letters 'CU' (on fin) & codes in range '520-530'

772 SQUADRON

BASE: UK Portland(HQ) & RFA Flights
ROLE: SAR; Fleet Requirements & Support
AIRCRAFT: Wessex HU.5
CODE MARKINGS: In white: deck letters eg 'PO' (on fin) & codes in ranges '510-517'(HQ);'332, 347, 436-437'(Ships' Flts)

781 SQUADRON

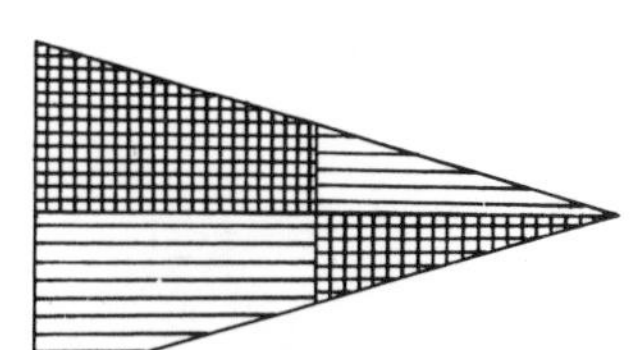

Fishery Protection Pennant worn by S/Devons

BASE: UK Lee-on-Solent (HMS Daedalus)
ROLE: Communications & Fishery Protection
AIRCRAFT: Sea Heron C.1, Sea Devon C.20, Chipmunk T.10, Wessex HU.5, Wasp HAS.1
CODE MARKINGS: Deck letters 'LS' on Chipmunk only. Callsigns '814-829'

1831 RNR SQUADRON

BASE: UK Lee-on-Solent (HMS Daedalus)
ROLE: Reserve Aircrew Re-familiarisation
AIRCRAFT: None; Chipmunk T.10 and Wasp HAS.1 of 781 Sqdn RNR Flight used.
CODE MARKINGS:

1832 RNR SQUADRON

BASE: UK
ROLE: Reserve Aircrew Type Familiarisation

None; aircrew train with current FAA rotary & fixed wing Sqdns.

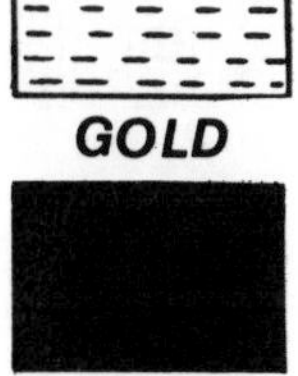
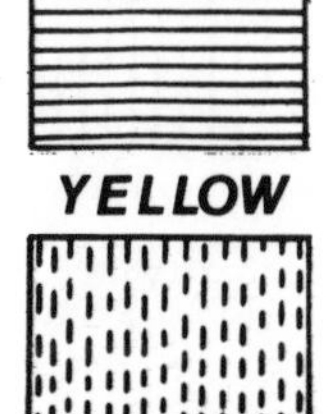

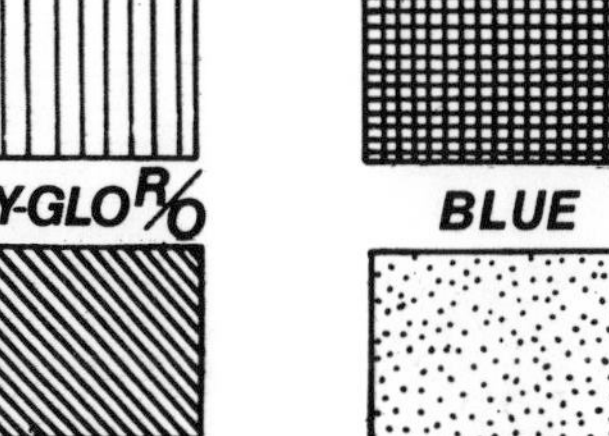

RED **GOLD** **YELLOW** **DAY-GLO R/O** **BLUE** **PALE BLUE**

WHITE **BLACK** **PURPLE** **BROWN** **GREY** **GREEN**

FRADU

BASE: UK RNAS Yeovilton (HMS Heron)
ROLE: Fleet Requirements & Air Direction
AIRCRAFT: Hunter GA.11, T.8C (Unit Canberra T.4, TT.18, T.22
CODE MARKINGS: In black or white: 'VL' on fin of some Hunters; codes '830-879'

BRNC

BASE: UK BRNC Dartmouth & Roborough
ROLE: Rotary & FW Air Experience Flying
AIRCRAFT: Wasp HAS.1, Chipmunk T.10
CODE MARKINGS: No deck letters worn. White: code '(8)95' on Wasp (prefix(8) not worn) Black: Chipmunk codes '901-912'

NAVAL HOVERCRAFT TRIALS UNIT

BASE: UK Lee-on-Solent (HMS Daedalus)
ROLE: Mine Counter-measures Trials
AIRCRAFT: SR.N6 Winchester Mk.2, Mk.6 BH.7 Wellington, VT.2
CODE MARKINGS: In black or white: no deck letters; codes 'RF','RJ','EX','RW'

FLEET TARGET GROUP

BASE: UK Portland(HQ) & RFA Detachments
ROLE: Pilotless drone aircraft & boats
AIRCRAFT: Shelduck D.1, Chukar D.2 Also operates Seaflash boats
CODE MARKINGS: None carried

FLEET AIR ARM HISTORIC FLIGHT

BASE: UK RNAS Yeovilton (HMS Heron) & *RNAS Culdrose (HMS Seahawk)
ROLE: The Flight is parented by 'Heron Flight' (ie Yeovilton Station Flight) and the aircraft are displayed at Air Days and Air Displays etc, to publicise the FAA.
AIRCRAFT: T8191, BB814 Tiger Moth T.2's, EZ407 Harvard T.3 (to be restored to (flying condition); LS326 '5A' Swordfish 2; TF956 'T/123' Sea Fury FB.11; WB271 'R/204' Firefly AS.6; WG655 'GN/910' Sea Fury T.20; *WV908 'A/188' Sea Hawk FGA.6

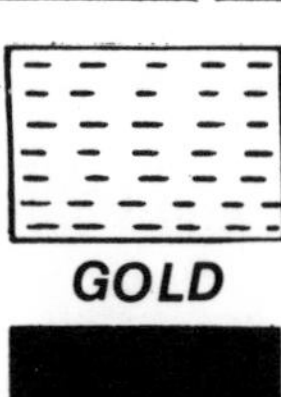

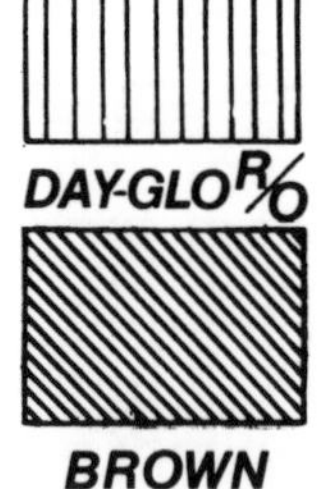
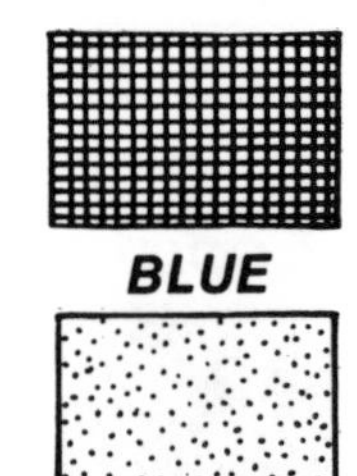
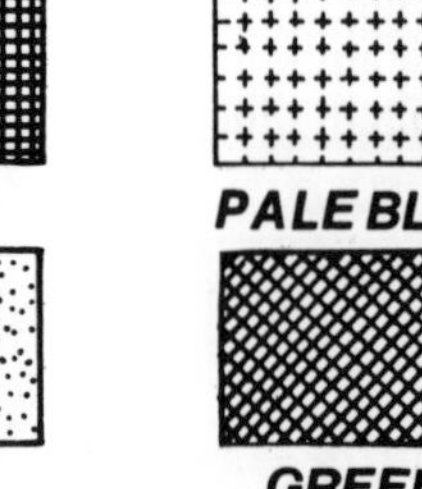

RED GOLD YELLOW DAY-GLO R/O BLUE PALE BLUE

WHITE BLACK PURPLE BROWN GREY GREEN

ARMY AIR CORPS SQUADRON & UNIT MARKINGS

651 SQUADRON

BASE: W.Germany Hildesheim
ROLE: Anti-tank/Utility, 1 Regt AAC
AIRCRAFT: Lynx AH.1, Scout AH.1

CODE MARKINGS: None

661 SQUADRON

BASE: W.Germany Hildesheim
ROLE: Observation/Liaison, 1 Regt AAC
AIRCRAFT: Gazelle AH.1

CODE MARKINGS: None

652 SQUADRON

BASE: W.Germany Bunde
ROLE: Anti-tank/Utility, 2 Regt AAC
AIRCRAFT: Lynx AH.1, Scout AH.1

CODE MARKINGS: None

662 SQUADRON

BASE: W.Germany Munster
ROLE: Observation/Liaison, 2 Regt AAC
AIRCRAFT: Gazelle AH.1

CODE MARKINGS: None

653 SQUADRON

BASE: W.Germany Soest
ROLE: Anti-tank/Utility, 3 Regt AAC
AIRCRAFT: Lynx AH.1, Scout AH.1

CODE MARKINGS: None

663 SQUADRON

BASE: W.Germany Soest
ROLE: Observation/Liaison, 3 Regt AAC
AIRCRAFT: Gazelle AH.1

CODE MARKINGS: None

RED GOLD YELLOW DAY-GLO R/O BLUE PALE BLUE

WHITE BLACK PURPLE BROWN GREY GREEN

654 SQUADRON

BASE: W.Germany Detmold
ROLE: Anti-tank/Utility, 4 Regt AAC
AIRCRAFT: Lynx AH.1, Scout AH.1

CODE MARKINGS: None

664 SQUADRON

BASE: W.Germany Minden
ROLE: Observation/Liaison, 4 Regt AAC
AIRCRAFT: Gazelle AH.1

CODE MARKINGS: None

659 SQUADRON

BASE: W.Germany Detmold
ROLE: Anti-tank/Utility, 9 Regt AAC
AIRCRAFT: Lynx AH.1, Scout AH.1

CODE MARKINGS: None

669 SQUADRON

BASE: W.Germany Detmold
ROLE: Observation/Liaison, 9 Regt AAC
AIRCRAFT: Gazelle AH.1

CODE MARKINGS: None

655 SQUADRON

BASE: UK Topcliffe
ROLE: Anti-tank/Utility/Observation/ Liaison, 5 Field Force
AIRCRAFT: Scout AH.1, Gazelle AH.1
CODE MARKINGS: None

656 SQUADRON

BASE: UK Farnborough
ROLE: Anti-tank/Utility/Observation/ Liaison, 6 Field Force
AIRCRAFT: Scout AH.1, Gazelle AH.1
CODE MARKINGS: None

RED GOLD YELLOW DAY-GLO R/O BLUE PALE BLUE
WHITE BLACK PURPLE BROWN GREY GREEN

657 SQUADRON

BASE: UK Oakington
ROLE: Anti-tank/Utility/Observation/Liaison, 7 Field Force
AIRCRAFT: Scout AH.1, Gazelle AH.1
CODE MARKINGS: None

658 SQUADRON

BASE: UK Netheravon
ROLE: Anti-tank/Utility/Observation/Liaison, 7 Regiment
AIRCRAFT: Scout AH.1, Gazelle AH.1
CODE MARKINGS: None

660 SQUADRON

BASE: Hong Kong Sek Kong (& Brunei)
ROLE: Utility/Liaison
AIRCRAFT: Scout AH.1

CODE MARKINGS: None

SQUADRON

BASE:
ROLE:
AIRCRAFT:

CODE MARKINGS:

3 CBAS

BASE: UK Coypool (Brunei, Dieppe, Kangow and Salerno Flights), Arbroath (Montfortebeek Flight)
ROLE: Utility
AIRCRAFT: Scout AH.1 (Brunei Flight), Gazelle AH.1 (all other Flights)
CODE MARKINGS: Single letter fin-code in white

RED
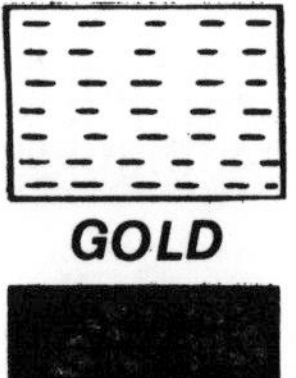
GOLD
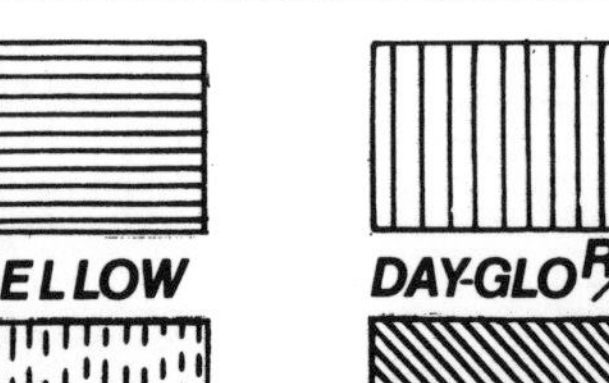
YELLOW
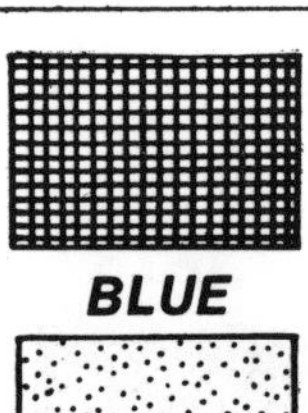
DAY-GLO R/O
BLUE
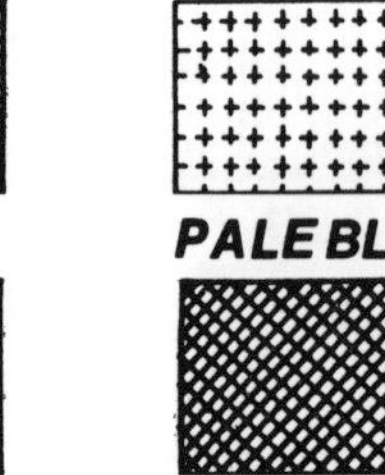
PALE BLUE
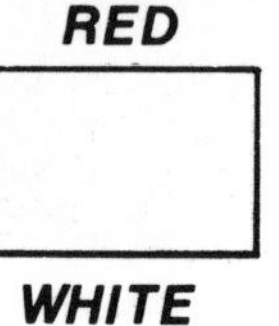
WHITE
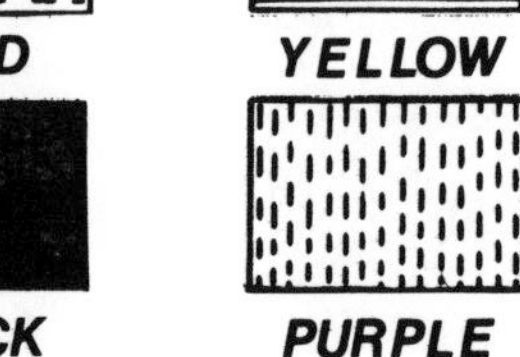
BLACK
PURPLE

BROWN
GREY
GREEN

2 FLIGHT

BASE: UK Netheravon
ROLE: Utility/Liaison
AIRCRAFT: Gazelle AH.1

CODE MARKINGS: None

3 FLIGHT

BASE: UK Omagh (N.Ireland)
ROLE: Observation/Liaison
AIRCRAFT: Gazelle AH.1

CODE MARKINGS: None

7 FLIGHT

BASE: W.Germany Berlin-Gatow
ROLE: Observation/Liaison
AIRCRAFT: Gazelle AH.1

CODE MARKINGS: None, although a large Union Jack is carried on the underside.

12 FLIGHT

BASE: W.Germany Wildenrath
ROLE: Liaison/Communications
AIRCRAFT: Gazelle AH.1

CODE MARKINGS: None

16 FLIGHT

BASE: Cyprus Dhekelia
ROLE: Utility/Liaison
AIRCRAFT: Alouette AH.2

CODE MARKINGS: None

UNFICYP FLIGHT

BASE: Cyprus Nicosia
ROLE: Utility/Observation/Liaison
AIRCRAFT: Alouette AH.2

CODE MARKINGS: None

RED
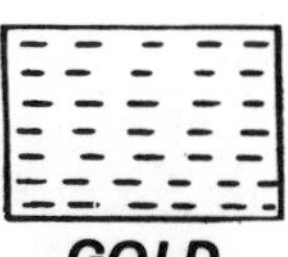
GOLD

YELLOW

DAY-GLO R/O
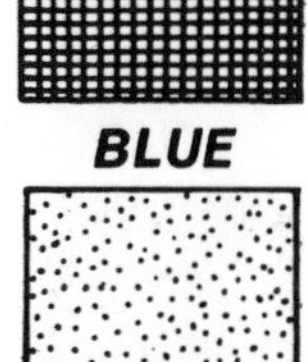
BLUE

PALE BLUE

WHITE
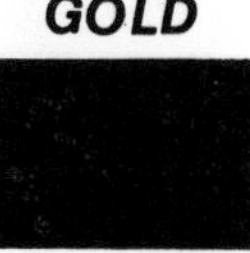
BLACK
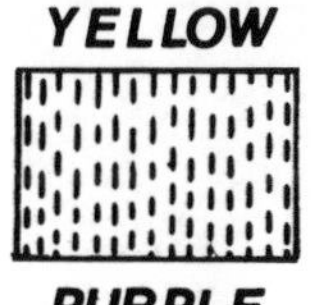
PURPLE
BROWN

GREY
GREEN

BATUS

BASE: Canada Suffield
ROLE: Training camp
AIRCRAFT: Beaver AL.1 (and helicopters detached from B.A.O.R. squadrons)
CODE MARKINGS: None

BEAVER FLT.

BASE: UK Belfast-Aldergrove
ROLE: Utility/Observation
AIRCRAFT: Beaver AL.1

CODE MARKINGS: None (although each has a different coloured spinner)

ARWS

BASE: UK Middle Wallop
ROLE: Training
AIRCRAFT: Gazelle AH.1

CODE MARKINGS: Black letter codes on dayglo panel.

ARW/LYNX CONV. FLT.

BASE: UK Middle Wallop
ROLE: Training
AIRCRAFT: Lynx AH.1

CODE MARKINGS: Black letter codes

ARW/SCOUT CONV. FLT.

BASE: UK Middle Wallop
ROLE: Training
AIRCRAFT: Scout AH.1

CODE MARKINGS: Black letter codes on dayglo panel.

BFWF

BASE: UK Middle Wallop
ROLE: Training
AIRCRAFT: Auster AOP.9, Chipmunk T.10

CODE MARKINGS: Single letter black fin-codes from 'A' (Chipmunk only).

RED GOLD YELLOW DAY-GLO R/O BLUE PALE BLUE
WHITE BLACK PURPLE BROWN GREY GREEN

BEAVER TRAINING FLIGHT	**D&T SQUADRON**
BASE: UK Middle Wallop **ROLE:** Training **AIRCRAFT:** Beaver AL.1 **CODE MARKINGS:** None	**BASE:** UK Middle Wallop **ROLE:** Evaluation/Trials/Demonstration **AIRCRAFT:** Gazelle AH.1, Lynx AH.1, Scout AH.1, Sioux AH.1, Skeeter AOP.12 **CODE MARKINGS:** None
AIRCREWMAN TRAINING FLT	**SQUADRON**
BASE: UK Middle Wallop **ROLE:** Training **AIRCRAFT:** Scout AH.1 **CODE MARKINGS:** None	**BASE:** **ROLE:** **AIRCRAFT:** **CODE MARKINGS:**
SQUADRON	**SQUADRON**
BASE: **ROLE:** **AIRCRAFT:** **CODE MARKINGS:**	**BASE:** **ROLE:** **AIRCRAFT:** **CODE MARKINGS:**

RED GOLD YELLOW DAY-GLO R/O BLUE PALE BLUE

WHITE BLACK PURPLE BROWN GREY GREEN

ADDITIONS & AMENDMENTS

SQUADRON	SQUADRON
BASE: ROLE: AIRCRAFT: CODE MARKINGS:	BASE: ROLE: AIRCRAFT: CODE MARKINGS:
SQUADRON	SQUADRON
BASE: ROLE: AIRCRAFT: CODE MARKINGS:	BASE: ROLE: AIRCRAFT: CODE MARKINGS:
BASE: ROLE: AIRCRAFT: CODE MARKINGS:	BASE: ROLE: AIRCRAFT: CODE MARKINGS:

RED GOLD YELLOW DAY-GLO R/O BLUE PALE BLUE

WHITE BLACK PURPLE BROWN GREY GREEN

SERIAL ALLOCATIONS XA100 - ZA999

XA100-XA172

serial	type	sqdn/unit	code	where&when seen	remarks

Initial contract for 53 Sea Vampire T.22 trainers for the RN built by de Havilland Aircraft Co Ltd at Christchurch. They were allotted the following c/ns: 15130-15131 15200-15223, 15404-15409, 15410-15413 & 15498-15514 respectively. They were delivered between 5.53 & 11.54. Some later transfers to Australia and sales to Chile.

serial	type	sqdn/unit	code	where&when seen	remarks
XA100	Sea Vampire T.22				
XA101	Sea Vampire T.22				To RAN Pr Camden NSW
XA102	Sea Vampire T.22				Used by INS 1960-61
XA103	Sea Vampire T.22				
XA104	Sea Vampire T.22				
XA105	Sea Vampire T.22				
XA106	Sea Vampire T.22				
XA107	Sea Vampire T.22				To ChAF 11.72
XA108	Sea Vampire T.22				
XA109	Sea Vampire T.22				Pr East Fortune
XA110	Sea Vampire T.22				
XA111	Sea Vampire T.22				
XA112	Sea Vampire T.22				
XA113	Sea Vampire T.22				
XA114	Sea Vampire T.22				
XA115	Sea Vampire T.22				
XA116	Sea Vampire T.22				
XA117	Sea Vampire T.22				
XA118	Sea Vampire T.22				
XA119	Sea Vampire T.22				
XA120	Sea Vampire T.22				
XA121	Sea Vampire T.22				
XA122	Sea Vampire T.22				
XA123	Sea Vampire T.22				
XA124	Sea Vampire T.22				
XA125	Sea Vampire T.22				
XA126	Sea Vampire T.22				
XA127	Sea Vampire T.22				Nose Pr FAAM
XA128	Sea Vampire T.22				To ChAF 11.72
XA129	Sea Vampire T.22				To FAAM
XA130	Sea Vampire T.22				
XA131	Sea Vampire T.22				
XA152	Sea Vampire T.22				
XA153	Sea Vampire T.22				
XA154	Sea Vampire T.22				
XA155	Sea Vampire T.22				
XA156	Sea Vampire T.22				
XA157	Sea Vampire T.22				
XA158	Sea Vampire T.22				
XA159	Sea Vampire T.22				
XA160	Sea Vampire T.22				
XA161	Sea Vampire T.22				
XA162	Sea Vampire T.22				
XA163	Sea Vampire T.22				
XA164	Sea Vampire T.22				
XA165	Sea Vampire T.22				To 8148M
XA166	Sea Vampire T.22				To ChAF 11.72
XA167	Sea Vampire T.22				To RAN
XA168	Sea Vampire T.22				
XA169	Sea Vampire T.22				
XA170	Sea Vampire T.22				
XA171	Sea Vampire T.22				
XA172	Sea Vampire T.22				

XA177-XA235

One Auster B.4 prototype built by Auster Aircraft Ltd at Rearsby in 1951 with the c/n 2983 and first-flown on 7.9.51 as G-25-2, later G-AMKL. Subsequently allotted military markings for evaluation at A&AEE Boscombe Down during 1952/53.

serial	type	sqdn/unit	code	where&when seen		remarks
XA177	Auster B.4					Ex G-AMKL/G-25-2

Two prototype Supermarine 545's developed from the Swift fighter to Spec F.105D2. Construction of XA181 took place at the Company's Hursley Park facility and was structurally complete when the programme was cancelled in 1955. Two developments were envisaged; a Mach 1.3 version and a Mach 2 version. XA186 was not built.

serial	type	sqdn/unit	code	where&when seen		remarks
XA181	Supermarine 545					To GI Cranfield
XA186	Supermarine 545					

Two Avro Yorks allotted military marks following a temporary trooping contract issued to Eagle Aviation Ltd. XA191 c/n 1356, ex G-AMGK; XA192 c/n 1215, ex G-AGNM.

serial	type	sqdn/unit	code	where&when seen		remarks
XA191	York 1					Restored to G-AMGK
XA192	York 1					Restored to G-AGNM

Initial batch of wing-controlled aerodynes built by Vickers-Armstrongs Ltd at Weybridge for use in the development of variable-geometric designs. The first successful launch of the radio-controlled model took place at Thurleigh on 19.1.50, but the aircraft crashed soon after leaving the launching trolley, due to 'pilot error'.

serial	type	sqdn/unit	code	where&when seen		remarks
XA197	Wild Goose					
XA198	Wild Goose					
XA199	Wild Goose					
XA200	Wild Goose					
XA201	Wild Goose					
XA202	Wild Goose					

XA203-XA204 Wild Goose (2 a/c) Cancelled and not built

Three Seamew AS.1 prototypes (c/ns SH1606-1608) built by Short Bros and Harland Ltd at Belfast to Spec M123D (later M123D&P - development and production). XA209 first flown on 13.8.53; XA216 not flown and retained at manufacturers for ground tests.

serial	type	sqdn/unit	code	where&when seen		remarks
XA209	Seamew AS.1					
XA213	Seamew AS.1					
XA216	Seamew AS.1					Structural Test Rig

Three Bristol Sycamore HR.50's (c/ns 13063-13065) built for direct transfer to RAN.

serial	type	sqdn/unit	code	where&when seen		remarks
XA219	Sycamore HR.50					To RAN
XA220	Sycamore HR.50					To RAN GI Sydney
XA221	Sycamore HR.50					To RAN

2nd production order for 20 Type 38 Grasshopper TX.1's built by Slingsby Sailplanes Ltd at Kirkbymoorside against Contract 7585 to follow WZ832. Allotted c/ns 858-877.

serial	type	sqdn/unit	code	where&when seen		remarks
XA225	Grasshopper TX.1					
XA226	Grasshopper TX.1					
XA227	Grasshopper TX.1					
XA228	Grasshopper TX.1					
XA229	Grasshopper TX.1					
XA230	Grasshopper TX.1					
XA231	Grasshopper TX.1					
XA232	Grasshopper TX.1					
XA233	Grasshopper TX.1					
XA234	Grasshopper TX.1					
XA235	Grasshopper TX.1					

XA236-XA292

serial	type	sqdn/unit	code	where&when seen		remarks
XA236	Grasshopper TX.1					
XA237	Grasshopper TX.1					
XA238	Grasshopper TX.1					
XA239	Grasshopper TX.1					
XA240	Grasshopper TX.1					
XA241	Grasshopper TX.1					
XA242	Grasshopper TX.1					
XA243	Grasshopper TX.1					
XA244	Grasshopper TX.1					

28 unsold Handley-Page Marathons diverted ex-storage to the RAF against Contract 8228 for use as navigational trainers. two others (G-AMHY/MHZ) were earmarked for RAF use as XA277/278 but were ntu, later being sold in Japan as JA6009/6010 resp. The oft used designation T.11 is wrong. C/ns were 101-111/113-126/131/132/135-137 resp.

serial	type	sqdn/unit	code	where&when seen		remarks
XA249	Marathon T.1					Ex G-ALUB
XA250	Marathon T.1					Ex G-ALVW
XA251	Marathon T.1					Ex G-ALVX
XA252	Marathon T.1					Ex G-ALVY
XA253	Marathon T.1					Ex G-ALXR
XA254	Marathon T.1					Ex G-AMAX
XA255	Marathon T.1					Ex G-AMAY To 7465M
XA256	Marathon T.1					Ex G-AMDH
XA257	Marathon T.1					Ex G-AMEK
XA258	Marathon T.1					Ex G-AMEL
XA259	Marathon T.1					Ex G-AMEM
XA260	Marathon T.1					Ex G-AMEP
XA261	Marathon T.1					Ex G-AMER To G-AMER
XA262	Marathon T.1					Ex G-AMET
XA263	Marathon T.1					Ex G-AMEU
XA264	Marathon T.1					Ex G-AMEV
XA265	Marathon T.1					Ex G-AMEW To G-AMEW
XA266	Marathon T.1					Ex G-AMGN
XA267	Marathon T.1					Ex G-AMGO
XA268	Marathon T.1					Ex G-AMGP
XA269	Marathon T.1					Ex G-AMGR
XA270	Marathon T.1					Ex G-AMGS
XA271	Marathon T.1					Ex G-AMGT
XA272	Marathon T.1					Ex G-AMGU
XA273	Marathon T.1					Ex G-AMGV
XA274	Marathon T.1					Ex G-AMHT To G-AMHT
XA275	Marathon T.1					Ex G-AMHU
XA276	Marathon T.1					Ex G-AMHX
XA277	Marathon T.1					ntu To JA6009
XA278	Marathon T.1					ntu To JA6010

2nd production order for 32 Type 31B Cadet TX.3 gliders built by Slingsby Sailplanes Ltd at Kirkbymoorside against Contract 6023 to follow WT919. Deliveries made to ATC units between June 1952 and March 1953. Allotted c/ns 824-855 incl.

serial	type	sqdn/unit	code	where&when seen		remarks
XA282	Cadet TX.3					
XA283	Cadet TX.3					
XA284	Cadet TX.3					
XA285	Cadet TX.3					
XA286	Cadet TX.3					
XA287	Cadet TX.3					
XA288	Cadet TX.3					
XA289	Cadet TX.3					
XA290	Cadet TX.3					
XA291	Cadet TX.3					
XA292	Cadet TX.3					

XA293-XA344

serial	type	sqdn/unit	code	where&when seen		remarks
XA293	Cadet TX.3					
XA294	Cadet TX.3					
XA295	Cadet TX.3					
XA296	Cadet TX.3					
XA297	Cadet TX.3					
XA298	Cadet TX.3					
XA299	Cadet TX.3					
XA300	Cadet TX.3					
XA301	Cadet TX.3					
XA302	Cadet TX.3					
XA303	Cadet TX.3					
XA304	Cadet TX.3					
XA305	Cadet TX.3					
XA306	Cadet TX.3					
XA307	Cadet TX.3					
XA308	Cadet TX.3					
XA309	Cadet TX.3					
XA310	Cadet TX.3					
XA311	Cadet TX.3					
XA312	Cadet TX.3					
XA313	Cadet TX.3					

2nd production order for 116 Gannet AS.1/4 anti-submarine aircraft and 24 T.2 training aircraft for the RN to follow on from WN464. Built by Fairey Aviation Ltd at Hayes (H) and Stockport (S). The final T.2 (XA531) was cancelled and replaced on contract by AS.1 XD898 (q.v.). Many diversions to RAN (including XA333 AS.1 which was later converted to T.2) and subsequent RN conversions of AS.4 to COD.4 and ECM.6 for Courier Onboard Delivery and Electronic Countermeasure roles respectively. Initial delivery configuration as follows:

AS.1	XA319-364/387-409/434/436	(71 a/c)	c/ns F.9211-9279/9304/9306
AS.4	XA410-433/435/454-473	(45 a/c)	c/ns F.9280-9303/9305/9307-9326
T.2	XA508-530	(23 a/c)	c/ns F.9328-9350

serial	type		sqdn/unit	code	where&when seen		remarks
XA319	Gannet AS.1	(H)					
XA320	Gannet AS.1	(S)					
XA321	Gannet AS.1	(S)					
XA322	Gannet AS.1	(S)					
XA323	Gannet AS.1	(S)					
XA324	Gannet AS.1	(H)					
XA325	Gannet AS.1	(H)					
XA326	Gannet AS.1	(H)					To RAN
XA327	Gannet AS.1	(H)					To RAN
XA328	Gannet AS.1	(H)					To RAN
XA329	Gannet AS.1	(H)					To RAN
XA330	Gannet AS.1	(H)					To RAN
XA331	Gannet AS.1	(H)					To RAN
XA332	Gannet AS.1	(H)					To RAN
XA333	Gannet T.2	(H)					To RAN
XA334	Gannet AS.1	(H)					To RAN Pr Camden NSW
XA335	Gannet AS.1	(H)					
XA336	Gannet AS.1	(S)					
XA337	Gannet AS.1	(S)					
XA338	Gannet AS.1	(S)					
XA339	Gannet AS.1	(S)					Parts to AS-05 - AS-11
XA340	Gannet AS.1	(H)					
XA341	Gannet AS.1	(H)					
XA342	Gannet AS.1	(H)					To A2471
XA343	Gannet AS.1	(H)					To RAN
XA344	Gannet AS.1	(S)					

XA345-XA424

serial	type		sqdn/unit	code	where&when seen		remarks
XA345	Gannet AS.1	(S)					
XA346	Gannet AS.1	(S)					
XA347	Gannet AS.1	(S)					
XA348	Gannet AS.1	(S)					Parts to AS-05 - AS-11
XA349	Gannet AS.1	(H)					
XA350	Gannet AS.1	(H)					To RAN
XA351	Gannet AS.1	(H)					To RAN
XA352	Gannet AS.1	(S)					
XA353	Gannet AS.1	(S)					
XA354	Gannet AS.1	(S)					
XA355	Gannet AS.1	(S)					
XA356	Gannet AS.1	(H)					To RAN
XA357	Gannet AS.1	(H)					
XA358	Gannet AS.1	(H)					
XA359	Gannet AS.1	(H)					To RAN
XA360	Gannet AS.1	(S)					
XA361	Gannet AS.1	(S)					Parts to AS-05 - AS-11
XA362	Gannet AS.1	(S)					
XA363	Gannet AS.1	(S)					To A2528
XA364	Gannet AS.1	(S)					
XA387	Gannet AS.1	(H)					
XA388	Gannet AS.1	(H)					
XA389	Gannet AS.1	(H)					To RAN
XA390	Gannet AS.1	(S)					
XA391	Gannet AS.1	(S)					
XA392	Gannet AS.1	(S)					
XA393	Gannet AS.1	(S)					
XA394	Gannet AS.1	(S)					
XA395	Gannet AS.1	(S)					
XA396	Gannet AS.1	(S)					
XA397	Gannet AS.1	(S)					To ANGK LAUT AS-03
XA398	Gannet AS.1	(S)					To ANGK LAUT AS-02
XA399	Gannet AS.1	(H)					
XA400	Gannet AS.1	(H)					
XA401	Gannet AS.1	(H)					
XA402	Gannet AS.1	(H)					
XA403	Gannet AS.1	(H)					To RAN
XA404	Gannet AS.1	(H)					
XA405	Gannet AS.1	(H)					
XA406	Gannet AS.1	(S)					
XA407	Gannet AS.1	(S)					
XA408	Gannet AS.1	(H)					
XA409	Gannet AS.1	(H)					To ANGK LAUT AS-01
XA410	Gannet AS.4	(S)					
XA411	Gannet AS.4	(S)					
XA412	Gannet AS.4	(H)					
XA413	Gannet AS.4	(H)					
XA414	Gannet ECM.6	(S)					
XA415	Gannet AS.4	(S)					
XA416	Gannet AS.4	(S)					
XA417	Gannet AS.4	(S)					
XA418	Gannet AS.4	(S)					
XA419	Gannet AS.4	(H)					
XA420	Gannet AS.4	(S)					
XA421	Gannet AS.4	(S)					
XA422	Gannet AS.4	(S)					
XA423	Gannet AS.4	(S)					
XA424	Gannet AS.4	(S)					

XA425-XA531

serial	type		sqdn/unit	code	where&when seen		remarks
XA425	Gannet AS.4	(S)					
XA426	Gannet AS.4	(S)					
XA427	Gannet AS.4	(H)					
XA428	Gannet AS.4	(S)					
XA429	Gannet AS.4	(H)					
XA430	Gannet COD.4	(S)					
XA431	Gannet AS.4	(S)					
XA432	Gannet AS.4	(S)					
XA433	Gannet AS.4	(S)					
XA434	Gannet AS.1	(H)					To RAN Pr Nowra NSW
XA435	Gannet AS.4	(S)					
XA436	Gannet AS.1	(H)					To RAN
XA454	Gannet COD.4	(S)					
XA455	Gannet AS.4	(S)					
XA456	Gannet AS.4	(S)					To A2533
XA457	Gannet AS.4	(S)					
XA458	Gannet AS.4	(S)					
XA459	Gannet ECM.6	(S)					To A2608 Pr Rhoose
XA460	Gannet ECM.6	(H)					To GI Connah's Quay
XA461	Gannet AS.4	(S)					
XA462	Gannet AS.4	(S)					
XA463	Gannet AS.4	(H)					
XA464	Gannet AS.4	(S)					
XA465	Gannet AS.4	(S)					
XA466	Gannet COD.4	(S)					To FAAM
XA467	Gannet AS.4	(S)					
XA468	Gannet AS.4	(S)					
XA469	Gannet AS.4	(S)					
XA470	Gannet COD.4	(H)					
XA471	Gannet AS.4	(H)					
XA472	Gannet AS.6	(S)					
XA473	Gannet AS.4	(S)					
XA508	Gannet T.2	(H)					To A2472 Pr FAAM
XA509	Gannet T.2	(H)					
XA510	Gannet T.2	(H)					
XA511	Gannet T.2	(H)					
XA512	Gannet T.2	(H)					
XA513	Gannet T.2	(H)					
XA514	Gannet T.2	(H)					To RAN
XA515	Gannet T.2	(H)					
XA516	Gannet T.2	(H)					
XA517	Gannet T.2	(H)					To RAN
XA518	Gannet T.2	(H)					
XA519	Gannet T.2	(H)					
XA520	Gannet T.2	(H)					
XA521	Gannet T.2	(H)					
XA522	Gannet T.2	(H)					
XA523	Gannet T.2	(H)					To A2459
XA524	Gannet T.2	(H)					
XA525	Gannet T.2	(H)					
XA526	Gannet T.2	(H)					
XA527	Gannet T.2	(H)					
XA528	Gannet T.2	(H)					
XA529	Gannet T.2	(H)					
XA530	Gannet T.2	(H)					

XA531 Gannet T.2 (1 a/c) Cancelled and not built (see XD898)

XA536-XA622

serial	type	sqdn/unit	code	where&when seen		remarks

One Canberra B.2 built by English Electric Co Ltd at Preston as a replacement for WD991 (which had crashed prior to delivery). Delivered in 4.53, it was subsequently converted by the manufacturer to T.11 and later T.19 standard.

serial	type	sqdn/unit	code	where&when seen		remarks
XA536	Canberra T.19					To 8605M

Prototype Sea Venom FAW.21 originally designated NF.21 prior to general designation changes. Built by de Havilland Aircraft Co Ltd at Christchurch and f/f 21.5.54. All production aircraft serialled in WM/WW/XG blocks for delivery to RN.

serial	type	sqdn/unit	code	where&when seen		remarks
XA539	Sea Venom FAW.21					

The main production order for 200 Javelin all-weather fighters was placed against Contract 6/Aircraft/8336 dated 14.7.52 and accounted for five variants, built by the Gloster Aircraft Co Ltd at Hucclecote, and by Sir W.G.Armstrong Whitworth Aircraft Ltd at Coventry as follows:

XA544-572/618-628	FAW.1	(40 a/c)	Gloster Aircraft	Dels.	7.54- 3.56
XA629-640/644	FAW.4	(13 a/c)	Gloster Aircraft	Dels.	9.55- 1.57
XA641-643/645-661	FAW.5	(20 a/c)	Gloster Aircraft	Dels.	9.56-10.57
XA662-667/688-719	FAW.5	(38 a/c)	Armstrong-Whitworth	Dels.	5.57- 8.57
XA720-737/749-762	FAW.4	(32 a/c)	Armstrong-Whitworth	Dels.	6.56- 4.57
XA763-767	FAW.4	(5 a/c)	Gloster Aircraft	Dels.	10.56- 2.57
XA768-781/799-814	FAW.2	(30 a/c)	Gloster Aircraft	Dels.	5.56-11.57
XA815-836	FAW.6	(22 a/c)	Gloster Aircraft	Dels.	9.57- 2.58

serial	type	sqdn/unit	code	where&when seen		remarks
XA544	Javelin FAW.1					To 7558M
XA545	Javelin FAW.1					
XA546	Javelin FAW.1					
XA547	Javelin FAW.1					
XA548	Javelin FAW.1					
XA549	Javelin FAW.1					To 7717M Pr Swinderby
XA550	Javelin FAW.1					To 7484M
XA551	Javelin FAW.1					To 7586M
XA552	Javelin FAW.1					
XA553	Javelin FAW.1					To 7470M Pr Stanmore
XA554	Javelin FAW.1					To 7662M
XA555	Javelin FAW.1					
XA556	Javelin FAW.1					
XA557	Javelin FAW.1					
XA558	Javelin FAW.1					
XA559	Javelin FAW.1					
XA560	Javelin FAW.1					To 7619M
XA561	Javelin FAW.1					
XA562	Javelin FAW.1					
XA563	Javelin FAW.1					To 7627M
XA564	Javelin FAW.1					To 7464M Pr Cosford
XA565	Javelin FAW.1					
XA566	Javelin FAW.1					
XA567	Javelin FAW.1					To 7551M
XA568	Javelin FAW.1					
XA569	Javelin FAW.1					
XA570	Javelin FAW.1					
XA571	Javelin FAW.1					To 7663M
XA572	Javelin FAW.1					
XA618	Javelin FAW.1					
XA619	Javelin FAW.1					
XA620	Javelin FAW.1					To 7667M ntu To 7723M
XA621	Javelin FAW.1					
XA622	Javelin FAW.1					

XA623-XA700

serial	type	sqdn/unit	code	where&when seen		remarks
XA623	Javelin FAW.1					
XA624	Javelin FAW.1					To 7664M ntu
XA625	Javelin FAW.1					
XA626	Javelin FAW.1					To 7666M
XA627	Javelin FAW.1					To 7661M
XA628	Javelin FAW.1					To 7665M ntu To 7720M
XA629	Javelin FAW.4					
XA630	Javelin FAW.4					
XA631	Javelin FAW.4					
XA632	Javelin FAW.4					
XA633	Javelin FAW.4					
XA634	Javelin FAW.4					To 7641M Pr Leeming
XA635	Javelin FAW.4					
XA636	Javelin FAW.4					
XA637	Javelin FAW.4					
XA638	Javelin FAW.4					
XA639	Javelin FAW.4					See XH764
XA640	Javelin FAW.4					
XA641	Javelin FAW.5					
XA642	Javelin FAW.5					
XA643	Javelin FAW.5					
XA644	Javelin FAW.4					
XA645	Javelin FAW.5					
XA646	Javelin FAW.5					
XA647	Javelin FAW.5					
XA648	Javelin FAW.5					
XA649	Javelin FAW.5					
XA650	Javelin FAW.5					
XA651	Javelin FAW.5					
XA652	Javelin FAW.5					
XA653	Javelin FAW.5					
XA654	Javelin FAW.5					
XA655	Javelin FAW.5					
XA656	Javelin FAW.5					
XA657	Javelin FAW.5					
XA658	Javelin FAW.5					
XA659	Javelin FAW.5					
XA660	Javelin FAW.5					
XA661	Javelin FAW.5					
XA662	Javelin FAW.5					
XA663	Javelin FAW.5					
XA664	Javelin FAW.5					
XA665	Javelin FAW.5					
XA666	Javelin FAW.5					
XA667	Javelin FAW.5					
XA688	Javelin FAW.5					
XA689	Javelin FAW.5					
XA690	Javelin FAW.5					
XA691	Javelin FAW.5					
XA692	Javelin FAW.5					
XA693	Javelin FAW.5					
XA694	Javelin FAW.5					
XA695	Javelin FAW.5					
XA696	Javelin FAW.5					
XA697	Javelin FAW.5					
XA698	Javelin FAW.5					
XA699	Javelin FAW.5					To 7809M
XA700	Javelin FAW.5					

XA701-XA769

serial	type	sqdn/unit	code	where&when seen		remarks
XA701	Javelin FAW.5					To 7765M
XA702	Javelin FAW.5					
XA703	Javelin FAW.5					
XA704	Javelin FAW.5					
XA705	Javelin FAW.5					
XA706	Javelin FAW.5					To 7649M
XA707	Javelin FAW.5					
XA708	Javelin FAW.5					
XA709	Javelin FAW.5					
XA710	Javelin FAW.5					
XA711	Javelin FAW.5					
XA712	Javelin FAW.5					
XA713	Javelin FAW.5					
XA714	Javelin FAW.5					
XA715	Javelin FAW.5					
XA716	Javelin FAW.5					
XA717	Javelin FAW.5					
XA718	Javelin FAW.5					
XA719	Javelin FAW.5					
XA720	Javelin FAW.4					
XA721	Javelin FAW.4					
XA722	Javelin FAW.4					
XA723	Javelin FAW.4					
XA724	Javelin FAW.4					
XA725	Javelin FAW.4					
XA726	Javelin FAW.4					
XA727	Javelin FAW.4					To 7744M ntu
XA728	Javelin FAW.4					
XA729	Javelin FAW.4					
XA730	Javelin FAW.4					
XA731	Javelin FAW.4					
XA732	Javelin FAW.4					
XA733	Javelin FAW.4					
XA734	Javelin FAW.4					
XA735	Javelin FAW.4					
XA736	Javelin FAW.4					
XA737	Javelin FAW.4					
XA749	Javelin FAW.4					
XA750	Javelin FAW.4					
XA751	Javelin FAW.4					
XA752	Javelin FAW.4					
XA753	Javelin FAW.4					
XA754	Javelin FAW.4					
XA755	Javelin FAW.4					To 7725M
XA756	Javelin FAW.4					
XA757	Javelin FAW.4					
XA758	Javelin FAW.4					
XA759	Javelin FAW.4					
XA760	Javelin FAW.4					
XA761	Javelin FAW.4					
XA762	Javelin FAW.4					
XA763	Javelin FAW.4					
XA764	Javelin FAW.4					
XA765	Javelin FAW.4					
XA766	Javelin FAW.4					
XA767	Javelin FAW.4					
XA768	Javelin FAW.2					
XA769	Javelin FAW.2					

'XA101' 'NW/805' Vampire T.22, preserved at RANAS Nowra, Australia 25.11.76. The true XA101 is preserved some 50 miles away at Camden, NSW and this example is believed to be XG770. (T.E. Stone)

XA110 'HF/599' Sea Vampire T.22, 750 Sqdn, at Hal Far, Malta during 10.64. (Flamingo).

XA177 Auster B.4 at A&AEE Boscombe Down 24.8.52. Ex G-25-2, it was evaluated at Boscombe Down during 1952/53 before becoming G-AMKL. (Crown)

XA181 Supermarine 545 prototype in use at the College of Aeronautics, Cranfield during 4.62 as an instructional airframe. As can be seen, the aircraft was all but completed when the project was cancelled in 1955. (D.A. Rough)

XA273/C Marathon T.1, 1 ANS, at Greenham Common during 5.56. (Flamingo)

XA293 Cadet TX.3, Central Gliding School, at Syerston 13.8.79. The old colour scheme of silver and dayglo contrasts sharply with the later red and white as worn by XN253 in the background. (R.A. Walker)

XA466 'LM/777' Gannet COD.4 of 849 Sqdn 'HQ' Flt at Lossiemouth in an unusual COD.4 colour scheme ie extra dark sea grey/sky and red/blue roundels. *(Crown)*

XA847 P.1B, RAE, at Farnborough in 1971 with a modified fin. The nose has also been altered to incorporate a ground-running intake specifically designed to prevent ingestion of foreign objects. *(P.J. Cooper)*

XA876 Sky, Central Gliding School, at Syerston in mid 1979. The Aircraft is painted in a red and white colour scheme. *(CGS)*

XA880 Devon C.2, RAE Llanbedr, at Upper Heyford 27.7.78 resplendent in the MoD (PE) colour scheme of red/white/blue. *(P. Dawe)*

XA913 Vulcan B.1, 101 Sqdn, at Finningley 15.9.62. The all-over white colour scheme with pale blue/red markings was worn to reflect the heat of any nuclear flash. *(I. MacFarlane)*

XA918 Victor B.1, with its undercarriage and airbrakes extended; probably at one of the type's first Farnborough Air Shows. *(via R.A. Walker)*

XA948 Wild Goose aerodynamic research model on a rocket-powered tracked trolley at Predannack in the early 1950's. Note the extra large serial presentation on the predominantly white fuselage. (via E.B. Morgan)

XB252 Dragonfly HR.4, date and location unknown. The type pioneered the casualty evacuation role in the RAF with 194 Sqdn in Malaya and this particular example served with that unit from 2.53. (via E. Myall)

XB265/A Beverley C.1, Abingdon Transport Wing (47 and 53 Sqdns), at Middleton St George 13.10.62. The Abingdon coat of arms is worn on the nose. (I. MacFarlane)

XB318 a straight TBM-3E Avenger of 824 Sqdn forming part of a line-up of the unit's aircraft in 11.53 whilst based at Lee-on-Solent. (FAA Museum)

XB446 '992' Avenger ECM.6B, Stn Flt, at Culdrose in 7.66. The RN's last airworthy Avenger, it was being retained for the Fleet Air Arm Museum. (R. Ward)

XD145, first prototype SR.53 landing at Farnborough and showing to advantage its clean lines enhanced by the all-white colour scheme. (British Hovercraft Corporation)

XD239 '613' Scimitar F.1, 736 Sqdn at Wethersfield 19.5.62. The unit marking on the fin consists of a blue lightning flash on a white background. Note the Sidewinder air-to-air missiles on the underwing pylons. (I. MacFarlane)

XD366/16 Varsity T.1, CFS, date and location unknown. This aircraft was a replacement for an earlier machine sold to Sweden. Note the CFS marking on the nose, the unit name along the roof and the small code above the fin flash. (via G.J. Cruikshank)

XD371 Mü 13A, over Bramcote in mid 1956 displaying the large 'ROYAL NAVY' inscription. Of pre 1943 origin, this sailplane was 'retrieved' from Germany at the end of the war. Initially unserialled in RN service. (RAF Museum)

XD614/62 Vampire T.11, 1 FTS, at Middleton St George 5.10.63. (I. MacFarlane)

XD632 Hermes 4A, Airwork, at Blackbushe during 1953. The serial is just forward of the tail-plane although the registration G-AKFP has been retained on the fin. The designation 4A was given following the Hermes' modification to take 100 octane fuel. (Flamingo)

XD662 Vickers V1000 prototype, during assembly at Wisley. As can be seen, this jet transport aircraft had reached an advanced stage of construction when the project was cancelled. (BAe)

The Vickers V1000 is shown here in model form to illustrate what it would have looked like had it entered service. Similarities with the Valiant bomber are quite noticcable. (BAe)

XD670 York 1 complete with roundels and fin flash whilst engaged on a trooping flight in the 1950's. Upon completion of the contract it reverted to the civil registration G-AGNU. (P. Spencer)

XD693/Z-Q Jet Provost T.1, 2 FTS, at Hullavington in the late 1950's. The tall undercarriage gives the type an ungainly look when compared with the later T.3. (via A.J. Cranston)

XD696 Avro 720, externally complete at Woodford. The project was cancelled before first flight could be achieved. (via E.B. Morgan)

XD759/S Sabre F.4, ex-92 Sqdn, in open storage at Stansted prior to disposal. This was not the only aircraft to wear this serial as can be seen overleaf! (via G.J. Cruikshank).

XD759 Jet Gyrodyne, hovers outside Fairey Aviation's White Waltham factory. To avoid confusion with the similarly serialled Sabre F.4, it was later reserialled XJ389. (Fairey Aviation)

XD763 Sabre F.4, believed to have been used by the Wing Commander (Flying) at Linton-on-Ouse where Sabre-equipped 66 and 92 Sqdns were based. The sword on the fin is taken from the station crest and 'EWW' are the Wg Cdr's initials. (via G.J. Cruikshank)

XD866 Valiant B.1, 138 Sqdn, at Leconfield 3.9.60. As with the other V-Bomber types, the white colour scheme was worn to reflect heat from nuclear flashes. (I. MacFarlane)

XD898 'M/847' Gannet AS.1, 816 Sqdn, RAN, on HMAS Melbourne is typical of the aircraft purchased by Australia in the 1950's that retained their British serials. Note the ship's deck letter on the aircraft's fin. (A. Bruce)

XE173 Seamew MR.2 (initial work had actually started to convert it to an AS.1) in open storage at Sydenham after cancellation of the AS.1 in 2.57 (RAF MR.2's cancelled 2.56). It is painted in Coastal Command overall grey. (G. Skillen)

XE179 'FD/507' Seamew AS.1, 700 Sqdn, at Lossiemouth 9.8.59. This was the sole example of the type to be painted in full unit markings and is seen here after withdrawal from service. (I. Stott)

XE280 Dakota 4 at Blackbushe in the early 1950's. This aircraft was registered G-AMRA and was given the service serial for trooping flight purposes. Note the swept fin flash. (via G.J. Cruikshank)

XE489 '026' Sea Hawk FGA.6, Airwork FRU, at Hurn in the early 1960's. The gloss black colour scheme was applied to aid identification and on retirement this aircraft was put on display at Southend in spurious markings. (C. Bruce)

XE521 Rotodyne approaches to land at Battersea Heliport. The bulges at the rotor blade tips are the jet efflux nozzles which contributed to the Rotodyne's notoriety as being one of the world's noisiest helicopters. (Fairey Aviation)

XE550 Hunter FGA.9 in Kuwait AF markings at Muharraq 21.11.67. It was officially transferred to that air arm 28.12.67, following the disbandment of 43 Sqdn. (D. Goodwin)

XE731 ML.130D Midget on its launching ramp during trials on Salisbury Plain. The serial of this early target drone is readable on the original photograph under the wings and on the rear fuselage. (M.L. Aviation)

XF124 Swift F.7, Guided Weapons Development Sqdn, at Odiham in 9.58. Note the Fireflash missiles under the wings, the last three of the serial on the nose-wheel door and the extremely neat nose radar installation. (Flamingo)

XF274 Meteor T.7, RAE Farnborough, at Hurn 3.9.73. Note the unit titling and crest. Following a crash, the wreckage of this aircraft was 'assembled' for display by the Accident Investigation Branch at Farnborough. (D. Spurgeon)

XF310 Hunter F.4 carrying a Fairey Fireflash AAM under each wing. Although firings were made, these were of no significance as the aircraft did not carry a radar to provide missile guidance. Note the re-profiled nose. (British Aerospace)

XF378 Hawker P.1109B, Hawker Aircraft Ltd, seen during flight trials. The underwing missiles and the lengthened nose are clearly visible on this modified Hunter F.6. (via G.J. Cruikshank)

XF537 Tudor 2 took up its military marks for a trooping contract awarded to its operator, Air Charter Ltd with whom it flew as G-AGRY. (K.J.H. Hearn)

XF619 Dakota 4, alias G-AMYX, undergoing maintenance at Blackbushe in 1953. Note the quite different application of serial and fin flash as well as the very large roundel compared to XE280 (see earlier). (Flamingo)

XF629 Viking 1B at Blackbushe 10.9.53. This aircraft was registered G-AJBO and was given the service serial for trooping flight purposes. (J. Robertson)

XF662 Bristol 170 Mk21 at Blackbushe in the early 1950's. This aircraft was registered to Silver City Airways as G-AIME and was given the service serial for trooping flight purposes. *(MAS)*

XF708/C Shackleton MR.3/3, 203 Sqdn, at Wattisham 5.8.67. The code is in red, outlined in white. *(R.A. Walker)*

*XF785 Bristol 173, in flight in the Bristol vicinity. This prototype aircraft was originally **G-ALBN** and subsequently became 7648M.* *(British Aerospace)*

XF828 DH.110 Mk.20X, during 8.56. The type was subsequently developed into the Sea Vixen naval all-weather fighter aircraft. *(British Aerospace)*

XF923 Bristol 188 at Filton (date unknown). Its gleaming polished stainless steel surface is most apparent. *(British Aerospace)*

XF907 Provost T.52, Sultan of Oman's AF, at Salalah in 4.66. Converted from an ex-RAF Provost T.1, it retained its former serial upon sale to the SOAF 17.5.65 and was camouflaged as shown. (Flamingo)

XF931 Balliol T.2, 288 Sqdn, late 1956/early 1957. In 1960 this aircraft became an instructional airframe at St Athan as 7654M. (via G.J. Cruikshank)

XG197/A Hunter F.6, Day Fighter Combat School, in the early 1960's. The DFCS was split into two Flights, one with yellow finned Hunters and the other, red. (via P.I. Ball)

XG354 was to have been the Bristol 191 anti-submarine helicopter but it was not completed. The aircraft was used instead by the manufacturer as a test-rig and inscribed 'Test Rig No 1'. (Avia Press)

XG455/B Belvedere HC.1, 72 Sqdn, in the mid 1960's. Interesting comparisons may be made between this type and the B.173 XF785 illustrated earlier. (via E. Myall)

XG502 Sycamore HR.14, 118 Sqdn, at Upavon 16.6.62. Note the fighter unit style of marking flanking the roundel. (R.A. Walker)

XG603 Heron C.2 British Air Attache, Saigon, in the Far East during mid 1966. (via A.J. Cranston)

XG737 'VL/737' Sea Venom FAW.22, Air Director School, at Yeovilton during 9.68. (Flamingo)

XG905 Short SC.1 VTOL test aircraft, at Farnborough 10.9.60 during the SBAC show. Note the effluxes for the centre mounted engines and the robust undercarriage. (P.G. Smith)

XH132 Short SC.9, Royal Radar Establishment, at Cottesmore 22.5.74. The unit badge is worn on the fin. Obvious external differences from the Canberra PR.9 are the nose configuration and the wing-tip stores. (R.A. Walker)

XH228/B Canberra B(I).8, 3 Sqdn, in the early 1970's. The unit fin badge is a red/grey cockatrice on a white disc, flanked by a green bar. (P.A. Tomlin)

XH469 Pioneer Srs 2, ex G-ANRG at Prestwick 9.54 while on loan to the War Office for trials. (via G.J. Cruikshank)

XH788/D Javelin FAW.7, 64 Sqdn, in a fine air-to-air study showing its underfuselage additional fuel tanks and the original rear fuselage shape before conversion to FAW.9 standard. (Flight)

XJ125 Javelin FAW.8 fitted with de Havilland Firestreak air-to-air missiles. This particular aircraft was used by Armstrong Siddeley for development flying of their Sapphire Sa.7R engines. (Flight)

The ultimate in wrong serial application is illustrated by this Sycamore HR.14 and Alouette AH.2 both wearing XJ384 in Cyprus in late 1961/early 1962. The Alouette serial was later corrected to XR384. (Sqdn Ldr E.B. Bywater)

XJ389 Jet Gyrodyne after withdrawal from use, outside the Southampton ATC headquarters 3.10.76. It has subsequently moved to Cosford. (R.A. Walker)

XJ409 Whirlwind HAR.2, 228 Sqdn, at Leconfield 3.9.60. In addition to the RESCUE marking it wears RAF Coastal Command titling. (I. MacFarlane)

XJ470 Bristol 170 Mk.31C, ex-A&AEE, at Lasham 9.3.69. It had been struck off charge at A&AEE and flown to Dan-Air Services at Lasham 30.12.68. (R.A. Walker)

XJ526 'R/248' Sea Vixen FAW.1, 890 Sqdn, takes-off from Yeovilton 27 6.64 in company with XN656 'R/251' of the same unit. *(P.J. Cooper)*

XJ633/K Hunter FR.10, 4 Sqdn, at Soesterberg, Holland 20.6.69. Of interest is this unit's unusual practice of applying its markings to both the nose and the fuselage flanking the roundel. *(J.D. Ragay)*

XJ924 Ultra-Light, Fairey Avn, at a Farnborough SBAC show in the 1950's. This promising design failed to achieve a production order. *(via Avia Press)*

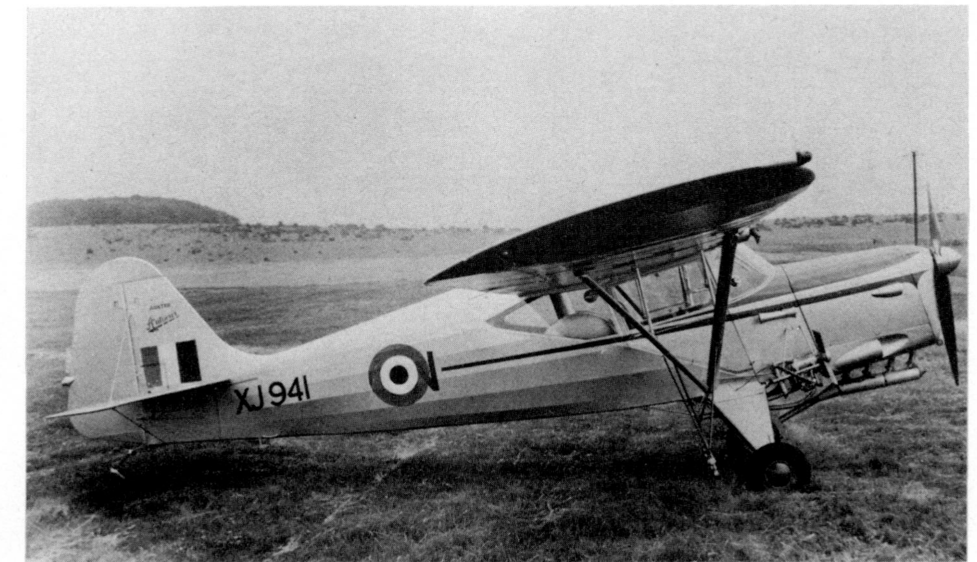

XJ941 J/5G Autocar, Colonial Insecticides Research Unit, date and location unknown. Note the under fuselage spray gear and the propeller-driven pump unit. Its ex-identity of G-ANVN is visible beside the roundel. *(Crown)*

XK375 Auster AOP.9, 656 Sqdn, over the Malayan jungle, date unknown. This aircraft remained in the Far East from the time of its issue to 656 Sqdn in 7.56 until it was struck off charge 1.7.64. *(via M.I. Draper)*

XK426 Rolls-Royce Thrust Measuring Rig proving that it could fly. The serial is painted down the right leg when looking at the photograph. It is understandable how it acquired the name 'Flying Bedstead.' (Rolls-Royce)

XK715 Comet C.2, 51 Sqdn, at Middleton St George 15.9.62. Although operated by this Signals Command unit the Transport Command titling was retained. (I. MacFarlane)

XK724 Gnat F.1, at Henlow in 8.64. This aircraft had been issued to the Technical College at Henlow in 2.62 for instructional purposes as 7715M. (Flamingo)

XK781 ML Utility Mk 2, at Boscombe Down 1.4.58. Each Utility had a number of detachable wings of varying designs and each wing was given a name. The above wing was named 'Gadfly'. (Crown)

Close-up of the pilot's gondola of ML Utility Mk1 XK776. This aircraft was fitted with the 'Puffin' wing and a folding chassis for transportation purposes. (Crown)

XK884 Pembroke C.1, 207 Sqdn, at Odiham 10.9.70. The non-standard colour scheme consists of a grey fuselage with a pale blue band. (R.A. Walker)

Above: An unidentified Swallow swing-wing research model on its launching trolley at Predannack during the development trials of the mid 1950's. (via E.B. Morgan)

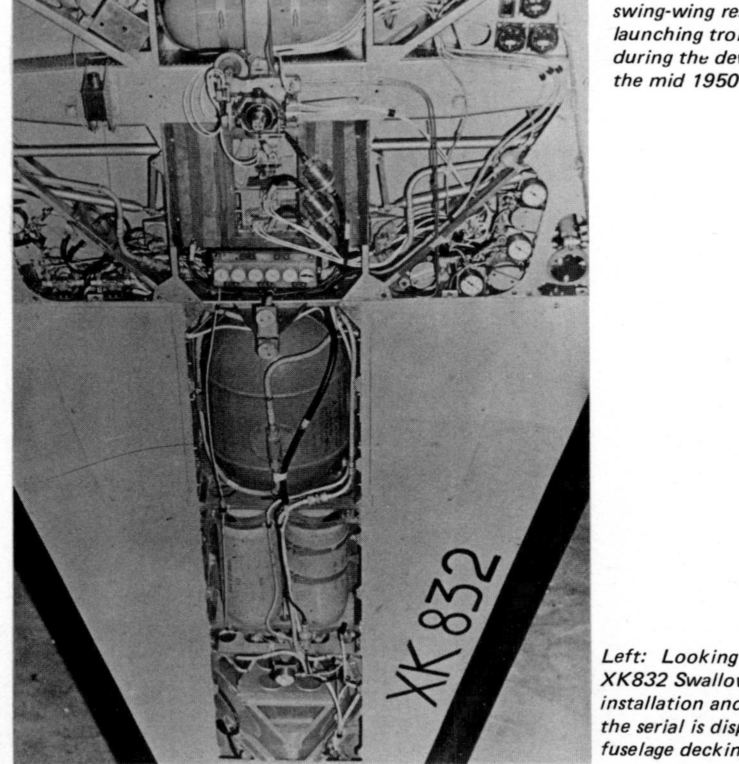

Left: Looking down on the top of XK832 Swallow, showing the engine installation and the only place where the serial is displayed -on top of the fuselage decking. (via E.B. Morgan)

XK889 P.74, Hunting Aircraft Co, at Luton in 1956. Besides being ungainly in appearance it was quite incapable of flight! (via Avia Press)

XL231 Victor B.2, 100/139 Sqdns, about to touch down in the mid 1960's. The Wittering Wing badge of a yellow lion is worn on the fin. (P.A. Tomlin)

XL471 'R/043' Gannet AEW.3, 849 Sqdn 'B' Flt (HMS Ark Royal), displays the Flight's yellow/black 'bee' markings on take-off from Yeovilton 28.6.77. (R.A. Walker)

XL517 Pioneer CC.1, 209 Sqdn, at Seletar in 9.66. Note how the camouflage has stripped around the nose due to the Far East weather elements. (Flamingo)

XL639 Britannia C.1, 99/511 Sqdns, at Gan in early 1972. Close study of the fuselage titling reveals the recent removal of 'Air Support Command' and the name 'Atria' appears beneath the cockpit window. (via T.E. Stone)

'XL698' Twin Pioneer CC.1, at Prestwick immediately after construction displaying an incorrect serial. The aircraft was repainted as XL968 prior to it being transferred to MoD charge in 2.59. (D. Reid)

XL710 Otter, 1956 Trans-Antarctic Expedition, seen on that Continent complete with a ski-undercarriage . (British Aerospace)

XL714 'VL' Tiger Moth T.2, Yeovilton Stn Flt, at Yeovilton 5.9.70. (R.A. Walker)

XL961 Heron Srs 2 was a civil aircraft (G-AMTS) hired from the manufacturer for use by HRH Princess Margaret during her West African tour of mid 1956. (British Aerospace)

XA770-XA842

serial	type	sqdn/unit	code	where&when seen		remarks
XA770	Javelin FAW.2					
XA771	Javelin FAW.2					
XA772	Javelin FAW.2					
XA773	Javelin FAW.2					
XA774	Javelin FAW.2					
XA775	Javelin FAW.2					
XA776	Javelin FAW.2					
XA777	Javelin FAW.2					
XA778	Javelin FAW.2					
XA779	Javelin FAW.2					
XA780	Javelin FAW.2					
XA781	Javelin FAW.2					
XA799	Javelin FAW.2					
XA800	Javelin FAW.2					
XA801	Javelin FAW.2					To 7739M Pr Stafford
XA802	Javelin FAW.2					
XA803	Javelin FAW.2					
XA804	Javelin FAW.2					
XA805	Javelin FAW.2					
XA806	Javelin FAW.2					
XA807	Javelin FAW.2					
XA808	Javelin FAW.2					
XA809	Javelin FAW.2					
XA810	Javelin FAW.2					
XA811	Javelin FAW.2					
XA812	Javelin FAW.2					
XA813	Javelin FAW.2					
XA814	Javelin FAW.2					
XA815	Javelin FAW.6					
XA816	Javelin FAW.6					
XA817	Javelin FAW.6					
XA818	Javelin FAW.6					
XA819	Javelin FAW.6					
XA820	Javelin FAW.6					To 7752M
XA821	Javelin FAW.6					To 7749M
XA822	Javelin FAW.6					
XA823	Javelin FAW.6					
XA824	Javelin FAW.6					
XA825	Javelin FAW.6					
XA826	Javelin FAW.6					
XA827	Javelin FAW.6					
XA828	Javelin FAW.6					
XA829	Javelin FAW.6					
XA830	Javelin FAW.6					
XA831	Javelin FAW.6					
XA832	Javelin FAW.6					
XA833	Javelin FAW.6					
XA834	Javelin FAW.6					
XA835	Javelin FAW.6					
XA836	Javelin FAW.6					

US-built Sikorsky S-55 (c/n 55016) (f/f UK 6.6.51) imported by Westlands as G-AMHK for use as Whirlwind production pattern aircraft. RN evaluation as WW339: back to G-AMHK: RAF evaluation as XA842: back to WW339: G-17-1 (1 day) and sold as LN-ORK.

serial	type	sqdn/unit	code	where&when seen		remarks
XA842	Sikorsky S-55					Ex G-AMHK To WW339

XA847-XA912

serial	type	sqdn/unit	code	where&when seen		remarks

Three English Electric P.1B prototypes to follow WG760/763 in the development of the BAC Lightning. Built at Preston with c/ns 95004-006 resp. XA847 f/f 4.4.57, XA853 f/f 5.9.57 and XA856 f/f 3.1.58.

serial	type	sqdn/unit	code	where&when seen		remarks
XA847	E.E. P.1B					To 8371M Pr Hendon
XA853	E.E. P.1B					
XA856	E.E. P.1B					

The first production batch of 10 Whirlwind HAR.1 helicopters for the FAA built by Westland Aircraft Ltd to Spec HR.127. XA862 f/f 15.8.53 (initially registered as G-AMJT). The batch was allotted the c/ns WA1-3/5-9/16-17 respectively.

serial	type	sqdn/unit	code	where&when seen		remarks
XA862	Whirlwind HAR.1					Ex G-AMJT ntu To A2542
XA863	Whirlwind HAR.1					
XA864	Whirlwind HAR.1					Ex G-17-1 Pr FAAM
XA865	Whirlwind HAR.1					
XA866	Whirlwind HAR.1					To A2550 Pr Donington
XA867	Whirlwind HAR.1					
XA868	Whirlwind HAR.1					To A2551 GI Crawley
XA869	Whirlwind HAR.1					To A2541
XA870	Whirlwind HAR.1					To A2543 Pr Helston
XA871	Whirlwind HAR.1					To A2468

One Slingsby T.34 Sky glider (c/n 672) built by Slingsby Sailplanes Ltd at Kirkbymoorside for the Empire Test Pilots School. Delivered to ETPS Farnborough on 18.8.52.

serial	type	sqdn/unit	code	where&when seen		remarks
XA876	Sky					

Two Devon C.1 communications aircraft built by de Havilland Aircraft Co Ltd at Hawarden against Contract 7383. They were delivered to the RAE: XA879 c/n 04374 delivered 21.10.52; XA880 c/n 04436 delivered 4.9.53, later to C.2 standard.

serial	type	sqdn/unit	code	where&when seen		remarks
XA879	Devon C.1					
XA880	Devon C.2					

1st production order for 25 Vulcan strategic bombers for the RAF to Spec B.129. Built by A.V.Roe & Co Ltd at Woodford, XA889 f/f 4.2.55 and the final delivery was made with XA913 on 19.12.57. Some aircraft subsequently converted to B.1A standard.

serial	type	sqdn/unit	code	where&when seen		remarks
XA889	Vulcan B.1					
XA890	Vulcan B.1					
XA891	Vulcan B.1					
XA892	Vulcan B.1					To 7746M
XA893	Vulcan B.1					To 8591M (nose)
XA894	Vulcan B.1					
XA895	Vulcan B.1					
XA896	Vulcan B.1					
XA897	Vulcan B.1					
XA898	Vulcan B.1					To 7856M
XA899	Vulcan B.1					To 7812M
XA900	Vulcan B.1A					To 7896M Pr Cosford
XA901	Vulcan B.1A					To 7897M
XA902	Vulcan B.1					
XA903	Vulcan B.1					
XA904	Vulcan B.1A					To 7738M
XA905	Vulcan B.1					To 7857M
XA906	Vulcan B.1A					
XA907	Vulcan B.1A					
XA908	Vulcan B.1					
XA909	Vulcan B.1A					
XA910	Vulcan B.1A					To 7995M
XA911	Vulcan B.1A					
XA912	Vulcan B.1A					

XA913-XB246

serial	type	sqdn/unit	code	where&when seen		remarks
XA913	Vulcan B.1A					

First production order for 25 Victor B.1 strategic bombers for the RAF against Contract 6/Aircraft/8441/CB6(a) to Spec B.128. Built by Handley-Page Ltd at Radlett, the first aircraft XA917 first flew 1.2.56. XA918 became the prototype tanker conversion, flying as such in 1964, while XA937 became the first 3-point conversion (K.1) and first flew as such 2.11.65.

serial	type	sqdn/unit	code	where&when seen		remarks
XA917	Victor B.1					To 7827M
XA918	Victor K.1					
XA919	Victor B.1					To 7724M
XA920	Victor B.1					
XA921	Victor B.1					
XA922	Victor B.1					
XA923	Victor B.1					To 7850M Pr Cosford
XA924	Victor B.1					To 7844M
XA925	Victor B.1					
XA926	Victor K.1					
XA927	Victor K.1					
XA928	Victor K.1					
XA929	Victor B.1					
XA930	Victor K.1					
XA931	Victor B.1					
XA932	Victor K.1					To 8517M Pr Marham
XA933	Victor B.1					
XA934	Victor B.1					
XA935	Victor B.1					
XA936	Victor K.1					
XA937	Victor K.1					
XA938	Victor K.1					
XA939	Victor K.1					
XA940	Victor B.1					
XA941	Victor K.1					

Following the early Wild Goose trials, a further batch was ordered from Vickers-Armstrongs Ltd in order to carry out further investigation into the ideas of Dr. Barnes Wallis. Built at Weybridge, these were twice as heavy as their predecessors and featured an auto-pilot, extra radio equipment and strengthened fuselage and wings. In mid-1951 trials moved to Predannack where a streamlined tracked trolley was installed for launching (see photograph). A successful launch was made at the first attempt on 29.4.52, but again the radio-controlled model crashed soon after due to pilot error on the ground, more aircraft crashing during subsequent trials.

serial	type	sqdn/unit	code	where&when seen		remarks
XA947	Wild Goose					
XA948	Wild Goose					
XA949	Wild Goose					
XA950	Wild Goose					
XA951	Wild Goose					
XA952	Wild Goose					

2nd production batch of 140 Swift F.2 aircraft but first to be sub-contracted to the Short Bros and Harland Ltd line at Belfast against 6/Aircraft/8509/CB5(b). The order was cancelled 2.55 when the entire Swift programme was terminated.

XA957-XA993	Swift F.2	(37 a/c)	Cancelled and not built
XB102-XB151	Swift F.2	(50 a/c)	Cancelled and not built
XB169-XB185	Swift F.2	(17 a/c)	Cancelled and not built
XB206-XB241	Swift F.2	(36 a/c)	Cancelled and not built

One Douglas Dakota 3 allotted military marks following a temporary trooping contract awarded to Airwork Ltd. Previously G-AMBW with c/n 13830/25275.

serial	type	sqdn/unit	code	where&when seen		remarks
XB246	Dakota 3					Restored to G-AMBW

XB251-XB310

serial	type	sqdn/unit	code	where&when seen		remarks

Six Dragonfly HC.4 helicopters built by Westland Helicopters Ltd at Yeovil 1952 with c/ns WA/H/124 to WA/H/129 resp. All were initially delivered to Seletar in two batches during 12.52 and 1.53 for 194 Squadron RAF.

serial	type	sqdn/unit	code	where&when seen		remarks
XB251	Dragonfly HC.4					
XB252	Dragonfly HC.4					
XB253	Dragonfly HC.4					
XB254	Dragonfly HC.4					
XB255	Dragonfly HC.4					
XB256	Dragonfly HC.4					

1st production contract for 20 Beverley C.1 aircraft for RAF Transport Command, and built by Blackburn and General Aircraft Ltd at Brough. XB259 f/f 29.1.55 and provisionally registered G-AOAI (ntu); XB260 temporarily registered G-AOEK. The final aircraft (XB291) f/f 3.10.56. The only c/ns allotted were 1002/1003 to XB259/XB260.

serial	type	sqdn/unit	code	where&when seen		remarks
XB259	Beverley C.1					To G-AOAI ntu Pr Paull
XB260	Beverley C.1					To G-AOEK Retd XB260
XB261	Beverley C.1					Pr Southend
XB262	Beverley C.1					
XB263	Beverley C.1					
XB264	Beverley C.1					
XB265	Beverley C.1					
XB266	Beverley C.1					
XB267	Beverley C.1					
XB268	Beverley C.1					
XB269	Beverley C.1					
XB283	Beverley C.1					
XB284	Beverley C.1					
XB285	Beverley C.1					
XB286	Beverley C.1					
XB287	Beverley C.1					
XB288	Beverley C.1					
XB289	Beverley C.1					
XB290	Beverley C.1					
XB291	Beverley C.1					

100 Grumman TBM-3E Avengers supplied to the RN under MDAP ex-US Navy stocks and delivered to UK between 3.53 and 10.53 to fulfil the anti-submarine role pending production of Fairey Gannets. The majority were converted to AS.4 and AS.5 by Scottish Aviation Ltd at Prestwick while some were converted to ECM.6/B radio and electronic counter measure duties by NARIU at RNAS Gosport.

Note that Avenger Mk.I/II/III's appear in JT/JZ/KE ranges etc.

serial	type	sqdn/unit	code	where&when seen		remarks
XB296	Avenger AS.4					Ex 53281 To Fr Govt
XB297	Avenger AS.4					Ex 53400 To Fr Govt
XB298	Avenger AS.4					Ex 53453 To Fr Govt
XB299	Avenger AS.4					Ex 53647 To Fr Govt
XB300	Avenger AS.5					Ex 53664 To FN 53664
XB301	Avenger AS.4					Ex 53665 To Fr Govt
XB302	Avenger AS.4					Ex 53667 To Fr Govt
XB303	Avenger AS.5					Ex 53906
XB304	Avenger AS.4					Ex 85614 To Fr Govt
XB305	Avenger AS.5					Ex 86228
XB306	Avenger AS.4					Ex 91324 To Fr Govt
XB307	Avenger AS.4					Ex 91696 To Fr Govt
XB308	Avenger AS.5					Ex 53107 To MLD 21-24
XB309	Avenger AS.5					Ex 69442 To FN 69442
XB310	Avenger AS.4					Ex 69447 To Fr Govt

XB311-XB390

serial	type	sqdn/unit	code	where&when seen		remarks
XB311	Avenger ECM.6					Ex 53221
XB312	Avenger AS.5					Ex 53815 To FN 53815
XB313	Avenger AS.4					Ex 53411 To Fr Govt
XB314	Avenger AS.4					Ex 69340
XB315	Avenger AS.5					Ex 85621
XB316	Avenger TBM-3E					Ex 85682
XB317	Avenger AS.4					Ex 53170
XB318	Avenger TBM-3E					Ex 85516
XB319	Avenger AS.4					Ex 85932 To Fr Govt
XB320	Avenger AS.5					Ex 53382
XB321	Avenger AS.5					Ex 53110 To FN 53110
XB322	Avenger AS.5					Ex 53127 To FN 53127
XB323	Avenger AS.5					Ex 53193
XB324	Avenger AS.4					Ex 53568 To Fr Govt
XB325	Avenger AS.4					Ex 53609 To Fr Govt
XB326	Avenger AS.4					Ex 53655 To Fr Govt
XB327	Avenger AS.4					Ex 69367 To Fr Govt
XB328	Avenger ECM.6					Ex 69506
XB329	Avenger AS.4					Ex 69523 To Fr Govt
XB330	Avenger AS.4					Ex 69533 To Fr Govt
XB331	Avenger AS.5					Ex 86174 To MLD 21-34
XB332	Avenger AS.4					Ex 86205 To Fr Govt
XB355	Avenger AS.5					Ex 53070
XB356	Avenger AS.4					Ex 85695 To Fr Govt
XB357	Avenger AS.5					Ex 53885
XB358	Avenger AS.5					Ex 53585
XB359	Avenger AS.4					Ex 91477 To Fr Govt
XB360	Avenger ECM.6					Ex 53493
XB361	Avenger AS.4					Ex 53220 To Fr Govt
XB362	Avenger AS.4					Ex 53065 To Fr Govt
XB363	Avenger AS.5					Ex 53287 To FN 53287
XB364	Avenger ECM.6					Ex 53389
XB365	Avenger AS.4					Ex 53590 To Fr Govt
XB366	Avenger AS.4					Ex 53634 To Fr Govt
XB367	Avenger AS.5					Ex 53636
XB368	Avenger AS.5					Ex 53672 To FN 53672
XB369	Avenger AS.5					Ex 53924 To MLD 21-33
XB370	Avenger AS.5					Ex 85686 To FN 85686
XB371	Avenger AS.5					Ex 53748 To FN 53748
XB372	Avenger AS.5					Ex 86235 To MLD 21-39
XB373	Avenger AS.5					Ex 91737 To FN 91737
XB374	Avenger AS.5					Ex 53294 To FN 53294
XB375	Avenger ECM.6					Ex 85974
XB376	Avenger ECM.6					Ex 53642
XB377	Avenger AS.5					Ex 53557 To MLD 21-27
XB378	Avenger AS.5					Ex 53142 To MLD 21-32
XB379	Avenger AS.5					Ex 91131 To MLD 21-30
XB380	Avenger AS.5					Ex 53790
XB381	Avenger AS.5					Ex 85899 To MLD 21-21
XB382	Avenger AS.5					Ex 53099 To MLD 21-29
XB383	Avenger AS.5					Ex 53796
XB384	Avenger AS.5					Ex 91723 To MLD 21-31
XB385	Avenger AS.5					Ex 53604 To MLD 21-28
XB386	Avenger AS.5					Ex 53676
XB387	Avenger AS.5					Ex 53399
XB388	Avenger AS.5					Ex 69452
XB389	Avenger AS.5					Ex 91547
XB390	Avenger TBM-3E					Ex 85628

XB391-XB524

serial	type	sqdn/unit	code	where&when seen		remarks
XB391	Avenger AS.5					Ex 91184 To FN 91184
XB392	Avenger AS.5					Ex 53053 To FN 53053
XB393	Avenger AS.5					Ex 53060 To MLD 21-37
XB394	Avenger AS.5					Ex 53438 To MLD 21-35
XB395	Avenger AS.5					Ex 53500
XB396	Avenger AS.5					Ex 53550 To MLD 21-23
XB397	Avenger AS.5					Ex 53167 To FN 53167
XB398	Avenger AS.5					Ex 53205 To FN 53205
XB399	Avenger AS.5					Ex 53367 To MLD 21-20
XB400	Avenger AS.5					Ex 53482
XB401	Avenger AS.5					Ex 53548 To MLD 21-38
XB402	Avenger AS.5					Ex 53595 To FN 53595
XB403	Avenger AS.5					Ex 85867
XB404	Avenger AS.5					Ex 86125 To FN 86125
XB437	Avenger AS.5					Ex 91355 To MLD 21-36
XB438	Avenger AS.4					Ex 91471 To Fr Govt
XB439	Avenger AS.5					Ex 91419
XB440	Avenger AS.5					Ex 91695
XB441	Avenger AS.4					Ex 53311 To Fr Govt
XB442	Avenger AS.5					Ex 53603 To FN 53603
XB443	Avenger AS.5					Ex 53678 To FN 53678
XB444	Avenger ECM.6					Ex 53797
XB445	Avenger AS.5					Ex 85549 To MLD 21-25
XB446	Avenger ECM.6B					Ex 69502 To FAAM
XB447	Avenger AS.5					Ex 85930 To MLD 21-26
XB448	Avenger AS.5					Ex 86154 To FN 86154
XB449	Avenger AS.5					Ex 86156 To MLD 21-22

78 Bell HSL-1 twin-rotor anti-submarine helicopters ordered by the USN of which 18 were due for delivery to the RN under MDAP. The first XHSL-1 129133 f/f 4.3.53 but the end of the Korean War meant the programme was cut to 50 aircraft. Unconfirmed reports suggest that serials XB453-XB470 were reserved for the RN aircraft.

20 Hiller UH-12B training helicopters built at Palo Alto 1953 and diverted to RN off USN contracts under MDAP. Delivered between 6.53 and 2.54, they were allotted BuAer serials 134724-743 respectively and c/ns 510-511/536-553. Although referred to by their USN designation HTE-2, all were actually styled as HT.1 in RN service.

serial	type	sqdn/unit	code	where&when seen		remarks
XB474	Hiller HT.1					To G-ASVH
XB475	Hiller HT.1					
XB476	Hiller HT.1					To G-ASVI
XB477	Hiller HT.1					To G-ASVJ
XB478	Hiller HT.1					To G-ASTM
XB479	Hiller HT.1					Parts to G-ASVK
XB480	Hiller HT.1					To A2577 To FAAM
XB481	Hiller HT.1					Parts to G-ASVL
XB513	Hiller HT.1					To G-ASTR
XB514	Hiller HT.1					
XB515	Hiller HT.1					
XB516	Hiller HT.1					
XB517	Hiller HT.1					
XB518	Hiller HT.1					
XB519	Hiller HT.1					
XB520	Hiller HT.1					
XB521	Hiller HT.1					
XB522	Hiller HT.1					Parts to G-ASVK
XB523	Hiller HT.1					Parts to G-ASVL
XB524	Hiller HT.1					

XB530-XB544

370 North American F-86E Sabre interceptor fighters built under licence by Canadair Ltd at Montreal, Canada with the maker's designation CL-13 Sabre Mk.2 and Mk.4, and supplied to the RAF through MDAP for use by 2 TAF Germany. It appears that the RAF retained the Canadair mark numbers but were translated into British nomenclature as F.2 and F.4 resp. The block of 370 Sabres was initially allotted serials as follows:

XB530-550 (21 a/c); XB575-603 (29); XB608-646 (39); XB664-713 (50); XB726-769 (44); XB790-839 (50 a/c); XB856-905 (50); XB941-990 (50); XD102-138 (37). Total 370.

At a later date a further 60 Canadair Sabre Mk.4's were delivered for use by Fighter Command, UK and funded through MDAP by the USA to bring total RAF procurement to 430 aircraft. These latter 60 were allotted RAF serials XD707-736 and XD753-781 (q.v.). To avoid any confusion between Canadian funded aircraft (2 TAF) and American funded aircraft (Fighter Command) all of the 2 TAF XD-series Sabres (between XD102 and 138) were re-serialled in the vacant blocks within the XB-series ie., XD102-105 became XB647-650; XD106-111 became XB770-775; XD112-116 became XB851-855; and XD117-138 became XB978-999. This last re-alignment in fact did not fill an existing gap in the XB-series - it simply compromised the already allocated XB941-990 block!

However, coincident with the rationalizing of the 2 TAF and UK-based aircraft, 55 2 TAF XB-serialled Sabres were re-serialled within the XB-series (reasons unknown) which ironed out the compromised block and generally tidied up the entire situation. That stated, the final result was as follows:

XB901-905 became XB912-916; and XB941-990 became XB917-977.

Deliveries of Sabres commenced with 3 Sabre F.2's and 9 Sabre F.4's during December 1952. One additional Sabre F.4 (XB551) was obtained to replace Sabre F.2 XB530 as the latter had been returned to Canada. An eventual total of 438 aircraft was involved in the RAF contract, the additional eight being mostly accounted for by those that had crashed prior to delivery and, in turn, were replaced. Deliveries by air took place between 8.12.52 and 19.12.53 in an operation known as 'Bechers Brook'.

Between 1956 and 1958, 302 RAF Sabres were returned to USAF charge (regaining their previous RCAF serials) for refurbishing by Aviation Traders at Stansted; Westland's at Merryfield; and Airwork General Trading Co at Gatwick, Dunsfold, Speke, and Ringway. Eventually 120 of these were delivered to the Jugoslavian Air Force (eg XB542 to USAF 19473, to JAF as 06-031, later 11-046) and 180 to the Italian Air Force for further service (eg XB733 to USAF 19607, to ItAF MM19607, to G-ATBF). The other two aircraft were XB775 to 19863 (cr at Naples on del) and XB982 transferred to BSE Ltd.

Note that in the serial listing where a serial is prefixed by (1) then that was the first instance that the serial was allotted. The remarks column provides the 'new' serial for that aircraft whilst the second and permanent allocation of the serial is prefixed by (2). The order for re-serialling of individual aircraft was issued in September 1953 to be physically undertaken as aircraft were camouflaged for RAF service, since all had arrived in an overall silver finish.

serial	type	sqdn/unit	code	where&when seen	remarks
XB530	Sabre F.2				Ex 19378 Returned
XB531	Sabre F.2				Ex 19384
XB532	Sabre F.2				Ex 19404 To USAF
XB533	Sabre F.4				Ex 19464 To USAF
XB534	Sabre F.4				Ex 19465
XB535	Sabre F.4				Ex 19466 To USAF
XB536	Sabre F.4				Ex 19467 To USAF
XB537	Sabre F.4				Ex 19468 To USAF
XB538	Sabre F.4				Ex 19469
XB539	Sabre F.4				Ex 19470 To USAF
XB540	Sabre F.4				Ex 19471 To USAF
XB541	Sabre F.4				Ex 19472
XB542	Sabre F.4				Ex 19473 To USAF
XB543	Sabre F.4				Ex 19474 To USAF
XB544	Sabre F.4				Ex 19475 To USAF

XB545-XB628

serial	type	sqdn/unit	code	where&when seen		remarks
XB545	Sabre F.4					Ex 19476 To USAF
XB546	Sabre F.4					Ex 19477 To USAF
XB547	Sabre F.4					Ex 19478
XB548	Sabre F.4					Ex 19479
XB549	Sabre F.4					Ex 19480
XB550	Sabre F.4					Ex 19481 To USAF
XB551	Sabre F.4					Ex 19663 To USAF
XB575	Sabre F.4					Ex 19482
XB576	Sabre F.4					Ex 19483 To USAF
XB577	Sabre F.4					Ex 19484 To USAF
XB578	Sabre F.4					Ex 19485 To USAF
XB579	Sabre F.4					Ex 19486
XB580	Sabre F.4					Ex 19487 To USAF
XB581	Sabre F.4					Ex 19488 To USAF
XB582	Sabre F.4					Ex 19489 To USAF
XB583	Sabre F.4					Ex 19490 To USAF
XB584	Sabre F.4					Ex 19491 To USAF
XB585	Sabre F.4					Ex 19492
XB586	Sabre F.4					Ex 19493 To USAF
XB587	Sabre F.4					Ex 19494 To USAF
XB588	Sabre F.4					Ex 19495
XB589	Sabre F.4					Ex 19496
XB590	Sabre F.4					Ex 19497
XB591	Sabre F.4					Ex 19498 To USAF
XB592	Sabre F.4					Ex 19499 To USAF
XB593	Sabre F.4					Ex 19500 To USAF
XB594	Sabre F.4					Ex 19501 To USAF
XB595	Sabre F.4					Ex 19502 To USAF
XB596	Sabre F.4					Ex 19503 To USAF
XB597	Sabre F.4					Ex 19504 To USAF
XB598	Sabre F.4					Ex 19505 To USAF
XB599	Sabre F.4					Ex 19506 To USAF
XB600	Sabre F.4					Ex 19507
XB601	Sabre F.4					Ex 19508 To USAF
XB602	Sabre F.4					Ex 19509 To USAF
XB603	Sabre F.4					Ex 19510
XB608	Sabre F.4					Ex 19511 To USAF
XB609	Sabre F.4					Ex 19512 To USAF
XB610	Sabre F.4					Ex 19513
XB611	Sabre F.4					Ex 19514 To USAF
XB612	Sabre F.4					Ex 19515
XB613	Sabre F.4					Ex 19516 To USAF
XB614	Sabre F.4					Ex 19517
XB615	Sabre F.4					Ex 19518
XB616	Sabre F.4					Ex 19519 To USAF
XB617	Sabre F.4					Ex 19520 To USAF
XB618	Sabre F.4					Ex 19521 To USAF
XB619	Sabre F.4					Ex 19522
XB620	Sabre F.4					Ex 19523 To USAF
XB621	Sabre F.4					Ex 19524 To USAF
XB622	Sabre F.4					Ex 19525 To USAF
XB623	Sabre F.4					Ex 19526
XB624	Sabre F.4					Ex 19527 To USAF
XB625	Sabre F.4					Ex 19528 To USAF
XB626	Sabre F.4					Ex 19529
XB627	Sabre F.4					Ex 19530
XB628	Sabre F.4					Ex 19531

XB629-XB699

serial	type	sqdn/unit	code	where&when seen		remarks
XB629	Sabre F.4					Ex 19532
XB630	Sabre F.4					Ex 19533
XB631	Sabre F.4					Ex 19534 To USAF
XB632	Sabre F.4					Ex 19535 To USAF
XB633	Sabre F.4					Ex 19536
XB634	Sabre F.4					Ex 19537
XB635	Sabre F.4					Ex 19538 To USAF
XB636	Sabre F.4					Ex 19539 To USAF
XB637	Sabre F.4					Ex 19540
XB638	Sabre F.4					Ex 19541
XB639	Sabre F.4					Ex 19542 To USAF
XB640	Sabre F.4					Ex 19543 To USAF
XB641	Sabre F.4					Ex 19544 To USAF
XB642	Sabre F.4					Ex 19545
XB643	Sabre F.4					Ex 19546
XB644	Sabre F.4					Ex 19547 To USAF
XB645	Sabre F.4					Ex 19548 To USAF
XB646	Sabre F.4					Ex 19549
XB647	Sabre F.4					Ex XD102
XB648	Sabre F.4					Ex XD103
XB649	Sabre F.4					Ex XD104 To USAF
XB650	Sabre F.4					Ex XD105 To USAF
XB664	Sabre F.4					Ex 19550 To USAF
XB665	Sabre F.4					Ex 19551 To USAF
XB666	Sabre F.4					Ex 19552 To USAF
XB667	Sabre F.4					Ex 19553
XB668	Sabre F.4					Ex 19554 To USAF
XB669	Sabre F.4					Ex 19555 To USAF
XB670	Sabre F.4					Ex 19556 To USAF
XB671	Sabre F.4					Ex 19557
XB672	Sabre F.4					Ex 19558 To USAF
XB673	Sabre F.4					Ex 19559
XB674	Sabre F.4					Ex 19560 To USAF
XB675	Sabre F.4					Ex 19561 To USAF
XB676	Sabre F.4					Ex 19562
XB677	Sabre F.4					Ex 19563
XB678	Sabre F.4					Ex 19564 To USAF
XB679	Sabre F.4					Ex 19565 To USAF
XB680	Sabre F.4					Ex 19566 To USAF
XB681	Sabre F.4					Ex 19567
XB682	Sabre F.4					Ex 19568 To USAF
XB683	Sabre F.4					Ex 19569
XB684	Sabre F.4					Ex 19570 To USAF
XB685	Sabre F.4					Ex 19571 To USAF
XB686	Sabre F.4					Ex 19572 To USAF
XB687	Sabre F.4					Ex 19573 To USAF
XB688	Sabre F.4					Ex 19574 To USAF
XB689	Sabre F.4					Ex 19457 To USAF
XB690	Sabre F.4					Ex 19576
XB691	Sabre F.4					Ex 19577 To USAF
XB692	Sabre F.4					Ex 19578 To USAF
XB693	Sabre F.4					Ex 19579 To USAF
XB694	Sabre F.4					Ex 19580 To USAF
XB695	Sabre F.4					Ex 19581 To USAF
XB696	Sabre F.4					Ex 19582 To USAF
XB697	Sabre F.4					Ex 19583 To USAF
XB698	Sabre F.4					Ex 19584 To USAF
XB699	Sabre F.4					Ex 19585

XB700-XB769

serial	type	sqdn/unit	code	where&when seen	remarks
XB700	Sabre F.4				Ex 19586
XB701	Sabre F.4				Ex 19587 To USAF
XB702	Sabre F.4				Ex 19588 To USAF
XB703	Sabre F.4				Ex 19589 To USAF
XB704	Sabre F.4				Ex 19590
XB705	Sabre F.4				Ex 19591 To USAF
XB706	Sabre F.4				Ex 19592 To USAF
XB707	Sabre F.4				Ex 19593 To USAF
XB708	Sabre F.4				Ex 19594 To USAF
XB709	Sabre F.4				Ex 19595 To USAF
XB710	Sabre F.4				Ex 19596 To USAF
XB711	Sabre F.4				Ex 19597
XB712	Sabre F.4				Ex 19598 To USAF
XB713	Sabre F.4				Ex 19599 To USAF
XB726	Sabre F.4				Ex 19600 To USAF
XB727	Sabre F.4				Ex 19601 To USAF
XB728	Sabre F.4				Ex 19602 To USAF
XB729	Sabre F.4				Ex 19603
XB730	Sabre F.4				Ex 19604
XB731	Sabre F.4				Ex 19605
XB732	Sabre F.4				Ex 19606 To USAF
XB733	Sabre F.4				Ex 19607 To USAF
XB734	Sabre F.4				Ex 19608
XB735	Sabre F.4				Ex 19609
XB736	Sabre F.4				Ex 19610 To USAF
XB737	Sabre F.4				Ex 19611 To USAF
XB738	Sabre F.4				Ex 19612 To USAF
XB739	Sabre F.4				Ex 19613 To USAF
XB740	Sabre F.4				Ex 19614 To USAF
XB741	Sabre F.4				Ex 19615 To USAF
XB742	Sabre F.4				Ex 19616 To USAF
XB743	Sabre F.4				Ex 19617 To USAF
XB744	Sabre F.4				Ex 19618 To USAF
XB745	Sabre F.4				Ex 19635 To USAF
XB746	Sabre F.4				Ex 19620 To USAF
XB747	Sabre F.4				Ex 19621 To USAF
XB748	Sabre F.4				Ex 19622 To USAF
XB749	Sabre F.4				Ex 19623 To USAF
XB750	Sabre F.4				Ex 19624
XB751	Sabre F.4				Ex 19625 To USAF
XB752	Sabre F.4				Ex 19626
XB753	Sabre F.4				Ex 19627 To USAF
XB754	Sabre F.4				Ex 19628 To USAF
XB755	Sabre F.4				Ex 19458 To USAF
XB756	Sabre F.4				Ex 19630 To USAF
XB757	Sabre F.4				Ex 19631 To USAF
XB758	Sabre F.4				Ex 19632 To USAF
XB759	Sabre F.4				Ex 19633 To USAF
XB760	Sabre F.4				Ex 19634
XB761	Sabre F.4				Ex 19459 To USAF
XB762	Sabre F.4				Ex 19636 To USAF
XB763	Sabre F.4				Ex 19629 To USAF
XB764	Sabre F.4				Ex 19638 To USAF
XB765	Sabre F.4				Ex 19639 To USAF
XB766	Sabre F.4				Ex 19640
XB767	Sabre F.4				Ex 19641 To USAF
XB768	Sabre F.4				Ex 19642
XB769	Sabre F.4				Ex 19460 To USAF

XB770-XB851

serial	type	sqdn/unit	code	where&when seen		remarks
XB770	Sabre F.4					Ex XD106 To USAF
XB771	Sabre F.4					Ex XD107 To USAF
XB772	Sabre F.4					Ex XD108 To USAF
XB773	Sabre F.4					Ex XD109 To USAF
XB774	Sabre F.4					Ex XD110 To USAF
XB775	Sabre F.4					Ex XD111 To USAF
XB790	Sabre F.4					Ex 19644 To USAF
XB791	Sabre F.4					Ex 19645 To USAF
XB792	Sabre F.4					Ex 19646 To USAF
XB793	Sabre F.4					Ex 19647 To USAF
XB794	Sabre F.4					Ex 19648 To USAF
XB795	Sabre F.4					Ex 19649 To USAF
XB796	Sabre F.4					Ex 19650 To USAF
XB797	Sabre F.4					Ex 19651 To USAF
XB798	Sabre F.4					Ex 19652 To USAF
XB799	Sabre F.4					Ex 19653 To USAF
XB800	Sabre F.4					Ex 19654 To USAF
XB801	Sabre F.4					Ex 19655 To USAF
XB802	Sabre F.4					Ex 19656
XB803	Sabre F.4					Ex 19657
XB804	Sabre F.4					Ex 19658 To USAF
XB805	Sabre F.4					Ex 19659 To USAF
XB806	Sabre F.4					Ex 19461 To USAF
XB807	Sabre F.4					Ex 19661 To USAF
XB808	Sabre F.4					Ex 19662
XB809	Sabre F.4					Ex 19453 To USAF
XB810	Sabre F.4					Ex 19664 To USAF
XB811	Sabre F.4					Ex 19665 To USAF
XB812	Sabre F.4					Ex 19666 To USAF
XB813	Sabre F.4					Ex 19667 To USAF
XB814	Sabre F.4					Ex 19668 To USAF
XB815	Sabre F.4					Ex 19669 To USAF
XB816	Sabre F.4					Ex 19454 To USAF
XB817	Sabre F.4					Ex 19671
XB818	Sabre F.4					Ex 19672 To USAF
XB819	Sabre F.4					Ex 19673
XB820	Sabre F.4					Ex 19674 To USAF
XB821	Sabre F.4					Ex 19675 To USAF
XB822	Sabre F.4					Ex 19676
XB823	Sabre F.4					Ex 19677 To USAF
XB824	Sabre F.4					Ex 19678 To USAF
XB825	Sabre F.4					Ex 19575 To USAF
XB826	Sabre F.4					Ex 19680 To USAF
XB827	Sabre F.4					Ex 19681 To USAF
XB828	Sabre F.4					Ex 19682 To USAF
XB829	Sabre F.4					Ex 19683 To USAF
XB830	Sabre F.4					Ex 19684 To USAF
XB831	Sabre F.4					Ex 19685 To USAF
XB832	Sabre F.4					Ex 19686 To USAF
XB833	Sabre F.4					Ex 19687 To USAF
XB834	Sabre F.4					Ex 19688 To USAF
XB835	Sabre F.4					Ex 19455 To USAF
XB836	Sabre F.4					Ex 19690 To USAF
XB837	Sabre F.4					Ex 19691 To USAF
XB838	Sabre F.4					Ex 19692 To USAF
XB839	Sabre F.4					Ex 19693
XB851	Sabre F.4					Ex XD112 To USAF

XB852-XB915

serial	type	sqdn/unit	code	where&when seen		remarks
XB852	Sabre F.4					Ex XD113
XB853	Sabre F.4					Ex XD114 To USAF
XB854	Sabre F.4					Ex XD115 To USAF
XB855	Sabre F.4					Ex XD116 To USAF
XB856	Sabre F.4					Ex 19694 To USAF
XB857	Sabre F.4					Ex 19695 To USAF
XB858	Sabre F.4					Ex 19696 To USAF
XB859	Sabre F.4					Ex 19697 To USAF
XB860	Sabre F.4					Ex 19698
XB861	Sabre F.4					Ex 19699
XB862	Sabre F.4					Ex 19700 To USAF
XB863	Sabre F.4					Ex 19701
XB864	Sabre F.4					Ex 19702 To USAF
XB865	Sabre F.4					Ex 19703
XB866	Sabre F.4					Ex 19704
XB867	Sabre F.4					Ex 19705
XB868	Sabre F.4					Ex 19706 To USAF
XB869	Sabre F.4					Ex 19732
XB870	Sabre F.4					Ex 19733 To USAF
XB871	Sabre F.4					Ex 19734
XB872	Sabre F.4					Ex 19735 To USAF
XB873	Sabre F.4					Ex 19736 To USAF
XB874	Sabre F.4					Ex 19737 To USAF
XB875	Sabre F.4					Ex 19738 To USAF
XB876	Sabre F.4					Ex 19739 To USAF
XB877	Sabre F.4					Ex 19740 To USAF
XB878	Sabre F.4					Ex 19741 To USAF
XB879	Sabre F.4					Ex 19742 To USAF
XB880	Sabre F.4					Ex 19743
XB881	Sabre F.4					Ex 19744 To USAF
XB882	Sabre F.4					Ex 19745
XB883	Sabre F.4					Ex 19746 To USAF
XB884	Sabre F.4					Ex 19747
XB885	Sabre F.4					Ex 19748 To USAF
XB886	Sabre F.4					Ex 19774 To USAF
XB887	Sabre F.4					Ex 19775 To USAF
XB888	Sabre F.4					Ex 19776 To USAF
XB889	Sabre F.4					Ex 19777
XB890	Sabre F.4					Ex 19778 To USAF
XB891	Sabre F.4					Ex 19779
XB892	Sabre F.4					Ex 19780 To USAF
XB893	Sabre F.4					Ex 19781 To USAF
XB894	Sabre F.4					Ex 19782 To USAF
XB895	Sabre F.4					Ex 19783 To USAF
XB896	Sabre F.4					Ex 19784 To USAF
XB897	Sabre F.4					Ex 19785 To USAF
XB898	Sabre F.4					Ex 19786
XB899	Sabre F.4					Ex 19787
XB900	Sabre F.4					Ex 19788
XB901	Sabre F.4					Ex 19789 To XB912
XB902	Sabre F.4					Ex 19790 To XB913
XB903	Sabre F.4					Ex 19791 To XB914
XB904	Sabre F.4					Ex 19792 To XB915
XB905	Sabre F.4					Ex 19803 To XB916
XB912	Sabre F.4					Ex XB901
XB913	Sabre F.4					Ex XB902
XB914	Sabre F.4					Ex XB903 To USAF
XB915	Sabre F.4					Ex XB904 To USAF

XB916-XB951

serial	type	sqdn/unit	code	where&when seen		remarks
XB916	Sabre F.4					Ex XB905 To USAF
XB917	Sabre F.4					Ex XB941 To USAF
XB918	Sabre F.4					Ex XB942
XB919	Sabre F.4					Ex XB943 To USAF
XB920	Sabre F.4					Ex XB944 To USAF
XB921	Sabre F.4					Ex XB945 To USAF
XB922	Sabre F.4					Ex XB946 To USAF
XB923	Sabre F.4					Ex XB947 To USAF
XB924	Sabre F.4					Ex XB948 To USAF
XB925	Sabre F.4					Ex XB949
XB926	Sabre F.4					Ex XB950 To USAF
XB927	Sabre F.4					Ex XB951
XB928	Sabre F.4					Ex XB952 To USAF
XB929	Sabre F.4					Ex XB953 To USAF
XB930	Sabre F.4					Ex XB954 To USAF
XB931	Sabre F.4					Ex XB955
XB932	Sabre F.4					Ex XB956
XB933	Sabre F.4					Ex XB957 To USAF
XB934	Sabre F.4					Ex XB958 To USAF
XB935	Sabre F.4					Ex XB959 To USAF
XB936	Sabre F.4					Ex XB960
XB937	Sabre F.4					Ex XB961
XB938	Sabre F.4					Ex XB962 To USAF
XB939	Sabre F.4					Ex XB963 To USAF
XB940	Sabre F.4					Ex XB964
(1)XB941	Sabre F.4					Ex 19804 To XB917
(2)XB941	Sabre F.4					Ex XB965 To USAF
(1)XB942	Sabre F.4					Ex 19805 To XB918
(2)XB942	Sabre F.4					Ex XB966 To USAF
(1)XB943	Sabre F.4					Ex 19806 To XB919
(2)XB943	Sabre F.4					Ex XB967 To USAF
(1)XB944	Sabre F.4					Ex 19807 To XB920
(2)XB944	Sabre F.4					Ex XB968
(1)XB945	Sabre F.4					Ex 19808 To XB921
(2)XB945	Sabre F.4					Ex XB969 To USAF
(1)XB946	Sabre F.4					Ex 19809 To XB922
(2)XB946	Sabre F.4					Ex XB970 To USAF
(1)XB947	Sabre F.4					Ex 19810 To XB923
(2)XB947	Sabre F.4					Ex XB971
(1)XB948	Sabre F.4					Ex 19811 To XB924
(2)XB948	Sabre F.4					Ex XB972 To USAF
(1)XB949	Sabre F.4					Ex 19812 To XB925 ntu
(2)XB949	Sabre F.4					Ex XB973 To USAF
(1)XB950	Sabre F.4					Ex 19813 To XB926
(2)XB950	Sabre F.4					Ex XB974
(1)XB951	Sabre F.4					Ex 19814 To XB927
(2)XB951	Sabre F.4					Ex XB975 To USAF

XB952-XB978

serial	type	sqdn/unit	code	where&when seen		remarks
(1)XB952	Sabre F.4					Ex 19815 To XB928
(2)XB952	Sabre F.4					Ex XB976 To USAF
(1)XB953	Sabre F.4					Ex 19816 To XB929
(2)XB953	Sabre F.4					Ex XB977 To USAF
(1)XB954	Sabre F.4					Ex 19817 To XB930
(2)XB954	Sabre F.4					Ex XB978 To USAF
(1)XB955	Sabre F.4					Ex 19818 To XB931
(2)XB955	Sabre F.4					Ex XB979 To USAF
(1)XB956	Sabre F.4					Ex 19819 To XB932
(2)XB956	Sabre F.4					Ex XB980 To USAF
(1)XB957	Sabre F.4					Ex 19820 To XB933
(2)XB957	Sabre F.4					Ex XB981 To USAF
(1)XB958	Sabre F.4					Ex 19821 To XB934
(2)XB958	Sabre F.4					Ex XB982 To USAF
(1)XB959	Sabre F.4					Ex 19822 To XB935
(2)XB959	Sabre F.4					Ex XB983 To USAF
(1)XB960	Sabre F.4					Ex 19823 To XB936
(2)XB960	Sabre F.4					Ex XB984 To USAF
(1)XB961	Sabre F.4					Ex 19824 To XB937
(2)XB961	Sabre F.4					Ex XB985 To USAF
XB962	Sabre F.4					Ex 19825 To XB938
XB963	Sabre F.4					Ex 19826 To XB939
XB964	Sabre F.4					Ex 19827 To XB940
XB965	Sabre F.4					Ex 19828 To XB941
XB966	Sabre F.4					Ex 19829 To XB942
XB967	Sabre F.4					Ex 19830 To XB943
XB968	Sabre F.4					Ex 19831 To XB944
XB969	Sabre F.4					Ex 19832 To XB945
XB970	Sabre F.4					Ex 19833 To XB946
XB971	Sabre F.4					Ex 19834 To XB947
XB972	Sabre F.4					Ex 19835 To XB948
(1)XB973	Sabre F.4					Ex 19836 To XB949
(2)XB973	Sabre F.4					Ex XB986 To USAF
(1)XB974	Sabre F.4					Ex 19837 To XB950
(2)XB974	Sabre F.4					Ex XB987 To USAF
(1)XB975	Sabre F.4					Ex 19838 To XB951
(2)XB975	Sabre F.4					Ex XB988 To USAF
(1)XB976	Sabre F.4					Ex 19839 To XB952
(2)XB976	Sabre F.4					Ex XB989 To USAF
(1)XB977	Sabre F.4					Ex 19840 To XB953
(2)XB977	Sabre F.4					Ex XB990 To USAF
(1)XB978	Sabre F.4					Ex 19841 To XB954
(2)XB978	Sabre F.4					Ex XD117 To USAF

XB979-XD114

serial	type	sqdn/unit	code	where&when seen		remarks
1)XB979	Sabre F.4					Ex 19842 To XB955
2)XB979	Sabre F.4					Ex XD118 To USAF
1)XB980	Sabre F.4					Ex 19843 To XB956
2)XB980	Sabre F.4					Ex XD119 To USAF
1)XB981	Sabre F.4					Ex 19844 To XB957
2)XB981	Sabre F.4					Ex XD120
1)XB982	Sabre F.4					Ex 19845 To XB958
2)XB982	Sabre F.4					Ex XD121 To USAF ntu
1)XB983	Sabre F.4					Ex 19846 To XB959
2)XB983	Sabre F.4					Ex XD122 To USAF
1)XB984	Sabre F.4					Ex 19847 To XB960
2)XB984	Sabre F.4					Ex XD123 To USAF
1)XB985	Sabre F.4					Ex 19848 To XB961
2)XB985	Sabre F.4					Ex XD124 To USAF
1)XB986	Sabre F.4					Ex 19849 To XB973
2)XB986	Sabre F.4					Ex XD125 To USAF
1)XB987	Sabre F.4					Ex 19850 To XB974
2)XB987	Sabre F.4					Ex XD126 To USAF
1)XB988	Sabre F.4					Ex 19851 To XB975
2)XB988	Sabre F.4					Ex XD127
1)XB989	Sabre F.4					Ex 19852 To XB976
2)XB989	Sabre F.4					Ex XD128
1)XB990	Sabre F.4					Ex 19853 To XB977
2)XB990	Sabre F.4					Ex XD129 To USAF
XB991	Sabre F.4					Ex XD130 To USAF
XB992	Sabre F.4					Ex XD131
XB993	Sabre F.4					Ex XD132 To USAF
XB994	Sabre F.4					Ex XD133 To USAF
XB995	Sabre F.4					Ex XD134
XB996	Sabre F.4					Ex XD135 To USAF
XB997	Sabre F.4					Ex XD136 To USAF
XB998	Sabre F.4					Ex XD137 To USAF
XB999	Sabre F.4					Ex XD138 To USAF
XD102	Sabre F.4					Ex 19854 To XB647
XD103	Sabre F.4					Ex 19855 To XB648
XD104	Sabre F.4					Ex 19856 To XB649
XD105	Sabre F.4					Ex 19857 To XB650
XD106	Sabre F.4					Ex 19858 To XB770
XD107	Sabre F.4					Ex 19859 To XB771
XD108	Sabre F.4					Ex 19860 To XB772
XD109	Sabre F.4					Ex 19861 To XB773
XD110	Sabre F.4					Ex 19862 To XB774
XD111	Sabre F.4					Ex 19863 To XB775
XD112	Sabre F.4					Ex 19864 To XB851
XD113	Sabre F.4					Ex 19865 To XB852
XD114	Sabre F.4					Ex 19866 To XB853

XD115-XD188

serial	type	sqdn/unit	code	where&when seen		remarks
XD115	Sabre F.4					Ex 19867 To XB854
XD116	Sabre F.4					Ex 19868 To XB855
XD117	Sabre F.4					Ex 19869 To XB978
XD118	Sabre F.4					Ex 19870 To XB979
XD119	Sabre F.4					Ex 19871 To XB980
XD120	Sabre F.4					Ex 19872 To XB981
XD121	Sabre F.4					Ex 19873 To XB982
XD122	Sabre F.4					Ex 19874 To XB983
XD123	Sabre F.4					Ex 19875 To XB984
XD124	Sabre F.4					Ex 19876 To XB985
XD125	Sabre F.4					Ex 19877 To XB986
XD126	Sabre F.4					Ex 19878 To XB987
XD127	Sabre F.4					Ex 19879 To XB988
XD128	Sabre F.4					Ex 19880 To XB989
XD129	Sabre F.4					Ex 19881 To XB990
XD130	Sabre F.4					Ex 19882 To XB991
XD131	Sabre F.4					Ex 19883 To XB992
XD132	Sabre F.4					Ex 19884 To XB993
XD133	Sabre F.4					Ex 19885 To XB994
XD134	Sabre F.4					Ex 19886 To XB995
XD135	Sabre F.4					Ex 19887 To XB996
XD136	Sabre F.4					Ex 19888 To XB997
XD137	Sabre F.4					Ex 19889 To XB998
XD138	Sabre F.4					Ex 19890 To XB999

Prototype Swift PR.6 contracted to Supermarine Division of Vickers-Armstrongs Ltd at South Marston, under maker's designation Type 550 to fulfil the role of unarmed strategic reconnaissance. Development was cancelled and the aircraft was not flown. Note that the serial XD143 is often mis-quoted as XD943.

serial	type	sqdn/unit	code	where&when seen		remarks
XD143	Swift PR.6					Not completed/7289M

Three SR.53 development prototypes contracted to Saunders-Roe Ltd at East Cowes IoW to Specification F.138D. XD145 and XD151 taken to Boscombe Down for assembly and f/f 16.5.57 and 8.12.57 respectively. XD153 was cancelled during January 1954.

serial	type	sqdn/unit	code	where&when seen		remarks
XD145	SR.53					Pr Cosford
XD151	SR.53					
XD153	SR.53					Cancelled 1.54

Prototype Javelin FAW.2 built by Gloster Aircraft Ltd at Hucclecote to test installation of US-designed radar as fitted to production FAW.2 aircraft. XD158 was first flown on 31.10.55.

serial	type	sqdn/unit	code	where&when seen		remarks
XD158	Javelin FAW.2					To 7592M

Initial production batch of 10 Whirlwind HAR.2/4's built for the Royal Air Force by the Westland Aircraft Co Ltd at Yeovil. XD163 f/f 15.7.54 as a HAR.4 and XD188 was delivered on 30.8.54 as a HAR.4. The aircraft were allocated the c/ns WA20-WA22 and WA25-WA31 inclusive. Seven of the batch were converted in 1960-64 to HAR.10's.

serial	type	sqdn/unit	code	where&when seen		remarks
XD163	Whirlwind HAR.10					To 8645M ntu
XD164	Whirlwind HAR.10					To 7853M
XD165	Whirlwind HAR.10					
XD182	Whirlwind HAR.10					To 8612M
XD183	Whirlwind HAR.10					
XD184	Whirlwind HAR.10					
XD185	Whirlwind HAR.4					
XD186	Whirlwind HAR.10					
XD187	Whirlwind HAR.4					
XD188	Whirlwind HAR.4					

XD196-XD273

serial	type	sqdn/unit	code	where&when seen	remarks

Two Sycamore HR.13 helicopters built by Bristol Aeroplane Co Ltd at Filton for ASR evaluation by RAF Fighter Command. Allocated c/ns 13066 and 13067 resp.

serial	type	sqdn/unit	code	where&when seen	remarks
XD196	Sycamore HR.13				
XD197	Sycamore HR.13				

Sole production contract for 100 Scimitar F.1 (to Spec N113P) for the RN, built by the Supermarine Division of Vickers-Armstrongs Ltd at South Marston. XD212 f/f on 11.1.57; XD333 del 10.1.61. Production terminated at 76th aircraft.

serial	type	sqdn/unit	code	where&when seen	remarks
XD212	Scimitar F.1				
XD213	Scimitar F.1				
XD214	Scimitar F.1				
XD215	Scimitar F.1				To A2573
XD216	Scimitar F.1				
XD217	Scimitar F.1				
XD218	Scimitar F.1				
XD219	Scimitar F.1				
XD220	Scimitar F.1				Pr FAAM Wroughton
XD221	Scimitar F.1				
XD222	Scimitar F.1				
XD223	Scimitar F.1				
XD224	Scimitar F.1				
XD225	Scimitar F.1				
XD226	Scimitar F.1				
XD227	Scimitar F.1				
XD228	Scimitar F.1				
XD229	Scimitar F.1				
XD230	Scimitar F.1				
XD231	Scimitar F.1				
XD232	Scimitar F.1				
XD233	Scimitar F.1				Static test airframe
XD234	Scimitar F.1				
XD235	Scimitar F.1				
XD236	Scimitar F.1				
XD237	Scimitar F.1				
XD238	Scimitar F.1				
XD239	Scimitar F.1				
XD240	Scimitar F.1				
XD241	Scimitar F.1				
XD242	Scimitar F.1				
XD243	Scimitar F.1				To A2588
XD244	Scimitar F.1				
XD245	Scimitar F.1				
XD246	Scimitar F.1				
XD247	Scimitar F.1				
XD248	Scimitar F.1				
XD249	Scimitar F.1				
XD250	Scimitar F.1				
XD264	Scimitar F.1				
XD265	Scimitar F.1				
XD266	Scimitar F.1				
XD267	Scimitar F.1				
XD268	Scimitar F.1				
XD269	Scimitar F.1				
XD270	Scimitar F.1				
XD271	Scimitar F.1				To A2589
XD272	Scimitar F.1				To A2585
XD273	Scimitar F.1				

XD274-XD381

serial	type	sqdn/unit	code	where&when seen		remarks
XD274	Scimitar F.1					To A2584
XD275	Scimitar F.1					To A2587
XD276	Scimitar F.1					To A2591
XD277	Scimitar F.1					
XD278	Scimitar F.1					To A2586
XD279	Scimitar F.1					
XD280	Scimitar F.1					To A2583
XD281	Scimitar F.1					
XD282	Scimitar F.1					
XD316	Scimitar F.1					
XD317	Scimitar F.1					Pr FAAM
XD318	Scimitar F.1					
XD319	Scimitar F.1					
XD320	Scimitar F.1					
XD321	Scimitar F.1					
XD322	Scimitar F.1					
XD323	Scimitar F.1					
XD324	Scimitar F.1					To A2590
XD325	Scimitar F.1					
XD326	Scimitar F.1					
XD327	Scimitar F.1					
XD328	Scimitar F.1					
XD329	Scimitar F.1					
XD330	Scimitar F.1					
XD331	Scimitar F.1					
XD332	Scimitar F.1					To A2574 Pr Helston
XD333	Scimitar F.1					

XD334 - XD357 Scimitar F.1 (24 a/c) Cancelled and not built

One Swift F.1 ordered as a replacement for WK198 which had been retained by the manufacturers for conversion to F.4 prototype. Believed not built.

serial	type	sqdn/unit	code	where&when seen		remarks
XD361	Swift F.1					

Unconfirmed reports suggest that Whirlwind HAR.3's XJ393-XJ402 were originally allocated serials XD363-XD372 of which XD363/4 were completed as such (NB: see XJ393 etc).

serial	type	sqdn/unit	code	where&when seen		remarks
XD363	Whirlwind HAR.3					To XJ393
XD364	Whirlwind HAR.3					To XJ394

One Varsity T.1 built by Vickers-Armstrongs Ltd at Hurn in 1953 as a replacement for WJ900 which was diverted off contract to the Swedish Air Force, serial Fv 82001.

serial	type	sqdn/unit	code	where&when seen		remarks
XD366	Varsity T.1					

Built pre-1943, this sailplane served with the WWII German NSFK. To UK 1945 for RN use retaining NSFK number 'LG-WZ' until 1947. XD371 allocated c1952 at Lee-on-Solent.

serial	type	sqdn/unit	code	where&when seen		remarks
XD371	Mü 13A					Ex LG-WZ

2nd production order for 160 Vampire T.11 trainers for the RAF built by de Havilland Aircraft Co Ltd at Christchurch, Hatfield, and Chester (Hawarden) against Contract 8981. Delivered between 9.53 and 10.55. Several assembled by sub-contractors, and others manufactured by Fairey Aviation Ltd at Ringway.

serial	type	sqdn/unit	code	where&when seen		remarks
XD375	Vampire T.11					To 7887M Pr Elsham
XD376	Vampire T.11					
XD377	Vampire T.11					To 8203M Pr B'ham
XD378	Vampire T.11					
XD379	Vampire T.11					
XD380	Vampire T.11					
XD381	Vampire T.11					

XD382-XD457

serial	type	sqdn/unit	code	where&when seen		remarks
XD382	Vampire T.11					To 8033M Pr Shawbury
XD383	Vampire T.11					
XD384	Vampire T.11					
XD385	Vampire T.11					
XD386	Vampire T.11					To 7629M
XD387	Vampire T.11					
XD388	Vampire T.11					
XD389	Vampire T.11					
XD390	Vampire T.11					
XD391	Vampire T.11					
XD392	Vampire T.11					
XD393	Vampire T.11					To 7732M
XD394	Vampire T.11					
XD395	Vampire T.11					To GI Chadderton
XD396	Vampire T.11					
XD397	Vampire T.11					
XD398	Vampire T.11					
XD399	Vampire T.11					
XD400	Vampire T.11					
XD401	Vampire T.11					
XD402	Vampire T.11					
XD403	Vampire T.11					Pr Strathallan
XD404	Vampire T.11					
XD405	Vampire T.11					
XD424	Vampire T.11					
XD425	Vampire T.11					Pr Tinwald Downs
XD426	Vampire T.11					
XD427	Vampire T.11					
XD428	Vampire T.11					
XD429	Vampire T.11					See XD542
XD430	Vampire T.11					To 7450M
XD431	Vampire T.11					
XD432	Vampire T.11					
XD433	Vampire T.11					
XD434	Vampire T.11					To GI Barton
XD435	Vampire T.11					Pr Wrexham
XD436	Vampire T.11					
XD437	Vampire T.11					
XD438	Vampire T.11					
XD439	Vampire T.11					
XD440	Vampire T.11					To SwAF U-1238
XD441	Vampire T.11					
XD442	Vampire T.11					
XD443	Vampire T.11					
XD444	Vampire T.11					To 7918M
XD445	Vampire T.11					Pr Huddersfield
XD446	Vampire T.11					
XD447	Vampire T.11					Pr Tattershall
XD448	Vampire T.11					
XD449	Vampire T.11					
XD450	Vampire T.11					
XD451	Vampire T.11					
XD452	Vampire T.11					7990M Pr London Colney
XD453	Vampire T.11					To 7890M Pr Salisbury
XD454	Vampire T.11					
XD455	Vampire T.11					
XD456	Vampire T.11					
XD457	Vampire T.11					To 7423M

XD458-XD589

serial	type	sqdn/unit	code	where&when seen		remarks
XD458	Vampire T.11					
XD459	Vampire T.11					
XD460	Vampire T.11					
XD461	Vampire T.11					
XD462	Vampire T.11					
XD463	Vampire T.11					To 8023M Pr Nottingham
XD506	Vampire T.11					To 7983M Pr Swinderby
XD507	Vampire T.11					
XD508	Vampire T.11					
XD509	Vampire T.11					
XD510	Vampire T.11					
XD511	Vampire T.11					To 7814M Pr Gorleston
XD512	Vampire T.11					
XD513	Vampire T.11					
XD514	Vampire T.11					
XD515	Vampire T.11					To 7998M Pr Nostell Py
XD516	Vampire T.11					
XD517	Vampire T.11					
XD518	Vampire T.11					
XD519	Vampire T.11					To 7651M
XD520	Vampire T.11					
XD521	Vampire T.11					
XD522	Vampire T.11					
XD523	Vampire T.11					
XD524	Vampire T.11					
XD525	Vampire T.11					To 7882M
XD526	Vampire T.11					
XD527	Vampire T.11					
XD528	Vampire T.11					To 8159M Pr W'hampton
XD529	Vampire T.11					
XD530	Vampire T.11					
XD531	Vampire T.11					
XD532	Vampire T.11					To IAF
XD533	Vampire T.11					
XD534	Vampire T.11					Pr Cheadle Hulme
XD535	Vampire T.11					GI Preston Tech
XD536	Vampire T.11					To 7734M Pr Reading
XD537	Vampire T.11					
XD538	Vampire T.11					To 7951M
XD539	Vampire T.11					
XD540	Vampire T.11					
XD541	Vampire T.11					
XD542	Vampire T.11					7604M Cranwell 'XD429'
XD543	Vampire T.11					
XD544	Vampire T.11					To SwAF
XD545	Vampire T.11					
XD546	Vampire T.11					
XD547	Vampire T.11					Pr Strathallan
XD548	Vampire T.11					To RJAF
XD549	Vampire T.11					
XD550	Vampire T.11					
XD551	Vampire T.11					
XD552	Vampire T.11					To RJAF
XD553	Vampire T.11					
XD554	Vampire T.11					
XD588	Vampire T.11					
XD589	Vampire T.11					

XD590-XD656

serial	type	sqdn/unit	code	where&when seen		remarks
XD590	Vampire T.11					
XD591	Vampire T.11					
XD592	Vampire T.11					
XD593	Vampire T.11					Pr Winthorpe
XD594	Vampire T.11					To SwAF
XD595	Vampire T.11					
XD596	Vampire T.11					To 7939M Pr Calmore
XD597	Vampire T.11					
XD598	Vampire T.11					To Austrian AF 5C-VA
XD599	Vampire T.11					To GI Staverton
XD600	Vampire T.11					
XD601	Vampire T.11					To 7878M
XD602	Vampire T.11					7737M Pr Sut Coldfield
XD603	Vampire T.11					
XD604	Vampire T.11					
XD605	Vampire T.11					
XD606	Vampire T.11					
XD607	Vampire T.11					
XD608	Vampire T.11					To SwAF
XD609	Vampire T.11					
XD610	Vampire T.11					
XD611	Vampire T.11					
XD612	Vampire T.11					
XD613	Vampire T.11					To 8122M Pr Cosford
XD614	Vampire T.11					8124M ntu To ChAF
XD615	Vampire T.11					
XD616	Vampire T.11					Pr Hoddesdon
XD617	Vampire T.11					To 7815M
XD618	Vampire T.11					
XD619	Vampire T.11					
XD620	Vampire T.11					
XD621	Vampire T.11					
XD622	Vampire T.11					To 8160M
XD623	Vampire T.11					
XD624	Vampire T.11					To GI Macclesfield
XD625	Vampire T.11					
XD626	Vampire T.11					To GI Bitteswell
XD627	Vampire T.11					

One Handley-Page Hermes and three Vickers Vikings allotted temporary military marks following a trooping contract awarded to Airwork Ltd. XD632 c/n HP81/1 ex G-AKFP; XD635 c/n 121 ex G-AHOT; XD636 c/n 124 ex G-AHOW; XD637 c/n 118 ex G-AHOR.

serial	type	sqdn/unit	code	where&when seen		remarks
XD632	HP.81 Hermes 4A					Restored to G-AKFP
XD635	V.498 Viking 1A					Restored to G-AHOT
XD636	V.498 Viking 1A					Restored to G-AHOW
XD637	V.498 Viking 1A					Restored to G-AHOR

The prototype Dragonfly (G-AKTW c/n WA/H/1) allotted military marks 3.52 for evaluation by the RAF. F/f as XD649 12.3.52, to Lympne 13.3 and back to Yeovil 24.3.

serial	type	sqdn/unit	code	where&when seen		remarks
XD649	WS.51 Dragonfly 1A					Restored to G-AKTW

Four Sycamore HR.51 helicopters built by Bristol Aeroplane Co Ltd at Filton in 1954, for direct transfer to RAN. Allotted c/ns 13071, 13145-13147. XD653 was originally allocated G-AMWJ (ntu). All initially to RN charge 3.54 & 8.54: to RAN 10.54.

serial	type	sqdn/unit	code	where&when seen		remarks
XD653	Sycamore HR.51					To RAN Pr Nowra NSW
XD654	Sycamore HR.51					To RAN
XD655	Sycamore HR.51					To RAN
XD656	Sycamore HR.51					To RAN

XD662-XD726

serial	type	sqdn/unit	code	where&when seen	remarks

The prototype Vickers V1000 jet transport ordered against Contract 6/Aircraft/8630/CB6(c). The V1000 programme was cancelled when the prototype was almost complete.

serial	type	sqdn/unit	code	where&when seen	remarks
XD662	V.1000				Cancelled

Four Avro Yorks allotted military marks following a temporary trooping contract issued to Air Charter Ltd. XD667 ex G-AMUN (and leased from Scottish Aviation Ltd) ; XD668 ex G-AMUU; XD669 ex G-AMUV; and XD670 c/n 1222 ex G-AGNU.

serial	type	sqdn/unit	code	where&when seen	remarks
XD667	Avro 685 York 1				Restored to G-AMUN
XD668	Avro 685 York 1				Restored to G-AMUU
XD669	Avro 685 York 1				Restored to G-AMUV
XD670	Avro 685 York 1				Restored to G-AGNU

Ten prototype and pre-production Jet Provosts for the RAF built by Hunting Percival Aircraft Ltd at Luton with c/ns PAC/84/001 to PAC/84/005 & PAC/84/007 to PAC/84/011 resp. T.1 XD674 f/f 26.6.54. XD694 completed as prototype T.2.

serial	type	sqdn/unit	code	where&when seen	remarks
XD674	Jet Provost T.1				To 7570M Pr St Athan
XD675	Jet Provost T.1				
XD676	Jet Provost T.1				
XD677	Jet Provost T.1				
XD678	Jet Provost T.1				
XD679	Jet Provost T.1				
XD680	Jet Provost T.1				
XD692	Jet Provost T.1				To 7369M
XD693	Jet Provost T.1				
XD694	Jet Provost T.2				

Two Avro 720 development prototypes built at Woodford to Spec F137D by A.V.Roe & Co Ltd to compete against Saunders-Roe SR.53. Both Avro 720's were cancelled in 1957 when the first (XD696) was virtually complete.

serial	type	sqdn/unit	code	where&when seen	remarks
XD696	Avro 720				
XD701	Avro 720				Cancelled

2nd block of Canadair F-86E Sabre F.4's built under licence at Montreal, Canada for RAF Fighter Command, to follow on from XD138. Funded through MDAP by the USA, these aircraft were initially designated F-86E-6-CAN and allocated USAF serials 52-10177 to 52-10236 respectively.

serial	type	sqdn/unit	code	where&when seen	remarks
XD706	Sabre F.4				Ex 19707
XD707	Sabre F.4				Ex 19708
XD708	Sabre F.4				Ex 19709 To USAF
XD709	Sabre F.4				Ex 19710 To USAF
XD710	Sabre F.4				Ex 19711
XD711	Sabre F.4				Ex 19712
XD712	Sabre F.4				Ex 19713
XD713	Sabre F.4				Ex 19714
XD714	Sabre F.4				Ex 19715 To USAF
XD715	Sabre F.4				Ex 19716 To USAF
XD716	Sabre F.4				Ex 19717
XD717	Sabre F.4				Ex 19718 To USAF
XD718	Sabre F.4				Ex 19719
XD719	Sabre F.4				Ex 19720 To USAF
XD720	Sabre F.4				Ex 19721 To USAF
XD721	Sabre F.4				Ex 19722 To USAF
XD722	Sabre F.4				Ex 19723
XD723	Sabre F.4				Ex 19724 To USAF
XD724	Sabre F.4				Ex 19725 To USAF
XD725	Sabre F.4				Ex 19726 To USAF
XD726	Sabre F.4				Ex 19727 To USAF

XD727-XD815

serial	type	sqdn/unit	code	where&when seen		remarks
XD727	Sabre F.4					Ex 19728
XD728	Sabre F.4					Ex 19729 To USAF
XD729	Sabre F.4					Ex 19730
XD730	Sabre F.4					Ex 19731
XD731	Sabre F.4					Ex 19749 To USAF
XD732	Sabre F.4					Ex 19750
XD733	Sabre F.4					Ex 19751
XD734	Sabre F.4					Ex 19752 To USAF
XD735	Sabre F.4					Ex 19753 To USAF
XD736	Sabre F.4					Ex 19754 To USAF
XD753	Sabre F.4					Ex 19755 To USAF
XD754	Sabre F.4					Ex 19756 To USAF
XD755	Sabre F.4					Ex 19757
XD756	Sabre F.4					Ex 19758 To USAF
XD757	Sabre F.4					Ex 19759 To USAF
XD758	Sabre F.4					Ex 19760
** XD759	Sabre F.4					Ex 19761
XD760	Sabre F.4					Ex 19762 To USAF
XD761	Sabre F.4					Ex 19763 To USAF
XD762	Sabre F.4					Ex 19764
XD763	Sabre F.4					Ex 19765
XD764	Sabre F.4					Ex 19766 To USAF
XD765	Sabre F.4					Ex 19767 To USAF
XD766	Sabre F.4					Ex 19768
XD767	Sabre F.4					Ex 19769 To USAF
XD768	Sabre F.4					Ex 19770
XD769	Sabre F.4					Ex 19771
XD770	Sabre F.4					Ex 19772
XD771	Sabre F.4					Ex 19773
XD772	Sabre F.4					Ex 19793
XD773	Sabre F.4					Ex 19794
XD774	Sabre F.4					Ex 19795 To USAF
XD775	Sabre F.4					Ex 19796
XD776	Sabre F.4					Ex 19797
** XD777	Sabre F.4					Ex 19798 To USAF
** XD778	Sabre F.4					Ex 19799 To USAF
** XD779	Sabre F.4					Ex 19800 To USAF
** XD780	Sabre F.4					Ex 19801
** XD781	Sabre F.4					Ex 19802 To USAF

Note that allocations marked (**) are compromised with the following aircraft. One Fairey Aviation Jet Gyrodyne (c/n F9420) which f/f January 1954 following conversion from Gyrodyne G-AJJP.

serial	type	sqdn/unit	code	where&when seen		remarks
XD759	Jet Gyrodyne					Ex G-AJJP To XJ389

20 RAF Whirlwind HAR.2/4's (Contract 6/Aircraft/9409). XD777 f/f 21.10.54 and XD784 24.11.54. This batch was delivered with these serials but was later re-allotted serials XJ407-XJ414. XJ426 f/f 14.12.54. C/ns believed to be WA33-38/40-53 resp.

serials	type		remarks
XD777-XD784	Whirlwind HAR.2	(8 a/c)	Re-allotted XJ407-XJ414 as HAR.4
XD795-XD806	Whirlwind HAR.2	(12 a/c)	Re-allotted XJ426-XJ437 as HAR.2/HAR.4

Third production order for 56 Valiant BK.1 bomber/tankers for the RAF built by Vickers-Armstrongs Ltd at Weybridge against Contract 6/Aircraft/9446/CB6(c). XD812 delivered 18.7.56. Production terminated with the 38th a/c (XD875) which f/f 27.8.57.

serial	type	sqdn/unit	code	where&when seen		remarks
XD812	Valiant BK.1					
XD813	Valiant BK.1					
XD814	Valiant BK.1					
XD815	Valiant BK.1					

XD816-XD915

serial	type	sqdn/unit	code	where&when seen		remarks
XD816	Valiant BK.1					Nose Pr Henlow
XD817	Valiant BK.1					
XD818	Valiant BK.1					To 7894M Pr Marham
XD819	Valiant BK.1					
XD820	Valiant BK.1					
XD821	Valiant BK.1					
XD822	Valiant BK.1					
XD823	Valiant BK.1					
XD824	Valiant BK.1					
XD825	Valiant BK.1					
XD826	Valiant BK.1					To 7872M
XD827	Valiant BK.1					
XD828	Valiant BK.1					
XD829	Valiant BK.1					
XD830	Valiant BK.1					
XD857	Valiant BK.1					
XD858	Valiant BK.1					
XD859	Valiant BK.1					
XD860	Valiant BK.1					
XD861	Valiant BK.1					
XD862	Valiant BK.1					
XD863	Valiant BK.1					
XD864	Valiant BK.1					
XD865	Valiant BK.1					
XD866	Valiant BK.1					
XD867	Valiant BK.1					
XD868	Valiant BK.1					
XD869	Valiant BK.1					
XD870	Valiant BK.1					
XD871	Valiant BK.1					
XD872	Valiant BK.1					
XD873	Valiant BK.1					
XD874	Valiant BK.1					
XD875	Valiant BK.1					

XD876-XD893 Valiant BK.1 (18 a/c) Cancelled and not built.

One Gannet AS.1 (c/n F.9327) built by Fairey Aviation Co Ltd at Stockport to replace T.2 XA531 (cancelled). It brought the total procurement of the XA-contract up to 140 units. After construction it was delivered to the Royal Australian Navy in 8.57.

serial	type	sqdn/unit	code	where&when seen		remarks
XD898	Gannet AS.1					To RAN

2nd production batch of Swift FR.5 fighter-reconnaissance aircraft for the RAF to be built by the Supermarine Division of Vickers-Armstrongs Ltd at South Marston 1956/57 under Type No.549. Production terminated with the 58th aircraft (XD977).

serial	type	sqdn/unit	code	where&when seen		remarks
XD903	Swift FR.5					
XD904	Swift FR.5					
XD905	Swift FR.5					
XD906	Swift FR.5					
XD907	Swift FR.5					
XD908	Swift FR.5					
XD909	Swift FR.5					
XD910	Swift FR.5					
XD911	Swift FR.5					
XD912	Swift FR.5					
XD913	Swift FR.5					
XD914	Swift FR.5					
XD915	Swift FR.5					

XD916-XE172

serial	type	sqdn/unit	code	where&when seen		remarks
XD916	Swift FR.5					
XD917	Swift FR.5					
XD918	Swift FR.5					
XD919	Swift FR.5					
XD920	Swift FR.5					
XD921	Swift FR.5					
XD922	Swift FR.5					
XD923	Swift FR.5					
XD924	Swift FR.5					
XD925	Swift FR.5					
XD926	Swift FR.5					
XD927	Swift FR.5					
XD928	Swift FR.5					
XD929	Swift FR.5					
XD930	Swift FR.5					
XD948	Swift FR.5					
XD949	Swift FR.5					
XD950	Swift FR.5					
XD951	Swift FR.5					To 7447M
XD952	Swift FR.5					
XD953	Swift FR.5					
XD954	Swift FR.5					
XD955	Swift FR.5					
XD956	Swift FR.5					
XD957	Swift FR.5					
XD958	Swift FR.5					
XD959	Swift FR.5					
XD960	Swift FR.5					
XD961	Swift FR.5					
XD962	Swift FR.5					
XD963	Swift FR.5					
XD964	Swift FR.5					
XD965	Swift FR.5					
XD966	Swift FR.5					
XD967	Swift FR.5					
XD968	Swift FR.5					
XD969	Swift FR.5					
XD970	Swift FR.5					
XD971	Swift FR.5					
XD972	Swift FR.5					
XD973	Swift FR.5					
XD974	Swift FR.5					
XD975	Swift FR.5					
XD976	Swift FR.5					
XD977	Swift FR.5					

XD978-XD988 Swift FR.5 (11 a/c) Cancelled and not built
XE105-XE116 Swift FR.5 (12 a/c) Cancelled and not built
XE133-XE164 Swift FR.5 (32 a/c) Cancelled and not built

60 Seamew AS.1's ordered for the RN from Short Bros & Harland, Belfast to Spec M.123 D&P issued in 2.52. In 2.55 the RAF ordered 30 MR.2's from the above production order, 5 being completed before cancellation in 2.56; the AS.1's were cancelled in 3.57. C/ns allocated were XE169-XE186 (SH1773-SH1790) & XE205-XE227 (SH1791-SH1813).

serial	type	sqdn/unit	code	where&when seen		remarks
XE169	Seamew AS.1					
XE170	Seamew AS.1					
XE171	Seamew AS.1					
XE172	Seamew AS.1					

XE173-XE319

serial	type	sqdn/unit	code	where&when seen		remarks
XE173	Seamew MR.2					
XE174	Seamew MR.2					
XE175	Seamew MR.2					
XE176	Seamew MR.2					
XE177	Seamew AS.1					
XE178	Seamew AS.1					
XE179	Seamew AS.1					
XE180	Seamew MR.2					To GI Shorts Belfast
XE181	Seamew AS.1					
XE182	Seamew AS.1					
XE183	Seamew AS.1					
XE184	Seamew AS.1					
XE185	Seamew AS.1					
XE186	Seamew AS.1					
XE205	Seamew AS.1					
XE206	Seamew AS.1					
XE207	Seamew AS.1					
XE208	Seamew AS.1					
XE209	Seamew AS.1					
XE210	Seamew AS.1					
XE211	Seamew AS.1					

XE212-XE231 Seamew AS.1 (20 a/c) Cancelled and not completed
XE263-XE277 Seamew AS.1 (15 a/c) Cancelled and not built

Two C-47B Dakota aircraft allocated military serials following a temporary trooping contract awarded to Airwork Ltd. XE280 c/n 15290/26735; XE281 c/n 16112/32860.

serial	type	sqdn/unit	code	where&when seen		remarks
XE280	C-47B Dakota 4					Restored to G-AMRA
XE281	C-47B Dakota 4					Restored to G-AMZD

Three Type 173 helicopters built by the Bristol Aeroplane Co Ltd at Weston-super-Mare in 1956/57. Allotted c/ns 13204-13206 resp, XE286-288 were originally registered as G-AMYF/MYG/MYH. XE286 f/f 9.11.56; construction of XE287/288 abandoned.

serial	type	sqdn/unit	code	where&when seen		remarks
XE286	Bristol 173 Mk.3					
XE287	Bristol 173 Mk.3					Not flown
XE288	Bristol 173 Mk.3					Not completed

Continued procurement of Valiant BK.1's against Contract 6/Aircraft/9446/CB6(c), all were later cancelled (see XD812 etc). These aircraft were not V1000's as often stated.

XE294-XE299 Valiant BK.1 (6 a/c) Cancelled and not built

17 Sycamore HR.14 helicopters built by the Bristol Aeroplane Co Ltd for the RAF with c/ns 13144-145/149-153/194-198/220-224 resp. XE313-317 were originally registered as Sycamore Mk.4's G-AMWK-MWO resp. The batch was delivered between 11.53 and 11.54.

serial	type	sqdn/unit	code	where&when seen		remarks
XE306	Sycamore HR.14					
XE307	Sycamore HR.14					
XE308	Sycamore HR.14					
XE309	Sycamore HR.14					
XE310	Sycamore HR.14					
XE311	Sycamore HR.14					
XE312	Sycamore HR.14					
XE313	Sycamore HR.14					Ex G-AMWK ntu
XE314	Sycamore HR.14					Ex G-AMWL ntu
XE315	Sycamore HR.14					Ex G-AMWM ntu
XE316	Sycamore HR.14					Ex G-AMWN ntu
XE317	Sycamore HR.14					Ex G-AMWO ntu Pr
XE318	Sycamore HR.14					
XE319	Sycamore HR.14					

XE320-XE393

serial	type	sqdn/unit	code	where&when seen		remarks
XE320	Sycamore HR.14					
XE321	Sycamore HR.14					
XE322	Sycamore HR.14					

107 Sea Hawk fighter aircraft for the RN, contracted to Sir W.G.Armstrong-Whitworth Aircraft Ltd at Coventry. XE327-338 were built as FGA.4's and the remainder as FGA.6's although all but two FGA.4's were upgraded to FGA.6's. Allotted c/ns AW6288-AW6394, deliveries took place between 3.55 and 1.56. Final eight aircraft cancelled.

serial	type	sqdn/unit	code	where&when seen		remarks
XE327	Sea Hawk FGA.6					To A2556
XE328	Sea Hawk FGA.6					
XE329	Sea Hawk FGA.4					
XE330	Sea Hawk FGA.6					To A2555
XE331	Sea Hawk FGA.6					
XE332	Sea Hawk FGA.4					
XE333	Sea Hawk FGA.6					To INS IN187
XE334	Sea Hawk FGA.6					
XE335	Sea Hawk FGA.6					To INS IN191
XE336	Sea Hawk FGA.6					
XE337	Sea Hawk FGA.6					
XE338	Sea Hawk FGA.6					
XE339	Sea Hawk FGA.6					To 8156M To A2635
XE340	Sea Hawk FGA.6					Pr FAAM Wroughton
XE341	Sea Hawk FGA.6					
XE342	Sea Hawk FGA.6					
XE343	Sea Hawk FGA.6					
XE344	Sea Hawk FGA.6					
XE362	Sea Hawk FGA.6					To INS IN185
XE363	Sea Hawk FGA.6					
XE364	Sea Hawk FGA.6					See XE489
XE365	Sea Hawk FGA.6					
XE366	Sea Hawk FGA.6					To A2515
XE367	Sea Hawk FGA.6					To INS IN193
XE368	Sea Hawk FGA.6					To A2534 Pr Helston
XE369	Sea Hawk FGA.6					To A2580/8158M/A2633
XE370	Sea Hawk FGA.6					
XE371	Sea Hawk FGA.6					To AWA 6.63 for INS?
XE372	Sea Hawk FGA.6					To INS IN192
XE373	Sea Hawk FGA.6					
XE374	Sea Hawk FGA.6					
XE375	Sea Hawk FGA.6					
XE376	Sea Hawk FGA.6					
XE377	Sea Hawk FGA.6					
XE378	Sea Hawk FGA.6					To INS IN181
XE379	Sea Hawk FGA.6					
XE380	Sea Hawk FGA.6					
XE381	Sea Hawk FGA.6					
XE382	Sea Hawk FGA.6					
XE383	Sea Hawk FGA.6					To INS IN183
XE384	Sea Hawk FGA.6					
XE385	Sea Hawk FGA.6					
XE386	Sea Hawk FGA.6					
XE387	Sea Hawk FGA.6					
XE388	Sea Hawk FGA.6					
XE389	Sea Hawk FGA.6					To AWA 6.63 for INS?
XE390	Sea Hawk FGA.6					To 8157M To A2636
XE391	Sea Hawk FGA.6					
XE392	Sea Hawk FGA.6					
XE393	Sea Hawk FGA.6					

XE394-XE506

serial	type	sqdn/unit	code	where&when seen		remarks
XE394	Sea Hawk FGA.6					To INS IN184
XE395	Sea Hawk FGA.6					
XE396	Sea Hawk FGA.6					
XE397	Sea Hawk FGA.6					To INS IN186
XE398	Sea Hawk FGA.6					
XE399	Sea Hawk FGA.6					
XE400	Sea Hawk FGA.6					
XE401	Sea Hawk FGA.6					
XE402	Sea Hawk FGA.6					
XE403	Sea Hawk FGA.6					
XE404	Sea Hawk FGA.6					
XE405	Sea Hawk FGA.6					
XE406	Sea Hawk FGA.6					
XE407	Sea Hawk FGA.6					
XE408	Sea Hawk FGA.6					
XE409	Sea Hawk FGA.6					
XE410	Sea Hawk FGA.6					
XE411	Sea Hawk FGA.6					
XE435	Sea Hawk FGA.6					
XE436	Sea Hawk FGA.6					
XE437	Sea Hawk FGA.6					
XE438	Sea Hawk FGA.6					To AWA 6.63 for INS?
XE439	Sea Hawk FGA.6					
XE440	Sea Hawk FGA.6					
XE441	Sea Hawk FGA.6					
XE442	Sea Hawk FGA.6					
XE443	Sea Hawk FGA.6					
XE444	Sea Hawk FGA.6					
XE445	Sea Hawk FGA.6					
XE446	Sea Hawk FGA.6					
XE447	Sea Hawk FGA.6					To AWA 6.63 for INS?
XE448	Sea Hawk FGA.6					
XE449	Sea Hawk FGA.6					
XE450	Sea Hawk FGA.6					
XE451	Sea Hawk FGA.6					
XE452	Sea Hawk FGA.6					
XE453	Sea Hawk FGA.6					
XE454	Sea Hawk FGA.6					To AWA 6.63 for INS?
XE455	Sea Hawk FGA.6					
XE456	Sea Hawk FGA.6					
XE457	Sea Hawk FGA.6					
XE458	Sea Hawk FGA.6					To INS IN182
XE459	Sea Hawk FGA.6					
XE460	Sea Hawk FGA.6					
XE461	Sea Hawk FGA.6					
XE462	Sea Hawk FGA.6					
XE463	Sea Hawk FGA.6					
XE489	Sea Hawk FGA.6					Pr Southend as 'XE364'
XE490	Sea Hawk FGA.6					

XE491-XE498 Sea Hawk FGA.6 (8 a/c) Cancelled and not built

One Provost T.1 training aircraft built by Hunting Percival Aircraft Ltd at Luton as a replacement aircraft for WV437 which had been transferred to the civil register. As such it formed part of Contract 6848 and was allocated c/n PAC/56/040. It was delivered to the Central Flying School in 9.53.

serial	type	sqdn/unit	code	where&when seen		remarks
XE506	Provost T.1					To G-23-5/FMAF FM1035

XE512-XE580

serial	type	sqdn/unit	code	where&when seen		remarks

Four Pioneer CC.1 communications aircraft built for the RAF by Scottish Aviation Ltd at Prestwick. XE512 was originally the Mk.1 prototype VL515 (c/n 101), later G-AKBF. XE514 f/f 3.9.53 as G-ANAZ (c/n 103, VL516 ntu). XE513 and XE515 had c/ns 102 and 104 respectively.

serial	type	sqdn/unit	code	where&when seen		remarks
XE512	Pioneer CC.1					Ex G-AKBF
XE513	Pioneer CC.1					
XE514	Pioneer CC.1					Ex G-ANAZ
XE515	Pioneer CC.1					

The prototype Fairey Rotodyne (Type Y) built at Hayes by Fairey Aviation Co Ltd and assembled at White Waltham for f/f 6.11.57. It was allotted c/n F9429 and the project was cancelled on 26.2.62.

serial	type	sqdn/unit	code	where&when seen		remarks
XE521	Rotodyne					Parts to Cranfield

The 2nd production order for 100 Hunter F.6 fighter aircraft for the RAF to follow WW598 and built by Hawker Aircraft Ltd at Kingston against Contract 6/Aircraft/7144/CB7(a). XE526 f/f 11.10.55; XE656 f/f 9.8.56. Subsequently many aircraft were converted to FGA.9 or FR.10 standard whilst XE531 was converted to 2-seat T.12 configuration for the RAE. In 1975/77 most surviving F.6's were modified to F.6A standard.

serial	type	sqdn/unit	code	where&when seen		remarks
XE526	Hunter F.6					To SwAF J-4008
XE527	Hunter F.6					To SwAF J-4006
XE528	Hunter F.6					To SwAF J-4009
XE529	Hunter F.6					To SwAF J-4005
XE530	Hunter FGA.9					To G-9-267/KuAF 220
XE531	Hunter T.12					
XE532	Hunter FGA.9					
XE533	Hunter F.6					To SwAF J-4002
XE534	Hunter F.6					To LeAF L-172
XE535	Hunter FGA.9					
XE536	Hunter F.6					To SwAF J-4001
XE537	Hunter F.6					To IAF BA233
XE538	Hunter F.6					To IAF BA234
XE539	Hunter F.6					To IAF BA235
XE540	Hunter F.6					To IAF BA236
XE541	Hunter F.6					To SwAF J-4003
XE542	Hunter F.6					To SwAF J-4004
XE543	Hunter F.6					To RJAF 707
XE544	Hunter FGA.9					
XE545	Hunter F.6					To SwAF J-4007
XE546	Hunter FGA.9					
XE547	Hunter F.6					To IAF BA237
XE548	Hunter F.6					To RRAF120
XE549	Hunter F.6					To IAF BA238
XE550	Hunter FGA.9					To KuAF
XE551	Hunter F.6					To RJAF 700/G-9-195/700
XE552	Hunter FGA.9					
XE553	Hunter F.6					To SwAF J-4012
XE554	Hunter F.6					To SwAF J-4010
XE555	Hunter F.6					To SwAF J-4011
XE556	Hunter FR.10					To G-9-353/IAF S1391
XE557	Hunter F.6					To G-9-319/ChAF J-727
XE558	Hunter F.6					To RJAF 701
XE559	Hunter F.6					To RRAF116
XE560	Hunter F.6					To RRAF126
XE561	Hunter F.6					To G-9-318/ChAF J-726
XE579	Hunter FR.10					
XE580	Hunter FR.10					To G-9-332/ChAF J-730

XE581-XE652

serial	type	sqdn/unit	code	where&when seen		remarks
XE581	Hunter FGA.9					
XE582	Hunter FGA.9					
XE583	Hunter F.6					
XE584	Hunter FGA.9					To G-9-450
XE585	Hunter FR.10					To G-9-354/IAF S1392
XE586	Hunter F.6					
XE587	Hunter F.6					
XE588	Hunter F.6					
XE589	Hunter FR.10					To G-9-270/ADAF 701
XE590	Hunter F.6					
XE591	Hunter F.6					To G-9-212/RSAF 602
XE592	Hunter FGA.9					
XE593	Hunter F.6					
XE594	Hunter F.6					
XE595	Hunter F.6					
XE596	Hunter FR.10					
XE597	Hunter FGA.9					
XE598	Hunter F.6					To LeAF L-170
XE599	Hunter FR.10					To G-9-376/SADC 535
XE600	Hunter FGA.9					
XE601	Hunter FGA.9					
XE602	Hunter F.6					
XE603	Hunter F.6					To G-9-209/RJAF 832
XE604	Hunter FGA.9					
XE605	Hunter FR.10					To G-9-360/SADC 523
XE606	Hunter F.6A					
XE607	Hunter FGA.9					
XE608	Hunter F.6A					
XE609	Hunter FGA.9					
XE610	Hunter FGA.9					
XE611	Hunter FGA.9					To G-9-295/SwAF J-4103
XE612	Hunter F.6					
XE613	Hunter F.6					To RRAF118
XE614	Hunter FR.10					To G-9-366/SADC 533
XE615	Hunter FGA.9					To G-9-305/SADC 508
XE616	Hunter FGA.9					
XE617	Hunter FGA.9					
XE618	Hunter FGA.9					To KuAF
XE619	Hunter F.6					
XE620	Hunter FGA.9					To G-9-273/IAF A967
XE621	Hunter FR.10					
XE622	Hunter FGA.9					
XE623	Hunter FGA.9					
XE624	Hunter FGA.9					
XE625	Hunter FR.10					To G-9-331/ChAF J-729
XE626	Hunter FR.10					To G-9-409/KAF 801
XE627	Hunter F.6A					
XE628	Hunter FGA.9					
XE643	Hunter FGA.9					To 8586M (nose)
XE644	Hunter F.6					To G-9-322/ChAF J-728
XE645	Hunter FGA.9					To RJAF 827
XE646	Hunter FGA.9					
XE647	Hunter FGA.9					
XE648	Hunter F.6					
XE649	Hunter FGA.9					
XE650	Hunter FGA.9					To G-9-449
XE651	Hunter FGA.9					
XE652	Hunter FGA.9					To G-9-323/SADC 519

XE653-XE716

serial	type	sqdn/unit	code	where&when seen		remarks
XE653	Hunter F.6A					
XE654	Hunter FGA.9					
XE655	Hunter FGA.9					To RJAF
XE656	Hunter F.6					

Continued production of 50 Hunter F.4 fighter aircraft for the RAF to follow WW665 and built by Hawker Aircraft Ltd at Blackpool against Contract 6/Aircraft/9817/CB7(a). Deliveries took place between 5.55 and 11.55. Eleven aircraft were subsequently upgraded to GA.11 standard for the RN and XE664/665 were converted to T.8/B configuration, also for the RN. Further production of Hunter F.4's followed with XF289.

serial	type	sqdn/unit	code	where&when seen		remarks
XE657	Hunter F.4					
XE658	Hunter F.4					
XE659	Hunter F.4					7785M/G-9-401/Sw J-4149
XE660	Hunter F.4					
XE661	Hunter F.4					
XE662	Hunter F.4					
XE663	Hunter F.4					
XE664	Hunter T.8B					To G-9-293/SADC 514
XE665	Hunter T.8C					
XE666	Hunter F.4					
XE667	Hunter F.4					
XE668	Hunter GA.11					
XE669	Hunter F.4					
XE670	Hunter F.4					7762M/8585M (nose)
XE671	Hunter F.4					
XE672	Hunter F.4					
XE673	Hunter GA.11					
XE674	Hunter GA.11					To G-9-340/SwAF J-4124
XE675	Hunter F.4					
XE676	Hunter F.4					
XE677	Hunter F.4					To GI Loughborough Col
XE678	Hunter F.4					7786M/G-9-404/Sw J-4145
XE679	Hunter F.4					7787M/G-9-370/SADC 541
XE680	Hunter GA.11					
XE681	Hunter F.4					
XE682	Hunter GA.11					
XE683	Hunter F.4					
XE684	Hunter F.4					
XE685	Hunter GA.11					
XE686	Hunter F.4					
XE687	Hunter F.4					
XE688	Hunter F.4					
XE689	Hunter GA.11					
XE702	Hunter F.4					7794M/G-9-375/Sw J-4204
XE703	Hunter F.4					
XE704	Hunter F.4					7788M/G-9-397/Ch J-736
XE705	Hunter F.4					
XE706	Hunter F.4					
XE707	Hunter GA.11					
XE708	Hunter F.4					
XE709	Hunter F.4					
XE710	Hunter F.4					
XE711	Hunter F.4					
XE712	Hunter GA.11					
XE713	Hunter F.4					
XE714	Hunter F.4					
XE715	Hunter F.4					To 7807M
XE716	Hunter GA.11					

XE717-XE805

serial	type	sqdn/unit	code	where&when seen		remarks
XE717	Hunter GA.11					To G-9-338/SwAF J-4122
XE718	Hunter F.4					

A batch of 20 ML-120D Midget piston-engined pilotless target aircraft produced to Spec U.120D by ML Aviation Ltd at White Waltham around 1953. Some, if not all, were launched at Larkhill ranges. Production continued with XG487 et seq.

serial	type	sqdn/unit	code	where&when seen		remarks
XE722	ML-120D Midget					
XE723	ML-120D Midget					
XE724	ML-120D Midget					
XE725	ML-120D Midget					
XE726	ML-120D Midget					
XE727	ML-120D Midget					
XE728	ML-120D Midget					
XE729	ML-120D Midget					
XE730	ML-120D Midget					
XE731	ML-120D Midget					
XE732	ML-120D Midget					
XE733	ML-120D Midget					
XE734	ML-120D Midget					
XE735	ML-120D Midget					
XE749	ML-120D Midget					
XE750	ML-120D Midget					
XE751	ML-120D Midget					
XE752	ML-120D Midget					
XE753	ML-120D Midget					
XE754	ML-120D Midget					

34 T.8/T.31B Cadet TX.2/3 gliders built by Slingsby Sailplanes Ltd at Kirkbymoorside against Contract 9708 for the Air Training Corps. The block was allocated c/ns 928-932 (XE758-XE762) and 897-925 (XE784-XE812). C/ns 928-932 were rebuilt aircraft.

serial	type	sqdn/unit	code	where&when seen		remarks
XE758	Cadet TX.2					Rebuild Ex VF181
XE759	Cadet TX.2					Rebuild Ex VM529
XE760	Cadet TX.2					Rebuild Ex VM539
XE761	Cadet TX.2					Rebuild Ex VM589
XE762	Cadet TX.2					Rebuild Ex VM594
XE784	Cadet TX.3					
XE785	Cadet TX.3					
XE786	Cadet TX.3					
XE787	Cadet TX.3					
XE788	Cadet TX.3					
XE789	Cadet TX.3					
XE790	Cadet TX.3					
XE791	Cadet TX.3					
XE792	Cadet TX.3					
XE793	Cadet TX.3					
XE794	Cadet TX.3					
XE795	Cadet TX.3					
XE796	Cadet TX.3					
XE797	Cadet TX.3					
XE798	Cadet TX.3					
XE799	Cadet TX.3					
XE800	Cadet TX.3					
XE801	Cadet TX.3					
XE802	Cadet TX.3					
XE803	Cadet TX.3					
XE804	Cadet TX.3					
XE805	Cadet TX.3					

XE806-XE876

serial	type	sqdn/unit	code	where&when seen		remarks
XE806	Cadet TX.3					
XE807	Cadet TX.3					
XE808	Cadet TX.3					
XE809	Cadet TX.3					
XE810	Cadet TX.3					
XE811	Cadet TX.3					
XE812	Cadet TX.3					

The third production batch of 135 Vampire T.11 training aircraft built for the RAF by the de Havilland Aircraft Co Ltd (Hatfield, Christchurch and Chester) against Contract 9751. Deliveries took place between 6.54 and 7.55.

serial	type	sqdn/unit	code	where&when seen		remarks
XE816	Vampire T.11					To SRAF SR116
XE817	Vampire T.11					To SRAF SR117
XE818	Vampire T.11					To SRAF SR118
XE819	Vampire T.11					To SRAF SR122
XE820	Vampire T.11					
XE821	Vampire T.11					
XE822	Vampire T.11					To 7585M
XE823	Vampire T.11					To SRAF SR119
XE824	Vampire T.11					To SRAF SR120
XE825	Vampire T.11					To SRAF SR121
XE826	Vampire T.11					To SRAF SR123
XE827	Vampire T.11					
XE828	Vampire T.11					To 7461M
XE829	Vampire T.11					
XE830	Vampire T.11					
XE831	Vampire T.11					
XE832	Vampire T.11					
XE833	Vampire T.11					
XE848	Vampire T.11					
XE849	Vampire T.11					To 7928M Pr Ware
XE850	Vampire T.11					
XE851	Vampire T.11					
XE852	Vampire T.11					To GI Hawarden
XE853	Vampire T.11					
XE854	Vampire T.11					
XE855	Vampire T.11					Pr Upton
XE856	Vampire T.11					Pr Welwyn Gdn City
XE857	Vampire T.11					8125M ntu To ChAF
XE858	Vampire T.11					
XE859	Vampire T.11					
XE860	Vampire T.11					
XE861	Vampire T.11					
XE862	Vampire T.11					
XE863	Vampire T.11					
XE864	Vampire T.11					
XE865	Vampire T.11					
XE866	Vampire T.11					
XE867	Vampire T.11					
XE868	Vampire T.11					
XE869	Vampire T.11					
XE870	Vampire T.11					
XE871	Vampire T.11					
XE872	Vampire T.11					Pr Long Itchington
XE873	Vampire T.11					
XE874	Vampire T.11					To 8582M Pr Valley
XE875	Vampire T.11					
XE876	Vampire T.11					

XE877-XE955

serial	type	sqdn/unit	code	where&when seen		remarks
XE877	Vampire T.11					
XE878	Vampire T.11					
XE879	Vampire T.11					
XE880	Vampire T.11					
XE881	Vampire T.11					
XE882	Vampire T.11					
XE883	Vampire T.11					
XE884	Vampire T.11					
XE885	Vampire T.11					
XE886	Vampire T.11					
XE887	Vampire T.11					To 7824M
XE888	Vampire T.11					
XE889	Vampire T.11					
XE890	Vampire T.11					To 7871M
XE891	Vampire T.11					
XE892	Vampire T.11					
XE893	Vampire T.11					
XE894	Vampire T.11					
XE895	Vampire T.11					
XE896	Vampire T.11					
XE897	Vampire T.11					
XE919	Vampire T.11					
XE920	Vampire T.11					To 8196M Pr Henlow
XE921	Vampire T.11					
XE922	Vampire T.11					
XE923	Vampire T.11					To 7446M
XE924	Vampire T.11					
XE925	Vampire T.11					
XE926	Vampire T.11					To 7472M
XE927	Vampire T.11					
XE928	Vampire T.11					
XE929	Vampire T.11					
XE930	Vampire T.11					
XE931	Vampire T.11					
XE932	Vampire T.11					To 7934M
XE933	Vampire T.11					
XE934	Vampire T.11					
XE935	Vampire T.11					Pr Hitchin
XE936	Vampire T.11					
XE937	Vampire T.11					
XE938	Vampire T.11					To SRAF SR124
XE939	Vampire T.11					To SRAF SR125
XE940	Vampire T.11					To SRAF SR126
XE941	Vampire T.11					To SRAF SR127
XE942	Vampire T.11					
XE943	Vampire T.11					
XE944	Vampire T.11					
XE945	Vampire T.11					To IAF
XE946	Vampire T.11					To 7473M
XE947	Vampire T.11					
XE948	Vampire T.11					
XE949	Vampire T.11					
XE950	Vampire T.11					To 8175M Pr Lightwater
XE951	Vampire T.11					
XE952	Vampire T.11					
XE953	Vampire T.11					
XE954	Vampire T.11					
XE955	Vampire T.11					

XE956-XF253

serial	type	sqdn/unit	code	where&when seen		remarks
XE956	Vampire T.11					To GI St Albans Tech
XE957	Vampire T.11					To IAF
XE958	Vampire T.11					
XE959	Vampire T.11					
XE960	Vampire T.11					
XE961	Vampire T.11					
XE975	Vampire T.11					
XE976	Vampire T.11					
XE977	Vampire T.11					To IAC GI 198
XE978	Vampire T.11					
XE979	Vampire T.11					Pr Standish
XE980	Vampire T.11					
XE981	Vampire T.11					
XE982	Vampire T.11					To 7564M Pr Hereford
XE983	Vampire T.11					To IAF
XE984	Vampire T.11					
XE985	Vampire T.11					Pr London Colney
XE986	Vampire T.11					
XE987	Vampire T.11					
XE988	Vampire T.11					
XE989	Vampire T.11					To 7296M
XE990	Vampire T.11					
XE991	Vampire T.11					
XE992	Vampire T.11					
XE993	Vampire T.11					To 8161M
XE994	Vampire T.11					
XE995	Vampire T.11					Pr Higher Blagdon
XE996	Vampire T.11					
XE997	Vampire T.11					
XE998	Vampire T.11					To GI Woodford

Further planned production of Vickers-Supermarine Swift fighters was drastically reduced following the cancellation of the programme. 6 F.4 aircraft (XF104-XF109) were cancelled and not built but production of 75 F.7 variants commenced with XF113. Initially 20 aircraft (XF203-XF217/XF244-XF248) were cancelled before construction was halted after XF124. XF114-XF124 were delivered to Valley in 4/5.57 for use by 1 Guided Weapon Development Squadron. Built against Contract 6/Aircraft/9757.

serial	type	sqdn/unit	code	where&when seen		remarks
XF104-XF109	Swift F.4	(6 a/c)		Cancelled and not built		
XF113	Swift F.7					
XF114	Swift F.7					Pr Connah's Quay
XF115	Swift F.7					
XF116	Swift F.7					
XF117	Swift F.7					
XF118	Swift F.7					
XF119	Swift F.7					
XF120	Swift F.7					
XF121	Swift F.7					
XF122	Swift F.7					
XF123	Swift F.7					
XF124	Swift F.7					
XF125-XF129	Swift F.7	(5 a/c)		Cancelled; construction abandoned		
XF155-XF180	Swift F.7	(26 a/c)		Cancelled and not built		
XF196-XF217	Swift F.7	(22 a/c)		Cancelled and not built		
XF244-XF253	Swift F.7	(10 a/c)		Cancelled and not built		

Three Dragonfly HC.4 helicopters built for the RAF by Westland Aircraft Ltd at Yeo-

XF259-XF311

serial	type	sqdn/unit	code	where&when seen	remarks

vil against Contract 9739. Details as follows:- XF259 c/n WA/H/105 f/f 18.3.54; XF260 c/n WA/H/106 f/f 23.3.54; XF261 c/n WA/H/107 f/f 24.3.54. All were delivered to the Central Flying School during 3/4.54.

serial	type	sqdn/unit	code	where&when seen	remarks
XF259	Dragonfly HC.4				
XF260	Dragonfly HC.4				
XF261	Dragonfly HC.4				

Five Sycamore HR.14 helicopters built for the RAF under Contract 9584 and produced by the Bristol Aeroplane Co Ltd at Filton. The block was allotted the c/n's 13225-13229 respectively. They were delivered in 1954-55.

serial	type	sqdn/unit	code	where&when seen	remarks
XF265	Sycamore HR.14				
XF266	Sycamore HR.14				
XF267	Sycamore HR.14				
XF268	Sycamore HR.14				
XF269	Sycamore HR.14				

The final batch of seven Meteor T.7 training aircraft built for the RAF by Gloster Aircraft Ltd at Hucclecote under Contract 6411. Meteor T.7 production for the RAF ceased with XF279 during July 1954.

serial	type	sqdn/unit	code	where&when seen	remarks
XF273	Meteor T.7				To BAF ED-37
XF274	Meteor T.7				Wreck Pr Farnborough
XF275	Meteor T.7				To KLu I-310 or 317
XF276	Meteor T.7				To KLu I-311 or 312
XF277	Meteor T.7				To KLu I-311 or 312
XF278	Meteor T.7				To KLu I-314
XF279	Meteor T.7				To KLu I-313

Two Avro Yorks allotted service serials following a temporary trooping contract awarded to Scottish Aviation Ltd. XF284 and 285 were previously G-AMUL/MUM resp.

serial	type	sqdn/unit	code	where&when seen	remarks
XF284	Avro 685 York 1				Restored to G-AMUL
XF285	Avro 685 York 1				Restored to G-AMUM

Continued production of 50 Hunter F.4 fighter aircraft built for the RAF by Hawker Aircraft Ltd at Blackpool. Deliveries took place between 11.55 and 3.56. Subsequent conversions to GA.11 (5) and T.8C (4) standard for the RN and 2 T.7's for the RAF.

serial	type	sqdn/unit	code	where&when seen	remarks
XF289	Hunter T.8C				
XF290	Hunter F.4				
XF291	Hunter GA.11				To G-9-334/SwAF J-4118
XF292	Hunter F.4				
XF293	Hunter F.4				
XF294	Hunter F.4				
XF295	Hunter F.4				
XF296	Hunter F.4				
XF297	Hunter GA.11				
XF298	Hunter F.4				
XF299	Hunter F.4				
XF300	Hunter GA.11				
XF301	Hunter GA.11				
XF302	Hunter F.4				7774M/G-9-382/Ch J-733
XF303	Hunter F.4				A2565/G-9-315/Sw J-4105
XF304	Hunter F.4				
XF305	Hunter F.4				
XF306	Hunter F.4				7776M/G-9-402/Sw J-4133
XF307	Hunter F.4				To 8002M
XF308	Hunter F.4				7777M/G-9-381/Sw J-4135
XF309	Hunter F.4				7771M/G-9-420/KAF 806
XF310	Hunter T.7				
XF311	Hunter F.4				A2566 to SAFTECH 11

XF312-XF421

serial	type	sqdn/unit	code	where&when seen		remarks
XF312	Hunter F.4					7848M/G-9-405/Sw J-4150
XF313	Hunter F.4					
XF314	Hunter F.4					
XF315	Hunter F.4					
XF316	Hunter F.4					7778M/G-9-403/Sw J-4134
XF317	Hunter F.4					7773M/G-9-383/Ch J-734
XF318	Hunter F.4					A2567/G-9-328/Sw J-4110
XF319	Hunter F.4					To 7849M
XF320	Hunter F.4					
XF321	Hunter T.7					
XF322	Hunter T.8					
XF323	Hunter F.4					8003M/G-9-380/Ch J-732
XF324	Hunter F.4					
XF357	Hunter T.8C					
XF358	Hunter T.8C					
XF359	Hunter F.4					
XF360	Hunter F.4					7942M/G-9-371/S ADC 542
XF361	Hunter F.4					To G-9-261/SwAF J-4117
XF362	Hunter F.4					To G-9-251/ADAF 705
XF363	Hunter F.4					To A2560 RSAF GI Pr
XF364	Hunter F.4					To G-9-262/RJAF 843
XF365	Hunter F.4					A2561/G-9-297/Sw J-4109
XF366	Hunter F.4					8004M/G-9-350/S ADC 537
XF367	Hunter F.4					To G-9-252/ADAF 706
XF368	Hunter GA.11					
XF369	Hunter F.4					7941M/G-9-351/S ADC 538
XF370	Hunter F.4					7772M/G-9-387/Sw J-4136

Continued production of 100 Hunter F.6 fighter aircraft built for the RAF by Sir W.G.Armstrong Whitworth Aircraft Ltd at Coventry. XF373 f/f 25.5.55 and subsequently many were converted to FGA.9 or FR.10 standard including the prototype of the latter mark, XF429. In 1975/77 most surviving F.6's were modified to F.6A standard.

serial	type	sqdn/unit	code	where&when seen		remarks
XF373	Hunter F.6					RJAF 703/G-9-205/703
XF374	Hunter F.6					To RRAF127
XF375	Hunter F.6					
XF376	Hunter FGA.9					
XF377	Hunter F.6					To LeAF L-173
XF378	Hunter F.6					
XF379	Hunter F.6					RJAF 705/G-9-200/705
XF380	Hunter F.6					RJAF 710/G-9-197/710
XF381	Hunter F.6					RJAF 702/G-9-201/702
XF382	Hunter F.6A					
XF383	Hunter F.6					
XF384	Hunter F.6					
XF385	Hunter F.6					To 7803M
XF386	Hunter F.6					
XF387	Hunter F.6					
XF388	Hunter FGA.9					
XF389	Hunter F.6					To G-9-271/RJAF 829
XF414	Hunter FGA.9					
XF415	Hunter F.6					To RJAF
XF416	Hunter FGA.9					
XF417	Hunter F.6					To RJAF
XF418	Hunter F.6A					
XF419	Hunter FGA.9					
XF420	Hunter F.6					
XF421	Hunter FGA.9					

XF422-XF510

serial	type	sqdn/unit	code	where&when seen		remarks
XF422	Hunter FR.10					To G-9-361/SADC 524
XF423	Hunter F.6					To RJAF
XF424	Hunter FGA.9					
XF425	Hunter F.6					
XF426	Hunter FR.10					To RJAF
XF427	Hunter F.6					
XF428	Hunter FR.10					To G-9-362/SADC 525
XF429	Hunter FR.10					To G-9-373/SwAF J-4131
XF430	Hunter FGA.9					To G-9-426/LeAF L-283
XF431	Hunter FGA.9					
XF432	Hunter FR.10					G-9-363/G-BABM/SADC 526
XF433	Hunter F.6					
XF434	Hunter F.6					
XF435	Hunter FGA.9					
XF436	Hunter FR.10					To G-9-321/SwAF J-4115
XF437	Hunter FGA.9					To G-9-324/SADC 503
XF438	Hunter FR.10					To G-9-333/SwAF J-4102
XF439	Hunter F.6A					
XF440	Hunter FGA.9					
XF441	Hunter FR.10					To G-9-377/SADC 545
XF442	Hunter FGA.9					
XF443	Hunter F.6					
XF444	Hunter F.6					RJAF 709/G-9-199/709
XF445	Hunter FGA.9					
XF446	Hunter FGA.9					To G-9-277/IAF A1010
XF447	Hunter F.6					To G-9-299/ChAF J-723
XF448	Hunter F.6					
XF449	Hunter F.6					
XF450	Hunter F.6					To G-9-211/RSAF 60-603
XF451	Hunter F.6					
XF452	Hunter F.6					RJAF 708/G-9-202/708
XF453	Hunter F.6					To G-9-233/ChAF J-716
XF454	Hunter FGA.9					To RJAF
XF455	Hunter FGA.9					
XF456	Hunter FGA.9					To G-9-301/SADC 509
XF457	Hunter FR.10					To G-9-422/LeAF L-281
XF458	Hunter FR.10					To G-9-364/SADC 527
XF459	Hunter FR.10					To G-9-355/IAF S1393
XF460	Hunter FR.10					To G-9-378/SADC 546
XF461	Hunter F.6					To LeAF L-171
XF462	Hunter FGA.9					To G-9-320/SwAF J-4107
XF463	Hunter F.6					To IAF BA241
XF495	Hunter F.6					To LeAF L-175
XF496	Hunter F.6					RJAF 706/G-9-196/706
XF497	Hunter F.6					To IAF BA242
XF498	Hunter F.6					RJAF 704/G-9-203/704
XF499	Hunter F.6					To IAF BA243
XF500	Hunter F.6					To IAF BA240
XF501	Hunter F.6					To IAF BA244
XF502	Hunter F.6					
XF503	Hunter F.6					To IAF BA245
XF504	Hunter F.6					To RRAF125
XF505	Hunter F.6					To IAF BA246
XF506	Hunter F.6					To RRAF119
XF507	Hunter F.6					
XF508	Hunter FGA.9					
XF509	Hunter F.6					
XF510	Hunter F.6					

XF511-XF594

serial	type	sqdn/unit	code	where&when seen		remarks
XF511	Hunter FGA.9					
XF512	Hunter F.6					To G-9-313/ChAF J-725
XF513	Hunter F.6					
XF514	Hunter F.6					To RJAF 718
XF515	Hunter F.6A					
XF516	Hunter F.6A					
XF517	Hunter FGA.9					
XF518	Hunter F.6					To RJAF 809
XF519	Hunter FGA.9					
XF520	Hunter F.6					To G-9-208/RJAF 814
XF521	Hunter F.6					To G-9-243/IAF A938
XF522	Hunter F.6					
XF523	Hunter FGA.9					
XF524	Hunter F.6					
XF525	Hunter F.6					
XF526	Hunter F.6					
XF527	Hunter F.6					

One Vickers Viking 1B allotted a military serial following a temporary trooping contract awarded to Airwork Ltd as follows:- XF532 c/n 246 ex G-AJBU.

serial	type	sqdn/unit	code	where&when seen		remarks
XF532	V.610 Viking 1B					Restored to G-AJBU

One Avro Tudor 2 allotted a military serial following a temporary trooping contract awarded to Air Charter Ltd as follows:- XF537 c/n 1262 ex G-AGRY.

serial	type	sqdn/unit	code	where&when seen		remarks
XF537	Avro 689 Tudor 2					Restored to G-AGRY

50 Provost T.1 trainers built by Hunting Percival Aircraft Ltd at Luton against Contract 9850. Allocated c/ns PAC/56/269-272, 275-308 & 311-312; del between 12.54 & 6.55.

serial	type	sqdn/unit	code	where&when seen		remarks
XF540	Provost T.1					
XF541	Provost T.1					
XF542	Provost T.1					
XF543	Provost T.1					
XF544	Provost T.1					
XF545	Provost T.1					To 7957M Pr Swinderby
XF546	Provost T.1					
XF547	Provost T.1					To G-23-1/FMAF FM1037
XF548	Provost T.1					
XF549	Provost T.1					
XF550	Provost T.1					
XF551	Provost T.1					
XF552	Provost T.1					
XF553	Provost T.1					
XF554	Provost T.1					To G-AWTD ntu/RhAF 3614
XF555	Provost T.1					To 8037M
XF556	Provost T.1					
XF557	Provost T.1					
XF558	Provost T.1					To FMAF
XF559	Provost T.1					
XF560	Provost T.1					
XF561	Provost T.1					
XF562	Provost T.1					
XF563	Provost T.1					
XF564	Provost T.1					
XF565	Provost T.1					
XF591	Provost T.1					
XF592	Provost T.1					
XF593	Provost T.1					
XF594	Provost T.1					

XF595-XF656

serial	type	sqdn/unit	code	where&when seen		remarks
XF595	Provost T.1					
XF596	Provost T.1					
XF597	Provost T.1					To GI Connah's Quay
XF598	Provost T.1					To 7466M
XF599	Provost T.1					
XF600	Provost T.1					
XF601	Provost T.1					To FMAF
XF602	Provost T.1					
XF603	Provost T.1					To GI Filton
XF604	Provost T.1					
XF605	Provost T.1					
XF606	Provost T.1					
XF607	Provost T.1					
XF608	Provost T.1					To 7954M
XF609	Provost T.1					
XF610	Provost T.1					
XF611	Provost T.1					To 7381M
XF612	Provost T.1					
XF613	Provost T.1					
XF614	Provost T.1					

Two Douglas Dakota 4's allotted military marks following a temporary trooping contract awarded to Silver City Airways Ltd. XF619 was previously G-AMYX with c/n 16294/33042; XF623 was previously G-AMYV with c/n 16195/32943.

serial	type	sqdn/unit	code	where&when seen		remarks
XF619	C-47D Dakota 4					Restored to G-AMYX
XF623	C-47D Dakota 4					Restored to G-AMYV

Five Vickers Vikings allotted military marks following a temporary trooping contract awarded to Eagle Aviation Ltd. Identities and c/ns as follows:- XF629 (G-AJBO 241); XF630 (G-AIVO 228); XF631 (G-AHPO 157); XF632 (G-AHPM 152); and XF633 (G-AJCD 255).

serial	type	sqdn/unit	code	where&when seen		remarks
XF629	V.610 Viking 1B					Restored to G-AJBO
XF630	V.610 Viking 1B					Restored to G-AIVO
XF631	V.610 Viking 1B					Restored to G-AHPO
XF632	V.610 Viking 1B					Restored to G-AHPM
XF633	V.610 Viking 1B					Restored to G-AJCD

Three Vickers Vikings allotted military marks following a temporary trooping contract awarded to Hunting-Clan Air Transport Ltd. Identities and c/ns as follows:- XF638 (G-AHPB 132); XF639 (G-AGRP 108); XF640 (G-AGRW 115).

serial	type	sqdn/unit	code	where&when seen		remarks
XF638	V.639 Viking 1					Restored to G-AHPB
XF639	V.639 Viking 1					Restored to G-AGRP
XF640	V.639 Viking 1					Restored to G-AGRW

Three Douglas Dakotas allotted military marks following a temporary trooping contract awarded to BKS Air Transport Ltd. Identities and c/ns XF645 (G-AMVC 16642/33390) XF646 (G-AMSF 14380/25825) and XF647 (G-AMVB 14637/26082).

serial	type	sqdn/unit	code	where&when seen		remarks
XF645	C-47D Dakota 4					Restored to G-AMVC
XF646	C-47B Dakota 4					Restored to G-AMSF
XF647	C-47B Dakota 4					Restored to G-AMVB

The entire Silver City Airways Ltd fleet of Bristol Freighters was allotted military marks for trooping contracts although it appears that most were not taken up.

serial	type	sqdn/unit	code	where&when seen		remarks
XF650	Bristol 170 Mk.32					Restored to G-AMWA
XF651	Bristol 170 Mk.32					Restored to G-AMWB
XF652	Bristol 170 Mk.32					Restored to G-AMWC
XF653	Bristol 170 Mk.32					Restored to G-AMWD
XF654	Bristol 170 Mk.32					Restored to G-AMWE
XF655	Bristol 170 Mk.32					Restored to G-AMWF
XF656	Bristol 170 Mk.21					Restored to G-AGVB

XF657-XF739

serial	type	sqdn/unit	code	where&when seen		remarks
XF657	Bristol 170 Mk.21					Restored to G-AGVC
XF658	Bristol 170 Mk.21E					Restored to G-AHJP
XF659	Bristol 170 Mk.21					Restored to G-AICS
XF660	Bristol 170 Mk.21					Restored to G-AIFM
XF661	Bristol 170 Mk.21					Restored to G-AIFV
XF662	Bristol 170 Mk.21					Restored to G-AIME
XF663	Bristol 170 Mk.21					Restored to G-AIMH

One BKS Air Transport Ltd Dakota allotted military marks for temporary trooping contracts (ex G-AMSH c/n 16583/33331) but may have carried XF648 in error.

serial	type	sqdn/unit	code	where&when seen		remarks
XF667	C-47B Dakota 4					Restored to G-AMSH

Two Balliol T.2 piston-engined training aircraft built by Boulton-Paul Aircraft Ltd at Wolverhampton against Contract 4869. Both aircraft were issued to 9 MU on 2.10.53 and placed in long-term storage. Built as replacements for diverted aircraft.

serial	type	sqdn/unit	code	where&when seen		remarks
XF672	Balliol T.2					
XF673	Balliol T.2					

Continued production of Provost T.1's by Hunting Percival Aircraft Ltd at Luton under Contract 9850. C/ns PAC/56/323-338 resp, they were delivered in 1954/55.

serial	type	sqdn/unit	code	where&when seen		remarks
XF678	Provost T.1					
XF679	Provost T.1					
XF680	Provost T.1					
XF681	Provost T.1					
XF682	Provost T.1					To SOAF
XF683	Provost T.1					To SOAF
XF684	Provost T.1					
XF685	Provost T.1					To G-AWPI
XF686	Provost T.1					
XF687	Provost T.1					
XF688	Provost T.1					To SOAF
XF689	Provost T.1					To 8038M
XF690	Provost T.1					To 8041M to G-BGKA
XF691	Provost T.1					To G-AWTE ntu To RhAF
XF692	Provost T.1					
XF693	Provost T.1					To G-AWTC ntu To RhAF

2nd production batch of 13 Shackleton MR.3 maritime reconnaissance aircraft built by A.V.Roe Ltd at Woodford under Contract 6408. Production ceased at XF730 after which all bar one (XF710) were upgraded to MR.3/Phase 3 standard. (See also XG912 etc).

serial	type	sqdn/unit	code	where&when seen		remarks
XF700	Shackleton MR.3/3					
XF701	Shackleton MR.3/3					
XF702	Shackleton MR.3/3					
XF703	Shackleton MR.3/3					To 8168M ntu
XF704	Shackleton MR.3/3					
XF705	Shackleton MR.3/3					
XF706	Shackleton MR.3/3					To 8089M
XF707	Shackleton MR.3/3					
XF708	Shackleton MR.3/3					Pr Duxford
XF709	Shackleton MR.3/3					
XF710	Shackleton MR.3/2					
XF711	Shackleton MR.3/3					
XF730	Shackleton MR.3/3					

One Avro Tudor allocated military marks following a trooping contract awarded to Air Charter Ltd. XF739 was previously G-AGRI with c/n 1257.

serial	type	sqdn/unit	code	where&when seen		remarks
XF739	Avro 688 Tudor 1					Restored to G-AGRI

XF746-XF799

serial	type	sqdn/unit	code	where&when seen	remarks

Four Douglas Dakotas allotted military marks following a trooping contract awarded to Transair Ltd. Identities and c/ns as follows:- XF746 (G-AMVL 16660/33408) ; XF747 (G-AMYJ 15968/32715); XF748 (G-AMZG 16668/33416); XF749 (G-AMZF 15633/27078).

serial	type	sqdn/unit	code	where&when seen	remarks
XF746	C-47B Dakota 4				Restored to G-AMVL
XF747	C-47D Dakota 4				Restored to G-AMYJ
XF748	C-47D Dakota 4				Restored to G-AMZG
XF749	C-47 Dakota 4				Restored to G-AMZF

Two Douglas Dakotas allotted military marks following a trooping contract awarded to Scottish Airlines Ltd. Identities and c/ns are: XF756 (G-AMPP 15272/26717), and XF757 (G-AMJU 14489/25934).

serial	type	sqdn/unit	code	where&when seen	remarks
XF756	C-47B Dakota 4				Restored to G-AMPP
XF757	C-47B Dakota 4				Restored to G-AMJU

Three Vikings and four Dakotas were allotted military marks for trooping duties on a temporary basis following a contract awarded to Hunting-Clan Air Transport Ltd. Identities and c/ns are as follows:- XF763 (G-AHPJ 147); XF764 (G-AHPC 133); XF765 (G-AHOY 128); XF766 (G-AMSL 14946/26391); XF767 (G-AMNL 16644/33392); XF768 (G-AMSJ 16477/33225); XF769 (G-AMSK 16206/32954).

serial	type	sqdn/unit	code	where&when seen	remarks
XF763	V.614 Viking 1				Restored to G-AHPJ
XF764	V.639 Viking 1				Restored to G-AHPC
XF765	V.639 Viking 1				Restored to G-AHOY
XF766	C-47 Dakota 4				Restored to G-AMSL
XF767	C-47 Dakota 4				Restored to G-AMNL
XF768	C-47 Dakota 4				Restored to G-AMSJ
XF769	C-47 Dakota 4				Restored to G-AMSK

Two prototype Swift variants built (as listed) by the Supermarine Division of Vickers Armstrongs Ltd at South Marston for development work, and both under the maker's designation Type 550. The F.7 variant was placed into limited production (See XF113 et seq) but development of the PR.6 variant was cancelled.

serial	type	sqdn/unit	code	where&when seen	remarks
XF774	Swift F.7				
XF780	Swift F.6/PR.6				

The prototype Bristol 173 twin-engined, tandem rotor helicopter f/f at Filton on 3.1.52 as G-ALBN (c/n 12871) and took up military marks (XF785) the following year for RAF and Royal Navy trials.

serial	type	sqdn/unit	code	where&when seen	remarks
XF785	Bristol 173				To 7648M Pr Henlow

Two Douglas Dakotas allotted military marks following a trooping contract awarded to Skyways Ltd. Identities and c/ns as follows:- XF791 (G-ANAE 14656/26101) and XF792 (G-AMWX 15846/32594)

serial	type	sqdn/unit	code	where&when seen	remarks
XF791	C-47 Dakota 4				Restored to G-ANAE
XF792	C-47 Dakota 4				Restored to G-AMWX

Four Pembroke C(PR).1 aircraft built by Hunting Percival Aircraft Ltd at Luton to follow on from WV754/755 against Contract 6/Aircraft/10009/CB5(a) dated 9.11.53. All were initially delivered to 81 Sqdn RAF in Malaya but were later returned to the UK and converted to C.1's for service in Europe. The C(PR).1 differed by having a camera in a transparent nose cone. C/ns are PAC/66/76-78 & 80 respectively.

serial	type	sqdn/unit	code	where&when seen	remarks
XF796	Pembroke C.1				To 8461M To G-BFKK
XF797	Pembroke C.1				
XF798	Pembroke C.1				
XF799	Pembroke C.1				

A block of twenty serials (XF804-XF823 inc.) was earmarked for an unspecified type, and in the event none was taken up. It is unconfirmed that they were intended to be the pre-production block of Lightnings which were subsequently allotted XG307 etc.

XF828-XF892

One semi-navalised pre-production Sea Vixen built to Spec N.139 by de Havilland Aircraft Co Ltd at Christchurch under the company designation DH.110 Mk 20X. XF828 made its first flight on 20.6.55 and spent much of its active life at RAE Bedford.

serial	type	sqdn/unit	code	where&when seen	remarks
XF828	DH.110 Mk.20X				To A2500

The sole prototype Hunter F.6 built by Hawker Aircraft Ltd at Kingston-upon-Thames under the company designation P.1099 and against Contract 6/Aircraft/10032/CB5(b). The nose, centre section and tail unit were derived from the cancelled P.1083 WN470.

serial	type	sqdn/unit	code	where&when seen	remarks
XF833	Hawker P.1109				

Continued production of Provost T.1 trainers built by Hunting Percival Aircraft Ltd at Luton against Contract 10088. They followed on from XF693 and production ceased with XF914 in April 1956. Some of the batch were diverted to Southern Rhodesia.

serial	type	sqdn/unit	code	where&when seen	remarks
XF836	Provost T.1				To 8043M Pr Old Warden
XF837	Provost T.1				To FMAF
XF838	Provost T.1				To G-AWTB ntu To RhAF
XF839	Provost T.1				To FMAF
XF840	Provost T.1				
XF841	Provost T.1				To 8039M
XF842	Provost T.1				
XF843	Provost T.1				
XF844	Provost T.1				To GI Farnborough
XF845	Provost T.1				To FMAF FM1038
XF846	Provost T.1				
XF847	Provost T.1				To FMAF FM1039
XF848	Provost T.1				To FMAF FM1040
XF849	Provost T.1				To SRAF SR140
XF850	Provost T.1				To SRAF SR141
XF851	Provost T.1				To SRAF SR142
XF852	Provost T.1				To SRAF SR143
XF853	Provost T.1				To FMAF FM1043
XF854	Provost T.1				To FMAF FM1044
XF868	Provost T.1				To SOAF
XF869	Provost T.1				
XF870	Provost T.1				To SRAF SR144
XF871	Provost T.1				To SRAF SR145
XF872	Provost T.1				To SRAF SR146
XF873	Provost T.1				To SRAF SR147
XF874	Provost T.1				
XF875	Provost T.1				
XF876	Provost T.1				
XF877	Provost T.1				To G-AWVF
XF878	Provost T.1				To SRAF SR148
XF879	Provost T.1				To SRAF SR149
XF880	Provost T.1				To SRAF SR150
XF881	Provost T.1				To SRAF SR151
XF882	Provost T.1				
XF883	Provost T.1				
XF884	Provost T.1				
XF885	Provost T.1				
XF886	Provost T.1				To RSAF as GI
XF887	Provost T.1				To Kenyan AF KAF969 Pr
XF888	Provost T.1				
XF889	Provost T.1				
XF890	Provost T.1				
XF891	Provost T.1				
XF892	Provost T.1				

XF893-XF945

serial	type	sqdn/unit	code	where&when seen		remarks
XF893	Provost T.1					
XF894	Provost T.1					
XF895	Provost T.1					
XF896	Provost T.1					To FMAF
XF897	Provost T.1					
XF898	Provost T.1					
XF899	Provost T.1					
XF900	Provost T.1					
XF901	Provost T.1					
XF902	Provost T.1					To 7425M
XF903	Provost T.1					
XF904	Provost T.1					
XF905	Provost T.1					
XF906	Provost T.1					
XF907	Provost T.1					To SOAF
XF908	Provost T.1					To G-ASMC
XF909	Provost T.1					
XF910	Provost T.1					
XF911	Provost T.1					
XF912	Provost T.1					
XF913	Provost T.1					
XF914	Provost T.1					Pr Castle Donington

One Avro York Mk.1 allotted military marks to carry out a temporary trooping contract awarded to Air Charter Ltd in 1955. Previously this aircraft was registered G-AMUS and reverted to that registration at the termination of the contract.

serial	type	sqdn/unit	code	where&when seen		remarks
XF919	Avro 685 York 1					Restored to G-AMUS

Two fully-equipped prototype Bristol 188 stainless steel research aircraft built by Bristol Aeroplane Co Ltd at Filton against Contract 6/Aircraft/10144 to meet Spec ER.134. XF923 c/n 13518 f/f 26.4.61; XF926 c/n 13519 f/f 29.4.63.

serial	type	sqdn/unit	code	where&when seen		remarks
XF923	Bristol 188					
XF926	Bristol 188					To 8368M Pr Cosford

The final production block of Balliol T.2 training aircraft built by Boulton-Paul Aircraft Ltd at Wolverhampton in 1954 against Contract 6/Aircraft/6251. The three aircraft were delivered in 4.54 and 5.54. as replacements for diverted aircraft.

serial	type	sqdn/unit	code	where&when seen		remarks
XF929	Balliol T.2					
XF930	Balliol T.2					
XF931	Balliol T.2					To 7654M

The final contract for Hunter F.4's (SP/6/Aircraft/10344/CB7(a)) accounted for 55 units between XF932 and XF999 plus 2 additional aircraft XG341/342. All were built by Hawker Aircraft Ltd at Blackpool, deliveries taking place between 3.56 & 7.56. Subsequent conversions included 1 to GA.11 standard and 11 to T.8B/C's for the RN.

serial	type	sqdn/unit	code	where&when seen		remarks
XF932	Hunter F.4					
XF933	Hunter F.4					7904M/G-9-392/Sw J-4132
XF934	Hunter F.4					
XF935	Hunter F.4					To G-9-253/ADAF 707
XF936	Hunter F.4					To G-9-255/RJAF 844
XF937	Hunter F.4					To G-9-256/SwAF J-4116
XF938	Hunter T.8C					
XF939	Hunter T.8C					
XF940	Hunter F.4					
XF941	Hunter F.4					8006M/G-9-374/Sw J-4139
XF942	Hunter T.8C					
XF943	Hunter F.4					
XF944	Hunter F.4					7907M/G-9-393/Sw J-4142
XF945	Hunter F.4					

XF946-XG137

serial	type	sqdn/unit	code	where&when seen		remarks
XF946	Hunter F.4					To 7804M Pr Jordan
XF947	Hunter F.4					A2568/G-9-317/Sw J-4104
XF948	Hunter F.4					
XF949	Hunter F.4					
XF950	Hunter F.4					7956M/G-9-349/SADC 536
XF951	Hunter F.4					7947M/G-9-389/Sw J-4202
XF952	Hunter F.4					To G-9-263/RJAF 848
XF953	Hunter F.4					
XF967	Hunter T.8C					
XF968	Hunter F.4					To G-9-264/RJAF 847
XF969	Hunter F.4					7935M/G-9-346/SADC 529
XF970	Hunter F.4					7936M/G-9-345/SADC 528
XF971	Hunter F.4					To G-9-257/ADAF 709
XF972	Hunter F.4					7948M/G-9-418/KAF 804
XF973	Hunter F.4					7908M/G-9-394/Sw J-4143
XF974	Hunter F.4					To 7949M
XF975	Hunter F.4					7945M/G-9-421
XF976	Hunter F.4					A2569/G-9-329/Sw J-4112
XF977	Hunter GA.11					
XF978	Hunter T.8B					
XF979	Hunter F.4					To G-9-258/RJAF 850
XF980	Hunter F.4					
XF981	Hunter F.4					To G-9-254/SwAF J-4114
XF982	Hunter F.4					7946M/G-9-391/Ch J-738
XF983	Hunter T.8C					
XF984	Hunter F.4					A2570/G-9-330/Sw J-4113
XF985	Hunter T.8C					
XF986	Hunter F.4					
XF987	Hunter F.4					To G-9-265/RJAF 842
XF988	Hunter F.4					
XF989	Hunter F.4					
XF990	Hunter F.4					8007M/G-9-408/Sw J-4141
XF991	Hunter T.8C					
XF992	Hunter T.8C					To G-9-269/SwAF J-4129
XF993	Hunter F.4					
XF994	Hunter T.8C					
XF995	Hunter T.8B					
XF996	Hunter F.4					
XF997	Hunter F.4					
XF998	Hunter F.4					7950M/G-9-390/Sw J-4140
XF999	Hunter F.4					

The 3rd production order for Hunter F.6's contracted to Hawker Aircraft Ltd totalled 110 aircraft to follow XE656. All were built at Kingston except XG150-XG168 which were subcontracted to Sir W.G.Armstrong Whitworth Aircraft Ltd at Coventry. Deliveries took place between 8.56 & 2.57. Many were subsequently converted to FGA.9 or FR.10 standard. In 1975/77 most surviving RAF F.6's were upgraded to F.6A standard.

serial	type	sqdn/unit	code	where&when seen		remarks
XG127	Hunter FR.10					To G-9-294/SwAF J-4101
XG128	Hunter FGA.9					
XG129	Hunter F.6					To G-9-240/IAF A936
XG130	Hunter FGA.9					
XG131	Hunter F.6					
XG132	Hunter F.6					To RJAF
XG133	Hunter F.6					
XG134	Hunter FGA.9					
XG135	Hunter FGA.9					
XG136	Hunter FGA.9					
XG137	Hunter F.6					To RJAF 813

XG150-XG231

serial	type	sqdn/unit	code	where&when seen		remarks
XG150	Hunter F.6					To IAF BA247
XG151	Hunter FGA.9					
XG152	Hunter F.6A					
XG153	Hunter FGA.9					To G-9-357/SADC 520
XG154	Hunter FGA.9					
XG155	Hunter FGA.9					
XG156	Hunter FGA.9					
XG157	Hunter F.6					
XG158	Hunter F.6A					
XG159	Hunter F.6					To RJAF 717
XG160	Hunter F.6A					
XG161	Hunter F.6					
XG162	Hunter F.6					
XG163	Hunter F.6					To IAF BA248
XG164	Hunter F.6					
XG165	Hunter F.6					
XG166	Hunter F.6					
XG167	Hunter F.6					To LeAF L-174
XG168	Hunter FR.10					To RJAF
XG169	Hunter FGA.9					
XG170	Hunter F.6					To G-9-241/IAF A940
XG171	Hunter F.6					To RJAF
XG172	Hunter F.6A					
XG185	Hunter F.6					
XG186	Hunter F.6					To G-9-237/IAF A941
XG187	Hunter F.6					To RJAF 811
XG188	Hunter F.6					
XG189	Hunter F.6					To G-9-238/IAF A942
XG190	Hunter F.6					To G-9-244/IAF A939
XG191	Hunter F.6A					
XG192	Hunter F.6					
XG193	Hunter F.6					
XG194	Hunter FGA.9					
XG195	Hunter FGA.9					To G-9-453
XG196	Hunter F.6A					
XG197	Hunter F.6A					
XG198	Hunter F.6					
XG199	Hunter F.6					To G-9-312/ChAF J-724
XG200	Hunter F.6					
XG201	Hunter F.6					To G-9-242/IAF A937
XG202	Hunter F.6					
XG203	Hunter F.6					
XG204	Hunter F.6					
XG205	Hunter FGA.9					To G-9-325/SADC 506
XG206	Hunter F.6					
XG207	Hunter FGA.9					
XG208	Hunter F.6					
XG209	Hunter F.6					
XG210	Hunter F.6					
XG211	Hunter F.6					To G-9-239/IAF A943
XG225	Hunter F.6A					
XG226	Hunter F.6A					
XG227	Hunter F.6					
XG228	Hunter FGA.9					
XG229	Hunter F.6					
XG230	Hunter F.6					
XG231	Hunter F.6					RJAF 715/G-9-207/715

XG232-XG311

serial	type	sqdn/unit	code	where&when seen		remarks
XG232	Hunter F.6					To G-9-216/ChAF J-714
XG233	Hunter F.6					
XG234	Hunter F.6					To G-9-272/RJAF 830
XG235	Hunter F.6					
XG236	Hunter F.6					
XG237	Hunter FGA.9					To G-9-268/RJAF 828
XG238	Hunter F.6					
XG239	Hunter F.6					
XG251	Hunter FGA.9					To G-9-304/SADC 507
XG252	Hunter FGA.9					
XG253	Hunter FGA.9					
XG254	Hunter FGA.9					
XG255	Hunter FGA.9					To RJAF 825
XG256	Hunter FGA.9					
XG257	Hunter F.6					To RJAF 812
XG258	Hunter F.6					
XG259	Hunter F.6					To RJAF GI
XG260	Hunter FGA.9					To G-9-300/SADC 501
XG261	Hunter FGA.9					
XG262	Hunter F.6					RJAF 712/G-9-198/712
XG263	Hunter F.6					To RJAF
XG264	Hunter FGA.9					
XG265	Hunter FGA.9					
XG266	Hunter FGA.9					To G-9-358/SADC 521
XG267	Hunter F.6					To RJAF 801
XG268	Hunter F.6					To RJAF 806
XG269	Hunter F.6					To RJAF 807
XG270	Hunter F.6					
XG271	Hunter FGA.9					
XG272	Hunter FGA.9					To G-9-310/SwAF J-4111
XG273	Hunter FGA.9					
XG274	Hunter F.6					
XG289	Hunter F.6					
XG290	Hunter F.6					
XG291	Hunter FGA.9					
XG292	Hunter FGA.9					To G-9-326/SADC 512
XG293	Hunter FGA.9					
XG294	Hunter F.6					To RRAF 122
XG295	Hunter F.6					To RRAF 121
XG296	Hunter FGA.9					To G-9-303/SADC 510
XG297	Hunter FGA.9					To G-9-452
XG298	Hunter FGA.9					To RJAF 826

The sole Skeeter Mk.5 prototype (G-AMTZ c/n SR.907) was built by Saunders-Roe Ltd at East Cowes during 1953. In March 1954 it was allotted military marks for trials at A&AEE Boscombe Down and the following year was modified to Mk.6 standard.

serial	type	sqdn/unit	code	where&when seen		remarks
XG303	Skeeter Mk.6					Ex G-AMTZ

The pre-production order for Lightning fighter aircraft accounted for 20 units built by English Electric Company Ltd at Preston with c/ns 95007-95026 respectively. XG307 f/f 3.4.58; XG337 f/f 1.8.59. All were engaged on tests and acceptance trials and numerous examples were up-graded to an 'interim Lightning F.3' configuration.

serial	type	sqdn/unit	code	where&when seen		remarks
XG307	Lightning F.1					
XG308	Lightning F.1/3					
XG309	Lightning F.1					
XG310	Lightning F.3 Prot					
XG311	Lightning F.1					

XG312-XG463

serial	type	sqdn/unit	code	where&when seen		remarks
XG312	Lightning F.1					
XG313	Lightning F.1					To G27-115 RSAF GI
XG325	Lightning F.1					Nose Pr HAM Southend
XG326	Lightning F.1					
XG327	Lightning F.1					To 8188M
XG328	Lightning F.1/3					
XG329	Lightning F.1/3					To 8050M
XG330	Lightning F.1/3					
XG331	Lightning F.1/3					Nose GI with Dowty's
XG332	Lightning F.1					
XG333	Lightning F.1/3					
XG334	Lightning F.1					
XG335	Lightning F.1/3					
XG336	Lightning F.1/3					To 8091M
XG337	Lightning F.1/3					To 8056M

The final two Hunter F.4 fighter aircraft for the RAF were built by Hawker Aircraft Ltd at Blackpool and placed against Contract SP/6/Aircraft/10344/CB7(a) to follow on from XF999. Both aircraft were delivered on 20.7.56.

serial	type	sqdn/unit	code	where&when seen		remarks
XG341	Hunter F.4					To G-9-260/ADAF 702
XG342	Hunter F.4					

Two Vickers Vikings allotted military serials following a temporary trooping contract awarded to Eagle Aviation Ltd as follows:- XG349 c/n 152 ex G-AHPM; and XG350 c/n 255 ex G-AJCD.

serial	type	sqdn/unit	code	where&when seen		remarks
XG349	V.610 Viking 1B					Restored to G-AHPM
XG350	V.610 Viking 1B					Restored to G-AJCD

Sole contract for Bristol Type 191 ship-based general purpose helicopters ordered for the RN in April 1956, and consisted of 3 Srs.1 prototypes (XG354-356) and 65 Srs 2 production helicopters (XG357 et seq) to meet Spec HR.146. The entire block was allocated c/ns 13274-13341 inclusive, but the contract was cancelled following the acceptance of the Wessex. The virtually complete XG354 was later used as a test-rig.

XG354-XG398	Bristol Type 191	(45 aircraft)	Cancelled and not built
XG419-XG441	Bristol Type 191	(23 aircraft)	Cancelled and not built

Sole production batch of 26 Type 192 helicopters built by the Bristol Aeroplane Co Ltd at Weston-super-Mare to meet Spec H.150. XG447 (prototype) f/f 5.7.58 and was followed by 9 pre-production helicopters (XG448-456). First production (XG457) made its f/f on 10.2.61 and all examples built entered service with the RAF as Belvedere HC.1's. The block of 26 Belvederes was allotted c/ns 13342-13367 respectively.

serial	type	sqdn/unit	code	where&when seen		remarks
XG447	Belvedere HC.1					
XG448	Belvedere HC.1					GI SAFTECH 4
XG449	Belvedere HC.1					
XG450	Belvedere HC.1					
XG451	Belvedere HC.1					
XG452	Belvedere HC.1					To 7997M Pr BRM W-s-M
XG453	Belvedere HC.1					
XG454	Belvedere HC.1					To 8366M Pr Henlow
XG455	Belvedere HC.1					
XG456	Belvedere HC.1					
XG457	Belvedere HC.1					
XG458	Belvedere HC.1					
XG459	Belvedere HC.1					
XG460	Belvedere HC.1					
XG461	Belvedere HC.1					
XG462	Belvedere HC.1					
XG463	Belvedere HC.1					

XG464-XG539

serial	type	sqdn/unit	code	where&when seen		remarks
XG464	Belvedere HC.1					
XG465	Belvedere HC.1					
XG466	Belvedere HC.1					
XG467	Belvedere HC.1					
XG468	Belvedere HC.1					
XG473	Belvedere HC.1					
XG474	Belvedere HC.1					To 8367M Pr Hendon
XG475	Belvedere HC.1					
XG476	Belvedere HC.1					

Five Vickers-Supermarine Swift F.4 fighter aircraft ordered for the RAF but not built following the cancellation of the entire Swift programme.

XG480-XG484	Swift F.4	(5 aircraft)	Cancelled and not built

Continued production of ML-120D Midget piston-engined pilotless target aircraft produced by ML Aviation Ltd at White Waltham. (See XE722 et seq).

XG487	ML-120D Midget					
XG488	ML-120D Midget					
XG489	ML-120D Midget					
XG490	ML-120D Midget					
XG491	ML-120D Midget					
XG492	ML-120D Midget					

One Devon C.1 built by de Havilland Aircraft Co Ltd at Chester in 1953 as a Dove 1B with c/n 04435 and initially registered as G-ANDX. It was sold to the MoD 28.6.54 and was handed-over on 21.7.54. It was later converted to Devon C.2 standard.

XG496	Devon C.2					Ex G-ANDX

36 Sycamore HR.14 helicopters built by Bristol Aeroplane Co Ltd at Filton (XG500-506/508-523/538-546) and Weston-super-Mare (XG507/547-549) for the RAF. The block was allocated c/ns 13245-247/264-265/267/203/402/239/269/268/271-273/368-389 resp.

XG500	Sycamore HR.14					
XG501	Sycamore HR.14					
XG502	Sycamore HR.14					Pr Middle Wallop
XG503	Sycamore HR.14					
XG504	Sycamore HR.14					Pr Nostell Priory
XG505	Sycamore HR.14					
XG506	Sycamore HR.14					To 7852M Pr Misson
XG507	Sycamore HR.14					
XG508	Sycamore HR.14					
XG509	Sycamore HR.14					To 7745M
XG510	Sycamore HR.14					
XG511	Sycamore HR.14					
XG512	Sycamore HR.14					
XG513	Sycamore HR.14					
XG514	Sycamore HR.14					
XG515	Sycamore HR.14					To 8008M
XG516	Sycamore HR.14					
XG517	Sycamore HR.14					
XG518	Sycamore HR.14					To 8009M Pr Balloch
XG519	Sycamore HR.14					
XG520	Sycamore HR.14					
XG521	Sycamore HR.14					
XG522	Sycamore HR.14					
XG523	Sycamore HR.14					To 7793M
XG538	Sycamore HR.14					
XG539	Sycamore HR.14					

XG540-XG597

serial	type	sqdn/unit	code	where&when seen		remarks
XG540	Sycamore HR.14					7899M/8345M Pr 'XJ385'
XG541	Sycamore HR.14					
XG542	Sycamore HR.14					
XG543	Sycamore HR.14					
XG544	Sycamore HR.14					Pr Higher Blagdon
XG545	Sycamore HR.14					
XG546	Sycamore HR.14					
XG547	Sycamore HR.14					To 8010M Pr BRM W-s-M
XG548	Sycamore HR.14					
XG549	Sycamore HR.14					

One Canberra B(I).6 built by English Electric Co Ltd at Preston against Contract 6445 for the RAF as a replacement aircraft. Delivered 3.56.

serial	type	sqdn/unit	code	where&when seen		remarks
XG554	Canberra B(I).6					

6 Pioneer CC.1 communications aircraft built by Scottish Aviation Ltd at Prestwick for the RAF. Allocated c/ns 106-111 respectively, delivered between 12.54 and 3.55.

serial	type	sqdn/unit	code	where&when seen		remarks
XG558	Pioneer CC.1					
XG559	Pioneer CC.1					
XG560	Pioneer CC.1					
XG561	Pioneer CC.1					
XG562	Pioneer CC.1					
XG563	Pioneer CC.1					

Two Vickers Vikings allotted military serials following a temporary trooping contract awarded to Eagle Aviation Ltd as follows:- XG567 c/n 264 ex G-AKBH; XG568 c/n 228 ex G-AIVO. Both aircraft carried these serials between 6.54 and 7.55.

serial	type	sqdn/unit	code	where&when seen		remarks
XG567	V.610 Viking 1B					Restored to G-AKBH
XG568	V.610 Viking 1B					Restored to G-AIVO

26 Whirlwind helicopters built by Westland Aircraft Ltd at Yeovil for the RN against Contract 10586 with c/ns WA67-92 resp. XG572-588 initially ordered as HAR.3 whilst XG589-597 built as HAS.7; XG586 modified with HAS.7 lower fuselage. XG572 f/f 9.9.55.

serial	type	sqdn/unit	code	where&when seen		remarks
XG572	Whirlwind HAR.3					
XG573	Whirlwind HAR.3					
XG574	Whirlwind HAR.3					To A2575 Pr Wroughton
XG575	Whirlwind HAR.3					
XG576	Whirlwind HAR.3					To G-AYNP
XG577	Whirlwind HAR.3					To A2571 Pr Duxford
XG578	Whirlwind HAR.3					
XG579	Whirlwind HAR.3					
XG580	Whirlwind HAR.3					
XG581	Whirlwind HAR.3					To A2469
XG582	Whirlwind HAR.3					
XG583	Whirlwind HAR.3					To G-BAGD
XG584	Whirlwind HAR.3					To A2487
XG585	Whirlwind HAR.3					
XG586	Whirlwind HAR.3/7					
XG587	Whirlwind HAR.3					To G-AYYI
XG588	Whirlwind HAR.3					To G-BAMH
XG589	Whirlwind HAS.7					
XG590	Whirlwind HAS.7					
XG591	Whirlwind HAS.7					
XG592	Whirlwind HAS.7					Pr SWAPS Rhoose
XG593	Whirlwind HAS.7					
XG594	Whirlwind HAS.7					Pr Wroughton
XG595	Whirlwind HAS.7					
XG596	Whirlwind HAS.7					To A2651 Pr BRM W-s-M
XG597	Whirlwind HAS.7					

XG603-XG666

serial	type	sqdn/unit	code	where&when seen		remarks

One Heron C.2 built by the de Havilland Aircraft Co Ltd at Hatfield for the British Joint Services Mission, Washington, USA. Allocated c/n 14058 and handed over at Benson on 13.9.54.

serial	type	sqdn/unit	code	where&when seen		remarks
XG603	Heron C.2					To OY-DNP

90 Sea Venom FAW.21/22 all-weather strike fighters built for the RN by the de Havilland Aircraft Co Ltd at Hatfield and Christchurch. XG606-638/653-680 were initially built as FAW.21 variant but some were subsequently converted to FAW.22 or ECM.21 as shown; XG681-702/721-737 built as FAW.22 from the outset. The last FAW.21 (XG680) f/f 6.6.57, and this contract finalised production of the Sea Venom.

serial	type	sqdn/unit	code	where&when seen		remarks
XG606	Sea Venom FAW.21					
XG607	Sea Venom FAW.21					
XG608	Sea Venom ECM.21					
XG609	Sea Venom FAW.21					
XG610	Sea Venom FAW.21					
XG611	Sea Venom FAW.21					
XG612	Sea Venom FAW.21					
XG613	Sea Venom FAW.21					Pr IWM Duxford
XG614	Sea Venom FAW.22					
XG615	Sea Venom FAW.21					
XG616	Sea Venom FAW.21					To A2492
XG617	Sea Venom FAW.21					
XG618	Sea Venom FAW.21					
XG619	Sea Venom FAW.21					
XG620	Sea Venom FAW.21					
XG621	Sea Venom FAW.21					To A2498
XG622	Sea Venom FAW.21					To A2504
XG623	Sea Venom FAW.21					
XG624	Sea Venom FAW.21					
XG625	Sea Venom FAW.21					
XG626	Sea Venom FAW.21					
XG627	Sea Venom FAW.21					
XG628	Sea Venom ECM.21					
XG629	Sea Venom FAW.22					Pr Higher Blagdon
XG630	Sea Venom FAW.21					
XG631	Sea Venom FAW.21					
XG632	Sea Venom FAW.21					
XG633	Sea Venom FAW.21					
XG634	Sea Venom FAW.21					
XG635	Sea Venom FAW.21					
XG636	Sea Venom FAW.21					
XG637	Sea Venom FAW.21					To A2512
XG638	Sea Venom FAW.21					
XG653	Sea Venom FAW.21					
XG654	Sea Venom FAW.21					
XG655	Sea Venom FAW.21					To A2506
XG656	Sea Venom FAW.21					
XG657	Sea Venom FAW.21					
XG658	Sea Venom FAW.21					
XG659	Sea Venom FAW.21					
XG660	Sea Venom FAW.21					
XG661	Sea Venom FAW.21					
XG662	Sea Venom FAW.21					
XG663	Sea Venom FAW.21					
XG664	Sea Venom FAW.21					
XG665	Sea Venom FAW.21					
XG666	Sea Venom FAW.21					

XG667-XG742

serial	type	sqdn/unit	code	where&when seen		remarks
XG667	Sea Venom FAW.21					
XG668	Sea Venom FAW.21					
XG669	Sea Venom FAW.21					
XG670	Sea Venom FAW.21					
XG671	Sea Venom FAW.21					
XG672	Sea Venom FAW.22					
XG673	Sea Venom FAW.22					
XG674	Sea Venom FAW.22					
XG675	Sea Venom FAW.21					
XG676	Sea Venom FAW.21					
XG677	Sea Venom FAW.21					
XG678	Sea Venom FAW.21					
XG679	Sea Venom FAW.21					
XG680	Sea Venom FAW.21					
XG681	Sea Venom FAW.22					
XG682	Sea Venom FAW.22					
XG683	Sea Venom FAW.22					
XG684	Sea Venom FAW.22					
XG685	Sea Venom FAW.22					
XG686	Sea Venom FAW.22					
XG687	Sea Venom FAW.22					
XG688	Sea Venom FAW.22					
XG689	Sea Venom FAW.22					
XG690	Sea Venom FAW.22					
XG691	Sea Venom FAW.22					Pr Chilton Cantelo
XG692	Sea Venom FAW.22					
XG693	Sea Venom FAW.22					
XG694	Sea Venom FAW.22					
XG695	Sea Venom FAW.22					
XG696	Sea Venom FAW.22					
XG697	Sea Venom FAW.22					
XG698	Sea Venom FAW.22					
XG699	Sea Venom FAW.22					
XG700	Sea Venom FAW.22					
XG701	Sea Venom FAW.22					
XG702	Sea Venom FAW.22					
XG721	Sea Venom FAW.22					
XG722	Sea Venom FAW.22					
XG723	Sea Venom FAW.22					
XG724	Sea Venom FAW.22					
XG725	Sea Venom FAW.22					
XG726	Sea Venom FAW.22					
XG727	Sea Venom FAW.22					
XG728	Sea Venom FAW.22					
XG729	Sea Venom FAW.22					
XG730	Sea Venom FAW.22					Pr London Colney
XG731	Sea Venom FAW.22					
XG732	Sea Venom FAW.22					
XG733	Sea Venom FAW.22					
XG734	Sea Venom FAW.22					
XG735	Sea Venom FAW.22					
XG736	Sea Venom FAW.22					
XG737	Sea Venom FAW.22					Pr FAAM

21 Sea Vampire T.22 trainers built for the RN by de Havilland Aircraft Co Ltd at Christchurch with c/ns 15633-15652. Delivered between 11.54 and 5.55, some aircraft were later transferred to Australia and others, at a later date, were sold to Chile.

serial	type	sqdn/unit	code	where&when seen		remarks
XG742	Sea Vampire T.22					

XG743-XG836

serial	type	sqdn/unit	code	where&when seen		remarks
XG743	Sea Vampire T.22					Pr IWM Duxford
XG744	Sea Vampire T.22					
XG745	Sea Vampire T.22					
XG746	Sea Vampire T.22					
XG747	Sea Vampire T.22					
XG748	Sea Vampire T.22					
XG749	Sea Vampire T.22					
XG765	Sea Vampire T.22					
XG766	Sea Vampire T.22					To RAN
XG767	Sea Vampire T.22					
XG768	Sea Vampire T.22					
XG769	Sea Vampire T.22					To ChAF 11.72
XG770	Sea Vampire T.22					To RAN
XG771	Sea Vampire T.22					
XG772	Sea Vampire T.22					To ChAF 11.72
XG773	Sea Vampire T.22					
XG774	Sea Vampire T.22					
XG775	Sea Vampire T.22					To GI Southall Tech
XG776	Sea Vampire T.22					
XG777	Sea Vampire T.22					To ChAF 11.72

47 Gannet anti-submarine search and strike aircraft all initially ordered as AS.1's for the RN to be built by Fairey Aviation Co Ltd at Hayes and at Stockport. 10 were built as AS.1 for the Royal Australian Navy; 12 were built as AS.4 at Hayes for the RN; 15 further AS.4 variants were built at Hayes for diversion to the West German Bundesmarine; whilst the remaining 10 were cancelled and not built. Several RN AS.4 Gannets were subsequently converted to COD.4, AS.6, and ECM.6 standard. Those aircraft built at Hayes are marked by (H) and those at Stockport by (S). XG783-798/825-855 were allocated c/ns F9351 to F9397 respectivly.

serial	type	sqdn/unit	code	where&when seen		remarks
XG783	Gannet AS.4 (H)					
XG784	Gannet AS.1 (S)					To RAN
XG785	Gannet AS.1 (S)					To RAN
XG786	Gannet COD.4 (H)					
XG787	Gannet AS.1 (S)					To RAN
XG788	Gannet AS.4 (H)					
XG789	Gannet AS.1 (S)					To RAN Pr Moorabbin
XG790	Gannet COD.4 (H)					
XG791	Gannet AS.1 (S)					To RAN
XG792	Gannet AS.1 (S)					To RAN
XG793	Gannet AS.4 (H)					
XG794	Gannet AS.4 (H)					
XG795	Gannet AS.1 (S)					To RAN
XG796	Gannet AS.1 (S)					To RAN
XG797	Gannet ECM.6 (H)					Pr IWM Duxford
XG798	Gannet AS.6 (H)					
XG825	Gannet AS.1 (S)					To RAN
XG826	Gannet AS.1 (S)					To RAN
XG827	Gannet AS.4 (H)					
XG828	Gannet AS.4 (H)					
XG829	Gannet AS.4 (H)					To WGN UA114
XG830	Gannet AS.4 (H)					To WGN UA115
XG831	Gannet ECM.6 (H)					To A2539 Pr Helston
XG832	Gannet ECM.6 (H)					
XG833	Gannet AS.4 (H)					To WGN UA101
XG834	Gannet AS.4 (H)					To WGN UA102
XG835	Gannet AS.4 (H)					To WGN UA103
XG836	Gannet AS.4 (H)					To WGN UA104

XG837-XG898

serial	type	sqdn/unit	code	where&when seen		remarks
XG837	Gannet AS.4					Cancelled not built
XG838	Gannet AS.4					Cancelled not built
XG839	Gannet AS.4 (H)					To WGN UA105
XG840	Gannet AS.4 (H)					To WGN UA106
XG841	Gannet AS.4					Cancelled not built
XG842	Gannet AS.4					Cancelled not built
XG843	Gannet AS.4 (H)					To WGN UA107
XG844	Gannet AS.4 (H)					To WGN UA108
XG845	Gannet AS.4					Cancelled not built
XG846	Gannet AS.4 (H)					To WGN UA109
XG847	Gannet AS.4					Cancelled not built
XG848	Gannet AS.4					Cancelled not built
XG849	Gannet AS.4 (H)					To WGN UA110
XG850	Gannet AS.4 (H)					To WGN UA111
XG851	Gannet AS.4					Cancelled not built
XG852	Gannet AS.4 (H)					To WGN UA112
XG853	Gannet AS.4 (H)					To WGN UA113
XG854	Gannet AS.4					Cancelled not built
XG855	Gannet AS.4					Cancelled not built

22 Gannet T.2/T.5 training aircraft for the RN and all built by Fairey Aviation Co Ltd at Hayes with c/ns F9398-F9419 resp. XG869-881 were initially built as T.2's and XG882-889 as T.5's. XG888 was diverted to RAN as a T.2 but returned to RN charge 1.67 and converted to T.5 standard 8.68; XG890 was diverted to the Bundesmarine as a T.2.

serial	type	sqdn/unit	code	where&when seen		remarks
XG869	Gannet T.2					
XG870	Gannet T.2					
XG871	Gannet T.2					To A2474
XG872	Gannet T.2					
XG873	Gannet T.5					
XG874	Gannet T.2					To ANGK LAUT LA-17
XG875	Gannet T.2					
XG876	Gannet T.2					
XG877	Gannet T.2					
XG878	Gannet T.2					
XG879	Gannet T.2					
XG880	Gannet T.2					
XG881	Gannet T.2					
XG882	Gannet T.5					
XG883	Gannet T.5					Pr FAAM
XG884	Gannet T.5					
XG885	Gannet T.5					
XG886	Gannet T.5					
XG887	Gannet T.5					
XG888	Gannet T.5					To RAN Returned to RN
XG889	Gannet T.5					
XG890	Gannet T.2					To WGN UA99

Two Vickers Vikings allotted military marks following a temporary trooping contract awarded to Eagle Aviation Ltd as follows:- XG895 c/n 241 ex G-AJBO; and XG896 c/n 221 ex G-AIVH.

serial	type	sqdn/unit	code	where&when seen		remarks
XG895	V.610 Viking 1B					Restored to G-AJBO
XG896	V.610 Viking 1B					Restored to G-AIVH

Two Avro Yorks allotted military serials for temporary trooping duties as follows:- XG897 ex G-AMRJ of Air Charter Ltd and XG898 ex G-ANRC of Scottish Aviation Ltd.

serial	type	sqdn/unit	code	where&when seen		remarks
XG897	Avro 685 York 1					Restored to G-AMRJ
XG898	Avro 685 York 1					Restored to G-ANRC

XG900-XH171

serial	type	sqdn/unit	code	where&when seen	remarks

Two Short SC.1 VTOL research aircraft built to Spec ER.143D; XG900 (c/n SH1814) f/f 2.4.57 and XG905 (SH1815) f/f 6.8.58. Both were issued to RAE Bedford for trials.

serial	type	sqdn/unit	code	where&when seen	remarks
XG900	Short SC.1				Science M St Wroughtn
XG905	Short SC.1				Pr Holywood Co Down

Planned production of Shackleton MR.3 maritime reconnaissance aircraft accounted for a further 13 units to follow on from XF730. The block was subsequently cancelled.

XG912-XG924 Shackleton MR.3 (13 aircraft) Cancelled and not built

One Avro York allotted a military serial following a temporary trooping contract awarded to Scottish Aviation Ltd. XG929 ex G-ANSY.

serial	type	sqdn/unit	code	where&when seen	remarks
XG929	Avro 685 York 1				Restored to G-ANSY

46 Sea Hawk FGA.4 ground-attack fighters contracted to Sir W.G. Armstrong-Whitworth Aircraft Ltd at Coventry, but the order was cancelled and none were built.

XG934-XG947 Sea Hawk FGA.4 (14 aircraft) Cancelled and not built
XG961-XG992 Sea Hawk FGA.4 (32 aircraft) Cancelled and not built

2nd production order for Beverley C.1 aircraft for the RAF to follow on from XB291, and built by Blackburn and General Aircraft Ltd at Brough. XH116 f/f 24.10.56 and the last (XH124) f/f 1.5.57. No c/ns allocated.

serial	type	sqdn/unit	code	where&when seen	remarks
XH116	Beverley C.1				
XH117	Beverley C.1				
XH118	Beverley C.1				
XH119	Beverley C.1				
XH120	Beverley C.1				
XH121	Beverley C.1				
XH122	Beverley C.1				To 8045M
XH123	Beverley C.1				
XH124	Beverley C.1				To 8025M Pr Hendon

23 Canberra PR.9 long-range photo-reconnaissance aircraft for the RAF, originally ordered as the PR.7 variant but built as PR.9's by Short Bros and Harland Ltd at Belfast with c/ns SH1719-SH1741 resp. Deliveries took place between 9.58 and 10.61. XH132 was converted to SC.9 standard (by Short Bros) between 12.59 and 5.61.

Unconfirmed reports suggest that XH138-151/158-163 were earmarked for Canberra B.6's (c/ns SH1742-SH1761 resp) and XH178-186 for further Canberra PR.9's, all cancelled.

serial	type	sqdn/unit	code	where&when seen	remarks
XH129	Canberra PR.9				
XH130	Canberra PR.9				
XH131	Canberra PR.9				
XH132	Short SC.9				
XH133	Canberra PR.9				
XH134	Canberra PR.9				
XH135	Canberra PR.9				
XH136	Canberra PR.9				
XH137	Canberra PR.9				
XH164	Canberra PR.9				
XH165	Canberra PR.9				
XH166	Canberra PR.9				
XH167	Canberra PR.9				
XH168	Canberra PR.9				
XH169	Canberra PR.9				
XH170	Canberra PR.9				
XH171	Canberra PR.9				

XH172-XH272

serial	type	sqdn/unit	code	where&when seen		remarks
XH172	Canberra PR.9					
XH173	Canberra PR.9					
XH174	Canberra PR.9					
XH175	Canberra PR.9					
XH176	Canberra PR.9					
XH177	Canberra PR.9					

25 Canberra B(I).8 bomber/interdictor aircraft built for the RAF by English Electric Co Ltd at Preston against Contract 11158. Deliveries took place between 8.56 & 9.58.

serial	type	sqdn/unit	code	where&when seen		remarks
XH203	Canberra B(I).8					To IAF IF896
XH204	Canberra B(I).8					
XH205	Canberra B(I).8					To IAF IF897
XH206	Canberra B(I).8					To PeAF 478, 479 or 480
XH207	Canberra B(I).8					
XH208	Canberra B(I).8					To 8167M
XH209	Canberra B(I).8					To 8201M
XH227	Canberra B(I).8					To IAF IF899
XH228	Canberra B(I).8					
XH229	Canberra B(I).8					To IAF IF900
XH230	Canberra B(I).8					To IAF IF901
XH231	Canberra B(I).8					
XH232	Canberra B(I).8					To IAF IF902
XH233	Canberra B(I).8					To IAF IF903
XH234	Canberra B(I).8					To G-52-7/PeAF 252
XH235	Canberra B(I).8					To IAF IF904
XH236	Canberra B(I).8					To IAF IF905
XH237	Canberra B(I).8					To IAF IF907
XH238	Canberra B(I).8					To IAF IF908
XH239	Canberra B(I).8					To IAF IF909
XH240	Canberra B(I).8					To IAF IF910
XH241	Canberra B(I).8					To PeAF 479 or IAF IF911
XH242	Canberra B(I).8					To PeAF 480 or IAF IF912
XH243	Canberra B(I).8					To PeAF 481 or IAF IF913
XH244	Canberra B(I).8					To PeAF 482 or VAF 4-A-39

The second prototype Fairey Rotodyne helicopter (to follow XE521) to be known as the Rotodyne 'Z' following classification of XE521 as 'Type Y' and allocated c/n F9430. However it was not built and all Rotodyne development was cancelled in 2.62.

serial	type	sqdn/unit	code	where&when seen		remarks
XH249	Rotodyne 'Z'					Not completed

Six prototype/pre-production Vickers V.1000 jet transport aircraft ordered to Spec C.132D and if built would have borne the Vickers Type number 1001. The order was announced during 6.54 against Contract 6/Aircraft/11190/CB6(c) but the programme was cancelled on 29.11.55 and the RAF received 6 Britannias in place of the V.1000's.

XH255 - XH260 Vickers V.1000 (6 a/c) Cancelled and not built

4th production order for 66 Vampire T.11 trainers for the RAF and built by the de Havilland Aircraft Co Ltd against Contract 11204. Deliveries were made between 7.55 and 5.56.

serial	type	sqdn/unit	code	where&when seen		remarks
XH264	Vampire T.11					
XH265	Vampire T.11					To RNZAF NZ5707
XH266	Vampire T.11					To RNZAF NZ5708
XH267	Vampire T.11					
XH268	Vampire T.11					To SRAF SR128
XH269	Vampire T.11					To SRAF SR129
XH270	Vampire T.11					To SRAF SR130
XH271	Vampire T.11					To RNZAF NZ5709
XH272	Vampire T.11					

XH273-XH368

serial	type	sqdn/unit	code	where&when seen		remarks
XH273	Vampire T.11					To 7830M
XH274	Vampire T.11					
XH275	Vampire T.11					To SRAF SR131
XH276	Vampire T.11					
XH277	Vampire T.11					
XH278	Vampire T.11					7866M/8595M Pr Henlow
XH292	Vampire T.11					Pr BAFM Brussels
XH293	Vampire T.11					
XH294	Vampire T.11					
XH295	Vampire T.11					
XH296	Vampire T.11					
XH297	Vampire T.11					
XH298	Vampire T.11					To 7760M
XH299	Vampire T.11					
XH300	Vampire T.11					
XH301	Vampire T.11					To SwAF
XH302	Vampire T.11					
XH303	Vampire T.11					
XH304	Vampire T.11					CFS Vintage Pair
XH305	Vampire T.11					
XH306	Vampire T.11					
XH307	Vampire T.11					
XH308	Vampire T.11					To SwAF
XH309	Vampire T.11					
XH310	Vampire T.11					
XH311	Vampire T.11					
XH312	Vampire T.11					Pr Knutsford
XH313	Vampire T.11					To GI St Albans Tech
XH314	Vanpire T.11					
XH315	Vampire T.11					
XH316	Vampire T.11					
XH317	Vampire T.11					To RNZAF NZ5710
XH318	Vampire T.11					To 7761M Pr Soton
XH319	Vampire T.11					
XH320	Vampire T.11					To Austrian AF 5C-VF
XH321	Vampire T.11					
XH322	Vampire T.11					
XH323	Vampire T.11					
XH324	Vampire T.11					
XH325	Vampire T.11					
XH326	Vampire T.11					
XH327	Vampire T.11					
XH328	Vampire T.11					
XH329	Vampire T.11					
XH330	Vampire T.11					
XH357	Vampire T.11					
XH358	Vampire T.11					To 7763M
XH359	Vampire T.11					
XH360	Vampire T.11					
XH361	Vampire T.11					
XH362	Vampire T.11					
XH363	Vampire T.11					
XH364	Vampire T.11					
XH365	Vampire T.11					
XH366	Vampire T.11					To RNZAF NZ5711
XH367	Vampire T.11					
XH368	Vampire T.11					

XH375-XH469

serial	type	sqdn/unit	code	where&when seen	remarks

One Heron Srs 2B (c/n 14059) built by the de Havilland Aircraft Co Ltd at Hatfield, and delivered to RAF Benson on 18.5.55. It was officially handed-over to the Queen's Flight on the following day as a Heron CC.3.

serial	type	sqdn/unit	code	where&when seen	remarks
XH375	Heron CC.3				Ex G-5-7 To G41-1-68

The 2nd prototype Type 173 helicopter built by the Bristol Aeroplane Co Ltd as a Mk.2 variant and initially flown as G-AMJI on 31.8.53. Subsequently it was converted to Mk.3 configuration with the serial XH379 for evaluation and test purposes. It was allocated the c/n 12872.

serial	type	sqdn/unit	code	where&when seen	remarks
XH379	Bristol 173				Ex G-AMJI

One Bristol 170 Mk.31E allotted a military serial following a temporary trooping contract awarded to Air Charter Ltd as follows:- XH385 c/n 13142 ex G-AMSA.

serial	type	sqdn/unit	code	where&when seen	remarks
XH385	Bristol 170 Mk.31E				Restored to G-AMSA

1st production order for 20 Javelin T.3 training aircraft for the RAF built by Gloster Aircraft Co Ltd at Hucclecote against Contract 11262, dated 27.9.54. XH390 f/f 6.1.58. See also XK577 and XM336 et seq.

serial	type	sqdn/unit	code	where&when seen	remarks
XH390	Javelin T.3				
XH391	Javelin T.3				
XH392	Javelin T.3				
XH393	Javelin T.3				
XH394	Javelin T.3				
XH395	Javelin T.3				
XH396	Javelin T.3				
XH397	Javelin T.3				
XH432	Javelin T.3				
XH433	Javelin T.3				
XH434	Javelin T.3				
XH435	Javelin T.3				
XH436	Javelin T.3				
XH437	Javelin T.3				
XH438	Javelin T.3				
XH443	Javelin T.3				
XH444	Javelin T.3				
XH445	Javelin T.3				
XH446	Javelin T.3				
XH447	Javelin T.3				

One prototype Vickers-Supermarine 'N.113' ordered 23.9.54 against Contract 6/Aircraft /11268/CB5(b) to Specification N.9/47 as a competitor to the de Havilland Sea Vixen. It was to be a two-seat version of the Scimitar strike aircraft but work was suspended on 27.4.55 and the project was cancelled.

serial	type	sqdn/unit	code	where&when seen	remarks
XH451	Vickers N.113				Cancelled

Two DHC.2 Beaver aircraft built by de Havilland Aircraft of Canada Ltd and imported for trials and evaluation as follows:- XH455 Srs.1 c/n 190 ex CF-CGR/G-AMVU and XH463 Srs.2 c/n 80 ex CF-GQE/G-ANAR.

serial	type	sqdn/unit	code	where&when seen	remarks
XH455	Beaver Srs.1				Ex G-AMVU To VR-LAV
XH463	Beaver Srs.2				Ex G-ANAR To G-ANAR

One Pioneer Srs.2 c/n 105 built by Scottish Aviation Ltd at Prestwick. Registered as G-ANRG on 15.5.54 and f/f on 24.6.54. Evaluated in Exercise 'Battle Royal' from 9.54 to 10.54 and was allocated the serial XH469 for the period, reverting to G-ANRG.

serial	type	sqdn/unit	code	where&when seen	remarks
XH469	Pioneer Srs.2				Ex G-ANRG To G-ANRG

XH475-XH584

serial	type	sqdn/unit	code	where&when seen		remarks

Second production contract for 37 Avro Vulcan strategic bombers built at Woodford for the RAF. The first 20 were built as B.1's while the remaining 17 were completed as B.2's, the first of which (XH533) f/f 19.8.58. All of the B.1's were subsequently converted to B.1A standard and 4 of the B.2's to SR.2 standard (later B.2(MRR)).

serial	type	sqdn/unit	code	where&when seen		remarks
XH475	Vulcan B.1A					To 7996M
XH476	Vulcan B.1A					
XH477	Vulcan B.1A					
XH478	Vulcan B.1A					To 8047M
XH479	Vulcan B.1A					To 7974M
XH480	Vulcan B.1A					
XH481	Vulcan B.1A					
XH482	Vulcan B.1A					
XH483	Vulcan B.1A					
XH497	Vulcan B.1A					
XH498	Vulcan B.1A					To 7993M
XH499	Vulcan B.1A					
XH500	Vulcan B.1A					To 7994M
XH501	Vulcan B.1A					
XH502	Vulcan B.1A					
XH503	Vulcan B.1A					
XH504	Vulcan B.1A					
XH505	Vulcan B.1A					
XH506	Vulcan B.1A					
XH532	Vulcan B.1A					
XH533	Vulcan B.2					To 8048M
XH534	Vulcan B.2(MRR)					
XH535	Vulcan B.2					
XH536	Vulcan B.2					
XH537	Vulcan B.2(MRR)					
XH538	Vulcan B.2					
XH539	Vulcan B.2					
XH554	Vulcan B.2					
XH555	Vulcan B.2					
XH556	Vulcan B.2					
XH557	Vulcan B.2					
XH558	Vulcan B.2					
XH559	Vulcan B.2					
XH560	Vulcan B.2(MRR)					
XH561	Vulcan B.2					
XH562	Vulcan B.2					
XH563	Vulcan B.2(MRR)					

4 Canberra B.6's and 2 T.4's built by English Electric Co Ltd at Preston against Contract 11313. Deliveries took place between 1.55 & 3.55. XH570 converted to B.16.

serial	type	sqdn/unit	code	where&when seen		remarks
XH567	Canberra B.6					
XH568	Canberra B.6					
XH569	Canberra B.6					
XH570	Canberra B.16					
XH583	Canberra T.4					
XH584	Canberra T.4					

2nd production contract for 34 Handley-Page Victor strategic bombers for the RAF and built at Radlett. The first 8 (XH587-594) were initially built as B.1's but later returned to the manufacturers for conversion to B.1A; the following 17 aircraft were

XH587-XH682

serial	type	sqdn/unit	code	where&when seen	remarks

built as B.1A's from the outset. XH668 was built to B.2 standard and f/f 20.2.59 and the following 7 aircraft (XH669-675) were all built as B.2's. Conversions involved many B.1A's to B(K).1A and K.1A standards, and B.2's to K.2 and SR.2 standards.

serial	type	sqdn/unit	code	where&when seen	remarks
XH587	Victor K.1A				
XH588	Victor K.1A				
XH589	Victor K.1A				
XH590	Victor K.1A				
XH591	Victor K.1A				
XH592	Victor B.1A				To 8429M
XH593	Victor B.1A				To 8428M
XH594	Victor B.1A				
XH613	Victor B.1A				
XH614	Victor K.1A				
XH615	Victor B(K).1A				
XH616	Victor K.1A				
XH617	Victor B.1				
XH618	Victor K.1A				
XH619	Victor K.1A				
XH620	Victor B(K).1A				
XH621	Victor K.1A				
XH645	Victor K.1A				
XH646	Victor B(K).1A				
XH647	Victor B(K).1A				
XH648	Victor B(K).1A				
XH649	Victor K.1A				
XH650	Victor K.1A				
XH651	Victor K.1A				
XH667	Victor B(K).1A				
XH668	Victor B.2				
XH669	Victor K.2				
XH670	Victor SR.2				
XH671	Victor K.2				
XH672	Victor SR.2				
XH673	Victor K.2				
XH674	Victor SR.2				
XH675	Victor K.2				

One Sycamore HR.14 acquired for the RAE in 7.54 and originally built by Bristol Aeroplane Co Ltd at Filton as a Type 171 Mk.3 with the registration G-ALSR (c/n 12886).

serial	type	sqdn/unit	code	where&when seen	remarks
XH682	Sycamore HR.14				Ex G-ALSR

Contract 6/Aircraft/11329/CB7(b) dated 19.10.54 accounted for 219 Gloster Javelins of various marks as follows:-

XH687-692	FAW.5	(6 a/c)	Armstrong-Whitworth	Dels	4.57-5.57
XH693-703	FAW.6	(11 a/c)	Gloster Aircraft	Dels	9.57-2.58
XH704-725/XH746-784	FAW.7	(61 a/c)	Gloster Aircraft	Dels	2.57-2.59
XH785-795/XH833-849	FAW.7	(28 a/c)	Armstrong-Whitworth	Dels	5.57-12.58
XH871-899	FAW.7	(29 a/c)	Armstrong-Whitworth	Dels	12.57-6.58
XH900-912/XH955-965	FAW.7	(24 a/c)	Gloster Aircraft	Dels	10.58-6.59
XH966-993/XJ113-130) XJ165-178)	FAW.8	(60 a/c)	Gloster Aircraft	Dels	7.58-8.60

Note that the final 13 aircraft (XJ166-XJ178) were cancelled in 8.60 and not built. Many FAW.7's were delivered directly into storage following a decision to update 116 of them to FAW.9 standard. The FAW.9 had many of the advanced features of the FAW.8

XH687-XH761

serial	type	sqdn/unit	code	where&when seen	remarks

but retained the British-built AI-17 radar. 40 aircraft were later fitted with a gigantic in-flight refuelling probe and designated FAW.9R's.

serial	type	sqdn/unit	code	where&when seen	remarks
XH687	Javelin FAW.5				
XH688	Javelin FAW.5				
XH689	Javelin FAW.5				
XH690	Javelin FAW.5				
XH691	Javelin FAW.5				
XH692	Javelin FAW.5				
XH693	Javelin FAW.6				
XH694	Javelin FAW.6				
XH695	Javelin FAW.6				
XH696	Javelin FAW.6				
XH697	Javelin FAW.6				
XH698	Javelin FAW.6				To 7743M
XH699	Javelin FAW.6				
XH700	Javelin FAW.6				
XH701	Javelin FAW.6				
XH702	Javelin FAW.6				
XH703	Javelin FAW.6				
XH704	Javelin FAW.7				
XH705	Javelin FAW.7				
XH706	Javelin FAW.7				
XH707	Javelin FAW.9R				
XH708	Javelin FAW.9R				
XH709	Javelin FAW.9R				
XH710	Javelin FAW.7				To 7748M
XH711	Javelin FAW.9				
XH712	Javelin FAW.9R				
XH713	Javelin FAW.9				
XH714	Javelin FAW.7				
XH715	Javelin FAW.9				
XH716	Javelin FAW.9				
XH717	Javelin FAW.9				
XH718	Javelin FAW.7				
XH719	Javelin FAW.9				
XH720	Javelin FAW.7				
XH721	Javelin FAW.9				
XH722	Javelin FAW.9				
XH723	Javelin FAW.9				
XH724	Javelin FAW.9				
XH725	Javelin FAW.9				
XH746	Javelin FAW.9				
XH747	Javelin FAW.9				
XH748	Javelin FAW.7				
XH749	Javelin FAW.9				
XH750	Javelin FAW.7				
XH751	Javelin FAW.9				
XH752	Javelin FAW.9				
XH753	Javelin FAW.9				
XH754	Javelin FAW.7				
XH755	Javelin FAW.9				
XH756	Javelin FAW.9				
XH757	Javelin FAW.9				To 7903M
XH758	Javelin FAW.9				
XH759	Javelin FAW.9R				
XH760	Javelin FAW.9				To 7892M
XH761	Javelin FAW.9				

XH762-XH876

serial	type	sqdn/unit	code	where&when seen		remarks
XH762	Javelin FAW.9R					
XH763	Javelin FAW.9R					
XH764	Javelin FAW.9R					To 7972M Pr Manston
XH765	Javelin FAW.9R					
XH766	Javelin FAW.9R					
XH767	Javelin FAW.9					To 7955M Pr Worcester
XH768	Javelin FAW.9					To 7929M Pr Southend
XH769	Javelin FAW.9					
XH770	Javelin FAW.9					
XH771	Javelin FAW.9					
XH772	Javelin FAW.9					
XH773	Javelin FAW.9					
XH774	Javelin FAW.9					
XH775	Javelin FAW.7					
XH776	Javelin FAW.9					
XH777	Javelin FAW.9					GI SAFTECH 9
XH778	Javelin FAW.9					
XH779	Javelin FAW.9					
XH780	Javelin FAW.9					
XH781	Javelin FAW.7					
XH782	Javelin FAW.7					To 7797M
XH783	Javelin FAW.7					To 7798M
XH784	Javelin FAW.7					To 7799M
XH785	Javelin FAW.9					
XH786	Javelin FAW.7					
XH787	Javelin FAW.9					
XH788	Javelin FAW.9					
XH789	Javelin FAW.7					
XH790	Javelin FAW.7					To 7808M
XH791	Javelin FAW.9					
XH792	Javelin FAW.9					
XH793	Javelin FAW.9R					GI SAFTECH 8
XH794	Javelin FAW.9					
XH795	Javelin FAW.7					To 7757M
XH833	Javelin FAW.9					
XH834	Javelin FAW.9					
XH835	Javelin FAW.9					
XH836	Javelin FAW.9					
XH837	Javelin FAW.7					To 8032M (nose)
XH838	Javelin FAW.7					
XH839	Javelin FAW.9					GI SAFTECH 10
XH840	Javelin FAW.9					To 7740M
XH841	Javelin FAW.9					
XH842	Javelin FAW.9					
XH843	Javelin FAW.9R					
XH844	Javelin FAW.9					
XH845	Javelin FAW.9R					
XH846	Javelin FAW.9					
XH847	Javelin FAW.9R					
XH848	Javelin FAW.9R					
XH849	Javelin FAW.9R					To 7975M
XH871	Javelin FAW.9R					
XH872	Javelin FAW.9R					GI SAFTECH 7
XH873	Javelin FAW.9R					
XH874	Javelin FAW.9R					
XH875	Javelin FAW.9					
XH876	Javelin FAW.9R					

XH877-XH976

serial	type	sqdn/unit	code	where&when seen		remarks
XH877	Javelin FAW.9R					
XH878	Javelin FAW.9					
XH879	Javelin FAW.9R					
XH880	Javelin FAW.9					
XH881	Javelin FAW.9					
XH882	Javelin FAW.9					
XH883	Javelin FAW.9					
XH884	Javelin FAW.9					
XH885	Javelin FAW.9R					
XH886	Javelin FAW.9R					
XH887	Javelin FAW.9R					
XH888	Javelin FAW.9R					
XH889	Javelin FAW.9R					
XH890	Javelin FAW.9R					
XH891	Javelin FAW.9R					
XH892	Javelin FAW.9R					To 7982M Pr Duxford
XH893	Javelin FAW.9R					GI SAFTECH 6
XH894	Javelin FAW.9R					
XH895	Javelin FAW.9R					GI SAFTECH 5
XH896	Javelin FAW.9R					
XH897	Javelin FAW.9					Pr IWM Duxford
XH898	Javelin FAW.9					
XH899	Javelin FAW.9R					
XH900	Javelin FAW.7					To 7811M
XH901	Javelin FAW.7					To 7800M
XH902	Javelin FAW.7					To 7801M
XH903	Javelin FAW.9					To 7938M Pr Innsworth
XH904	Javelin FAW.9					
XH905	Javelin FAW.9					
XH906	Javelin FAW.9					
XH907	Javelin FAW.9					
XH908	Javelin FAW.9R					
XH909	Javelin FAW.9					
XH910	Javelin FAW.9					
XH911	Javelin FAW.9					
XH912	Javelin FAW.9					
XH955	Javelin FAW.9R					
XH956	Javelin FAW.9					
XH957	Javelin FAW.9					
XH958	Javelin FAW.9					
XH959	Javelin FAW.9R					
XH960	Javelin FAW.9					
XH961	Javelin FAW.9R					
XH962	Javelin FAW.9					
XH963	Javelin FAW.9					
XH964	Javelin FAW.9					
XH965	Javelin FAW.9					
XH966	Javelin FAW.8					
XH967	Javelin FAW.8					
XH968	Javelin FAW.8					
XH969	Javelin FAW.8					
XH970	Javelin FAW.8					
XH971	Javelin FAW.8					
XH972	Javelin FAW.8					To 7834M
XH973	Javelin FAW.8					
XH974	Javelin FAW.8					
XH975	Javelin FAW.8					
XH976	Javelin FAW.8					

XH977-XJ264

serial	type	sqdn/unit	code	where&when seen		remarks
XH977	Javelin FAW.8					
XH978	Javelin FAW.8					
XH979	Javelin FAW.8					
XH980	Javelin FAW.8					To 7867M Pr W Raynham
XH981	Javelin FAW.8					
XH982	Javelin FAW.8					
XH983	Javelin FAW.8					
XH984	Javelin FAW.8					
XH985	Javelin FAW.8					
XH986	Javelin FAW.8					To 7842M
XH987	Javelin FAW.8					
XH988	Javelin FAW.8					
XH989	Javelin FAW.8					
XH990	Javelin FAW.8					
XH991	Javelin FAW.8					To 7831M
XH992	Javelin FAW.8					To 7829M
XH993	Javelin FAW.8					
XJ113	Javelin FAW.8					
XJ114	Javelin FAW.8					
XJ115	Javelin FAW.8					
XJ116	Javelin FAW.8					To 7832M
XJ117	Javelin FAW.8					To 7833M
XJ118	Javelin FAW.8					
XJ119	Javelin FAW.8					
XJ120	Javelin FAW.8					
XJ121	Javelin FAW.8					
XJ122	Javelin FAW.8					To 7836M
XJ123	Javelin FAW.8					
XJ124	Javelin FAW.8					
XJ125	Javelin FAW.8					
XJ126	Javelin FAW.8					To 7837M
XJ127	Javelin FAW.8					
XJ128	Javelin FAW.8					
XJ129	Javelin FAW.8					
XJ130	Javelin FAW.8					
XJ165	Javelin FAW.8					

XJ166 - XJ178 Javelin FAW.8 (13 a/c) Cancelled and not built

Twenty Swift F.4 fighter aircraft ordered against Contract 8509 to be built at South Marston by Vickers-Armstrongs (Supermarine Division). All were cancelled.

XJ183 - XJ188 Swift F.4 (6 a/c) Cancelled and not built
XJ217 - XJ226 Swift F.4 (10 a/c) Cancelled and not built
XJ241 - XJ244 Swift F.4 (4 a/c) Cancelled and not built

Two Canberra B.6's built by English Electric Co Ltd at Preston against Contract 5786 to replace WJ779 and WJ784 (diverted to France). Deliveries took place 4/5.56.

serial	type	sqdn/unit	code	where&when seen		remarks
XJ249	Canberra B.6					
XJ257	Canberra B.6					

One Avro York allotted military marks following a temporary trooping contract awarded to Scottish Aviation Ltd.

serial	type	sqdn/unit	code	where&when seen		remarks
XJ264	Avro 685 York 1					Restored to G-ANVO

The final block of military serials allotted for temporary trooping purposes was allocated to five Hermes 4's (of Britavia Ltd) and one Viking 1B (of Eagle Aircraft

XJ269-XJ355

serial	type	sqdn/unit	code	where&when seen	remarks

Services Ltd), although it is possible that the Viking was sub-leased on this occasion. Aircraft details as follows:- XJ269 (c/n HP81/17 ex G-ALDP); XJ276 (c/n HP81/24 ex G-ALDX); XJ281 (c/n HP81/12 ex G-ALDK); XJ288 (c/n HP81/21 ex G-ALDU); XJ309 (c/n HP81/10 ex G-ALDI). Note that the designation 4A refers to aircraft modified to use 100 octane fuel as used on trooping flights. The Viking was allotted XJ304 (c/n 207 ex G-AJPH) but has frequently been mis-recorded as 'XJ804'.

serial	type	sqdn/unit	code	where&when seen	remarks
XJ269	HP.81 Hermes 4A				Restored to G-ALDP
XJ276	HP.81 Hermes 4A				Restored to G-ALDX
XJ281	HP.81 Hermes 4A				Restored to G-ALDK
XJ288	HP.81 Hermes 4A				Restored to G-ALDU
XJ304	V.610 Viking 1B				Restored to G-AJPH
XJ309	HP.81 Hermes 4A				Restored to G-ALDI

The first prototype Thrust Measuring Rig built by Rolls-Royce at Hucknall and nicknamed 'Flying Bedstead' was designed to test the Nene 101 engine in VTOL configuration. XJ314 f/f 9.7.53 (tethered) and 3.8.54 (free).

serial	type	sqdn/unit	code	where&when seen	remarks
XJ314	Thrust Measuring Rig				Pr Science Museum

Ten Sea Devon C.20 communications aircraft built by the de Havilland Aircraft Co Ltd during 1953, they were originally earmarked (and registered) as Doves of various marks for export to American civil customers. All (except XJ350) were initially stored at Hatfield and Panshanger until Sept/Oct 1954 when they were sold to the Royal Navy. Details are as follows:- XJ319 (c/n 04420 ex Mk.2A G-AMXP); XJ320 (c/n 04441 ex Mk.6A G-ANDY); XJ321 (c/n 04415 ex Mk.2A XB-TAN); XJ322 (c/n 04421 ex Mk.2A G-AMYP); XJ323 (c/n 04409 ex Mk.2A G-AMXY), XJ324 (c/n 04410 ex Mk.2A G-AMXZ); XJ347 (c/n 04392 ex Mk.2A G-AMXT); XJ348 (c/n 04406 ex Mk.2A G-AMXX); XJ349 (c/n 04401 ex Mk.2A G-AMXW); XJ350 (c/n 04453 new aircraft).

serial	type	sqdn/unit	code	where&when seen	remarks
XJ319	Sea Devon C.20				
XJ320	Sea Devon C.20				Restored to G-ANDY
XJ321	Sea Devon C.20				To G-AROH
XJ322	Sea Devon C.20				
XJ323	Sea Devon C.20				Restored to G-AMXY
XJ324	Sea Devon C.20				
XJ347	Sea Devon C.20				
XJ348	Sea Devon C.20				
XJ349	Sea Devon C.20				Restored to G-AMXW
XJ350	Sea Devon C.20				

The third prototype Skeeter 6 helicopter built by Saunders Roe Ltd allotted military marks for evaluation during November 1954. It was originally registered as G-ANMH with c/n SR.905 and first flown as such on 29.8.54.

serial	type	sqdn/unit	code	where&when seen	remarks
XJ355	Skeeter Mk.6				Ex G-ANMH

10 Sycamore HR.14 helicopters built by the Bristol Aeroplane Co Ltd for the RAF. XJ361 was allotted the c/n 13248 whilst the remainder were allotted c/ns as follows: XJ362 (13266), XJ363 (13240), XJ364 (13241), XJ380 (13242), XJ381 (13243), XJ382 (13244), XJ383 (13390), XJ384 (13391) and XJ385 (13392). This batch was delivered between 3.55 and 10.56.

Note that several Alouette helicopters were delivered to the United Kingdom with serials ranging in the XJ3xx blocks (eg XJ376). These serials were in fact mis-painted at the manufacturers and were later corrected to read XR376 etc.

XJ361-XJ437

serial	type	sqdn/unit	code	where&when seen		remarks
XJ361	Sycamore HR.14					
XJ362	Sycamore HR.14					
XJ363	Sycamore HR.14					
XJ364	Sycamore HR.14					
XJ380	Sycamore HR.14					Pr Finningley
XJ381	Sycamore HR.14					
XJ382	Sycamore HR.14					
XJ383	Sycamore HR.14					
XJ384	Sycamore HR.14					
XJ385	Sycamore HR.14					See XG540

The prototype Fairey Jet Gyrodyne (XD759) was re-allocated the marks XJ389 due to the former serial being 'compromised' with a Canadair Sabre F.4 (qv).

serial	type	sqdn/unit	code	where&when seen		remarks
XJ389	Jet Gyrodyne					Ex XD759 Pr Cosford

10 RN Whirlwind HAR.3's built by Westland Aircraft Ltd, at Yeovil with c/ns WA57-66. The batch is believed to have been initially allocated 'compromise' serials XD763 to XD772. This is borne out by the fact that an 'XD763' f/f on 24.9.54 at Yeovil (NB: batch also reported as being XD363-XD372). XJ396 and XJ398 were converted to HAR.5 standard and at a much later date, brought up to virtually HAR.10's.

serial	type	sqdn/unit	code	where&when seen		remarks
XJ393	Whirlwind HAR.3					To A2538 Pr H Blagdon
XJ394	Whirlwind HAR.3					
XJ395	Whirlwind HAR.3					
XJ396	Whirlwind HAR.5/10					
XJ397	Whirlwind HAR.3					To A2485
XJ398	Whirlwind HAR.5/10					To G-BDBZ
XJ399	Whirlwind HAR.3					To A2578
XJ400	Whirlwind HAR.3					
XJ401	Whirlwind HAR.3					To G-AYTK
XJ402	Whirlwind HAR.3					To A2572 Pr FAAM

20 Whirlwind HAR.2 and HAR.4 helicopters built by Westland Aircraft Ltd at Yeovil for the RAF with the c/ns WA33-38/40-53 resp. XJ429/430/432-436 were built as HAR.2's and the remainder as HAR.4's. All were initially allotted 'compromised' serials in the XD range (XD777-784/795-806). The batch XJ407-414 was test flown and delivered as XD777-784. XJ426 f/f 14.12.54. Some later conversions to HAR.10 standard.

serial	type	sqdn/unit	code	where&when seen		remarks
XJ407	Whirlwind HAR.10					Ex XD777
XJ408	Whirlwind HAR.4					Ex XD778
XJ409	Whirlwind HAR.10					Ex XD779
XJ410	Whirlwind HAR.10					Ex XD780
XJ411	Whirlwind HAR.10					Ex XD781
XJ412	Whirlwind HAR.10					Ex XD782
XJ413	Whirlwind HAR.4					Ex XD783
XJ414	Whirlwind HAR.10					Ex XD784
XJ426	Whirlwind HAR.10					
XJ427	Whirlwind HAR.4					
XJ428	Whirlwind HAR.10					To 7821M
XJ429	Whirlwind HAR.10					
XJ430	Whirlwind HAR.10					
XJ431	Whirlwind HAR.4					
XJ432	Whirlwind HAR.10					
XJ433	Whirlwind HAR.10					
XJ434	Whirlwind HAR.2					
XJ435	Whirlwind HAR.10					
XJ436	Whirlwind HAR.2					
XJ437	Whirlwind HAR.10					

XJ440-XJ523

serial	type	sqdn/unit	code	where&when seen	remarks

Prototype Gannet AEW.3 built to Spec AEW.154D by Fairey Aviation Co Ltd at Hayes to Contract 6/AIR/11497/CB9(a) with c/n F9431. It first flew at Northolt on 20.8.58.

serial	type	sqdn/unit	code	where&when seen	remarks
XJ440	Gannet AEW.3				

Planned to have been the Whirlwind Mk.6 prototype for the RAF, XJ445 (c/n WA93) was in fact built by Westland Aircraft Ltd at Yeovil as a HAR.5 for the RN. F/f 10.57.

serial	type	sqdn/unit	code	where&when seen	remarks
XJ445	Whirlwind HAR.5				

4 Pioneer CC.1 communications aircraft built by Scottish Aviation Ltd at Prestwick for the RAF. Allocated c/ns 112-114 & 117 resp. XJ450 was delivered 3.5.55.

serial	type	sqdn/unit	code	where&when seen	remarks
XJ450	Pioneer CC.1				
XJ451	Pioneer CC.1				
XJ465	Pioneer CC.1				
XJ466	Pioneer CC.1				

The sole Type 170 Mk.31C Freighter built by the Bristol Aeroplane Co Ltd at Filton with c/n 13217. Ordered for the A&AEE, it was delivered to Boscombe Down 21.2.55.

serial	type	sqdn/unit	code	where&when seen	remarks
XJ470	Bristol 170 Mk.31C				Ex G-18-193

The first production order for Sea Vixen FAW.1 carrier-borne all-weather fighters for the RN built by de Havilland Aircraft Co Ltd. The first of 78 aircraft (XJ474) f/f at Christchurch 20.3.57, and the block was allotted c/ns 10001-10078 inclusive. Later, most aircraft were converted to FAW.2 standard at Chester (C) and RNAY Belfast (B). Flight Refuelling Ltd, Tarrant Rushton later reworked some to D.3's.

serial	type	sqdn/unit	code	where&when seen	remarks
XJ474	Sea Vixen FAW.1				
XJ475	Sea Vixen FAW.1				
XJ476	Sea Vixen FAW.1				Nose Pr Southampton
XJ477	Sea Vixen FAW.1				To A2601 Pr Arbroath
XJ478	Sea Vixen FAW.1				
XJ479	Sea Vixen FAW.1				
XJ480	Sea Vixen FAW.1				
XJ481	Sea Vixen FAW.1				Pr FAAM
XJ482	Sea Vixen FAW.1				To A2598
XJ483	Sea Vixen FAW.1				
XJ484	Sea Vixen FAW.1				To A2535
XJ485	Sea Vixen FAW.1				
XJ486	Sea Vixen FAW.1				To A2599
XJ487	Sea Vixen FAW.1				To A2544
XJ488	Sea Vixen FAW.1				
XJ489	Sea Vixen FAW.2 (C)				
XJ490	Sea Vixen FAW.2 (C)				
XJ491	Sea Vixen FAW.2 (C)				
XJ492	Sea Vixen FAW.1				
XJ493	Sea Vixen FAW.1				
XJ494	Sea Vixen FAW.2 (B)				
XJ513	Sea Vixen FAW.1				Pr FAAM
XJ514	Sea Vixen FAW.1				
XJ515	Sea Vixen FAW.1				
XJ516	Sea Vixen FAW.2 (C)				
XJ517	Sea Vixen FAW.2 (C)				
XJ518	Sea Vixen FAW.2 (C)				
XJ519	Sea Vixen FAW.1				
XJ520	Sea Vixen FAW.1				
XJ521	Sea Vixen FAW.2 (C)				To A2612
XJ522	Sea Vixen FAW.1				
XJ523	Sea Vixen FAW.1				

XJ524-XJ627

serial	type	sqdn/unit	code	where&when seen		remarks
XJ524	Sea Vixen FAW.2 (C)					TT version used by FR
XJ525	Sea Vixen FAW.1					
XJ526	Sea Vixen FAW.2 (C)					To 8145M
XJ527	Sea Vixen FAW.1					
XJ528	Sea Vixen FAW.1					
XJ556	Sea Vixen FAW.1					
XJ557	Sea Vixen FAW.1					
XJ558	Sea Vixen FAW.2 (B)					
XJ559	Sea Vixen FAW.2 (B)					
XJ560	Sea Vixen FAW.2 (B)					To 8142M
XJ561	Sea Vixen FAW.2 (C)					
XJ562	Sea Vixen FAW.1					
XJ563	Sea Vixen FAW.1					
XJ564	Sea Vixen FAW.2 (B)					
XJ565	Sea Vixen FAW.2 (C)					Pr London Colney
XJ566	Sea Vixen FAW.1					
XJ567	Sea Vixen FAW.1					
XJ568	Sea Vixen FAW.1					
XJ569	Sea Vixen FAW.1					
XJ570	Sea Vixen FAW.2 (B)					
XJ571	Sea Vixen FAW.2 (C)					To 8140M
XJ572	Sea Vixen FAW.2 (C)					
XJ573	Sea Vixen FAW.1					
XJ574	Sea Vixen FAW.2 (B)					
XJ575	Sea Vixen FAW.2 (B)					To A2611 Pr Helston
XJ576	Sea Vixen FAW.2 (B)					
XJ577	Sea Vixen FAW.1					
XJ578	Sea Vixen FAW.2 (C)					
XJ579	Sea Vixen FAW.2 (B)					
XJ580	Sea Vixen FAW.2 (C)					
XJ581	Sea Vixen FAW.2 (B)					
XJ582	Sea Vixen FAW.2 (C)					To 8139M
XJ583	Sea Vixen FAW.1					To A2507
XJ584	Sea Vixen FAW.2 (B)					To A2621 Pr Helston
XJ585	Sea Vixen FAW.1					
XJ586	Sea Vixen FAW.1					
XJ602	Sea Vixen FAW.2 (C)					To A2622 To XJ602
XJ603	Sea Vixen FAW.1					
XJ604	Sea Vixen FAW.2 (B)					To 8222M
XJ605	Sea Vixen FAW.1					
XJ606	Sea Vixen FAW.2 (C)					
XJ607	Sea Vixen FAW.2 (C)					To 8171M
XJ608	Sea Vixen FAW.2 (B)					
XJ609	Sea Vixen FAW.2 (B)					To 8172M
XJ610	Sea Vixen FAW.2 (B)					
XJ611	Sea Vixen FAW.1					

Two Hawker P.1101 prototypes built by Hawker Aircraft Co Ltd at Kingston to meet RAF Spec T.157D. XJ615 f/f 8.7.55; XJ627 f/f 17.11.56. Production aircraft (Hunter T7) commence with XL563. Both prototypes built to Contract 6/Aircraft/11595/CB7(a).

serial	type	sqdn/unit	code	where&when seen		remarks
XJ615	Hunter T.7					
XJ627	Hunter T.7					To G-9-296/ChAF J-721

The 4th production order for Hunter F.6's to be built at Kingston by Hawker Aircraft Ltd totalled 45 aircraft to follow XG298. Deliveries took place between 1.57 & 5.57. Subsequent conversions to FGA.9, FR.10 and F.6A standards took place as shown over.

XJ632-XJ729

serial	type	sqdn/unit	code	where&when seen		remarks
XJ632	Hunter FGA.9					To G-9-302/SADC 505
XJ633	Hunter FR.10					To G-9-356/SADC 534
XJ634	Hunter F.6A					
XJ635	Hunter FGA.9					
XJ636	Hunter FGA.9					
XJ637	Hunter F.6A					
XJ638	Hunter F.6					To RRAF123
XJ639	Hunter F.6A					
XJ640	Hunter FGA.9					To G-9-425/LeAF L-285
XJ641	Hunter F.6					
XJ642	Hunter FGA.9					To G-9-311/SADC 518
XJ643	Hunter FGA.9					To G-9-309/SADC 515
XJ644	Hunter FGA.9					To G-9-427/LeAF L-284
XJ645	Hunter FGA.9					To G-9-274/RJAF 831
XJ646	Hunter FGA.9					To G-9-275/IAF A968
XJ673	Hunter FGA.9					
XJ674	Hunter FGA.9					
XJ675	Hunter F.6					
XJ676	Hunter F.6A					
XJ677	Hunter F.6					To Iraq AF 394
XJ678	Hunter F.6					To Iraq AF 395
XJ679	Hunter F.6					To Iraq AF 396
XJ680	Hunter FGA.9					To G-9-307/SADC 511
XJ681	Hunter F.6					To Iraq AF 397
XJ682	Hunter F.6					To Iraq AF 398
XJ683	Hunter FGA.9					
XJ684	Hunter FGA.9					To G-9-308/SADC 513
XJ685	Hunter FGA.9					To G-9-306/SADC 502
XJ686	Hunter FGA.9					
XJ687	Hunter FGA.9					
XJ688	Hunter FGA.9					
XJ689	Hunter FGA.9					To G-9-327/SADC 517
XJ690	Hunter FGA.9					To G-9-451
XJ691	Hunter FGA.9					
XJ692	Hunter FGA.9					To G-9-276/IAF A969
XJ693	Hunter F.6					
XJ694	Hunter FR.10					To G-9-344/IAF S1389
XJ695	Hunter FGA.9					
XJ712	Hunter F.6					To G-9-210/RSAF 60-601
XJ713	Hunter F.6					To G-9-298/ChAF J-722
XJ714	Hunter FR.10					To G-9-365/SADC 531
XJ715	Hunter F.6					To G-9-213/RSAF 60-604
XJ716	Hunter F.6					To RRAF124
XJ717	Hunter F.6					To G-9-234/ChAF J-717
XJ718	Hunter F.6					To RRAF117

19 Whirlwind HAR.2 helicopters contracted to Westland Aircraft Ltd at Yeovil for RAF service and built as such except XJ723/724 and XJ761 which were built to HAR.4 standard. The batch was allocated c/ns WA94-112 resp and was delivered to the RAF between 9.55 and 4.56. Some conversions to HAR.10 standard between 1962 and 1964.

serial	type	sqdn/unit	code	where&when seen		remarks
XJ723	Whirlwind HAR.10					
XJ724	Whirlwind HAR.10					To 8613M
XJ725	Whirlwind HAR.2					
XJ726	Whirlwind HAR.10					
XJ727	Whirlwind HAR.10					
XJ728	Whirlwind HAR.2					
XJ729	Whirlwind HAR.10					

XJ730-XJ898

serial	type	sqdn/unit	code	where&when seen		remarks
XJ730	Whirlwind HAR.2					
XJ756	Whirlwind HAR.2					
XJ757	Whirlwind HAR.10					To 7921M
XJ758	Whirlwind HAR.10					To 8464M
XJ759	Whirlwind HAR.2					
XJ760	Whirlwind HAR.10					
XJ761	Whirlwind HAR.4					
XJ762	Whirlwind HAR.10					
XJ763	Whirlwind HAR.10					
XJ764	Whirlwind HAR.10					
XJ765	Whirlwind HAR.2					
XJ766	Whirlwind HAR.2					

Six Vampire T.11 trainers originally built by de Havilland Aircraft Co Ltd for the Royal Norwegian AF. Presented to the UK by the Norwegian Govt, they were subsequently refurbished by Marshall of Cambridge from 3.56. In RNoAF service c/ns were used as serials; 15018, 15027, 15051 becoming XJ771-XJ773 (not necessarily in that order) and 15016, 15028, 15033 becoming XJ774-XJ776 (not necessarily in that order).

serial	type	sqdn/unit	code	where&when seen		remarks
XJ771	Vampire T.11					
XJ772	Vampire T.11					To GI Brooklands
XJ773	Vampire T.11					To SwAF
XJ774	Vampire T.11					To ChAF J-05
XJ775	Vampire T.11					
XJ776	Vampire T.11					

Continued production of 8 Vulcan B.2 strategic bombers built by A.V.Roe & Co Ltd at Woodford to follow on from XH563. Falling within this allocation is the oft reported Viking XJ804 (G-AJPH) which was actually allocated XJ304.

serial	type	sqdn/unit	code	where&when seen		remarks
XJ780	Vulcan B.2					
XJ781	Vulcan B.2					
XJ782	Vulcan B.2					
XJ783	Vulcan B.2					
XJ784	Vulcan B.2					
XJ823	Vulcan B.2					
XJ824	Vulcan B.2					
XJ825	Vulcan B.2					

Two Marathon 1A communications aircraft acquired for the RAE in March 1955, having been originally built by Handley-Page (Reading) Ltd as G-AMHS (c/n 130) and G-AMHV (c/n 133). Both were initially leased to West African Airways during October 1952 as VR-NAS and 'NAT respectively prior to RAE service. During September 1958 XJ830/1 were both sold to Air Navigation & Trading Co.

serial	type	sqdn/unit	code	where&when seen		remarks
XJ830	Marathon 1A					Ex VR-NAS To G-AMHS
XJ831	Marathon 1A					Ex VR-NAT To G-AMHV

18 Gloster Type P.376 subsonic/transonic aircraft designed as a successor to the Javelin to meet Spec F.153D and often referred to as the 'Thin-wing' Javelin. The project was cancelled during July 1956 and no aircraft were built.

XJ836 - XJ842	Gloster P.376 (F.153D)	(7 a/c)	Cancelled and not built
XJ877 - XJ887	Gloster P.376 (F.153D)	(11 a/c)	Cancelled and not built

9 Sycamore HR.14 helicopters built by Bristol Aeroplane Co Ltd at Weston-super-Mare for the RAF. Allocated c/ns 13404-406/408-410/412-414, del between 10.56 and 1.57.

serial	type	sqdn/unit	code	where&when seen		remarks
XJ895	Sycamore HR.14					
XJ896	Sycamore HR.14					
XJ897	Sycamore HR.14					
XJ898	Sycamore HR.14					

XJ915-XK224

serial	type	sqdn/unit	code	where&when seen		remarks
XJ915	Sycamore HR.14					To 7910M ntu To 7915M
XJ916	Sycamore HR.14					
XJ917	Sycamore HR.14					Pr Helston
XJ918	Sycamore HR.14					To 8190M
XJ919	Sycamore HR.14					

Four prototype Ultra-Light helicopters built by Fairey Aviation Co Ltd to meet Spec H.144T. XJ924 (c/n F9423) f/f at White Waltham 14.8.55, followed by XJ928 (F9424), XJ930 (F9425) and XJ936 (F9426). XJ928 and XJ936 were registered as G-AOUJ and 'OUK following the withdrawal of Ministry support.

serial	type	sqdn/unit	code	where&when seen		remarks
XJ924	Fairey Ultra-Light					
XJ928	Fairey Ultra-Light					To G-AOUJ Pr W-s-M
XJ930	Fairey Ultra-Light					
XJ936	Fairey Ultra-Light					To G-AOUK

One J/5G Autocar built by Auster Aircraft Ltd at Rearsby 1955 with c/n 3153 and registered to the Secretary of State for the Colonies as G-ANVN. It was delivered to the Colonial Insecticides Research Unit for use in Malaya as XJ941 for spray tests.

serial	type	sqdn/unit	code	where&when seen		remarks
XJ941	J/5G Autocar					Ex G-ANVN

The final production contract for Hunter F.6's was drastically curtailed. 50 aircraft (between XJ945 & XK111) were originally to have been built by Hawker Aircraft Co Ltd at Blackpool but were cancelled. Allocations from XK136 were to be constructed at the Company's main Kingston facility but 100 of these were also cancelled, and 32 of the remainder were converted to F.56's for diversion to India as BA201-232 (XK157-175/215 f/f as such, XK213/214/216-232 f/f in dual RAF/IAF marks). 21 were delivered to the RAF of which (XK143-147/152-156) were subsequently diverted to Iraq as 400-409 between 21.8.57 & 1.10.57. Most RAF aircraft converted to FGA.9 or F.6A.

XJ945 - XJ958 Hunter F.6 (14 a/c) Cancelled and not built
XJ971 - XJ997 Hunter F.6 (27 a/c) Cancelled and not built
XK103 - XK111 Hunter F.6 (9 a/c) Cancelled and not built

serial	type	sqdn/unit	code	where&when seen		remarks
XK136	Hunter FGA.9					
XK137	Hunter FGA.9					
XK138	Hunter FGA.9					
XK139	Hunter FGA.9					
XK140	Hunter FGA.9					
XK141	Hunter F.6A					
XK142	Hunter FGA.9					To G-9-359/SADC 522
XK143	Hunter F.6					To Iraq AF 400
XK144	Hunter F.6					To Iraq AF 401
XK145	Hunter F.6					To Iraq AF 402
XK146	Hunter F.6					To Iraq AF 403
XK147	Hunter F.6					To Iraq AF 404
XK148	Hunter F.6					To G-9-235/ChAF J-715
XK149	Hunter F.6A					
XK150	Hunter FGA.9					To RJAF
XK151	Hunter FGA.9					
XK152	Hunter F.6					To Iraq AF 405
XK153	Hunter F.6					To Iraq AF 406
XK154	Hunter F.6					To Iraq AF 407
XK155	Hunter F.6					To Iraq AF 408
XK156	Hunter F.6					To Iraq AF 409

XK157 - XK176 Hunter F.6 Diverted off contract to India as BA201 - BA220 (F.56A)
XK213 - XK224 Hunter F.6 Diverted off contract to India as BA221 - BA232 (F.56A)

XK225-XK436

serial	type	sqdn/unit	code	where&when seen	remarks
XK225 - XK241	Hunter F.6		(17 a/c)		Cancelled and not built
XK257 - XK306	Hunter F.6		(50 a/c)		Cancelled and not built
XK323 - XK355	Hunter F.6		(33 a/c)		Cancelled and not built

Continued production of four Pioneer CC.1 communications aircraft built for the RAF by Scottish Aviation Ltd at Prestwick to follow on from XJ466. This block was allocated the c/ns 121 - 124 respectively and were delivered between 10.55 and 12.55. Allocations continue with XL517.

serial	type	sqdn/unit	code	where&when seen	remarks
XK367	Pioneer CC.1				
XK368	Pioneer CC.1				
XK369	Pioneer CC.1				
XK370	Pioneer CC.1				To SOAF Returned RAF

The second production order for 25 Auster AOP.9 aircraft for the RAF was built at Rearsby by Auster Aircraft Ltd against Contract 6/Aircraft/11436/CB5(c). Deliveries were made between 1.2.56 and 7.3.57.

serial	type	sqdn/unit	code	where&when seen	remarks
XK374	Auster AOP.9				
XK375	Auster AOP.9				
XK376	Auster AOP.9				
XK377	Auster AOP.9				
XK378	Auster AOP.9				To TA200
XK379	Auster AOP.9				
XK380	Auster AOP.9				
XK381	Auster AOP.9				
XK382	Auster AOP.9				
XK406	Auster AOP.9				
XK407	Auster AOP.9				
XK408	Auster AOP.9				
XK409	Auster AOP.9				
XK410	Auster AOP.9				
XK411	Auster AOP.9				
XK412	Auster AOP.9				
XK413	Auster AOP.9				
XK414	Auster AOP.9				
XK415	Auster AOP.9				
XK416	Auster AOP.9				To 7855M To G-AYUA
XK417	Auster AOP.9				To G-AVXY
XK418	Auster AOP.9				To 7976M Pr Lasham
XK419	Auster AOP.9				To 8058M
XK420	Auster AOP.9				
XK421	Auster AOP.9				To 8365M GI Brunel Un

The second prototype Thrust Measuring Rig built by Rolls-Royce at Hucknall to follow XJ314. XK426 made its first tethered flight on 17.10.55 and during November 1956 attained initial free flight. On 28.11.57 it was destroyed in a crash at Hucknall.

serial	type	sqdn/unit	code	where&when seen	remarks
XK426	Thrust Measuring Rig				

Six Bristol 188 prototypes were originally ordered to meet Spec ER.134, two of which were serialled XF923 and 926 (qv) and a third constructed for ground tests only. The remaining three prototypes (XK429/434/436) were cancelled and not built.

serial	type	sqdn/unit	code	where&when seen	remarks
XK429	Bristol 188				Cancelled
XK434	Bristol 188				Cancelled
XK436	Bristol 188				Cancelled

XK440-XK585

serial	type	sqdn/unit	code	where&when seen	remarks

Planned production of the Canberra PR.9 accounted for a further eleven aircraft to be built by Short Bros & Harland Ltd at Belfast against Contract 12164 and to follow on from XH177. However this contract was cancelled and none was built.

XK440 - XK443	Canberra PR.9	(4 a/c)	Cancelled and not built
XK467 - XK473	Canberra PR.9	(7 a/c)	Cancelled and not built

The first production order for Skeeter AOP.10 helicopters accounted for 4 examples built by Saunders-Roe Ltd at East Cowes to Spec.162. The block was allotted c/ns S2/3012, 3036, 3051 & 3070 resp. XK479 was designated T.11 and delivered to CFS 1957.

serial	type	sqdn/unit	code	where&when seen	remarks
XK479	Skeeter T.11				
XK480	Skeeter AOP.10				
XK481	Skeeter AOP.10				
XK482	Skeeter AOP.10				To 7840M Pr Ottershaw

Twenty prototype and pre-production Buccaneer S.1 shipboard strike aircraft were built by Blackburn Aircraft Ltd at Brough. Initially the type was designated NA.39 derived from Naval ASR NA.39; the Admiralty also issued the Spec M.148T to cover the design. XK486 f/f 9.7.58. XK526/527 became the prototype S.2's; XK526 f/f as S.2 18.4.63.

serial	type	sqdn/unit	code	where&when seen	remarks
XK486	Buccaneer S.1				
XK487	Buccaneer S.1				
XK488	Buccaneer S.1				Pr FAAM
XK489	Buccaneer S.1				
XK490	Buccaneer S.1				
XK491	Buccaneer S.1				
XK523	Buccaneer S.1				
XK524	Buccaneer S.1				
XK525	Buccaneer S.1				
XK526	Buccaneer S.2				To 8648M
XK527	Buccaneer S.2D				
XK528	Buccaneer S.1				
XK529	Buccaneer S.1				
XK530	Buccaneer S.1				
XK531	Buccaneer S.1				To 8403M Pr Honington
XK532	Buccaneer S.1				To A2581
XK533	Buccaneer S.1				
XK534	Buccaneer S.1				To A2582
XK535	Buccaneer S.1				
XK536	Buccaneer S.1				To A&AEE test airframe

Planned production of Type 38 Grasshopper gliders accounted for a further 10 units to be built by Slingsby Sailplanes Ltd at Kirkbymoorside to follow on from XA244. However the contract was subsequently cancelled before construction commenced.

XK542 - XK548	Grasshopper TX.1	(7 a/c)	Cancelled and not built
XK569 - XK571	Grasshopper TX.1	(3 a/c)	Cancelled and not built

One Javelin T.3 built by Gloster Aircraft Co Ltd at Hucclecote against Contract 6/Aircraft/11262 (dated 27.9.54) to Spec T.118. It was delivered to A&AEE, Boscombe Down for use as a trials aircraft.

serial	type	sqdn/unit	code	where&when seen	remarks
XK577	Javelin T.3				

24 Vampire T.11 trainers built by de Havilland Aircraft Co Ltd at Hawarden, Chester against Contract 12203. Deliveries commenced with XK582 during 5.56 and terminated with XK637 on 27.11.56.

serial	type	sqdn/unit	code	where&when seen	remarks
XK582	Vampire T.11				
XK583	Vampire T.11				
XK584	Vampire T.11				
XK585	Vampire T.11				

XK586-XK720

serial	type	sqdn/unit	code	where&when seen		remarks
XK586	Vampire T.11					
XK587	Vampire T.11					
XK588	Vampire T.11					
XK589	Vampire T.11					
XK590	Vampire T.11					Pr Witney
XK623	Vampire T.11					To GI Moston Tech
XK624	Vampire T.11					Pr Lytham St Annes
XK625	Vampire T.11					Pr HAM Southend
XK626	Vampire T.11					
XK627	Vampire T.11					Pr Bacup
XK628	Vampire T.11					
XK629	Vampire T.11					To 7553M
XK630	Vampire T.11					To 7560M
XK631	Vampire T.11					
XK632	Vampire T.11					
XK633	Vampire T.11					
XK634	Vampire T.11					To Austrian AF 5C-VE
XK635	Vampire T.11					
XK636	Vampire T.11					
XK637	Vampire T.11					Pr Royton

One Canberra B.6 and two T.4's built by English Electric Co Ltd at Preston against Contract 12265. XK641 was delivered 5.56. XK647 and XK650 were subsequently diverted to the Indian Air Force with serials IQ994 and IQ995 respectively.

serial	type	sqdn/unit	code	where&when seen		remarks
XK641	Canberra B.6					
XK647	Canberra T.4					To IAF IQ994
XK650	Canberra T.4					To IAF IQ995

Three ex-civil DH.106 Comet 2 aircraft acquired for use by 192 Squadron against Contract 6/Aircraft/11808/CB10(d). XK655 c/n 06023 f/f 27.8.53 as G-AMXA; XK659 c/n 06025 f/f 25.11.53 as G-AMXC; XK663 c/n 06027 f/f 18.7.55 (G-AMXE ntu).

serial	type	sqdn/unit	code	where&when seen		remarks
XK655	Comet R.2					Ex G-AMXA Pr Strath'l'n
XK659	Comet C(RCM).2					Ex G-AMXC Bar Pomona Dk
XK663	Comet C(RCM).2					Ex G-AMXE

Ten DH.106 Comet 2's originally laid down as civil aircraft but aquired for use by 216 Squadron against Contract 6/Aircraft/11809/CB10(d). The block was allotted c/ns as follows:- 06024/06028/06029/06030/06031/06032/06034/06035/06037 and 06045 respectively. XK669 and XK670 were initially delivered as T.2's. Deliveries 6.56 to 6.57.

serial	type	sqdn/unit	code	where&when seen		remarks
XK669	Comet C.2					Ex G-AMXB
XK670	Comet C.2					Ex G-AMXF To 7926M
XK671	Comet C.2					Ex G-AMXG To 7927M
XK695	Comet R.2					Ex G-AMXH Pr Duxford
XK696	Comet C.2					Ex G-AMXI
XK697	Comet C.2					Ex G-AMXJ Pr Wyton
XK698	Comet C.2					Ex G-AMXL To 8031M
XK699	Comet C.2					Ex G-AMXM To 7971M Pr
XK715	Comet C.2					To 7905M
XK716	Comet C.2					To 7958M

No other information is known about this allocation. (3rd R-R Thrust Measuring Rig?)

serial	type	sqdn/unit	code	where&when seen		remarks
XK720	VTOL Test-bed					

XK724-XK854

serial	type	sqdn/unit	code	where&when seen	remarks

Six Gnat F.1 fighter aircraft built by Folland Aircraft Ltd at Hamble to Spec F.163 for MoS trials. Allocated the c/ns FL2 to FL7 respectively, they f/f from Chilbolton as follows: 26.5.56; 4.12.56; 6.3.57; 15.5.57; 28.6.57 and 14.8.57 (as G-39-3).

serial	type	sqdn/unit	code	where&when seen	remarks
XK724	Gnat F.1				Ex G-39-2 To 7715M
XK739	Gnat F.1				
XK740	Gnat F.1				To 8396M Pr Cosford
XK741	Gnat F.1				Pr Baginton
XK767	Gnat F.1				
XK768	Gnat F.1				ntu To G-39-3/IE1059

The first prototype Skeeter 6 built by Saunders-Roe Ltd at East Cowes as G-ANMG with c/n SR.904 was allotted military marks during mid-1955 for trials and evaluation purposes.

serial	type	sqdn/unit	code	where&when seen	remarks
XK773	Skeeter 6				Ex G-ANMG

3 ML Utility inflatable wing aircraft built by ML Aviation Ltd at White Waltham and flight tested between 1954 and 1960 under a MoS contract on behalf of the War Office.

serial	type	sqdn/unit	code	where&when seen	remarks
XK776	M.L. Utility Mk.1				
XK781	M.L. Utility Mk.2				
XK784	M.L. Utility Proto				Initially unserialled

Ten Type 38 Grasshopper TX.1 gliders built by Slingsby Sailplanes Ltd at Kirkbymoorside against Contract 12291 for use by the Air Training Corps and School Combined Cadet Forces. The batch was allocated c/ns 1034-1043 inclusive.

serial	type	sqdn/unit	code	where&when seen	remarks
XK788	Grasshopper TX.1				
XK789	Grasshopper TX.1				
XK790	Grasshopper TX.1				
XK791	Grasshopper TX.1				
XK819	Grasshopper TX.1				
XK820	Grasshopper TX.1				
XK821	Grasshopper TX.1				
XK822	Grasshopper TX.1				
XK823	Grasshopper TX.1				
XK824	Grasshopper TX.1				

Advanced, supersonic successor to Wild Goose, built by Vickers-Armstrongs at Weybridge. The first subsonic model turned turtle on its maiden flight (mid 1954) but during 1955, a rocket-powered model achieved Mach 2.5 at great altitude at Larkhill.

serial	type	sqdn/unit	code	where&when seen	remarks
XK831	Swallow				
XK832	Swallow				
XK833	Swallow				
XK834	Swallow				
XK835	Swallow				
XK850	Swallow				
XK851	Swallow				
XK852	Swallow				
XK853	Swallow				
XK854	Swallow				

Six Pembroke C.1 communications aircraft built by Hunting Percival Aircraft Ltd at Luton for the RAF against Contract No. 6/Aircraft/12518/CB.5(a). The batch was allocated c/ns PAC/66/071, 072, 073, 081, 082 and 083 respectively.

XK859-XK959

serial	type	sqdn/unit	code	where&when seen		remarks
XK859	Pembroke C.1					
XK860	Pembroke C.1					
XK861	Pembroke C.1					
XK862	Pembroke C.1					To 8191M to 8194M
XK884	Pembroke C.1					
XK885	Pembroke C.1					To 8452M

One prototype Hunting Percival P.74 ten-seat helicopter built for research and test purposes in an effort to develop the Napier Twin-Oryx engine. However the helicopter failed to fly despite several hours of ground running between April and July 1956 following which all further work was cancelled.

serial	type	sqdn/unit	code	where&when seen		remarks
XK889	Percival P.74					

Three Sea Devon C.20 communications aircraft built by the de Havilland Aircraft Co Ltd for the RN. XK895/896 allocated c/ns 04472/04473 and both handed over 17.4.56; XK897 c/n 04474 handed over 18.4.56.

serial	type	sqdn/unit	code	where&when seen		remarks
XK895	Sea Devon C.20					
XK896	Sea Devon C.20					
XK897	Sea Devon C.20					To G-AROI

Two Sycamore HR.51 helicopters built by the Bristol Aeroplane Co Ltd at Weston-super-Mare for direct transfer to the RAN. XK902 and 903 were allocated c/ns 13401/13407 respectively and XK903 appears to have been re-serialled XL507. XK902 del 3.56.

serial	type	sqdn/unit	code	where&when seen		remarks
XK902	Sycamore HR.51					To RAN
XK903	Sycamore HR.51					See XL507

20 Whirlwind HAS.7 anti-submarine helicopters built by Westland Aircraft Ltd at Yeovil for the Royal Navy, to follow on from XG597. The batch was allocated the c/ns WA153-WA172 respectively and delivered to the RN between 7.57 and 10.57.

serial	type	sqdn/unit	code	where&when seen		remarks
XK906	Whirlwind HAS.7					To G-AYXT ntu
XK907	Whirlwind HAS.7					
XK908	Whirlwind HAS.7					To A2442
XK909	Whirlwind HAS.7					
XK910	Whirlwind HAS.7					
XK911	Whirlwind HAS.7					To A2603
XK912	Whirlwind HAS.7					Pr Lacock
XK933	Whirlwind HAS.7					To A2496
XK934	Whirlwind HAS.7					
XK935	Whirlwind HAS.7					
XK936	Whirlwind HAS.7					Pr IWM Duxford
XK937	Whirlwind HAS.7					To 8432M
XK938	Whirlwind HAS.7					
XK939	Whirlwind HAS.7					
XK940	Whirlwind HAS.7					To G-AYXT
XK941	Whirlwind HAS.7					
XK942	Whirlwind HAS.7					
XK943	Whirlwind HAS.7					To A2653
XK944	Whirlwind HAS.7					To A2607 GI Brunel Un
XK945	Whirlwind HAS.7					

4 Canberra B(I).8 bomber/interdictor aircraft built by English Electric Co Ltd at Preston against Contract 6445 (XK951-953) and 11158 (XK959). Deliveries in 9/10.56.

serial	type	sqdn/unit	code	where&when seen		remarks
XK951	Canberra B(I).8					To G-52-3/PeAF 248
XK952	Canberra B(I).8					
XK953	Canberra B(I).8					To IAF IF895
XK959	Canberra B(I).8					To IAF IF898

XK964-XL164

serial	type	sqdn/unit	code	where&when seen		remarks

The third Skeeter Mk 6 prototype allocated military marks during January 1956 for service trials. Originally registered G-ANMI with c/n SR.906, XK964 was restored to Saunders-Roe during the Spring of 1956. Two other prototypes were allocated XJ355 and XK773.

serial	type	sqdn/unit	code	where&when seen		remarks
XK964	Skeeter 6					Ex G-ANMI To G-ANMI

Nine Whirlwind HAR.2 helicopters built by Westland Aircraft Ltd at Yeovil for the RAF and five HAR.4 variants also built for the RAF all against Contract 6/Aircraft/12881/CB9(b). The block was allocated c/ns WA139-WA152 inclusive with dels. between 5.56 and 12.56. Conversions to HAR.10 configuration later took place as listed.

serial	type	sqdn/unit	code	where&when seen		remarks
XK968	Whirlwind HAR.10					To 8445M
XK969	Whirlwind HAR.10					To 8646M
XK970	Whirlwind HAR.10					
XK986	Whirlwind HAR.10					
XK987	Whirlwind HAR.10					To 8393M
XK988	Whirlwind HAR.10					To A2646
XK989	Whirlwind HAR.2					To 7415M
XK990	Whirlwind HAR.10					
XK991	Whirlwind HAR.10					To 7810M
XL109	Whirlwind HAR.10					
XL110	Whirlwind HAR.10					
XL111	Whirlwind HAR.10					To 8000M
XL112	Whirlwind HAR.10					
XL113	Whirlwind HAR.2					

The third production order for 8 Beverley C.1 transport aircraft built by Blackburn and General Aircraft Ltd at Brough for RAF Transport Command against Contract 6/Aircraft/12264 to follow on from XH124. XL130 f/f 7.4.57; XL152 f/f 27.9.57. XL130-XL132 were originally allotted serials XL117-XL119 respectively but were re-serialled prior to completion in order to avoid confusion with XH117-XH119. No c/ns were allocated to these aircraft.

serial	type	sqdn/unit	code	where&when seen		remarks
XL117	Beverley C.1					To XL130
XL118	Beverley C.1					To XL131
XL119	Beverley C.1					To XL132
XL130	Beverley C.1					
XL131	Beverley C.1					
XL132	Beverley C.1					
XL148	Beverley C.1					
XL149	Beverley C.1					To 7988M
XL150	Beverley C.1					
XL151	Beverley C.1					
XL152	Beverley C.1					

The second production order for 18 Victor B.2 strategic bombers built by Handley-Page Ltd at Radlett for the RAF against Contract 6/Aircraft/12305/CB6. Examples were later converted to SR.2 configuration for strategic reconnaissance, including the prototype SR.2 XL165 which f/f 23.2.65, and subsequently to K.2 standard.

serial	type	sqdn/unit	code	where&when seen		remarks
XL158	Victor K.2					
XL159	Victor B.2					
XL160	Victor K.2					
XL161	Victor K.2					
XL162	Victor K.2					
XL163	Victor K.2					
XL164	Victor K.2					

XL165-XL384

serial	type	sqdn/unit	code	where&when seen		remarks
XL165	Victor SR.2					
XL188	Victor K.2					
XL189	Victor K.2					
XL190	Victor K.2					
XL191	Victor K.2					
XL192	Victor K.2					
XL193	Victor SR.2					
XL230	Victor SR.2					
XL231	Victor K.2					
XL232	Victor K.2					
XL233	Victor K.2					

22 Sea Hawk FB.50 shipboard fighters built by Sir W.G. Armstrong Whitworth Aircraft Ltd at Coventry against Contract 6/Aircraft/13024 for direct transfer to the Royal Netherlands Navy (MLD). The block was allocated c/ns 6621-6642 and f/flts ranged between 13.5.57 and 2.1.58, prior to adopting Dutch serials 6-50 to 6-71. (It has been reported that the batches emerged as XL237-241/269-275/305-314 despite the block being allotted serials as listed). Note that six Victor B.2's were noted at Radlett in 3.62 virtually complete and serialled XL250-XL255 - presumed reserialled.

serial	type	sqdn/unit	code	where&when seen		remarks
XL237	Sea Hawk FB.50					To MLD 6-50
XL238	Sea Hawk FB.50					To MLD 6-51
XL239	Sea Hawk FB.50					To MLD 6-52
XL240	Sea Hawk FB.50					To MLD 6-53
XL241	Sea Hawk FB.50					To MLD 6-54
XL269	Sea Hawk FB.50					To MLD 6-55
XL270	Sea Hawk FB.50					To MLD 6-56
XL271	Sea Hawk FB.50					To MLD 6-57
XL272	Sea Hawk FB.50					To MLD 6-58
XL273	Sea Hawk FB.50					To MLD 6-59
XL274	Sea Hawk FB.50					To MLD 6-60
XL275	Sea Hawk FB.50					To MLD 6-61
XL276	Sea Hawk FB.50					To MLD 6-62?
XL305	Sea Hawk FB.50					To MLD 6-63?
XL306	Sea Hawk FB.50					To MLD 6-64?
XL307	Sea Hawk FB.50					To MLD 6-65?
XL308	Sea Hawk FB.50					To MLD 6-66?
XL309	Sea Hawk FB.50					To MLD 6-67?
XL310	Sea Hawk FB.50					To MLD 6-68?
XL311	Sea Hawk FB.50					To MLD 6-69?
XL312	Sea Hawk FB.50					To MLD 6-70?
XL313	Sea Hawk FB.50					To MLD 6-71?

The third production order for 24 Vulcan B.2 strategic bombers built by A.V.Roe & Co Ltd at Woodford for the RAF.

serial	type	sqdn/unit	code	where&when seen		remarks
XL317	Vulcan B.2					
XL318	Vulcan B.2					
XL319	Vulcan B.2					
XL320	Vulcan B.2					
XL321	Vulcan B.2					
XL359	Vulcan B.2					
XL360	Vulcan B.2					
XL361	Vulcan B.2					
XL384	Vulcan B.2					To 8505M

XL385-XL507

serial	type	sqdn/unit	code	where&when seen		remarks
XL385	Vulcan B.2					
XL386	Vulcan B.2					
XL387	Vulcan B.2					
XL388	Vulcan B.2					
XL389	Vulcan B.2					
XL390	Vulcan B.2					
XL391	Vulcan B.2					
XL392	Vulcan B.2					
XL425	Vulcan B.2					
XL426	Vulcan B.2					
XL427	Vulcan B.2					
XL443	Vulcan B.2					
XL444	Vulcan B.2					
XL445	Vulcan B.2					
XL446	Vulcan B.2					

The first production order for 31 Gannet AEW.3's built to Spec AEW.154P by Fairey Aviation Co Ltd at Hayes against Contract 6/AIR/12876/CB9(a). The batch was allotted c/ns F9432-F9462 respectively. XL449 first flew at Northolt on 2.10.58.

serial	type	sqdn/unit	code	where&when seen		remarks
XL449	Gannet AEW.3					Pr SWAPS Rhoose
XL450	Gannet AEW.3					To 8601M
XL451	Gannet AEW.3					
XL452	Gannet AEW.3					
XL453	Gannet AEW.3					
XL454	Gannet AEW.3					
XL455	Gannet AEW.3					
XL456	Gannet AEW.3					
XL471	Gannet AEW.3					To GI Farnborough
XL472	Gannet AEW.3					To GI A&AEE
XL473	Gannet AEW.3					
XL474	Gannet AEW.3					
XL475	Gannet AEW.3					
XL476	Gannet AEW.3					
XL477	Gannet AEW.3					
XL478	Gannet AEW.3					
XL479	Gannet AEW.3					
XL480	Gannet AEW.3					
XL481	Gannet AEW.3					
XL482	Gannet AEW.3					
XL493	Gannet AEW.3					
XL494	Gannet AEW.3					
XL495	Gannet AEW.3					
XL496	Gannet AEW.3					
XL497	Gannet AEW.3					Pr Prestwick
XL498	Gannet AEW.3					
XL499	Gannet AEW.3					
XL500	Gannet AEW.3					
XL501	Gannet AEW.3					
XL502	Gannet AEW.3					To 8610M
XL503	Gannet AEW.3					Pr FAAM

One Sycamore HR.51 (c/n 13407) built by the Bristol Aeroplane Co Ltd at Weston-super Mare for direct transfer to the RAN (del 3.56). It was originally allotted XK903.

serial	type	sqdn/unit	code	where&when seen		remarks
XL507	Sycamore HR.51					To RAN

XL511-XL593

serial	type	sqdn/unit	code	where&when seen		remarks

Three Victor B.2 strategic bombers built by Handley-Page Ltd at Radlett for the RAF against Contract 6/Aircraft/12305/CB6 and to follow XL233. These three aircraft may have been reserialled from the incorrect block XL250 etc. Subsequent conversions to K.2 standard by Hawker Siddeley Aviation Ltd at Woodford.

serial	type	sqdn/unit	code	where&when seen		remarks
XL511	Victor K.2					
XL512	Victor K.2					
XL513	Victor K.2					

10 Pioneer CC.1 communications aircraft built by Scottish Aviation Ltd at Prestwick for the RAF to follow XK370. The block was allocated c/ns 125-134 incl. XL517 was initially registered as G-AOGK and f/f as such on 29.1.56. XL558 delivered 28.6.56.

serial	type	sqdn/unit	code	where&when seen		remarks
XL517	Pioneer CC.1					Ex G-AOGK
XL518	Pioneer CC.1					To SOAF Returned RAF
XL519	Pioneer CC.1					
XL520	Pioneer CC.1					
XL553	Pioneer CC.1					
XL554	Pioneer CC.1					To SOAF
XL555	Pioneer CC.1					
XL556	Pioneer CC.1					
XL557	Pioneer CC.1					
XL558	Pioneer CC.1					

The sole production order for Hunter trainers accounted for some 55 T.7's for the RAF to be built by Hawker Aircraft Co Ltd at Kingston-upon-Thames, although originally all were to have been built at Blackpool. The first aircraft (XL563) f/f 11.10.57 by which time it had been decided to transfer 10 aircraft to the Royal Navy as T.8's, some of which were subsequently upgraded to T.8A, T.8C and T.8M standard. Deliveries took place between 12.57 and 2.59. All built against Contract 11626.

serial	type	sqdn/unit	code	where&when seen		remarks
XL563	Hunter T.7					
XL564	Hunter T.7					
XL565	Hunter T.7					
XL566	Hunter T.7					
XL567	Hunter T.7					
XL568	Hunter T.7					
XL569	Hunter T.7					
XL570	Hunter T.7					
XL571	Hunter T.7					
XL572	Hunter T.7					
XL573	Hunter T.7					
XL574	Hunter T.7					
XL575	Hunter T.7					
XL576	Hunter T.7					
XL577	Hunter T.7					
XL578	Hunter T.7					
XL579	Hunter T.7					
XL580	Hunter T.8M					
XL581	Hunter T.8					
XL582	Hunter T.8					
XL583	Hunter T.7					
XL584	Hunter T.8C					
XL585	Hunter T.8C					
XL586	Hunter T.7					
XL587	Hunter T.7					
XL591	Hunter T.7					
XL592	Hunter T.7					
XL593	Hunter T.7					

XL594-XL666

serial	type	sqdn/unit	code	where&when seen		remarks
XL594	Hunter T.7					
XL595	Hunter T.7					
XL596	Hunter T.7					
XL597	Hunter T.7					
XL598	Hunter T.8C					
XL599	Hunter T.8					
XL600	Hunter T.7					
XL601	Hunter T.7					
XL602	Hunter T.8M					
XL603	Hunter T.8M					
XL604	Hunter T.8C					To G-9-416/KAF 802
XL605	Hunter T.7					G-9-214/RS&RJAF/XX467
XL609	Hunter T.7					
XL610	Hunter T.7					
XL611	Hunter T.7					
XL612	Hunter T.7					
XL613	Hunter T.7					
XL614	Hunter T.7					
XL615	Hunter T.7					
XL616	Hunter T.7					
XL617	Hunter T.7					
XL618	Hunter T.7					
XL619	Hunter T.7					
XL620	Hunter T.7					G-9-215/RS&RJAF/XX466
XL621	Hunter T.7					
XL622	Hunter T.7					
XL623	Hunter T.7					

Two Lightning T.4 prototypes (2-seat equivalent of F.1A) built by English Electric Co Ltd at Preston for the RAF with c/ns 95049 and 95050 resp. XL628 f/f 6.5.59 and XL629 f/f 21.10.59. Production aircraft commenced with XM966 (qv).

serial	type	sqdn/unit	code	where&when seen		remarks
XL628	Lightning T.4					
XL629	Lightning T.4					Pr Boscombe Down

Ten Britannia C.1's built under manufacturer's designation Bristol 175 Srs 253 and sub-contracted to Short Bros & Harland Ltd at Belfast with c/ns 13397-13400/13448/13449/13454-13457 respectively. XL635 f/f 29.12.59 and Transport Command allotted names to its Britannia fleet as follows:- XL635 (Bellatrix); XL636 (Argo); XL637 (Vega); XL638 (Sirius); XL639 (Atria); XL640 (Antares); XL657 (Rigel); XL658 (Adhara); XL659 (Polaris); XL660 (Alphard).

serial	type	sqdn/unit	code	where&when seen		remarks
XL635	Britannia C.1					To OO-YCA
XL636	Britannia C.1					To OO-YCE
XL637	Britannia C.1					To OO-YCH
XL638	Britannia C.1					
XL639	Britannia C.1					To EI-BDC
XL640	Britannia C.1					To EI-BCI
XL657	Britannia C.1					To 9U-BAD
XL658	Britannia C.1					To EI-BBY
XL659	Britannia C.1					To OO-YCB
XL660	Britannia C.1					To G-BEMZ

12 Pioneer CC.1 communications aircraft built by Scottish Aviation Ltd at Prestwick for the RAF to follow XL558 against Contract 6/Aircraft/13670. XL664 f/f 29.8.56; XL706 f/f 25.1.57. The block was allocated c/ns 135-144/146-147 respectively.

serial	type	sqdn/unit	code	where&when seen		remarks
XL664	Pioneer CC.1					
XL665	Pioneer CC.1					
XL666	Pioneer CC.1					

XL667-XL771

serial	type	sqdn/unit	code	where&when seen		remarks
XL667	Pioneer CC.1					
XL699	Pioneer CC.1					
XL700	Pioneer CC.1					
XL701	Pioneer CC.1					
XL702	Pioneer CC.1					
XL703	Pioneer CC.1					To 8034M Pr Henlow
XL704	Pioneer CC.1					
XL705	Pioneer CC.1					
XL706	Pioneer CC.1					

One DHC.3 Otter STOL aircraft built at Downsview and allotted military marks for use by the 1956 British Commonwealth Trans-Antarctic Expedition. XL710 (c/n 126) had originally been allocated Bu.Aer number 147574. Subsequently it passed to the Royal New Zealand Air Force.

serial	type	sqdn/unit	code	where&when seen		remarks
XL710	DHC.3 Otter					To RNZAF NZ6081

Four ex-civilian Tiger Moth T.2's purchased by the RN circa 8.56 mainly for use by BRNC Flight at Roborough. They should have been allocated their old serials (see listing) but instead were allotted new ones. Delivered to the RN between 7.56 & 7.57.

serial	type	sqdn/unit	code	where&when seen		remarks
XL714	Tiger Moth T.2					Ex G-AOGR/T6099 To G-GR
XL715	Tiger Moth T.2					Ex G-AOIK/DE395
XL716	Tiger Moth T.2					Ex G-AOIL/T7363
XL717	Tiger Moth T.2					Ex G-AOXG/T7291 Pr FAAM

One US-built Sikorsky HSS-1 (S-58) imported by Westland Aircraft Ltd as a pattern helicopter prior to Westland Wessex production at Yeovil. Previously allocated the Bu Aer number 141602 (c/n 58-265) it f/f at Yeovil 11.8.56 initially as G-17-1 before embarking on development trials as XL722. The Spec No was HAS.170.

serial	type	sqdn/unit	code	where&when seen		remarks
XL722	Sikorsky S-58					Ex G-17-1 To A2514

Three pre-production Wessex HAS.1 helicopters built by Westland Aircraft Ltd at Yeovil with c/ns WA.1 to WA.3 resp. XL727 f/f 20.6.58 and all three were employed on manufacturer's development trials. XL728 later refurbished to near Mk.5 standard.

serial	type	sqdn/unit	code	where&when seen		remarks
XL727	Wessex HAS.1					
XL728	Wessex Mk5 (hybrid)					
XL729	Wessex HAS.1					To A2641

27 Skeeter AOP.12 helicopters built by Saunders-Roe Ltd for the Army Air Corps against Contract 6/Aircraft/13919. The block was allocated c/ns (prefixed S2/xxxx) 5064/5066-69/5071-72/5074-76/5078-80/5084-90/5093-99 resp. First deliveries in 6.58.

serial	type	sqdn/unit	code	where&when seen		remarks
XL734	Skeeter AOP.12					
XL735	Skeeter AOP.12					
XL736	Skeeter AOP.12					
XL737	Skeeter AOP.12					
XL738	Skeeter AOP.12					To 7860M Pr MW 'XL769'
XL739	Skeeter AOP.12					Pr Detmold
XL740	Skeeter AOP.12					
XL762	Skeeter AOP.12					To 8017M Pr E Fortune
XL763	Skeeter AOP.12					To GI Southall Tech
XL764	Skeeter AOP.12					To 7940M Pr Nstl Priory
XL765	Skeeter AOP.12					To GI Leeds University
XL766	Skeeter AOP.12					
XL767	Skeeter AOP.12					
XL768	Skeeter AOP.12					
XL769	Skeeter AOP.12					To 7981M To G-BDNS
XL770	Skeeter AOP.12					To 8046M Pr Shrivenham
XL771	Skeeter AOP.12					

XL772-XL872

serial	type	sqdn/unit	code	where&when seen		remarks
XL772	Skeeter AOP.12					
XL806	Skeeter AOP.12					
XL807	Skeeter AOP.12					
XL808	Skeeter AOP.12					
XL809	Skeeter AOP.12					To PH-HOF
XL810	Skeeter AOP.12					
XL811	Skeeter AOP.12					Pr HAM Southend
XL812	Skeeter AOP.12					To G-SARO
XL813	Skeeter AOP.12					Pr Middle Wallop
XL814	Skeeter AOP.12					AAC Historic Flight

Final production order for 10 Sycamore HR.14 helicopters built by Bristol Aeroplane Co Ltd at Weston-super-Mare against Contract 13888. Allocated c/ns 13415/13417/13438/13441/13444/13447/13460/13468/13471/13474 resp and del between 2.57 and 12.57.

serial	type	sqdn/unit	code	where&when seen		remarks
XL820	Sycamore HR.14					
XL821	Sycamore HR.14					
XL822	Sycamore HR.14					
XL823	Sycamore HR.14					
XL824	Sycamore HR.14					To 8021M Pr Henlow
XL825	Sycamore HR.14					
XL826	Sycamore HR.14					To 7909M ntu To 7916M
XL827	Sycamore HR.14					
XL828	Sycamore HR.14					
XL829	Sycamore HR.14					Pr Bristol Ind Museum

45 Whirlwind HAS.7 helicopters built by Westland Aircraft Ltd at Yeovil for the RN to follow XK945 against Contract 6/Aircraft/13955/CB9(b). The block was allocated c/ns WA195-WA239 respectively, deliveries taking place between 12.57 and 11.58. Some were converted to HAR.9 standard in 1965/66. XL833 f/f 15.10.57.

serial	type	sqdn/unit	code	where&when seen		remarks
XL833	Whirlwind HAS.7					
XL834	Whirlwind HAS.7					
XL835	Whirlwind HAS.7					To 8356M ntu
XL836	Whirlwind HAS.7					To A2642 Pr Fleetlands
XL837	Whirlwind HAS.7					
XL838	Whirlwind HAS.7					
XL839	Whirlwind HAR.9					To A2665
XL840	Whirlwind HAS.7					Pr Blackpool
XL841	Whirlwind HAS.7					
XL842	Whirlwind HAS.7					
XL843	Whirlwind HAS.7					
XL844	Whirlwind HAS.7					
XL845	Whirlwind HAS.7					
XL846	Whirlwind HAS.7					To A2625
XL847	Whirlwind HAS.7					To A2626
XL848	Whirlwind HAS.7					
XL849	Whirlwind HAS.7					
XL850	Whirlwind HAS.7					
XL851	Whirlwind HAS.7					
XL852	Whirlwind HAS.7					
XL853	Whirlwind HAS.7					To A2630
XL854	Whirlwind HAS.7					
XL867	Whirlwind HAS.7					
XL868	Whirlwind HAS.7					To A2595
XL869	Whirlwind HAS.7					
XL870	Whirlwind HAS.7					
XL871	Whirlwind HAS.7					
XL872	Whirlwind HAS.7					

XL873-XL969

serial	type	sqdn/unit	code	where&when seen		remarks
XL873	Whirlwind HAS.7					
XL874	Whirlwind HAS.7					
XL875	Whirlwind HAR.9					To GI Perth
XL876	Whirlwind HAS.7					
XL877	Whirlwind HAS.7					
XL878	Whirlwind HAS.7					
XL879	Whirlwind HAS.7					
XL880	Whirlwind HAR.9					
XL881	Whirlwind HAS.7					
XL882	Whirlwind HAS.7					
XL883	Whirlwind HAS.7					
XL884	Whirlwind HAS.7					
XL896	Whirlwind HAS.7					
XL897	Whirlwind HAS.7					
XL898	Whirlwind HAR.9					To 8654M
XL899	Whirlwind HAR.9					
XL900	Whirlwind HAR.9					

Nine pre-production Saunders-Roe SR.177 mixed-power interceptors designed to meet Naval requirement NA.47 and RAF Operational Requirement OR.337. Spec F.177D was issued to meet these two requirements and from this the aircraft designation was derived. On 4.9.56 a formal contract was placed for 9 development aircraft, 9 RAF aircraft and 9 RN aircraft. The RAF programme was terminated in early 1957, in that year's infamous Defence White Paper and the whole programme was abandoned in 12.57, no aircraft being completed.

XL905-XL907	Saunders-Roe SR.177	(3 a/c)	Cancelled and not completed
XL920-XL925	Saunders-Roe SR.177	(6 a/c)	Cancelled and not completed

The final production order for 7 Pembroke communications aircraft built by Hunting Percival Aircraft Ltd at Luton against Contract 13975 dated 25.9.56, originally all as C.1's. However XL953-956 were actually built as C(PR).1 standard, later being converted to C.1 configuration. The block was allocated c/ns PAC/66/087; 92; 95; 98; 101; 104; 107. The last aircraft (XL956) was delivered to the RAF in 2.58.

serial	type	sqdn/unit	code	where&when seen		remarks
XL929	Pembroke C.1					Pr Kemble (for RAFM)
XL930	Pembroke C.1					
XL931	Pembroke C.1					
XL953	Pembroke C.1					
XL954	Pembroke C.1					
XL955	Pembroke C.1					
XL956	Pembroke C.1					

One Heron Srs.2 (c/n 14007) originally built by the de Havilland Aircraft Co Ltd at Hatfield as a demonstrator and registered G-AMTS. During 1956 it was allotted the serial XL961 especially for the use of HRH Princess Margaret during her tour of Africa. Upon completion of the tour, during October 1956, XL961 reverted to its previous civilian marks.

serial	type	sqdn/unit	code	where&when seen		remarks
XL961	Heron Srs.2					Restored to G-AMTS

The first production order for Twin Pioneer CC.1 communications aircraft for the RAF was against Contract 6/Aircraft/14074 which accounted for 20 aircraft, 12 of which were serialled XL966 et seq. The block was allocated c/ns by Scottish Aviation Ltd as follows:- 514/518/520/522/524/525/527/528/530/531/534 and 535. XL966 f/f 29.8.57 XL997 f/f 1.7.58.

serial	type	sqdn/unit	code	where&when seen		remarks
XL966	Twin Pioneer CC.1					
XL967	Twin Pioneer CC.1					
XL968	Twin Pioneer CC.1					
XL969	Twin Pioneer CC.1					

XL970-XM147

serial	type	sqdn/unit	code	where&when seen		remarks
XL970	Twin Pioneer CC.1					
XL991	Twin Pioneer CC.1					
XL992	Twin Pioneer CC.1					
XL993	Twin Pioneer CC.1					To 8388M Pr Cosford
XL994	Twin Pioneer CC.1					
XL995	Twin Pioneer CC.1					
XL996	Twin Pioneer CC.1					
XL997	Twin Pioneer CC.1					

The fourth and final production order for 10 Beverley C.1 aircraft built by Blackburn and General Aircraft Ltd at Brough to follow XL152. XM103 f/f 23.10.57; XM112 f/f 15.5.58. No c/ns were allocated to these aircraft.

serial	type	sqdn/unit	code	where&when seen		remarks
XM103	Beverley C.1					
XM104	Beverley C.1					
XM105	Beverley C.1					
XM106	Beverley C.1					
XM107	Beverley C.1					
XM108	Beverley C.1					
XM109	Beverley C.1					
XM110	Beverley C.1					
XM111	Beverley C.1					
XM112	Beverley C.1					

The second production order for 10 Hunter T.7 trainers for the RAF was originally to replace those aircraft that had been transferred to the RN from the block XL563 etc. The order was subsequently cancelled and the aircraft were transferred to part of an order placed on behalf of the Royal Netherlands Air Force with whom they were allotted serials N311 to N320 resp.

XM117 - XM126 Hunter T.7 (10 a/c) Cancelled and diverted to R.Netherlands AF

One Jet Provost T.1 originally built by Hunting Percival Aircraft Ltd at Luton 1954 and registered G-AOBU (c/n PAC/84/006) for use as a company demonstrator. During 1956 this aircraft was loaned to the Controller of Aircraft for trials and allocated the serial XM129 for six months although the serial G-42-1 was probably carried in lieu.

serial	type	sqdn/unit	code	where&when seen		remarks
XM129	Jet Provost T.1					Returned to G-AOBU

The first production contract for Lightning F.1/F.1A supersonic fighters for the RAF accounted for some 50 aircraft built by English Electric Co Ltd at Preston. XM134 f/f 30.10.59 and production of the F.1 variant continued to XM167 which f/f 14.7.60 and this block was allocated c/ns 95030-95048 resp. Lightning F.1A production commenced with XM169 which f/f 16.8.60 and the final F.1A (XM216) f/f 24.7.61. XM169-XM192 were allocated c/ns 95056-95070/95082-95090; XM213-216 c/ns 95091-95093/95095. One F.1 airframe (XM168) was employed as a static test unit and never flown, whilst two F.1A's (XM217/218) were not built.

serial	type	sqdn/unit	code	where&when seen		remarks
XM134	Lightning F.1					
XM135	Lightning F.1					Pr IWM Duxford
XM136	Lightning F.1					
XM137	Lightning F.1					
XM138	Lightning F.1					
XM139	Lightning F.1					To 8411M
XM140	Lightning F.1					
XM141	Lightning F.1					
XM142	Lightning F.1					
XM143	Lightning F.1					
XM144	Lightning F.1					To 8417M Pr Leuchars
XM145	Lightning F.1					
XM146	Lightning F.1					
XM147	Lightning F.1					To 8412M

XM163-XM265

serial	type	sqdn/unit	code	where&when seen		remarks
XM163	Lightning F.1					
XM164	Lightning F.1					
XM165	Lightning F.1					
XM166	Lightning F.1					
XM167	Lightning F.1					
XM168	Lightning F.1					Static test airframe
XM169	Lightning F.1A					To 8422M
XM170	Lightning F.1A					To 7877M
XM171	Lightning F.1A					
XM172	Lightning F.1A					To 8427M Pr Coltishall
XM173	Lightning F.1A					To 8414M Pr Bentley Pry
XM174	Lightning F.1A					
XM175	Lightning F.1A					
XM176	Lightning F.1A					
XM177	Lightning F.1A					
XM178	Lightning F.1A					To 8418M
XM179	Lightning F.1A					
XM180	Lightning F.1A					To 8424M
XM181	Lightning F.1A					To 8415M
XM182	Lightning F.1A					To 8425M
XM183	Lightning F.1A					To 8416M
XM184	Lightning F.1A					
XM185	Lightning F.1A					
XM186	Lightning F.1A					
XM187	Lightning F.1A					To 7838M
XM188	Lightning F.1A					
XM189	Lightning F.1A					To 8423M
XM190	Lightning F.1A					
XM191	Lightning F.1A					To 7854M/8590M (nose)
XM192	Lightning F.1A					To 8413M Pr Wattisham
XM213	Lightning F.1A					
XM214	Lightning F.1A					To 8420M
XM215	Lightning F.1A					To 8421M
XM216	Lightning F.1A					To 8426M
XM217	Lightning F.1A					Not built
XM218	Lightning F.1A					Not built

One Devon C.1 communications aircraft built by the de Havilland Aircraft Co Ltd for the RAF with c/n 04498. Handed over on 19.12.57 it was subsequently operated by the RAE at Farnborough and later converted to C.2 standard.

XM223	Devon C.2					

Two Canberra T.4 aircraft to be built by English Electric Co Ltd at Preston for the RAF but were subsequently cancelled.

XM228 - XM229 Canberra T.4 (2 a/c) Cancelled and not built

20 Canberra B(I).8 bomber/interdictor aircraft built by English Electric Co Ltd at Preston. Essentially this batch was ordered as replacement aircraft for those aircraft diverted off contract to overseas customers. Deliveries took place between 8.58 and 4.59.

XM244	Canberra B(I).8					To 8202M
XM245	Canberra B(I).8					
XM262	Canberra B(I).8					
XM263	Canberra B(I).8					To G-52-10/PeAF 255
XM264	Canberra B(I).8					To 8227M
XM265	Canberra B(I).8					To 8199M

XM266-XM341

serial	type	sqdn/unit	code	where&when seen		remarks
XM266	Canberra B(I).8					
XM267	Canberra B(I).8					
XM268	Canberra B(I).8					
XM269	Canberra B(I).8					
XM270	Canberra B(I).8					
XM271	Canberra B(I).8					To 8204M
XM272	Canberra B(I).8					
XM273	Canberra B(I).8					To G-52-8/PeAF 253
XM274	Canberra B(I).8					To 8170M
XM275	Canberra B(I).8					
XM276	Canberra B(I).8					To G-52-11/PeAF 256
XM277	Canberra B(I).8					
XM278	Canberra B(I).8					
XM279	Canberra B(I).8					To G-52-12/PeAF 257

Eight Twin Pioneer CC.1 communications aircraft built by Scottish Aviation Ltd at Prestwick for the RAF and placed against Contract 6/Aircraft/14074 with XL966 et seq. XM284 f/f 9.7.58; XM291 f/f 17.9.58; both delivered to 22 MU 30.7.58, 16.10.58 resp. This block was allocated c/ns 536/538/539/541/542/543/544 and 545.

serial	type	sqdn/unit	code	where&when seen		remarks
XM284	Twin Pioneer CC.1					
XM285	Twin Pioneer CC.1					To G-31-15/G-AYFA
XM286	Twin Pioneer CC.1					
XM287	Twin Pioneer CC.1					
XM288	Twin Pioneer CC.1					
XM289	Twin Pioneer CC.1					
XM290	Twin Pioneer CC.1					
XM291	Twin Pioneer CC.1					

Two Heron CC.4 VIP aircraft built by de Havilland Aircraft Co Ltd at Chester against Contract 6/Aircraft/14194 especially for the use of RAF Queen's Flight. XM295 was delivered to Benson on 17.4.58 together with XM296. C/ns allocated were 14129 and 14130 respectively. XM296 passed to the RN in 7.72 as a C.4 to replace C.1 XR444.

serial	type	sqdn/unit	code	where&when seen		remarks
XM295	Heron CC.4					To G41-2-68/CF-XOK
XM296	Heron C.4					

The first pre-production order for 9 Wessex HAS.1 helicopters built by Westland Aircraft Ltd at Yeovil for RN and manufacturer's trials. The block was allocated the c/ns WA4-WA12 respectively. XM299 f/f 19.12.58 and was subsequently developed as the HC.2 prototype whilst several others were later converted to HAS.3 standard.

serial	type	sqdn/unit	code	where&when seen		remarks
XM299	Wessex HC.2					
XM300	Wessex HAS.1					
XM301	Wessex HAS.1					
XM326	Wessex HAS.1					
XM327	Wessex HAS.3					
XM328	Wessex HAS.3					
XM329	Wessex HAS.1					To A2609
XM330	Wessex HAS.1					
XM331	Wessex HAS.3					

The final production batch of 6 Javelin T.3 trainers for the RAF was later reduced to only one aircraft (XM336) which was built by Gloster Aircraft Co Ltd at Hucclecote and placed against Contract 6/Aircraft/11262 with XH390 et seq.

serial	type	sqdn/unit	code	where&when seen		remarks
XM336	Javelin T.3					

XM337 - XM341 Javelin T.3 (5 a/c) Cancelled and not built

The first production contract for 100 Jet Provost T.3 basic trainers for the RAF was built by Hunting Aircraft Ltd at Luton against Contract 6/Aircraft/14157. XM346 f/f

XM346-XM412

serial	type	sqdn/unit	code	where&when seen	remarks

22.6.58 and deliveries to the RAF commenced 7.59. From 6.73 most surviving aircraft were updated to T.3A's by BAC at Warton against Contract KA5(c)/466/CBA.5(c), the last being completed in 1976.

serial	type	sqdn/unit	code	where&when seen	remarks
XM346	Jet Provost T.3				
XM347	Jet Provost T.3				
XM348	Jet Provost T.3				
XM349	Jet Provost T.3A				
XM350	Jet Provost T.3A				
XM351	Jet Provost T.3				To 8078M
XM352	Jet Provost T.3A				
XM353	Jet Provost T.3				
XM354	Jet Provost T.3				
XM355	Jet Provost T.3				To 8229M
XM356	Jet Provost T.3				
XM357	Jet Provost T.3A				
XM358	Jet Provost T.3A				
XM359	Jet Provost T.3				
XM360	Jet Provost T.3				
XM361	Jet Provost T.3				
XM362	Jet Provost T.3				To 8230M
XM363	Jet Provost T.3				
XM364	Jet Provost T.3				
XM365	Jet Provost T.3A				
XM366	Jet Provost T.3A				
XM367	Jet Provost T.3				To 8083M
XM368	Jet Provost T.3				
XM369	Jet Provost T.3				To 8084M
XM370	Jet Provost T.3A				
XM371	Jet Provost T.3A				
XM372	Jet Provost T.3A				
XM373	Jet Provost T.3				To 7726M
XM374	Jet Provost T.3A				
XM375	Jet Provost T.3				To 8231M
XM376	Jet Provost T.3A				
XM377	Jet Provost T.3				
XM378	Jet Provost T.3A				
XM379	Jet Provost T.3				
XM380	Jet Provost T.3				
XM381	Jet Provost T.3				To 8232M
XM382	Jet Provost T.3				
XM383	Jet Provost T.3A				
XM384	Jet Provost T.3				
XM385	Jet Provost T.3				
XM386	Jet Provost T.3				To 8076M
XM387	Jet Provost T.3A				
XM401	Jet Provost T.3A				
XM402	Jet Provost T.3				To 8055AM
XM403	Jet Provost T.3A				
XM404	Jet Provost T.3				To 8055BM
XM405	Jet Provost T.3A				
XM406	Jet Provost T.3				
XM407	Jet Provost T.3				
XM408	Jet Provost T.3				To 8333M wears 8233M
XM409	Jet Provost T.3				To 8082M
XM410	Jet Provost T.3				To 8054AM
XM411	Jet Provost T.3				To 8434M/'XM811'
XM412	Jet Provost T.3A				

XM413-XM491

serial	type	sqdn/unit	code	where&when seen		remarks
XM413	Jet Provost T.3					
XM414	Jet Provost T.3A					
XM415	Jet Provost T.3					
XM416	Jet Provost T.3					
XM417	Jet Provost T.3					To 8054BM
XM418	Jet Provost T.3					To 8593M
XM419	Jet Provost T.3A					
XM420	Jet Provost T.3					
XM421	Jet Provost T.3					
XM422	Jet Provost T.3					
XM423	Jet Provost T.3					
XM424	Jet Provost T.3A					
XM425	Jet Provost T.3A					
XM426	Jet Provost T.3					
XM427	Jet Provost T.3					
XM428	Jet Provost T.3					
XM451	Jet Provost T.3					
XM452	Jet Provost T.3					
XM453	Jet Provost T.3A					
XM454	Jet Provost T.3					
XM455	Jet Provost T.3A					
XM456	Jet Provost T.3					
XM457	Jet Provost T.3					
XM458	Jet Provost T.3A					
XM459	Jet Provost T.3A					
XM460	Jet Provost T.3					
XM461	Jet Provost T.3A					
XM462	Jet Provost T.3					
XM463	Jet Provost T.3A					
XM464	Jet Provost T.3A					
XM465	Jet Provost T.3A					
XM466	Jet Provost T.3A					
XM467	Jet Provost T.3					To 8085M
XM468	Jet Provost T.3					To 8081M
XM469	Jet Provost T.3					
XM470	Jet Provost T.3A					
XM471	Jet Provost T.3A					
XM472	Jet Provost T.3A					
XM473	Jet Provost T.3A					
XM474	Jet Provost T.3					To 8121M
XM475	Jet Provost T.3A					
XM476	Jet Provost T.3					
XM477	Jet Provost T.3					
XM478	Jet Provost T.3A					
XM479	Jet Provost T.3A					
XM480	Jet Provost T.3					To 8080M

The second batch of 10 Britannia C.1 aircraft for RAF Transport Command was built by Short Bros & Harland Ltd at Belfast (XM489-491/496-497) and by Bristol Aeroplane Co Ltd at Filton (XM498/517-520). XM489-491 were built against Contract 6/Aircraft/14293 with the remainder against 6/Aircraft/15527. The entire block was allotted c/ns 13434-13436/13508-13514. RAF Transport Command named the aircraft as follows:- XM489 (Denebola); XM490 (Aldebaran); XM491 (Procyon); XM496 (Regulus); XM497 (Schedar); XM498 (Hadar); XM517 (Avior); XM518 (Spica); XM519 (Capella); XM520 (Arcturus).

serial	type	sqdn/unit	code	where&when seen		remarks
XM489	Britannia C.1					To OO-YCC
XM490	Britannia C.1					To G-BDLZ
XM491	Britannia C.1					To EI-BBH

XM496-XM606

serial	type	sqdn/unit	code	where&when seen		remarks
XM496	Britannia C.1					To G-BDUP
XM497	Britannia C.1					To OO-YCF ntu
XM498	Britannia C.1					To OO-YCG
XM517	Britannia C.1					To 9Q-CAJ
XM518	Britannia C.1					To OO-YCD
XM519	Britannia C.1					To G-BDUR
XM520	Britannia C.1					To 9G-ACE

The third production order for 20 Skeeter AOP.12 helicopters built by Saunders-Roe Ltd for the Army Air Corps against Contract 6/Aircraft/15410. The block was allocated c/ns (prefixed S2/xxxx) 5100-5110/5112-5120 resp. XM524 delivered 1.4.59.

serial	type	sqdn/unit	code	where&when seen		remarks
XM524	Skeeter AOP.12					
XM525	Skeeter AOP.12					
XM526	Skeeter AOP.12					
XM527	Skeeter AOP.12					To 7820M
XM528	Skeeter AOP.12					
XM529	Skeeter AOP.12					To 7979M
XM530	Skeeter AOP.12					
XM553	Skeeter AOP.12					To G-AWSV
XM554	Skeeter AOP.12					
XM555	Skeeter AOP.12					To 8027M Pr Shawbury
XM556	Skeeter AOP.12					To 7870M Pr W-s-M
XM557	Skeeter AOP.12					
XM558	Skeeter AOP.12					
XM559	Skeeter AOP.12					
XM560	Skeeter AOP.12					
XM561	Skeeter AOP.12					To 7980M GI Moston
XM562	Skeeter AOP.12					
XM563	Skeeter AOP.12					
XM564	Skeeter AOP.12					Pr RACM Bovington
XM565	Skeeter AOP.12					To 7861M

The fourth production batch of 40 Vulcan B.2 strategic bombers built for the RAF by A.V.Roe Co Ltd at Woodford to follow on from XL446. The last production Vulcan B.2 (XM657) was delivered to the RAF on 14.1.65.

serial	type	sqdn/unit	code	where&when seen		remarks
XM569	Vulcan B.2					
XM570	Vulcan B.2					
XM571	Vulcan B.2					
XM572	Vulcan B.2					
XM573	Vulcan B.2					
XM574	Vulcan B.2					
XM575	Vulcan B.2					
XM576	Vulcan B.2					
XM594	Vulcan B.2					
XM595	Vulcan B.2					
XM596	Vulcan B.2					
XM597	Vulcan B.2					
XM598	Vulcan B.2					
XM599	Vulcan B.2					
XM600	Vulcan B.2					
XM601	Vulcan B.2					
XM602	Vulcan B.2					
XM603	Vulcan B.2					
XM604	Vulcan B.2					
XM605	Vulcan B.2					
XM606	Vulcan B.2					

serial	type	sqdn/unit	code	where&when seen		remarks
XM607	Vulcan B.2					
XM608	Vulcan B.2					
XM609	Vulcan B.2					
XM610	Vulcan B.2					
XM611	Vulcan B.2					
XM612	Vulcan B.2					
XM645	Vulcan B.2					
XM646	Vulcan B.2					
XM647	Vulcan B.2					
XM648	Vulcan B.2					
XM649	Vulcan B.2					
XM650	Vulcan B.2					
XM651	Vulcan B.2					
XM652	Vulcan B.2					
XM653	Vulcan B.2					
XM654	Vulcan B.2					
XM655	Vulcan B.2					
XM656	Vulcan B.2					
XM657	Vulcan B.2					

15 Whirlwind HAS.7 helicopters built by Westland Aircraft Ltd at Yeovil for the RN against Contract 6/Aircraft/15633/CB9(b). Allotted c/ns WA251-WA265 resp XM660 f/f 20.11.58 and del 9.12.58. In 1966 XM666 was converted to HAR.9 standard at W-s-M.

serial	type	sqdn/unit	code	where&when seen		remarks
XM660	Whirlwind HAS.7					Pr Almondbank
XM661	Whirlwind HAS.7					
XM662	Whirlwind HAS.7					
XM663	Whirlwind HAS.7					
XM664	Whirlwind HAS.7					
XM665	Whirlwind HAS.7					Pr Thorpe Water Park
XM666	Whirlwind HAR.9					
XM667	Whirlwind HAS.7					To A2629
XM668	Whirlwind HAS.7					
XM669	Whirlwind HAS.7					
XM683	Whirlwind HAS.7					
XM684	Whirlwind HAS.7					
XM685	Whirlwind HAS.7					To G-AYZJ ntu
XM686	Whirlwind HAS.7					
XM687	Whirlwind HAS.7					

Sole contract for development Gnat T.1 advanced trainers for the RAF built by Folland Aircraft Ltd at Hamble against Contract 15434 to Spec T.185. Test flown from Chilbolton and Dunsfold; allotted c/ns FL501 to FL514 resp. Deliveries commenced 2.62.

serial	type	sqdn/unit	code	where&when seen		remarks
XM691	Gnat T.1					
XM692	Gnat T.1					
XM693	Gnat T.1					To 7891M
XM694	Gnat T.1					
XM695	Gnat T.1					
XM696	Gnat T.1					
XM697	Gnat T.1					Pr Woking
XM698	Gnat T.1					To 8090M & 8497M
XM704	Gnat T.1					To 7992M (nose)
XM705	Gnat T.1					To 8574M
XM706	Gnat T.1					To 8572M
XM707	Gnat T.1					
XM708	Gnat T.1					To 8573M
XM709	Gnat T.1					To 8617M

XM714-XM874

serial	type	sqdn/unit	code	where&when seen		remarks

The final contract for Victor B.2 strategic bombers accounted for 30 aircraft to be built by Handley-Page Ltd at Radlett for the RAF. Production, however, terminated with the 5th aircraft from this order (XM718) which was delivered on 2.5.63. The remaining 25 aircraft were cancelled and not built. Conversions to strategic reconnaissance (SR.2) and tanker (K.2) roles subsequently took place.

serial	type	sqdn/unit	code	where&when seen		remarks
XM714	Victor B.2					
XM715	Victor K.2					
XM716	Victor SR.2					
XM717	Victor K.2					
XM718	Victor SR.2					

XM719 - XM721	Victor B.2	(3 a/c)	Cancelled and not built
XM745 - XM756	Victor B.2	(12 a/c)	Cancelled and not built
XM785 - XM794	Victor B.2	(10 a/c)	Cancelled and not built

Two EP.9 utility aircraft built by Edgar Percival Aircraft Ltd at Stapleford with c/ns 38 and 39, and delivered to the Army Air Corps during March 1958 for evaluation purposes. Both aircraft were subsequently sold to Steels (Aviation) Ltd and delivered Middle Wallop to Staverton on 26.10.61.

serial	type	sqdn/unit	code	where&when seen		remarks
XM797	E.P.9					To G-ARTU
XM819	E.P.9					To G-ARTV

One DH.106 Comet 1XB acquired by the MoS for use by RAE Farnborough against Contract 6/Aircraft/15321/CB10(d). It was allotted c/n 06022 and was originally built for Air France at Hatfield as F-BGNZ in 1953 before returning to the UK as G-APAS.

serial	type	sqdn/unit	code	where&when seen		remarks
XM823	Comet Srs.1XB					Ex G-APAS To 8351M Pr

One DH.106 Comet 1XB acquired by the MoS for use by the A&AEE in August 1961 against Contract 6/Aircraft/15417/CB10(d). It was allotted c/n 06021 and was originally built for Air France as F-BGNY in 1953 before returning to the UK as G-AOJU.

serial	type	sqdn/unit	code	where&when seen		remarks
XM829	Comet Srs.1XB					Ex G-AOJU

First production contract for 40 Wessex HAS.1 helicopters built for the RN by Westland Aircraft Ltd at Yeovil with c/ns WA.13 to WA.52 respectively. XM832 was delivered to 700H Squadron on 6.4.60. Subsequently conversions to HAS.3 took place.

serial	type	sqdn/unit	code	where&when seen		remarks
XM832	Wessex HAS.1					
XM833	Wessex HAS.3					
XM834	Wessex HAS.3					
XM835	Wessex HAS.1					To A2516
XM836	Wessex HAS.3					
XM837	Wessex HAS.3					
XM838	Wessex HAS.3					
XM839	Wessex HAS.1					
XM840	Wessex HAS.1					
XM841	Wessex HAS.1					
XM842	Wessex HAS.1					
XM843	Wessex HAS.1					
XM844	Wessex HAS.3					
XM845	Wessex HAS.1					To A2682
XM868	Wessex HAS.1					
XM869	Wessex HAS.1					
XM870	Wessex HAS.3					
XM871	Wessex HAS.3					
XM872	Wessex HAS.3					
XM873	Wessex HAS.1					
XM874	Wessex HAS.1					To A2689

XM875-XM974

serial	type	sqdn/unit	code	where&when seen		remarks
XM875	Wessex HAS.1					
XM876	Wessex HAS.1					
XM915	Wessex HAS.1					
XM916	Wessex HAS.3					
XM917	Wessex HAS.1					
XM918	Wessex HAS.3					
XM919	Wessex HAS.3					
XM920	Wessex HAS.3					
XM921	Wessex HAS.1					
XM922	Wessex HAS.1					
XM923	Wessex HAS.3					
XM924	Wessex HAS.1					
XM925	Wessex HAS.1					
XM926	Wessex HAS.1					
XM927	Wessex HAS.3					
XM928	Wessex HAS.1					
XM929	Wessex HAS.1					
XM930	Wessex HAS.1					
XM931	Wessex HAS.1					

One Canberra B(I).8 built for the RAF by English Electric Co Ltd at Preston against Contract KD/E/01 presumably as a replacement for an earlier aircraft diverted to the Indian Air Force. It was delivered in 4.59.

serial	type	sqdn/unit	code	where&when seen		remarks
XM936	Canberra B(I).8					To G-52-9/PeAF 254

Continued production of 12 Twin Pioneer CC.1 communication aircraft built for the RAF by Scottish Aviation Ltd at Prestwick. XM939 f/f 24.9.58 and the final Mk CC.1 (XM963) f/f 20.1.59 and was delivered to 22 MU 30.1.59. The block was allotted c/ns 546/549/550/551/552/553/554/555/557/558/559 and 560 resp. Twin Pioneer allocations continued with the CC.2 variant XN318 et seq.

serial	type	sqdn/unit	code	where&when seen		remarks
XM939	Twin Pioneer CC.1					
XM940	Twin Pioneer CC.1					
XM941	Twin Pioneer CC.1					
XM942	Twin Pioneer CC.1					
XM943	Twin Pioneer CC.1					
XM957	Twin Pioneer CC.1					
XM958	Twin Pioneer CC.1					
XM959	Twin Pioneer CC.1					
XM960	Twin Pioneer CC.1					
XM961	Twin Pioneer CC.1					To 7978M
XM962	Twin Pioneer CC.1					
XM963	Twin Pioneer CC.1					

The first production order for 30 Lightning T.4 two-seat training and conversion aircraft was subsequently cut back to 20. All were built at Preston by English Electric Company Ltd with c/ns 95051-95055/95071-95080/95100/95101/95104/95103/95111 resp. XM966 f/f 15.7.60 and was subsequently converted at Filton to become the second T.5 prototype, the first (XM967) having been completed as such and f/f 29.3.62.

serial	type	sqdn/unit	code	where&when seen		remarks
XM966	Lightning T.5					
XM967	Lightning T.5					To 8433M
XM968	Lightning T.4					To 8541M ntu
XM969	Lightning T.4					To 8592M
XM970	Lightning T.4					To 8529M
XM971	Lightning T.4					
XM972	Lightning T.4					
XM973	Lightning T.4					To 8528M
XM974	Lightning T.4					

XM987-XN152

serial	type	sqdn/unit	code	where&when seen		remarks
XM987	Lightning T.4					
XM988	Lightning T.4					
XM989	Lightning T.4					To RSAF 54-650
XM990	Lightning T.4					
XM991	Lightning T.4					To 8456M
XM992	Lightning T.4					To RSAF 54-651
XM993	Lightning T.4					
XM994	Lightning T.4					
XM995	Lightning T.4					To 8542M
XM996	Lightning T.4					
XM997	Lightning T.4					

XN103 - XN112 Lightning T.4 (10 a/c) Cancelled and not built

The Jet Provost T.3 prototype, converted in 1958 by Hunting Aircraft Ltd at Luton from T.2 G-23-1 with the c/n PAC/84/013. Took part in trials in Aden in 8/9.58.

serial	type	sqdn/unit	code	where&when seen		remarks
XN117	Jet Provost T.3					Ex G-23-1

One Gnat F.1 built by Folland Aircraft Ltd at Hamble with c/n FL.18. F/f 29.7.58 and delivered to Khormaksar for trials to select a replacement for the Venom. These trials commenced on 14.8.58. Sold to Indian AF as IE1064 and delivered 8.9.58.

serial	type	sqdn/unit	code	where&when seen		remarks
XN122	Gnat F.1					

Two Whirlwind HCC.8 helicopters built by Westland Aircraft Ltd at Yeovil for the RAF Queen's Flight against Contract KC/2N/01. They were allotted c/ns WA266 and 267 respectively. Delivered in 8.59 and 11.59 respectively, both were subsequently converted to HAR.10 standard for normal RAF squadron use.

serial	type	sqdn/unit	code	where&when seen		remarks
XN126	Whirlwind HAR.10					
XN127	Whirlwind HAR.10					

Two Alouette AH.2 helicopters built by Sud Aviation with c/ns 1185 and 1186 respectively and delivered Le Bourget to Middle Wallop 18.9.58 as F-WIPG and F-WIPH. Both were part of a batch of five Alouettes ordered by the Army Air Corps for trials and evaluational purposes. See also XP966-967 and XR232.

serial	type	sqdn/unit	code	where&when seen		remarks
XN132	Alouette AH.2					Ex F-WIPG
XN133	Alouette AH.2					Ex F-WIPH To 7702M

One Jet Provost T.3 built by Hunting Aircraft Ltd at Luton for the RAF against the Contract 6/Aircraft/14157 which covered the 100 production aircraft in the XM3xx range. The aircraft was delivered in 8.60 as a replacement for the crashed XM348.

serial	type	sqdn/unit	code	where&when seen		remarks
XN137	Jet Provost T.3					

Following the completion of RAF evaluation trials as XH463 (qv) and restoration to civil marks as G-ANAR, the DHC.2 Beaver Srs 2 was evaluated by the AAC during 1958 as XN142. As a result of these tests a production order for 36 Beaver AL.1's was placed with the manufacturer (See XP769 et seq.).

serial	type	sqdn/unit	code	where&when seen		remarks
XN142	Beaver Srs 2					Ex G-ANAR To G-ANAR

Production of the Type 21B Sedbergh TX.1 glider was resumed by Slingsby Sailplanes Ltd at Kirkbymoorside when a final 19 were built against Contract KF/2R/04 for use by the Air Training Corps. The block was allotted c/ns 1150-1168 respectively.

serial	type	sqdn/unit	code	where&when seen		remarks
XN146	Sedbergh TX.1					To BGA1110
XN147	Sedbergh TX.1					To BGA1482
XN148	Sedbergh TX.1					
XN149	Sedbergh TX.1					
XN150	Sedbergh TX.1					
XN151	Sedbergh TX.1					
XN152	Sedbergh TX.1					

XN153-XN298

serial	type	sqdn/unit	code	where&when seen		remarks
XN153	Sedbergh TX.1					
XN154	Sedbergh TX.1					To BGA1465
XN155	Sedbergh TX.1					
XN156	Sedbergh TX.1					
XN157	Sedbergh TX.1					
XN183	Sedbergh TX.1					To BGA1354
XN184	Sedbergh TX.1					
XN185	Sedbergh TX.1					
XN186	Sedbergh TX.1					
XN187	Sedbergh TX.1					
XN188	Sedbergh TX.1					To BGA1588
XN189	Sedbergh TX.1					To BGA1144

The fourth and final production order for 24 Type 31B Cadet TX.3 gliders built by Slingsby Sailplanes Ltd at Kirkbymoorside against Contract KF/2R/05 for use by the Air Training Corps. The block was allotted c/ns 1169-1192 respectively.

serial	type	sqdn/unit	code	where&when seen		remarks
XN194	Cadet TX.3					
XN195	Cadet TX.3					To 7845M
XN196	Cadet TX.3					
XN197	Cadet TX.3					
XN198	Cadet TX.3					
XN199	Cadet TX.3					
XN236	Cadet TX.3					
XN237	Cadet TX.3					
XN238	Cadet TX.3					
XN239	Cadet TX.3					
XN240	Cadet TX.3					
XN241	Cadet TX.3					
XN242	Cadet TX.3					
XN243	Cadet TX.3					
XN244	Cadet TX.3					
XN245	Cadet TX.3					
XN246	Cadet TX.3					
XN247	Cadet TX.3					
XN248	Cadet TX.3					
XN249	Cadet TX.3					
XN250	Cadet TX.3					
XN251	Cadet TX.3					
XN252	Cadet TX.3					
XN253	Cadet TX.3					

The fifth and final order for Whirlwind HAS.7 helicopters for the RN by Westland Aircraft Ltd at Yeovil against Contract KF/2N/015/CB25(a). This order covered 40 helicopters in two serial blocks, the first (XN258-264/297-314) being allotted c/ns WA270-WA294 (see XN357 etc for second block). XN258 f/f 29.8.59 and deliveries took place between 9.59 and 3.60. During 1965/66 several were converted to turbine powered HAR.9 standard at Weston-super-Mare.

serial	type	sqdn/unit	code	where&when seen		remarks
XN258	Whirlwind HAR.9					Pr Helston
XN259	Whirlwind HAS.7					To A2604
XN260	Whirlwind HAS.7					
XN261	Whirlwind HAS.7					To A2652
XN262	Whirlwind HAS.7					
XN263	Whirlwind HAS.7					To GI Middle Wallop
XN264	Whirlwind HAS.7					Pr Christchurch
XN297	Whirlwind HAS.7					
XN298	Whirlwind HAR.9					

XN299-XN355

serial	type	sqdn/unit	code	where&when seen		remarks
XN299	Whirlwind HAS.7					
XN300	Whirlwind HAS.7					
XN301	Whirlwind HAS.7					
XN302	Whirlwind HAS.7					To A2654
XN303	Whirlwind HAS.7					
XN304	Whirlwind HAS.7					To GI Shrivenham
XN305	Whirlwind HAS.7					To A2606
XN306	Whirlwind HAR.9					
XN307	Whirlwind HAS.7					To A2501
XN308	Whirlwind HAS.7					To A2605
XN309	Whirlwind HAR.9					To A2663
XN310	Whirlwind HAR.9					
XN311	Whirlwind HAR.9					To A2643
XN312	Whirlwind HAS.7					
XN313	Whirlwind HAS.7					
XN314	Whirlwind HAS.7					To A2614

Four Twin Pioneer CC.2 communications aircraft built by Scottish Aviation Ltd at Prestwick for the RAF as follows:- XN318 c/n 573 f/f 29.5.59; XN319 c/n 574; XN320 c/n 575; and XN321 c/n 576 f/f 27.7.59. Allocations continue with XP293.

serial	type	sqdn/unit	code	where&when seen		remarks
XN318	Twin Pioneer CC.2					
XN319	Twin Pioneer CC.2					
XN320	Twin Pioneer CC.2					
XN321	Twin Pioneer CC.2					

One Gnat F.1 transferred from the Finnish AF order and f/f 27.10.58 as G-39-11 at Chilbolton. Delivered to A&AEE as XN326 24.2.59, later returning to Folland Aircraft Co in 1960 for nose-mounted camera mods prior to delivery to Finland as GN113.

serial	type	sqdn/unit	code	where&when seen		remarks
XN326	Gnat F.1					Ex G-39-11 To FiAF GN113

Private venture development of the Skeeter by Saro, the prototype P.531-O/N G-APNU (c/n S2/5267) f/f 20.7.58 at Eastleigh. It was followed by G-APNV (S2/5268) f/f 30.9 which was subsequently del. to the RN 2.10.59 as XN332, following the decision to evaluate the type (Contract KF/2Q/01/CB25(a)). XN333 d/d 20.10.59, XN334 d/d 6.11.59.

serial	type	sqdn/unit	code	where&when seen		remarks
XN332	Saro P.531 O/N					Ex G APNV To A2579 Pr
XN333	Saro P.531 O/N					To A2519
XN334	Saro P.531 O/N					To A2525 Pr FAAM

The third and final order for 17 Skeeter AOP.12 helicopters built by Saunders-Roe Ltd for the AAC against Contract KF/C/021, to follow on from XM565. The block was allotted c/ns S2/7145 to S2/7161 resp and deliveries took place between 12.59 and 9.60.

serial	type	sqdn/unit	code	where&when seen		remarks
XN339	Skeeter AOP.12					
XN340	Skeeter AOP.12					
XN341	Skeeter AOP.12					To 8022M Pr St Athan
XN342	Skeeter AOP.12					
XN343	Skeeter AOP.12					
XN344	Skeeter AOP.12					To 8018M Pr Science M
XN345	Skeeter AOP.12					
XN346	Skeeter AOP.12					
XN347	Skeeter AOP.12					
XN348	Skeeter AOP.12					To 8024M Pr Buckeburg
XN349	Skeeter AOP.12					
XN350	Skeeter AOP.12					
XN351	Skeeter AOP.12					Pr Higher Blagdon
XN352	Skeeter AOP.12					
XN353	Skeeter AOP.12					
XN354	Skeeter AOP.12					
XN355	Skeeter AOP.12					

XN357-XN443

The second part of Contract KF/2N/015/CB25(a) accounted for 15 Whirlwind HAS.7 helicopters built for the RN by Westland Aircraft Ltd at Yeovil to follow on from XN258 et seq. This block was allotted c/ns WA303-WA317 resp, XN357 first flew 10.3.60.

serial	type	sqdn/unit	code	where&when seen		remarks
XN357	Whirlwind HAS.7					
XN358	Whirlwind HAS.7					To A2644
XN359	Whirlwind HAR.9					
XN360	Whirlwind HAS.7					
XN361	Whirlwind HAS.7					
XN362	Whirlwind HAS.7					
XN379	Whirlwind HAS.7					
XN380	Whirlwind HAS.7					Pr Headcorn
XN381	Whirlwind HAS.7					
XN382	Whirlwind HAS.7					To GI Middle Wallop
XN383	Whirlwind HAS.7					
XN384	Whirlwind HAR.9					
XN385	Whirlwind HAS.7					
XN386	Whirlwind HAR.9					
XN387	Whirlwind HAR.9					To 8564M

Three Britannia C.2's built under the manufacturer's designation Bristol 175 Srs 252 and sub-contracted to Short Bros & Harland Ltd at Belfast with c/ns 13450-13452 and against Contract 6/Aircraft/11804. Originally all had been ordered by the Ministry of Supply in a mixed-traffic configuration for lease to charter operators and were initially registered as G-APPE/PPF/PPG respectively. However they were later delivered to RAF Transport Command as Britannia C.2 aircraft on 19.3.59, 8.4.59 and 28.10.59 resp and allotted names: XN392 (Accrux), XN398 (Altair) and XN404 (Canopus).

serial	type	sqdn/unit	code	where&when seen		remarks
XN392	Britannia C.2					Ex G-APPE
XN398	Britannia C.2					Ex G-APPF To 9Q-CPX
XN404	Britannia C.2					Ex G-APPG

The third production order for 15 Auster AOP.9 aircraft built by Auster Aircraft Ltd at Rearsby against Contract KC/N/034/CB5(c). Deliveries to the Army Air Corps were made between 9.9.59 and 7.4.60.

serial	type	sqdn/unit	code	where&when seen		remarks
XN407	Auster AOP.9					To HKG-6
XN408	Auster AOP.9					
XN409	Auster AOP.9					
XN410	Auster AOP.9					To HKG-
XN411	Auster AOP.9					
XN412	Auster AOP.9					
XN435	Auster AOP.9					To G-BGBU
XN436	Auster AOP.9					
XN437	Auster AOP.9					To G-AXWA
XN438	Auster AOP.9					
XN439	Auster AOP.9					
XN440	Auster AOP.9					
XN441	Auster AOP.9					To G-BGKT
XN442	Auster AOP.9					
XN443	Auster AOP.9					To 7977M

Three Type 171 Sycamore HR.51 helicopters built by the Bristol Aeroplane Co Ltd at Filton (XN448) and Weston-super-Mare (XN449/450) and allotted serials for direct transfer to the Royal Australian Navy. XN448 was originally built in 1955 with c/n 13270 and registered G-AOBM for delivery to Canada where it was registered CF-HVX. During 1956 it was returned to the UK for overhaul and sale; to RAN 6.58. XN449 (c/n

XN448-XN550

13504) and XN450 (c/n 13505) were delivered in 6.59, the last Sycamores to be built.

serial	type	sqdn/unit	code	where&when seen	remarks
XN448	Sycamore HR.51				Ex G-18-5 To RAN
XN449	Sycamore HR.51				Ex G-18-177 To RAN
XN450	Sycamore HR.51				Ex G-18-178 To RAN Pr

One DH.106 Comet Srs 2E originally built by de Havilland Aircraft Co Ltd at Hatfield for BOAC as G-AMXD and f/f as such on 20.8.54. After conversion to Srs 2E it was allotted the serial XN453 for use by RAE Farnborough to whom it was delivered on 15.7.60 as a radio trials development aircraft.

serial	type	sqdn/unit	code	where&when seen	remarks
XN453	Comet Srs 2E				Ex G-AMXD

The second production order for 100 Jet Provost T.3 training aircraft built for the RAF by Hunting Aircraft Ltd at Luton against Contract KC/E/031 and to follow on from XM480, deliveries taking place during 1960/61. From 1973 most surviving examples were converted to T.3A standard by BAC against Contract KA5(c)/466/CBA.5(c).

serial	type	sqdn/unit	code	where&when seen	remarks
XN458	Jet Provost T.3				To 8334M wears 8234M
XN459	Jet Provost T.3A				
XN460	Jet Provost T.3				
XN461	Jet Provost T.3A				
XN462	Jet Provost T.3A				
XN463	Jet Provost T.3				
XN464	Jet Provost T.3				
XN465	Jet Provost T.3				
XN466	Jet Provost T.3A				
XN467	Jet Provost T.4				T.4 proto To 8559M
XN468	Jet Provost T.4				T.4 prototype
XN469	Jet Provost T.3				
XN470	Jet Provost T.3A				
XN471	Jet Provost T.3A				
XN472	Jet Provost T.3A				
XN473	Jet Provost T.3A				
XN492	Jet Provost T.3				To 8079M
XN493	Jet Provost T.3				
XN494	Jet Provost T.3A				
XN495	Jet Provost T.3A				
XN496	Jet Provost T.3				To RSAF GI
XN497	Jet Provost T.3A				
XN498	Jet Provost T.3A				
XN499	Jet Provost T.3A				
XN500	Jet Provost T.3A				
XN501	Jet Provost T.3A				
XN502	Jet Provost T.3A				
XN503	Jet Provost T.3				
XN504	Jet Provost T.3				
XN505	Jet Provost T.3A				
XN506	Jet Provost T.3A				
XN507	Jet Provost T.3				
XN508	Jet Provost T.3A				
XN509	Jet Provost T.3A				
XN510	Jet Provost T.3A				
XN511	Jet Provost T.3				
XN512	Jet Provost T.3				To 8435M
XN547	Jet Provost T.3A				
XN548	Jet Provost T.3A				
XN549	Jet Provost T.3				To 8335M wears 8235M
XN550	Jet Provost T.3				

XN551-XN639

serial	type	sqdn/unit	code	where&when seen		remarks
XN551	Jet Provost T.3A					
XN552	Jet Provost T.3A					
XN553	Jet Provost T.3A					
XN554	Jet Provost T.3					To 8436M
XN555	Jet Provost T.3					
XN556	Jet Provost T.3					
XN557	Jet Provost T.3					
XN558	Jet Provost T.3					
XN559	Jet Provost T.3					
XN573	Jet Provost T.3					
XN574	Jet Provost T.3A					
XN575	Jet Provost T.3					
XN576	Jet Provost T.3					
XN577	Jet Provost T.3A					
XN578	Jet Provost T.3					
XN579	Jet Provost T.3A					
XN580	Jet Provost T.3					
XN581	Jet Provost T.3A					
XN582	Jet Provost T.3A					
XN583	Jet Provost T.3					
XN584	Jet Provost T.3A					
XN585	Jet Provost T.3A					
XN586	Jet Provost T.3A					
XN587	Jet Provost T.3					
XN588	Jet Provost T.3					
XN589	Jet Provost T.3A					
XN590	Jet Provost T.3A					
XN591	Jet Provost T.3					
XN592	Jet Provost T.3					
XN593	Jet Provost T.3A					
XN594	Jet Provost T.3					To 8077M
XN595	Jet Provost T.3A					
XN596	Jet Provost T.3					To SAFTECH.1
XN597	Jet Provost T.3					To 7984M (Nose)
XN598	Jet Provost T.3A					
XN599	Jet Provost T.3					
XN600	Jet Provost T.3					
XN601	Jet Provost T.3					
XN602	Jet Provost T.3					To 8088M
XN603	Jet Provost T.3					
XN604	Jet Provost T.3					
XN605	Jet Provost T.3A					
XN606	Jet Provost T.3A					
XN607	Jet Provost T.3					
XN629	Jet Provost T.3A					
XN630	Jet Provost T.3					
XN631	Jet Provost T.3					
XN632	Jet Provost T.3					To 8352M
XN633	Jet Provost T.3					To 8353M
XN634	Jet Provost T.3A					
* XN635	Jet Provost T.3					
XN636	Jet Provost T.3A					
XN637	Jet Provost T.3					Pr Duxford
XN638	Jet Provost T.3					
XN639	Jet Provost T.3					

* Compromised serial allocation. See under XN635 on the following page.

*XN635-XN710

serial	type	sqdn/unit	code	where&when seen		remarks
XN640	Jet Provost T.3A					
XN641	Jet Provost T.3A					
XN642	Jet Provost T.3					
XN643	Jet Provost T.3A					

One Type 171 Sycamore HR.51 helicopter built by the Bristol Aeroplane Co Ltd at Weston-super-Mare originally as a Mk.4 G-AMWI. Converted for the RAN, it was initially allocated the 'compromised' serial XN635 before being re-allocated the serial XR592.

serial	type	sqdn/unit	code	where&when seen		remarks
* XN635	Sycamore HR.51					To XR592

Second production order for 40 Sea Vixen FAW.1 shipboard all-weather fighters built by Hawker Siddeley Ltd for the RN. The block was allotted the c/ns 10079-10118 resp; deliveries took place between 3.61 and 10.62. Later most aircraft were converted to FAW.2 standard at Chester (C) and RNAY Belfast (B). Flight Refuelling Ltd at Tarrant Rushton/Hurn are reworking some to D.3's (first conversion XN657 f/f as D.3 11.5.79).

serial	type	sqdn/unit	code	where&when seen		remarks
XN647	Sea Vixen FAW.2 (C)					To A2610 Pr Helston
XN648	Sea Vixen FAW.1					
XN649	Sea Vixen FAW.2 (C)					
XN650	Sea Vixen FAW.2 (B)					To A2639 Pr Rhoose
XN651	Sea Vixen FAW.2 (C)					A2616 Nose Pr Bristol
XN652	Sea Vixen FAW.2 (B)					
XN653	Sea Vixen FAW.2 (B)					
XN654	Sea Vixen FAW.2 (C)					
XN655	Sea Vixen FAW.2 (C)					
XN656	Sea Vixen FAW.2 (C)					
XN657	Sea Vixen D.3 (B)					
XN658	Sea Vixen FAW.2 (C)					To 8223M
XN683	Sea Vixen FAW.2 (B)					
XN684	Sea Vixen FAW.2 (C)					
XN685	Sea Vixen FAW.2 (C)					To 8173M
XN686	Sea Vixen FAW.2 (B)					
XN687	Sea Vixen FAW.2 (B)					
XN688	Sea Vixen FAW.2 (C)					To 8141M
XN689	Sea Vixen FAW.2 (B)					
XN690	Sea Vixen FAW.2 (C)					
XN691	Sea Vixen FAW.2 (C)					To 8143M
XN692	Sea Vixen FAW.2 (C)					To A2624
XN693	Sea Vixen FAW.2 (B)					
XN694	Sea Vixen FAW.2 (C)					
XN695	Sea Vixen FAW.1					
XN696	Sea Vixen FAW.2 (C)					
XN697	Sea Vixen FAW.2 (C)					To A2623
XN698	Sea Vixen FAW.1					
XN699	Sea Vixen FAW.2 (B)					To 8224M
XN700	Sea Vixen FAW.2 (B)					To 8138M
XN701	Sea Vixen FAW.1					
XN702	Sea Vixen FAW.2 (C)					
XN703	Sea Vixen FAW.1					
XN704	Sea Vixen FAW.1					
XN705	Sea Vixen FAW.2 (B)					To 8225M
XN706	Sea Vixen FAW.2 (B)					To A2613 To XN706
XN707	Sea Vixen FAW.2 (B)					To 8144M
XN708	Sea Vixen FAW.1					
XN709	Sea Vixen FAW.1					
XN710	Sea Vixen FAW.1					

XN714-XN797

serial	type	sqdn/unit	code	where&when seen		remarks

Two jet flap research aircraft ordered from Hunting Aircraft Co Ltd under the manufacturer's designation H.126 to Spec ER.189. Only XN714 was completed, making its first flight from Luton on 26.3.63. Used by RAE in the UK and by NASA in the USA.

serial	type	sqdn/unit	code	where&when seen		remarks
XN714	Hunting H.126					Pr Cosford
XN719	Hunting H.126					Canx before completn

The sole production order for 50 Lightning F.2 fighter aircraft for the RAF was subsequently reduced to 44. All were built by English Electric Company Ltd at Preston with c/ns 95096/95094/95097-95099/95105-95110/95113-95115/95121-95150 respectively and against Contract KC/2D/03/CB7(b). The first F.2 (XN723) f/f 11.7.61, and many were later reworked to F.6 standard under the designation F.2A. Several were also diverted to the Royal Saudi Air Force as F.52 variants.

serial	type	sqdn/unit	code	where&when seen		remarks
XN723	Lightning F.2					
XN724	Lightning F.2A					To 8513M
XN725	Lightning F.2A					
XN726	Lightning F.2A					To 8545M ntu
XN727	Lightning F.2A					To 8547M ntu
XN728	Lightning F.2A					To 8546M
XN729	Lightning F.2					To G27-1/RSAF/52-659
XN730	Lightning F.2A					To 8496M
XN731	Lightning F.2A					To 8518M
XN732	Lightning F.2A					To 8519M
XN733	Lightning F.2A					To 8520M
XN734	Lightning F.2A					To 8346M
XN735	Lightning F.2A					To 8552M
XN767	Lightning F.2					To RSAF 52-655
XN768	Lightning F.2					To 8347M
XN769	Lightning F.2					To 8402M Pr W Drayton
XN770	Lightning F.2					To RSAF 52-656
XN771	Lightning F.2A					
XN772	Lightning F.2A					
XN773	Lightning F.2A					To 8521M
XN774	Lightning F.2A					To 8551M
XN775	Lightning F.2A					To 8448M
XN776	Lightning F.2A					
XN777	Lightning F.2A					To 8536M
XN778	Lightning F.2A					To 8537M
XN779	Lightning F.2					To 8348M
XN780	Lightning F.2A					
XN781	Lightning F.2A					To 8538M
XN782	Lightning F.2A					To 8539M
XN783	Lightning F.2A					To 8526M
XN784	Lightning F.2A					To 8540M
XN785	Lightning F.2					
XN786	Lightning F.2A					To 8500M
XN787	Lightning F.2A					To 8522M
XN788	Lightning F.2A					To 8543M
XN789	Lightning F.2A					To 8527M
XN790	Lightning F.2A					To 8523M
XN791	Lightning F.2A					To 8524M
XN792	Lightning F.2A					To 8525M
XN793	Lightning F.2A					To 8544M
XN794	Lightning F.2					To 8349M
XN795	Lightning F.2A					
XN796	Lightning F.2					To RSAF 52-657
XN797	Lightning F.2					To RSAF 52-658

XN798-XN902

serial	type	sqdn/unit	code	where&when seen	remarks
XN798 - XN803	Lightning F.2 (6 a/c)			Cancelled and not built	

The first production order for 20 Argosy C.1 aircraft built for RAF Transport Command by Sir W.G.Armstrong Whitworth Aircraft Ltd at Bitteswell with c/ns 6743 to 6762 resp. The block was ordered against two Contracts (i) KU/K/031 for seven aircraft (XN814-XN820) and (ii) KD/2K/01 for 13 (XN821, XN847-XN858). The first Argosy C.1 (XN814) f/f 4.3.61. Three aircraft were later modified to E.1 calibration aircraft.

serial	type	sqdn/unit	code	where&when seen	remarks
XN814	Argosy E.1				
XN815	Argosy C.1				
XN816	Argosy E.1				To 8489M
XN817	Argosy C.1				
XN818	Argosy C.1				
XN819	Argosy C.1				To 8205M
XN820	Argosy C.1				
XN821	Argosy C.1				
XN847	Argosy C.1				To 8220M ntu
XN848	Argosy C.1				To 8195M ntu
XN849	Argosy C.1				
XN850	Argosy C.1				
XN851	Argosy C.1				
XN852	Argosy C.1				
XN853	Argosy C.1				
XN854	Argosy C.1				
XN855	Argosy E.1				To 8556M
XN856	Argosy C.1				
XN857	Argosy C.1				
XN858	Argosy C.1				

The first contract placed with the Northrop Corporation for 40 Shelduck D.1 training target drones and built by the company's Ventura Division (previously the Radioplane Company facility) for the RN. They were the equivalent of the USN KD2R-5 (re-styled MQM-36A on 18.9.62) and delivered in 1959. Procurement continued with XR148.

serial	type	sqdn/unit	code	where&when seen	remarks
XN862	Shelduck D.1				
XN863	Shelduck D.1				
XN864	Shelduck D.1				
XN865	Shelduck D.1				
XN866	Shelduck D.1				
XN867	Shelduck D.1				
XN868	Shelduck D.1				
XN869	Shelduck D.1				
XN870	Shelduck D.1				
XN871	Shelduck D.1				
XN872	Shelduck D.1				
XN873	Shelduck D.1				
XN874	Shelduck D.1				
XN875	Shelduck D.1				
XN876	Shelduck D.1				
XN893	Shelduck D.1				
XN894	Shelduck D.1				
XN895	Shelduck D.1				
XN896	Shelduck D.1				
XN897	Shelduck D.1				
XN898	Shelduck D.1				
XN899	Shelduck D.1				
XN900	Shelduck D.1				
XN901	Shelduck D.1				
XN902	Shelduck D.1				

XN903-XN960

serial	type	sqdn/unit	code	where&when seen		remarks
XN903	Shelduck D.1					
XN904	Shelduck D.1					
XN905	Shelduck D.1					
XN906	Shelduck D.1					
XN907	Shelduck D.1					
XN908	Shelduck D.1					
XN909	Shelduck D.1					
XN910	Shelduck D.1					
XN911	Shelduck D.1					
XN912	Shelduck D.1					
XN913	Shelduck D.1					
XN914	Shelduck D.1					
XN915	Shelduck D.1					
XN916	Shelduck D.1					
XN917	Shelduck D.1					

The first true production order for Buccaneer shipboard strike aircraft for the RN was placed during September 1958 and accounted for 40 S.1 (to follow on from XK536) and 10 S.2 variants, all to be built by Blackburn Aircraft Ltd at Brough. The first production S.1 (XN922) first flewat Holme-on-Spalding Moor on 23.1.62 and production continued to XN973 by which time the company had been absorbed into the Hawker-Siddeley Group (during May 1963) and become known as Hawker Siddeley Aviation Ltd, Hawker-Blackburn Division. The first production S.2 (XN974) f/f 5.6.64. Following the adoption of the Buccaneer by the RAF and conversion of both RAF and RN aircraft to carry the Matra/Hawker Siddeley Dynamics Martel missile system, the undermentioned designation changes apply:- (NOTE: all RN S.2C/D's transferred to RAF in 11.78).

- S.2A Ex-RN S.2/S.2C's modified for RAF use (non-Martel equipped)
- S.2B New build and modified ex-RN aircraft for RAF use (Martel equipped)
- S.2C Updated S.2's for RN service (non-Martel equipped)
- S.2D Updated S.2's for RN service (Martel equipped)

serial	type	sqdn/unit	code	where&when seen		remarks
XN922	Buccaneer S.1					
XN923	Buccaneer S.1					Trials airframe A&AEE
XN924	Buccaneer S.1					To A2553
XN925	Buccaneer S.1					To A2602 To 8087M
XN926	Buccaneer S.1					
XN927	Buccaneer S.1					
XN928	Buccaneer S.1					To 8179M Pr Rhoose
XN929	Buccaneer S.1					To 8051M Nose Pr
XN930	Buccaneer S.1					To 8180M
XN931	Buccaneer S.1					
XN932	Buccaneer S.1					To A2552
XN933	Buccaneer S.1					
XN934	Buccaneer S.1					To A2600
XN935	Buccaneer S.1					
XN948	Buccaneer S.1					
XN949	Buccaneer S.1					
XN950	Buccaneer S.1					
XN951	Buccaneer S.1					
XN952	Buccaneer S.1					
XN953	Buccaneer S.1					To 8182M To A2655
XN954	Buccaneer S.1					To A2617
XN955	Buccaneer S.1					
XN956	Buccaneer S.1					To 8059M
XN957	Buccaneer S.1					Pr FAAM
XN958	Buccaneer S.1					
XN959	Buccaneer S.1					
XN960	Buccaneer S.1					

XN961-XP150

serial	type	sqdn/unit	code	where&when seen	remarks
XN961	Buccaneer S.1				
XN962	Buccaneer S.1				To 8183M Nose only
XN963	Buccaneer S.1				
XN964	Buccaneer S.1				To GI BAe Brough
XN965	Buccaneer S.1				To GI Farnborough
XN966	Buccaneer S.1				
XN967	Buccaneer S.1				To A2627 Pr Helston
XN968	Buccaneer S.1				
XN969	Buccaneer S.1				
XN970	Buccaneer S.1				
XN971	Buccaneer S.1				
XN972	Buccaneer S.1				To 8181M To Warton
XN973	Buccaneer S.1				
XN974	Buccaneer S.2A				
XN975	Buccaneer S.2A				
XN976	Buccaneer S.2B				
XN977	Buccaneer S.2A				
XN978	Buccaneer S.2B				
XN979	Buccaneer S.2A				
XN980	Buccaneer S.2				
XN981	Buccaneer S.2B				
XN982	Buccaneer S.2A				
XN983	Buccaneer S.2B				

The second production contract for 40 Wessex HAS.1 helicopters built by Westland Aircraft Ltd at Yeovil for the RN to follow on from XM931. XP103 f/f 20.1.62; and XP160 f/f 14.12.62. Subsequent conversions to HAS.3 configuration took place and the block was allotted c/ns WA.54 to WA.93 respectively.

serial	type	sqdn/unit	code	where&when seen	remarks
XP103	Wessex HAS.3				
XP104	Wessex HAS.3				
XP105	Wessex HAS.3				
XP106	Wessex HAS.1				
XP107	Wessex HAS.1				To A2527
XP108	Wessex HAS.1				
XP109	Wessex HAS.1				
XP110	Wessex HAS.3				
XP111	Wessex HAS.1				
XP112	Wessex HAS.1				
XP113	Wessex HAS.1				
XP114	Wessex HAS.1				
XP115	Wessex HAS.1				
XP116	Wessex HAS.3				To A2618
XP117	Wessex HAS.1				To A2681
XP118	Wessex HAS.3				
XP137	Wessex HAS.3				
XP138	Wessex HAS.3				
XP139	Wessex HAS.3				
XP140	Wessex HAS.3				
XP141	Wessex HAS.1				
XP142	Wessex HAS.3				
XP143	Wessex HAS.3				
XP144	Wessex HAS.1				
XP145	Wessex HAS.1				
XP146	Wessex HAS.1				
XP147	Wessex HAS.3				
XP148	Wessex HAS.1				
XP149	Wessex HAS.1				To A2669
XP150	Wessex HAS.3				

XP151-XP246

serial	type	sqdn/unit	code	where&when seen		remarks
XP151	Wessex HAS.1					To A2684
XP152	Wessex HAS.1					
XP153	Wessex HAS.3					
XP154	Wessex HAS.1					
XP155	Wessex HAS.1					To A2640
XP156	Wessex HAS.3					
XP157	Wessex HAS.1					To A2680
XP158	Wessex HAS.1					To A2688
XP159	Wessex HAS.1					TI Leatherhead
XP160	Wessex HAS.1					To A2650

Pre-production order for 8 P.531/2 Sprite helicopters built at Eastleigh by Saunders-Roe Ltd for AAC evaluation and trials. During the construction of this batch the company was absorbed by Westland Aircraft Ltd and at the same time the type became known as the Scout AH.1. C/ns are S2/8437, S2/5311, S2/8438, S2/8440, S2/8441, S2/8443, S2/8446 and S2/8447 respectively. XP165 f/f 29.8.60; XP192 f/f 23.2.62.

serial	type	sqdn/unit	code	where&when seen		remarks
XP165	Scout AH.1					Pr HAM Southend
XP166	Scout AH.1					Ex G-APVL
XP167	Scout AH.1					
XP188	Scout AH.1					
XP189	Scout AH.1					
XP190	Scout AH.1					To GI Arborfield
XP191	Scout AH.1					
XP192	Scout AH.1					

9 Gannet AEW.3's built to Spec AEW.154P by Westland Aircraft Ltd at Hayes against Contract KC/L/017/CB9(a). Allotted c/ns F9463-F9471 resp, dels between 10.61 & 12.62.

serial	type	sqdn/unit	code	where&when seen		remarks
XP197	Gannet AEW.3					
XP198	Gannet AEW.3					
XP199	Gannet AEW.3					
XP224	Gannet AEW.3					
XP225	Gannet AEW.3					
XP226	Gannet AEW.3					To A2667 Pr HMS Dryad
XP227	Gannet AEW.3					
XP228	Gannet AEW.3					
XP229	Gannet AEW.3					

The 4th production order for 33 Auster AOP.9 aircraft built at Rearsby by Beagle-Auster Aircraft Ltd for the AAC against Contract KC/N/047/CB5(c). Deliveries were made between November 1960 and November 1961. XP254 was diverted off contract and retained by the manufacturer for conversion to AOP.11 standard and was not issued to the AAC, being replaced on contract by XS238.

serial	type	sqdn/unit	code	where&when seen		remarks
XP232	Auster AOP.9					
XP233	Auster AOP.9					
XP234	Auster AOP.9					
XP235	Auster AOP.9					
XP236	Auster AOP.9					
XP237	Auster AOP.9					
XP238	Auster AOP.9					
XP239	Auster AOP.9					
XP240	Auster AOP.9					
XP241	Auster AOP.9					Pr Rableyheath
XP242	Auster AOP.9					
XP243	Auster AOP.9					
XP244	Auster AOP.9					To 7864M wears 7922M
XP245	Auster AOP.9					
XP246	Auster AOP.9					

XP247-XP349

serial	type	sqdn/unit	code	where&when seen		remarks
XP247	Auster AOP.9					
XP248	Auster AOP.9					To 7822M Pr Marlboro'
XP249	Auster AOP.9					
XP250	Auster AOP.9					To 7823M
XP251	Auster AOP.9					
XP252	Auster AOP.9					
XP253	Auster AOP.9					
XP254	Auster AOP.11					To G-ASCC
XP277	Auster AOP.9					
XP278	Auster AOP.9					
XP279	Auster AOP.9					To G-BWKK
XP280	Auster AOP.9					Pr Leicester
XP281	Auster AOP.9					Pr IWM Duxford
XP282	Auster AOP.9					To G-BGTC
XP283	Auster AOP.9					To 7859M
XP284	Auster AOP.9					
XP285	Auster AOP.9					Pr Oakey Australia
XP286	Auster AOP.9					To 8044M

The second order for Twin Pioneer CC.2 aircraft built for the RAF by Scottish Aviation Ltd at Prestwick accounted for three aircraft against Contract KC/K/030. XP293 (c/n 571) f/f 5.10.60; XP294 (c/n 572) f/f 22.3.61; and XP295 (c/n 577) f/f 28.11.60.

serial	type	sqdn/unit	code	where&when seen		remarks
XP293	Twin Pioneer CC.2					
XP294	Twin Pioneer CC.2					
XP295	Twin Pioneer CC.2					To G-31-16/G-AZHJ

The first production order for 52 Whirlwind HAR.10 helicopters built for the RAF by Westland Aircraft Ltd at Yeovil was against two Contracts:- KF/2N/037/CB25(a) for 12 helicopters (XP299-303/327-333) and KF/2N/042/CB25(a) for 40 (XP338-363/392-405). The entire block was allotted c/ns WA342 to WA393 respectively but, following the crash of XP392 (WA380) prior to delivery, XS412 was built as a replacement with the same c/n. XP299 f/f 28.3.61 and the batch was delivered between 7.61 and 11.62.

serial	type	sqdn/unit	code	where&when seen		remarks
XP299	Whirlwind HAR.10					
XP300	Whirlwind HAR.10					
XP301	Whirlwind HAR.10					
XP302	Whirlwind HAR.10					To 8443M
XP303	Whirlwind HAR.10					
XP327	Whirlwind HAR.10					
XP328	Whirlwind HAR.10					
XP329	Whirlwind HAR.10					
XP330	Whirlwind HAR.10					
XP331	Whirlwind HAR.10					To 8649M
XP332	Whirlwind HAR.10					
XP333	Whirlwind HAR.10					To 8650M
XP338	Whirlwind HAR.10					To 8647M
XP339	Whirlwind HAR.10					
XP340	Whirlwind HAR.10					
XP341	Whirlwind HAR.10					To 8340M
XP342	Whirlwind HAR.10					
XP343	Whirlwind HAR.10					
XP344	Whirlwind HAR.10					
XP345	Whirlwind HAR.10					
XP346	Whirlwind HAR.10					
XP347	Whirlwind HAR.10					
XP348	Whirlwind HAR.10					
XP349	Whirlwind HAR.10					

XP350-XP450

serial	type	sqdn/unit	code	where&when seen		remarks
XP350	Whirlwind HAR.10					
XP351	Whirlwind HAR.10					
XP352	Whirlwind HAR.10					
XP353	Whirlwind HAR.10					
XP354	Whirlwind HAR.10					
XP355	Whirlwind HAR.10					To 8463M To G-BEBC
XP356	Whirlwind HAR.10					
XP357	Whirlwind HAR.10					To 8499M
XP358	Whirlwind HAR.10					GI Bruggen
XP359	Whirlwind HAR.10					To 8447M
XP360	Whirlwind HAR.10					Pr Lasham
XP361	Whirlwind HAR.10					
XP362	Whirlwind HAR.10					
XP363	Whirlwind HAR.10					To 8228M
XP392	Whirlwind HAR.10					
XP393	Whirlwind HAR.10					
XP394	Whirlwind HAR.10					
XP395	Whirlwind HAR.10					
XP396	Whirlwind HAR.10					
XP397	Whirlwind HAR.10					
XP398	Whirlwind HAR.10					
XP399	Whirlwind HAR.10					
XP400	Whirlwind HAR.10					To 8444M
XP401	Whirlwind HAR.10					
XP402	Whirlwind HAR.10					
XP403	Whirlwind HAR.10					
XP404	Whirlwind HAR.10					
XP405	Whirlwind HAR.10					

The second production order for 20 Argosy C.1 aircraft was built for RAF Transport Command by Sir W.G.Armstrong Whitworth Aircraft Ltd (later Whitworth-Gloster Aircraft Ltd within the Hawker Siddeley Group) at Bitteswell. This order was placed against Contract KD/2K/011 and was allotted c/ns 6763-6782 resp. Batch delivered 1962-63 and later several aircraft were modified to E.1 and T.2 standard.

serial	type	sqdn/unit	code	where&when seen		remarks
XP408	Argosy C.1					
XP409	Argosy C.1					To 8221M
XP410	Argosy C.1					
XP411	Argosy C.1					To 8442M
XP412	Argosy C.1					To G-BDCV
XP413	Argosy E.1					
XP437	Argosy C.1					
XP438	Argosy C.1					
XP439	Argosy E.1					To 8558M
XP440	Argosy C.1					
XP441	Argosy C.1					
XP442	Argosy T.2					To 8454M
XP443	Argosy C.1					
XP444	Argosy C.1					To 8455M
XP445	Argosy C.1					
XP446	Argosy C.1					To 9Q-COE
XP447	Argosy T.2					To N1430Z
XP448	Argosy E.1					
XP449	Argosy E.1					
XP450	Argosy C.1					To RP-C-1192

The final order for 20 Type 38 Grasshopper TX.1 primary training gliders built by Slingsby Sailplanes Ltd at Kirkbymoorside was placed against Contract KF/2R/012 for

XP454-XP540

the Air Training Corps and School Combined Cadet Forces. The block was allotted the c/ns 1253 to 1272 respectively and was delivered during 1962-63.

serial	type	sqdn/unit	code	where&when seen	remarks
XP454	Grasshopper TX.1				
XP455	Grasshopper TX.1				
XP456	Grasshopper TX.1				
XP457	Grasshopper TX.1				
XP458	Grasshopper TX.1				
XP459	Grasshopper TX.1				
XP460	Grasshopper TX.1				
XP461	Grasshopper TX.1				
XP462	Grasshopper TX.1				
XP463	Grasshopper TX.1				
XP464	Grasshopper TX.1				
XP487	Grasshopper TX.1				
XP488	Grasshopper TX.1				
XP489	Grasshopper TX.1				
XP490	Grasshopper TX.1				
XP491	Grasshopper TX.1				
XP492	Grasshopper TX.1				
XP493	Grasshopper TX.1				
XP494	Grasshopper TX.1				
XP495	Grasshopper TX.1				

The first production order for 30 Gnat T.1 advanced training aircraft for the RAF was placed against Contract KC/2B/05 and built by Hawker Siddeley Aviation Ltd at Hamble and test flown from Dunsfold. The block was allocated c/ns FL515 to FL544 respectively. Deliveries took place between 6.11.62 (XP501) and 3.7.63 (XP542), although XP500 was retained by the manufacturers and not delivered until 28.2.64.

serial	type	sqdn/unit	code	where&when seen	remarks
XP500	Gnat T.1				To 8557M
XP501	Gnat T.1				
XP502	Gnat T.1				To 8576M
XP503	Gnat T.1				To 8568M
XP504	Gnat T.1				To 8618M
XP505	Gnat T.1				
XP506	Gnat T.1				
XP507	Gnat T.1				
XP508	Gnat T.1				
XP509	Gnat T.1				
XP510	Gnat T.1				
XP511	Gnat T.1				To 8619M
XP512	Gnat T.1				
XP513	Gnat T.1				
XP514	Gnat T.1				To 8635M
XP515	Gnat T.1				To 8614M
XP516	Gnat T.1				To 8580M
XP530	Gnat T.1				To 8606M
XP531	Gnat T.1				
XP532	Gnat T.1				To 8577M/8615M ntu
XP533	Gnat T.1				To 8632M
XP534	Gnat T.1				To 8620M
XP535	Gnat T.1				To A2679
XP536	Gnat T.1				
XP537	Gnat T.1				
XP538	Gnat T.1				To 8607M
XP539	Gnat T.1				
XP540	Gnat T.1				To 8608M

XP541-XP621

serial	type	sqdn/unit	code	where&when seen		remarks
XP541	Gnat T.1					To 8616M
XP542	Gnat T.1					To 8575M

The first production order for Jet Provost T.4 basic training aircraft for the RAF was placed against Contract KC/E/041 and accounted for 100 aircraft. Deliveries from Luton commenced during November 1961 by which time Hunting Aircraft Ltd had been absorbed into the British Aircraft Corporation group. Dels between 10.61 and 12.62.

serial	type	sqdn/unit	code	where&when seen		remarks
XP547	Jet Provost T.4					
XP548	Jet Provost T.4					To 8404M ntu
XP549	Jet Provost T.4					
XP550	Jet Provost T.4					
XP551	Jet Provost T.4					
XP552	Jet Provost T.4					
XP553	Jet Provost T.4					
XP554	Jet Provost T.4					
XP555	Jet Provost T.4					
XP556	Jet Provost T.4					
XP557	Jet Provost T.4					To 8494M
XP558	Jet Provost T.4					To A2628 To 8627M
XP559	Jet Provost T.4					
XP560	Jet Provost T.4					
XP561	Jet Provost T.4					
XP562	Jet Provost T.4					
XP563	Jet Provost T.4					
XP564	Jet Provost T.4					
XP565	Jet Provost T.4					
XP566	Jet Provost T.4					
XP567	Jet Provost T.4					To 8510M
XP568	Jet Provost T.4					
XP569	Jet Provost T.4					
XP570	Jet Provost T.4					
XP571	Jet Provost T.4					
XP572	Jet Provost T.4					
XP573	Jet Provost T.4					To 8336M wears 8236M
XP574	Jet Provost T.4					
XP575	Jet Provost T.4					
XP576	Jet Provost T.4					
XP577	Jet Provost T.4					
XP578	Jet Provost T.4					
XP579	Jet Provost T.4					
XP580	Jet Provost T.4					
XP581	Jet Provost T.4					
XP582	Jet Provost T.4					
XP583	Jet Provost T.4					To 8400M
XP584	Jet Provost T.4					
XP585	Jet Provost T.4					To 8407M
XP586	Jet Provost T.4					
XP587	Jet Provost T.4					
XP588	Jet Provost T.4					
XP589	Jet Provost T.4					
XP614	Jet Provost T.4					
XP615	Jet Provost T.4					
XP616	Jet Provost T.4					
XP617	Jet Provost T.4					
XP618	Jet Provost T.4					
XP619	Jet Provost T.4					
XP620	Jet Provost T.4					
XP621	Jet Provost T.4					

XP622-XP694

serial	type	sqdn/unit	code	where&when seen		remarks
XP622	Jet Provost T.4					
XP623	Jet Provost T.4					
XP624	Jet Provost T.4					
XP625	Jet Provost T.4					
XP626	Jet Provost T.4					
XP627	Jet Provost T.4					
XP628	Jet Provost T.4					
XP629	Jet Provost T.4					
XP630	Jet Provost T.4					
XP631	Jet Provost T.4					
XP632	Jet Provost T.4					
XP633	Jet Provost T.4					
XP634	Jet Provost T.4					
XP635	Jet Provost T.4					
XP636	Jet Provost T.4					
XP637	Jet Provost T.4					
XP638	Jet Provost T.4					
XP639	Jet Provost T.4					
XP640	Jet Provost T.4					To 8501M
XP641	Jet Provost T.4					
XP642	Jet Provost T.4					
XP661	Jet Provost T.4					To 7819M To 8594M
XP662	Jet Provost T.4					
XP663	Jet Provost T.4					
XP664	Jet Provost T.4					
XP665	Jet Provost T.4					
XP666	Jet Provost T.4					To G-27-92/S Yemen 105
XP667	Jet Provost T.4					
XP668	Jet Provost T.4					
XP669	Jet Provost T.4					
XP670	Jet Provost T.4					
XP671	Jet Provost T.4					
XP672	Jet Provost T.4					To 8458M
XP673	Jet Provost T.4					
XP674	Jet Provost T.4					
XP675	Jet Provost T.4					
XP676	Jet Provost T.4					
XP677	Jet Provost T.4					To 8587M (Nose)
XP678	Jet Provost T.4					
XP679	Jet Provost T.4					
XP680	Jet Provost T.4					To 8460M
XP681	Jet Provost T.4					
XP682	Jet Provost T.4					
XP683	Jet Provost T.4					
XP684	Jet Provost T.4					To G-27-93/S Yemen 106
XP685	Jet Provost T.4					
XP686	Jet Provost T.4					To 8401M ntu/ 8502M
XP687	Jet Provost T.4					
XP688	Jet Provost T.4					

The first contract for Lightning F.3 fighter aircraft for the RAF accounted for 47 aircraft following the conversion of numerous P.1B development aircraft (XG310 etc). All were built by the British Aircraft Corporation (Preston Division) and the first production F.3 (XP693) f/f 16.6.62 with deliveries commencing in January 1964. The block was allotted c/ns 95116-95117/95119-95120/95151-95197, although there has been some confusion over certain aircraft. XP693 & XP697 later converted to F.6 standard.

serial	type	sqdn/unit	code	where&when seen		remarks
XP693	Lightning F.6					
XP694	Lightning F.3					

XP695-XP773

serial	type	sqdn/unit	code	where&when seen		remarks
XP695	Lightning F.3					
XP696	Lightning F.3					
XP697	Lightning F.6					
XP698	Lightning F.3					
XP699	Lightning F.3					
XP700	Lightning F.3					
XP701	Lightning F.3					
XP702	Lightning F.3					
XP703	Lightning F.3					
XP704	Lightning F.3					
XP705	Lightning F.3					
XP706	Lightning F.3					
XP707	Lightning F.3					
XP708	Lightning F.3					
XP735	Lightning F.3					
XP736	Lightning F.3					
XP737	Lightning F.3					
XP738	Lightning F.3					
XP739	Lightning F.3					
XP740	Lightning F.3					
XP741	Lightning F.3					
XP742	Lightning F.3					
XP743	Lightning F.3					
XP744	Lightning F.3					
XP745	Lightning F.3					To 8453M Pr Boulmer
XP746	Lightning F.3					
XP747	Lightning F.3					
XP748	Lightning F.3					To 8446M Pr Binbrook
XP749	Lightning F.3					
XP750	Lightning F.3					
XP751	Lightning F.3					
XP752	Lightning F.3					To 8166M
XP753	Lightning F.3					
XP754	Lightning F.3					
XP755	Lightning F.3					
XP756	Lightning F.3					
XP757	Lightning F.3					
XP758	Lightning F.3					
XP759	Lightning F.3					
XP760	Lightning F.3					
XP761	Lightning F.3					To 8438M
XP762	Lightning F.3					
XP763	Lightning F.3					
XP764	Lightning F.3					
XP765	Lightning F.3					

Following the evaluation of XN142 (qv), a contract was placed with de Havilland Aircraft of Canada Ltd for 36 Beaver AL.1 utility aircraft for the Army Air Corps. All were built at Downsview, Toronto and test-flown prior to being crated and shipped to Hawarden (Chester) via Liverpool docks for re-assembly. Deliveries commenced to the AAC during September 1961 and were completed with XP827 in February 1962. The block was allotted c/ns 1421/1440-1446/1448-1451/1453-1455/1457-1458/1463-1464/1466/1468-1469/1473-1474/1476/1478-1479/1482-1484/1486/1488-1489/1491/1493 and 1495 resp.

serial	type	sqdn/unit	code	where&when seen		remarks
XP769	Beaver AL.1					
XP770	Beaver AL.1					To GI
XP771	Beaver AL.1					
XP772	Beaver AL.1					
XP773	Beaver AL.1					

XP774-XP852

serial	type	sqdn/unit	code	where&when seen		remarks
XP774	Beaver AL.1					
XP775	Beaver AL.1					
XP776	Beaver AL.1					
XP777	Beaver AL.1					
XP778	Beaver AL.1					
XP779	Beaver AL.1					
XP780	Beaver AL.1					
XP804	Beaver AL.1					
XP805	Beaver AL.1					
XP806	Beaver AL.1					To GI Arborfield
XP807	Beaver AL.1					
XP808	Beaver AL.1					
XP809	Beaver AL.1					
XP810	Beaver AL.1					
XP811	Beaver AL.1					
XP812	Beaver AL.1					To 7735M/XP000
XP813	Beaver AL.1					
XP814	Beaver AL.1					
XP815	Beaver AL.1					
XP816	Beaver AL.1					
XP817	Beaver AL.1					
XP818	Beaver AL.1					
XP819	Beaver AL.1					
XP820	Beaver AL.1					
XP821	Beaver AL.1					
XP822	Beaver AL.1					
XP823	Beaver AL.1					
XP824	Beaver AL.1					
XP825	Beaver AL.1					
XP826	Beaver AL.1					
XP827	Beaver AL.1					

Two prototype P.1127 single-seat V/STOL strike fighters designed by Hawker Aircraft Ltd but built under the aegis of Hawker Siddeley Aviation Ltd at Kingston and developed (via the Kestrel) into the Harrier series. The first prototype (XP831) f/f at Dunsfold 21.10.60 (tethered flight) and on 19.11.60 (free hover). The second prototype (XP836) f/f 7.7.61 (tethered flight) and on 12.9.61 (free hover). A development batch of P.1127 aircraft follows with XP972.

serial	type	sqdn/unit	code	where&when seen		remarks
XP831	Hawker P.1127					To 8406M Pr Hendon
XP836	Hawker P.1127					

One low-speed slender delta development prototype built to Spec ER.197D by Handley-Page Ltd at Radlett under the designation HP.115. XP841 f/f 17.8.61 at RAE Bedford and was engaged on trials, particularly in connection with the Concorde project.

serial	type	sqdn/unit	code	where&when seen		remarks
XP841	HP.115					Pr Yeovilton

First production order for 40 Scout AH.1 helicopters built for the Army Air Corps by Westland Aircraft Ltd at the original Fairey Aviation facility at Hayes against Contract KF/2Q/06/CB25(a). Flight testing was conducted at White Waltham and the block was allotted c/ns F9472-F9511 respectively. XP846 f/f 20.10.61.

serial	type	sqdn/unit	code	where&when seen		remarks
XP846	Scout AH.1					
XP847	Scout AH.1					To GI Middle Wallop
XP848	Scout AH.1					
XP849	Scout AH.1					
XP850	Scout AH.1					
XP851	Scout AH.1					
XP852	Scout AH.1					

XP853-XP925

serial	type	sqdn/unit	code	where&when seen		remarks
XP853	Scout AH.1					
XP854	Scout AH.1					To 7898M To TAD043
XP855	Scout AH.1					
XP856	Scout AH.1					To GI Middle Wallop
XP857	Scout AH.1					
XP883	Scout AH.1					
XP884	Scout AH.1					
XP885	Scout AH.1					
XP886	Scout AH.1					
XP887	Scout AH.1					
XP888	Scout AH.1					
XP889	Scout AH.1					
XP890	Scout AH.1					
XP891	Scout AH.1					
XP892	Scout AH.1					
XP893	Scout AH.1					
XP894	Scout AH.1					
XP895	Scout AH.1					
XP896	Scout AH.1					
XP897	Scout AH.1					
XP898	Scout AH.1					
XP899	Scout AH.1					
XP900	Scout AH.1					
XP901	Scout AH.1					
XP902	Scout AH.1					
XP903	Scout AH.1					
XP904	Scout AH.1					
XP905	Scout AH.1					
XP906	Scout AH.1					
XP907	Scout AH.1					
XP908	Scout AH.1					
XP909	Scout AH.1					To GI Middle Wallop
XP910	Scout AH.1					

The sole DH.106 Comet 3 (c/n 06100) was built by de Havilland Aircraft Co Ltd at Hatfield and f/f as G-ANLO on 19.7.54. It was engaged on development trials for the Comet 4 for many years and, following the go-ahead for the medium-range 4B version, was converted to Srs 3B standard during 1958. Transferred to military marks in 1.61, it was delivered to the Blind Landing Experimental Unit at RAE Bedford on 20.6.61. At the end of its flying hours it was used for foam arrester trials until it was transferred to Woodford 22.8.73 for use in the Nimrod development programme.

serial	type	sqdn/unit	code	where&when seen		remarks
XP915	Comet 3B					Ex G-ANLO

The third production order for Sea Vixen carrier-borne fighters originally accounted for 15 FAW.1's but only XP918 was built to that standard, the remainder emerging as FAW.2's (XP919 f/f 8.3.63). All aircraft in this contract were built at Chester by Hawker Siddeley Aviation Ltd and the block was allotted c/ns 10119 (XP918) and 10120 to 10133 (XP919-925/953-959). XP918 converted to FAW.2 standard at Chester (C). Flight Refuelling Ltd will be reworking some to D.3 drones over the next few years.

serial	type	sqdn/unit	code	where&when seen		remarks
XP918	Sea Vixen FAW.2 (C)					
XP919	Sea Vixen FAW.2					To 8163M Pr Thorpe W Pk
XP920	Sea Vixen FAW.2					
XP921	Sea Vixen FAW.2					To 8226M
XP922	Sea Vixen FAW.2					
XP923	Sea Vixen FAW.2					
XP924	Sea Vixen D.3					
XP925	Sea Vixen FAW.2					

XP953-XR149

serial	type	sqdn/unit	code	where&when seen		remarks
XP953	Sea Vixen FAW.2					
XP954	Sea Vixen FAW.2					
XP955	Sea Vixen FAW.2					
XP956	Sea Vixen FAW.2					
XP957	Sea Vixen FAW.2					
XP958	Sea Vixen FAW.2					
XP959	Sea Vixen FAW.2					

Two Alouette AH.2 helicopters built by Sud Aviation with c/ns 1499 and 1500 respectively and delivered to the AAC at Middle Wallop during December 1960, forming part of an evaluation order placed just prior to their arrival. This order for five Alouettes also included XR232 and two earlier helicopters (XN132/XN133) which had been on loan since 1958.

serial	type	sqdn/unit	code	where&when seen		remarks
XP966	Alouette AH.2					
XP967	Alouette AH.2					

Four development prototype P.1127 V/STOL strike fighters built by Hawker Siddeley Aviation Ltd at Kingston to follow the two initial prototypes XP831 and XP836. The first aircraft (XP972) f/f at Dunsfold on 5.5.62 with a Bristol Siddeley Pegasus 2 engine; XP976 f/f 12.7.62 and was used for flight-testing the Pegasus 4; XP980 was employed on systems/performance trials and f/f 24.1.63; and XP984 f/f 13.2.64 and emerged with a Pegasus 5 engine and was built to Hawker Siddeley Kestrel standard.

serial	type	sqdn/unit	code	where&when seen		remarks
XP972	Hawker P.1127					
XP976	Hawker P.1127					GI Wittering
XP980	Hawker P.1127					
XP984	Hawker P.1127					To A2658

The third and final production batch of 16 Argosy C.1 aircraft was built at Bitteswell by the Avro Whitworth Division of Hawker Siddeley Aviation (as Whitworth Gloster Aircraft Ltd had been renamed during 1963). The order was placed against Contract KU/K/01 and followed on from XP450. The block was allotted the c/ns 6783-6798 and was delivered in 1963-64. Subsequent conversions to E.1 and T.2 standard.

serial	type	sqdn/unit	code	where&when seen		remarks
XR105	Argosy C.1					
XR106	Argosy C.1					
XR107	Argosy C.1					To 8441M
XR108	Argosy C.1					
XR109	Argosy C.1					
XR133	Argosy C.1					
XR134	Argosy C.1					
XR135	Argosy C.1					
XR136	Argosy T.2					To 9Q-COA
XR137	Argosy E.1					
XR138	Argosy C.1					
XR139	Argosy C.1					
XR140	Argosy E.1					To 8579M
XR141	Argosy C.1					
XR142	Argosy C.1					
XR143	Argosy E.1					To G-BFVT

The 2nd contract placed with the Northrop Corporation for 40 Shelduck D.1 training target drones. All were built at the company's Ventura Division (previously known as the Radioplane Company facility) for the RN, being the equivalent of the US Navy KD2R-5 which was re-styled MQM-36A on 18.9.62. This batch delivered during 1960.

serial	type	sqdn/unit	code	where&when seen		remarks
XR148	Shelduck D.1					
XR149	Shelduck D.1					

XR150-XR223

serial	type	sqdn/unit	code	where&when seen		remarks
XR150	Shelduck D.1					
XR151	Shelduck D.1					
XR152	Shelduck D.1					
XR153	Shelduck D.1					
XR154	Shelduck D.1					
XR155	Shelduck D.1					
XR156	Shelduck D.1					
XR157	Shelduck D.1					
XR158	Shelduck D.1					
XR159	Shelduck D.1					
XR160	Shelduck D.1					
XR161	Shelduck D.1					
XR162	Shelduck D.1					
XR185	Shelduck D.1					
XR186	Shelduck D.1					
XR187	Shelduck D.1					
XR188	Shelduck D.1					
XR189	Shelduck D.1					
XR190	Shelduck D.1					
XR191	Shelduck D.1					
XR192	Shelduck D.1					
XR193	Shelduck D.1					
XR194	Shelduck D.1					
XR195	Shelduck D.1					
XR196	Shelduck D.1					
XR197	Shelduck D.1					
XR198	Shelduck D.1					
XR199	Shelduck D.1					
XR200	Shelduck D.1					
XR201	Shelduck D.1					
XR202	Shelduck D.1					
XR203	Shelduck D.1					
XR204	Shelduck D.1					
XR205	Shelduck D.1					
XR206	Shelduck D.1					
XR207	Shelduck D.1					
XR208	Shelduck D.1					
XR209	Shelduck D.1					

Four Beaver AL.1 utility aircraft ordered on behalf of the Air Force of the Sultan of Oman and built by de Havilland Aircraft of Canada Ltd at Downsview, Toronto. All were test-flown prior to being crated and shipped to the UK where they were taken to Hawarden for re-assembly, as follows:- XR213 c/n 1447 f/f 3.3.61; XR214 c/n 1460 f/f 11.5.61; XR215 c/n 1471 f/f 17.7.61; and XR216 c/n 1481 f/f 8.9.61.

serial	type	sqdn/unit	code	where&when seen		remarks
XR213	Beaver AL.1					Ex G-5-11 To SOAF
XR214	Beaver AL.1					To SOAF
XR215	Beaver AL.1					To SOAF
XR216	Beaver AL.1					To SOAF

Nine BAC TSR-2 Type 571 prototypes ordered on 6.10.60 under Contract KD/2L/02/CB42(a) to be built by BAC (Weybridge Division) to Spec RB.192. XR219 f/f at Boscombe Down on 27.9.64 and XR220 was completed but not flown. Production stopped following the TSR-2 cancellation on 6.4.65. Most of the almost complete airframes were scrapped.

serial	type	sqdn/unit	code	where&when seen		remarks
XR219	BAC TSR-2					
XR220	BAC TSR-2					To 7933M Pr Cosford
XR221	BAC TSR-2					
XR222	BAC TSR-2					Pr IWM Duxford
XR223	BAC TSR-2					

XR224-XR310

serial	type	sqdn/unit	code	where&when seen		remarks
XR224	BAC TSR-2					
XR225	BAC TSR-2					
XR226	BAC TSR-2					
XR227	BAC TSR-2					

The final Alouette AH.2 of an evaluational batch of five helicopters built by Sud Aviation for the Army Air Corps. XR232 (c/n 1503) was delivered to Middle Wallop on 15.12.60 as F-WEIP. An order followed the successful trials and these helicopters were allocated serials commencing XR376 (qv).

serial	type	sqdn/unit	code	where&when seen		remarks
XR232	Alouette AH.2					Ex F-WEIP

The final order for 16 Auster AOP.9 aircraft built at Rearsby by Beagle-Auster Aircraft Ltd for the AAC against Contract KC/N/058/CB5(c). Deliveries were made from November 1961 to April 1962.

serial	type	sqdn/unit	code	where&when seen		remarks
XR236	Auster AOP.9					
XR237	Auster AOP.9					
XR238	Auster AOP.9					
XR239	Auster AOP.9					
XR240	Auster AOP.9					To G-BDFH
XR241	Auster AOP.9					To G-AXRR Pr O Warden
XR242	Auster AOP.9					
XR243	Auster AOP.9					To 8057M Pr St Athan
XR244	Auster AOP.9					
XR245	Auster AOP.9					
XR246	Auster AOP.9					To 7862M To G-AZBU
XR267	Auster AOP.9					Pr Innsworth
XR268	Auster AOP.9					
XR269	Auster AOP.9					To G-BDXY
XR270	Auster AOP.9					
XR271	Auster AOP.9					Pr RAM Woolwich

The third contract placed with the Northrop Corporation for 44 training target drones for RN and Army issue. In British use all are referred to as Shelduck D.1 drones although from observation it is possible that the blocks XR290-315/331-336 are in reality Falconer D.1 drones and based upon the Northrop AN/USD-1 drone which was restyled MQM-57A on 18.9.62. Procurement continued with XR404.

serial	type	sqdn/unit	code	where&when seen		remarks
XR290	Shelduck D.1					
XR291	Shelduck D.1					
XR292	Shelduck D.1					
XR293	Shelduck D.1					
XR294	Shelduck D.1					
XR295	Shelduck D.1					
XR296	Shelduck D.1					
XR297	Shelduck D.1					
XR298	Shelduck D.1					
XR299	Shelduck D.1					
XR300	Shelduck D.1					
XR301	Shelduck D.1					
XR302	Shelduck D.1					
XR303	Shelduck D.1					
XR304	Shelduck D.1					
XR305	Shelduck D.1					
XR306	Shelduck D.1					
XR307	Shelduck D.1					
XR308	Shelduck D.1					
XR309	Shelduck D.1					
XR310	Shelduck D.1					

XR311-XR385

serial	type	sqdn/unit	code	where&when seen		remarks
XR311	Shelduck D.1					
XR312	Shelduck D.1					
XR313	Shelduck D.1					
XR314	Shelduck D.1					
XR315	Shelduck D.1					
XR331	Shelduck D.1					
XR332	Shelduck D.1					
XR333	Shelduck D.1					
XR334	Shelduck D.1					
XR335	Shelduck D.1					
XR336	Shelduck D.1					
XR345	Shelduck D.1					
XR346	Shelduck D.1					
XR347	Shelduck D.1					
XR348	Shelduck D.1					
XR349	Shelduck D.1					
XR350	Shelduck D.1					
XR351	Shelduck D.1					
XR352	Shelduck D.1					
XR353	Shelduck D.1					
XR354	Shelduck D.1					
XR355	Shelduck D.1					
XR356	Shelduck D.1					

The sole order for 10 Belfast C.1 long-range strategic freighter aircraft was contracted to Short Bros & Harland Ltd at Belfast. XR362 f/f 5.1.64 (later G-ASKE) and all were delivered to 53 Sqdn at Brize Norton starting in 1.66. Allotted c/ns were SH1816 to SH1825 and Transport Command allotted the aircraft the following names:- XR362 (Samson); XR363 (Goliath); XR364 (Pallus); XR365 (Hector); XR366 (Atlas); XR367 (Heracles); XR368 (Theseus); XR369 (Spartacus); XR370 (Ajax); XR371 (Enceladus).

serial	type	sqdn/unit	code	where&when seen		remarks
XR362	Belfast C.1					Ex G-ASKE To G-BEPE
XR363	Belfast C.1					
XR364	Belfast C.1					
XR365	Belfast C.1					
XR366	Belfast C.1					
XR367	Belfast C.1					To G-BFYU
XR368	Belfast C.1					To G-BEPS/G
XR369	Belfast C.1					To G-BEPL
XR370	Belfast C.1					
XR371	Belfast C.1					Pr Cosford

The second order for 12 Alouette AH.2 helicopters and placed with Sud Aviation during January 1961. First deliveries to the Army Air Corps at Middle Wallop were made by XR376 & XR377 on 24.4.61 although these and probably all the others within the block were initially delivered with XJ-prefixed serials in error. All were allotted c/ns 1558/1567/1582/1583/1596/1606/1607/1621/1644/1645/1663 and 1664 respectively, and the final delivery was made to Middle Wallop by XR387 during December 1961.

serial	type	sqdn/unit	code	where&when seen		remarks
XR376	Alouette AH.2					Ex XJ376
XR377	Alouette AH.2					Ex XJ377
XR378	Alouette AH.2					Ex F-WIEM Ex XJ378
XR379	Alouette AH.2					Ex F-WIEN
XR380	Alouette AH.2					Ex XJ380
XR381	Alouette AH.2					
XR382	Alouette AH.2					
XR383	Alouette AH.2					
XR384	Alouette AH.2					Ex XJ384
XR385	Alouette AH.2					Ex XJ385

XR386-XR433

serial	type	sqdn/unit	code	where&when seen		remarks
XR386	Alouette AH.2					
XR387	Alouette AH.2					

One de Havilland DH.114 Heron Srs 4 built at Hawarden, Chester for the RAF Queen's Flight under Contract KU/J/01 and handed over at Benson on 25.6.61. During June 1970 it was issued to 60 Sqdn (after having served with the RN in 1969/70) with whom it remained until December 1971 when it was sold to Saunders Aircraft Co of Canada for conversion to ST-27 configuration. Its original DH c/n 14141 was amended to 27-007.

serial	type	sqdn/unit	code	where&when seen		remarks
XR391	Heron C.4					To CF-CNT

Five de Havilland DH.106 Comet C.4 transport aircraft built at Hawarden, Chester for RAF Transport Command against Contract KD/G/054 as follows:- XR395 c/n 06467 f/f 15.11.61; XR396 c/n 06468 f/f 28.12.61; XR397 c/n 06469 f/f 18.1.62; XR398 c/n 06470 f/f 13.2.62; and XR399 c/n 06471 f/f 20.3.62. All were used exclusively by 216 Squadron until September 1975 when the fleet was sold to Dan Air Services Ltd.

serial	type	sqdn/unit	code	where&when seen		remarks
XR395	Comet C.4					To G-BDIT
XR396	Comet C.4					To G-BDIU
XR397	Comet C.4					To G-BDIV
XR398	Comet C.4					To G-BDIW
XR399	Comet C.4					To G-BDIX

25 Radioplane OQ-19 (re-styled MQM-33 18.9.62) training target drones built by the Ventura Division of the Northrop Corporation for the British Army and being a direct equivalent of the US Army variant. In British service the OQ-19 was known as the Shelduck D.1. Procurement continued with XR447.

serial	type	sqdn/unit	code	where&when seen		remarks
XR404	Shelduck D.1					
XR405	Shelduck D.1					
XR406	Shelduck D.1					
XR407	Shelduck D.1					
XR408	Shelduck D.1					
XR409	Shelduck D.1					
XR410	Shelduck D.1					
XR411	Shelduck D.1					
XR412	Shelduck D.1					
XR413	Shelduck D.1					
XR414	Shelduck D.1					
XR415	Shelduck D.1					
XR416	Shelduck D.1					
XR417	Shelduck D.1					
XR418	Shelduck D.1					
XR419	Shelduck D.1					
XR420	Shelduck D.1					
XR421	Shelduck D.1					
XR422	Shelduck D.1					
XR423	Shelduck D.1					
XR424	Shelduck D.1					
XR425	Shelduck D.1					
XR426	Shelduck D.1					
XR427	Shelduck D.1					
XR428	Shelduck D.1					

Third, and last production batch of 3 Gannet AEW.3's built to Spec AEW.154P for the RN by Westland Aircraft Ltd at Hayes against Contract KC/L/037/CB9(a). They were allotted c/ns F9514-F9516 respectively. XR433 was delivered to the RN on 6.6.63.

serial	type	sqdn/unit	code	where&when seen		remarks
XR431	Gannet AEW.3					
XR432	Gannet AEW.3					
XR433	Gannet AEW.3					

XR436-XR493

serial	type	sqdn/unit	code	where&when seen		remarks

One P.531/2 helicopter built by Saunders-Roe Ltd at Eastleigh originally for evaluation by the Indian Government. It was allocated the c/n S2/8444 and first flew at White Waltham 2.62. As a result of diminishing Indian interest, it was diverted to the Army Air Corps. Saunders-Roe by this time had become part of Westland A/c Ltd.

serial	type	sqdn/unit	code	where&when seen		remarks
XR436	Scout AH.1					

Five second-hand de Havilland DH.114 Heron Srs 2B aircraft were purchased during March 1961 for use by the RN in the communications role. All were originally built by de Havilland at Hawarden, Chester as follows:- XR441 c/n 14101 ex- G-AORG Airlines (Jersey) Ltd; XR442 c/n 14102 ex- G-AORH Airlines (Jersey) Ltd; XR443 c/n 14072 ex- G-ARKU Overseas Aviation Ltd/VR-NAQ West African Airways Corp; XR444 c/n 14091 ex- G-ARKV Overseas Aviation Ltd/VR-NCE West African Airways Corp; XR445 c/n 14092 ex- G-ARKW Overseas Aviation Ltd/VR-NCF West African Airways Corp.

serial	type	sqdn/unit	code	where&when seen		remarks
XR441	Sea Heron C.1					Ex G-AORG
XR442	Sea Heron C.1					Ex G-AORH
XR443	Sea Heron C.1					Ex G-ARKU
XR444	Sea Heron C.1					Ex G-ARKV GI M.Mowbray
XR445	Sea Heron C.1					Ex G-ARKW

Four Shelduck D.1 training target drones built by the Ventura Division of the Northrop Corporation for the Royal Navy, being a direct equivalent of the US Navy KD2R-5 (re-styled MQM-36A on 18.9.62). Procurement continued with XR818.

serial	type	sqdn/unit	code	where&when seen		remarks
XR447	Shelduck D.1					
XR448	Shelduck D.1					
XR449	Shelduck D.1					
XR450	Shelduck D.1					

The second and final production order for 15 Whirlwind HAR.10 helicopters and two HCC.12 variants for the RAF and Queen's Flight resp, all built against Contract KK/K/04/CB25(a) by Westland Aircraft Ltd at Yeovil. The block was allotted c/ns WA403 to WA419 resp. XR453 was delivered on 29.11.62; XR487 delivered 7.5.64. XR486 eventually joined 32 Sqdn at Northolt on communications duties.

serial	type	sqdn/unit	code	where&when seen		remarks
XR453	Whirlwind HAR.10					
XR454	Whirlwind HAR.10					
XR455	Whirlwind HAR.10					To 8219M
XR456	Whirlwind HAR.10					
XR457	Whirlwind HAR.10					To 8644M
XR458	Whirlwind HAR.10					
XR477	Whirlwind HAR.10					
XR478	Whirlwind HAR.10					GI Winterbourne Gunner
XR479	Whirlwind HAR.10					GI Farnborough
XR480	Whirlwind HAR.10					
XR481	Whirlwind HAR.10					
XR482	Whirlwind HAR.10					GI Winterbourne Gunner
XR483	Whirlwind HAR.10					
XR484	Whirlwind HAR.10					
XR485	Whirlwind HAR.10					
XR486	Whirlwind HCC.12					
XR487	Whirlwind HCC.12					

One Saunders-Roe P.531/2 helicopter originally built at Eastleigh in 1959 and registered as G-APVM with the c/n S2/5312. Subsequently it was re-worked at Hayes during 1960 to become the true forerunner to the Westland Scout. It was allocated XR493 for some Army Air Corps trials and subsequently remained on AAC charge.

serial	type	sqdn/unit	code	where&when seen		remarks
XR493	Scout AH.1					Ex G-APVM To 8040M

XR497-XR572

serial	type	sqdn/unit	code	where&when seen	remarks

The first production order for 30 Wessex HC.2 helicopters built by Westland Aircraft Ltd at Yeovil for the RAF. Deliveries were made between 28.2.63 and 31.12.64. The prototype Wessex HC.2 was allocated the serial XR588 (qv). The block was allotted c/ns WA122 to WA151 respectively and was built against Contract KF/N/019/CB25(b).

serial	type	sqdn/unit	code	where&when seen	remarks
XR497	Wessex HC.2				
XR498	Wessex HC.2				
XR499	Wessex HC.2				
XR500	Wessex HC.2				
XR501	Wessex HC.2				
XR502	Wessex HC.2				
XR503	Wessex HC.2				
XR504	Wessex HC.2				
XR505	Wessex HC.2				
XR506	Wessex HC.2				
XR507	Wessex HC.2				
XR508	Wessex HC.2				
XR509	Wessex HC.2				
XR510	Wessex HC.2				
XR511	Wessex HC.2				
XR515	Wessex HC.2				
XR516	Wessex HC.2				
XR517	Wessex HC.2				
XR518	Wessex HC.2				
XR519	Wessex HC.2				
XR520	Wessex HC.2				
XR521	Wessex HC.2				
XR522	Wessex HC.2				
XR523	Wessex HC.2				
XR524	Wessex HC.2				
XR525	Wessex HC.2				
XR526	Wessex HC.2				To 8147M
XR527	Wessex HC.2				GI Sherborne, Dorset
XR528	Wessex HC.2				
XR529	Wessex HC.2				

The second order for 20 Gnat T.1 advanced trainers for the RAF was built by Hawker Siddeley Aviation Ltd at Hamble against Contract KC/2B/05 with XP500 et seq. Initial flights took place at Dunsfold; XR534 f/f 24.5.63. Allotted c/ns FL545-FL564 resp.

serial	type	sqdn/unit	code	where&when seen	remarks
XR534	Gnat T.1				To 8578M Pr Valley
XR535	Gnat T.1				To 8569M
XR536	Gnat T.1				
XR537	Gnat T.1				To 8642M
XR538	Gnat T.1				To 8621M
XR539	Gnat T.1				
XR540	Gnat T.1				To 8636M
XR541	Gnat T.1				To 8602M
XR542	Gnat T.1				
XR543	Gnat T.1				
XR544	Gnat T.1				
XR545	Gnat T.1				
XR567	Gnat T.1				
XR568	Gnat T.1				To 7874M
XR569	Gnat T.1				To 8560M
XR570	Gnat T.1				
XR571	Gnat T.1				To 8493M Pr Kemble
XR572	Gnat T.1				To A2676

XR573-XR655

serial	type	sqdn/unit	code	where&when seen		remarks
XR573	Gnat T.1					
XR574	Gnat T.1					To 8631M

The first true prototype Wessex HC.2 helicopter (to follow the converted XM299) was built by Westland Aircraft Ltd at Yeovil and f/f 5.10.62. It was allotted c/n WA121 and preceded production helicopters commencing at XR497 et seq.

serial	type	sqdn/unit	code	where&when seen		remarks
XR588	Wessex HC.2					

One Type 171 Sycamore HR.51 helicopter built by the Bristol Aeroplane Co Ltd originally as a Mk 4 G-AMWI. It was subsequently converted to HR.51 standard for direct issue to the Royal Australian Navy but was allocated a 'compromised' serial XN635. Later it was re-allocated XR592. It retained its original c/n 13070. Del 6.61.

serial	type	sqdn/unit	code	where&when seen		remarks
XR592	Sycamore HR.51					Ex XN635 ntu Pr NSW

The second production order for 24 Scout AH.1 helicopters built by Westland Aircraft Ltd at Hayes for the Army Air Corps against Contract KF/2Q/09/CB25(a), and to follow on from XP910. The block was allotted c/ns F9517 to F9540 resp. XR595 f/f 12.12.63.

serial	type	sqdn/unit	code	where&when seen		remarks
XR595	Scout AH.1					
XR596	Scout AH.1					
XR597	Scout AH.1					
XR598	Scout AH.1					
XR599	Scout AH.1					
XR600	Scout AH.1					
XR601	Scout AH.1					
XR602	Scout AH.1					
XR603	Scout AH.1					
XR604	Scout AH.1					
XR627	Scout AH.1					
XR628	Scout AH.1					
XR629	Scout AH.1					
XR630	Scout AH.1					
XR631	Scout AH.1					
XR632	Scout AH.1					
XR633	Scout AH.1					
XR634	Scout AH.1					
XR635	Scout AH.1					
XR636	Scout AH.1					
XR637	Scout AH.1					
XR638	Scout AH.1					
XR639	Scout AH.1					
XR640	Scout AH.1					

The second production order for 50 Jet Provost T.4 basic training aircraft for the RAF was placed against Contract KC/E/057 to follow on from XP688. All were built at Luton by the British Aircraft Corporation (Luton Division) and delivered in 1962-63.

serial	type	sqdn/unit	code	where&when seen		remarks
XR643	Jet Provost T.4					To 8516M
XR644	Jet Provost T.4					
XR645	Jet Provost T.4					
XR646	Jet Provost T.4					
XR647	Jet Provost T.4					
XR648	Jet Provost T.4					
XR649	Jet Provost T.4					
XR650	Jet Provost T.4					To 8459M
XR651	Jet Provost T.4					To 8431M
XR652	Jet Provost T.4					To G-27-94/S Yemen 107
XR653	Jet Provost T.4					
XR654	Jet Provost T.4					Fuselage Pr Baginton
XR655	Jet Provost T.4					

XR656-XR718

serial	type	sqdn/unit	code	where&when seen		remarks
XR656	Jet Provost T.4					
XR657	Jet Provost T.4					
XR658	Jet Provost T.4					To 8192M
XR659	Jet Provost T.4					
XR660	Jet Provost T.4					To 8374M ntu
XR661	Jet Provost T.4					To G-27-95/S Yemen 108
XR662	Jet Provost T.4					To 8410M
XR663	Jet Provost T.4					
XR664	Jet Provost T.4					
XR665	Jet Provost T.4					
XR666	Jet Provost T.4					
XR667	Jet Provost T.4					
XR668	Jet Provost T.4					
XR669	Jet Provost T.4					To 8062M
XR670	Jet Provost T.4					To 8498M
XR671	Jet Provost T.4					
XR672	Jet Provost T.4					To 8495M
XR673	Jet Provost T.4					
XR674	Jet Provost T.4					
XR675	Jet Provost T.4					
XR676	Jet Provost T.4					
XR677	Jet Provost T.4					
XR678	Jet Provost T.4					
XR679	Jet Provost T.4					
XR680	Jet Provost T.4					
XR681	Jet Provost T.4					To 8588M (Nose)
XR697	Jet Provost T.4					
XR698	Jet Provost T.4					
XR699	Jet Provost T.4					
XR700	Jet Provost T.4					To 8589M (Nose)
XR701	Jet Provost T.4					
XR702	Jet Provost T.4					
XR703	Jet Provost T.4					
XR704	Jet Provost T.4					To 8506M
XR705	Jet Provost T.4					
XR706	Jet Provost T.4					
XR707	Jet Provost T.4					To 8193M

The second production order for Lightning F.3 fighter aircraft originally accounted for 44 units. The first ten aircraft (XR711-XR720) were issued to RAF squadrons whilst the following 13 (XR721-728/747-751) were initially flown to Warton for storage. XR752 emerged during May 1965 to interim F.6 standard (and known as the F.3A) and aircraft up to XR765 were similarly built, lacking only the overwing tank that was standard to the F.6. XR766-773 were built from the outset as production F.6 aircraft being the first production order for that variant. Subsequently most of the stored F.3 Lightnings were up-graded to F.6 standard, whilst XR722 was converted to F.53 for the Royal Saudi Air Force and f/f as such on 19.10.66. All were built by the British Aircraft Corporation (Preston Division) and allotted c/ns 95194-95211 (XR711-XR728) and 95212-95238 (XR747-XR773), although there has been some confusion over certain aircraft. Unconfirmed reports suggest that XR774-XR795 were cancelled.

serial	type	sqdn/unit	code	where&when seen		remarks
XR711	Lightning F.3					
XR712	Lightning F.3					
XR713	Lightning F.3					
XR714	Lightning F.3					
XR715	Lightning F.3					
XR716	Lightning F.3					
XR717	Lightning F.3					
XR718	Lightning F.3					

XR719-XR809

serial	type	sqdn/unit	code	where&when seen		remarks
XR719	Lightning F.3					
XR720	Lightning F.3					
XR721	Lightning F.3					
XR722	Lightning F.3					To G-27-2/RSAF 53-666
XR723	Lightning F.6					
XR724	Lightning F.6					
XR725	Lightning F.6					
XR726	Lightning F.6					
XR727	Lightning F.6					
XR728	Lightning F.6					
XR747	Lightning F.6					
XR748	Lightning F.3					
XR749	Lightning F.3					
XR750	Lightning F.3					
XR751	Lightning F.3					
XR752	Lightning F.6					
XR753	Lightning F.6					
XR754	Lightning F.6					
XR755	Lightning F.6					
XR756	Lightning F.6					
XR757	Lightning F.6					
XR758	Lightning F.6					
XR759	Lightning F.6					
XR760	Lightning F.6					
XR761	Lightning F.6					
XR762	Lightning F.6					
XR763	Lightning F.6					
XR764	Lightning F.6					
XR765	Lightning F.6					
XR766	Lightning F.6					
XR767	Lightning F.6					
XR768	Lightning F.6					
XR769	Lightning F.6					
XR770	Lightning F.6					
XR771	Lightning F.6					
XR772	Lightning F.6					
XR773	Lightning F.6					

Two second-hand Vickers Viscounts purchased for use by the Empire Test Pilots School at Farnborough (later Boscombe Down) during January 1962. Both had originally been built by Vickers-Armstrongs (Aircraft) Ltd at Hurn for Capital Airlines of America as follows:- XR801 Type 744 c/n 89 f/f as N7403 30.6.55, returned to UK and registered G-APKK January 1958 to the manufacturer; XR802 Type 745 c/n 198 f/f as N7442 24.9.56, returned to UK and registered G-ARUU June 1961 to the manufacturer.

XR801	V.744 Viscount					Ex G-APKK
XR802	V.745 Viscount					Ex G-ARUU

The first production order for 5 VC.10 C.1 long-range strategic transport aircraft to Spec C.239 was contracted to BAC (Weybridge Division). All were built under the original Vickers designation Type 1106 and allotted c/ns 826 to 830 respectively. XR806 f/f 26.11.65 and XR810 f/f 29.11.66. RAF Transport Command allocated names to its VC.10 fleet as follows:- XR806 (George Thompson VC); XR807 (Donald Garland VC & Thomas Gray VC); XR808 (Kenneth Campbell VC); XR809 (Hugh Malcolm VC); XR810 (David Lord VC). XR809 became the flying test-bed for the RB.211 as G-AXLR.

XR806	VC.10 C.1					
XR807	VC.10 C.1					
XR808	VC.10 C.1					
XR809	VC.10 C.1					G-AXLR(G-1-1/G-37-6 ntu)

XR810-XR879

serial	type	sqdn/unit	code	where&when seen		remarks
XR810	VC.10 C.1					

One Cushioncraft CC-2 (c/n 001) built by the Hovercraft Division of Britten-Norman Ltd in the Isle of Wight. Evaluated at RAE Bedford from 8.61 to 4.69 when it was transferred to HDL.

serial	type	sqdn/unit	code	where&when seen		remarks
XR814	Cushioncraft CC.2					

Continued procurement of 80 Shelduck D.1 training target drones built by the Ventura Division of the Northrop Corporation for both the British Army and the RN and being the equivalent of the US Navy KD2R-5 (re-styled MQM-36A 18.9.62). However, as three separate contracts were issued to cover this block (in batches of 55, 13 and 12), it is possible that drones within the range XR894 to XR938 are in reality Falconer drones based upon the Northrop AN/USD-1 variant which was procured for the US Army Signal Corps and re-styled MQM-57A on 18.9.62 (see XT580-589).

serial	type	sqdn/unit	code	where&when seen		remarks
XR818	Shelduck D.1					
XR819	Shelduck D.1					
XR820	Shelduck D.1					
XR821	Shelduck D.1					
XR822	Shelduck D.1					
XR823	Shelduck D.1					
XR824	Shelduck D.1					
XR825	Shelduck D.1					
XR826	Shelduck D.1					
XR827	Shelduck D.1					
XR828	Shelduck D.1					
XR829	Shelduck D.1					
XR830	Shelduck D.1					
XR831	Shelduck D.1					
XR832	Shelduck D.1					
XR833	Shelduck D.1					
XR834	Shelduck D.1					
XR835	Shelduck D.1					
XR836	Shelduck D.1					
XR837	Shelduck D.1					
XR838	Shelduck D.1					
XR839	Shelduck D.1					
XR840	Shelduck D.1					
XR841	Shelduck D.1					
XR842	Shelduck D.1					
XR861	Shelduck D.1					
XR862	Shelduck D.1					
XR863	Shelduck D.1					
XR864	Shelduck D.1					
XR865	Shelduck D.1					
XR866	Shelduck D.1					
XR867	Shelduck D.1					
XR868	Shelduck D.1					
XR869	Shelduck D.1					
XR870	Shelduck D.1					
XR871	Shelduck D.1					
XR872	Shelduck D.1					
XR873	Shelduck D.1					
XR874	Shelduck D.1					
XR875	Shelduck D.1					
XR876	Shelduck D.1					
XR877	Shelduck D.1					
XR878	Shelduck D.1					
XR879	Shelduck D.1					

XR880-XR950

serial	type	sqdn/unit	code	where&when seen		remarks
XR880	Shelduck D.1					
XR881	Shelduck D.1					
XR882	Shelduck D.1					
XR883	Shelduck D.1					
XR884	Shelduck D.1					
XR885	Shelduck D.1					
XR886	Shelduck D.1					
XR887	Shelduck D.1					
XR888	Shelduck D.1					
XR889	Shelduck D.1					
XR890	Shelduck D.1					
XR894	Shelduck D.1					
XR895	Shelduck D.1					
XR896	Shelduck D.1					
XR897	Shelduck D.1					
XR898	Shelduck D.1					
XR916	Shelduck D.1					
XR917	Shelduck D.1					
XR918	Shelduck D.1					
XR919	Shelduck D.1					
XR920	Shelduck D.1					
XR921	Shelduck D.1					
XR922	Shelduck D.1					
XR923	Shelduck D.1					
XR927	Shelduck D.1					
XR928	Shelduck D.1					
XR929	Shelduck D.1					
XR930	Shelduck D.1					
XR931	Shelduck D.1					
XR932	Shelduck D.1					
XR933	Shelduck D.1					
XR934	Shelduck D.1					
XR935	Shelduck D.1					
XR936	Shelduck D.1					
XR937	Shelduck D.1					
XR938	Shelduck D.1					

Three Type WA.116 gyrocopters supplied to the Army Air Corps for evaluation during 1962 following construction at Shoreham by Beagle Aircraft Ltd. XR942 c/n B.201 f/f 10.5.62 but was written-off whilst taxying at Shoreham two days later. The serial was transferred to c/n B.202 which f/f 13.7.62 with dual identity G-ARZA/XR942. XR943 c/n B.203 f/f 18.10.62 and registered G-ARZB, and XR944 c/n B.204 followed although initially registered G-ARZC (ntu) and later G-ASDY. After evaluation all were returned to Beagle Aircraft Ltd.

serial	type	sqdn/unit	code	where&when seen		remarks
XR942	WA.116					Ex G-ARZA To G-ARZA
XR943	WA.116					Ex G-ARZB To G-ARZB
XR944	WA.116					To G-ASDY

The final order for 41 Gnat T.1 advanced trainers for the RAF was built by Hawker Siddeley Aviation Ltd at Hamble and test flown from Dunsfold against Contract KC/2B/031. The block was allotted c/ns FL565 to FL605 respectively. XS111 f/f 9.4.65 and delivered to the RAF on 14.5.65. Several Gnats from this block spent their operational lives with the "RED ARROWS" aerobatic team.

serial	type	sqdn/unit	code	where&when seen		remarks
XR948	Gnat T.1					
XR949	Gnat T.1					
XR950	Gnat T.1					

XR951-XS127

serial	type	sqdn/unit	code	where&when seen		remarks
XR951	Gnat T.1					To 8603M
XR952	Gnat T.1					
XR953	Gnat T.1					To 8609M
XR954	Gnat T.1					To 8570M
XR955	Gnat T.1					To A2678
XR976	Gnat T.1					
XR977	Gnat T.1					To 8640M
XR978	Gnat T.1					
XR979	Gnat T.1					
XR980	Gnat T.1					To 8622M
XR981	Gnat T.1					
XR982	Gnat T.1					
XR983	Gnat T.1					
XR984	Gnat T.1					To 8571M
XR985	Gnat T.1					To 7886M (nose)
XR986	Gnat T.1					
XR987	Gnat T.1					To 8641M
XR991	Gnat T.1					To 8637M
XR992	Gnat T.1					
XR993	Gnat T.1					To A2677
XR994	Gnat T.1					
XR995	Gnat T.1					
XR996	Gnat T.1					
XR997	Gnat T.1					
XR998	Gnat T.1					To 8623M
XR999	Gnat T.1					
XS100	Gnat T.1					To 8561M
XS101	Gnat T.1					To 8638M
XS102	Gnat T.1					To 8624M
XS103	Gnat T.1					
XS104	Gnat T.1					To 8604M
XS105	Gnat T.1					To 8625M
XS106	Gnat T.1					
XS107	Gnat T.1					To 8639M
XS108	Gnat T.1					
XS109	Gnat T.1					To 8626M
XS110	Gnat T.1					To 8562M
XS111	Gnat T.1					

The third production contract for 20 Wessex HAS.1 helicopters built by Westland Aircraft Ltd at Yeovil for the RN to follow on from XP160. XS115 f/f 20.3.63 and delivered to RNAY Fleetlands 3.4.63; XS154 f/f 19.11.63 and delivered to Fleetlands on 3.12.63. The block was allotted c/ns WA.94 to WA.113 respectively. Subsequently several examples were converted to HAS.3 standard.

serial	type	sqdn/unit	code	where&when seen		remarks
XS115	Wessex HAS.1					
XS116	Wessex HAS.1					
XS117	Wessex HAS.1					
XS118	Wessex HAS.1					
XS119	Wessex HAS.3					
XS120	Wessex HAS.1					To 8653M
XS121	Wessex HAS.3					
XS122	Wessex HAS.3					
XS123	Wessex HAS.1					
XS124	Wessex HAS.1					
XS125	Wessex HAS.1					To A2648
XS126	Wessex HAS.3					
XS127	Wessex HAS.3					

XS128-XS218

serial	type	sqdn/unit	code	where&when seen		remarks
XS128	Wessex HAS.1					To A2670
XS149	Wessex HAS.3					
XS150	Wessex HAS.1					
XS151	Wessex HAS.1					
XS152	Wessex HAS.1					
XS153	Wessex HAS.3					
XS154	Wessex HAS.1					

Fourteen Hiller HT.2 basic-training helicopters were ordered for the RN during May 1962 direct from United Helicopters of Palo Alto, USA. Deliveries (by sea) commenced with XS159 to RNAY Fleetlands on 16.8.62, and the last of this batch (XS172) arrived on 8.1.63. The block was allotted c/ns 2199/2208/2216/2253-2255/2261-2264/2270 to 2273 respectively.

serial	type	sqdn/unit	code	where&when seen		remarks
XS159	Hiller HT.2					To ZS-HFU
XS160	Hiller HT.2					To G-BDOH
XS161	Hiller HT.2					
XS162	Hiller HT.2					
XS163	Hiller HT.2					
XS164	Hiller HT.2					
XS165	Hiller HT.2					To G-BEFX
XS166	Hiller HT.2					To G-BDOI
XS167	Hiller HT.2					To ZS-HGW
XS168	Hiller HT.2					To ZS-HFV
XS169	Hiller HT.2					To G-BEFY
XS170	Hiller HT.2					To ZS-HFY
XS171	Hiller HT.2					
XS172	Hiller HT.2					To G-BDRY

The final production order for 35 Jet Provost T.4 basic training aircraft for the RAF was placed against Contract KC/E/070/CB5(a) and built by the British Aircraft Corporation (Luton Division) to follow on from XR707. Deliveries took place between 10.63 & 9.64. XS230/231 were subsequently converted to prototype T.5 standard; XS230 f/f as T.5 (from Warton) 28.2.67; XS231 f/f as interim T.5 (at Luton) 16.3.65 (registration G-ATAJ ntu), f/f after full conversion 7.67. Production Jet Provost T.5 aircraft commence with XW287.

serial	type	sqdn/unit	code	where&when seen		remarks
XS175	Jet Provost T.4					
XS176	Jet Provost T.4					To 8514M
XS177	Jet Provost T.4					
XS178	Jet Provost T.4					
XS179	Jet Provost T.4					To 8337M wears 8237M
XS180	Jet Provost T.4					To 8338M wears 8238M
XS181	Jet Provost T.4					
XS182	Jet Provost T.4					
XS183	Jet Provost T.4					
XS184	Jet Provost T.4					
XS185	Jet Provost T.4					
XS186	Jet Provost T.4					To 8408M
XS209	Jet Provost T.4					To 8409M
XS210	Jet Provost T.4					To 8339M wears 8239M
XS211	Jet Provost T.4					
XS212	Jet Provost T.4					
XS213	Jet Provost T.4					To 8097M/Kenyan AF GI
XS214	Jet Provost T.4					
XS215	Jet Provost T.4					To 8507M
XS216	Jet Provost T.4					
XS217	Jet Provost T.4					
XS218	Jet Provost T.4					To 8508M

XS219-XS285

serial	type	sqdn/unit	code	where&when seen		remarks
XS219	Jet Provost T.4					
XS220	Jet Provost T.4					
XS221	Jet Provost T.4					
XS222	Jet Provost T.4					
XS223	Jet Provost T.4					To G-27-4/S Yemen 101
XS224	Jet Provost T.4					To G-27-5/S Yemen 102
XS225	Jet Provost T.4					
XS226	Jet Provost T.4					
XS227	Jet Provost T.4					To G-27-6/S Yemen 103
XS228	Jet Provost T.4					To G-27-7/S Yemen 104
XS229	Jet Provost T.4					
XS230	Jet Provost T.5					
XS231	Jet Provost T.5					To G-ATAJ ntu

One DH.106 Comet 4C built by Hawker Siddeley Aviation Ltd at Hawarden, Chester for use by the A&AEE Boscombe Down as a navigational trials aircraft. It was allotted c/n 06473 and f/f 26.9.63; delivered to Boscombe Down 2.12.63 and named 'Canopus'.

serial	type	sqdn/unit	code	where&when seen		remarks
XS235	Comet 4C					

One Auster AOP.9 built for the Army Air Corps by Beagle-Auster Aircraft Ltd at Rearsby against Contract KC/N/047 as a replacement for XP254 which had been diverted off contract for conversion to AOP.11 standard.

serial	type	sqdn/unit	code	where&when seen		remarks
XS238	Auster AOP.9					

The prototype Wessex HU.5 built by Westland Aircraft Ltd at Yeovil and f/f 31.5.63. It was allotted c/n WA.152. Production helicopters for the RN commence with XS479.

serial	type	sqdn/unit	code	where&when seen		remarks
XS241	Wessex HU.5					

Sixty Shelduck D.1 training target drones built by the Ventura Division of the Northrop Corporation for both the British Army and the RN. From observation RN-issued drones are based upon the KD2R-5 (MQM-36A) variant whilst those issued directly to British Army units appear to have been the equivalent of the Falconer AN/USD-1 drone and which was re-styled MQM-57A on 18.9.62 with the US Army.

serial	type	sqdn/unit	code	where&when seen		remarks
XS246	Shelduck D.1					
XS247	Shelduck D.1					
XS248	Shelduck D.1					
XS249	Shelduck D.1					
XS250	Shelduck D.1					
XS251	Shelduck D.1					
XS252	Shelduck D.1					
XS253	Shelduck D.1					
XS254	Shelduck D.1					
XS255	Shelduck D.1					
XS256	Shelduck D.1					
XS257	Shelduck D.1					
XS273	Shelduck D.1					
XS274	Shelduck D.1					
XS275	Shelduck D.1					
XS276	Shelduck D.1					
XS277	Shelduck D.1					
XS278	Shelduck D.1					
XS279	Shelduck D.1					
XS280	Shelduck D.1					
XS281	Shelduck D.1					
XS282	Shelduck D.1					
XS283	Shelduck D.1					
XS284	Shelduck D.1					
XS285	Shelduck D.1					

XL905 was to have been a SR.177 mixed-power interceptor but the project was cancelled in 1957 before the prototype was completed. This model of the type clearly illustrates the unique lines of the project. (British Hovercraft Corporation)

XM562 Skeeter AOP.12, 651 Sqdn/13 Flt, at Newcastle 13.2.61. The insignia of 3 Division is painted on the nose. (I. MacFarlane)

The SR.177 mock-up in the factory at Cowes, highlights the squat appearance of the type when compared to the SR.53. (British Hovercraft Corporation)

XM597 Vulcan B.2, Waddington Wing, about to land during 1972. This aircraft was the first to be fitted with the ECM attachment on the fin. (P.A. Tomlin)

XM819 EP.9 at A&AEE Boscombe Down 1958/59. The extra large 'ARMY' titling on the fuselage was later reduced in size to that of the serial. (Crown)

XM837 'NF/407' Wessex HAS.3, 737 Sqdn, HMS Norfolk Flt, at Lee-on-Solent on 26.6.77 in readiness to take part in the Queen's Silver Jubilee Naval Review flypast. (R.A.Walker)

XM991/T Lightning T.4, 19 Sqdn, at Hannover in the late 1960's. The unit markings consist of a dolphin motif on the fin and blue/white nose checks. (P.A. Tomlin)

XN117 Jet Provost T.3 prototype, at Khormaksar in 6/8.57 while being evaluated along with Gnat F.1 XN122 and Hunter F.6's XK150 & XK151 as Venom FB.4 replacement. The Hunter FGA.9 was developed as a result of the trials. (via R.A. Walker)

XN148 Sedbergh TX.1, on display in Horse Guards Parade, London 16.9.60 as part of the Capital's Battle of Britain Week celebrations. (P.G. Smith)

XN305 'PO/516' Whirlwind HAS.7, 771 Sqdn, at Portland 9.8.69. The rescue winch can be seen above the open door. (R.A. Walker)

XN320 Twin Pioneer CC.1, 209 Sqdn, climbs slowly over Johore, Malaysia on 17.12.66. (Crown)

XN332 '759' Saunders-Roe P.531-O/N, ex 771 Sqdn, at Plymouth in 7.63. (Flamingo)

XN691 'E/131' Sea Vixen FAW.2, 899 Sqdn. The unit's white mailed fist marking is painted boldly on the fin. The extended booms of the Sea Vixen FAW.2 are clearly visible. (FAA Museum)

XN714 Hunting H.126 jet-flap research aircraft. As can be seen from this airborne view, its appearance was purely functional. Upon completion of trials it was moved to Cosford for display. (British Aerospace)

XN732/H Lightning F.2, 92 Sqdn, at Hannover in the late 1960's. The unit markings consist of a cobra motif on a royal blue fin and a red/yellow arrowhead on the nose. (P.A. Tomlin)

XN934 'LM/631' Buccaneer S.1, ex 736 Sqdn, at Lee-on-Solent in the late 1960's. Used as an instructional airframe, it was given the 'A' serial A2600. (via. D.J. Rose)

XN981 Buccaneer S.2B, 12 Sqdn, in the early 1970's. The unit's fox head badge is on the engine intake. This aircraft later returned to the RN as a S.2D. (P.A. Tomlin)

'XP000' Beaver AL.1, AETW, at Middle Wallop 28.7.73. This aircraft is in reality 7735M (a composite airframe built from XP812 & XP815), but was actually TOC as XP000, eventually being SOC on 29.3.76. (R.A. Walker)

XP254 AOP.11, at Farnborough 7.9.61 during the SBAC show. Developed as a replacement for the AOP.9, it was foresaken for a helicopter type. (R.A. Walker)

XP331/T Whirlwind HAR.10, 2 FTS, at Valley 18.8.79. The unit motif consists of a red winged torch of learning on a white disc. (R. Plimmer/MCAS)

XP408 Argosy C.1, 114/267 Sqdns, at Southend 24.3.68. One of the first Argosies to be camouflaged, it wears Air Support Command titling. (I. MacFarlane)

XP841 HP.115 slender delta research aircraft, at Farnborough 9.9.61 during the SBAC show. This aircraft was transferred to Yeovilton from Cosford during 1979 for display in the Concorde Museum. (P.G. Smith)

XP972 Hawker P.1127, banks over Southern England during a test flight in the mid 1960's. Although the aircraft wears the Tri-partite fin flash it never served with that Evaluation Unit. (British Aerospace)

XR216 Beaver AL.1, Sultan of Oman's AF, at Sharjah in 12.66 is another example of an aircraft wearing a British serial while in foreign service. It was subsequently re-serialled 216. (Flamingo)

XR219 TSR-2, BAC, turns finals to land at Boscombe Down and illustrates well its somewhat unusual looking undercarriage layout. (British Aerospace)

XR226 TSR-2 lies at Weybridge in mid 1965 after being removed from the production line and scrapped as a result of the project cancellation. The serial is just discernable under 'FUEL' on the rear fuselage section. (via E.B. Morgan)

XR369 Belfast C.1, 53 Sqdn, at Finningley 20.9.69. Note the then current 'Air Support Command' titling and the name 'Spartacus' beneath the cockpit. (R.A. Walker)

XR385 Alouette AH.2 6 Flt, at Middle Wallop 24.7.75. Note the white serial and the inscription 'ARMY' in use at the time and also the small unit badge beneath the rotor pylon. (R.A. Walker)

XR399 Comet C.4, 216 Sqdn, at Newcastle 15.9.74. (I. MacFarlane)

XR511 Wessex HC.2, in Sultan of Oman's AF marks. A number of these helicopters were seconded to the SOAF from the RAF in the late 1960's/early 1970's and repainted in this desert style camouflage. (via A.J. Cranston)

XR534/93 Gnat T.1, CFS, at Middleton St George 5.10.63. The CFS crest is worn on the nose and almost half the tail code has been removed. The Gnat colour scheme of silver/dayglo later gave way to one of red/white. (I. MacFarlane)

XR603 Scout AH.1, 653 Sqdn, at Middle Wallop 4.8.77. (R.A. Walker)

XR770 Lightning F.6, BAC, in flight preparatory to the Farnborough SBAC Show in 9.66. It was painted in R. Saudi AF colours to represent an F.53 and on completion of the show, entered RAF service. (British Aerospace)

XR770/C Lightning F.6, 74 Sqdn, at Tengah in 7.67. The overwing ferry tanks were fitted for the deployment from the UK to Singapore and were removed upon arrival. (Flamingo)

XR801 Viscount 744, Empire Test Pilots School, at Farnborough 7.9.62. An ex-civil airliner, it was initially painted in a silver/white/blue colour scheme. *(I. MacFarlane)*

XR808 VC.10 C.1, 10 Sqdn, at Brize Norton 3.7.76. Just aft of the cockpit can be seen the unit crest and the aircraft name 'Kenneth Campbell VC'. *(R.A. Walker)*

'XR847' Scout AH.1, AETW, at Middle Wallop 11.1.78. This instructional airframe had its correct serial, XP847, corrupted during a re-paint. *(M.I. Draper)*

XR944 WA.116 autogyro, at Biggin Hill 4.5.63. The poles at the front and rear are rotor blade supports for use when the aircraft is at rest. *(R.A. Walker)*

XS100/57 Gnat T.1, 4 FTS, at Bentwaters 16.5.70. This particular aircraft is one of the few that has been issued a '100' serial. The red/white colour scheme had only just been introduced when this photograph was taken. *(P. Spencer)*

XS162 '48' Hiller HT.2, 705 Sqdn, at Culdrose 31.7.74. The full code '548' is not worn, the 'last two' appearing on both the fuselage and the nose. (D.A. Rough)

XS349 Hughes 269A, at Middle Wallop 6.7.62. Imported in 6.62 (as G-ASBL), this helicopter was being demonstrated to the Army by the agents, Westland Helicopters Ltd. In a subsequent trial at A&AEE in 1963 it was serialled XS684. (Flamingo)

XS597 Andover C.1, 32 Sqdn, at Newcastle 1.6.77. Developed from the Avro 748, the Andover has a 'kneeling' undercarriage capability and a ramp/rear fuselage doors combination to aid loading, as is well illustrated above. (I. MacFarlane)

XS655 SR.N3 of the Interservice Hovercraft Trials Unit being demonstrated to service personnel on the Solent off Browndown. (British Hovercraft Corporation)

XS681 Brantly B2A at Idris, Libya in 7/8.63 whilst under evaluation by 'D' Sqdn A&AEE. It had been loaned for the trials by BEAS of Oxford to whom it returned in 10.63 and reverted to its previous civil markings, G-ASHK. (Crown)

XS684 Hughes 269A also photographed at Idris, Libya, in 7/8.63 whilst under 'D' Sqdn A&AEE evaluation. It had been loaned from Westland Helicopters Ltd for the trials and on restoration became G-ASBL (See XS349). (Crown)

XS688 Kestrel FGA.1 in formation with XL564 Hunter T.7 over Southern England in the mid 1960's. Note the Kestrel's tripartite markings representing the UK, USA and W.German national markings. (Crown)

XS735 Dominie T.1, at Odiham 19.9.68 displays the full name of its operator 'Royal Air Force College of Air Warfare' along the roof. (R.A. Walker)

XS765 Basset C.1, Northern Comms Sqdn, takes-off from Upper Heyford in the late 1960's. (via M.I. Draper)

XS793 Andover CC.2, Queen's Flight, at Newcastle 15.7.77. The Royal Cypher is visible on the nose of this superbly maintained aircraft. (I. MacFarlane)

G-15-252 Vickers VA-1 battling through choppy seas and producing a considerable amount of spray. This hovercraft did carry the serial XS798 for trials but no photographs appear to have been taken at the time. (British Hovercraft Corporation)

XS856 Vickers VA-2 negotiates some rough and rocky terrain during its military trials in the Libyan desert in 1963. (British Hovercraft Corporation)

XS941 Student, at Shoreham, date unknown. At the time it was painted in a black and white colour scheme. (via G.J. Cruikshank)

XT160/B Sioux AH.1, 658 Sqdn, at Middle Wallop 24.7.75. The simple construction of the type is most apparent. (R.A. Walker)

'XT193' - not a Sioux AH.1, but a hovercraft mock-up built on a Landrover and looking very convincing at a Portsmouth Dockyard open day in the late 1960's. (P. Spencer)

XT287 'H/230' Buccaneer S.2, 801 Sqdn, at Lossiemouth in the late 1960's. It was subsequently converted to S.2D standard. (P.A. Tomlin)

XT439 'ZU/442' Wasp HAS.1, 829 Sqdn, HMS Zulu Flt, takes off from RNAY Fleetlands 11.6.79. (R.A. Walker)

XT492 SR.N5, Interservice Hovercraft Unit, climbs up the slipway to its home base at Lee-on-Solent 14.10.74. Of special interest is the apparent red, white and blue fin flash. (R.A. Walker)

GH9011 SR.N6 Mk.5A, British Hovercraft Corporation, at Lee-on-Solent 21.7.79. Formerly XT493, the modifications from a standard SR.N6 are apparent and the flat vehicle/cargo space can be clearly seen. (R.A. Walker)

XT581 Shelduck D.1 of the Army on its handling trolley at the Aldershot Army Show in 6.68. Beneath the wings can be seen the rocket motor used for launching. Note the black outline to the fin flash plus the white stencilling. (P. Spencer)

XT653 Swallow TX.1 at Swanton Morley in the original silver and dayglo colour scheme with black 'Air Cadets' titling. The Swallow is used primarily to enable instructors to maintain proficiency in soaring. (P. Spencer)

XT752 (Ex G-APYO/AS-14/WN365) 'BY/772' Gannet T.5, 849 Sqdn, 'HQ' Flt (date and location unknown). It started life as the prototype Gannet T.2. (Flamingo)

XV208 Hercules W.2, RAE Farnborough, takes-off from Greenham Common 25.6.79. Extensively modified by Marshall of Cambridge from a C.1, it is employed on meteorological research duties. (R.A. Walker)

XV211 Hercules C.1, 70 Sqdn, at Luqa 19.11.70. Unlike the UK based Hercules units, this Sqdn displayed its badge on the fins of its aircraft. (M. Pace)

XV230/30 Nimrod MR.1, St Mawgan Wing, climbs away from Yeovilton 8.7.72. From 1979 onwards the Nimrod fleet is being repainted in a camouflage colour scheme. (R.A. Walker)

XV285 CC-2, at Browndown Camp during 6.66 whilst undergoing trials. (Flamingo)

XV329/T Lightning T.5, 74 Sqdn, at Tengah during 1968. The unit tiger head emblem is clearly visible on the fin, as is the yellow/black nose flash. The Sqdn had re-instated its black fin colour scheme prior to disbandment in 1971. (via A.J. Cranston)

XV432/L Phantom FGR.2, 54 Sqdn, at Coningsby during 1972. The unit marking consists of blue and yellow checks and yellow fin codes. (via D.J. Rose)

XV589 'R/006' Phantom FG.1, 892 Sqdn, about to be catapulted from HMS Ark Royal during 4.74. Of interest is the extended nose undercarriage leg and the jet blast deflector on the flight deck. (Crown)

G-15-253 Vickers VA-3 during trial services with British United Airways between Rhyl and Wallasey. The hovercraft carried out military trials as XV366 but again no photographs appear to have been taken). *(British Hovercraft Corporation)*

XV617/RJ SR.N6 Mk.2, Naval Hovercraft Trials Unit, moving out to sea from the slipway at Lee-on-Solent 24.1.79. The differences in the cabin/deck area between this craft and XV859 are readily apparent. *(Lovelock/Long)*

XV657 'CU/580' Sea King HAS.2A, 824 Sqdn, at Fleetlands 11.6.79 with the unit's stylised yellow bird painted along the fuselage. The HAS 2/2A can be discerned from the HAS.1 by its six bladed tail rotor. *(R.A. Walker)*

XV859/EX SR.N6 Mk.6, Naval Hovercraft Trials Unit, at RNAY Fleetlands 10.6.78. The code appears on the bow door. *(R.A. Walker)*

XV902 was to have been the RAF's first F-111K but had not been completed at the time of the project cancellation. For publicity purposes the above photograph of an F-111A was re-touched to represent the RAF version. *(General Dynamics)*

'XV916' Sea King HAS.2, in primer colour scheme at Yeovil circa 2.79. It was correctly repainted as XZ916 prior to delivery as were 'XV915' and 'XV917' to XZ915 and XZ917. This aircraft subsequently became the prototype HAS.5. *(Avia Press)*

XV951 Slingsby T.53B in 'Air Cadets' markings shows off its elegant lines over Yorkshire during a pre-delivery flight. (Vickers-Slingsby)

XW211/CH Puma HC.1, 33 Sqdn, at Odiham 14.5.77. The white snow camouflage had been applied for an exercise in Norway and provides an interesting comparison with the colour scheme of XW210. (R.A. Walker)

XW210/CG Puma HC.1, 33 Sqdn, in the early 1970's. The unit emblem of a stag's head can be seen beneath the cockpit. (P.A. Tomlin)

XW249 CC-7, date and location unknown. This hovercraft was ordered from Cushioncraft for trials by the National Physical Laboratory Hovercraft Unit. (Flight)

XW255 BH-7, IHU, at speed on the Solent in late 1970. A considerable amount of equipment had still to be fitted. *(British Hovercraft Corporation)*

XW255/RW BH-7, Naval Hovercraft Trials Unit, speeds across the Solent 21.8.79 and makes an interesting comparison with the earlier photograph of the same craft. Re-classified a ship in 9.79, pennant number P235 was applied. *(G. Long)*

XW370/49 Jet Provost T.5, 3 FTS, at North Weald 24.5.72. At the time it was used by the "Gemini Pair" aerobatic team. *(R.A. Walker)*

XW555 HM-2, Department of Trade and Industry, travels up Southampton Water displaying its smart but simple colour scheme. *(Crown)*

XW626 Comet 4 AEW test-bed, BAe, at Farnborough 3.9.78. It was converted from a standard Comet 4 to the aerodynamic test prototype for the Nimrod AEW.3 programme. *(R.A. Walker)*

XW635 D5/180 Husky, 5 AEF, at Cambridge in 4.70. The name on the nose is 'Spirit of Butlins', after the organisation that donated the aircraft to the Air Cadets. (Flamingo)

XW640 Schleicher Ka 6CR, ETPS, at Boscombe Down 9.7.73. It subsequently reverted to civilian guise as BGA 1348. (Crown)

XW660 Hoverhawk Mk.III was evaluated by the MoD prior to being noted in storage at Bedford in 11.72. Information and a photograph of this craft have been elusive and an example of an unidentified Mk.III is reproduced above. (via D.A. Rough)

XW665 Nimrod R.1 is seen, prior to delivery, at Woodford. Note the shorter rear fuselage extension which distinguishes this variant. (P.A. Tomlin)

XW750 HS.748 Srs 107, RAE, at Leuchars 18.9.71. The colour scheme consists of a white top, grey undersides and light blue cheat line outlined in white and black. (R.A. Walker)

XW784 'LS' Kittiwake Mk 1, at Lee-on-Solent, 24.7.71. Construction was initiated by Navy apprentices at Arbroath (and completed at Lee) as part of their training in aircraft structures. It was to have been used as a glider tug. (R.A. Walker)

XS286-XS362

serial	type	sqdn/unit	code	where&when seen		remarks
XS286	Shelduck D.1					
XS287	Shelduck D.1					
XS288	Shelduck D.1					
XS289	Shelduck D.1					
XS290	Shelduck D.1					
XS294	Shelduck D.1					
XS295	Shelduck D.1					
XS296	Shelduck D.1					
XS297	Shelduck D.1					
XS298	Shelduck D.1					
XS299	Shelduck D.1					
XS300	Shelduck D.1					
XS301	Shelduck D.1					
XS302	Shelduck D.1					
XS303	Shelduck D.1					
XS304	Shelduck D.1					
XS305	Shelduck D.1					
XS306	Shelduck D.1					
XS307	Shelduck D.1					
XS308	Shelduck D.1					
XS309	Shelduck D.1					
XS310	Shelduck D.1					
XS311	Shelduck D.1					
XS335	Shelduck D.1					
XS336	Shelduck D.1					
XS337	Shelduck D.1					
XS338	Shelduck D.1					
XS339	Shelduck D.1					
XS340	Shelduck D.1					
XS341	Shelduck D.1					
XS342	Shelduck D.1					
XS343	Shelduck D.1					
XS344	Shelduck D.1					
XS345	Shelduck D.1					
XS346	Shelduck D.1					

One Hughes 269A helicopter originally built by the Hughes Tool Co at Culver City, California USA with c/n 42-0066 and registered G-ASBL in June 1962. Later during 1962 it was allocated military marks XS349 for evaluation at Boscombe Down to meet an Army Air Corps requirement for an Ultra Light Helicopter (Spec H.240). G-ASBL was later allocated the serial XS684 for further trials.

serial	type	sqdn/unit	code	where&when seen		remarks
XS349	Hughes 269A					Ex G-ASBL To G-ASBL

41 Shelduck D.1 training target drones built by the Ventura Division of the Northrop Corporation for both the British Army and the RN, to follow on from XS346. Comments against the block commencing XS246 apply equally to this procurement.

serial	type	sqdn/unit	code	where&when seen		remarks
XS352	Shelduck D.1					
XS353	Shelduck D.1					
XS354	Shelduck D.1					
XS355	Shelduck D.1					
XS356	Shelduck D.1					
XS357	Shelduck D.1					
XS358	Shelduck D.1					
XS359	Shelduck D.1					
XS360	Shelduck D.1					
XS361	Shelduck D.1					
XS362	Shelduck D.1					

XS363-XS454

serial	type	sqdn/unit	code	where&when seen		remarks
XS363	Shelduck D.1					
XS364	Shelduck D.1					
XS365	Shelduck D.1					
XS366	Shelduck D.1					
XS367	Shelduck D.1					
XS368	Shelduck D.1					
XS369	Shelduck D.1					
XS370	Shelduck D.1					
XS371	Shelduck D.1					
XS372	Shelduck D.1					
XS373	Shelduck D.1					
XS374	Shelduck D.1					
XS375	Shelduck D.1					
XS376	Shelduck D.1					
XS377	Shelduck D.1					
XS378	Shelduck D.1					
XS379	Shelduck D.1					
XS380	Shelduck D.1					
XS381	Shelduck D.1					
XS398	Shelduck D.1					
XS399	Shelduck D.1					
XS400	Shelduck D.1					
XS401	Shelduck D.1					
XS402	Shelduck D.1					
XS403	Shelduck D.1					
XS404	Shelduck D.1					
XS405	Shelduck D.1					
XS406	Shelduck D.1					
XS407	Shelduck D.1					
XS408	Shelduck D.1					

One Whirlwind HAR.10 helicopter built by Westland Aircraft Ltd at Yeovil for the RAF and placed against Contract KF/2N/042/CB25(a) as a replacement for XP392. It was allotted the c/n WA.380 and f/f 8.10.62, being delivered 29.10.62.

serial	type	sqdn/unit	code	where&when seen		remarks
XS412	Whirlwind HAR.10					To 8030M

The first production contract for 20 Lightning T.5 two-seat trainer version of the Lightning F.3 followed the two prototypes XM966 and XM967. Most of this batch was built by the British Aircraft Corporation (Filton Division) - formerly Bristol Aircraft Ltd - who had previously converted XM966 to T.5 standard. XS416 f/f 20.8.64 at Filton; XS417 f/f 17.7.64 at Samlesbury. XS460 was subsequently converted to a T.55 for the Royal Saudi Air Force (See XV328/329). The block was allotted the c/ns 95001 to 95020 respectively.

serial	type	sqdn/unit	code	where&when seen		remarks
XS416	Lightning T.5					
XS417	Lightning T.5					
XS418	Lightning T.5					To 8531M
XS419	Lightning T.5					
XS420	Lightning T.5					
XS421	Lightning T.5					
XS422	Lightning T.5					
XS423	Lightning T.5					To 8532M
XS449	Lightning T.5					To 8533M
XS450	Lightning T.5					To 8534M
XS451	Lightning T.5					To 8503M
XS452	Lightning T.5					
XS453	Lightning T.5					
XS454	Lightning T.5					To 8535M

XS455-XS522

serial	type	sqdn/unit	code	where&when seen		remarks
XS455	Lightning T.5					
XS456	Lightning T.5					
XS457	Lightning T.5					
XS458	Lightning T.5					
XS459	Lightning T.5					
XS460	Lightning T.5					To RSAF 55-710

Two prototype/development Wasp HAS.1 helicopters built to Spec HAS.216D&P for the RN by Westland Aircraft Ltd at Hayes under Contract KK/N/014/CB25(a). XS463 first flew at White Waltham on 28.10.62. The two helicopters were allotted c/ns F9541 & F9542 respectively. Production Wasp HAS.1's for the RN commence with XS527.

serial	type	sqdn/unit	code	where&when seen		remarks
XS463	Wasp HAS.1					Ex G-17-1 To A2647
XS476	Wasp HAS.1					Ex G-17-2 To A2656

The first production order for 40 Wessex HU.5 helicopters for the RN was built by Westland Aircraft Ltd at Yeovil. XS479 f/f 17.11.63 at Yeovil and the first delivery of Wessex HU.5 helicopters was made on 5.12.63. The block was allotted the c/ns WA.153 to WA.192 respectively. Allocations continue with XT448.

serial	type	sqdn/unit	code	where&when seen		remarks
XS479	Wessex HU.5					
XS480	Wessex HU.5					
XS481	Wessex HU.5					
XS482	Wessex HU.5					
XS483	Wessex HU.5					
XS484	Wessex HU.5					
XS485	Wessex HU.5					
XS486	Wessex HU.5					
XS487	Wessex HU.5					
XS488	Wessex HU.5					
XS489	Wessex HU.5					
XS490	Wessex HU.5					
XS491	Wessex HU.5					
XS492	Wessex HU.5					
XS493	Wessex HU.5					
XS494	Wessex HU.5					
XS495	Wessex HU.5					
XS496	Wessex HU.5					
XS497	Wessex HU.5					
XS498	Wessex HU.5					
XS499	Wessex HU.5					
XS500	Wessex HU.5					
XS506	Wessex HU.5					
XS507	Wessex HU.5					
XS508	Wessex HU.5					
XS509	Wessex HU.5					To A2597
XS510	Wessex HU.5					
XS511	Wessex HU.5					
XS512	Wessex HU.5					
XS513	Wessex HU.5					
XS514	Wessex HU.5					
XS515	Wessex HU.5					
XS516	Wessex HU.5					
XS517	Wessex HU.5					
XS518	Wessex HU.5					
XS519	Wessex HU.5					
XS520	Wessex HU.5					
XS521	Wessex HU.5					
XS522	Wessex HU.5					

XS523-XS588

serial	type	sqdn/unit	code	where&when seen		remarks
XS523	Wessex HU.5					

Thirty production Wasp HAS.1 helicopters built to Spec HAS.216D&P for the RN by Westland Aircraft Ltd at Hayes under Contract KK/N/011/CB25(a). XS527 first flew 1.63 at White Waltham. The block was allotted c/ns F9543-F9544/F9556-F9583 respectively.

serial	type	sqdn/unit	code	where&when seen		remarks
XS527	Wasp HAS.1					Ex G-17-3
XS528	Wasp HAS.1					
XS529	Wasp HAS.1					
XS530	Wasp HAS.1					To G-17-7/BzN N-7040
XS531	Wasp HAS.1					
XS532	Wasp HAS.1					
XS533	Wasp HAS.1					
XS534	Wasp HAS.1					
XS535	Wasp HAS.1					
XS536	Wasp HAS.1					
XS537	Wasp HAS.1					To A2672
XS538	Wasp HAS.1					
XS539	Wasp HAS.1					
XS540	Wasp HAS.1					
XS541	Wasp HAS.1					
XS542	Wasp HAS.1					To G-17-30/BzN N-7042
XS543	Wasp HAS.1					
XS544	Wasp HAS.1					
XS545	Wasp HAS.1					
XS562	Wasp HAS.1					
XS563	Wasp HAS.1					
XS564	Wasp HAS.1					To G-17-22/BzN N-7038
XS565	Wasp HAS.1					
XS566	Wasp HAS.1					
XS567	Wasp HAS.1					
XS568	Wasp HAS.1					
XS569	Wasp HAS.1					
XS570	Wasp HAS.1					
XS571	Wasp HAS.1					
XS572	Wasp HAS.1					

In order to display a Northrop-Radioplanes Shelduck D.1 target drone at the FAA Museum at Yeovilton one non-flyable example was constructed from the remnants of other damaged drones. For near authenticity an unused serial XS574 was applied.

serial	type	sqdn/unit	code	where&when seen		remarks
XS574	Shelduck D.1					

The final production contract for 15 Sea Vixen FAW.2 carrier-borne fighters for the RN built by Hawker Siddeley Aviation Ltd at Chester. Production of the Sea Vixen ceased during 1966 with this batch which was allotted c/ns 10134-10148 respectively. Flight Refuelling at Tarrant Rushton/Hurn are now re-working some to D.3 standard.

serial	type	sqdn/unit	code	where&when seen		remarks
XS576	Sea Vixen FAW.2					Pr IWM Duxford
XS577	Sea Vixen D.3					
XS578	Sea Vixen FAW.2					
XS579	Sea Vixen FAW.2					
XS580	Sea Vixen FAW.2					
XS581	Sea Vixen FAW.2					
XS582	Sea Vixen FAW.2					
XS583	Sea Vixen FAW.2					To 8397M ntu
XS584	Sea Vixen FAW.2					
XS585	Sea Vixen FAW.2					
XS586	Sea Vixen FAW.2					
XS587	Sea Vixen D.3					
XS588	Sea Vixen FAW.2					

XS589-XS655

serial	type	sqdn/unit	code	where&when seen		remarks
XS589	Sea Vixen FAW.2					
XS590	Sea Vixen FAW.2					Pr FAAM

The sole production order for 31 Andover C.1 tactical transport aircraft was contracted to Hawker Siddeley Aviation Ltd at Woodford and built under the maker's designation HS.780. The prototype (XS594) f/f 9.7.65 and the type entered service with 46 Squadron in July 1966. Only the initial four aircraft were allotted c/ns within the normal sequence:- XS594-XS597 c/ns 1572-1575 resp. The remainder are known by their 'build numbers' as follows:- XS598-XS613 Sets 5 to 20; XS637-XS647 Sets 21 to 31. Several were subsequently converted to E.3 and E.3A standard for 115 Sqdn while 10 were sold to the RNZAF.

serial	type	sqdn/unit	code	where&when seen		remarks
XS594	Andover C.1					
XS595	Andover C.1					
XS596	Andover C.1					
XS597	Andover C.1					
XS598	Andover C.1					
XS599	Andover C.1					To NZ7620
XS600	Andover C.1					To NZ7621
XS601	Andover C.1					
XS602	Andover C.1					To NZ7622
XS603	Andover E.3					
XS604	Andover C.1					To NZ7623
XS605	Andover E.3					
XS606	Andover C.1					
XS607	Andover C.1					To G-BEBY Rtnd XS607
XS608	Andover C.1					To NZ7624
XS609	Andover C.1					
XS610	Andover E.3					
XS611	Andover C.1					To NZ7625
XS612	Andover C.1					To NZ7626
XS613	Andover C.1					To NZ7627
XS637	Andover C.1					
XS638	Andover C.1					To NZ7628
XS639	Andover E.3A					
XS640	Andover E.3					
XS641	Andover E.3A					
XS642	Andover C.1					
XS643	Andover C.1					
XS644	Andover C.1(mod)					
XS645	Andover C.1					To NZ7629
XS646	Andover C.1					
XS647	Andover C.1					

Three Type 45 Swallow gliders built by Slingsby Sailplanes Ltd at Kirkbymoorside and acquired for evaluation with the Air Training Corps. XS650 and XS651 were new gliders and allotted c/ns 1386 and 1387 respectively while XS652 (c/n 1373) had originally been allotted the serial BGA1107.

serial	type	sqdn/unit	code	where&when seen		remarks
XS650	Swallow TX.1					
XS651	Swallow TX.1					
XS652	Swallow TX.1					Ex BGA1107

One SR.N3 hovercraft (c/n 001) laid down by Westland Aircraft Ltd at East Cowes in 8.62 to meet Spec RG.234. First hover 25.11.63, first sea hover 4.12.63. It was handed over to the IHTU at Lee-on-Solent on 2.6.64 and made its 570th and last sortie with the Unit on 21.2.74 after which it was withdrawn from use and broken up.

serial	type	sqdn/unit	code	where&when seen		remarks
XS655	SR.N3					

Eleven BAC TSR-2 Type 579 aircraft ordered on 28.6.63 to be built by BAC (Preston

XS660-XS700

serial	type	sqdn/unit	code	where&when seen	remarks

Division) against Contract KD/2L/13/CB42(a). Allocated c/ns XO.10-XO.20, none were completed by the time the TSR-2 programme was cancelled on 6.4.65. The incomplete airframes were later scrapped on the orders of the Government.

serial	type	sqdn/unit	code	where&when seen	remarks
XS660	BAC TSR-2				
XS661	BAC TSR-2				
XS662	BAC TSR-2				
XS663	BAC TSR-2				
XS664	BAC TSR-2				
XS665	BAC TSR-2				
XS666	BAC TSR-2				
XS667	BAC TSR-2				
XS668	BAC TSR-2				
XS669	BAC TSR-2				
XS670	BAC TSR-2				

The second production batch of six Wessex HC.2 helicopters built for the RAF by Westland Aircraft Ltd at Yeovil. XS674 f/f 16.2.65 del 2.3.65; XS679 f/f 28.4.65 and del 5.5.65. The block was allotted c/ns WA193 to WA198 inclusive.

serial	type	sqdn/unit	code	where&when seen	remarks
XS674	Wessex HC.2				
XS675	Wessex HC.2				
XS676	Wessex HC.2				
XS677	Wessex HC.2				
XS678	Wessex HC.2				To HdeH Australia TI
XS679	Wessex HC.2				

Three Brantly and two Hughes helicopters were allocated service markings for evaluation purposes (6.63 to 10.63) in connection with the AAC Unit Light Helicopter concept (Spec H.240) as follows:- XS681 Brantly B2A c/n 315 ex G-ASHK; XS682 Brantly B2A c/n 303 ex G-ASEH; XS683 Brantly B2B c/n 319 ex G-ASHJ; XS684 Hughes 269A c/n 42-0066 ex G-ASBL; XS685 Hughes 269A c/n 42-0081 ex G-ASBD. G-ASEH did not take up the marks XS682 and XS684 was previously evaluated as XS349.

serial	type	sqdn/unit	code	where&when seen	remarks
XS681	Brantly B2A				Ex G-ASHK To G-ASHK
XS682	Brantly B2A				
XS683	Brantly B2B				Ex G-ASHJ To G-ASHJ
XS684	Hughes 269A				Ex G-ASBL To G-ASBL
XS685	Hughes 269A				Ex G-ASBD To G-ASBD

Nine Kestrel FGA.1 VTOL strike fighters (Spec FGA.236) ordered against Contract KC/2Q/016 and built by Hawker Siddeley Aviation Ltd at Kingston for service with the special tripartite trials squadron (British, German and American crews) which operated from West Raynham from 15.10.64 to 30.11.65. The nine aircraft first flew on the following respective dates:- 7.3.64; 28.5.64; 5.8.64; 5.9.64; 7.11.64; 25.11.64; 10.12.64; 17.2.65 and 5.3.65. XS693/695/696 rumoured to be allocated 64-18267/9/70.

serial	type	sqdn/unit	code	where&when seen	remarks
XS688	Kestrel FGA.1				To 64-18262 Pr USAFM
XS689	Kestrel FGA.1				To 64-18263 Pr DC
XS690	Kestrel FGA.1				To 64-18264
XS691	Kestrel FGA.1				To 64-18265
XS692	Kestrel FGA.1				To 64-18266 Pr VA
XS693	Kestrel FGA.1				
XS694	Kestrel FGA.1				To 64-18268
XS695	Kestrel FGA.1				To A2619
XS696	Kestrel FGA.1				

The second and final order for seven Hiller HT.2 basic training helicopters was placed with United Helicopters Inc during August 1963 on behalf of the RN, and to follow on from XS172. Deliveries were made by sea to RNAY Fleetlands between 22.10.63 and 5.12.63. The block was allotted c/ns 2299/2280/2289-2292/2300 respectively.

serial	type	sqdn/unit	code	where&when seen	remarks
XS700	Hiller HT.2				To ZS-HFX

XS701-XS780

serial	type	sqdn/unit	code	where&when seen		remarks
XS701	Hiller HT.2					To ZS-HFW
XS702	Hiller HT.2					
XS703	Hiller HT.2					To G-BDFO
XS704	Hiller HT.2					
XS705	Hiller HT.2					To G-BDYY
XS706	Hiller HT.2					To G-BEDK

20 Dominie T.1 advanced navigation training aircraft built for the RAF by the Chester Division of Hawker Siddeley Aviation Ltd as a replacement for the Meteor NF(T).14. XS709 f/f in 12.64 and the type entered service with 1 ANS at Stradishall 12 months later. The block was allotted c/ns 25011/25012/25024/25040/25041/25054/25044/25045/25048/25049/25050/25055/25056/25059/25061/25071/25072/25076/25077 and 25081 resp.

serial	type	sqdn/unit	code	where&when seen		remarks
XS709	Dominie T.1					Ex G-37-65
XS710	Dominie T.1					
XS711	Dominie T.1					
XS712	Dominie T.1					
XS713	Dominie T.1					
XS714	Dominie T.1					
XS726	Dominie T.1					
XS727	Dominie T.1					
XS728	Dominie T.1					
XS729	Dominie T.1					
XS730	Dominie T.1					
XS731	Dominie T.1					
XS732	Dominie T.1					
XS733	Dominie T.1					
XS734	Dominie T.1					
XS735	Dominie T.1					
XS736	Dominie T.1					
XS737	Dominie T.1					
XS738	Dominie T.1					
XS739	Dominie T.1					

Two B.206Z prototypes and 20 Basset CC.1 communications aircraft built to Spec C.238 by Beagle Aircraft Ltd at Rearsby against Contract KU/S/02. XS742 c/n B.003 (designated B.206Z1 by Beagle) f/f 24.1.64; XS743 c/n B.004 (B.206Z2) f/f 20.2.64. The first Basset (XS765) f/f 28.12.64 and deliveries were made between 23.2.65 and 2.9.66. The twenty Bassets were allotted c/ns B.006/B.008/B.010/B.011/B.012/B.014/B.016/B.017/B.018/B.020/B.021/B.024/B.025/B.030/B.034/B.031/B.033/B.036/B.042 & B.045 resp.

serial	type	sqdn/unit	code	where&when seen		remarks
XS742	Beagle B.206Z					
XS743	Beagle B.206Z					
XS765	Basset CC.1					
XS766	Basset CC.1					To G-BCJE
XS767	Basset CC.1					To G-BCIS
XS768	Basset CC.1					To G-BCJT
XS769	Basset CC.1					
XS770	Basset CC.1					
XS771	Basset CC.1					To G-BCJA
XS772	Basset CC.1					To G-BCJB
XS773	Basset CC.1					To G-BCJF
XS774	Basset CC.1					To G-BCMW
XS775	Basset CC.1					
XS776	Basset CC.1					To G-BCJG
XS777	Basset CC.1					To G-BCIV
XS778	Basset CC.1					To G-BCIX
XS779	Basset CC.1					To G-BCJC
XS780	Basset CC.1					To G-BCIU

XS781-XS878

serial	type	sqdn/unit	code	where&when seen		remarks
XS781	Basset CC.1					To G-BCIY
XS782	Basset CC.1					To G-BCJD
XS783	Basset CC.1					
XS784	Basset CC.1					To G-BCIZ

Six Andover CC.2 passenger-carrying transport aircraft built at Woodford by Hawker Siddeley Aviation Ltd for the Queen's Flight (XS789 and XS790) and for RAF Middle East & Far East Communications Flights plus the Metropolitan Communications Squadron in the UK (later 32 Sqdn). This variant has the manufacturer's designation HS.748 Srs 206 and was allotted c/ns 1561-1566 resp. Deliveries between 10.7.64 and 9.9.65.

serial	type	sqdn/unit	code	where&when seen		remarks
XS789	Andover CC.2					
XS790	Andover CC.2					
XS791	Andover CC.2					
XS792	Andover CC.2					
XS793	Andover CC.2					
XS794	Andover CC.2					

One Vickers-Armstrongs VA.1 hovercraft (c/n 001) built at Southampton and carried the B-Class registration G-15-252. Evaluated by the IHTU at Lee-on-Solent between 5.62 and 2.63. The serial was allocated but believed not carried.

serial	type	sqdn/unit	code	where&when seen		remarks
XS798	VA-1					

Thirty Wasp HAS.1 helicopters ordered for the RN and to be built by Westland Aircraft Ltd at Hayes, but the order was subsequently cancelled and none was built.

serials	type	quantity	remarks
XS802 - XS812	Wasp HAS.1	(11 a/c)	Cancelled and not built
XS834 - XS852	Wasp HAS.1	(19 a/c)	Cancelled and not built

One VA.2 hovercraft built by Vickers-Armstrongs Ltd at Southampton (c/n 001). After initial trials as VA.2-001 it was delivered to the IHTU Lee-on-Solent c4.63 and allocated the serial XS856 for overland trials carried out in Libya between 4.63 & 5.63.

serial	type	sqdn/unit	code	where&when seen		remarks
XS856	VA-2					

One Type 45 Swallow glider built by Slingsby Sailplanes Ltd at Kirkbymoorside and acquired by the Air Training Corps. It was allotted the c/n 1397 and was originally allocated the serial BGA1136.

serial	type	sqdn/unit	code	where&when seen		remarks
XS859	Swallow TX.1					Ex BGA1136

The fourth and final production contract for 28 Wessex HAS.1 helicopters built by Westland Aircraft Ltd at Yeovil for the RN and to follow on from XS154. XS862 f/f 15.4.65 and delivered to Culdrose 5.5.65; XS889 f/f 20.4.66 and delivered to RNAY Fleetlands 6.5.66. The block was allotted c/ns WA242 -WA269 respectively. Only XS862 from this batch was converted to HAS.3 configuration.

serial	type	sqdn/unit	code	where&when seen		remarks
XS862	Wessex HAS.3					
XS863	Wessex HAS.1					
XS864	Wessex HAS.1					
XS865	Wessex HAS.1					
XS866	Wessex HAS.1					
XS867	Wessex HAS.1					To A2671
XS868	Wessex HAS.1					To A2691
XS869	Wessex HAS.1					To A2649
XS870	Wessex HAS.1					
XS871	Wessex HAS.1					To 8457M
XS872	Wessex HAS.1					To A2666
XS873	Wessex HAS.1					To A2686
XS874	Wessex HAS.1					
XS875	Wessex HAS.1					
XS876	Wessex HAS.1					
XS877	Wessex HAS.1					To A2687
XS878	Wessex HAS.1					To A2683

XS879-XS941

serial	type	sqdn/unit	code	where&when seen		remarks
XS879	Wessex HAS.1					
XS880	Wessex HAS.1					
XS881	Wessex HAS.1					A2675 Pr FAAM
XS882	Wessex HAS.1					
XS883	Wessex HAS.1					
XS884	Wessex HAS.1					
XS885	Wessex HAS.1					To A2668
XS886	Wessex HAS.1					To A2685
XS887	Wessex HAS.1					To A2690
XS888	Wessex HAS.1					
XS889	Wessex HAS.1					

The main production order for 33 Lightning F.6 fighter aircraft for the RAF to follow XR766-773, and built by the British Aircraft Corporation (Preston Division). The block was allotted c/ns 95239-95271 respectively and formed the end of Lightning production for the RAF, the final aircraft (XS938) f/f 30.6.67 and was del 25.8.67.

serial	type	sqdn/unit	code	where&when seen		remarks
XS893	Lightning F.6					
XS894	Lightning F.6					
XS895	Lightning F.6					
XS896	Lightning F.6					
XS897	Lightning F.6					
XS898	Lightning F.6					
XS899	Lightning F.6					
XS900	Lightning F.6					
XS901	Lightning F.6					
XS902	Lightning F.6					
XS903	Lightning F.6					
XS904	Lightning F.6					
XS918	Lightning F.6					
XS919	Lightning F.6					
XS920	Lightning F.6					
XS921	Lightning F.6					
XS922	Lightning F.6					
XS923	Lightning F.6					
XS924	Lightning F.6					
XS925	Lightning F.6					
XS926	Lightning F.6					
XS927	Lightning F.6					
XS928	Lightning F.6					
XS929	Lightning F.6					
XS930	Lightning F.6					
XS931	Lightning F.6					
XS932	Lightning F.6					
XS933	Lightning F.6					
XS934	Lightning F.6					
XS935	Lightning F.6					
XS936	Lightning F.6					
XS937	Lightning F.6					
XS938	Lightning F.6					

The sole M.100 Student Mk.2, originally built (as a Mk.1) at Shoreham by F.G.Miles Ltd as a private-venture jet trainer and f/f 14.5.57 as G-35-4, later G-APLK. It was allotted c/n 100/1008. After a period of storage it was fitted with an uprated turbojet (to become Mk.2) and f/f 22.4.64 as XS941.

serial	type	sqdn/unit	code	where&when seen		remarks
XS941	M.100 Student Mk.2					Ex G-APLK To G-APLK

Thirty BAC TSR-2 Type 594 aircraft ordered on 20.3.64 under Contract KD/2L/16/CB42(a) to be built by the British Aircraft Corporation Ltd at Weybridge and Preston. Pro-

serial	type	sqdn/unit	code	where&when seen	remarks

duction was terminated on 6.4.65 when the TSR-2 programme was cancelled.

XS944 - XS954	BAC TSR-2	(11 a/c)	Cancelled and not built
XS977 - XS995	BAC TSR-2	(19 a/c)	Cancelled and not built

The first order for Sioux AH.1 helicopters for the AAC to Spec H.240 accounted for 200 units against Contract KK/191/033/CB25(a) and with 150 allotted consecutive serials XT101-XT250. The first 50 (XT101-150) were built by Costruzioni Aeronautiche Giovanni Agusta Spa (Agusta-Bell) at Gallerate, Italy under the manufacturer's designation Agusta-Bell 47G-3B-1 and allotted c/ns within the range 1535-1592. The remaining 100 Sioux from this block were built by Westland Aircraft Ltd at Yeovil. The first delivery to the UK was made by XT127/128 on 4.6.64 followed by Sioux up to XT150 which was delivered to Middle Wallop 5.3.65. The next batch (XT101-126) was delivered to overseas-based AAC units. Westland-built Sioux (XT151-250) were delivered between 2.4.65 and 6.10.66 and were allotted c/ns WA310-WA409 respectively.

serial	type	sqdn/unit	code	where&when seen	remarks
XT101	Sioux AH.1				
XT102	Sioux AH.1				To G-BGHN
XT103	Sioux AH.1				
XT104	Sioux AH.1				
XT105	Sioux AH.1				To G-BGHO
XT106	Sioux AH.1				
XT107	Sioux AH.1				To 9M-AUN
XT108	Sioux AH.1				Pr Middle Wallop
XT109	Sioux AH.1				To D-HAHS
XT110	Sioux AH.1				To G-BEHK
XT111	Sioux AH.1				To HB-XHS
XT112	Sioux AH.1				
XT113	Sioux AH.1				
XT114	Sioux AH.1				
XT115	Sioux AH.1				
XT116	Sioux AH.1				
XT117	Sioux AH.1				To G-BEHL
XT118	Sioux AH.1				
XT119	Sioux AH.1				
XT120	Sioux AH.1				To D-HAFC
XT121	Sioux AH.1				
XT122	Sioux AH.1				
XT123	Sioux AH.1				
XT124	Sioux AH.1				To G-BFFV
XT125	Sioux AH.1				
XT126	Sioux AH.1				To G-BFTS
XT127	Sioux AH.1				
XT128	Sioux AH.1				
XT129	Sioux AH.1				
XT130	Sioux AH.1				
XT131	Sioux AH.1				AAC Historic Flt
XT132	Sioux AH.1				To G-BFEF
XT133	Sioux AH.1				To 7923M
XT134	Sioux AH.1				To HB-XIH
XT135	Sioux AH.1				To G-MACD
XT136	Sioux AH.1				
XT137	Sioux AH.1				
XT138	Sioux AH.1				To G-BFBK
XT139	Sioux AH.1				To G-BHBX
XT140	Sioux AH.1				To GI Perth
XT141	Sioux AH.1				To 8509M
XT142	Sioux AH.1				
XT143	Sioux AH.1				To G-BFEJ
XT144	Sioux AH.1				

XT145-XT203

serial	type	sqdn/unit	code	where&when seen		remarks
XT145	Sioux AH.1					To G-BFRW
XT146	Sioux AH.1					To USA
XT147	Sioux AH.1					
XT148	Sioux AH.1					
XT149	Sioux AH.1					
XT150	Sioux AH.1					To GI Arborfield
XT151	Sioux AH.1					To GI Shrivenham
XT152	Sioux AH.1					
XT153	Sioux AH.1					To D-HOFD
XT154	Sioux AH.1					
XT155	Sioux AH.1					To D-HFFF
XT156	Sioux AH.1					To G-BFEI
XT157	Sioux AH.1					
XT158	Sioux AH.1					
XT159	Sioux AH.1					
XT160	Sioux AH.1					To G-BGAM
XT161	Sioux AH.1					
XT162	Sioux AH.1					To G-BFJN
XT163	Sioux AH.1					
XT164	Sioux AH.1					
XT165	Sioux AH.1					To G-BHOI
XT166	Sioux AH.1					
XT167	Sioux AH.1					To G-BFYI
XT168	Sioux AH.1					
XT169	Sioux AH.1					
XT170	Sioux AH.1					To G-BHBU
XT171	Sioux AH.1					
XT172	Sioux AH.1					To D-HAFK
XT173	Sioux AH.1					
XT174	Sioux AH.1					
XT175	Sioux AH.1					To TAD175 GI Oxford
XT176	Sioux AH.1					Pr Eastney
XT177	Sioux AH.1					
XT178	Sioux AH.1					
XT179	Sioux AH.1					To G-BFYF
XT180	Sioux AH.1					To G-BFEG
XT181	Sioux AH.1					To G-BGID
XT182	Sioux AH.1					To D-HAFD
XT183	Sioux AH.1					To ZS-HGZ
XT184	Sioux AH.1					
XT185	Sioux AH.1					
XT186	Sioux AH.1					To G-BEBV
XT187	Sioux AH.1					
XT188	Sioux AH.1					To D-HOWD
XT189	Sioux AH.1					
XT190	Sioux AH.1					
XT191	Sioux AH.1					To G-BGXP
XT192	Sioux AH.1					
XT193	Sioux AH.1					To D-HAFM
XT194	Sioux AH.1					To G-BHAR
XT195	Sioux AH.1					To G-BEHN
XT196	Sioux AH.1					
XT197	Sioux AH.1					To SE-HIF
XT198	Sioux AH.1					To ZS-HHX
XT199	Sioux AH.1					
XT200	Sioux AH.1					Pr Winthorpe
XT201	Sioux AH.1					
XT202	Sioux AH.1					To D-HEEE
XT203	Sioux AH.1					

XT204-XT257

serial	type	sqdn/unit	code	where&when seen		remarks
XT204	Sioux AH.1					
XT205	Sioux AH.1					To D-HGGG
XT206	Sioux AH.1					To D-HAFQ
XT207	Sioux AH.1					To D-HMHF
XT208	Sioux AH.1					
XT209	Sioux AH.1					
XT210	Sioux AH.1					
XT211	Sioux AH.1					To G-BFOH
XT212	Sioux AH.1					To D-HAFG
XT213	Sioux AH.1					To G-BFLS
XT214	Sioux AH.1					To G-BFJU
XT215	Sioux AH.1					
XT216	Sioux AH.1					
XT217	Sioux AH.1					To 9M-AUO
XT218	Sioux AH.1					
XT219	Sioux AH.1					
XT220	Sioux AH.1					To D-HDDD
XT221	Sioux AH.1					To G-CHOP
XT222	Sioux AH.1					To D-HIII
XT223	Sioux AH.1					To G-BGZK
XT224	Sioux AH.1					To G-BEBW
XT225	Sioux AH.1					
XT226	Sioux AH.1					To A O Hong Kong TV Co
XT227	Sioux AH.1					To G-BHKB
XT228	Sioux AH.1					To D-HAFR
XT229	Sioux AH.1					
XT230	Sioux AH.1					
XT231	Sioux AH.1					
XT232	Sioux AH.1					
XT233	Sioux AH.1					
XT234	Sioux AH.1					To G-BFVM
XT235	Sioux AH.1					
XT236	Sioux AH.1					Pr Sek Kong HK
XT237	Sioux AH.1					To D-HAFL
XT238	Sioux AH.1					
XT239	Sioux AH.1					
XT240	Sioux AH.1					
XT241	Sioux AH.1					
XT242	Sioux AH.1					
XT243	Sioux AH.1					
XT244	Sioux AH.1					To D-HATW
XT245	Sioux AH.1					To D-HHRK
XT246	Sioux AH.1					
XT247	Sioux AH.1					
XT248	Sioux AH.1					
XT249	Sioux AH.1					To G-BHBV
XT250	Sioux AH.1					

Three Wessex HAS.3 helicopters built by Westland Aircraft Ltd at Yeovil to serve as development 'prototypes' in connection with the conversion programme of RN HAS.1 to HAS.3 standard. The block was allotted c/ns WA239-WA241 resp. XT255 f/f 3.11.64.

serial	type	sqdn/unit	code	where&when seen		remarks
XT255	Wessex HAS.3					
XT256	Wessex HAS.3					To A2615
XT257	Wessex HAS.3					

The second production order for 20 Buccaneer S.2 carrier-borne strike aircraft for the RN. The batch was built by Hawker Siddeley Aviation Ltd, Brough and test flown at Holme-on-Spalding Moor between 3.65 and 1.66. (For details relating to subsequent conversions see explanation under XN922-935/XN948-983).

XT269-XT359

serial	type	sqdn/unit	code	where&when seen	remarks
XT269	Buccaneer S.2				
XT270	Buccaneer S.2B				
XT271	Buccaneer S.2A				
XT272	Buccaneer S.2				
XT273	Buccaneer S.2A				
XT274	Buccaneer S.2A				
XT275	Buccaneer S.2B				
XT276	Buccaneer S.2B				
XT277	Buccaneer S.2A				
XT278	Buccaneer S.2A				
XT279	Buccaneer S.2A				
XT280	Buccaneer S.2A				
XT281	Buccaneer S.2B				
XT282	Buccaneer S.2				
XT283	Buccaneer S.2A				
XT284	Buccaneer S.2A				
XT285	Buccaneer S.2				
XT286	Buccaneer S.2A				
XT287	Buccaneer S.2D				
XT288	Buccaneer S.2B				

85 Shelduck D.1 training target drones built by the Ventura Division of the Northrop Corporation for the RN PTA squadrons. All are a direct equivalent of the US Navy MQM-36A (previously known as the KD2R-5) and are marked as such.

serial	type	sqdn/unit	code	where&when seen	remarks
XT293	Shelduck D.1				
XT294	Shelduck D.1				
XT295	Shelduck D.1				
XT296	Shelduck D.1				
XT297	Shelduck D.1				
XT298	Shelduck D.1				
XT299	Shelduck D.1				
XT300	Shelduck D.1				
XT301	Shelduck D.1				
XT302	Shelduck D.1				
XT303	Shelduck D.1				
XT304	Shelduck D.1				
XT305	Shelduck D.1				
XT306	Shelduck D.1				
XT307	Shelduck D.1				
XT308	Shelduck D.1				
XT309	Shelduck D.1				
XT310	Shelduck D.1				
XT311	Shelduck D.1				
XT312	Shelduck D.1				
XT313	Shelduck D.1				
XT314	Shelduck D.1				
XT315	Shelduck D.1				
XT316	Shelduck D.1				
XT317	Shelduck D.1				
XT318	Shelduck D.1				
XT319	Shelduck D.1				
XT320	Shelduck D.1				
XT321	Shelduck D.1				
XT322	Shelduck D.1				
XT323	Shelduck D.1				
XT357	Shelduck D.1				
XT358	Shelduck D.1				
XT359	Shelduck D.1				

XT360-XT417

serial	type	sqdn/unit	code	where&when seen		remarks
XT360	Shelduck D.1					
XT361	Shelduck D.1					
XT362	Shelduck D.1					
XT363	Shelduck D.1					
XT364	Shelduck D.1					
XT365	Shelduck D.1					
XT366	Shelduck D.1					
XT367	Shelduck D.1					
XT368	Shelduck D.1					
XT369	Shelduck D.1					
XT370	Shelduck D.1					
XT371	Shelduck D.1					
XT372	Shelduck D.1					
XT373	Shelduck D.1					
XT374	Shelduck D.1					
XT375	Shelduck D.1					
XT376	Shelduck D.1					
XT377	Shelduck D.1					
XT378	Shelduck D.1					
XT379	Shelduck D.1					
XT380	Shelduck D.1					
XT381	Shelduck D.1					
XT382	Shelduck D.1					
XT383	Shelduck D.1					
XT384	Shelduck D.1					
XT385	Shelduck D.1					
XT386	Shelduck D.1					
XT387	Shelduck D.1					
XT388	Shelduck D.1					
XT389	Shelduck D.1					
XT390	Shelduck D.1					
XT391	Shelduck D.1					
XT392	Shelduck D.1					
XT393	Shelduck D.1					
XT394	Shelduck D.1					
XT395	Shelduck D.1					
XT396	Shelduck D.1					
XT397	Shelduck D.1					
XT398	Shelduck D.1					
XT399	Shelduck D.1					
XT400	Shelduck D.1					
XT401	Shelduck D.1					
XT402	Shelduck D.1					
XT403	Shelduck D.1					
XT404	Shelduck D.1					
XT405	Shelduck D.1					
XT406	Shelduck D.1					
XT407	Shelduck D.1					
XT408	Shelduck D.1					
XT409	Shelduck D.1					
XT410	Shelduck D.1					

Second production order (excluding XS802 etc) for 30 Wasp HAS.1 helicopters built to Spec HAS.216D&P for the RN by Westland Aircraft Ltd at Hayes under Contract KK/N/49/CB25(a) with c/ns F9584-F9613 respectively. XT414 first flew on 26.9.64.

serial	type	sqdn/unit	code	where&when seen		remarks
XT414	Wasp HAS.1					
XT415	Wasp HAS.1					
XT416	Wasp HAS.1					
XT417	Wasp HAS.1					NZ3904/XT417/NZ3904

XT418-XT476

serial	type	sqdn/unit	code	where&when seen		remarks
XT418	Wasp HAS.1					
XT419	Wasp HAS.1					To G-17-1/BzN N-7018
XT420	Wasp HAS.1					
XT421	Wasp HAS.1					
XT422	Wasp HAS.1					
XT423	Wasp HAS.1					
XT424	Wasp HAS.1					
XT425	Wasp HAS.1					
XT426	Wasp HAS.1					
XT427	Wasp HAS.1					
XT428	Wasp HAS.1					
XT429	Wasp HAS.1					
XT430	Wasp HAS.1					
XT431	Wasp HAS.1					
XT432	Wasp HAS.1					
XT433	Wasp HAS.1					To G-17-6/BzN N-7039
XT434	Wasp HAS.1					
XT435	Wasp HAS.1					
XT436	Wasp HAS.1					
XT437	Wasp HAS.1					
XT438	Wasp HAS.1					
XT439	Wasp HAS.1					
XT440	Wasp HAS.1					
XT441	Wasp HAS.1					
XT442	Wasp HAS.1					
XT443	Wasp HAS.1					

The second production order for 40 Wessex HU.5 helicopters for the RN built by Westland Aircraft Ltd at Yeovil. They were allocated c/ns WA270 to WA309 respectively. XT448 f/f 17.2.65 and the last of the batch (XT487) was delivered to the RN 21.6.66.

serial	type	sqdn/unit	code	where&when seen		remarks
XT448	Wessex HU.5					To A2596
XT449	Wessex HU.5					
XT450	Wessex HU.5					
XT451	Wessex HU.5					
XT452	Wessex HU.5					To Bangladesh AF WA274
XT453	Wessex HU.5					
XT454	Wessex HU.5					
XT455	Wessex HU.5					
XT456	Wessex HU.5					
XT457	Wessex HU.5					
XT458	Wessex HU.5					
XT459	Wessex HU.5					
XT460	Wessex HU.5					
XT461	Wessex HU.5					
XT462	Wessex HU.5					
XT463	Wessex HU.5					
XT464	Wessex HU.5					
XT465	Wessex HU.5					
XT466	Wessex HU.5					
XT467	Wessex HU.5					
XT468	Wessex HU.5					
XT469	Wessex HU.5					
XT470	Wessex HU.5					
XT471	Wessex HU.5					
XT472	Wessex HU.5					
XT473	Wessex HU.5					
XT474	Wessex HU.5					
XT475	Wessex HU.5					
XT476	Wessex HU.5					

XT477-XT553

serial	type	sqdn/unit	code	where&when seen		remarks
XT477	Wessex HU.5					
XT478	Wessex HU.5					To Bangladesh AF WA300
XT479	Wessex HU.5					
XT480	Wessex HU.5					
XT481	Wessex HU.5					
XT482	Wessex HU.5					
XT483	Wessex HU.5					
XT484	Wessex HU.5					
XT485	Wessex HU.5					
XT486	Wessex HU.5					
XT487	Wessex HU.5					

Two SR.N5 Warden hovercraft (c/ns 002 and 003) built by Westland Aircraft Co Ltd at East Cowes and delivered to the Interservice Hovercraft Trials Unit (Far East) at Lee-on-Solent on 19.8.64 and 21.10.64 respectively. XT492 handed over to the FAA Museum on 9.11.76. XT493 was converted to an SR.N6 Winchester Mk.5 and delivered to 200 HTS RCT in 6.72. It was sold back to British Hovercraft Corporation on 5.12.75.

serial	type	sqdn/unit	code	where&when seen		remarks
XT492	SR.N5 Warden					To FAAM To GH....
XT493	SR.N6 Winchester 5					To GH9011

The second block of serial allocations placed against Contract KK/191/033/CB25(a) to account for 50 Sioux AH.1 helicopters for the AAC to follow on from XT101-250 (qv). Deliveries commenced with XT499 on 6.10.66 (prior to XT498) and ended with XT570 on 9.6.67. The block was allotted c/ns WA410 to WA459 respectively. All were built by Westland Aircraft Ltd at Yeovil.

serial	type	sqdn/unit	code	where&when seen		remarks
XT498	Sioux AH.1					
XT499	Sioux AH.1					
XT500	Sioux AH.1					To G-BEWJ
XT501	Sioux AH.1					To G-BEHO
XT502	Sioux AH.1					
XT503	Sioux AH.1					
XT504	Sioux AH.1					
XT505	Sioux AH.1					To D-HHHH
XT506	Sioux AH.1					To GI Arborfield
XT507	Sioux AH.1					To G-BEBX
XT508	Sioux AH.1					To G-BGAI
XT509	Sioux AH.1					
XT510	Sioux AH.1					To G-BHBE
XT511	Sioux AH.1					
XT512	Sioux AH.1					To G-BEPA
XT513	Sioux AH.1					
XT514	Sioux AH.1					To D-HAFN
XT515	Sioux AH.1					
XT516	Sioux AH.1					To 9M-AUP
XT540	Sioux AH.1					
XT541	Sioux AH.1					
XT542	Sioux AH.1					To D-HAFH
XT543	Sioux AH.1					To G-BFSJ
XT544	Sioux AH.1					
XT545	Sioux AH.1					To G-BGOZ
XT546	Sioux AH.1					
XT547	Sioux AH.1					
XT548	Sioux AH.1					To GI Arborfield
XT549	Sioux AH.1					
XT550	Sioux AH.1					To GI Middle Wallop
XT551	Sioux AH.1					
XT552	Sioux AH.1					
XT553	Sioux AH.1					

XT554-XT607

serial	type	sqdn/unit	code	where&when seen		remarks
XT554	Sioux AH.1					
XT555	Sioux AH.1					
XT556	Sioux AH.1					To D-HATA
XT557	Sioux AH.1					To ZS-HHB
XT558	Sioux AH.1					
XT559	Sioux AH.1					
XT560	Sioux AH.1					To D-HAFF
XT561	Sioux AH.1					To D-H...
XT562	Sioux AH.1					To ZS-HHA
XT563	Sioux AH.1					
XT564	Sioux AH.1					
XT565	Sioux AH.1					
XT566	Sioux AH.1					To D-HAFB
XT567	Sioux AH.1					
XT568	Sioux AH.1					To G-BGTZ
XT569	Sioux AH.1					
XT570	Sioux AH.1					

One second-hand Vickers Viscount purchased by the Ministry of Technology during 1964 for use by the Radar Research Establishment. It was originally built by Vickers-Armstrongs (Aircraft) Ltd at Weybridge for Austrian Airlines as a Type 837 and allotted c/n 438. It f/f 17.2.60 as OE-LAG and del 1.3.60. Subsequently it was delivered to the RRE on 31.10.64.

serial	type	sqdn/unit	code	where&when seen		remarks
XT575	V.837 Viscount					Ex OE-LAG

Ten MQM-57A training target drones built by the Ventura Division of the Northrop Corporation for the British Army. All are a direct equivalent of the US Army Signal Corps MQM-57A drone and known in British service as the SD-1 Shelduck D.1, the designation being a corruption of the previous US designation AN/USD-1.

serial	type	sqdn/unit	code	where&when seen		remarks
XT580	Shelduck D.1					
XT581	Shelduck D.1					Pr Duxford
XT582	Shelduck D.1					
XT583	Shelduck D.1					Pr Arborfield
XT584	Shelduck D.1					GI Larkhill
XT585	Shelduck D.1					
XT586	Shelduck D.1					
XT587	Shelduck D.1					
XT588	Shelduck D.1					
XT589	Shelduck D.1					

Two YF-4K prototypes (XT595/596) and two pre-production F-4K Phantom FG.1 variants (XT597/598) built by McDonnell Douglas Aircraft Corporation at St. Louis, Missouri for the RN. XT595 f/f 27.6.66. The block had line numbers 1449/1527/1611 and 1669 respectively. Production aircraft for the RN commence with XT857.

serial	type	sqdn/unit	code	where&when seen		remarks
XT595	Phantom FG.1					To 8550M
XT596	Phantom FG.1					
XT597	Phantom FG.1					
XT598	Phantom FG.1					

The third production batch of seven Wessex HC.2 helicopters built by Westland Aircraft Ltd at Yeovil for the RAF. XT601 f/f 13.5.66 del 18.6.66; XT607 f/f 8.9.66 del 18.9.66. The block was allotted c/ns WA528 to WA534 inclusive.

serial	type	sqdn/unit	code	where&when seen		remarks
XT601	Wessex HC.2					
XT602	Wessex HC.2					
XT603	Wessex HC.2					
XT604	Wessex HC.2					
XT605	Wessex HC.2					
XT606	Wessex HC.2					
XT607	Wessex HC.2					

XT610-XT657

serial	type	sqdn/unit	code	where&when seen	remarks

One Twin Pioneer CC.2 originally built by Scottish Aviation Ltd at Prestwick with c/n 561 and registered G-APRS; f/f as such on 13.9.59. Following a succession of leases to various civilian operators, it was sold to the Ministry of Technology for use by the Empire Test Pilots School and delivered as XT610 on 16.3.65.

serial	type	sqdn/unit	code	where&when seen	remarks
XT610	Twin Pioneer CC.2				Ex G-APRS To G-BCWF

The third production order for 36 Scout AH.1 helicopters built by Westland Aircraft Ltd at Hayes, for the AAC against Contract KK/N/80/CB25(a). The block was allotted c/ns F9620 to F9655 inclusive. XT614 f/f 18.10.65; XT649 delivered 5.12.66.

serial	type	sqdn/unit	code	where&when seen	remarks
XT614	Scout AH.1				
XT615	Scout AH.1				
XT616	Scout AH.1				
XT617	Scout AH.1				
XT618	Scout AH.1				
XT619	Scout AH.1				
XT620	Scout AH.1				
XT621	Scout AH.1				
XT622	Scout AH.1				
XT623	Scout AH.1				
XT624	Scout AH.1				
XT625	Scout AH.1				To TAD625 Pr 'XR625'
XT626	Scout AH.1				
XT627	Scout AH.1				
XT628	Scout AH.1				
XT629	Scout AH.1				
XT630	Scout AH.1				
XT631	Scout AH.1				
XT632	Scout AH.1				
XT633	Scout AH.1				
XT634	Scout AH.1				
XT635	Scout AH.1				
XT636	Scout AH.1				To GI Middle Wallop
XT637	Scout AH.1				
XT638	Scout AH.1				
XT639	Scout AH.1				
XT640	Scout AH.1				
XT641	Scout AH.1				
XT642	Scout AH.1				
XT643	Scout AH.1				
XT644	Scout AH.1				
XT645	Scout AH.1				
XT646	Scout AH.1				
XT647	Scout AH.1				
XT648	Scout AH.1				
XT649	Scout AH.1				

One Type 45 Swallow TX.1 glider built by Slingsby Sailplanes Ltd at Kirkbymoorside with c/n 1420 for use by the Air Training Corps.

serial	type	sqdn/unit	code	where&when seen	remarks
XT653	Swallow TX.1				

One SR.N5 Warden hovercraft (c/n 005) built by Westland Aircraft Co Ltd, East Cowes and delivered to the Interservice Hovercraft Trials Unit at Lee-on-Solent on 5.3.65. Converted to SR.N6 Winchester Mk.5; delivered to 200 HTS RCT 6.72. To BHC 12.4.75.

serial	type	sqdn/unit	code	where&when seen	remarks
XT657	SR.N6 Winchester 5				To GH9008

One Vickers Type 838 Viscount originally built at Weybridge for Ghana Airways with c/n 371 and first flew 6.9.61 as 9G-AAV and delivered as such on 3.10.61. During February 1965 it was delivered to the Ministry of Technology for use by the RRE.

XT661-XT730

serial	type	sqdn/unit	code	where&when seen		remarks
XT661	V.838 Viscount					Ex 9G-AAV

Continued production of 15 Wessex HC.2 helicopters built by Westland Aircraft Ltd at Yeovil for the RAF to follow on from XT607. XT667 f/f 23.9.66; XT681 f/f 17.4.67 and deliveries took place between 3.10.66 and 5.7.67. The block was allotted c/ns WA535 to WA549 respectively.

serial	type	sqdn/unit	code	where&when seen		remarks
XT667	Wessex HC.2					
XT668	Wessex HC.2					
XT669	Wessex HC.2					
XT670	Wessex HC.2					
XT671	Wessex HC.2					
XT672	Wessex HC.2					
XT673	Wessex HC.2					
XT674	Wessex HC.2					
XT675	Wessex HC.2					
XT676	Wessex HC.2					
XT677	Wessex HC.2					To 8016M
XT678	Wessex HC.2					
XT679	Wessex HC.2					
XT680	Wessex HC.2					
XT681	Wessex HC.2					

Continued procurement of 50 Northrop KD2R-5/MQM-36A pilotless target drones for the RN PTA Squadrons to follow on from XT410. All are known as the Shelduck D.1 and allocations continue with XT931.

serial	type	sqdn/unit	code	where&when seen		remarks
XT685	Shelduck D.1					
XT686	Shelduck D.1					
XT687	Shelduck D.1					
XT688	Shelduck D.1					
XT689	Shelduck D.1					
XT690	Shelduck D.1					
XT691	Shelduck D.1					
XT692	Shelduck D.1					
XT693	Shelduck D.1					
XT694	Shelduck D.1					
XT695	Shelduck D.1					
XT696	Shelduck D.1					
XT697	Shelduck D.1					
XT698	Shelduck D.1					
XT699	Shelduck D.1					
XT700	Shelduck D.1					
XT701	Shelduck D.1					
XT702	Shelduck D.1					
XT703	Shelduck D.1					
XT717	Shelduck D.1					
XT718	Shelduck D.1					
XT719	Shelduck D.1					
XT720	Shelduck D.1					
XT721	Shelduck D.1					
XT722	Shelduck D.1					
XT723	Shelduck D.1					
XT724	Shelduck D.1					
XT725	Shelduck D.1					
XT726	Shelduck D.1					
XT727	Shelduck D.1					
XT728	Shelduck D.1					
XT729	Shelduck D.1					
XT730	Shelduck D.1					

XT731-XT782

serial	type	sqdn/unit	code	where&when seen		remarks
XT731	Shelduck D.1					
XT732	Shelduck D.1					
XT733	Shelduck D.1					
XT734	Shelduck D.1					
XT735	Shelduck D.1					
XT736	Shelduck D.1					
XT737	Shelduck D.1					
XT738	Shelduck D.1					
XT739	Shelduck D.1					
XT740	Shelduck D.1					
XT741	Shelduck D.1					
XT742	Shelduck D.1					
XT743	Shelduck D.1					
XT744	Shelduck D.1					
XT745	Shelduck D.1					
XT746	Shelduck D.1					
XT747	Shelduck D.1					

One Gannet T.5 originally built by Fairey Aviation Ltd at Hayes as an AS.1 with the serial WN365 but converted to become the T.2 prototype and f/f as such on 16.8.54. It was subsequently re-worked to T.5 standard and registered as G-APYO on 17.2.60 and delivered to White Waltham on 3.3.60 to participate in the training of crews for the Indonesian Navy, for which task it was serialled AS-14. Following a period of storage it was again re-worked at Hayes during 1966 to full RN standard and issued for service with a new serial. It was allotted the c/n F9137.

serial	type	sqdn/unit	code	where&when seen		remarks
XT752	Gannet T.5					Ex AS-14

The third and final batch of 20 Wessex HU.5 helicopters built by Westland Aircraft Ltd at Yeovil for the RN to follow on from XT487. The block was allotted the c/ns WA477-WA489/WA550-WA556 respectively. Delivered to RN between 7.66 and 9.67.

serial	type	sqdn/unit	code	where&when seen		remarks
XT755	Wessex HU.5					
XT756	Wessex HU.5					
XT757	Wessex HU.5					
XT758	Wessex HU.5					
XT759	Wessex HU.5					
XT760	Wessex HU.5					
XT761	Wessex HU.5					
XT762	Wessex HU.5					
XT763	Wessex HU.5					
XT764	Wessex HU.5					
XT765	Wessex HU.5					
XT766	Wessex HU.5					
XT767	Wessex HU.5					
XT768	Wessex HU.5					
XT769	Wessex HU.5					
XT770	Wessex HU.5					
XT771	Wessex HU.5					
XT772	Wessex HU.5					
XT773	Wessex HU.5					
XT774	Wessex HU.5					

Third production order for 18 Wasp HAS.1 helicopters built for the RN by Westland Helicopters Ltd, Hayes under Contract KK/N/93/CB25(a) with c/ns F9660-F9677 respectively. XT778 f/f at Yeovil on 12.5.66 and XT795 was delivered to the RN on 5.10.67.

serial	type	sqdn/unit	code	where&when seen		remarks
XT778	Wasp HAS.1					
XT779	Wasp HAS.1					
XT780	Wasp HAS.1					
XT781	Wasp HAS.1					
XT782	Wasp HAS.1					

XT783-XT836

serial	type	sqdn/unit	code	where&when seen		remarks
XT783	Wasp HAS.1					
XT784	Wasp HAS.1					
XT785	Wasp HAS.1					
XT786	Wasp HAS.1					
XT787	Wasp HAS.1					
XT788	Wasp HAS.1					
XT789	Wasp HAS.1					
XT790	Wasp HAS.1					
XT791	Wasp HAS.1					
XT792	Wasp HAS.1					
XT793	Wasp HAS.1					
XT794	Wasp HAS.1					
XT795	Wasp HAS.1					

The third production block of 49 Sioux AH.1 helicopters was built by Westland Aircraft Ltd at Yeovil against two contracts. XT798-XT820 were originally assigned to the Royal Marines against Contract KK/2C/2/CB25(a) but many were subsequently diverted to AAC units. XT824-XT849 were placed against Contract KK/191/033/CB25(a) and effectively replaced XT101-XT126 which had been diverted to overseas-based units of which many were attached to the Royal Marines. All were built concurrently with other Sioux blocks between XT196 and XV323 and were allotted c/ns WA505-WA527 and WA586-WA611 respectively. XT798 delivered 26.11.65; XT849 delivered 4.3.68.

serial	type	sqdn/unit	code	where&when seen		remarks
XT798	Sioux AH.1					
XT799	Sioux AH.1					
XT800	Sioux AH.1					
XT801	Sioux AH.1					To D-HHRW
XT802	Sioux AH.1					
XT803	Sioux AH.1					
XT804	Sioux AH.1					To G-BHBY
XT805	Sioux AH.1					
XT806	Sioux AH.1					To G-SOLY
XT807	Sioux AH.1					To G-BGMU
XT808	Sioux AH.1					
XT809	Sioux AH.1					
XT810	Sioux AH.1					To D-H...
XT811	Sioux AH.1					To G-BFOI
XT812	Sioux AH.1					To D-H...
XT813	Sioux AH.1					
XT814	Sioux AH.1					To D-H...
XT815	Sioux AH.1					To OE-AXX
XT816	Sioux AH.1					
XT817	Sioux AH.1					
XT818	Sioux AH.1					
XT819	Sioux AH.1					
XT820	Sioux AH.1					
XT824	Sioux AH.1					
XT825	Sioux AH.1					
XT826	Sioux AH.1					To G-BJAM
XT827	Sioux AH.1					To GI Arborfield
XT828	Sioux AH.1					
XT829	Sioux AH.1					To D-H...
XT830	Sioux AH.1					
XT831	Sioux AH.1					To G-BENG
XT832	Sioux AH.1					
XT833	Sioux AH.1					
XT834	Sioux AH.1					To G-BHBW
XT835	Sioux AH.1					To ZS-HGX
XT836	Sioux AH.1					

XT837-XT898

serial	type	sqdn/unit	code	where&when seen		remarks
XT837	Sioux AH.1					To ZS-HGY
XT838	Sioux AH.1					
XT839	Sioux AH.1					To G-BEBD
XT840	Sioux AH.1					
XT841	Sioux AH.1					To G-BFJT
XT842	Sioux AH.1					To G-BHKC
XT843	Sioux AH.1					
XT844	Sioux AH.1					To G-BERO
XT845	Sioux AH.1					
XT846	Sioux AH.1					To D-HLLL
XT847	Sioux AH.1					
XT848	Sioux AH.1					To G-BHKD
XT849	Sioux AH.1					

Two YF-4M prototypes built by McDonnell Douglas Aircraft Corporation at St. Louis, Missouri for the RAF as the Phantom FGR.2 variant with the line numbers 1950 and 2020 respectively. XT852 f/f 17.2.67.

serial	type	sqdn/unit	code	where&when seen		remarks
XT852	Phantom FGR.2					
XT853	Phantom FGR.2					

The first production batch of 20 Phantom FG.1 all-weather, ground attack and fighter reconnaissance aircraft for the RN and built by McDonnell Douglas Aircraft Corporation at St. Louis, Missouri. Initial delivery was made by XT858-860 to Yeovilton on 25.4.68. The block had line numbers 2097/2225/2279/2336/2383/2426/2463/2475/2502/2526/2546/2602/2623/2646/2666/2706/2738/2775/2813 and 2856 respectively.

serial	type	sqdn/unit	code	where&when seen		remarks
XT857	Phantom FG.1					
XT858	Phantom FG.1					
XT859	Phantom FG.1					
XT860	Phantom FG.1					
XT861	Phantom FG.1					
XT862	Phantom FG.1					
XT863	Phantom FG.1					
XT864	Phantom FG.1					
XT865	Phantom FG.1					
XT866	Phantom FG.1					
XT867	Phantom FG.1					
XT868	Phantom FG.1					
XT869	Phantom FG.1					
XT870	Phantom FG.1					
XT871	Phantom FG.1					
XT872	Phantom FG.1					
XT873	Phantom FG.1					
XT874	Phantom FG.1					
XT875	Phantom FG.1					
XT876	Phantom FG.1					

The first production batch of F-4M Phantom FGR.2 variants built by McDonnell Douglas Aircraft Corporation at St. Louis, Missouri for the RAF originally accounted for 38 aircraft, but was subsequently cut back to 24. XT891 was delivered to Aldergrove on 20.7.68. The block had line numbers 2250/2285/2333/2370/2417/2456/2471/2485/2507/2516/2536/2567/2592/2616/2636/2657/2665/2684/2696/2709/2727/2742/2754/2771 resp.

serial	type	sqdn/unit	code	where&when seen		remarks
XT891	Phantom FGR.2					
XT892	Phantom FGR.2					
XT893	Phantom FGR.2					
XT894	Phantom FGR.2					
XT895	Phantom FGR.2					
XT896	Phantom FGR.2					
XT897	Phantom FGR.2					
XT898	Phantom FGR.2					

XT899-XT971

serial	type	sqdn/unit	code	where&when seen		remarks
XT899	Phantom FGR.2					
XT900	Phantom FGR.2					
XT901	Phantom FGR.2					
XT902	Phantom FGR.2					
XT903	Phantom FGR.2					
XT904	Phantom FGR.2					
XT905	Phantom FGR.2					
XT906	Phantom FGR.2					
XT907	Phantom FGR.2					
XT908	Phantom FGR.2					
XT909	Phantom FGR.2					
XT910	Phantom FGR.2					
XT911	Phantom FGR.2					
XT912	Phantom FGR.2					
XT913	Phantom FGR.2					
XT914	Phantom FGR.2					

XT915 - XT928 Phantom FGR.2 (14 a/c) Cancelled and not built

Continued procurement of 50 Northrop KD2R-5/MQM-36A pilotless target drones for the RN Fleet Target Group to follow on from XT747. All are known as the Shelduck D.1 and allocations continue with XV818.

serial	type	sqdn/unit	code	where&when seen		remarks
XT931	Shelduck D.1					
XT932	Shelduck D.1					
XT933	Shelduck D.1					
XT934	Shelduck D.1					
XT935	Shelduck D.1					
XT936	Shelduck D.1					
XT937	Shelduck D.1					
XT938	Shelduck D.1					
XT939	Shelduck D.1					
XT940	Shelduck D.1					
XT941	Shelduck D.1					
XT942	Shelduck D.1					
XT943	Shelduck D.1					
XT944	Shelduck D.1					
XT945	Shelduck D.1					
XT946	Shelduck D.1					
XT947	Shelduck D.1					
XT953	Shelduck D.1					
XT954	Shelduck D.1					
XT955	Shelduck D.1					
XT956	Shelduck D.1					
XT957	Shelduck D.1					
XT958	Shelduck D.1					
XT959	Shelduck D.1					
XT960	Shelduck D.1					
XT961	Shelduck D.1					
XT962	Shelduck D.1					
XT963	Shelduck D.1					
XT964	Shelduck D.1					
XT965	Shelduck D.1					
XT966	Shelduck D.1					
XT967	Shelduck D.1					
XT968	Shelduck D.1					
XT969	Shelduck D.1					
XT970	Shelduck D.1					
XT971	Shelduck D.1					

XT972-XV140

serial	type	sqdn/unit	code	where&when seen		remarks
XT972	Shelduck D.1					
XT973	Shelduck D.1					
XT974	Shelduck D.1					
XT975	Shelduck D.1					
XT976	Shelduck D.1					
XT977	Shelduck D.1					
XT978	Shelduck D.1					
XT979	Shelduck D.1					
XT980	Shelduck D.1					
XT981	Shelduck D.1					
XT982	Shelduck D.1					
XT983	Shelduck D.1					
XT984	Shelduck D.1					
XT985	Shelduck D.1					

The second and final production batch of 9 VC.10 C.1 long-range strategic transport aircraft for the RAF was built by British Aircraft Corporation (Weybridge Division). All were built under the original Vickers designation Type 1106 and allocated c/ns 831-839 respectively. XV101 f/f 11.1.67; XV109 f/f 18.7.68. The RAF allocated names to its VC.10 fleet as follows:- XV101 (Lanoe Hawker VC); XV102 (Guy Gibson VC); XV103 (Edward Mannock VC); XV104 (James McCudden VC); XV105 (Albert Ball VC); XV106 (Thomas Mottershead VC); XV107 (James Nicolson VC); XV108 (William Rhodes-Moorhouse VC); XV109 (Arthur Scarfe VC).

serial	type	sqdn/unit	code	where&when seen		remarks
XV101	VC.10 C.1					
XV102	VC.10 C.1					
XV103	VC.10 C.1					
XV104	VC.10 C.1					
XV105	VC.10 C.1					
XV106	VC.10 C.1					
XV107	VC.10 C.1					
XV108	VC.10 C.1					
XV109	VC.10 C.1					

The fourth production order for 24 Scout AH.1 helicopters built by Westland Aircraft Ltd at Hayes for the AAC, and against Contract KK/N/102/CB25(a). The block was allotted c/ns F9693-F9716 respectively. Delivered to AAC between 1.67 and 2.68.

serial	type	sqdn/unit	code	where&when seen		remarks
XV118	Scout AH.1					
XV119	Scout AH.1					
XV120	Scout AH.1					
XV121	Scout AH.1					
XV122	Scout AH.1					
XV123	Scout AH.1					
XV124	Scout AH.1					
XV125	Scout AH.1					To GI Shrivenham
XV126	Scout AH.1					
XV127	Scout AH.1					
XV128	Scout AH.1					
XV129	Scout AH.1					
XV130	Scout AH.1					
XV131	Scout AH.1					
XV132	Scout AH.1					
XV133	Scout AH.1					
XV134	Scout AH.1					
XV135	Scout AH.1					
XV136	Scout AH.1					
XV137	Scout AH.1					
XV138	Scout AH.1					
XV139	Scout AH.1					
XV140	Scout AH.1					

XV141-XV182

serial	type	sqdn/unit	code	where&when seen		remarks
XV141	Scout AH.1					

One DH.106 Comet 2E acquired by the RAE Bedford Blind Landing Experimental Unit for Smiths Autoland System trials. Originally built by the de Havilland Aircraft Co Ltd at Hatfield with c/n 06033 for BOAC but cancelled, it was subsequently purchased by the Ministry of Supply and registered G-AMXK and f/f as such on 10.7.57. It was delivered to RAE Bedford as XV144 on 18.11.66.

XV144	Comet 2E					Ex G-AMXK

The final two Comet 4C airframes were initially built as such but converted to HS.801 Nimrod configuration for prototype trials purposes. The first prototype (XV148) was built at Chester with c/n 06477 and f/f 23.5.67 with Spey turbofan engines; XV147 was built at Woodford and f/f 31.7.67 with Avon engines and was allotted c/n 06476.

XV147	HS.801 (Nimrod)					
XV148	HS.801 (Nimrod)					

The third production order for 17 Buccaneer S.2 strike aircraft for the RN built by Hawker Siddeley Aviation Ltd at Brough to follow on from XT288. All the aircraft were test flown from Holme-on-Spalding Moor between 3.66 and 11.66. For conversion details see XN922 etc.

XV152	Buccaneer S.2A					
XV153	Buccaneer S.2					
XV154	Buccaneer S.2A					
XV155	Buccaneer S.2B					
XV156	Buccaneer S.2A					
XV157	Buccaneer S.2B					
XV158	Buccaneer S.2					
XV159	Buccaneer S.2					
XV160	Buccaneer S.2B					
XV161	Buccaneer S.2A					
XV162	Buccaneer S.2B					
XV163	Buccaneer S.2A					
XV164	Buccaneer S.2					
XV165	Buccaneer S.2B					
XV166	Buccaneer S.2B					
XV167	Buccaneer S.2					
XV168	Buccaneer S.2B					

One Cushioncraft CC-2 (c/n 002) built by the Hovercraft Division of Britten-Norman Ltd in the Isle of Wight. After evaluation by MVEE Chertsey, it underwent further trials at RAE Bedford from 1.66 to 4.69.

XV172	CC-2					

The first procurement of 48 Hercules C.1 transport aircraft built by the Lockheed Georgia Company at Marietta, Georgia for the RAF. All UK aircraft were built under the type designation C-130K-130-LM, being the equivalent of the USAF C-130E, US serials were allocated (but not carried) as follows: XV176-XV199 65-13021 to 65-13044; XV200-XV223 66-8850 to 66-8873 respectively. Deliveries commenced with XV177 on 19.12.66 and ended with XV223 in January 1968. The block of 48 was allotted the c/ns (prefixed 382-) 4169/4182/4188/4195/4196/4198-4201/4203-4207/4210-4214/4216-4220/4223/4224/4226-4228/4230-4233/4235-4238/4240-4247/4251-4253 respectively. XV208 was converted to W.2 standard and XV223 was the first C.3 conversion.

XV176	Hercules C.1					
XV177	Hercules C.1					
XV178	Hercules C.1					
XV179	Hercules C.1					
XV180	Hercules C.1					
XV181	Hercules C.1					
XV182	Hercules C.1					

XV183-XV239

serial	type	sqdn/unit	code	where&when seen		remarks
XV183	Hercules C.1					
XV184	Hercules C.1					
XV185	Hercules C.1					
XV186	Hercules C.1					
XV187	Hercules C.1					
XV188	Hercules C.1					
XV189	Hercules C.1					
XV190	Hercules C.1					
XV191	Hercules C.1					
XV192	Hercules C.1					
XV193	Hercules C.1					
XV194	Hercules C.1					
XV195	Hercules C.1					
XV196	Hercules C.1					
XV197	Hercules C.3					
XV198	Hercules C.1					
XV199	Hercules C.1					
XV200	Hercules C.1					
XV201	Hercules C.1					
XV202	Hercules C.1					
XV203	Hercules C.1					
XV204	Hercules C.1					
XV205	Hercules C.1					
XV206	Hercules C.1					
XV207	Hercules C.1					
XV208	Hercules W.2					
XV209	Hercules C.1					
XV210	Hercules C.1					
XV211	Hercules C.1					
XV212	Hercules C.1					
XV213	Hercules C.1					
XV214	Hercules C.1					
XV215	Hercules C.1					
XV216	Hercules C.1					
XV217	Hercules C.1					
XV218	Hercules C.1					
XV219	Hercules C.1					
XV220	Hercules C.1					
XV221	Hercules C.1					
XV222	Hercules C.1					
XV223	Hercules C.3					

First production contract for 38 Nimrod MR.1 long-range reconnaissance aircraft for the RAF built by Hawker Siddeley Aviation Ltd at Woodford with c/ns 8001-8038 resp. XV226 f/f 28.6.68 and XV262 del. 8.72. Subsequent conversions to MR.2/AEW.3 standard.

serial	type	sqdn/unit	code	where&when seen		remarks
XV226	Nimrod MR.1					
XV227	Nimrod MR.1					
XV228	Nimrod MR.1					
XV229	Nimrod MR.2					
XV230	Nimrod MR.1					
XV231	Nimrod MR.1					
XV232	Nimrod MR.1					
XV233	Nimrod MR.1					
XV234	Nimrod MR.1					
XV235	Nimrod MR.1					
XV236	Nimrod MR.2					
XV237	Nimrod MR.2					
XV238	Nimrod MR.1					
XV239	Nimrod MR.1					

XV240-XV290

serial	type	sqdn/unit	code	where&when seen		remarks
XV240	Nimrod MR.1					
XV241	Nimrod MR.1					
XV242	Nimrod MR.1					
XV243	Nimrod MR.1					
XV244	Nimrod MR.1					
XV245	Nimrod MR.1					
XV246	Nimrod MR.1					
XV247	Nimrod MR.1					
XV248	Nimrod MR.1					
XV249	Nimrod MR.1					
XV250	Nimrod MR.1					
XV251	Nimrod MR.1					
XV252	Nimrod MR.1					
XV253	Nimrod MR.1					
XV254	Nimrod MR.1					
XV255	Nimrod MR.2					
XV256	Nimrod MR.2					
XV257	Nimrod MR.1					
XV258	Nimrod MR.1					
XV259	Nimrod MR.2					
XV260	Nimrod MR.1					
XV261	Nimrod MR.1					
XV262	Nimrod MR.1					
XV263	Nimrod MR.1					

Six Beaver AL.1 utility aircraft built by de Havilland Aircraft of Canada Ltd at Downsview, Toronto for the AAC. All were shipped to the UK and assembled at the Hawker Siddeley Aviation facility at Hawarden (Chester) with deliveries being made between 20.12.66 and 20.3.67. The block was allotted c/ns 1648/1620/1621/1624/1651/ and 1654 respectively.

serial	type	sqdn/unit	code	where&when seen		remarks
XV268	Beaver AL.1					
XV269	Beaver AL.1					To 8011M
XV270	Beaver AL.1					
XV271	Beaver AL.1					
XV272	Beaver AL.1					
XV273	Beaver AL.1					

Six pre-production Harrier V/STOL strike fighters built by Hawker Siddeley Aviation Ltd at Kingston for continued evaluation prior to full production allocations which commence with XV738. All of this batch f/f at Dunsfold on 31.8.66/9.11.66/13.12.66/ 4.3.67/4.4.67/14.7.67 respectively.

serial	type	sqdn/unit	code	where&when seen		remarks
XV276	Harrier GR.1					
XV277	Harrier GR.1					
XV278	Harrier GR.1					
XV279	Harrier GR.1					To 8566M
XV280	Harrier GR.1					
XV281	Harrier GR.1					

One Cushioncraft CC-2 (c/n 003) built by the Hovercraft Division of Britten-Norman Ltd in the Isle of Wight. Evaluated by FVRDE at Long Valley from 8.3.65 until 4.65. Later to RAE Bedford as a spares source for CC-2's XR814 and XV172.

serial	type	sqdn/unit	code	where&when seen		remarks
XV285	Cushioncraft CC-2					

The second allocation of 18 Hercules C.1 transport aircraft built by the Lockheed Georgia Company at Marietta, Georgia for the RAF to follow on from XV223. Deliveries of this batch commenced with XV290 during January 1968 and ended with XV307 on 31.5.68. C/ns (prefixed 382-) were allotted as follows: 4254/4256-4259/4261-4264/ 4266-4268/4270/4272-4275 and 4277. Allocated US serials 66-13533-13550(not carried).

serial	type	sqdn/unit	code	where&when seen		remarks
XV290	Hercules C.1					

XV291-XV341

serial	type	sqdn/unit	code	where&when seen		remarks
XV291	Hercules C.1					
XV292	Hercules C.1					
XV293	Hercules C.1					
XV294	Hercules C.1					
XV295	Hercules C.1					
XV296	Hercules C.1					
XV297	Hercules C.1					
XV298	Hercules C.1					
XV299	Hercules C.1					
XV300	Hercules C.1					
XV301	Hercules C.1					
XV302	Hercules C.1					
XV303	Hercules C.1					
XV304	Hercules C.1					
XV305	Hercules C.1					
XV306	Hercules C.1					
XV307	Hercules C.1					

15 Sioux HT.2 helicopters built for the RAF by Westland Aircraft Ltd at Yeovil against Contract KK/2C/12/CB25(a). Originally this variant was to be designated AH.1A but, all entered service with the CFS as HT.2's. Several were subsequently loaned to the AAC(XV312, XV321 & XV322 c11.69 - 2.72). The block was allocated c/ns WA564-WA578.

serial	type	sqdn/unit	code	where&when seen		remarks
XV310	Sioux HT.2					
XV311	Sioux HT.2					To G-BDIA
XV312	Sioux HT.2					To 8430M & A2631
XV313	Sioux HT.2					To G-BCZJ
XV314	Sioux HT.2					To G-BDEE
XV315	Sioux HT.2					To G-BDHY
XV316	Sioux HT.2					
XV317	Sioux HT.2					To A2638
XV318	Sioux HT.2					To G-BCYY
XV319	Sioux HT.2					To G-BCYZ
XV320	Sioux HT.2					To G-BDHZ
XV321	Sioux HT.2					To G-BCZK
XV322	Sioux HT.2					
XV323	Sioux HT.2					To G-BCZL
XV324	Sioux HT.2					

Two Lightning T.5 advanced-training aircraft built for the RAF by the British Aircraft Corporation (Preston Division) to replace XS453 which had crashed on 1.7.66 and XS460 which had been diverted to Saudi Arabia. They were allotted c/ns 95021 and 95022 respectively and both made first flights during December 1966.

serial	type	sqdn/unit	code	where&when seen		remarks
XV328	Lightning T.5					
XV329	Lightning T.5					

The fourth production order for 30 Buccaneer S.2 strike aircraft for the RN built by Hawker Siddeley Aviation Ltd at Brough to follow on from XV168. XV332-XV352 were test flown from Holme-on-Spalding Moor between 11.66 and 10.67. XV353-XV361 were test flown from Driffield between 10.67 and 3.68. (Conversion details see XN922 etc)

serial	type	sqdn/unit	code	where&when seen		remarks
XV332	Buccaneer S.2B					
XV333	Buccaneer S.2B					
XV334	Buccaneer S.2B					
XV335	Buccaneer S.2					
XV336	Buccaneer S.2A					
XV337	Buccaneer S.2C					
XV338	Buccaneer S.2A					
XV339	Buccaneer S.2A					
XV340	Buccaneer S.2B					
XV341	Buccaneer S.2A					

XV342-XV396

serial	type	sqdn/unit	code	where&when seen		remarks
XV342	Buccaneer S.2B					
XV343	Buccaneer S.2					
XV344	Buccaneer S.2C					
XV345	Buccaneer S.2A					
XV346	Buccaneer S.2					
XV347	Buccaneer S.2B					
XV348	Buccaneer S.2B					
XV349	Buccaneer S.2B					
XV350	Buccaneer S.2B					
XV351	Buccaneer S.2D					
XV352	Buccaneer S.2B					
XV353	Buccaneer S.2B					
XV354	Buccaneer S.2A					
XV355	Buccaneer S.2A					
XV356	Buccaneer S.2A					
XV357	Buccaneer S.2A					
XV358	Buccaneer S.2C					
XV359	Buccaneer S.2C					
XV360	Buccaneer S.2A					
XV361	Buccaneer S.2C					

One VA.3 hovercraft built by Vickers-Armstrongs Ltd at Southampton (c/n 001) which wore the B-Class registration G-15-253. It was used by British United Airways for scheduled services and was also evaluated in the USA by Republic Aircraft Corp. It was allocated the serial XV366, presumably for MoD trials, but believed not carried.

serial	type	sqdn/unit	code	where&when seen		remarks
XV366	VA-3					

Four Sikorsky-built S-61's (c/ns 61-393 to 61-396) supplied to Westland Aircraft Co Ltd as trials and pattern aircraft. The first aircraft was carried as deck cargo to Avonmouth, where it was assembled on the quayside and then flown to Yeovil on 11.10.66 as G-ATYU, subsequently becoming XV370.

serial	type	sqdn/unit	code	where&when seen		remarks
XV370	Sikorsky SH-3D					Ex G-ATYU
XV371	Sea King HAS.1					
XV372	Sea King HAS.1					
XV373	Sea King HAS.1					

One SR.N5 Warden hovercraft to be built by the British Hovercraft Corporation for continued evaluation of the type by the IHTU at Lee-on-Solent. The order was subsequently cancelled.

serial	type	sqdn/unit	code	where&when seen		remarks
XV377	SR.N5 Warden					Cancelled

Planned procurement of a further 12 Northrop AN/USD-1 (MQM-57A) pilotless battlefield surveillance drones for the Army to follow on from XT589 was subsequently cancelled. Allocations continue with XW571.

XV378 - XV389 Northrop AN/USD-1 Shelduck D.1 (12 a/c) Cancelled

The second production batch of 124 F-4M Phantom FGR.2 aircraft was subsequently cut back to 92. All were built by McDonnell Douglas Aircraft Corporation at St. Louis, Missouri for the RAF with the line numbers: (XV393-442) 2791/2803/2822/2834/2850/2864/2869/2877/2885/2893/2901/2910/2919/2928/2937/2946/2955/2964/2973/2981/2990/2999 3007/3017/3026/3036/3045/3053/3061/3068/3075/3084/3093/3100/3106/3115/3124/3131/3140 3149/3158/3167/3174/3183/3195/3201/3208/3214/3220 and 3226. (XV460-501) 3231/3237/3243/3249/3255/3261/3266/3270/3276/3282/3288/3293/3298/3304/3309/3314/3321/3329/3336 3344/3350/3355/3361/3367/3373/3377/3382/3386/3392/3396/3401/3407/3413/3420/3428/3434 3442/3454/3466/3477/3491 and 3507 respectively.

serial	type	sqdn/unit	code	where&when seen		remarks
XV393	Phantom FGR.2					
XV394	Phantom FGR.2					
XV395	Phantom FGR.2					
XV396	Phantom FGR.2					

XV397-XV471

serial	type	sqdn/unit	code	where&when seen		remarks
XV397	Phantom FGR.2					
XV398	Phantom FGR.2					
XV399	Phantom FGR.2					
XV400	Phantom FGR.2					
XV401	Phantom FGR.2					
XV402	Phantom FGR.2					
XV403	Phantom FGR.2					
XV404	Phantom FGR.2					
XV405	Phantom FGR.2					
XV406	Phantom FGR.2					
XV407	Phantom FGR.2					
XV408	Phantom FGR.2					
XV409	Phantom FGR.2					
XV410	Phantom FGR.2					
XV411	Phantom FGR.2					
XV412	Phantom FGR.2					
XV413	Phantom FGR.2					
XV414	Phantom FGR.2					
XV415	Phantom FGR.2					
XV416	Phantom FGR.2					
XV417	Phantom FGR.2					
XV418	Phantom FGR.2					
XV419	Phantom FGR.2					
XV420	Phantom FGR.2					
XV421	Phantom FGR.2					
XV422	Phantom FGR.2					
XV423	Phantom FGR.2					
XV424	Phantom FGR.2					
XV425	Phantom FGR.2					
XV426	Phantom FGR.2					
XV427	Phantom FGR.2					
XV428	Phantom FGR.2					
XV429	Phantom FGR.2					
XV430	Phantom FGR.2					
XV431	Phantom FGR.2					
XV432	Phantom FGR.2					
XV433	Phantom FGR.2					
XV434	Phantom FGR.2					
XV435	Phantom FGR.2					
XV436	Phantom FGR.2					
XV437	Phantom FGR.2					
XV438	Phantom FGR.2					
XV439	Phantom FGR.2					
XV440	Phantom FGR.2					
XV441	Phantom FGR.2					
XV442	Phantom FGR.2					
XV460	Phantom FGR.2					
XV461	Phantom FGR.2					
XV462	Phantom FGR.2					
XV463	Phantom FGR.2					
XV464	Phantom FGR.2					
XV465	Phantom FGR.2					
XV466	Phantom FGR.2					
XV467	Phantom FGR.2					
XV468	Phantom FGR.2					
XV469	Phantom FGR.2					
XV470	Phantom FGR.2					
XV471	Phantom FGR.2					

XV472-XV584

serial	type	sqdn/unit	code	where&when seen		remarks
XV472	Phantom FGR.2					
XV473	Phantom FGR.2					
XV474	Phantom FGR.2					
XV475	Phantom FGR.2					
XV476	Phantom FGR.2					
XV477	Phantom FGR.2					
XV478	Phantom FGR.2					
XV479	Phantom FGR.2					
XV480	Phantom FGR.2					
XV481	Phantom FGR.2					
XV482	Phantom FGR.2					
XV483	Phantom FGR.2					
XV484	Phantom FGR.2					
XV485	Phantom FGR.2					
XV486	Phantom FGR.2					
XV487	Phantom FGR.2					
XV488	Phantom FGR.2					
XV489	Phantom FGR.2					
XV490	Phantom FGR.2					
XV491	Phantom FGR.2					
XV492	Phantom FGR.2					
XV493	Phantom FGR.2					
XV494	Phantom FGR.2					
XV495	Phantom FGR.2					
XV496	Phantom FGR.2					
XV497	Phantom FGR.2					
XV498	Phantom FGR.2					
XV499	Phantom FGR.2					
XV500	Phantom FGR.2					
XV501	Phantom FGR.2					

XV520 - XV551 Phantom FGR.2 (32 a/c) Cancelled and not delivered

The second production batch of 35 F-4K Phantom FG.1 aircraft was subsequently cut back to 28. All were built by McDonnell Douglas Aircraft Corporation at St. Louis, Missouri for the RN with the line numbers: (XV565-592) 2872/2896/2922/2943/2970/2995 3020/3042/3065/3087/3112/3134/3155/3180/3204/3218/3235/3253/3268/3286/3302/3317/3331 3346/3363/3394/3409 and 3424 respectively. All the remaining RN FG.1's in the 'XT' and 'XV' ranges were transferred to the RAF in 11.78 with the demise of HMS Ark Royal.

serial	type	sqdn/unit	code	where&when seen		remarks
XV565	Phantom FG.1					
XV566	Phantom FG.1					
XV567	Phantom FG.1					
XV568	Phantom FG.1					
XV569	Phantom FG.1					
XV570	Phantom FG.1					
XV571	Phantom FG.1					
XV572	Phantom FG.1					
XV573	Phantom FG.1					
XV574	Phantom FG.1					
XV575	Phantom FG.1					
XV576	Phantom FG.1					
XV577	Phantom FG.1					
XV578	Phantom FG.1					
XV579	Phantom FG.1					
XV580	Phantom FG.1					
XV581	Phantom FG.1					
XV582	Phantom FG.1					
XV583	Phantom FG.1					
XV584	Phantom FG.1					

XV585-XV654

serial	type	sqdn/unit	code	where&when seen		remarks
XV585	Phantom FG.1					
XV586	Phantom FG.1					
XV587	Phantom FG.1					
XV588	Phantom FG.1					
XV589	Phantom FG.1					
XV590	Phantom FG.1					
XV591	Phantom FG.1					
XV592	Phantom FG.1					

XV604 - XV610 Phantom FG.1 (7 a/c) Cancelled and not built

Four SR.N6 Winchester Mk.2 hovercraft (c/ns 032/033/034/?) built by BHC, East Cowes to Spec G.262. XV614 d/d to IHTU 12.67 and returned to BHC 18.12.74; sold to Egypt 1976 with XV616, as Mk.2F's. XV615-617 were delivered to 200 HTS RCT between 12.67 & 2.68.

serial	type	sqdn/unit	code	where&when seen		remarks
XV614	SR.N6 Winchester 2					To GH9006
XV615	SR.N6 Winchester 2					
XV616	SR.N6 Winchester 2					To GH9007
XV617	SR.N6 Winchester 2					

Fourth production order for 18 Wasp HAS.1 helicopters built for the RN by Westland Helicopters Ltd, Hayes under Contract KK/N/142/CB25(a) to follow on from XT795. The block was allotted c/ns F9717-F9734 respectively. The first of the batch, XV622 f/f at Yeovil on 17.1.68 and the last RN Wasp XV639 was delivered on 17.12.69.

serial	type	sqdn/unit	code	where&when seen		remarks
XV622	Wasp HAS.1					
XV623	Wasp HAS.1					
XV624	Wasp HAS.1					
XV625	Wasp HAS.1					
XV626	Wasp HAS.1					
XV627	Wasp HAS.1					
XV628	Wasp HAS.1					
XV629	Wasp HAS.1					
XV630	Wasp HAS.1					
XV631	Wasp HAS.1					
XV632	Wasp HAS.1					
XV633	Wasp HAS.1					
XV634	Wasp HAS.1					
XV635	Wasp HAS.1					
XV636	Wasp HAS.1					
XV637	Wasp HAS.1					
XV638	Wasp HAS.1					
XV639	Wasp HAS.1					

The first production contract for 56 Sea King HAS.1 helicopters to meet Spec HAS.261 was built for the RN by Westland Aircraft Ltd at Yeovil (c/ns WA630-WA685). XV642 f/f 7.5.69 and the majority of this production batch have subsequently been reworked to HAS.2A standard by WHL(Yeovil), RNAY Fleetlands and NASU RNAS Culdrose.

serial	type	sqdn/unit	code	where&when seen		remarks
XV642	Sea King HAS.2A					
XV643	Sea King HAS.2A					
XV644	Sea King HAS.1					To A2664
XV645	Sea King HAS.1					
XV646	Sea King HAS.1					
XV647	Sea King HAS.2A					
XV648	Sea King HAS.2A					
XV649	Sea King HAS.2A					
XV650	Sea King HAS.2A					
XV651	Sea King HAS.1					
XV652	Sea King HAS.2A					
XV653	Sea King HAS.2A					
XV654	Sea King HAS.2A					

XV655-XV726

serial	type	sqdn/unit	code	where&when seen		remarks
XV655	Sea King HAS.2A					
XV656	Sea King HAS.2A					
XV657	Sea King HAS.2A					
XV658	Sea King HAS.2A					
XV659	Sea King HAS.2A					
XV660	Sea King HAS.2A					
XV661	Sea King HAS.2A					
XV662	Sea King HAS.1					
XV663	Sea King HAS.2A					
XV664	Sea King HAS.2A					
XV665	Sea King HAS.2A					
XV666	Sea King HAS.2A					
XV667	Sea King HAS.1					
XV668	Sea King HAS.2A					
XV669	Sea King HAS.1					To A2659
XV670	Sea King HAS.2A					
XV671	Sea King HAS.2A					
XV672	Sea King HAS.2A					
XV673	Sea King HAS.2A					
XV674	Sea King HAS.2A					
XV675	Sea King HAS.2A					
XV676	Sea King HAS.2A					
XV677	Sea King HAS.2A					
XV695	Sea King HAS.1					
XV696	Sea King HAS.2A					
XV697	Sea King HAS.2A					
XV698	Sea King HAS.2A					
XV699	Sea King HAS.2A					
XV700	Sea King HAS.2A					
XV701	Sea King HAS.2A					
XV702	Sea King HAS.1					
XV703	Sea King HAS.2A					
XV704	Sea King HAS.2A					
XV705	Sea King HAS.2A					
XV706	Sea King HAS.2A					
XV707	Sea King HAS.2A					
XV708	Sea King HAS.2A					
XV709	Sea King HAS.2A					
XV710	Sea King HAS.2A					
XV711	Sea King HAS.2A					
XV712	Sea King HAS.2A					
XV713	Sea King HAS.2A					
XV714	Sea King HAS.2A					

The final production contract for Wessex helicopters built by Westland Aircraft Ltd for the RAF accounted for 13 HC.2's (to follow on from XT681) and two HCC.4's for the RAF Queen's Flight to replace Whirlwind HCC.12's XR486 and XR487. Deliveries commenced with XV719 on 19.12.67 and ended with XV731 on 3.7.68. XV732 and XV733 f/f 17.3.69 and 13.5.69 respectively. The entire block was allotted c/ns WA614 to WA628 inclusive.

serial	type	sqdn/unit	code	where&when seen		remarks
XV719	Wessex HC.2					
XV720	Wessex HC.2					
XV721	Wessex HC.2					
XV722	Wessex HC.2					
XV723	Wessex HC.2					
XV724	Wessex HC.2					
XV725	Wessex HC.2					
XV726	Wessex HC.2					

XV727-XV796

serial	type	sqdn/unit	code	where&when seen		remarks
XV727	Wessex HC.2					
XV728	Wessex HC.2					
XV729	Wessex HC.2					
XV730	Wessex HC.2					
XV731	Wessex HC.2					
XV732	Wessex HCC.4					
XV733	Wessex HCC.4					

The first production contract for Harrier GR.1 V/STOL fighter aircraft for the RAF accounted for 60 units, and was built by Hawker Siddeley Aviation Ltd at Kingston. The first aircraft (XV738) f/f at Dunsfold on 28.12.67 and deliveries of the block continued until April 1971. Most were subsequently uprated to GR.1A's and GR.3's.

serial	type	sqdn/unit	code	where&when seen		remarks
XV738	Harrier GR.3					
XV739	Harrier GR.1A					
XV740	Harrier GR.3					
XV741	Harrier GR.3					
XV742	Harrier GR.3					To G-VSTO Rtnd XV742
XV743	Harrier GR.1					
XV744	Harrier GR.3					
XV745	Harrier GR.3					
XV746	Harrier GR.3					
XV747	Harrier GR.3					
XV748	Harrier GR.3					
XV749	Harrier GR.1					
XV750	Harrier GR.3					
XV751	Harrier GR.3					
XV752	Harrier GR.3					
XV753	Harrier GR.3					
XV754	Harrier GR.3					
XV755	Harrier GR.3					
XV756	Harrier GR.3					
XV757	Harrier GR.3					
XV758	Harrier GR.3					
XV759	Harrier GR.3					
XV760	Harrier GR.3					
XV761	Harrier GR.3					
XV762	Harrier GR.3					
XV776	Harrier GR.3					
XV777	Harrier GR.1					
XV778	Harrier GR.3					
XV779	Harrier GR.3					
XV780	Harrier GR.1A					
XV781	Harrier GR.3					
XV782	Harrier GR.3					
XV783	Harrier GR.3					
XV784	Harrier GR.3					
XV785	Harrier GR.3					
XV786	Harrier GR.3					
XV787	Harrier GR.3					
XV788	Harrier GR.3					
XV789	Harrier GR.3					
XV790	Harrier GR.3					
XV791	Harrier GR.3					
XV792	Harrier GR.3					
XV793	Harrier GR.3					
XV794	Harrier GR.1					
XV795	Harrier GR.3					
XV796	Harrier GR.1					

XV797-XV859

serial	type	sqdn/unit	code	where&when seen		remarks
XV797	Harrier GR.3					
XV798	Harrier GR.1					
XV799	Harrier GR.1					
XV800	Harrier GR.3					
XV801	Harrier GR.3					
XV802	Harrier GR.1					
XV803	Harrier GR.1					
XV804	Harrier GR.3					
XV805	Harrier GR.3					
XV806	Harrier GR.3					
XV807	Harrier GR.3					
XV808	Harrier GR.3					
XV809	Harrier GR.3					
XV810	Harrier GR.3					

One DH.106 Comet 4 originally built at Hatfield by the de Havilland Aircraft Co Ltd for BOAC and f/f 11.12.58 as G-APDF (c/n 06407). During 1970 it was purchased by the Ministry of Technology for use by the RAE at Farnborough.

serial	type	sqdn/unit	code	where&when seen		remarks
XV814	Comet 4					Ex G-APDF

Continued procurement of 20 Northrop KD2R-5/MQM-36A pilotless target drones for the RN Fleet Target Group to follow on from XT985. All are known as the Shelduck D.1 and allocations continue with XW101.

serial	type	sqdn/unit	code	where&when seen		remarks
XV818	Shelduck D.1					
XV819	Shelduck D.1					
XV820	Shelduck D.1					
XV821	Shelduck D.1					
XV822	Shelduck D.1					
XV823	Shelduck D.1					
XV824	Shelduck D.1					
XV825	Shelduck D.1					
XV826	Shelduck D.1					
XV827	Shelduck D.1					
XV828	Shelduck D.1					
XV829	Shelduck D.1					
XV830	Shelduck D.1					
XV831	Shelduck D.1					
XV832	Shelduck D.1					
XV833	Shelduck D.1					
XV834	Shelduck D.1					
XV835	Shelduck D.1					
XV836	Shelduck D.1					
XV837	Shelduck D.1					

Fifteen Chinook helicopters ordered for the RAF as a replacement for the Belvedere HC.1 from the Boeing Company, Vertol Division during March 1967. However the contract was subsequently cancelled during November 1967 as part of a widespread programme of defence cuts. The planned RAF purchase was of the US CH-47B variant.

XV841 - XV855 Chinook HC.1 (15 a/c) Cancelled and not delivered

One SR.N6 Winchester hovercraft (c/n 027) brought up to Mk.6 standard by BHC at East Cowes and delivered to the Interservice Hovercraft Unit at Lee-on-Solent in 12.73.

serial	type	sqdn/unit	code	where&when seen		remarks
XV859	SR.N6 Winchester 6					Ex GH9001

The fifth production order for 15 Buccaneer S.2 strike aircraft for the RN was subsequently reduced to seven aircraft following some defence cuts. They were built to Martel standard (later called S.2D's) by Hawker Siddeley Aviation Ltd at Brough and test flown from Holme-on-Spalding Moor between 5.68 and 12.68. Following the withdrawal of Ark Royal from service they were issued to the RAF as S.2B's.

XV863-XW128

serial	type	sqdn/unit	code	where&when seen		remarks
XV863	Buccaneer S.2B					
XV864	Buccaneer S.2B					
XV865	Buccaneer S.2B					
XV866	Buccaneer S.2B					
XV867	Buccaneer S.2B					
XV868	Buccaneer S.2B					
XV869	Buccaneer S.2B					

XV870 - XV877 Buccaneer S.2 (8 a/c) Cancelled and not built

Following the cancellation of the TSR-2 programme an order was subsequently placed with the General Dynamics Corporation, Fort Worth Division for 50 advanced F-111A strike and reconnaissance aircraft under the general designation F-111K. The order accounted for 46 F-111K variants and 4 TF-111K examples for training purposes. Ultimately the entire programme was cancelled shortly after XV902 was rolled-out as 'UK-1'. US serials were allotted as follows: XV884-887 67-0151/0152/0153/0155. XV902-947 67-0149/0150/0154/0156-0158, 68-0181 to 68-0210/68-0229 to 68-0238 resp.

XV884 - XV887 TF-111K (4 a/c) Cancelled and not delivered

XV902 - XV947 F-111K (46 a/c) Cancelled and not delivered

40 Type T.53B all-metal two-seat training gliders were ordered for use by the Air Training Corps, to have been built by Slingsby Sailplanes Ltd at Kirkbymoorside against Contract KK/D/2735. The contract was cancelled after only the first aircraft had been completed. XV951 (c/n 1574) was awaiting collection 29.5.68.

serial	type	sqdn/unit	code	where&when seen		remarks
XV951	T.53B					

XV952 - XV990 T-53B (39 a/c) Cancelled and not built

Continued procurement of 60 Northrop KD2R-5/MQM-36A pilotless target drones for the RN Fleet Target Group to follow on from XV837. All are known as the Shelduck D.1 and allocations continue with XW444.

serial	type	sqdn/unit	code	where&when seen		remarks
XW101	Shelduck D.1					
XW102	Shelduck D.1					
XW103	Shelduck D.1					
XW104	Shelduck D.1					
XW105	Shelduck D.1					
XW106	Shelduck D.1					
XW107	Shelduck D.1					
XW108	Shelduck D.1					
XW109	Shelduck D.1					
XW110	Shelduck D.1					
XW111	Shelduck D.1					
XW112	Shelduck D.1					
XW113	Shelduck D.1					
XW114	Shelduck D.1					
XW115	Shelduck D.1					
XW116	Shelduck D.1					
XW117	Shelduck D.1					
XW118	Shelduck D.1					
XW119	Shelduck D.1					
XW120	Shelduck D.1					
XW121	Shelduck D.1					
XW122	Shelduck D.1					
XW123	Shelduck D.1					
XW124	Shelduck D.1					
XW125	Shelduck D.1					
XW126	Shelduck D.1					
XW127	Shelduck D.1					
XW128	Shelduck D.1					

XW129-XW195

serial	type	sqdn/unit	code	where&when seen		remarks
XW129	Shelduck D.1					
XW130	Shelduck D.1					
XW131	Shelduck D.1					
XW132	Shelduck D.1					
XW133	Shelduck D.1					
XW134	Shelduck D.1					
XW135	Shelduck D.1					
XW136	Shelduck D.1					
XW137	Shelduck D.1					
XW138	Shelduck D.1					
XW139	Shelduck D.1					
XW140	Shelduck D.1					
XW141	Shelduck D.1					
XW142	Shelduck D.1					
XW143	Shelduck D.1					
XW144	Shelduck D.1					
XW145	Shelduck D.1					
XW146	Shelduck D.1					
XW147	Shelduck D.1					
XW148	Shelduck D.1					
XW149	Shelduck D.1					
XW150	Shelduck D.1					
XW161	Shelduck D.1					
XW162	Shelduck D.1					
XW163	Shelduck D.1					
XW164	Shelduck D.1					
XW165	Shelduck D.1					
XW166	Shelduck D.1					
XW167	Shelduck D.1					
XW168	Shelduck D.1					
XW169	Shelduck D.1					
XW170	Shelduck D.1					

Two Harrier T.2 prototypes built by Hawker Siddeley Aviation at Kingston upon Thames, XW174 making its maiden flight at Dunsfold on 24.4.69.

serial	type	sqdn/unit	code	where&when seen		remarks
XW174	Harrier T.2					
XW175	Harrier T.2					

The final order for 17 Sioux AH.1 helicopters built for the AAC by Westland Aircraft Ltd at Yeovil against Contract KK/2C/22/CB25(b). XW179 was delivered on 5.11.68. The batch was allotted the c/ns WA699-WA715 respectively.

serial	type	sqdn/unit	code	where&when seen		remarks
XW179	Sioux AH.1					
XW180	Sioux AH.1					To G-BHNV
XW181	Sioux AH.1					To D-HAFJ
XW182	Sioux AH.1					To D-HAFO
XW183	Sioux AH.1					To D-HMNI
XW184	Sioux AH.1					To G-BEHP
XW185	Sioux AH.1					To G-BEGA
XW186	Sioux AH.1					
XW187	Sioux AH.1					To G-BGJC
XW188	Sioux AH.1					To D-HKKK
XW189	Sioux AH.1					
XW190	Sioux AH.1					To G-BFKM
XW191	Sioux AH.1					
XW192	Sioux AH.1					To G-BGFS
XW193	Sioux AH.1					To G-BHKW
XW194	Sioux AH.1					
XW195	Sioux AH.1					

XW198-XW246

serial	type	sqdn/unit	code	where&when seen	remarks

The first contract placed with Westland Aircraft Ltd for the SNIAS/Westland Puma HC.1 tactical assault helicopter accounted for 40 units. All were built for the RAF at Hayes with deliveries commencing with XW198 and XW199 on 29.1.71. The block was allotted c/ns 1039/1042/1048/1054/1061/1068/1074/1080/1086/1091/1095/1096/1101/1106/1111/1116/1120/1125/1129/1134/1139/1144/1148/1152/1157/1161/1166/1170/1175/1178/1183/1185/1191/1195/1199/1205/1206/1213/1217 & 1220 resp. (See also XW241). XW198-205/209/210 were also allocated 'Westland-Fairey' c/ns F9745-F9752/F9772/F9773 resp.

serial	type	sqdn/unit	code	where&when seen	remarks
XW198	Puma HC.1				
XW199	Puma HC.1				
XW200	Puma HC.1				
XW201	Puma HC.1				
XW202	Puma HC.1				
XW203	Puma HC.1				
XW204	Puma HC.1				
XW205	Puma HC.1				
XW206	Puma HC.1				
XW207	Puma HC.1				
XW208	Puma HC.1				
XW209	Puma HC.1				
XW210	Puma HC.1				
XW211	Puma HC.1				
XW212	Puma HC.1				
XW213	Puma HC.1				
XW214	Puma HC.1				
XW215	Puma HC.1				
XW216	Puma HC.1				
XW217	Puma HC.1				
XW218	Puma HC.1				
XW219	Puma HC.1				
XW220	Puma HC.1				
XW221	Puma HC.1				
XW222	Puma HC.1				
XW223	Puma HC.1				
XW224	Puma HC.1				
XW225	Puma HC.1				
XW226	Puma HC.1				
XW227	Puma HC.1				
XW228	Puma HC.1				
XW229	Puma HC.1				
XW230	Puma HC.1				
XW231	Puma HC.1				
XW232	Puma HC.1				
XW233	Puma HC.1				
XW234	Puma HC.1				
XW235	Puma HC.1				
XW236	Puma HC.1				
XW237	Puma HC.1				

One pre-production SA.330 transport helicopter (c/n 08) built by Sud Aviation at Marignane. First flight 30.7.68 as F-ZJUX and delivered to Westland Helicopters Ltd at Yeovil on 19.10.68 as XW241 for use as a pattern aircraft.

serial	type	sqdn/unit	code	where&when seen	remarks
XW241	SA.330E (Puma)				Ex F-ZJUX

One SR.N5 Warden hovercraft built by BHC at East Cowes (c/n 006). F/f 17.11.64 as SR.N5-006 until d/d to IHU on 5.11.68. Disposed of to Hoverwork Ltd on 30.9.74.

serial	type	sqdn/unit	code	where&when seen	remarks
XW246	SR.N5 Warden				To GH2041

One Cushioncraft CC-7 8-10 seat hovercraft (c/n 001) built by Cushioncraft Ltd (later part of BHC) in 3.68 for MinTech. Evaluated by the NPL Hovercraft Unit.

XW249-XW299

serial	type	sqdn/unit	code	where&when seen		remarks
XW249	CC-7					Pr Helston

One BH.7 Wellington hovercraft built by BHC at East Cowes (c/n 001) and delivered to the IHU at Lee-on-Solent on 28.9.70 prior to official handover in 3.71.

serial	type	sqdn/unit	code	where&when seen		remarks
XW255	BH-7 Wellington					

One HM-2 hovercraft (high-speed, rigid sidewall craft) built by Hovermarine Transport Ltd at Woolston, Southampton for evaluation purposes.

serial	type	sqdn/unit	code	where&when seen		remarks
XW260	HM-2					

The first production contract for 11 Harrier T.2 V/STOL training aircraft to be built by Hawker Siddeley Aviation Ltd at Kingston. The first (XW264) f/f at Dunsfold on 3.10.69. Most were later uprated to T.4's. XW273 was registered to Hawker Siddeley Aviation Ltd on 27.7.70 with c/n B3/41H/735795, initially as a T.2 and later as a T.52.

serial	type	sqdn/unit	code	where&when seen		remarks
XW264	Harrier T.2					
XW265	Harrier T.4					
XW266	Harrier T.4					
XW267	Harrier T.4					
XW268	Harrier T.4					
XW269	Harrier T.4					
XW270	Harrier T.4					
XW271	Harrier T.4					
XW272	Harrier T.4					
XW273	Harrier T.2					To G-VTOL
XW274	Harrier T.2					Static test airframe

The third of four French-built pre-production SA.341 helicopters (c/n 03) was shipped to Yeovil (as F-ZWRI) and assembled by Westland Helicopters Ltd in order to serve as the British Gazelle prototype. As XW276 it f/f at Yeovil on 28.4.70. Production Gazelle allocations commence with XW842.

serial	type	sqdn/unit	code	where&when seen		remarks
XW276	SA.341					Ex F-ZWRI

The fifth production batch of Scout AH.1 helicopters for the AAC were built by Westland Helicopters Ltd at Hayes under Contract KK/N/155/CB25(a). All were delivered during 1969 and were allotted c/ns F9735-F9739 respectively. XW280 f/f 9.5.69.

serial	type	sqdn/unit	code	where&when seen		remarks
XW280	Scout AH.1					
XW281	Scout AH.1					
XW282	Scout AH.1					
XW283	Scout AH.1					
XW284	Scout AH.1					

Initial order for 110 Jet Provost T.5 basic training aircraft for the RAF, built by BAC (Preston Division). XW287 was handed over to the CFS at Little Rissington on 3.9.69. The batch was allotted c/ns EEP/JP/951-1060 resp. Between 10.10.73 and 21.1.76 93 aircraft were returned to Warton for up-grading to T.5A standard with additional avionics. 13 T.5's fitted with tip-tanks are used as navigational trainers.

serial	type	sqdn/unit	code	where&when seen		remarks
XW287	Jet Provost T.5					
XW288	Jet Provost T.5A					
XW289	Jet Provost T.5A					
XW290	Jet Provost T.5A					
XW291	Jet Provost T.5					
XW292	Jet Provost T.5A					
XW293	Jet Provost T.5					
XW294	Jet Provost T.5A					
XW295	Jet Provost T.5A					
XW296	Jet Provost T.5					
XW297	Jet Provost T.5					
XW298	Jet Provost T.5					
XW299	Jet Provost T.5A					

XW300-XW371

serial	type	sqdn/unit	code	where&when seen		remarks
XW300	Jet Provost T.5					
XW301	Jet Provost T.5A					
XW302	Jet Provost T.5					
XW303	Jet Provost T.5A					
XW304	Jet Provost T.5					
XW305	Jet Provost T.5A					
XW306	Jet Provost T.5					
XW307	Jet Provost T.5					
XW308	Jet Provost T.5A					
XW309	Jet Provost T.5					
XW310	Jet Provost T.5A					
XW311	Jet Provost T.5					
XW312	Jet Provost T.5A					
XW313	Jet Provost T.5A					
XW314	Jet Provost T.5A					
XW315	Jet Provost T.5A					
XW316	Jet Provost T.5A					
XW317	Jet Provost T.5A					
XW318	Jet Provost T.5A					
XW319	Jet Provost T.5A					
XW320	Jet Provost T.5A					
XW321	Jet Provost T.5A					
XW322	Jet Provost T.5A					
XW323	Jet Provost T.5A					
XW324	Jet Provost T.5					
XW325	Jet Provost T.5A					
XW326	Jet Provost T.5A					
XW327	Jet Provost T.5A					
XW328	Jet Provost T.5A					
XW329	Jet Provost T.5A					
XW330	Jet Provost T.5A					
XW331	Jet Provost T.5					
XW332	Jet Provost T.5A					
XW333	Jet Provost T.5A					
XW334	Jet Provost T.5A					
XW335	Jet Provost T.5A					
XW336	Jet Provost T.5A					
XW351	Jet Provost T.5A					
XW352	Jet Provost T.5					
XW353	Jet Provost T.5A					
XW354	Jet Provost T.5A					
XW355	Jet Provost T.5A					
XW356	Jet Provost T.5					
XW357	Jet Provost T.5A					
XW358	Jet Provost T.5A					
XW359	Jet Provost T.5A					
XW360	Jet Provost T.5A					
XW361	Jet Provost T.5A					
XW362	Jet Provost T.5A					
XW363	Jet Provost T.5A					
XW364	Jet Provost T.5A					
XW365	Jet Provost T.5A					
XW366	Jet Provost T.5A					
XW367	Jet Provost T.5A					
XW368	Jet Provost T.5A					
XW369	Jet Provost T.5A					
XW370	Jet Provost T.5A					
XW371	Jet Provost T.5A					

XW372-XW458

serial	type	sqdn/unit	code	where&when seen		remarks
XW372	Jet Provost T.5A					
XW373	Jet Provost T.5A					
XW374	Jet Provost T.5A					
XW375	Jet Provost T.5A					
XW404	Jet Provost T.5A					
XW405	Jet Provost T.5A					
XW406	Jet Provost T.5A					
XW407	Jet Provost T.5A					
XW408	Jet Provost T.5A					
XW409	Jet Provost T.5A					
XW410	Jet Provost T.5A					
XW411	Jet Provost T.5A					
XW412	Jet Provost T.5A					
XW413	Jet Provost T.5A					
XW414	Jet Provost T.5A					
XW415	Jet Provost T.5A					
XW416	Jet Provost T.5A					
XW417	Jet Provost T.5A					
XW418	Jet Provost T.5A					
XW419	Jet Provost T.5A					
XW420	Jet Provost T.5A					
XW421	Jet Provost T.5A					
XW422	Jet Provost T.5A					
XW423	Jet Provost T.5A					
XW424	Jet Provost T.5A					
XW425	Jet Provost T.5A					
XW426	Jet Provost T.5A					
XW427	Jet Provost T.5A					
XW428	Jet Provost T.5A					
XW429	Jet Provost T.5A					
XW430	Jet Provost T.5A					
XW431	Jet Provost T.5A					
XW432	Jet Provost T.5A					
XW433	Jet Provost T.5A					
XW434	Jet Provost T.5A					
XW435	Jet Provost T.5A					
XW436	Jet Provost T.5A					
XW437	Jet Provost T.5A					
XW438	Jet Provost T.5A					

Continued procurement of 73 Northrop KD2R-5/MQM-36A pilotless target drones for the RN Fleet Target Group to follow on from XW170. All are known as the Shelduck D.1 and allocations continue with XW670.

serial	type	sqdn/unit	code	where&when seen		remarks
XW444	Shelduck D.1					
XW445	Shelduck D.1					
XW446	Shelduck D.1					
XW447	Shelduck D.1					
XW448	Shelduck D.1					
XW449	Shelduck D.1					
XW450	Shelduck D.1					
XW451	Shelduck D.1					
XW452	Shelduck D.1					
XW453	Shelduck D.1					
XW454	Shelduck D.1					
XW455	Shelduck D.1					
XW456	Shelduck D.1					
XW457	Shelduck D.1					
XW458	Shelduck D.1					

XW459-XW516

serial	type	sqdn/unit	code	where&when seen		remarks
XW459	Shelduck D.1					
XW460	Shelduck D.1					
XW461	Shelduck D.1					
XW462	Shelduck D.1					
XW463	Shelduck D.1					
XW464	Shelduck D.1					
XW465	Shelduck D.1					
XW466	Shelduck D.1					
XW467	Shelduck D.1					
XW468	Shelduck D.1					
XW469	Shelduck D.1					
XW470	Shelduck D.1					
XW471	Shelduck D.1					
XW472	Shelduck D.1					
XW473	Shelduck D.1					
XW474	Shelduck D.1					
XW475	Shelduck D.1					
XW476	Shelduck D.1					
XW477	Shelduck D.1					
XW478	Shelduck D.1					
XW479	Shelduck D.1					
XW480	Shelduck D.1					
XW481	Shelduck D.1					
XW482	Shelduck D.1					
XW483	Shelduck D.1					
XW484	Shelduck D.1					
XW485	Shelduck D.1					
XW486	Shelduck D.1					
XW487	Shelduck D.1					
XW488	Shelduck D.1					
XW489	Shelduck D.1					
XW490	Shelduck D.1					
XW491	Shelduck D.1					
XW492	Shelduck D.1					
XW493	Shelduck D.1					
XW494	Shelduck D.1					
XW495	Shelduck D.1					
XW496	Shelduck D.1					
XW497	Shelduck D.1					
XW498	Shelduck D.1					
XW499	Shelduck D.1					
XW500	Shelduck D.1					
XW501	Shelduck D.1					
XW502	Shelduck D.1					
XW503	Shelduck D.1					
XW504	Shelduck D.1					
XW505	Shelduck D.1					
XW506	Shelduck D.1					
XW507	Shelduck D.1					
XW508	Shelduck D.1					
XW509	Shelduck D.1					
XW510	Shelduck D.1					
XW511	Shelduck D.1					
XW512	Shelduck D.1					
XW513	Shelduck D.1					
XW514	Shelduck D.1					
XW515	Shelduck D.1					
XW516	Shelduck D.1					

XW525-XW580

serial	type	sqdn/unit	code	where&when seen	remarks

26 Buccaneer S.2B strike aircraft for the RAF built by Hawker Siddeley Aviation Ltd at Brough from 1970 with initial flights from Holme. XW525 first flew 8.1.70.

serial	type	sqdn/unit	code	where&when seen	remarks
XW525	Buccaneer S.2B				
XW526	Buccaneer S.2B				
XW527	Buccaneer S.2B				
XW528	Buccaneer S.2B				
XW529	Buccaneer S.2B				
XW530	Buccaneer S.2B				
XW531	Buccaneer S.2B				
XW532	Buccaneer S.2B				
XW533	Buccaneer S.2B				
XW534	Buccaneer S.2B				
XW535	Buccaneer S.2B				
XW536	Buccaneer S.2B				
XW537	Buccaneer S.2B				
XW538	Buccaneer S.2B				
XW539	Buccaneer S.2B				
XW540	Buccaneer S.2B				
XW541	Buccaneer S.2B				
XW542	Buccaneer S.2B				
XW543	Buccaneer S.2B				
XW544	Buccaneer S.2B				
XW545	Buccaneer S.2B				
XW546	Buccaneer S.2B				
XW547	Buccaneer S.2B				
XW548	Buccaneer S.2B				
XW549	Buccaneer S.2B				
XW550	Buccaneer S.2B				

One HM-2 hovercraft (high speed, rigid sidewall craft) built by Hovermarine Transport Ltd at Woolston, Southampton for evaluation. Later used by the NMI at Hythe.

serial	type	sqdn/unit	code	where&when seen	remarks
XW555	HM-2				

Three prototype SEPECAT Jaguar tactical strike aircraft built at Warton by the British Aircraft Corporation (Preston Division). Built jointly with France, Breguet Aviation being the French partner, the British prototypes were the last to fly: S.06 f/f 12.10.69; B.08 (the two-seat prototype) f/f 30.8.71.

serial	type	sqdn/unit	code	where&when seen	remarks
XW560	Jaguar S.06				
XW563	Jaguar S.07				To 8563M
XW566	Jaguar B.08				

Continued procurement of 20 Northrop AN/USD-1 (MQM-57A) pilotless battlefield surveillance drones for the Army. Although known in US Army Signal Corps service as the Northrop Falconer, all were later referred to in UK service as the Shelduck D.1. This block follows on from XT589 apart from the cancelled batch XV378-XV389.

serial	type	sqdn/unit	code	where&when seen	remarks
XW571	Shelduck D.1				
XW572	Shelduck D.1				
XW573	Shelduck D.1				
XW574	Shelduck D.1				
XW575	Shelduck D.1				
XW576	Shelduck D.1				
XW577	Shelduck D.1				
XW578	Shelduck D.1				
XW579	Shelduck D.1				
XW580	Shelduck D.1				

XW594-XW664

serial	type	sqdn/unit	code	where&when seen		remarks
XW594	Shelduck D.1					
XW595	Shelduck D.1					
XW596	Shelduck D.1					
XW597	Shelduck D.1					
XW598	Shelduck D.1					
XW599	Shelduck D.1					
XW600	Shelduck D.1					
XW601	Shelduck D.1					
XW602	Shelduck D.1					
XW603	Shelduck D.1					

The sixth production order for five Scout AH.1 helicopters for the AAC was placed against Contract KK/N/182/CB25(a), to follow on from XW284. All were built by Westland Aircraft Ltd at Hayes and delivered between February and May 1970. The block was allotted c/ns F9740-F9744 respectively, and allocations continue with XW795.

XW612	Scout AH.1					
XW613	Scout AH.1					
XW614	Scout AH.1					
XW615	Scout AH.1					
XW616	Scout AH.1					

One DH.106 Comet 4, originally built at Chester by the de Havilland Aircraft Co Ltd for BOAC and f/f 6.8.59 as G-APDS (c/n 06419). It was acquired by the Ministry of Technology on 30.1.69 and subsequently converted as an AEW Nimrod development aircraft and fitted with Nimrod nose radar housing. F/f as such on 28.6.77.

XW626	Comet 4					Ex G-APDS

One Harrier GR.1 built by Hawker Siddeley Aviation Ltd at Kingston for the RAF as a replacement aircraft for XV743 which had crashed on 27.1.69 prior to delivery to the RAF. XW630 was modified later to a GR.1A and subsequently to GR.3 standard.

XW630	Harrier GR.3					

One Beagle D5/180 Husky originally built by Beagle Aircraft Ltd at Rearsby for the National Society for the Mentally Handicapped as G-AWSW (c/n 3690) and f/f as such on 24.2.69. After being successfully raffled in London it was presented to the Air Training Corps for use by 5 Air Experience Flight at Cambridge.

XW635	D5/180 Husky					Ex G-AWSW

High-performance sailplane built in Germany in 1966 (c/n 6525). It was delivered to the Empire Test Pilots School at Boscombe Down 16.7.69, remaining there until it was delivered to RAFGSA at Abingdon 12.4.75. The BGA number was restored in 1976.

XW640	Schleicher Ka 6CR					Ex BGA1348 To BGA1348

Twelve Harrier Mk.50 aircraft built by Hawker Siddeley Aviation Ltd at Kingston for direct transfer to the USMC under the designation AV-8A. It is believed that this batch were allotted the USMC serials 158384-158395 respectively and thus forming the initial procurement batch for the USMC. At the time of press no further export Harriers had been allocated UK serials.

XW644 - XW655 Harrier Mk 50 (AV-8A) (12 a/c) Diverted to US Marine Corps

One HA5 Hover-Air Hoverhawk Mk.III (c/n 058) two-seat light hovercraft built by Hover-Air of Crowland, Lincolnshire for Service evaluation. It was temporarily stored at RAE Bedford in November 1972.

XW660	Hoverhawk Mk.III					

Three Nimrod R.1 electronic surveillance aircraft built by Hawker Siddeley Aviation Ltd at Woodford for use by 51 Sqdn as a replacement for that unit's Comet aircraft. It is believed that this block was allotted c/ns 8039-8041 resp. XW664 d/d 7.7.71.

XW664	Nimrod R.1					

XW665-XW737

serial	type	sqdn/unit	code	where&when seen		remarks
XW665	Nimrod R.1					
XW666	Nimrod R.1					

Continued procurement of 60 Northrop KD2R-5/MQM-36A pilotless target drones for the RN Fleet Target Group to follow on from XW516. All are known as the Shelduck D.1 and allocations continue with XW803.

serial	type	sqdn/unit	code	where&when seen		remarks
XW670	Shelduck D.1					
XW671	Shelduck D.1					
XW672	Shelduck D.1					
XW673	Shelduck D.1					
XW674	Shelduck D.1					
XW675	Shelduck D.1					
XW676	Shelduck D.1					
XW677	Shelduck D.1					
XW678	Shelduck D.1					
XW679	Shelduck D.1					
XW680	Shelduck D.1					
XW681	Shelduck D.1					
XW682	Shelduck D.1					
XW683	Shelduck D.1					
XW684	Shelduck D.1					
XW685	Shelduck D.1					
XW686	Shelduck D.1					
XW687	Shelduck D.1					
XW688	Shelduck D.1					
XW689	Shelduck D.1					
XW690	Shelduck D.1					
XW691	Shelduck D.1					
XW692	Shelduck D.1					
XW693	Shelduck D.1					
XW694	Shelduck D.1					
XW695	Shelduck D.1					
XW696	Shelduck D.1					
XW697	Shelduck D.1					
XW698	Shelduck D.1					
XW699	Shelduck D.1					
XW700	Shelduck D.1					
XW701	Shelduck D.1					
XW702	Shelduck D.1					
XW703	Shelduck D.1					
XW704	Shelduck D.1					
XW705	Shelduck D.1					
XW706	Shelduck D.1					
XW707	Shelduck D.1					
XW724	Shelduck D.1					
XW725	Shelduck D.1					
XW726	Shelduck D.1					
XW727	Shelduck D.1					
XW728	Shelduck D.1					
XW729	Shelduck D.1					
XW730	Shelduck D.1					
XW731	Shelduck D.1					
XW732	Shelduck D.1					
XW733	Shelduck D.1					
XW734	Shelduck D.1					
XW735	Shelduck D.1					
XW736	Shelduck D.1					
XW737	Shelduck D.1					

XW738-XW791

serial	type	sqdn/unit	code	where&when seen		remarks
XW738	Shelduck D.1					
XW739	Shelduck D.1					
XW740	Shelduck D.1					
XW741	Shelduck D.1					
XW742	Shelduck D.1					
XW743	Shelduck D.1					
XW744	Shelduck D.1					
XW745	Shelduck D.1					

One HS.748 Srs 107 originally built by Hawker Siddeley Aviation Ltd at Woodford for Smiths Aviation Division and registered G-ASJT (c/n 1559). It f/f as such 11.10.63 and was delivered on 20.10.63. Subsequently it was procured for the RAE as XW750 and delivered on 13.1.70.

serial	type	sqdn/unit	code	where&when seen		remarks
XW750	HS.748 Srs 107					Ex G-ASJT

The second production contract for Harrier V/STOL aircraft for the RAF accounted for 17 GR.1's (XW754-XW770) and 3 T.2's (XW778-780). It is reported that due to possible confusion between the serials XW754 et seq and the allocations within the initial production batch (XV754 etc) some re-allocations took place. This involved XW754-XW762 being re-issued as XW916-XW924 and the T.2's XW778-XW780 being re-issued as XW925-XW927 resp. All were built by Hawker Siddeley Aviation Ltd at Kingston. XW763-XW770 were later updated to GR.1A and GR.3 standard. XW763 delivered 5.11.71.

serial	type	sqdn/unit	code	where&when seen		remarks
XW754	Harrier GR.1					ntu To XW916
XW755	Harrier GR.1					ntu To XW917
XW756	Harrier GR.1					ntu To XW918
XW757	Harrier GR.1					ntu To XW919
XW758	Harrier GR.1					ntu To XW920
XW759	Harrier GR.1					ntu To XW921
XW760	Harrier GR.1					ntu To XW922
XW761	Harrier GR.1					ntu To XW923
XW762	Harrier GR.1					ntu To XW924
XW763	Harrier GR.3					
XW764	Harrier GR.3					
XW765	Harrier GR.3					
XW766	Harrier GR.3					
XW767	Harrier GR.3					
XW768	Harrier GR.3					
XW769	Harrier GR.3					
XW770	Harrier GR.3					
XW778	Harrier T.2					ntu To XW925
XW779	Harrier T.2					ntu To XW926
XW780	Harrier T.2					ntu To XW927

One Mitchell-Procter Kittiwake Mk.1 all-metal single-seat glider tug built by Royal Navy apprentices at Arbroath but completed at Lee-on-Solent. Allotted c/ns 02 and PFA.1352 it f/f at Lee on 21.10.71. On 20.11.73 it took up the civil regn. G-BBRN.

serial	type	sqdn/unit	code	where&when seen		remarks
XW784	Kittiwake Mk 1					To G-BBRN

Four HS.125 CC.1 executive transport aircraft built for the RAF by Hawker Siddeley Aviation Ltd at Chester for use by 32 Squadron at Northolt. All were allotted c/ns 25255/25264/25266 and 25268 respectively and are a direct equivalent of the civil Model 400B. Deliveries to the RAF were as follows: XW788 20.4.71; XW789 7.4.71; XW790 18.5.71; and XW791 27.5.71.

serial	type	sqdn/unit	code	where&when seen		remarks
XW788	HS.125 CC.1					
XW789	HS.125 CC.1					
XW790	HS.125 CC.1					
XW791	HS.125 CC.1					

XW795-XW839

serial	type	sqdn/unit	code	where&when seen		remarks

The seventh and final production order for five Scout AH.1 helicopters for the Army Air Corps was placed against Contract K25A/223/SW/CB25(a), to follow on from XW616. All were built by Westland Helicopters Ltd, Hayes and delivered between 4.5.72 and 13.10.72. The block was allotted c/ns F9758-F9762 respectively.

serial	type	sqdn/unit	code	where&when seen		remarks
XW795	Scout AH.1					
XW796	Scout AH.1					
XW797	Scout AH.1					
XW798	Scout AH.1					
XW799	Scout AH.1					

Continued procurement of 30 Northrop KD2R-5/MQM-36A pilotless target drones for the RN Fleet Target Group to follow on from XW745. All are known as the Shelduck D.1 and allocations continue with XW941.

serial	type	sqdn/unit	code	where&when seen		remarks
XW803	Shelduck D.1					
XW804	Shelduck D.1					
XW805	Shelduck D.1					
XW806	Shelduck D.1					
XW807	Shelduck D.1					
XW808	Shelduck D.1					
XW809	Shelduck D.1					
XW810	Shelduck D.1					
XW811	Shelduck D.1					
XW812	Shelduck D.1					
XW813	Shelduck D.1					
XW814	Shelduck D.1					
XW815	Shelduck D.1					
XW816	Shelduck D.1					
XW817	Shelduck D.1					
XW818	Shelduck D.1					
XW819	Shelduck D.1					
XW820	Shelduck D.1					
XW821	Shelduck D.1					
XW822	Shelduck D.1					
XW823	Shelduck D.1					
XW824	Shelduck D.1					
XW825	Shelduck D.1					
XW826	Shelduck D.1					
XW827	Shelduck D.1					
XW828	Shelduck D.1					
XW829	Shelduck D.1					
XW830	Shelduck D.1					
XW831	Shelduck D.1					
XW832	Shelduck D.1					

The first five prototype WG.13 helicopters built by Westland Helicopters Ltd, Yeovil all to a basic configuration. XW835 (Build No 1/02) f/f 21.3.71 and was rebuilt as G-BEAD and f/f as such 19.7.76. XW836 (Build No 1/04) f/f 24.3.72; XW837 (Build No 1/06) f/f 28.9.71; XW838 (Build No 1/03) f/f 8.3.72; XW839 (Build No 2/09) f/f 19.6.74. Subsequent Lynx prototypes were built to naval or utility configuration and allocations continue with XX153 and XX469. The Lynx was built to Spec H.273.

serial	type	sqdn/unit	code	where&when seen		remarks
XW835	Lynx					To G-BEAD
XW836	Lynx					
XW837	Lynx					
XW838	Lynx					
XW839	Lynx					

The first production contract for Aerospatiale/Westland Gazelle helicopters accounted for 60 units for all three British Services as follows: 29 Mk AH.1 for the AAC

XW842-XW904

serial	type	sqdn/unit	code	where&when seen	remarks

and Royal Marines; 21 Mk HT.2 for the Royal Navy; and 10 Mk HT.3 for the RAF. All were built by Westland Helicopters Ltd, Yeovil and were allotted c/ns as follows: 1002/1004/1005/1007/1009/1011/1013/1016/1019/1021/1024/1033/1045/1050/1078/1081/1089 1091/1100/1102/1104/1114/1116/1119/1120/1128/1130/1139/1146/1148/1150/1152/1157/1158 1159/1160/1161/1163/1165/1167/1173/1174/1177/1178/1191/1192/1195/1196/1199/1208/1209 1212/1213/1216/1217/1227/1228/1230/1231 and 1233. Delivered between 4.73 and 9.74.

serial	type	sqdn/unit	code	where&when seen	remarks
XW842	Gazelle AH.1				
XW843	Gazelle AH.1				
XW844	Gazelle AH.1				To F-ZKCW Rtnd XW844
XW845	Gazelle HT.2				
XW846	Gazelle AH.1				
XW847	Gazelle AH.1				
XW848	Gazelle AH.1				
XW849	Gazelle AH.1				
XW850	Gazelle AH.1				
XW851	Gazelle AH.1				
XW852	Gazelle HT.3				
XW853	Gazelle HT.2				
XW854	Gazelle HT.2				
XW855	Gazelle HT.3				
XW856	Gazelle HT.2				
XW857	Gazelle HT.2				
XW858	Gazelle HT.3				
XW859	Gazelle HT.2				
XW860	Gazelle HT.2				
XW861	Gazelle HT.2				
XW862	Gazelle HT.3				
XW863	Gazelle HT.2				
XW864	Gazelle HT.2				
XW865	Gazelle AH.1				
XW866	Gazelle HT.3				
XW867	Gazelle HT.2				
XW868	Gazelle HT.2				
XW869	Gazelle AH.1				
XW870	Gazelle HT.3				
XW871	Gazelle HT.2				
XW884	Gazelle HT.2				
XW885	Gazelle AH.1				
XW886	Gazelle HT.2				
XW887	Gazelle HT.2				
XW888	Gazelle AH.1				
XW889	Gazelle AH.1				
XW890	Gazelle HT.2				
XW891	Gazelle HT.2				
XW892	Gazelle AH.1				
XW893	Gazelle AH.1				
XW894	Gazelle HT.2				
XW895	Gazelle HT.2				
XW896	Gazelle AH.1				
XW897	Gazelle AH.1				
XW898	Gazelle HT.3				
XW899	Gazelle AH.1				
XW900	Gazelle AH.1				
XW901	Gazelle AH.1				
XW902	Gazelle HT.3				
XW903	Gazelle AH.1				
XW904	Gazelle AH.1				

XW905-XW948

serial	type	sqdn/unit	code	where&when seen		remarks
XW905	Gazelle AH.1					
XW906	Gazelle HT.3					
XW907	Gazelle HT.2					
XW908	Gazelle AH.1					
XW909	Gazelle AH.1					
XW910	Gazelle HT.3					
XW911	Gazelle AH.1					
XW912	Gazelle AH.1					
XW913	Gazelle AH.1					

Twelve Harrier V/STOL aircraft built by Hawker Siddeley Aviation Ltd at Kingston for the RAF, XW916-XW924 to GR.1 standard and XW925-XW927 to T.2 standard, both with the Pegasus 101 engine. All are reported to have been re-serialled from XW754-XW762 and XW778-XW780 resp (qv). Subsequent upgrading to GR.1A and T.2A standard (Pegasus 102) and GR.3 and T.4 standard (Pegasus 103). XW916 d/d 19.11.71; XW927 d/d 28.7.72.

serial	type	sqdn/unit	code	where&when seen		remarks
XW916	Harrier GR.3					
XW917	Harrier GR.3					
XW918	Harrier GR.1					
XW919	Harrier GR.3					
XW920	Harrier GR.1A					
XW921	Harrier GR.3					
XW922	Harrier GR.3					
XW923	Harrier GR.3					
XW924	Harrier GR.3					
XW925	Harrier T.4					
XW926	Harrier T.4					
XW927	Harrier T.4					

One HS.125 Srs 1B originally built by Hawker Siddeley Aviation Ltd at Chester in 1965 for the John Bloom empire of Rolls-Razor as a Srs 1 with c/n 25009. After a lengthy period of storage it was registered as G-ATPC to the Ministry of Aviation on 11.2.66 for use by the CAFU at Stansted. During March 1971 it was transferred to RAE Bedford as XW930.

serial	type	sqdn/unit	code	where&when seen		remarks
XW930	HS.125 Srs 1B					Ex G-ATPC

Two Harrier T.4 V/STOL training aircraft built by Hawker Siddeley Aviation Ltd at Kingston for the RAF as replacements for XW273 (retained by the manufacturer as G-VTOL) and XW274 (retained as a static test rig). The first (XW933) was delivered 22.8.73.

serial	type	sqdn/unit	code	where&when seen		remarks
XW933	Harrier T.4					
XW934	Harrier T.4					

One Piper PA-30 Twin Comanche 160 originally built at Lock Haven during 1964 and registered as N7385Y with c/n 30-439. Imported to the UK and registered as G-ATMT on 10.1.66 to Airways Aviation Ltd, it was delivered to the College of Aeronautics Cranfield on 19.1.71 for experimental flying. The aircraft left Cranfield 29.3.74.

serial	type	sqdn/unit	code	where&when seen		remarks
XW938	Twin Comanche 160					Ex G-ATMT To G-ATMT

Continued procurement of 40 Northrop KD2R-5/MQM-36A pilotless target drones for the RN Fleet Target Group to follow on from XW832. All are known as the Shelduck D.1 and allocations continue with XX850.

serial	type	sqdn/unit	code	where&when seen		remarks
XW941	Shelduck D.1					
XW942	Shelduck D.1					
XW943	Shelduck D.1					
XW944	Shelduck D.1					
XW945	Shelduck D.1					
XW946	Shelduck D.1					
XW947	Shelduck D.1					
XW948	Shelduck D.1					

XW949-XW998

serial	type	sqdn/unit	code	where&when seen		remarks
XW949	Shelduck D.1					
XW950	Shelduck D.1					
XW951	Shelduck D.1					
XW952	Shelduck D.1					
XW953	Shelduck D.1					
XW954	Shelduck D.1					
XW955	Shelduck D.1					
XW956	Shelduck D.1					
XW957	Shelduck D.1					
XW958	Shelduck D.1					
XW959	Shelduck D.1					
XW960	Shelduck D.1					
XW961	Shelduck D.1					
XW962	Shelduck D.1					
XW963	Shelduck D.1					
XW964	Shelduck D.1					
XW965	Shelduck D.1					
XW966	Shelduck D.1					
XW967	Shelduck D.1					
XW968	Shelduck D.1					
XW969	Shelduck D.1					
XW970	Shelduck D.1					
XW971	Shelduck D.1					
XW972	Shelduck D.1					
XW973	Shelduck D.1					
XW974	Shelduck D.1					
XW975	Shelduck D.1					
XW976	Shelduck D.1					
XW977	Shelduck D.1					
XW978	Shelduck D.1					
XW979	Shelduck D.1					
XW980	Shelduck D.1					

One Type T61A Falke motor-glider built at Kirkbymoorside by Slingsby Sailplanes Ltd although the manufacturer had since been absorbed into the Vickers group. Originally registered as G-AYUP on 19.3.71 with c/n 1735 it was immediately transferred to military marks for evaluation purposes. Production motor-gliders for the Air Training Corps commence with XZ550.

serial	type	sqdn/unit	code	where&when seen		remarks
XW983	Venture T.1					Ex G-AYUP

Three Buccaneer S.2B's built by Hawker Siddeley Aviation Ltd at Brough, specifically for trials use by the RAE at Farnborough and West Freugh. The aircraft were test flown from Holme-on-Spalding Moor and were delivered in 1973/74.

serial	type	sqdn/unit	code	where&when seen		remarks
XW986	Buccaneer S.2B					
XW987	Buccaneer S.2B					
XW988	Buccaneer S.2B					

The first order for 10 Chukar D.1 jet-powered pilotless target drones for the Royal Navy Fleet Target Group. All were built by the Ventura Division of the Northrop Corporation and are a direct equivalent of the MQM-74A in US Navy service.

serial	type	sqdn/unit	code	where&when seen		remarks
XW990	Chukar D.1					
XW991	Chukar D.1					
XW992	Chukar D.1					
XW993	Chukar D.1					
XW994	Chukar D.1					To FAAM
XW995	Chukar D.1					
XW996	Chukar D.1					
XW997	Chukar D.1					
XW998	Chukar D.1					

XW999-XX153

serial	type	sqdn/unit	code	where&when seen		remarks
XW999	Chukar D.1					

Two CC-7 8-10 seat hovercraft (c/ns 004/005) built by BHC in the Isle of Wight and delivered to 200 HTS RCT at Browndown, Hants c7.72.

serial	type	sqdn/unit	code	where&when seen		remarks
XX101	CC-7					Pr Yeovilton
XX102	CC-7					

One BAC-111 Srs 201AC originally built by the British Aircraft Corporation Ltd at Hurn for British United Airways Ltd and registered as G-ASJD 6.6.63, f/f as such on 6.7.64. Subsequently procured for the Royal Aircraft Establishment, it was delivered to Bedford on 21.9.71. It was allotted the c/n 008.

serial	type	sqdn/unit	code	where&when seen		remarks
XX105	BAC-111 Srs 201AC					Ex G-ASJD

The first production order for 30 SEPECAT/BAC Jaguar aircraft accounted for 15 GR.1 tactical support and ground attack aircraft (XX108-XX122 c/ns S.1-S.15) and 15 T.2 operational advanced training aircraft (XX136-XX150 c/ns B.1-B.15). All were built for the RAF by British Aircraft Corporation (Military Aircraft Division) at Preston. XX108 f/f 11.10.72; XX136 f/f 28.3.73. Subsequent loans to the Indian AF.

serial	type	sqdn/unit	code	where&when seen		remarks
XX108	Jaguar GR.1					
XX109	Jaguar GR.1					
XX110	Jaguar GR.1					
XX111	Jaguar GR.1					To G-27-314/IAF JI011
XX112	Jaguar GR.1					
XX113	Jaguar GR.1					
XX114	Jaguar GR.1					
XX115	Jaguar GR.1					To G-27-315/IAF JI005
XX116	Jaguar GR.1					To G-27-316/IAF JI008
XX117	Jaguar GR.1					To G-27-317/IAF JI004
XX118	Jaguar GR.1					To G-27-318/IAF JI018
XX119	Jaguar GR.1					
XX120	Jaguar GR.1					
XX121	Jaguar GR.1					
XX122	Jaguar GR.1					
XX136	Jaguar T.2					
XX137	Jaguar T.2					
XX138	Jaguar T.2					To G-27-319/IAF JI001
XX139	Jaguar T.2					
XX140	Jaguar T.2					
XX141	Jaguar T.2					
XX142	Jaguar T.2					
XX143	Jaguar T.2					To G-27-321/IAF JI002
XX144	Jaguar T.2					
XX145	Jaguar T.2					
XX146	Jaguar T.2					
XX147	Jaguar T.2					
XX148	Jaguar T.2					
XX149	Jaguar T.2					
XX150	Jaguar T.2					

One Lynx prototype (to follow on from XW835-XW839) and built to utility (Army) configuration by Westland Aircraft Ltd at Yeovil to act as the Mk AH.1 development helicopter. XX153 f/f 12.4.72 and was allotted build number 2/11.

serial	type	sqdn/unit	code	where&when seen		remarks
XX153	Lynx AH.1					

The first order for HS.1182 Hawk advanced/weapons training aircraft was contracted to Hawker Siddeley Aviation Ltd at Kingston. The block accounted for one prototype (XX154, f/f at Dunsfold 21.8.74) and 175 production aircraft (XX156 f/f 19.5.75). A small number were assembled and test-flown at Bitteswell.

XX154-XX222

serial	type	sqdn/unit	code	where&when seen		remarks
XX154	Hawk T.1					
XX156	Hawk T.1					
XX157	Hawk T.1					
XX158	Hawk T.1					
XX159	Hawk T.1					
XX160	Hawk T.1					
XX161	Hawk T.1					
XX162	Hawk T.1					
XX163	Hawk T.1					
XX164	Hawk T.1					
XX165	Hawk T.1					
XX166	Hawk T.1					
XX167	Hawk T.1					
XX168	Hawk T.1					
XX169	Hawk T.1					
XX170	Hawk T.1					
XX171	Hawk T.1					
XX172	Hawk T.1					
XX173	Hawk T.1					
XX174	Hawk T.1					
XX175	Hawk T.1					
XX176	Hawk T.1					
XX177	Hawk T.1					
XX178	Hawk T.1					
XX179	Hawk T.1					
XX180	Hawk T.1					
XX181	Hawk T.1					
XX182	Hawk T.1					
XX183	Hawk T.1					
XX184	Hawk T.1					
XX185	Hawk T.1					
XX186	Hawk T.1					
XX187	Hawk T.1					
XX188	Hawk T.1					
XX189	Hawk T.1					
XX190	Hawk T.1					
XX191	Hawk T.1					
XX192	Hawk T.1					
XX193	Hawk T.1					
XX194	Hawk T.1					
XX195	Hawk T.1					
XX196	Hawk T.1					
XX197	Hawk T.1					
XX198	Hawk T.1					
XX199	Hawk T.1					
XX200	Hawk T.1					
XX201	Hawk T.1					
XX202	Hawk T.1					
XX203	Hawk T.1					
XX204	Hawk T.1					
XX205	Hawk T.1					
XX217	Hawk T.1					
XX218	Hawk T.1					
XX219	Hawk T.1					
XX220	Hawk T.1					
XX221	Hawk T.1					
XX222	Hawk T.1					

XX223-XX291

serial	type	sqdn/unit	code	where&when seen		remarks
XX223	Hawk T.1					
XX224	Hawk T.1					
XX225	Hawk T.1					
XX226	Hawk T.1					
XX227	Hawk T.1					
XX228	Hawk T.1					
XX229	Hawk T.1					
XX230	Hawk T.1					
XX231	Hawk T.1					
XX232	Hawk T.1					
XX233	Hawk T.1					
XX234	Hawk T.1					
XX235	Hawk T.1					
XX236	Hawk T.1					
XX237	Hawk T.1					
XX238	Hawk T.1					
XX239	Hawk T.1					
XX240	Hawk T.1					
XX241	Hawk T.1					
XX242	Hawk T.1					
XX243	Hawk T.1					
XX244	Hawk T.1					
XX245	Hawk T.1					
XX246	Hawk T.1					
XX247	Hawk T.1					
XX248	Hawk T.1					
XX249	Hawk T.1					
XX250	Hawk T.1					
XX251	Hawk T.1					
XX252	Hawk T.1					
XX253	Hawk T.1					
XX254	Hawk T.1					
XX255	Hawk T.1					
XX256	Hawk T.1					
XX257	Hawk T.1					
XX258	Hawk T.1					
XX259	Hawk T.1					
XX260	Hawk T.1					
XX261	Hawk T.1					
XX262	Hawk T.1					
XX263	Hawk T.1					
XX264	Hawk T.1					
XX265	Hawk T.1					
XX266	Hawk T.1					
XX278	Hawk T.1					
XX279	Hawk T.1					
XX280	Hawk T.1					
XX281	Hawk T.1					
XX282	Hawk T.1					
XX283	Hawk T.1					
XX284	Hawk T.1					
XX285	Hawk T.1					
XX286	Hawk T.1					
XX287	Hawk T.1					
XX288	Hawk T.1					
XX289	Hawk T.1					
XX290	Hawk T.1					
XX291	Hawk T.1					

XX292-XX360

serial	type	sqdn/unit	code	where&when seen		remarks
XX292	Hawk T.1					
XX293	Hawk T.1					
XX294	Hawk T.1					
XX295	Hawk T.1					
XX296	Hawk T.1					
XX297	Hawk T.1					
XX298	Hawk T.1					
XX299	Hawk T.1					
XX300	Hawk T.1					
XX301	Hawk T.1					
XX302	Hawk T.1					
XX303	Hawk T.1					
XX304	Hawk T.1					
XX305	Hawk T.1					
XX306	Hawk T.1					
XX307	Hawk T.1					
XX308	Hawk T.1					
XX309	Hawk T.1					
XX310	Hawk T.1					
XX311	Hawk T.1					
XX312	Hawk T.1					
XX313	Hawk T.1					
XX314	Hawk T.1					
XX315	Hawk T.1					
XX316	Hawk T.1					
XX317	Hawk T.1					
XX318	Hawk T.1					
XX319	Hawk T.1					
XX320	Hawk T.1					
XX321	Hawk T.1					
XX322	Hawk T.1					
XX323	Hawk T.1					
XX324	Hawk T.1					
XX325	Hawk T.1					
XX326	Hawk T.1					
XX327	Hawk T.1					
XX339	Hawk T.1					
XX340	Hawk T.1					
XX341	Hawk T.1					
XX342	Hawk T.1					
XX343	Hawk T.1					
XX344	Hawk T.1					
XX345	Hawk T.1					
XX346	Hawk T.1					
XX347	Hawk T.1					
XX348	Hawk T.1					
XX349	Hawk T.1					
XX350	Hawk T.1					
XX351	Hawk T.1					
XX352	Hawk T.1					
XX353	Hawk T.1					
XX354	Hawk T.1					
XX355	Hawk T.1					
XX356	Hawk T.1					
XX357	Hawk T.1					
XX358	Hawk T.1					
XX359	Hawk T.1					
XX360	Hawk T.1					

XX361-XX408

serial	type	sqdn/unit	code	where&when seen		remarks
XX361	Hawk T.1					
XX362	Hawk T.1					
XX363	Hawk T.1					

One B.175 Britannia Srs 312F originally built by the Bristol Aeroplane Co Ltd at Filton as a Srs 312 for BOAC and f/f 29.4.58 as G-AOVM (c/n 13421). Subsequently converted to freighter configuration and operated by Air Spain (as EC-BSY), it was procured for the A&AEE and delivered to Boscombe Down on 28.4.72.

serial	type	sqdn/unit	code	where&when seen		remarks
XX367	Britannia Srs 312F					Ex EC-BSY

The second production order for 82 Aerospatiale/Westland Gazelle helicopters (to follow on from XW913) and built by Westland Helicopters Ltd, Yeovil for all three UK armed services as follows: 69 Mk AH.1 for the AAC and Royal Marines; 9 Mk HT.2 for the RN; and 4 Mk HT.3 variants for the RAF. XX370 f/f 20.8.74; XX462 f/f 11.6.76. The block was allotted c/ns as follows: 1236/1237/1240/1241/1244/1253/1254/1257/1258/1261/1268/1269/1272/1273/1276/1283/1284/1287/1288/1291/1298/1299/1302/1303/1306/1313/1314/1317/1318/1321/1328/1329/1332/1333/1336/1343/1344/1347/1279/1351/1358/1359/1362/1309/1366/1367/1370/1371/1324/1381/1382/1385/1386/1389/1401/1402/1405/1406/1409/1184/1418/1221/1235/1248/1435/1436/1439/1440/1443/1449/1450/1453/1454/1457/1464/1465/1468/1469/1472/1484/1485 and 1488. Allocations continue with XZ290.

serial	type	sqdn/unit	code	where&when seen		remarks
XX370	Gazelle AH.1					
XX371	Gazelle AH.1					
XX372	Gazelle AH.1					
XX373	Gazelle AH.1					
XX374	Gazelle HT.3					
XX375	Gazelle AH.1					
XX376	Gazelle AH.1					
XX377	Gazelle AH.1					
XX378	Gazelle AH.1					
XX379	Gazelle AH.1					
XX380	Gazelle AH.1					
XX381	Gazelle AH.1					
XX382	Gazelle HT.3					
XX383	Gazelle AH.1					
XX384	Gazelle AH.1					
XX385	Gazelle AH.1					
XX386	Gazelle AH.1					
XX387	Gazelle AH.1					
XX388	Gazelle AH.1					
XX389	Gazelle AH.1					
XX390	Gazelle AH.1					
XX391	Gazelle HT.2					
XX392	Gazelle AH.1					
XX393	Gazelle AH.1					
XX394	Gazelle AH.1					
XX395	Gazelle AH.1					
XX396	Gazelle HT.3					
XX397	Gazelle HT.2					
XX398	Gazelle AH.1					
XX399	Gazelle AH.1					
XX400	Gazelle AH.1					
XX401	Gazelle AH.1					
XX402	Gazelle AH.1					
XX403	Gazelle AH.1					
XX404	Gazelle AH.1					
XX405	Gazelle AH.1					
XX406	Gazelle HT.3					
XX407	Gazelle AH.1					
XX408	Gazelle AH.1					

XX409-XX469

serial	type	sqdn/unit	code	where&when seen		remarks
XX409	Gazelle AH.1					
XX410	Gazelle HT.2					
XX411	Gazelle AH.1					
XX412	Gazelle AH.1					
XX413	Gazelle AH.1					
XX414	Gazelle AH.1					
XX415	Gazelle HT.2					
XX416	Gazelle AH.1					
XX417	Gazelle AH.1					
XX418	Gazelle AH.1					
XX419	Gazelle AH.1					
XX431	Gazelle HT.2					
XX432	Gazelle AH.1					
XX433	Gazelle AH.1					
XX434	Gazelle AH.1					
XX435	Gazelle AH.1					
XX436	Gazelle HT.2					
XX437	Gazelle AH.1					
XX438	Gazelle AH.1					
XX439	Gazelle AH.1					
XX440	Gazelle AH.1					
XX441	Gazelle HT.2					
XX442	Gazelle AH.1					
XX443	Gazelle AH.1					
XX444	Gazelle AH.1					
XX445	Gazelle AH.1					
XX446	Gazelle HT.2					
XX447	Gazelle AH.1					
XX448	Gazelle AH.1					
XX449	Gazelle AH.1					
XX450	Gazelle AH.1					
XX451	Gazelle HT.2					
XX452	Gazelle AH.1					
XX453	Gazelle AH.1					
XX454	Gazelle AH.1					
XX455	Gazelle AH.1					
XX456	Gazelle AH.1					
XX457	Gazelle AH.1					
XX458	Gazelle AH.1					
XX459	Gazelle AH.1					
XX460	Gazelle AH.1					
XX461	Gazelle AH.1					
XX462	Gazelle AH.1					

Two second-hand Hunter T.7 operational training aircraft acquired from the Jordanian Air Force as replacements for FR.10 variants XG168 and XF426, both of which were diverted to Jordan. XX466 and XX467 were both delivered to Chivenor on 4.5.72.

serial	type	sqdn/unit	code	where&when seen		remarks
XX466	Hunter T.7					
XX467	Hunter T.7					

One Lynx HAS.2 prototype built by Westland Helicopters Ltd at Yeovil to full naval configuration and given the build number 1/07. XX469 first flew on 25.5.72.

serial	type	sqdn/unit	code	where&when seen		remarks
XX469	Lynx HAS.2					

The first contract for 26 Jetstream T.1 navigational training aircraft was placed with Scottish Aviation (Jetstream) Ltd on behalf of the RAF. The first seven had originally been built by Handley-Page Ltd at Radlett but following that company's liquidation (on 8.8.69) all were subsequently acquired by Scottish Aviation and re-

XX475-XX513

serial	type	sqdn/unit	code	where&when seen	remarks

worked as Jetstream T.1's as follows:- XX475 (c/n 206) ex G-AWVJ/N1036S; XX476 (216) ex G-AXGL/N1037S; and five unflown examples XX477 (249) ex G-AXXS; XX478 (261) ex-G-AXXT; XX479 (259) ex G-AXUR; XX480 (262) ex G-AXXU; and XX481 (251) ex G-AXUP. Fourteen additional aircraft were built by Scottish Aviation by using uncompleted Handley-Page airframes as follows:- XX482-XX493/XX496-XX497 c/ns 263/264/266/268/265 269/267/279/271/275/274/278/276 and 280 respectively. The final five aircraft were built (from scratch) by Scottish Aviation at Prestwick as follows:. XX494-XX495/XX498-XX500 c/ns 422-426 respectively. XX475 f/f 13.4.73; XX500 f/f 2.12.76. 14 ex-RAF T.1's to RN for conversion to T.2's. First delivery to RN (XX480) on 21.10.78.

serial	type	sqdn/unit	code	where&when seen	remarks
XX475	Jetstream T.2				Ex N1036S
XX476	Jetstream T.2				Ex N1037S
XX477	Jetstream T.1				Ex G-AXXS To 8462M
XX478	Jetstream T.2				Ex G-AXXT
XX479	Jetstream T.2				Ex G-AXUR
XX480	Jetstream T.2				Ex G-AXXU
XX481	Jetstream T.2				Ex G-AXUP
XX482	Jetstream T.1				
XX483	Jetstream T.2				
XX484	Jetstream T.2				
XX485	Jetstream T.2				
XX486	Jetstream T.2				
XX487	Jetstream T.2				
XX488	Jetstream T.2				
XX489	Jetstream T.2				
XX490	Jetstream T.2				
XX491	Jetstream T.1				
XX492	Jetstream T.1				
XX493	Jetstream T.1				
XX494	Jetstream T.1				
XX495	Jetstream T.1				
XX496	Jetstream T.1				
XX497	Jetstream T.1				
XX498	Jetstream T.1				
XX499	Jetstream T.1				
XX500	Jetstream T.1				

Four Hawker Siddeley HS.125 executive jet aircraft acquired for 32 Squadron RAF as follows:- HS.125 Srs 400B XX505 (c/n 25252) and XX506 (25271 ex G-BABL) and both delivered to Northolt on 5.9.72 and 23.10.72 respectively, and operated until the delivery of two HS.125 Srs 600B variants XX507 (c/n 256006) and XX508 (256008) on 26.4.73 and 27.4.73 respectively. XX505 and XX506 were then returned to Hawker Siddeley.

serial	type	sqdn/unit	code	where&when seen	remarks
XX505	HS.125 CC.1				Ex G-5-17 To G-BAZB
XX506	HS.125 CC.1				Ex G-BABL To G-BABL
XX507	HS.125 CC.2				
XX508	HS.125 CC.2				

One Lynx prototype built by Westland Helicopters Ltd, Yeovil to full naval configuration and to act as the definitive RN prototype. XX510 f/f 5.3.73 and was allotted the build number 3/13.

serial	type	sqdn/unit	code	where&when seen	remarks
XX510	Lynx HAS.2				

The Bulldog T.1 single-engine training aircraft was conceived by Beagle Aircraft Ltd who produced one prototype, but following the liquidation of this company all design and manufacturing rights passed to Scottish Aviation (Bulldog) Ltd at Prestwick. 130 aircraft were built for the RAF as successors to the Chipmunk T.10's. XX513 f/f 30.1.73 and deliveries extended into 1976. The block was allotted c/ns as follows:- 199-223/230-238/240-249/253-261/272-277/285-297/303-337/341-363 respectively.

serial	type	sqdn/unit	code	where&when seen	remarks
XX513	Bulldog T.1				

XX514-XX619

serial	type	sqdn/unit	code	where&when seen		remarks
XX514	Bulldog T.1					
XX515	Bulldog T.1					
XX516	Bulldog T.1					
XX517	Bulldog T.1					
XX518	Bulldog T.1					
XX519	Bulldog T.1					
XX520	Bulldog T.1					
XX521	Bulldog T.1					
XX522	Bulldog T.1					
XX523	Bulldog T.1					
XX524	Bulldog T.1					
XX525	Bulldog T.1					
XX526	Bulldog T.1					
XX527	Bulldog T.1					
XX528	Bulldog T.1					
XX529	Bulldog T.1					
XX530	Bulldog T.1					
XX531	Bulldog T.1					
XX532	Bulldog T.1					
XX533	Bulldog T.1					
XX534	Bulldog T.1					
XX535	Bulldog T.1					
XX536	Bulldog T.1					
XX537	Bulldog T.1					
XX538	Bulldog T.1					
XX539	Bulldog T.1					
XX540	Bulldog T.1					
XX541	Bulldog T.1					
XX542	Bulldog T.1					
XX543	Bulldog T.1					
XX544	Bulldog T.1					
XX545	Bulldog T.1					
XX546	Bulldog T.1					
XX547	Bulldog T.1					
XX548	Bulldog T.1					
XX549	Bulldog T.1					
XX550	Bulldog T.1					
XX551	Bulldog T.1					
XX552	Bulldog T.1					
XX553	Bulldog T.1					
XX554	Bulldog T.1					
XX555	Bulldog T.1					
XX556	Bulldog T.1					
XX557	Bulldog T.1					
XX558	Bulldog T.1					
XX559	Bulldog T.1					
XX560	Bulldog T.1					
XX561	Bulldog T.1					
XX562	Bulldog T.1					
XX611	Bulldog T.1					
XX612	Bulldog T.1					
XX613	Bulldog T.1					
XX614	Bulldog T.1					
XX615	Bulldog T.1					
XX616	Bulldog T.1					
XX617	Bulldog T.1					
XX618	Bulldog T.1					
XX619	Bulldog T.1					

XX620-XX700

serial	type	sqdn/unit	code	where&when seen		remarks
XX620	Bulldog T.1					
XX621	Bulldog T.1					
XX622	Bulldog T.1					
XX623	Bulldog T.1					
XX624	Bulldog T.1					
XX625	Bulldog T.1					
XX626	Bulldog T.1					
XX627	Bulldog T.1					
XX628	Bulldog T.1					
XX629	Bulldog T.1					
XX630	Bulldog T.1					
XX631	Bulldog T.1					
XX632	Bulldog T.1					
XX633	Bulldog T.1					
XX634	Bulldog T.1					
XX635	Bulldog T.1					
XX636	Bulldog T.1					
XX637	Bulldog T.1					
XX638	Bulldog T.1					
XX639	Bulldog T.1					
XX640	Bulldog T.1					
XX653	Bulldog T.1					
XX654	Bulldog T.1					
XX655	Bulldog T.1					
XX656	Bulldog T.1					
XX657	Bulldog T.1					
XX658	Bulldog T.1					
XX659	Bulldog T.1					
XX660	Bulldog T.1					
XX661	Bulldog T.1					
XX662	Bulldog T.1					
XX663	Bulldog T.1					
XX664	Bulldog T.1					
XX665	Bulldog T.1					
XX666	Bulldog T.1					
XX667	Bulldog T.1					
XX668	Bulldog T.1					
XX669	Bulldog T.1					
XX670	Bulldog T.1					
XX671	Bulldog T.1					
XX672	Bulldog T.1					
XX685	Bulldog T.1					
XX686	Bulldog T.1					
XX687	Bulldog T.1					
XX688	Bulldog T.1					
XX689	Bulldog T.1					
XX690	Bulldog T.1					
XX691	Bulldog T.1					
XX692	Bulldog T.1					
XX693	Bulldog T.1					
XX694	Bulldog T.1					
XX695	Bulldog T.1					
XX696	Bulldog T.1					
XX697	Bulldog T.1					
XX698	Bulldog T.1					
XX699	Bulldog T.1					
XX700	Bulldog T.1					

XX701-XX758

serial	type	sqdn/unit	code	where&when seen		remarks
XX701	Bulldog T.1					
XX702	Bulldog T.1					
XX703	Bulldog T.1					
XX704	Bulldog T.1					
XX705	Bulldog T.1					
XX706	Bulldog T.1					
XX707	Bulldog T.1					
XX708	Bulldog T.1					
XX709	Bulldog T.1					
XX710	Bulldog T.1					
XX711	Bulldog T.1					
XX712	Bulldog T.1					
XX713	Bulldog T.1					
XX714	Bulldog T.1					

The second production contract for Jaguar tactical support/ground-attack aircraft and operational training aircraft accounted for 61 GR.1 (c/ns S.16-S.76) and 20 T.2 (c/ns B.16-B.35) variants to follow on from XX122 and XX150 resp. All were built by BAC (Preston Division). XX719 f/f 31.1.74; XX847 f/f 23.10.75. Later loans to India.

serial	type	sqdn/unit	code	where&when seen		remarks
XX719	Jaguar GR.1					
XX720	Jaguar GR.1					To G-27-320/IAF JI003
XX721	Jaguar GR.1					
XX722	Jaguar GR.1					
XX723	Jaguar GR.1					
XX724	Jaguar GR.1					
XX725	Jaguar GR.1					To G-27-325/IAF JI010
XX726	Jaguar GR.1					
XX727	Jaguar GR.1					
XX728	Jaguar GR.1					To G-27-324/IAF JI009
XX729	Jaguar GR.1					To G-27-326/IAF JI012
XX730	Jaguar GR.1					
XX731	Jaguar GR.1					
XX732	Jaguar GR.1					
XX733	Jaguar GR.1					
XX734	Jaguar GR.1					To G-27-328/IAF JI014
XX735	Jaguar GR.1					
XX736	Jaguar GR.1					To G-27-327/IAF JI013
XX737	Jaguar GR.1					To G-27-330/IAF JI015
XX738	Jaguar GR.1					To G-27-329/IAF JI016
XX739	Jaguar GR.1					
XX740	Jaguar GR.1					To G-27-331/IAF JI017
XX741	Jaguar GR.1					
XX742	Jaguar GR.1					
XX743	Jaguar GR.1					
XX744	Jaguar GR.1					
XX745	Jaguar GR.1					
XX746	Jaguar GR.1					
XX747	Jaguar GR.1					
XX748	Jaguar GR.1					
XX749	Jaguar GR.1					
XX750	Jaguar GR.1					
XX751	Jaguar GR.1					
XX752	Jaguar GR.1					
XX753	Jaguar GR.1					
XX754	Jaguar GR.1					
XX755	Jaguar GR.1					
XX756	Jaguar GR.1					
XX757	Jaguar GR.1					
XX758	Jaguar GR.1					

XX759-XX862

serial	type	sqdn/unit	code	where&when seen		remarks
XX759	Jaguar GR.1					
XX760	Jaguar GR.1					
XX761	Jaguar GR.1					To 8600M (nose)
XX762	Jaguar GR.1					
XX763	Jaguar GR.1					
XX764	Jaguar GR.1					
XX765	Jaguar GR.1					
XX766	Jaguar GR.1					
XX767	Jaguar GR.1					
XX768	Jaguar GR.1					
XX817	Jaguar GR.1					
XX818	Jaguar GR.1					
XX819	Jaguar GR.1					
XX820	Jaguar GR.1					
XX821	Jaguar GR.1					
XX822	Jaguar GR.1					
XX823	Jaguar GR.1					
XX824	Jaguar GR.1					
XX825	Jaguar GR.1					
XX826	Jaguar GR.1					
XX827	Jaguar GR.1					
XX828	Jaguar T.2					
XX829	Jaguar T.2					
XX830	Jaguar T.2					
XX831	Jaguar T.2					
XX832	Jaguar T.2					
XX833	Jaguar T.2					
XX834	Jaguar T.2					
XX835	Jaguar T.2					
XX836	Jaguar T.2					
XX837	Jaguar T.2					
XX838	Jaguar T.2					
XX839	Jaguar T.2					
XX840	Jaguar T.2					
XX841	Jaguar T.2					
XX842	Jaguar T.2					
XX843	Jaguar T.2					
XX844	Jaguar T.2					
XX845	Jaguar T.2					
XX846	Jaguar T.2					
XX847	Jaguar T.2					

Continued procurement of 30 Northrop KD2R-5/MQM-36A pilotless target drones for the RN Fleet Target Group to follow on from XW980. All are known as the Shelduck D.1 and allocations continue with XX923.

serial	type	sqdn/unit	code	where&when seen		remarks
XX850	Shelduck D.1					
XX851	Shelduck D.1					
XX852	Shelduck D.1					
XX853	Shelduck D.1					
XX854	Shelduck D.1					
XX855	Shelduck D.1					
XX856	Shelduck D.1					
XX857	Shelduck D.1					
XX858	Shelduck D.1					
XX859	Shelduck D.1					
XX860	Shelduck D.1					
XX861	Shelduck D.1					
XX862	Shelduck D.1					

XX863-XX916

serial	type	sqdn/unit	code	where&when seen		remarks
XX863	Shelduck D.1					
XX864	Shelduck D.1					
XX865	Shelduck D.1					
XX866	Shelduck D.1					
XX867	Shelduck D.1					
XX868	Shelduck D.1					
XX869	Shelduck D.1					
XX870	Shelduck D.1					
XX871	Shelduck D.1					
XX872	Shelduck D.1					
XX873	Shelduck D.1					
XX874	Shelduck D.1					
XX875	Shelduck D.1					
XX876	Shelduck D.1					
XX877	Shelduck D.1					
XX878	Shelduck D.1					
XX879	Shelduck D.1					

The penultimate contract for Buccaneer S.2B aircraft for the RAF accounted for 17 units to follow on from XW988. All were built by Hawker Siddeley Aviation Ltd at Brough and test-flown from Holme-on-Spalding Moor. XX885 delivered c2.74.

serial	type	sqdn/unit	code	where&when seen		remarks
XX885	Buccaneer S.2B					
XX886	Buccaneer S.2B					
XX887	Buccaneer S.2B					
XX888	Buccaneer S.2B					
XX889	Buccaneer S.2B					
XX890	Buccaneer S.2B					
XX891	Buccaneer S.2B					
XX892	Buccaneer S.2B					
XX893	Buccaneer S.2B					
XX894	Buccaneer S.2B					
XX895	Buccaneer S.2B					
XX896	Buccaneer S.2B					
XX897	Buccaneer S.2B					
XX898	Buccaneer S.2B					
XX899	Buccaneer S.2B					
XX900	Buccaneer S.2B					
XX901	Buccaneer S.2B					

Four prototype/pre-production Lynx helicopters built by Westland Helicopters Ltd at Yeovil to naval configuration. Build numbers and f/f dates are as follows:- XX904 (3/18) 6.7.73; XX907 (1/08) 20.5.73; XX910 (3/16) 23.4.74; and XX911 (4/20) 18.9.73.

serial	type	sqdn/unit	code	where&when seen		remarks
XX904	Lynx HAS.2 (FN)					To F-ZKCU
XX907	Lynx AH.1					
XX910	Lynx HAS.2					
XX911	Lynx HAS.2 (FN)					To F-ZKCV

One VC.10 Type 1103 originally built by the British Aircraft Corporation at Weybridge for British United Airways as G-ATDJ (c/n 825) and f/f as such on 18.6.65. During 2.73 it was bought by the Ministry of Technology for RAE Bedford.

serial	type	sqdn/unit	code	where&when seen		remarks
XX914	VC.10 Srs 1103					Ex G-ATDJ

Two Jaguar T.2 operational training aircraft (c/ns B.36-B.37) built by SEPECAT and assembled at Warton by the British Aircraft Corporation. These two aircraft were ordered for use by the Empire Test Pilots School at Boscombe Down. XX915 f/f 22.6.76.

serial	type	sqdn/unit	code	where&when seen		remarks
XX915	Jaguar T.2					
XX916	Jaguar T.2					

XX919-XX965

serial	type	sqdn/unit	code	where&when seen		remarks

One BAC-111 Srs 402AP originally built by the British Aircraft Corporation at Hurn for Philippine Airlines as PI-C1121 (c/n 091) and f/f 7.4.66. During December 1971 it was returned to BAC and re-worked for use by RAE Farnborough as XX919 and was delivered on 16.5.74.

serial	type	sqdn/unit	code	where&when seen		remarks
XX919	BAC-111 Srs 402AP					Ex PI-C1121

Continued procurement of 19 Northrop KD2R-5/MQM-36A pilotless target drones for the RN Fleet Target Group to follow on from XX879. All are known as the Shelduck D.1 and allocations continue with XZ410.

serial	type	sqdn/unit	code	where&when seen		remarks
XX923	Shelduck D.1					
XX924	Shelduck D.1					
XX925	Shelduck D.1					
XX926	Shelduck D.1					
XX927	Shelduck D.1					
XX928	Shelduck D.1					
XX929	Shelduck D.1					
XX930	Shelduck D.1					
XX931	Shelduck D.1					
XX932	Shelduck D.1					
XX933	Shelduck D.1					
XX934	Shelduck D.1					
XX935	Shelduck D.1					
XX936	Shelduck D.1					
XX937	Shelduck D.1					
XX938	Shelduck D.1					
XX939	Shelduck D.1					
XX940	Shelduck D.1					
XX941	Shelduck D.1					

One DH.106 Comet 4 originally built by the de Havilland Aircraft Co Ltd at Chester for BOAC as G-APDP (c/n 06417) and f/f 29.5.59. Subsequently operated by Malaysia-Singapore Airlines (as 9V-BBH) and Dan-Air (as G-APDP), it was acquired by the RAE for use by the Radio Department at Farnborough, to whom it was delivered on 19.7.73.

serial	type	sqdn/unit	code	where&when seen		remarks
XX944	Comet 4					Ex G-APDP

Four prototype Panavia MRCA aircraft (later named Tornado) and built by the British Aircraft Corporation (Preston Division). XX946 (c/n P.02) f/f 30.10.74; XX947 (c/n P.03) f/f 5.8.75; XX948 (c/n P.06) f/f 19.12.75; XX950 (c/n P.08) f/f 15.7.76.

serial	type	sqdn/unit	code	where&when seen		remarks
XX946	Tornado					
XX947	Tornado (T)					
XX948	Tornado					
XX950	Tornado (T)					

The third production contract for 45 Jaguar GR.1 tactical support/ground-attack aircraft was contracted to BAC (Preston Division) to follow on from XX827. The block was allotted c/ns S.77-S.121 resp. XX955 f/f 18.9.75; XZ120 f/f 19.5.76.

serial	type	sqdn/unit	code	where&when seen		remarks
XX955	Jaguar GR.1					
XX956	Jaguar GR.1					
XX957	Jaguar GR.1					
XX958	Jaguar GR.1					
XX959	Jaguar GR.1					
XX960	Jaguar GR.1					
XX961	Jaguar GR.1					
XX962	Jaguar GR.1					
XX963	Jaguar GR.1					
XX964	Jaguar GR.1					
XX965	Jaguar GR.1					

XX966-XZ137

serial	type	sqdn/unit	code	where&when seen		remarks
XX966	Jaguar GR.1					
XX967	Jaguar GR.1					
XX968	Jaguar GR.1					
XX969	Jaguar GR.1					
XX970	Jaguar GR.1					
XX971	Jaguar GR.1					
XX972	Jaguar GR.1					
XX973	Jaguar GR.1					
XX974	Jaguar GR.1					
XX975	Jaguar GR.1					
XX976	Jaguar GR.1					
XX977	Jaguar GR.1					
XX978	Jaguar GR.1					
XX979	Jaguar GR.1					
XZ101	Jaguar GR.1					
XZ102	Jaguar GR.1					
XZ103	Jaguar GR.1					
XZ104	Jaguar GR.1					
XZ105	Jaguar GR.1					
XZ106	Jaguar GR.1					
XZ107	Jaguar GR.1					
XZ108	Jaguar GR.1					
XZ109	Jaguar GR.1					
XZ110	Jaguar GR.1					
XZ111	Jaguar GR.1					
XZ112	Jaguar GR.1					
XZ113	Jaguar GR.1					
XZ114	Jaguar GR.1					
XZ115	Jaguar GR.1					
XZ116	Jaguar GR.1					
XZ117	Jaguar GR.1					
XZ118	Jaguar GR.1					
XZ119	Jaguar GR.1					
XZ120	Jaguar GR.1					

One Hawker Siddeley AV-8A (Harrier) was temporarily diverted off contract for demonstration to the French Aeronavale on 10-11.10.73. The trials took place upon the French vessel 'Jeanne D'Arc' and due to the very nature of the flights a British military serial was officially allotted but outside the normal sequence. However a stipulation made by the MoD demanded that the AV-8A was not to land in a foreign country. After the flight trials were complete the aircraft reverted to its USMC serial 158969.

XY125	AV-8A					Ex 158969 To 158969

Continued procurement of Harrier V/STOL aircraft accounted for 12 GR.3's and three T.4 trainers, being uprated versions of the GR.1 and T.2 respectively. Built by Hawker Siddeley Aviation Ltd at Kingston and test flown at Dunsfold, deliveries commenced with T.4 XZ145 and GR.3 XZ128 on 8.3.76 and 15.3.76 respectively.

XZ128	Harrier GR.3					
XZ129	Harrier GR.3					
XZ130	Harrier GR.3					
XZ131	Harrier GR.3					
XZ132	Harrier GR.3					
XZ133	Harrier GR.3					
XZ134	Harrier GR.3					
XZ135	Harrier GR.3					
XZ136	Harrier GR.3					
XZ137	Harrier GR.3					

XZ138-XZ195

serial	type	sqdn/unit	code	where&when seen		remarks
XZ138	Harrier GR.3					
XZ139	Harrier GR.3					
XZ145	Harrier T.4					
XZ146	Harrier T.4					
XZ147	Harrier T.4					

The second order for 13 Northrop MQM-74A Chukar pilotless target drones for the Royal Navy Fleet Target Group, to follow on from XW999. All were built by the Ventura Division of the Northrop Corporation, being amongst the last of this variant to be built before production ended during 1973.

serial	type	sqdn/unit	code	where&when seen		remarks
XZ152	Chukar D.1					
XZ153	Chukar D.1					
XZ154	Chukar D.1					
XZ155	Chukar D.1					
XZ156	Chukar D.1					
XZ157	Chukar D.1					
XZ158	Chukar D.1					
XZ159	Chukar D.1					
XZ160	Chukar D.1					
XZ161	Chukar D.1					
XZ162	Chukar D.1					
XZ163	Chukar D.1					
XZ164	Chukar D.1					

The final pre-production Lynx helicopter built by Westland Helicopters Ltd, Yeovil to full naval configuration as a replacement for XX469 which had crashed during its early flight trials. XZ166 f/f 5.3.75. To Rolls-Royce, Filton 4.79 as G-1-2.

serial	type	sqdn/unit	code	where&when seen		remarks
XZ166	Lynx HAS.2					To G-1-2

The first production order for 50 Lynx AH.1 helicopters built by Westland Helicopters Ltd at Yeovil for the Army Air Corps. XZ170 (c/n WA008) f/f 11.2.77. Allocations continue with XZ605.

serial	type	sqdn/unit	code	where&when seen		remarks
XZ170	Lynx AH.1					
XZ171	Lynx AH.1					
XZ172	Lynx AH.1					
XZ173	Lynx AH.1					
XZ174	Lynx AH.1					
XZ175	Lynx AH.1					
XZ176	Lynx AH.1					
XZ177	Lynx AH.1					
XZ178	Lynx AH.1					
XZ179	Lynx AH.1					
XZ180	Lynx AH.1					
XZ181	Lynx AH.1					
XZ182	Lynx AH.1					
XZ183	Lynx AH.1					
XZ184	Lynx AH.1					
XZ185	Lynx AH.1					
XZ186	Lynx AH.1					
XZ187	Lynx AH.1					
XZ188	Lynx AH.1					
XZ189	Lynx AH.1					
XZ190	Lynx AH.1					
XZ191	Lynx AH.1					
XZ192	Lynx AH.1					
XZ193	Lynx AH.1					
XZ194	Lynx AH.1					
XZ195	Lynx AH.1					

XZ196-XZ256

serial	type	sqdn/unit	code	where&when seen		remarks
XZ196	Lynx AH.1					
XZ197	Lynx AH.1					
XZ198	Lynx AH.1					
XZ199	Lynx AH.1					
XZ203	Lynx AH.1					
XZ204	Lynx AH.1					
XZ205	Lynx AH.1					
XZ206	Lynx AH.1					
XZ207	Lynx AH.1					
XZ208	Lynx AH.1					
XZ209	Lynx AH.1					
XZ210	Lynx AH.1					
XZ211	Lynx AH.1					
XZ212	Lynx AH.1					
XZ213	Lynx AH.1					
XZ214	Lynx AH.1					
XZ215	Lynx AH.1					
XZ216	Lynx AH.1					
XZ217	Lynx AH.1					
XZ218	Lynx AH.1					
XZ219	Lynx AH.1					
XZ220	Lynx AH.1					
XZ221	Lynx AH.1					
XZ222	Lynx AH.1					

The first production order for 30 Lynx HAS.2 helicopters built by Westland Helicopters Ltd at Yeovil for the Royal Navy. XZ227 (c/n WA001) f/f 28.5.76; XZ257 delivered 5.3.79. Allocations continue with XZ689.

serial	type	sqdn/unit	code	where&when seen		remarks
XZ227	Lynx HAS.2					
XZ228	Lynx HAS.2					
XZ229	Lynx HAS.2					
XZ230	Lynx HAS.2					
XZ231	Lynx HAS.2					
XZ232	Lynx HAS.2					
XZ233	Lynx HAS.2					
XZ234	Lynx HAS.2					
XZ235	Lynx HAS.2					
XZ236	Lynx HAS.2					
XZ237	Lynx HAS.2					
XZ238	Lynx HAS.2					
XZ239	Lynx HAS.2					
XZ240	Lynx HAS.2					
XZ241	Lynx HAS.2					
XZ242	Lynx HAS.2					
XZ243	Lynx HAS.2					
XZ244	Lynx HAS.2					
XZ245	Lynx HAS.2					
XZ246	Lynx HAS.2					
XZ247	Lynx HAS.2					
XZ248	Lynx HAS.2					
XZ249	Lynx HAS.2					
XZ250	Lynx HAS.2					
XZ251	Lynx HAS.2					
XZ252	Lynx HAS.2					
XZ254	Lynx HAS.2					
XZ255	Lynx HAS.2					
XZ256	Lynx HAS.2					

serial	type	sqdn/unit	code	where&when seen		remarks
XZ257	Lynx HAS.2					

The first production order for 18 Lynx HAS.2(FN) helicopters for the French Aeronavale. Built by Westland Helicopters Ltd at Yeovil, they were fitted out by Aerospatiale at Marignane. XZ260 (c/n WA015) f/f 4.5.77.

serial	type	sqdn/unit	code	where&when seen		remarks
XZ260	Lynx HAS.2(FN)					To F-ZARL
XZ261	Lynx HAS.2(FN)					
XZ262	Lynx HAS.2(FN)					
XZ263	Lynx HAS.2(FN)					
XZ264	Lynx HAS.2(FN)					
XZ265	Lynx HAS.2(FN)					
XZ266	Lynx HAS.2(FN)					
XZ267	Lynx HAS.2(FN)					
XZ269	Lynx HAS.2(FN)					
XZ270	Lynx HAS.2(FN)					
XZ271	Lynx HAS.2(FN)					
XZ272	Lynx HAS.2(FN)					
XZ273	Lynx HAS.2(FN)					
XZ274	Lynx HAS.2(FN)					
XZ275	Lynx HAS.2(FN)					
XZ276	Lynx HAS.2(FN)					
XZ277	Lynx HAS.2(FN)					
XZ278	Lynx HAS.2(FN)					

Follow on order for 8 Nimrod MR.1's announced 1.72 and built at Woodford with the c/ns 8042-8049. Only five were completed as MR.1's and of these XZ281 & XZ285 later joined the other three in the MR.2/AEW.3 conversion programmes. XZ280 del early 1975.

serial	type	sqdn/unit	code	where&when seen		remarks
XZ280	Nimrod MR.1					
XZ281	Nimrod AEW.3					
XZ282	Nimrod MR.1					
XZ283	Nimrod MR.1					
XZ284	Nimrod MR.2					
XZ285	Nimrod AEW.3					
XZ286	Nimrod AEW.3					
XZ287	Nimrod AEW.3					

Sixty Gazelle AH.1 helicopters built for the AAC by Westland Helicopters Ltd, Yeovil (XZ290-XZ337) and at Weston-super-Mare (XZ338-XZ349), to follow on from XX462. XZ290 f/f 21.6.76. The block was allotted c/ns as follows:- 1489/1492/1502/1503/1506/1507/1510/1520/1521/1524/1525/1528/1538/1539/1542/1543/1559/1560/1563/1564/1577/1578/1581/1582/1595/1596/1599/1600/1609/1610/1613/1614/1630/1631/1634/1635/1647/1648/1651/1652/1661/1662/1665/1666/1673/1674/1676/1677/1682/1683/1691/1692/1697/1698/1704/1705/1712/1713/1719 and 1720.

serial	type	sqdn/unit	code	where&when seen		remarks
XZ290	Gazelle AH.1					
XZ291	Gazelle AH.1					
XZ292	Gazelle AH.1					
XZ293	Gazelle AH.1					
XZ294	Gazelle AH.1					
XZ295	Gazelle AH.1					
XZ296	Gazelle AH.1					
XZ297	Gazelle AH.1					
XZ298	Gazelle AH.1					
XZ299	Gazelle AH.1					
XZ300	Gazelle AH.1					
XZ301	Gazelle AH.1					
XZ302	Gazelle AH.1					
XZ303	Gazelle AH.1					
XZ304	Gazelle AH.1					

XZ305-XZ363

serial	type	sqdn/unit	code	where&when seen		remarks
XZ305	Gazelle AH.1					
XZ306	Gazelle AH.1					
XZ307	Gazelle AH.1					
XZ308	Gazelle AH.1					
XZ309	Gazelle AH.1					
XZ310	Gazelle AH.1					
XZ311	Gazelle AH.1					
XZ312	Gazelle AH.1					
XZ313	Gazelle AH.1					
XZ314	Gazelle AH.1					
XZ315	Gazelle AH.1					
XZ316	Gazelle AH.1					
XZ317	Gazelle AH.1					
XZ318	Gazelle AH.1					
XZ319	Gazelle AH.1					
XZ320	Gazelle AH.1					
XZ321	Gazelle AH.1					
XZ322	Gazelle AH.1					
XZ323	Gazelle AH.1					
XZ324	Gazelle AH.1					
XZ325	Gazelle AH.1					
XZ326	Gazelle AH.1					
XZ327	Gazelle AH.1					
XZ328	Gazelle AH.1					
XZ329	Gazelle AH.1					
XZ330	Gazelle AH.1					
XZ331	Gazelle AH.1					
XZ332	Gazelle AH.1					
XZ333	Gazelle AH.1					
XZ334	Gazelle AH.1					
XZ335	Gazelle AH.1					
XZ336	Gazelle AH.1					
XZ337	Gazelle AH.1					To F-WXFX Rtnd XZ337
XZ338	Gazelle AH.1					
XZ339	Gazelle AH.1					
XZ340	Gazelle AH.1					
XZ341	Gazelle AH.1					
XZ342	Gazelle AH.1					
XZ343	Gazelle AH.1					
XZ344	Gazelle AH.1					
XZ345	Gazelle AH.1					
XZ346	Gazelle AH.1					
XZ347	Gazelle AH.1					
XZ348	Gazelle AH.1					
XZ349	Gazelle AH.1					

Continued production of 44 Jaguar GR.1 tactical support/ground-attack aircraft built for the RAF by BAC (Preston Division) to follow on from XZ120. The block was allotted c/ns S.122-S.165 respectively. XZ355 f/f 10.6.76; XZ400 f/f 29.6.79. Diversions to the Indian AF (on loan pending delivery of their own production aircraft).

serial	type	sqdn/unit	code	where&when seen		remarks
XZ355	Jaguar GR.1					
XZ356	Jaguar GR.1					
XZ357	Jaguar GR.1					
XZ358	Jaguar GR.1					
XZ359	Jaguar GR.1					
XZ360	Jaguar GR.1					
XZ361	Jaguar GR.1					
XZ362	Jaguar GR.1					
XZ363	Jaguar GR.1					

XZ364-XZ424

serial	type	sqdn/unit	code	where&when seen		remarks
XZ364	Jaguar GR.1					
XZ365	Jaguar GR.1					
XZ366	Jaguar GR.1					
XZ367	Jaguar GR.1					
XZ368	Jaguar GR.1					
XZ369	Jaguar GR.1					
XZ370	Jaguar GR.1					
XZ371	Jaguar GR.1					
XZ372	Jaguar GR.1					
XZ373	Jaguar GR.1					
XZ374	Jaguar GR.1					
XZ375	Jaguar GR.1					
XZ376	Jaguar GR.1					
XZ377	Jaguar GR.1					
XZ378	Jaguar GR.1					
XZ381	Jaguar GR.1					
XZ382	Jaguar GR.1					
XZ383	Jaguar GR.1					
XZ384	Jaguar GR.1					
XZ385	Jaguar GR.1					
XZ386	Jaguar GR.1					
XZ387	Jaguar GR.1					
XZ388	Jaguar GR.1					
XZ389	Jaguar GR.1					
XZ390	Jaguar GR.1					
XZ391	Jaguar GR.1					
XZ392	Jaguar GR.1					
XZ393	Jaguar GR.1					
XZ394	Jaguar GR.1					
XZ395	Jaguar GR.1					
XZ396	Jaguar GR.1					
XZ397	Jaguar GR.1					To G-27-322/IAF JI006
XZ398	Jaguar GR.1					To G-27-323/IAF JI007
XZ399	Jaguar GR.1					
XZ400	Jaguar GR.1					

Sailplane built by Schempp-Hirth in Germany in 1968 (c/n 21). Del. from Cranfield to ETPS Boscombe Down 17.6.74, leaving for Lambourn 19.4.75. BGA No. restored in 1976.

serial	type	sqdn/unit	code	where&when seen		remarks
XZ405	Cirrus					Ex BGA1473 To BGA1473

Continued procurement of 16 Northrop KD2R-5/MQM-36A pilotless target drones for the RN Fleet Target Group to follow on from XX941. All are known as the Shelduck D.1 and allocations continue with XZ505.

serial	type	sqdn/unit	code	where&when seen		remarks
XZ410	Shelduck D.1					
XZ411	Shelduck D.1					
XZ412	Shelduck D.1					
XZ413	Shelduck D.1					
XZ414	Shelduck D.1					
XZ415	Shelduck D.1					
XZ416	Shelduck D.1					
XZ417	Shelduck D.1					
XZ418	Shelduck D.1					
XZ419	Shelduck D.1					
XZ420	Shelduck D.1					
XZ421	Shelduck D.1					
XZ422	Shelduck D.1					
XZ423	Shelduck D.1					
XZ424	Shelduck D.1					

XZ425-XZ518

serial	type	sqdn/unit	code	where&when seen		remarks
XZ425	Shelduck D.1					

The final production order for Buccaneer S.2B long-range strike aircraft accounted for three aircraft for the RAF to follow on from XX901. All were built by Hawker Siddeley Aviation Ltd at Brough. XZ432 delivered 6.10.77.

serial	type	sqdn/unit	code	where&when seen		remarks
XZ430	Buccaneer S.2B					
XZ431	Buccaneer S.2B					
XZ432	Buccaneer S.2B					

The first contract for Sea Harrier FRS.1 shipboard fighter aircraft for the RN accounted for three 'prototypes' (XZ438-XZ440), 21 production aircraft (XZ450 etc) and one Harrier T.4 conversion trainer. XZ450 f/f 21.8.78 at Dunsfold, followed by the prototype XZ438 on 30.12.78.

serial	type	sqdn/unit	code	where&when seen		remarks
XZ438	Sea Harrier FRS.1					
XZ439	Sea Harrier FRS.1					
XZ440	Sea Harrier FRS.1					
XZ445	Harrier T.4					
XZ450	Sea Harrier FRS.1					
XZ451	Sea Harrier FRS.1					
XZ452	Sea Harrier FRS.1					
XZ453	Sea Harrier FRS.1					
XZ454	Sea Harrier FRS.1					
XZ455	Sea Harrier FRS.1					
XZ456	Sea Harrier FRS.1					
XZ457	Sea Harrier FRS.1					
XZ458	Sea Harrier FRS.1					
XZ459	Sea Harrier FRS.1					
XZ460	Sea Harrier FRS.1					
XZ491	Sea Harrier FRS.1					
XZ492	Sea Harrier FRS.1					
XZ493	Sea Harrier FRS.1					
XZ494	Sea Harrier FRS.1					
XZ495	Sea Harrier FRS.1					
XZ496	Sea Harrier FRS.1					
XZ497	Sea Harrier FRS.1					
XZ498	Sea Harrier FRS.1					
XZ499	Sea Harrier FRS.1					
XZ500	Sea Harrier FRS.1					

Continued procurement of 30 Northrop KD2R-5/MQM-36A pilotless target drones for the RN Fleet Target Group to follow on from XZ425. All are known as the Shelduck D.1 and allocations continue with XZ745.

serial	type	sqdn/unit	code	where&when seen		remarks
XZ505	Shelduck D.1					
XZ506	Shelduck D.1					
XZ507	Shelduck D.1					
XZ508	Shelduck D.1					
XZ509	Shelduck D.1					
XZ510	Shelduck D.1					
XZ511	Shelduck D.1					
XZ512	Shelduck D.1					
XZ513	Shelduck D.1					
XZ514	Shelduck D.1					
XZ515	Shelduck D.1					
XZ516	Shelduck D.1					
XZ517	Shelduck D.1					
XZ518	Shelduck D.1					

XZ531-XZ586

serial	type	sqdn/unit	code	where&when seen		remarks
XZ531	Shelduck D.1					
XZ532	Shelduck D.1					
XZ533	Shelduck D.1					
XZ534	Shelduck D.1					
XZ535	Shelduck D.1					
XZ536	Shelduck D.1					
XZ537	Shelduck D.1					
XZ538	Shelduck D.1					
XZ539	Shelduck D.1					
XZ540	Shelduck D.1					
XZ541	Shelduck D.1					
XZ542	Shelduck D.1					
XZ543	Shelduck D.1					
XZ544	Shelduck D.1					
XZ545	Shelduck D.1					
XZ546	Shelduck D.1					

First production order for 15 Venture T.2 motor-gliders to be built by Slingsby Sailplanes Ltd at Kirkbymoorside, this following the successful evaluation of T.1 XW983. Batch was allotted c/ns 1870-1884 resp; XZ550 f/f 3.7.77. XZ551 later to T.3.

serial	type	sqdn/unit	code	where&when seen		remarks
XZ550	Venture T.2					
XZ551	Venture T.3					
XZ552	Venture T.2					
XZ553	Venture T.2					
XZ554	Venture T.2					
XZ555	Venture T.2					
XZ556	Venture T.2					
XZ557	Venture T.2					
XZ558	Venture T.2					
XZ559	Venture T.2					
XZ560	Venture T.2					
XZ561	Venture T.2					
XZ562	Venture T.2					
XZ563	Venture T.2					
XZ564	Venture T.2					

The second batch of Sea King anti-submarine helicopters for the RN was built to HAS.2 standard, featuring uprated engines and six-bladed tail rotor. The 13 aircraft were allotted c/ns WA838-WA850, XZ570 f/f on 18.6.76 and XZ582 was delivered 12.9.77.

serial	type	sqdn/unit	code	where&when seen		remarks
XZ570	Sea King HAS.2					
XZ571	Sea King HAS.2					
XZ572	Sea King HAS.2					
XZ573	Sea King HAS.2					
XZ574	Sea King HAS.2					
XZ575	Sea King HAS.2					
XZ576	Sea King HAS.2					
XZ577	Sea King HAS.2					
XZ578	Sea King HAS.2					
XZ579	Sea King HAS.2					
XZ580	Sea King HAS.2					
XZ581	Sea King HAS.2					
XZ582	Sea King HAS.2					

15 Sea King HAR.3 rescue helicopters for the RAF built by Westland Helicopters Ltd at Yeovil. XZ585 first flew on 6.9.77 and XZ589 was delivered 2.2.79. The batch was allotted the c/ns WA851-WA865

serial	type	sqdn/unit	code	where&when seen		remarks
XZ585	Sea King HAR.3					
XZ586	Sea King HAR.3					

XZ587-XZ640

serial	type	sqdn/unit	code	where&when seen		remarks
XZ587	Sea King HAR.3					
XZ588	Sea King HAR.3					
XZ589	Sea King HAR.3					
XZ590	Sea King HAR.3					
XZ591	Sea King HAR.3					
XZ592	Sea King HAR.3					
XZ593	Sea King HAR.3					
XZ594	Sea King HAR.3					
XZ595	Sea King HAR.3					
XZ596	Sea King HAR.3					
XZ597	Sea King HAR.3					
XZ598	Sea King HAR.3					
XZ599	Sea King HAR.3					

Thirteen Lynx helicopters originally ordered as training aircraft for the RAF but, following an early policy change, the order was transferred to the AAC and the aircraft built as AH.1's. XZ605 (c/n WA149) f/f 21.11.79; XZ617 (WA168) f/f 14.3.80.

serial	type	sqdn/unit	code	where&when seen		remarks
XZ605	Lynx AH.1					
XZ606	Lynx AH.1					
XZ607	Lynx AH.1					
XZ608	Lynx AH.1					
XZ609	Lynx AH.1					
XZ610	Lynx AH.1					
XZ611	Lynx AH.1					
XZ612	Lynx AH.1					
XZ613	Lynx AH.1					
XZ614	Lynx AH.1					
XZ615	Lynx AH.1					
XZ616	Lynx AH.1					
XZ617	Lynx AH.1					

The second production order for 8 Lynx HAS.2(FN)'s placed with Westland Helicopters Ltd at Yeovil on behalf of the French Aeronavale. Final fitting out was carried out at Aerospatiale's Marignane plant. XZ620 (c/n WA087) first flew on 24.10.78.

serial	type	sqdn/unit	code	where&when seen		remarks
XZ620	Lynx HAS.2(FN)					
XZ621	Lynx HAS.2(FN)					
XZ622	Lynx HAS.2(FN)					
XZ623	Lynx HAS.2(FN)					
XZ624	Lynx HAS.2(FN)					
XZ625	Lynx HAS.2(FN)					
XZ626	Lynx HAS.2(FN)					
XZ627	Lynx HAS.2(FN)					

Two pre-production Tornados built by British Aerospace Corporation at Warton. XZ630 (c/n P.12) f/f 14.3.77 and XZ631 (P.15) f/f 24.11.78. XZ630 became the first aircraft to be handed over to the customer when it was delivered on 3.2.78.

serial	type	sqdn/unit	code	where&when seen		remarks
XZ630	Tornado.					
XZ631	Tornado					
XZ635						
XZ636						
XZ637						
XZ638						
XZ639						

Further production order for 37 Lynx AH.1 helicopters for the Army Air Corps to be built by Westland Helicopters Ltd at Yeovil. XZ640 (c/n WA171) first flew 7.5.80.

serial	type	sqdn/unit	code	where&when seen		remarks
XZ640	Lynx AH.1					

XZ641-XZ703

serial	type	sqdn/unit	code	where&when seen		remarks
XZ641	Lynx AH.1					
XZ642	Lynx AH.1					
XZ643	Lynx AH.1					
XZ644	Lynx AH.1					
XZ645	Lynx AH.1					
XZ646	Lynx AH.1					
XZ647	Lynx AH.1					
XZ648	Lynx AH.1					
XZ649	Lynx AH.1					
XZ650	Lynx AH.1					
XZ651	Lynx AH.1					
XZ652	Lynx AH.1					
XZ653	Lynx AH.1					
XZ654	Lynx AH.1					
XZ655	Lynx AH.1					
XZ661	Lynx AH.1					
XZ662	Lynx AH.1					
XZ663	Lynx AH.1					
XZ664	Lynx AH.1					
XZ665	Lynx AH.1					
XZ666	Lynx AH.1					
XZ667	Lynx AH.1					
XZ668	Lynx AH.1					
XZ669	Lynx AH.1					
XZ670	Lynx AH.1					
XZ671	Lynx AH.1					
XZ672	Lynx AH.1					
XZ673	Lynx AH.1					
XZ674	Lynx AH.1					
XZ675	Lynx AH.1					
XZ676	Lynx AH.1					
XZ677	Lynx AH.1					
XZ678	Lynx AH.1					
XZ679	Lynx AH.1					
XZ680	Lynx AH.1					
XZ681	Lynx AH.1					

Second production order for 12 Lynx HAS.2 anti-submarine helicopters for the Royal Navy to be built by Westland Helicopters Ltd at Yeovil. XZ689 (c/n WA091) first flew 15.12.78, before several of the previous batch, XZ690 (WA113) not flying until 14.5.79; XZ700 (WA163) first flew 1.4.80.

serial	type	sqdn/unit	code	where&when seen		remarks
XZ689	Lynx HAS.2					
XZ690	Lynx HAS.2					
XZ691	Lynx HAS.2					
XZ692	Lynx HAS.2					
XZ693	Lynx HAS.2					
XZ694	Lynx HAS.2					
XZ695	Lynx HAS.2					
XZ696	Lynx HAS.2					
XZ697	Lynx HAS.2					
XZ698	Lynx HAS.2					
XZ699	Lynx HAS.2					
XZ700	Lynx HAS.2					
XZ701						
XZ702						
XZ703						

XZ704-XZ757

serial	type	sqdn/unit	code	where&when seen		remarks
XZ704						
XZ705						
XZ706						
XZ707						
XZ708						
XZ709						
XZ710						
XZ711						
XZ712						
XZ713						
XZ714						
XZ715						
XZ716						
XZ717						
XZ718						

Eighteen Lynx HAS.2 anti-submarine helicopters built for the Royal Navy by Westland Helicopters Ltd at Yeovil. XZ719 (c/n WA164) first flew on 16.4.80 and was delivered on 2.5.80. Some aircraft may later be modified to HAS.3 standard.

serial	type	sqdn/unit	code	where&when seen		remarks
XZ719	Lynx HAS.2					
XZ720	Lynx HAS.2					
XZ721	Lynx HAS.2					
XZ722	Lynx HAS.2					
XZ723	Lynx HAS.2					
XZ724	Lynx HAS.2					
XZ725	Lynx HAS.2					
XZ726	Lynx HAS.2					
XZ727	Lynx HAS.2					
XZ728	Lynx HAS.2					
XZ729	Lynx HAS.2					
XZ730	Lynx HAS.2					
XZ731	Lynx HAS.2					
XZ732	Lynx HAS.2					
XZ733	Lynx HAS.2					
XZ734	Lynx HAS.2					
XZ735	Lynx HAS.2					
XZ736	Lynx HAS.2					

VIP Westland Commando 2B built at Yeovil for Egypt. It f/f 13.3.75 as WA805/G-17-14 (c/n WA805) being del. on 21.5.75. To UK for mods 17.3.76 using temporary transit serial XZ741. Became G-17-14 and then G-BDVL for return to Egypt 3.6.76. To WA805.

serial	type	sqdn/unit	code	where&when seen		remarks
XZ741	Commando 2B					To G-17-14 To G-BDVL

Continued procurement of 52 Northrop KD2R-5/MQM-36A pilotless target drones for the RN Fleet Target Group to follow on from XZ546. All are known as the Shelduck D.1 This batch covers the latest known Shelduck allocations.

serial	type	sqdn/unit	code	where&when seen		remarks
XZ745	Shelduck D.1					
XZ746	Shelduck D.1					
XZ747	Shelduck D.1					
XZ748	Shelduck D.1					
XZ749	Shelduck D.1					
XZ750	Shelduck D.1					
XZ751	Shelduck D.1					
XZ752	Shelduck D.1					
XZ753	Shelduck D.1					
XZ754	Shelduck D.1					
XZ755	Shelduck D.1					
XZ756	Shelduck D.1					
XZ757	Shelduck D.1					

XZ758-XZ828

serial	type	sqdn/unit	code	where&when seen		remarks
XZ758	Shelduck D.1					
XZ759	Shelduck D.1					
XZ760	Shelduck D.1					
XZ761	Shelduck D.1					
XZ762	Shelduck D.1					
XZ763	Shelduck D.1					
XZ764	Shelduck D.1					
XZ765	Shelduck D.1					
XZ766	Shelduck D.1					
XZ767	Shelduck D.1					
XZ768	Shelduck D.1					
XZ769	Shelduck D.1					
XZ770	Shelduck D.1					
XZ771	Shelduck D.1					
XZ772	Shelduck D.1					
XZ773	Shelduck D.1					
XZ774	Shelduck D.1					
XZ790	Shelduck D.1					
XZ791	Shelduck D.1					
XZ792	Shelduck D.1					
XZ793	Shelduck D.1					
XZ794	Shelduck D.1					
XZ795	Shelduck D.1					
XZ796	Shelduck D.1					
XZ797	Shelduck D.1					
XZ798	Shelduck D.1					
XZ799	Shelduck D.1					
XZ800	Shelduck D.1					
XZ801	Shelduck D.1					
XZ802	Shelduck D.1					
XZ803	Shelduck D.1					
XZ804	Shelduck D.1					
XZ805	Shelduck D.1					
XZ806	Shelduck D.1					
XZ807	Shelduck D.1					
XZ808	Shelduck D.1					
XZ809	Shelduck D.1					
XZ810	Shelduck D.1					
XZ811	Shelduck D.1					

MATS-B is a small, piston-engined, pneumatically launched target drone developed and produced by Short Bros Ltd at Belfast under an MoD contract. Test flights commenced in 6.75. The first order accounted for 50 units for use as a target for practice firings of short-range surface-to-air missiles and guns.

serial	type	sqdn/unit	code	where&when seen		remarks
XZ815	MATS-B					
XZ816	MATS-B					
XZ817	MATS-B					
XZ818	MATS-B					
XZ819	MATS-B					
XZ820	MATS-B					
XZ821	MATS-B					
XZ822	MATS-B					
XZ823	MATS-B					
XZ824	MATS-B					
XZ825	MATS-B					
XZ826	MATS-B					
XZ827	MATS-B					
XZ828	MATS-B					

XZ829-XZ882

serial	type	sqdn/unit	code	where&when seen		remarks
XZ829	MATS-B					
XZ830	MATS-B					
XZ831	MATS-B					
XZ832	MATS-B					
XZ833	MATS-B					
XZ834	MATS-B					
XZ835	MATS-B					
XZ836	MATS-B					
XZ837	MATS-B					
XZ838	MATS-B					
XZ839	MATS-B					
XZ840	MATS-B					
XZ841						
XZ842						
XZ843						
XZ844						
XZ845						
XZ846						
XZ847						
XZ848						
XZ849						
XZ850						
XZ851						
XZ852						
XZ853						
XZ854						
XZ855						
XZ856						
XZ857						
XZ858						
XZ859						
XZ860						

Further allocations for MATS-B target drones to complete the initial production order for 50 aircraft. Allocations continue with ZA200.

serial	type	sqdn/unit	code	where&when seen		remarks
XZ861	MATS-B					
XZ862	MATS-B					
XZ863	MATS-B					
XZ864	MATS-B					
XZ865	MATS-B					
XZ866	MATS-B					
XZ867	MATS-B					
XZ868	MATS-B					
XZ869	MATS-B					
XZ870	MATS-B					
XZ871	MATS-B					
XZ872	MATS-B					
XZ873	MATS-B					
XZ874	MATS-B					
XZ875	MATS-B					
XZ876	MATS-B					
XZ877	MATS-B					
XZ878	MATS-B					
XZ879	MATS-B					
XZ880	MATS-B					
XZ881	MATS-B					
XZ882	MATS-B					

XZ883-XZ933

serial	type	sqdn/unit	code	where&when seen		remarks
XZ883	MATS-B					
XZ884	MATS-B					
XZ885						
XZ886						
XZ887						
XZ888						
XZ889						
XZ890						
XZ891						
XZ892						
XZ893						
XZ894						
XZ895						
XZ896						
XZ897						
XZ898						
XZ899						
XZ900						
XZ901						
XZ902						
XZ903						
XZ904						
XZ905						
XZ906						
XZ907						
XZ908						
XZ909						
XZ910						
XZ911						
XZ912						
XZ913						
XZ914						

The third batch of 8 Sea King HAS.2 anti-submarine helicopters for the Royal Navy built by Westland Helicopters Ltd at Yeovil. The first three aircraft flew with incorrect serials applied; XZ915 f/f 7.2.79 (as'XV915'). The batch was allotted the c/ns WA875-WA882 respectively. XZ916 became the prototype HAS.5, with other conversions to follow.

serial	type	sqdn/unit	code	where&when seen		remarks
XZ915	Sea King HAS.2					Ex 'XV915'
XZ916	Sea King HAS.5					Ex 'XV916'
XZ917	Sea King HAS.2					Ex 'XV917'
XZ918	Sea King HAS.2					
XZ919	Sea King HAS.2					
XZ920	Sea King HAS.2					
XZ921	Sea King HAS.2					
XZ922	Sea King HAS.2					

Further batch of 13 Gazelle helicopters for the Royal Air Force (XZ930-XZ935), MoD(PE) (XZ936) and the Royal Navy (XZ937-XZ942), built by Westland Helicopters Ltd at Weston-super-Mare. The batch was allotted the c/ns 1727/1728/1734/1735/1736/1742/1743/1746/1747/1750/1757/1758 and 1761 respectively. First flights took place on 3.5.78 (XZ930), 18.4.78 (XZ936) and 18.8.78 (XZ937). During 1979/80 some HT.2's were taken from storage, modified to HT.3 standard and delivered to the RAF.

serial	type	sqdn/unit	code	where&when seen		remarks
XZ930	Gazelle HT.3					
XZ931	Gazelle HT.3					
XZ932	Gazelle HT.3					
XZ933	Gazelle HT.3					

XZ934-XZ999

serial	type	sqdn/unit	code	where&when seen		remarks
XZ934	Gazelle HT.3					
XZ935	Gazelle HT.3					
XZ936	Gazelle HT.3					
XZ937	Gazelle HT.3					
XZ938	Gazelle HT.2					
XZ939	Gazelle HT.3					
XZ940	Gazelle HT.3					
XZ941	Gazelle HT.3					
XZ942	Gazelle HT.2					

The third order for 10 Northrop Chukar jet-powered pilotless target drones for the Royal Navy Fleet Target Group. The MQM-74A had not been a great success and was replaced on the Ventura Division production line by the MQM-74C which was given the UK designation Chukar D.2.

serial	type	sqdn/unit	code	where&when seen		remarks
XZ950	Chukar D.2					
XZ951	Chukar D.2					
XZ952	Chukar D.2					
XZ953	Chukar D.2					
XZ954	Chukar D.2					
XZ955	Chukar D.2					
XZ956	Chukar D.2					
XZ957	Chukar D.2					
XZ958	Chukar D.2					
XZ959	Chukar D.2					

24 Harrier GR.3 V/STOL aircraft for the RAF, ordered for attrition replacement. Built by British Aerospace (Kingston-Brough Division), final assembly and test flying took place at Dunsfold. Deliveries commenced early in 1980.

serial	type	sqdn/unit	code	where&when seen		remarks
XZ963	Harrier GR.3					
XZ964	Harrier GR.3					
XZ965	Harrier GR.3					
XZ966	Harrier GR.3					
XZ967	Harrier GR.3					
XZ968	Harrier GR.3					
XZ969	Harrier GR.3					
XZ970	Harrier GR.3					
XZ971	Harrier GR.3					
XZ972	Harrier GR.3					
XZ973	Harrier GR.3					
XZ987	Harrier GR.3					
XZ988	Harrier GR.3					
XZ989	Harrier GR.3					
XZ990	Harrier GR.3					
XZ991	Harrier GR.3					
XZ992	Harrier GR.3					
XZ993	Harrier GR.3					
XZ994	Harrier GR.3					
XZ995	Harrier GR.3					
XZ996	Harrier GR.3					
XZ997	Harrier GR.3					
XZ998	Harrier GR.3					
XZ999	Harrier GR.3					

This Harrier GR.3 allocation brings to an end the 'X' serial range. Although aircraft from this order only appeared in 1980, the first 'Z' serial, Hawk T.50 ZA101 had appeared by June 1977.

ZA101-ZA143

serial	type	sqdn/unit	code	where&when seen	remarks

The British Aerospace Hawk T.50 demonstrator G-HAWK (c/n 41H/4020010) was issued the serial ZA101 to enable it to carry out live weapons firing demonstrations which are not permitted by civil aircraft.

serial	type	sqdn/unit	code	where&when seen	remarks
ZA101	Hawk T.50				G-HAWK

Following the fifteen search and rescue Sea King HAR.3's, an extra aircraft was ordered to RAF standard in 1977. Allocated c/n WA886, ZA105 will be delivered to the Empire Test Pilots School at Boscombe Down. This aircraft is scheduled to be ready for delivery in mid-1980.

serial	type	sqdn/unit	code	where&when seen	remarks
ZA105	Sea King HAR.3				

In addition to the aircraft transferred from RAF stocks, two ex-civil aircraft have been acquired as part of the Royal Navy's Jetstream T.2 programme. The c/ns are ZA110 (248) and ZA111 (211).

serial	type	sqdn/unit	code	where&when seen	remarks
ZA110	Jetstream T.2				Ex F-BTMI
ZA111	Jetstream T.2				Ex 9Q-CTC
ZA112					
ZA113					
ZA114					
ZA115					
ZA116					
ZA117					
ZA118					
ZA119					
ZA120					
ZA121					
ZA122					
ZA123					
ZA124					
ZA125					

The Royal Navy's fourth batch of Sea King anti-submarine helicopters will be the first to be completed to HAS.5 standard. Deliveries from the production line at Westland's Yeovil factory are due to commence in mid-1980. The c/ns are WA887-WA898

serial	type	sqdn/unit	code	where&when seen	remarks
ZA126	Sea King HAS.5				
ZA127	Sea King HAS.5				
ZA128	Sea King HAS.5				
ZA129	Sea King HAS.5				
ZA130	Sea King HAS.5				
ZA131	Sea King HAS.5				
ZA132	Sea King HAS.5				
ZA133	Sea King HAS.5				
ZA134	Sea King HAS.5				
ZA135	Sea King HAS.5				
ZA136	Sea King HAS.5				
ZA137	Sea King HAS.5				

Nine ex-civil VC.10 transports are being converted by British Aerospace at Filton into tanker aircraft, specifically to support the RAF's Tornado F.2's. The c/ns are as follows; ZA140 (814), ZA141 (809), ZA142 (811), ZA143 (813), ZA144 (806) all VC.10 series 1112 and ZA147 (882), ZA148 (883), ZA149 (884), ZA150 (885) all Super VC.10 series 1164.

serial	type	sqdn/unit	code	where&when seen	remarks
ZA140	VC.10 K.2				Ex A40-VL
ZA141	VC.10 K.2				Ex A40-VG
ZA142	VC.10 K.2				Ex A40-VI
ZA143	VC.10 K.2				Ex A40-VK

ZA144-ZA209

serial	type	sqdn/unit	code	where&when seen		remarks
ZA144	VC.10 K.2					Ex A40-VC
ZA147	VC.10 K.3					Ex 5H-MMT
ZA148	VC.10 K.3					Ex 5Y-ADA
ZA149	VC.10 K.3					Ex 5X-UVJ
ZA150	VC.10 K.3					Ex 5H-MOG

The fourth order for 10 Northrop Chukar pilotless target drones for the Royal Navy Fleet Target Group. Following on from XZ959, this batch again covered the MQM-74C version (UK designation Chukar D.2) and was built by the company's Ventura Division.

serial	type	sqdn/unit	code	where&when seen		remarks
ZA155	Chukar D.2					
ZA156	Chukar D.2					
ZA157	Chukar D.2					
ZA158	Chukar D.2					
ZA159	Chukar D.2					
ZA160	Chukar D.2					
ZA161	Chukar D.2					
ZA162	Chukar D.2					
ZA163	Chukar D.2					
ZA164	Chukar D.2					

Further production of Sea King HAS.5 anti-submarine helicopters for the RN. To be built by Westland Helicopters Ltd at Yeovil, the batch is allotted c/ns WA899-WA903.

serial	type	sqdn/unit	code	where&when seen		remarks
ZA166	Sea King HAS.5					
ZA167	Sea King HAS.5					
ZA168	Sea King HAS.5					
ZA169	Sea King HAS.5					
ZA170	Sea King HAS.5					

Follow-on order for 10 Sea Harrier FRS.1 ship-borne V/STOL fighter aircraft to be built by British Aerospace for the Royal Navy. The aircraft will be built at Kingston and Brough with final assembly and test flying taking place at Dunsfold.

serial	type	sqdn/unit	code	where&when seen		remarks
ZA174	Sea Harrier FRS.1					
ZA175	Sea Harrier FRS.1					
ZA176	Sea Harrier FRS.1					
ZA177	Sea Harrier FRS.1					
ZA190	Sea Harrier FRS.1					
ZA191	Sea Harrier FRS.1					
ZA192	Sea Harrier FRS.1					
ZA193	Sea Harrier FRS.1					
ZA194	Sea Harrier FRS.1					
ZA195	Sea Harrier FRS.1					

A further production order for 25 MATS-B target drones built by Short Bros at Belfast. The initials appear to stand for either 'Military Aircraft Target System' or 'Miniature Aerial Target System'. The dimensions are: wing span 11ft; fuselage length 8ft and it is powered by an 18hp Weslake 274-6 engine. Undamaged aircraft can be recovered either by a skid landing or a parachute.

serial	type	sqdn/unit	code	where&when seen		remarks
ZA200	MATS-B					
ZA201	MATS-B					
ZA202	MATS-B					
ZA203	MATS-B					
ZA204	MATS-B					
ZA205	MATS-B					
ZA206	MATS-B					
ZA207	MATS-B					
ZA208	MATS-B					
ZA209	MATS-B					

ZA210-ZA283

serial	type	sqdn/unit	code	where&when seen		remarks
ZA210	MATS-B					
ZA211	MATS-B					
ZA212	MATS-B					
ZA213	MATS-B					
ZA214	MATS-B					
ZA215						
ZA216						
ZA217						
ZA218						
ZA219						
ZA220						
ZA221						
ZA222						
ZA223						
ZA224						
ZA225						
ZA226						
ZA227						
ZA228						
ZA229						
ZA230						
ZA231						
ZA232						
ZA233						
ZA234						
ZA235						
ZA236						

Further allocations for MATS-B target drones to complete the second production order for 25 aircraft. This batch was initially painted up incorrectly with serials running on from the previous allocation (ZA215 etc). The error was later rectified. Production continues with twenty additional aircraft.

serial	type	sqdn/unit	code	where&when seen		remarks
ZA237	MATS-B					Ex 'ZA215'
ZA238	MATS-B					Ex 'ZA216'
ZA239	MATS-B					Ex 'ZA217'
ZA240	MATS-B					Ex 'ZA218'
ZA241	MATS-B					Ex 'ZA219'
ZA242	MATS-B					Ex 'ZA220'
ZA243	MATS-B					Ex 'ZA221'
ZA244	MATS-B					Ex 'ZA222'
ZA245	MATS-B					Ex 'ZA223'
ZA246	MATS-B					Ex 'ZA224'

The Hawker Siddeley/British Aerospace Harrier T.52 demonstrator G-VTOL (c/n 735795) was issued the serial ZA250 to enable it to carry out live weapons firing demonstrations which are not permitted by civil aircraft. First flew (as G-VTOL) 16.9.71.

serial	type	sqdn/unit	code	where&when seen		remarks
ZA250	Harrier T.52					G-VTOL Ex XW273

Three prototypes of the UK-only, air defence variant of the Panavia Tornado multi-role aircraft. ZA254 was rolled out at Warton on 9.8.79 and made its maiden flight on 28.10.79. The RAF has a requirement for 165 of these long-range fighters and the first production order is expected to be placed in 1980.

serial	type	sqdn/unit	code	where&when seen		remarks
ZA254	Tornado F.2					
ZA267	Tornado F.2					
ZA283	Tornado F.2					

ZA290-ZA365

serial	type	sqdn/unit	code	where&when seen	remarks

The Sea King HC.4 is a navalised version of the Commando assault helicopter, the first four aircraft being originally built on spec as Commandos. Built by Westland Helicopters Ltd at Yeovil, ZA290 f/f 26.9.79 and deliveries to the Royal Navy commenced with ZA291 on 13.11.79. C/ns are WA904-WA913 (ZA290-ZA299) and WA914-WA918 (ZA310-ZA314) respectively.

serial	type	sqdn/unit	code	where&when seen	remarks
ZA290	Sea King HC.4				
ZA291	Sea King HC.4				
ZA292	Sea King HC.4				
ZA293	Sea King HC.4				
ZA294	Sea King HC.4				
ZA295	Sea King HC.4				
ZA296	Sea King HC.4				
ZA297	Sea King HC.4				
ZA298	Sea King HC.4				
ZA299	Sea King HC.4				
ZA310	Sea King HC.4				
ZA311	Sea King HC.4				
ZA312	Sea King HC.4				
ZA313	Sea King HC.4				
ZA314	Sea King HC.4				

The first production order for Panavia Tornado strike aircraft was placed in 1977 and totalled 40 aircraft; 23 for the RAF and 17 for West Germany(Bundesmarine and Luftwaffe). The RAF total is made-up of 12 dual-control conversion trainers (indicated by (T) in listing) and 11 strike aircraft. ZA319, the first production Tornado to be completed was rolled out at Warton on 5.6.79 and first flew on 10.7.79. The build number of ZA319 (BT001) indicates that it is the first British Trainer aircraft.

serial	type	sqdn/unit	code	where&when seen	remarks
ZA319	Tornado GR.1 (T)				
ZA320	Tornado GR.1 (T)				
ZA321	Tornado GR.1				
ZA322	Tornado GR.1				
ZA323	Tornado GR.1 (T)				
ZA324	Tornado GR.1 (T)				
ZA325	Tornado GR.1 (T)				
ZA326	Tornado GR.1 (T)				
ZA327	Tornado GR.1				
ZA328	Tornado GR.1				
ZA329	Tornado GR.1				
ZA330	Tornado GR.1 (T)				
ZA352	Tornado GR.1 (T)				
ZA353	Tornado GR.1				
ZA354	Tornado GR.1				
ZA355	Tornado GR.1				
ZA356	Tornado GR.1 (T)				
ZA357	Tornado GR.1 (T)				
ZA358	Tornado GR.1 (T)				
ZA359	Tornado GR.1				
ZA360	Tornado GR.1				
ZA361	Tornado GR.1				
ZA362	Tornado GR.1 (T)				

The third production order for Panavia Tornados was placed in 1979 and totalled 164 aircraft comprising 68 for the RAF, 68 for West Germany and 28 for Italy. The RAF total is made-up of 8 conversion trainers and 60 strike aircraft. The serials for the second and third batches are reversed, this allocation continuing on from ZA614.

serial	type	sqdn/unit	code	where&when seen	remarks
ZA365	Tornado GR.1				

ZA366-ZA470

serial	type	sqdn/unit	code	where&when seen		remarks
ZA366	Tornado GR.1					
ZA367	Tornado GR.1					
ZA368	Tornado GR.1					
ZA369	Tornado GR.1					
ZA370	Tornado GR.1					
ZA371	Tornado GR.1					
ZA372	Tornado GR.1					
ZA373	Tornado GR.1					
ZA374	Tornado GR.1					
ZA375	Tornado GR.1					
ZA376	Tornado GR.1					
ZA392	Tornado GR.1					
ZA393	Tornado GR.1					
ZA394	Tornado GR.1					
ZA395	Tornado GR.1					
ZA396	Tornado GR.1					
ZA397	Tornado GR.1					
ZA398	Tornado GR.1					
ZA399	Tornado GR.1					
ZA400	Tornado GR.1					
ZA401	Tornado GR.1					
ZA402	Tornado GR.1					
ZA403	Tornado GR.1					
ZA404	Tornado GR.1					
ZA405	Tornado GR.1					
ZA406	Tornado GR.1					
ZA407	Tornado GR.1					
ZA408	Tornado GR.1					
ZA409	Tornado GR.1 (T)					
ZA410	Tornado GR.1 (T)					
ZA411	Tornado GR.1 (T)					
ZA412	Tornado GR.1 (T)					
ZA446	Tornado GR.1					
ZA447	Tornado GR.1					
ZA448	Tornado GR.1					
ZA449	Tornado GR.1					
ZA450	Tornado GR.1					
ZA451	Tornado GR.1					
ZA452	Tornado GR.1					
ZA453	Tornado GR.1					
ZA454	Tornado GR.1					
ZA455	Tornado GR.1					
ZA456	Tornado GR.1					
ZA457	Tornado GR.1					
ZA458	Tornado GR.1					
ZA459	Tornado GR.1					
ZA460	Tornado GR.1					
ZA461	Tornado GR.1					
ZA462	Tornado GR.1					
ZA463	Tornado GR.1					
ZA464	Tornado GR.1 (T)					
ZA465	Tornado GR.1 (T)					
ZA466	Tornado GR.1 (T)					
ZA467	Tornado GR.1 (T)					
ZA468	Tornado GR.1					
ZA469	Tornado GR.1					
ZA470	Tornado GR.1					

ZA471-ZA539

serial	type	sqdn/unit	code	where&when seen		remarks
ZA471	Tornado GR.1					
ZA472	Tornado GR.1					
ZA473	Tornado GR.1					
ZA474	Tornado GR.1					
ZA475	Tornado GR.1					
ZA490	Tornado GR.1					
ZA491	Tornado GR.1					
ZA492	Tornado GR.1					
ZA493	Tornado GR.1					
ZA494	Tornado GR.1					

Westland Helicopters' civil Lynx demonstrater G-LYNX (c/n WA102) was allocated the serial ZA500 to enable it to carry out live rocket firing during a demonstration to the Spanish Armed Forces in 6.79 and later in the UK. Wrong serial: to ZB500 5.80.

serial	type	sqdn/unit	code	where&when seen		remarks
ZA500	Lynx					G-LYNX To ZB500

One BN.2A-21 Islander (c/n 2011) acquired by the RAF in 1979 for parachute training. It has been allocated the serial ZA503 but wears the civil registration G-DIVE. It is reported that the JSPA Islander G-AYRU (c/n 181) also has a 'shadow' serial.

serial	type	sqdn/unit	code	where&when seen		remarks
ZA503	Islander					G-DIVE
ZA504						
ZA505						
ZA506						
ZA507						
ZA508						
ZA509						
ZA510						
ZA511						
ZA512						
ZA513						
ZA514						
ZA515						
ZA516						
ZA517						
ZA518						
ZA519						
ZA520						
ZA521						
ZA522						
ZA523						
ZA524						
ZA525						
ZA526						
ZA527						
ZA528						
ZA529						
ZA530						
ZA531						
ZA532						
ZA533						
ZA534						
ZA535						
ZA536						
ZA537						
ZA538						
ZA539						

ZA540-ZA611

serial	type	sqdn/unit	code	where&when seen	remarks

The second production order for Panavia Tornado multi-role aircraft was placed in 1978 and totalled 110 aircraft comprising 55 for the RAF, 40 for West Germany and 15 for Italy. The RAF total is made-up of 16 dual-control conversion trainers and 39 strike aircraft. The serials for the second and third Tornado orders appear to be out of sequence, production continuing with ZA365.

serial	type	sqdn/unit	code	where&when seen	remarks
ZA540	Tornado GR.1 (T)				
ZA541	Tornado GR.1 (T)				
ZA542	Tornado GR.1				
ZA543	Tornado GR.1				
ZA544	Tornado GR.1 (T)				
ZA545	Tornado GR.1				
ZA546	Tornado GR.1				
ZA547	Tornado GR.1				
ZA548	Tornado GR.1 (T)				
ZA549	Tornado GR.1 (T)				
ZA550	Tornado GR.1				
ZA551	Tornado GR.1 (T)				
ZA552	Tornado GR.1 (T)				
ZA553	Tornado GR.1				
ZA554	Tornado GR.1				
ZA555	Tornado GR.1 (T)				
ZA556	Tornado GR.1				
ZA557	Tornado GR.1				
ZA558	Tornado GR.1				
ZA559	Tornado GR.1				
ZA560	Tornado GR.1				
ZA561	Tornado GR.1				
ZA562	Tornado GR.1 (T)				
ZA563	Tornado GR.1				
ZA564	Tornado GR.1				
ZA585	Tornado GR.1				
ZA586	Tornado GR.1				
ZA587	Tornado GR.1				
ZA588	Tornado GR.1				
ZA589	Tornado GR.1				
ZA590	Tornado GR.1				
ZA591	Tornado GR.1				
ZA592	Tornado GR.1				
ZA593	Tornado GR.1				
ZA594	Tornado GR.1 (T)				
ZA595	Tornado GR.1 (T)				
ZA596	Tornado GR.1				
ZA597	Tornado GR.1				
ZA598	Tornado GR.1 (T)				
ZA599	Tornado GR.1 (T)				
ZA600	Tornado GR.1				
ZA601	Tornado GR.1				
ZA602	Tornado GR.1 (T)				
ZA603	Tornado GR.1				
ZA604	Tornado GR.1 (T)				
ZA605	Tornado GR.1				
ZA606	Tornado GR.1				
ZA607	Tornado GR.1				
ZA608	Tornado GR.1				
ZA609	Tornado GR.1				
ZA610	Tornado GR.1				
ZA611	Tornado GR.1				

ZA612-ZA708

serial	type	sqdn/unit	code	where&when seen		remarks
ZA612	Tornado GR.1 (T)					
ZA613	Tornado GR.1					
ZA614	Tornado GR.1					

25 Venture T.3 motor-gliders built by Slingsby Sailplanes Ltd at Kirkbymoorside. ZA625 (c/n 1961) first flew 4.10.79. The T.3 features electric engine starting.

serial	type	sqdn/unit	code	where&when seen		remarks
ZA625	Venture T.3					
ZA626	Venture T.3					
ZA627	Venture T.3					
ZA628	Venture T.3					
ZA629	Venture T.3					
ZA630	Venture T.3					
ZA631	Venture T.3					
ZA632	Venture T.3					
ZA633	Venture T.3					
ZA634	Venture T.3					
ZA652	Venture T.3					
ZA653	Venture T.3					
ZA654	Venture T.3					
ZA655	Venture T.3					
ZA656	Venture T.3					
ZA657	Venture T.3					
ZA658	Venture T.3					
ZA659	Venture T.3					
ZA660	Venture T.3					
ZA661	Venture T.3					
ZA662	Venture T.3					
ZA663	Venture T.3					
ZA664	Venture T.3					
ZA665	Venture T.3					
ZA666	Venture T.3					

33 Chinook HC.1 twin-rotor transport helicopters ordered to meet the RAF's long-standing medium-lift requirement. Built by Boeing-Vertol Co, Ridley, Philadelphia PA, they are allocated TAB Block Nos (equivalent to c/ns) M/A 001-M/A 033. The RAF's HC.1 is based on the US Army CH-47C variant but incorporates some advanced features of the CH-47D and some British-built equipment. ZA670 first flew 23.3.80.

serial	type	sqdn/unit	code	where&when seen		remarks
ZA670	Chinook HC.1					
ZA671	Chinook HC.1					
ZA672	Chinook HC.1					
ZA673	Chinook HC.1					
ZA674	Chinook HC.1					
ZA675	Chinook HC.1					
ZA676	Chinook HC.1					
ZA677	Chinook HC.1					
ZA678	Chinook HC.1					
ZA679	Chinook HC.1					
ZA680	Chinook HC.1					
ZA681	Chinook HC.1					
ZA682	Chinook HC.1					
ZA683	Chinook HC.1					
ZA684	Chinook HC.1					
ZA704	Chinook HC.1					
ZA705	Chinook HC.1					
ZA706	Chinook HC.1					
ZA707	Chinook HC.1					
ZA708	Chinook HC.1					

ZA709-ZA764

serial	type	sqdn/unit	code	where&when seen		remarks
ZA709	Chinook HC.1					
ZA710	Chinook HC.1					
ZA711	Chinook HC.1					
ZA712	Chinook HC.1					
ZA713	Chinook HC.1					
ZA714	Chinook HC.1					
ZA715	Chinook HC.1					
ZA716	Chinook HC.1					
ZA717	Chinook HC.1					
ZA718	Chinook HC.1					
ZA719	Chinook HC.1					
ZA720	Chinook HC.1					
ZA721	Chinook HC.1					

Twelve Gazelle AH.1 helicopters for the AAC built by Westland Helicopters Ltd at Weston-super-Mare. Allotted c/ns 1795-1806 resp; ZA727 delivered 14.12.79.

serial	type	sqdn/unit	code	where&when seen		remarks
ZA726	Gazelle AH.1					
ZA727	Gazelle AH.1					
ZA728	Gazelle AH.1					
ZA729	Gazelle AH.1					
ZA730	Gazelle AH.1					
ZA731	Gazelle AH.1					
ZA732	Gazelle AH.1					
ZA733	Gazelle AH.1					
ZA734	Gazelle AH.1					
ZA735	Gazelle AH.1					
ZA736	Gazelle AH.1					
ZA737	Gazelle AH.1					
ZA738						
ZA739						
ZA740						
ZA741						
ZA742						
ZA743						
ZA744						
ZA745						
ZA746						
ZA747						
ZA748						
ZA749						
ZA750						
ZA751						
ZA752						
ZA753						
ZA754						
ZA755						
ZA756						
ZA757						
ZA758						
ZA759						
ZA760						
ZA761						
ZA762						
ZA763						
ZA764						

Thirteen Gazelle AH.1 helicopters for the Army Air Corps to be built by Westland

ZA765-ZA812

Helicopters Ltd at Weston-super-Mare. This batch forms second part of the 1979 order, following on from ZA726 etc. The batch is allotted the c/ns 1807-1819 resp.

serial	type	sqdn/unit	code	where&when seen	remarks
ZA765	Gazelle AH.1				
ZA766	Gazelle AH.1				
ZA767	Gazelle AH.1				
ZA768	Gazelle AH.1				
ZA769	Gazelle AH.1				
ZA770	Gazelle AH.1				
ZA771	Gazelle AH.1				
ZA772	Gazelle AH.1				
ZA773	Gazelle AH.1				
ZA774	Gazelle AH.1				
ZA775	Gazelle AH.1				
ZA776	Gazelle AH.1				
ZA777	Gazelle AH.1				
ZA778					
ZA779					
ZA780					
ZA781					
ZA782					
ZA783					
ZA784					
ZA785					
ZA786					
ZA787					
ZA788					
ZA789					
ZA790					
ZA791					
ZA792					
ZA793					
ZA794					
ZA795					
ZA796					
ZA797					
ZA798					
ZA799					
ZA800					

A further batch of four Gazelle HT.3 training helicopters for the Royal Air Force built by Westland Helicopters Ltd at Weston-super-Mare. The batch was allotted the c/ns 1791-1794 resp. ZA801 first flew on 24.7.79 and was delivered on 26.8.79.

serial	type	sqdn/unit	code	where&when seen	remarks
ZA801	Gazelle HT.3				
ZA802	Gazelle HT.3				
ZA803	Gazelle HT.3				
ZA804	Gazelle HT.3				
ZA805					
ZA806					
ZA807					
ZA808					
ZA809					
ZA810					
ZA811					
ZA812					

ZA813-ZA871

serial	type	sqdn/unit	code	where&when seen		remarks
ZA813						
ZA814						
ZA815						
ZA816						
ZA817						
ZA818						
ZA819						
ZA820						
ZA821						
ZA822						
ZA823						
ZA824						
ZA825						
ZA826						
ZA827						
ZA828						
ZA829						
ZA830						
ZA831						
ZA832						
ZA833						
ZA834						
ZA835						
ZA836						
ZA837						
ZA838						
ZA839						
ZA840						
ZA841						
ZA842						
ZA843						
ZA844						
ZA845						
ZA846						
ZA847						
ZA848						
ZA849						
ZA850						
ZA851						
ZA852						
ZA853						
ZA854						
ZA855						
ZA856						
ZA857						
ZA858						
ZA859						
ZA860						
ZA861						
ZA862						
ZA863						
ZA864						
ZA865						
ZA866						
ZA867						
ZA868						
ZA869						
ZA870						
ZA871						

ZA872-ZA930

serial	type	sqdn/unit	code	where&when seen		remarks
ZA872						
ZA873						
ZA874						
ZA875						
ZA876						
ZA877						
ZA878						
ZA879						
ZA880						
ZA881						
ZA882						
ZA883						
ZA884						
ZA885						
ZA886						
ZA887						
ZA888						
ZA889						
ZA890						
ZA891						
ZA892						
ZA893						
ZA894						
ZA895						
ZA896						
ZA897						
ZA898						
ZA899						
ZA900						
ZA901						
ZA902						
ZA903						
ZA904						
ZA905						
ZA906						
ZA907						
ZA908						
ZA909						
ZA910						
ZA911						
ZA912						
ZA913						
ZA914						
ZA915						
ZA916						
ZA917						
ZA918						
ZA919						
ZA920						
ZA921						
ZA922						
ZA923						
ZA924						
ZA925						
ZA926						
ZA927						
ZA928						
ZA929						
ZA930						

ZA931-ZA983

serial	type	sqdn/unit	code	where&when seen		remarks
ZA931						
ZA932						
ZA933						

A further batch of 7 Puma HC.1 assault helicopters (later increased to 8) built by Westland Helicopters Ltd for attrition replacement. The UK assembly line was re-instated at Weston-super-Mare in 1979 and ZA934 first flew on 7.5.80.

serial	type	sqdn/unit	code	where&when seen		remarks
ZA934	Puma HC.1					
ZA935	Puma HC.1					
ZA936	Puma HC.1					
ZA937	Puma HC.1					
ZA938	Puma HC.1					
ZA939	Puma HC.1					
ZA940	Puma HC.1					
ZA941	Puma HC.1					

Ex RCAF C-47A 661 (c/n 10200) acquired by the MoD. After overhaul by Scottish Aviation, it was delivered to RAE West Freugh in 5.71 wearing its supposed ex-RAF serial KG661. In fact the real KG661 (c/n 13478) had crashed in 12.44. This case of mistaken identity was finally recognised in 6.79 when a new serial (ZA947) was allotted.

serial	type	sqdn/unit	code	where&when seen		remarks
ZA947	Dakota C.3					
ZA948						
ZA949						
ZA950						
ZA951						
ZA952						
ZA953						
ZA954						
ZA955						
ZA956						
ZA957						
ZA958						
ZA959						
ZA960						
ZA961						
ZA962						
ZA963						
ZA964						
ZA965						
ZA966						
ZA967						
ZA968						
ZA969						
ZA970						
ZA971						
ZA972						
ZA973						
ZA974						
ZA975						
ZA976						
ZA977						
ZA978						
ZA979						
ZA980						
ZA981						
ZA982						
ZA983						

ZA984-ZB143

serial	type	sqdn/unit	code	where&when seen		remarks
ZA984						
ZA985						
ZA986						
ZA987						
ZA988						
ZA989						
ZA990						
ZA991						
ZA992						
ZA993						
ZA994						
ZA995						
ZA996						
ZA997						
ZA998						
ZA999						
ZB101						
ZB102						
ZB103						
ZB104						
ZB105						
ZB106						
ZB107						
ZB108						
ZB109						
ZB110						
ZB111						
ZB112						
ZB113						
ZB114						
ZB115						
ZB116						
ZB117						
ZB118						
ZB119						
ZB120						
ZB121						
ZB122						
ZB123						
ZB124						
ZB125						
ZB126						
ZB127						
ZB128						
ZB129						
ZB130						
ZB131						
ZB132						
ZB133						
ZB134						
ZB135						
ZB136						
ZB137						
ZB138						
ZB139						
ZB140						
ZB141						
ZB142						
ZB143						

ZB144-ZB202

serial	type	sqdn/unit	code	where&when seen		remarks
ZB144						
ZB145						
ZB146						
ZB147						
ZB148						
ZB149						
ZB150						
ZB151						
ZB152						
ZB153						
ZB154						
ZB155						
ZB156						
ZB157						
ZB158						
ZB159						
ZB160						
ZB161						
ZB162						
ZB163						
ZB164						
ZB165						
ZB166						
ZB167						
ZB168						
ZB169						
ZB170						
ZB171						
ZB172						
ZB173						
ZB174						
ZB175						
ZB176						
ZB177						
ZB178						
ZB179						
ZB180						
ZB181						
ZB182						
ZB183						
ZB184						
ZB185						
ZB186						
ZB187						
ZB188						
ZB189						
ZB190						
ZB191						
ZB192						
ZB193						
ZB194						
ZB195						
ZB196						
ZB197						
ZB198						
ZB199						
ZB200						
ZB201						
ZB202						

ZB203-ZB261

serial	type	sqdn/unit	code	where&when seen		remarks
ZB203						
ZB204						
ZB205						
ZB206						
ZB207						
ZB208						
ZB209						
ZB210						
ZB211						
ZB212						
ZB213						
ZB214						
ZB215						
ZB216						
ZB217						
ZB218						
ZB219						
ZB220						
ZB221						
ZB222						
ZB223						
ZB224						
ZB225						
ZB226						
ZB227						
ZB228						
ZB229						
ZB230						
ZB231						
ZB232						
ZB233						
ZB234						
ZB235						
ZB236						
ZB237						
ZB238						
ZB239						
ZB240						
ZB241						
ZB242						
ZB243						
ZB244						
ZB245						
ZB246						
ZB247						
ZB248						
ZB249						
ZB250						
ZB251						
ZB252						
ZB253						
ZB254						
ZB255						
ZB256						
ZB257						
ZB258						
ZB259						
ZB260						
ZB261						

ZB262-ZB320

serial	type	sqdn/unit	code	where&when seen		remarks
ZB262						
ZB263						
ZB264						
ZB265						
ZB266						
ZB267						
ZB268						
ZB269						
ZB270						
ZB271						
ZB272						
ZB273						
ZB274						
ZB275						
ZB276						
ZB277						
ZB278						
ZB279						
ZB280						
ZB281						
ZB282						
ZB283						
ZB284						
ZB285						
ZB286						
ZB287						
ZB288						
ZB289						
ZB290						
ZB291						
ZB292						
ZB293						
ZB294						
ZB295						
ZB296						
ZB297						
ZB298						
ZB299						
ZB300						
ZB301						
ZB302						
ZB303						
ZB304						
ZB305						
ZB306						
ZB307						
ZB308						
ZB309						
ZB310						
ZB311						
ZB312						
ZB313						
ZB314						
ZB315						
ZB316						
ZB317						
ZB318						
ZB319						
ZB320						

ZB321-ZB379

serial	type	sqdn/unit	code	where&when seen		remarks
ZB321						
ZB322						
ZB323						
ZB324						
ZB325						
ZB326						
ZB327						
ZB328						
ZB329						
ZB330						
ZB331						
ZB332						
ZB333						
ZB334						
ZB335						
ZB336						
ZB337						
ZB338						
ZB339						
ZB340						
ZB341						
ZB342						
ZB343						
ZB344						
ZB345						
ZB346						
ZB347						
ZB348						
ZB349						
ZB350						
ZB351						
ZB352						
ZB353						
ZB354						
ZB355						
ZB356						
ZB357						
ZB358						
ZB359						
ZB360						
ZB361						
ZB362						
ZB363						
ZB364						
ZB365						
ZB366						
ZB367						
ZB368						
ZB369						
ZB370						
ZB371						
ZB372						
ZB373						
ZB374						
ZB375						
ZB376						
ZB377						
ZB378						
ZB379						

ZB380-ZB438

serial	type	sqdn/unit	code	where&when seen		remarks
ZB380						
ZB381						
ZB382						
ZB383						
ZB384						
ZB385						
ZB386						
ZB387						
ZB388						
ZB389						
ZB390						
ZB391						
ZB392						
ZB393						
ZB394						
ZB395						
ZB396						
ZB397						
ZB398						
ZB399						
ZB400						
ZB401						
ZB402						
ZB403						
ZB404						
ZB405						
ZB406						
ZB407						
ZB408						
ZB409						
ZB410						
ZB411						
ZB412						
ZB413						
ZB414						
ZB415						
ZB416						
ZB417						
ZB418						
ZB419						
ZB420						
ZB421						
ZB422						
ZB423						
ZB424						
ZB425						
ZB426						
ZB427						
ZB428						
ZB429						
ZB430						
ZB431						
ZB432						
ZB433						
ZB434						
ZB435						
ZB436						
ZB437						
ZB438						

ZB439-ZB497

serial	type	sqdn/unit	code	where&when seen		remarks
ZB439						
ZB440						
ZB441						
ZB442						
ZB443						
ZB444						
ZB445						
ZB446						
ZB447						
ZB448						
ZB449						
ZB450						
ZB451						
ZB452						
ZB453						
ZB454						
ZB455						
ZB456						
ZB457						
ZB458						
ZB459						
ZB460						
ZB461						
ZB462						
ZB463						
ZB464						
ZB465						
ZB466						
ZB467						
ZB468						
ZB469						
ZB470						
ZB471						
ZB472						
ZB473						
ZB474						
ZB475						
ZB476						
ZB477						
ZB478						
ZB479						
ZB480						
ZB481						
ZB482						
ZB483						
ZB484						
ZB485						
ZB486						
ZB487						
ZB488						
ZB489						
ZB490						
ZB491						
ZB492						
ZB493						
ZB494						
ZB495						
ZB496						
ZB497						

ZB498-ZB550

serial	type	sqdn/unit	code	where&when seen		remarks
ZB498						
ZB499						
ZB500	Lynx					G-LYNX Ex ZA500
ZB501						
ZB502						
ZB503						
ZB504						
ZB505						

One Sea King Mk.4X to be built by Westland Helicopters Ltd at Yeovil as a test airframe for use in the forthcoming WG.34 Sea King Replacement programme. The aircraft is a Sea King HC.4 airframe with the transmission and rotor system from the WG.34.

serial	type	sqdn/unit	code	where&when seen		remarks
ZB506	Sea King Mk.4X					
ZB507						
ZB508						
ZB509						
ZB510						
ZB511						
ZB512						
ZB513						
ZB514						
ZB515						
ZB516						
ZB517						
ZB518						
ZB519						
ZB520						
ZB521						
ZB522						
ZB523						
ZB524						
ZB525						
ZB526						
ZB527						
ZB528						
ZB529						
ZB530						
ZB531						
ZB532						
ZB533						
ZB534						
ZB535						
ZB536						
ZB537						
ZB538						
ZB539						
ZB540						
ZB541						
ZB542						
ZB543						
ZB544						
ZB545						
ZB546						
ZB547						
ZB548						
ZB549						
ZB550						

ZB551-ZB608

serial	type	sqdn/unit	code	where&when seen		remarks
ZB551						
ZB552						
ZB553						
ZB554						
ZB555						
ZB556						
ZB557						
ZB558						
ZB559						
ZB560						
ZB561						
ZB562						
ZB563						
ZB564						
ZB565						
ZB566						
ZB567						
ZB568						
ZB569						
ZB570						
ZB571						
ZB572						
ZB573						
ZB574						
ZB575						
ZB576						
ZB577						
ZB578						
ZB579						
ZB580						
ZB581						
ZB582						
ZB583						
ZB584						
ZB585						
ZB586						
ZB587						
ZB588						
ZB589						
ZB590						
ZB591						
ZB592						
ZB593						
ZB594						
ZB595						
ZB596						
ZB597						
ZB598						
ZB599						
ZB600						
ZB601						
ZB602						
ZB603						
ZB604						
ZB605						
ZB606						
ZB607						
ZB608						

ZB609-ZB661

serial	type	sqdn/unit	code	where&when seen	remarks

One Hawk T.52 strike/trainer built by British Aerospace for the Kenyan AF and assembled and test flown at Dunsfold. During 1.80 it was allotted the serial ZB609 for live weapons firing. It was delivered to Kenya (as 1001) in 4.80.

serial	type	sqdn/unit	code	where&when seen		remarks
ZB609	Hawk T.52					Ex G-9-454 To G-9-454
ZB610						
ZB611						
ZB612						
ZB613						
ZB614						
ZB615						
ZB616						
ZB617						
ZB618						
ZB619						
ZB620						
ZB621						
ZB622						
ZB623						
ZB624						
ZB625						
ZB626						
ZB627						
ZB628						
ZB629						
ZB630						
ZB631						
ZB632						
ZB633						
ZB634						
ZB635						
ZB636						
ZB637						
ZB638						
ZB639						
ZB640						
ZB641						
ZB642						
ZB643						
ZB644						
ZB645						
ZB646						
ZB647						
ZB648						
ZB649						
ZB650						
ZB651						
ZB652						
ZB653						
ZB654						
ZB655						
ZB656						
ZB657						
ZB658						
ZB659						
ZB660						
ZB661						

ZB662-ZB720

serial	type	sqdn/unit	code	where&when seen		remarks
ZB662						
ZB663						
ZB664						
ZB665						
ZB666						
ZB667						
ZB668						
ZB669						
ZB670						
ZB671						
ZB672						
ZB673						
ZB674						
ZB675						
ZB676						
ZB677						
ZB678						
ZB679						
ZB680						
ZB681						
ZB682						
ZB683						
ZB684						
ZB685						
ZB686						
ZB687						
ZB688						
ZB689						
ZB690						
ZB691						
ZB692						
ZB693						
ZB694						
ZB695						
ZB696						
ZB697						
ZB698						
ZB699						
ZB700						
ZB701						
ZB702						
ZB703						
ZB704						
ZB705						
ZB706						
ZB707						
ZB708						
ZB709						
ZB710						
ZB711						
ZB712						
ZB713						
ZB714						
ZB715						
ZB716						
ZB717						
ZB718						
ZB719						
ZB720						

ZB721-ZB779

serial	type	sqdn/unit	code	where&when seen		remarks
ZB721						
ZB722						
ZB723						
ZB724						
ZB725						
ZB726						
ZB727						
ZB728						
ZB729						
ZB730						
ZB731						
ZB732						
ZB733						
ZB734						
ZB735						
ZB736						
ZB737						
ZB738						
ZB739						
ZB740						
ZB741						
ZB742						
ZB743						
ZB744						
ZB745						
ZB746						
ZB747						
ZB748						
ZB749						
ZB750						
ZB751						
ZB752						
ZB753						
ZB754						
ZB755						
ZB756						
ZB757						
ZB758						
ZB759						
ZB760						
ZB761						
ZB762						
ZB763						
ZB764						
ZB765						
ZB766						
ZB767						
ZB768						
ZB769						
ZB770						
ZB771						
ZB772						
ZB773						
ZB774						
ZB775						
ZB776						
ZB777						
ZB778						
ZB779						

ZB780-ZB838

serial	type	sqdn/unit	code	where&when seen		remarks
ZB780						
ZB781						
ZB782						
ZB783						
ZB784						
ZB785						
ZB786						
ZB787						
ZB788						
ZB789						
ZB790						
ZB791						
ZB792						
ZB793						
ZB794						
ZB795						
ZB796						
ZB797						
ZB798						
ZB799						
ZB800						
ZB801						
ZB802						
ZB803						
ZB804						
ZB805						
ZB806						
ZB807						
ZB808						
ZB809						
ZB810						
ZB811						
ZB812						
ZB813						
ZB814						
ZB815						
ZB816						
ZB817						
ZB818						
ZB819						
ZB820						
ZB821						
ZB822						
ZB823						
ZB824						
ZB825						
ZB826						
ZB827						
ZB828						
ZB829						
ZB830						
ZB831						
ZB832						
ZB833						
ZB834						
ZB835						
ZB836						
ZB837						
ZB838						

ZB839-ZB897

serial	type	sqdn/unit	code	where&when seen		remarks
ZB839						
ZB840						
ZB841						
ZB842						
ZB843						
ZB844						
ZB845						
ZB846						
ZB847						
ZB848						
ZB849						
ZB850						
ZB851						
ZB852						
ZB853						
ZB854						
ZB855						
ZB856						
ZB857						
ZB858						
ZB859						
ZB860						
ZB861						
ZB862						
ZB863						
ZB864						
ZB865						
ZB866						
ZB867						
ZB868						
ZB869						
ZB870						
ZB871						
ZB872						
ZB873						
ZB874						
ZB875						
ZB876						
ZB877						
ZB878						
ZB879						
ZB880						
ZB881						
ZB882						
ZB883						
ZB884						
ZB885						
ZB886						
ZB887						
ZB888						
ZB889						
ZB890						
ZB891						
ZB892						
ZB893						
ZB894						
ZB895						
ZB896						
ZB897						

ZB898-ZB956

serial	type	sqdn/unit	code	where&when seen		remarks
ZB898						
ZB899						
ZB900						
ZB901						
ZB902						
ZB903						
ZB904						
ZB905						
ZB906						
ZB907						
ZB908						
ZB909						
ZB910						
ZB911						
ZB912						
ZB913						
ZB914						
ZB915						
ZB916						
ZB917						
ZB918						
ZB919						
ZB920						
ZB921						
ZB922						
ZB923						
ZB924						
ZB925						
ZB926						
ZB927						
ZB928						
ZB929						
ZB930						
ZB931						
ZB932						
ZB933						
ZB934						
ZB935						
ZB936						
ZB937						
ZB938						
ZB939						
ZB940						
ZB941						
ZB942						
ZB943						
ZB944						
ZB945						
ZB946						
ZB947						
ZB948						
ZB949						
ZB950						
ZB951						
ZB952						
ZB953						
ZB954						
ZB955						
ZB956						

ZB957-ZB999

serial	type	sqdn/unit	code	where&when seen		remarks
ZB957						
ZB958						
ZB959						
ZB960						
ZB961						
ZB962						
ZB963						
ZB964						
ZB965						
ZB966						
ZB967						
ZB968						
ZB969						
ZB970						
ZB971						
ZB972						
ZB973						
ZB974						
ZB975						
ZB976						
ZB977						
ZB978						
ZB979						
ZB980						
ZB981						
ZB982						
ZB983						
ZB984						
ZB985						
ZB986						
ZB987						
ZB988						
ZB989						
ZB990						
ZB991						
ZB992						
ZB993						
ZB994						
ZB995						
ZB996						
ZB997						
ZB998						
ZB999						

ADDITIONS & AMENDMENTS

serial	type	sqdn/unit	code	where&when seen		remarks

ADDITIONS & AMENDMENTS

serial	type	sqdn/unit	code	where&when seen		remarks

PRE "XA100" APPENDICES

The following three appendices cover the Pre-XA100 allocations which are still in existance, whether in service, preserved, or derelict, each compiled to cover a different aspect of the topic. The format of the main text has been continued, adapted to suit each appendix.

PRE 'XA100' STILL IN SERVICE *, as the title suggests this appendix lists the allocations prior to XA100 still currently in service. The first examples listed are aircraft in flying condition belonging to the Historical Flights of the British armed forces. Each entry is placed under its ordered batch, with full details of the batch being given. Some types in this appendix are not covered in the main text, the prime example being the Chipmunk T.10 which still fulfills an important role in all three of the Services today. The main bulk of the allocations listed constituted the backbone of the armed forces when ordered, but today these types, such as the Canberra, Hunter and the odd Meteor, are assigned to tasks with second-line units. Also worthy of a note are the glider allocations for the Air Cadets which once again still play an important part in the training role.*

At the time of compilation this appendix was a true picture of the status, but we must point out that as time goes by the situation is always changing and for this reason it should only be used as a guide.

PRE 'XA100' PRESERVED & DERELICT IN THE U.K. *has been added to complement the previous Pre-XA100 appendix, by listing the aircraft that are extant, though not in service at the time of printing. These are basically preserved machines, gate guardians, those aircraft allocated to Service establishments for fire fighting duties, those merely left derelict and civil registered aircraft flying with British military identities and markings. It must be stressed from the start that the information contained in this appendix is not necessarily complete, and is provided purely as a guide to what older aircraft can still be seen around the United Kingdom.*

The aircraft have been listed in alphabetical/numerical order with the remarks column being completed with details of location and state of aircraft known at the time of writing, ranging from Cody Biplane 304 to Grasshopper TX.1 WZ821. One of the most noticeable points in this appendix is the use of Roman and Arabic numerals to depict the marks of aircraft and the following explanation may be of interest:-

In 1944 certain aircraft types had been in production for many years and with the rapid development of aircraft in that era many had been produced in a number of variants (for example, the Spitfire). It was decided that rather than continue allocating all variant mark numbers in Roman numerals, all these over twenty would be represented in Arabic (thus the Spitfire F.XXII became the F.22, the Mosquito NF.XXX the NF.30 etc). In early 1948 the decision to standardise on Arabic numerals was made, all types then in service being so designated. It should be pointed out, however, that the dates quoted are those when the designations officially changed and that anomalies continued to arise for some while thereafter.

PRE 'XA100' OVERSEAS *lists aircraft flying, preserved and derelict still displaying British military identities, resident overseas. Under each country, which is placed in alphabetic order, is a run-down of aircraft known to us, their locations being added in the remarks column. This appendix completes the Pre-XA100 appendices and like the two before must only be used as a guide. We feel we must point out that this appendix is probably the most incomplete, due to the great complexities of trying to obtain and verify every airframe which falls into this category, and we must reiterate that this series of appendices must be only used as a guide. If you have any additions or amendments to these appendices we will be glad to hear them.*

PRE XA100 SERIAL ALLOCATIONS STILL IN CURRENT USE

serial	type	sqdn/unit	code	where&when seen	remarks

The Fleet Air Arm and the Royal Air Force maintain a number of historic aircraft in flying condition for display purposes. The Harvard T.2B's are operated by A&AEE, Boscombe Down for low-speed photographic and calibration duties.

serial	type	sqdn/unit	code	where&when seen	remarks
P7350	Spitfire IIA				BoB Memorial Flight
T8191	Tiger Moth T.2				FAA Historic Flight
AB910	Spitfire V				BoB Memorial Flight
BB814	Tiger Moth T.2				FAA Historic Flight
EZ407	Harvard T.3				To/Ex PAF1656 FAAHF
FT375	Harvard T.2B				
KF183	Harvard T.2B				
KF314	Harvard T.2B				
LF363	Hurricane IIC				BoB Memorial Flight
LS326	Swordfish II				FAA Historic Flight
PA474	Lancaster B.I				BoB Memorial Flight
PM631	Spitfire PR.19				BoB Memorial Flight
PS853	Spitfire PR.19				BoB Memorial Flight
PZ865	Hurricane IIC				BoB Memorial Flight
TF956	Sea Fury FB.11				FAA Historic Flight

The Devon C.1 was a military version of the DH.104 Dove light transport. The initial order totalled 30 aircraft (cut back from 50) built by de Havilland Aircraft Co Ltd at Hatfield against Contract 235. Serialled VP952-VP981, deliveries commenced in 1948. From 1965 most were modified to the equivalent standard of the civil Dove 8 and redesignated Devon C.2's.

serial	type	sqdn/unit	code	where&when seen	remarks
VP952	Devon C.2				
VP955	Devon C.2				
VP957	Devon C.2				
VP958	Devon C.2				
VP959	Devon C.2				
VP961	Devon C.2				
VP962	Devon C.2				
VP965	Devon C.2				
VP967	Devon C.2				
VP968	Devon C.2				
VP971	Devon C.2				
VP975	Devon C.2				
VP976	Devon C.2				
VP977	Devon C.2				
VP981	Devon C.2				

One ex civil Sedbergh TX.1, built by Slingsby Sailplanes Ltd at Kirkbymoorside in 1947, was later purchased for Air Training Corps use and allocated the serial VX275.

serial	type	sqdn/unit	code	where&when seen	remarks
VX275	Sedbergh TX.1				

A number of ex FAA Sea Fury T.20's were sold to Germany in 1958/9 for use as target tugs and on 15.10.74 one was returned to the UK and restored to its previous marks.

serial	type	sqdn/unit	code	where&when seen	remarks
VZ345	Sea Fury T.20				Ex D-CATA

The first production batch of Meteor F.8's totalled 128 aircraft and was built at both Hucclecote (VZ438-VZ485, VZ493-VZ517) and Coventry (VZ518-VZ532, VZ540-VZ569) against Contract 2430. Deliveries took place between 12.49 and 10.50, several being converted to F(TT).8 standard at a later date.

serial	type	sqdn/unit	code	where&when seen	remarks
VZ467	Meteor F(TT).8				

The third production batch of Meteor T.7's totalled 137 aircraft (WA590-WA639, WA649-WA698, WA709-WA743) and was built at Hucclecote in 1948/49, deliveries taking place between 9.49 and 2.51 against Contract 2982. Some were converted to T.7 Specials for ejector seat trials.

XW868 'CU/50' Gazelle HT.2, 705 Sqdn, over Cornwall in the late 1970's. The helicopter is painted in the "Sharks" aerobatic team colour scheme. *(Crown)*

XW902 Gazelle HT.3 in the special markings of the 'British Tri-Service Team' which was to have taken part in the 1978 World Helicopter Championships in the USSR. The fin marking is the well known 'Combined Operations' emblem. *(Crown)*

XW938 Twin Comanche 160, Cranfield Institute of Technology, seen at its base during 9.71. *(via P.G. Smith)*

XW983 Venture T.1, Central Gliding School, at Syerston 13.8.79. Used to evaluate the type's suitability for Air Cadet flying, this aircraft was retained following the introduction of the Venture T.2. *(R.A. Walker)*

XW991 Chukar D.1, RN PTAS, at Portland 14.7.73. It is displayed 'suspended' from its recovery parachute and wears a red and white colour scheme. *(R.A. Walker)*

XX102 CC-7, 200 HTS RCT, being loaded onto an Army lorry at Lee-on-Solent on 11.7.72. The skirt folds up vertically for transport as illustrated. *(R.A. Walker)*

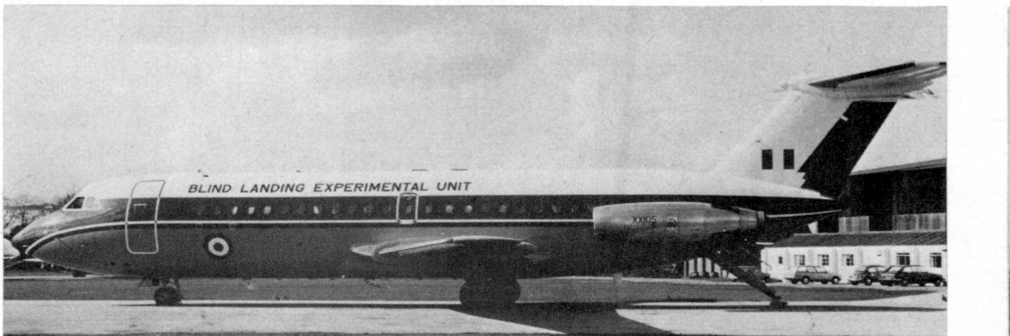

XX105 BAC 1-11 Srs 201 Blind Landing Experimental Unit, at Hurn in the early 1970's. The colour scheme is a striking yellow/red/white combination. (D.J. Rose)

XX185/185 Hawk T.1, CFS, at Wattisham 16.5.79. (R.A. Walker)

XX228/228 Hawk T.1, 1 TWU, at Yeovilton 4.8.79. All TWU Hawks were delivered in all-over camouflage scheme and most took up the markings of one of the unit shadow squadrons, in this case the black and yellow checks of 63 Sqdn. (R.A. Walker)

XX367 Britannia 312F, A&AEE, at Kinloss during 2.73. The cheat line and fin are red. (Flamingo)

XX376/K Gazelle AH.1, 3CBAS, Royal Marines, at Middle Wallop 24.7.75. The code on the fin is painted white, in variance to the other low visibility markings. (D.A. Rough)

XX467/92 Hunter T.7, 229 OCU, at Chivenor in 1974 following service with the RSAF and RJAF. It had originally been in RAF service as XL605. (P.J. Cooper)

XX479 'CU/563' Jetstream T.2, 750 Sqdn, at Culdrose 28.3.79. The 'thimble' nose makes this aircraft easily identifiable when compared with the RAF's T.1. (D.A. Rough)

XX630/'gamma' Bulldog T.1, East Midlands UAS, at Bicester 19.7.75. The unit subsequently discarded Greek letters for more conventional aircraft codes. (F. Tyler)

XX494/71 Jetstream T.1, Multi-Engine Training Sqdn, at Teesside 3.3.78. After very limited service, the Jetstreams were stored for several years prior to the forming of the METS and transfers to the Royal Navy for modification to T.2. (I. MacFarlane)

XX821/BF Jaguar GR.1, 17 Sqdn, lands at Nellis AFB 7.11.78. The aircraft had been participating in a "Red Flag" mission. (S. Hill)

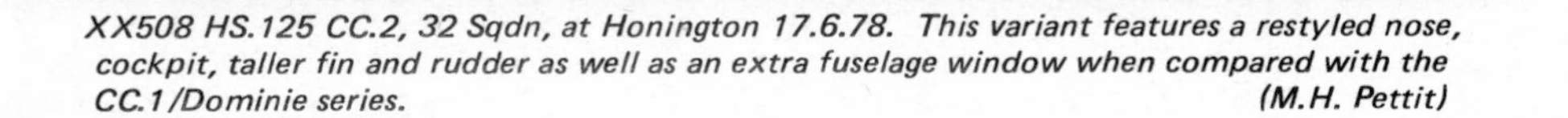

XX508 HS.125 CC.2, 32 Sqdn, at Honington 17.6.78. This variant features a restyled nose, cockpit, taller fin and rudder as well as an extra fuselage window when compared with the CC.1/Dominie series. (M.H. Pettit)

XX829 Jaguar T.2, 54 Sqdn, at Coltishall 3.8.78. (G.J. Glover)

XX853 Shelduck D.1, Royal Navy Pilotless Target Aircraft Sqdn (PTAS), at Portland 3.8.74. The launch boost rocket is attached to its rear fuselage. (R.A. Walker)

XX914 VC.10 Srs 1103, RAE Bedford, at Heathrow in 4.74. Aft of the cockpit is the 'Aero Flight Bedford' inscription. Its colour scheme owes much to its former British Caledonian livery. (Flamingo)

XX915 Jaguar T.2, ETPS, at Farnborough 8.9.76. The MoD(PE) aircraft colour scheme of red, white and blue contrasts sharply with the camouflaged examples of this type that serve with the RAF. (R.A. Walker)

XX944 Comet 4, RAE, at Farnborough 21.7.73. Note the under-fuselage pannier for the carriage of test equipment. (P.J. Cooper)

XX946 Tornado prototype was the first of the type to be built in the UK and is seen here in the original red and white colour scheme. Note the positioning of the serial under the tail-plane and the German cross under the starboard wing. (British Aerospace)

XY125 AV-8A, on board the French helicopter carrier 'Jeanne d'Arc' during demonstrations to the Aeronavale 10/11.10.73. Note that it wears both roundels and a fin flash. The dorsal aerial easily distinguishes the type from the Harrier. It also carries an underwing serial. (British Aerospace)

XZ133/A Harrier GR.3, 233 OCU, at Middle Wallop 4.8.77. This batch of XZ-serialled aircraft was the first to come off the production line equipped with lasar nose and radar warning receivers. (R.A. Walker)

XZ178 Lynx AH.1, Advanced Rotary Wing Flight, at Middle Wallop 26.7.79. This particular example, whilst having the dayglo spine and door, does not have the dayglo nose of the other aircraft of the Flight. (R.A. Walker)

XZ232 'BM/333' Lynx HAS.2, HMS Birmingham Flt, at Culdrose 27.7.77. At the time it was 'parented' by 700L Sqdn, pending the official re-forming of 702 Sqdn. (D. Allen)

XZ260 Lynx HAS.2(FN), Aeronavale, at Hurn 20.6.77 for customs clearance prior to onward delivery to France. The serial is retained in French service, although in some cases the two letters are deleted. (D. Spurgeon)

XZ405 Standard Cirrus sailplane appears to have eluded photographers whilst with ETPS. It is shown above in its previous civil guise as BGA 1473 '82'. The turned rudder hides part of its competition number. (Cranfield Institute of Technology)

XZ451 'VL/100' Sea Harrier FRS.1, 700A Sqdn IFTU at Yeovilton 4.8.79. The unit badge consists of a grey harrier superimposed on a red 'A'. The IFTU did not actually officially commission until 19.9.79. (R.A. Walker)

XZ555 Venture T.2, Central Gliding School, at Syerston 13.8.79. The difference in the nose shape is readily apparent between the T.2 and T.1 XW983. (R.A. Walker)

XZ594 Sea King HAR.3, 202 Sqdn, at Newcastle 2.2.79. The unit badge consists of a mallard on a white disc and is painted just aft of the cockpit. (I. MacFarlane)

XZ741 Commando 2B, Egyptian Govt, at Hurn 18.3.76 for customs clearance on returning to Yeovil for mods. Transit problems dictated that the aircraft be given a British serial to expedite its flight to the UK. (D.A. Spurgeon)

XZ958 Chukar D.2, Fleet Target Group, at Portland 22.7.78. It is painted in a day-glo orange and white colour scheme. (M.I. Draper)

ZA101/G-HAWK Hawk T.50 owned by British Aerospace seen here in U.S. Navy two-tone grey scheme in 6.79. Note the military serial under the tail-plane and the civil registration under the wings. (British Aerospace)

A Shorts MATS-B target drone being recovered by parachute after a sortie (serial unknown). XZ815, the first MATS-B first flew in June 1975. (Shorts)

The Shorts Skeet target drone was developed from the MATS-B and f/f 10.10.78. No 002 is shown here on its launching ramp. (Shorts)

3/5th scale model of Flight Refuelling's ASAT drone. A development batch of eight was ordered in 1979. (Flight Refuelling)

ZA250 Harrier T.52, British Aerospace, at Farnborough 3.9.78. Although privately owned and registered as G-VTOL, the serial is worn to enable live weapons to be carried. (R.A. Walker)

ZA254 Tornado F.2 prototype at Warton in 7.79. It wears a light grey and black colour scheme. Note the lengthened fuselage, forward of the wing, and the re-profiled nose which will house the new Marconi/Ferranti radar. (British Aerospace)

ZA291 Sea King HC.4, during its first flight from Yeovil 6.11.79. As can be seen, it is painted in full Royal Navy markings. (via Inter Avia)

ZA319 Tornado GR.1, the first production aircraft, pictured on an early test flight in 7.79. The serial is visible on the original photograph in the shadow area behind and beneath the wing. (British Aerospace)

ZA503 Islander 2A did not wear its military marks upon sale to the MoD and was re-registered from G-BEXA to G-DIVE for service parachuting work. It is seen here at Weston-on-the-Green 11.9.79. (M.J. Hockley)

ZA670 Chinook HC.1, during its first flight at Ridley, Pennsylvania 23.3.80. The first of thirty-three aircraft on order, it was due to be delivered to the UK in 8.80. (Boeing-Vertol)

ZA801/V Gazelle HT.3, CFS, at Abingdon 15.9.79. This Gazelle was the first of a new batch of HT.3's to be built at Weston-super-Mare for the RAF. (Bushell/MCAS)

ZA947 Dakota C.3, RAE Farnborough, Abingdon 15.9.79. It was previously operated by the RAE with the incorrect serial 'KG661' which was itself a corruption of its former CAF serial 661. (R.A. Walker)

Finally, a view of the Hawker P.1121 supersonic fighter under construction at Kingston, with the full scale mock-up in the rear. Although construction began, no serial was ever allocated to the prototype. (British Aerospace)

TAD01 Gazelle CIM, AETW, at Middle Wallop 26.7.79. A purpose built training aid, it was constructed by Westland Helicopters using many Gazelle components. Colour scheme is light grey overall. (R.A. Walker)

TAD009 Lynx CIM, AETW, at Middle Wallop 26.7.79. Another purpose built training aid, it is here surrounded by work stands to enable trainees to be taught the elements of Lynx maintenance. (R.A. Walker)

D8096 Bristol F.2B, Shuttleworth Collection, at Upavon 16.6.62. Ex G-AEPH, it is the only airworthy example of the type. (via C. Howland)

J9941 Hart, HSA, at Dunsfold 12.6.71. This aircraft was subsequently presented to the RAFM Hendon for display. (R.A. Walker)

K3215 Tutor, Shuttleworth Collection, at Upavon 16.6.62. The only example of the type extant, it is painted training yellow overall. (via C. Howland)

K8032 Gladiator I, Shuttleworth Collection, at Upavon 16.6.62. It was subsequently restored to its correct serial L8032. (Via C. Howland)

L8353 Magister painted as 0/8 EFTS in the Museum of Transport and Technology in Auckland, NZ in 5.76. It was previously L8353/G-AMMC/ZK-AYW. (P. Hellier)

N220/4 Supermarine S.5 replica seen flying over White Waltham 6.77. This superb replica is owned by Leisure Sport and can usually be found at Thorpe Water Park. (P. Hellier)

P7350/QV-B Spitfire IIA, Battle of Britain Memorial Flight, at Brawdy 31.5.79. The code 'QV' represents a 19 Sqdn aircraft. (P. Hellier)

R9003 Lysander III, NACC, at Trenton, Canada during 1970. It was restored to flying condition with components from three different airframes and first flew 29.12.67. (Flamingo)

FF860 Bermuda I, at the Military Aircraft Restoration Corporation compound, Barstow Daggett, California 23.10.78 and ex-New Guinea. (P. Dawe)

FT375 Harvard T.2B, A&AEE, at Bassingbourn 27.5.78. The colour scheme is all over yellow and the A&AEE crest can be seen on a small plaque beneath the cockpit. Note the last digit of the serial on the undercarriage hub. (R.A. Walker)

HB751 Fairchild Argus II, at Bassingbourn 27.5.78. Typical of many civil aircraft being re-painted to represent earlier military careers, this aircraft is actually G-BCBL and is operated by 'After the Battle' magazine. (R.A. Walker)

HM579 Moth Minor, alias ZK-BFP at Ardmore, NZ in 5.76, shows that the trend of painting civil aircraft to represent their earlier military career is not limited to the United Kingdom. (P. Hellier)

KB336/U Mosquito B.20, NACC, at Trenton, Canada, during 6.67. This aircraft was built by de Havilland A/c of Canada and is one of the few examples of its type to be preserved. (Flamingo)

KK995/E Hoverfly I, on display at Abingdon 15.6.68. It was subsequently moved to the RAFM Hendon for display. (R.A. Walker)

LB312 Taylorcraft Plus D, at Middle Wallop 4.8.77. On permanent loan to the Army Air Corps Historic Flight at Middle Wallop, it is actually G-AHXE and is a further example of a civil aircraft being re-painted in its old identity. (R.A. Walker)

LF363/LE-D Hurricane IIC, Battle of Britain Memorial Flt, at Lee-on-Solent on 23.7.78. The code 'LE' represents a 242 Sqdn aircraft. (R.A. Walker)

LS326/5A Swordfish II, Fleet Air Arm Historic Flight, at Lee-on-Solent 23.7.78. It is the only airworthy example of its type. (R.A. Walker)

MF628 Wellington T.10, on display at Abingdon 15.6.68. The only known complete example, it was subsequently moved to the RAFM Hendon for display. (C. Thomas)

MV154 Spitfire VIII at Bankstown, NSW in 1970. One of many British serialled aircraft to be preserved abroad, it once served with the Royal Australian Air Force as A58-671. (Flamingo)

PA474/KM-B Lancaster B.I, Battle of Britain Memorial Flt, at Bentwaters 26.5.73 being prepared for flight. The code 'KM' represents a 44 Sqdn aircraft. (R.A. Walker)

SL542 Spitfire LF.16 on display just inside the main gate at Coltishall on 12.6.75. (R.A. Walker)

SN219/SR-F Tempest TT.5 on display by the main gate at Middleton St George in the late 1950's Restored from parts of several airframes, it was re-serialled NV778 in the mid 1960's and was subsequently displayed at the RAFM. (D.A. Rough)

SX137 Seafire F.17, at Yeovilton 29.6.63. This aircraft now forms part of the Fleet Air Arm Museum. *(R.A. Walker)*

TG503 Hastings T.5, 230 OCU, at Coningsby 4.6.77 shortly before being retired to permanent exhibition status at Gatow, Berlin in commemoration of the airlift of supplies to that city in 1948/49. *(R.A. Walker)*

TX228 Anson C.19, Western Comms Sqdn, at Odiham 6.9.66. Upon the type's withdrawal from service this particular aircraft was used for instructional purposes by Crawley Technical College. It was subsequently moved to Duxford. *(R.A. Walker)*

VN485/DW-X Spitfire F.24, on display in Hong Kong during 1966. After RAF service this aircraft was operated by the Hong Kong Auxilliary AF. *(via C. Thomas)*

VT812/N Vampire F.3, on display at Abingdon 15.6.68 in 601 Sqdn markings. It was subsequently moved to the RAFM Hendon for display. *(C. Thomas)*

VT935 Boulton-Paul P.111A at the College of Aeronautics, Cranfield in use as an instructional airframe. One of the many interesting prototypes to be produced by the UK industry during the 50's, it has since been preserved. *(via D.A. Rough)*

VX574 Valetta C.2, RAF Malta Comms Flt, at Luqa date unknown. This aircraft remained in Malta after it was withdrawn from service. (D. Robinson)

VZ345 Sea Fury T.20, A&AEE, on a flight from Boscombe Down shortly after arrival in 1974. At this time it was still painted in the overall red colour scheme with day-glo rudder that was applied by its previous W. German owners. (Crown)

WD955/Q Canberra T.17, 360 Sqdn, at Wyton 21.8.79. One of the longest serving Canberras, this aircraft entered service as a B.2 in 1951. (J.B.E. Hale)

WF125 'CU/576' Sea Prince T.1, 750 Sqdn, at Yeovilton 28.6.77 about to be refuelled. Although over twenty-five years old, the aircraft still looks immaculate in its light grey and dayglo colour scheme. (R.A. Walker)

WG630 Sea Fury FB.11, at the Commonwealth Experimental Building Station, Ryde, Sydney in 12.76 shows a novel use for a redundant aircraft. Ex RAN, it is in use as a wind generator for airflow tests of building materials. (M.J. Stone)

WG768/28 Short SB.5 on display at Finningley 20.9.69. The code stems from its earlier use with the ETPS. This aircraft was subsequently transferred to Cosford for display. (R.A. Walker)

WG774 BAC 221, taking off from Farnborough 10.9.66. This aircraft was converted from the FD.2 and incorporated many features related to development of the Concorde. The drooped nose is apparent in this photograph. (R.A. Walker)

WH666 Canberra B.2, 75 Sqdn, RNZAF, at Tengah, Singapore during 1961. The badge on the fin is the unit's greenstone Tiki marking. This is one of the aircraft that were leased to New Zealand to equip the unit. (Flamingo)

WJ109 'K/238' Firefly TT.6, on display by the main gate at Nowra, NSW 25.11.76. This aircraft has been re-painted in the markings of 816 Sqdn, RAN and was originally delivered to Australia in 1.53. (T.E. Stone)

WK635 'LS' Chipmunk T.10, Lee-on-Solent Stn Flt, at L-o-S in the mid 1960's. Parented by 781 Sqdn, it was in use as a glider tug. (P.J. Cooper)

WK800/Z Meteor D.16, RAE Llanbedr, at Valley 18.8.79. One of the very last Meteor drones, it was converted from an F.8 by Flight Refuelling. (R. Plimmer/MCAS)

WK935 Meteor Prone Pilot, on display at St Athan in the mid 1970's. Converted from a Meteor F.8 by Armstrong Whitworth Aircraft, it first flew in this configuration 10.2.54 from Baginton. (D.A. Rough)

WA638-WB937

serial	type	sqdn/unit	code	where&when seen		remarks
WA638	Meteor T.7 Special					
WA662	Meteor T.7					
WA669	Meteor T.7					

Between 1949 & 1953 over 100 Firefly Mk.5/6's were supplied to the RAN and in 6.67 one aircraft (converted in Australia for TT work) was returned to the UK by sea.

serial	type	sqdn/unit	code	where&when seen		remarks
WB271	Firefly AS.6					FAA Historic Flight

The second batch of Devon C.1's was serialled WB530-WB535, deliveries taking place in 1949. From 1965 onwards most were converted to C.2's.

serial	type	sqdn/unit	code	where&when seen		remarks
WB530	Devon C.2					
WB531	Devon C.2					
WB533	Devon C.2					
WB534	Devon C.2					

The first production batch of Chipmunk T.10's totalled 200 aircraft against Contract 2508. Serialled WB549-WB588, WB600-WB635, WB638-WB662, WB665-WB706, WB709-WB739, WB743-WB768, deliveries to the RAF took place between 11.49 and 12.50. Some aircraft were later transferred to the Royal Navy and the Army Air Corps.

serial	type	sqdn/unit	code	where&when seen		remarks
WB550	Chipmunk T.10					
WB555	Chipmunk T.10					
WB560	Chipmunk T.10					
WB565	Chipmunk T.10					
WB567	Chipmunk T.10					
WB569	Chipmunk T.10					
WB575	Chipmunk T.10					
WB586	Chipmunk T.10					
WB615	Chipmunk T.10					
WB627	Chipmunk T.10					
WB647	Chipmunk T.10					
WB652	Chipmunk T.10					
WB654	Chipmunk T.10					
WB657	Chipmunk T.10					
WB671	Chipmunk T.10					
WB693	Chipmunk T.10					
WB697	Chipmunk T.10					
WB739	Chipmunk T.10					
WB754	Chipmunk T.10					

The first production batch of Sedbergh TX.1's totalled 69 aircraft and was built by both Slingsby (WB919-WB948, WB955-WB973) and Martin Hearn (WB974-WB993). Deliveries from Slingsby commenced in 6.49 and the contract was completed by early 1950.

serial	type	sqdn/unit	code	where&when seen		remarks
WB919	Sedbergh TX.1					
WB920	Sedbergh TX.1					
WB922	Sedbergh TX.1					
WB923	Sedbergh TX.1					
WB924	Sedbergh TX.1					
WB926	Sedbergh TX.1					
WB927	Sedbergh TX.1					
WB929	Sedbergh TX.1					
WB931	Sedbergh TX.1					
WB932	Sedbergh TX.1					
WB934	Sedbergh TX.1					
WB935	Sedbergh TX.1					
WB937	Sedbergh TX.1					

WB938-WD790

serial	type	sqdn/unit	code	where&when seen		remarks
WB938	Sedbergh TX.1					
WB939	Sedbergh TX.1					
WB941	Sedbergh TX.1					
WB942	Sedbergh TX.1					
WB943	Sedbergh TX.1					
WB944	Sedbergh TX.1					
WB946	Sedbergh TX.1					
WB947	Sedbergh TX.1					
WB958	Sedbergh TX.1					
WB959	Sedbergh TX.1					
WB960	Sedbergh TX.1					
WB961	Sedbergh TX.1					
WB962	Sedbergh TX.1					
WB963	Sedbergh TX.1					
WB971	Sedbergh TX.1					
WB972	Sedbergh TX.1					
WB973	Sedbergh TX.1					
WB974	Sedbergh TX.1					
WB975	Sedbergh TX.1					
WB976	Sedbergh TX.1					
WB978	Sedbergh TX.1					
WB979	Sedbergh TX.1					
WB980	Sedbergh TX.1					
WB981	Sedbergh TX.1					
WB983	Sedbergh TX.1					
WB985	Sedbergh TX.1					
WB986	Sedbergh TX.1					
WB987	Sedbergh TX.1					
WB988	Sedbergh TX.1					
WB989	Sedbergh TX.1					
WB990	Sedbergh TX.1					
WB991	Sedbergh TX.1					
WB992	Sedbergh TX.1					
WB993	Sedbergh TX.1					

The second production batch of Chipmunk T.10's for the RAF totalled 100 aircraft and was given the serials WD282-WD310, WD318-WD338, WD344-WD365, WD370-WD397. Deliveries commenced in 12.50 and were completed in 4.51. Some aircraft were later transferred to the Royal Navy and the Army Air Corps.

WD310	Chipmunk T.10					
WD325	Chipmunk T.10					
WD331	Chipmunk T.10					
WD373	Chipmunk T.10					
WD374	Chipmunk T.10					
WD390	Chipmunk T.10					

The first production batch of Meteor NF.11 night-fighters totalled 200 aircraft and was built by AWA at Coventry during 1950/52 against Contract 6/Aircraft/3433/CB5(b). Serialled WD585-WD634, WD640-WD689, WD696-WD745, WD751-WD800, deliveries took place between 11.50 and 7.52 with several later being modified as trials aircraft.

WD790	Meteor NF.11 (mod)					

The first production batch of Canberra B.2's totalled 70 aircraft (WD929-WD966, WD980-WD999, WE111-WE122) and was built by the English Electric Co at Preston against Contract 3520. WD929 f/f 8.10.50 and the type entered service in 5.51. Several aircraft were later converted to T.4's, T.17's and TT.18's.

WD955-WF916

serial	type	sqdn/unit	code	where&when seen		remarks
WD955	Canberra T.17					
WE113	Canberra B.2					
WE121	Canberra B.2					
WE122	Canberra TT.18					

The first production batch of Canberra PR.3's totalled 27 aircraft (WE135-WE151, WE166-WE175) and was built by English Electric Co at Preston against Contract 3520. WE135 f/f 31.7.52 and the type entered service with 540 Squadron at Benson in 1953.

serial	type	sqdn/unit	code	where&when seen		remarks
WE173	Canberra PR.3					

The first production batch of Canberra T.4's totalled 8 aircraft (WE188-WE195) and was built by the English Electric Co at Preston against Contract 3520. The type first entered service with 231 OCU at Bassingbourn in 1954.

serial	type	sqdn/unit	code	where&when seen		remarks
WE188	Canberra T.4					
WE192	Canberra T.4					

The only production batch of Slingsby Prefect TX.1 gliders for the RAF was built by Slingsby Sailplanes Ltd at Kirkbymoorside against Contract 3926. Delivery of the 15 aircraft (WE979-WE993) took place between 2.50 and 4.51.

serial	type	sqdn/unit	code	where&when seen		remarks
WE981	Prefect TX.1					
WE982	Prefect TX.1					
WE983	Prefect TX.1					
WE985	Prefect TX.1					
WE987	Prefect TX.1					
WE990	Prefect TX.1					
WE992	Prefect TX.1					
WE993	Prefect TX.1					

The first production batch of Hunting Sea Prince T.1's totalled 16 aircraft (WF118-WF133) and was built at Luton in 1951. WF118 f/f 28.6.51 and the type entered service in 2.53 with 750 Sqdn at St Merryn. The type was withdrawn from service in 1979 and the survivors either placed in storage or allocated for ground instruction.

serial	type	sqdn/unit	code	where&when seen		remarks
WF118	Sea Prince T.1					To G-DACA
WF122	Sea Prince T.1					A2673 GI Culdrose
WF128	Sea Prince T.1					8611M
WF131	Sea Prince T.1					
WF133	Sea Prince T.1					

The first production batch of Varsity T.1's totalled 60 aircraft against Contract 6/Aircraft/4816/CB6(b). They were built by Vickers-Armstrongs Ltd at Weybridge (WF324-WF335, WF369-WF385, WF387-WF391) and Hurn (WF386, WF392-WF394, WF408-WF429) with WF324 making its first flight on 21.5.51. Deliveries took place between 9.51 and 10.52, several aircraft later being modified for trials.

serial	type	sqdn/unit	code	where&when seen		remarks
WF379	Varsity T.1 (mod)					

The fourth production batch of Meteor T.7's totalled 89 aircraft (WF766-WF795, WF813-WF862, WF875-WF883) and was built at Hucclecote by Gloster Aircraft Co Ltd against Contract 6/Aircraft/5044/CB7(b). Deliveries took place between 1.51 & 9.51.

serial	type	sqdn/unit	code	where&when seen		remarks
WF791	Meteor T.7					

The second production batch of Canberra B.2's totalled 18 aircraft (WF886-WF892, WF907-WF917) and was built by English Electric Co Ltd at Preston against Contract 3520. Some aircraft were later converted by British Aircraft Corporation (into which English Electric had merged) to T.17 ECM trainers.

serial	type	sqdn/unit	code	where&when seen		remarks
WF890	Canberra T.17					
WF916	Canberra T.17					

WG308-WH670

serial	type	sqdn/unit	code	where&when seen	remarks

The third production batch of Chipmunk T.10's for the RAF totalled 150 aircraft (WG271-WG281, WG299-WG336, WG348-WG364, WG392-WG432, WG457-WG491), deliveries taking place between 4.51 and 1.52. Some aircraft were later transferred to the RN and the AAC.

serial	type	sqdn/unit	code	where&when seen	remarks
WG308	Chipmunk T.10				
WG321	Chipmunk T.10				
WG323	Chipmunk T.10				
WG362	Chipmunk T.10				8630M
WG403	Chipmunk T.10				
WG407	Chipmunk T.10				
WG430	Chipmunk T.10				
WG432	Chipmunk T.10				
WG458	Chipmunk T.10				
WG466	Chipmunk T.10				
WG469	Chipmunk T.10				
WG478	Chipmunk T.10				
WG479	Chipmunk T.10				
WG480	Chipmunk T.10				
WG486	Chipmunk T.10				

A small batch of production Sedbergh TX.1's (WG496-WG499) was built by Slingsby Sailplanes Ltd at Kirkbymoorside in 1951 and delivered for Air Training Corps use.

serial	type	sqdn/unit	code	where&when seen	remarks
WG496	Sedbergh TX.1				
WG497	Sedbergh TX.1				
WG498	Sedbergh TX.1				
WG499	Sedbergh TX.1				

The first Shackleton MR.2's followed the MR.1A's on the Woodford production line, the first ten (WG530-WG533, WG553-WG558) being built and delivered in 1952. Most were updated to Phase 1, Phase 2 and in a few cases Phase 3 standard.

serial	type	sqdn/unit	code	where&when seen	remarks
WG556	Shackleton MR.2/3				8651M

A number of ex-FAA Sea Fury T.20's were sold to Germany in 1958/59 for use as target tugs and in 6.76 one was returned to the UK and restored to its previous marks.

serial	type	sqdn/unit	code	where&when seen	remarks
WG655	Sea Fury T.20				FAAHF Ex D-CACU

Two Canberra B.2's (WG788-WG789) were built by the English Electric Co as replacement aircraft for others sold abroad. They were both delivered in 8.52.

serial	type	sqdn/unit	code	where&when seen	remarks
WG789	Canberra B.2				

The fifth production batch of Meteor F.8's totalled 200 aircraft (WH249-WH263, WH272-WH320, WH342-WH386, WH395-WH426, WH442-WH484, WH498-WH513) and was built by AWA at Coventry against Contract 6/Aircraft/5621/CB7(b). Deliveries took place between 9.51 and 3.52 and several were later converted to U.16/D.16 standard.

serial	type	sqdn/unit	code	where&when seen	remarks
WH453	Meteor D.16				

The fourth production batch of Canberra B.2's totalled 86 aircraft (WH637-WH674, WH695-WH742) and was built by English Electric Co Ltd at Preston against Contract 5786. Deliveries took place between 8.52 and 8.53. Later some aircraft were converted by BAC to T.17 and TT.18 standard.

serial	type	sqdn/unit	code	where&when seen	remarks
WH646	Canberra T.17				
WH664	Canberra T.17				
WH665	Canberra T.17				
WH666	Canberra B.2				
WH667	Canberra B.2				
WH670	Canberra B.2				

WH703-WH964

serial	type	sqdn/unit	code	where&when seen		remarks
WH703	Canberra B.2					8490M
WH718	Canberra TT.18					
WH734	Canberra B.2(mod)					
WH740	Canberra T.17					

The Canberra PR.7 was the photo-reconnaissance version of the B.6 and followed the PR.3 into service. The first batch totalled 23 aircraft (WH773-WH780, WH790-WH804) and was built by English Electric Company at Preston against Contract 5786. WH773 f/f 28.10.53, with deliveries taking place between 11.53 and 7.54. Some aircraft were later converted to T.22's for the Royal Navy by BAC at Samlesbury.

serial	type	sqdn/unit	code	where&when seen		remarks
WH773	Canberra PR.7					
WH774	Canberra PR.7					
WH775	Canberra PR.7					8128M ntu
WH777	Canberra PR.7					
WH779	Canberra PR.7					8129M ntu
WH780	Canberra T.22					
WH794	Canberra PR.7					8652M
WH796	Canberra PR.7					
WH797	Canberra T.22					
WH798	Canberra PR.7					
WH801	Canberra T.22					
WH803	Canberra T.22					

The second production batch of Canberra T.4's totalled 12 aircraft (WH839-WH850) and was built by the English Electric Co at Preston against Contract 5786. Deliveries took place between 1.54 and 7.54.

serial	type	sqdn/unit	code	where&when seen		remarks
WH844	Canberra T.4					
WH846	Canberra T.4					
WH848	Canberra T.4					
WH849	Canberra T.4					
WH850	Canberra T.4					

The first production batch of Canberra B.2's built by Short Bros and Harland at Sydenham totalled 60 aircraft against Contract 5790 (WH853-WH887, WH902-WH925, WH944). WH853 f/f 30.10.52 with deliveries taking place between 11.52 and 9.54. Several aircraft were later converted by BAC to T.17's, TT.18's and T.11/19's.

serial	type	sqdn/unit	code	where&when seen		remarks
WH856	Canberra TT.18					
WH863	Canberra T.17					
WH869	Canberra B.2					8515M
WH872	Canberra T.17					
WH876	Canberra B.2(mod)					
WH887	Canberra TT.18					
WH902	Canberra T.17					
WH904	Canberra T.19					
WH911	Canberra B.2					
WH914	Canberra B.2					
WH919	Canberra B.2					

The first production batch of Canberra B.6's totalled 40 aircraft against Contract 5790 (WH945-WH984) and was built by Short Bros & Harland at Sydenham, deliveries taking place between 10.54 and 10.55. Several were later converted to B.15's for service with FEAF and from 1970 to E.15's for the high-level calibration role.

serial	type	sqdn/unit	code	where&when seen		remarks
WH953	Canberra B.6					
WH957	Canberra E.15					
WH960	Canberra B.15					8344M
WH964	Canberra E.15					

WH972-WJ756

serial	type	sqdn/unit	code	where&when seen		remarks
WH972	Canberra E.15					
WH981	Canberra E.15					
WH983	Canberra E.15					
WH984	Canberra B.15					8101M

A single Sedbergh TX.1 built by Slingsby Sailplanes Ltd at Kirkbymoorside in 1951 was issued with the serial WJ306.

serial	type	sqdn/unit	code	where&when seen		remarks
WJ306	Sedbergh TX.1					

The only production batch of Canberra B.2's built by Handley-Page Ltd at Cricklewood and Radlett totalled 75 aircraft against Contract 5943 (WJ564-WJ582, WJ603-WJ649, WJ674-WJ682). WJ564 first flew on 5.1.53 and deliveries took place between 3.53 and 4.55. Several aircraft were later converted by BAC to T.4's, T.17's and TT.18's while others were modified for trials (eg WJ643). Note that the original order placed with Handley-Page called for 150 aircraft but the following 75 were cancelled:- WJ683-WJ707, WS960-WS999, WT113-WT122.

serial	type	sqdn/unit	code	where&when seen		remarks
WJ565	Canberra T.17					
WJ567	Canberra T.4					
WJ574	Canberra TT.18					
WJ576	Canberra T.17					
WJ581	Canberra T.17					
WJ603	Canberra B.2					
WJ607	Canberra T.17					
WJ614	Canberra TT.18					
WJ625	Canberra T.17					
WJ629	Canberra TT.18					
WJ630	Canberra T.17					
WJ633	Canberra T.17					
WJ636	Canberra TT.18					
WJ637	Canberra B.2					
WJ639	Canberra TT.18					
WJ640	Canberra B.2					
WJ643	Canberra B.2/8					
WJ678	Canberra B.2					
WJ680	Canberra TT.18					
WJ681	Canberra B.2					
WJ682	Canberra TT.18					

The fifth production batch of Canberra B.2's built by English Electric totalled 25 aircraft (WJ712-WJ733, WJ751-WJ753 against Contract 5786, deliveries taking place between 8.53 and 1.54. Several aircraft were later converted by BAC to TT.18's.

serial	type	sqdn/unit	code	where&when seen		remarks
WJ715	Canberra TT.18					
WJ717	Canberra TT.18					
WJ721	Canberra TT.18					
WJ722	Canberra B.2					
WJ731	Canberra B.2					
WJ753	Canberra B.2					

The first production batch of Canberra B.6's built by English Electric totalled 31 aircraft (WJ754-WJ784) against Contract 5786; WJ754 f/f 26.1.54. Deliveries took place between 2.54 and 11.54 and from 1960 onwards several aircraft were modified by BAC to B.15's and B.16's for service with the RAF's FEAF and NEAF resp. From 1970 further conversions were made of B.15's to E.15's to fulfil the high-level calibration role.

serial	type	sqdn/unit	code	where&when seen		remarks
WJ756	Canberra E.15					

WJ775-WK163

serial	type	sqdn/unit	code	where&when seen		remarks
WJ775	Canberra B.6(mod)					8581M

The second production batch of Canberra PR.7's totalled 11 aircraft (WJ815-WJ825) and was built by English Electric at Preston against Contract 5786. Deliveries took place between 6.54 and 10.54.

serial	type	sqdn/unit	code	where&when seen		remarks
WJ815	Canberra PR.7					
WJ817	Canberra PR.7					
WJ821	Canberra PR.7					
WJ825	Canberra PR.7					

The third production batch of Canberra T.4's built by English Electric totalled 25 aircraft against Contract 5786 (WJ857-WJ881). Deliveries took place between 6.54 and 3.55.

serial	type	sqdn/unit	code	where&when seen		remarks
WJ861	Canberra T.4					
WJ865	Canberra T.4					
WJ866	Canberra T.4					
WJ867	Canberra T.4					
WJ869	Canberra T.4					
WJ870	Canberra T.4					
WJ872	Canberra T.4					8492M
WJ874	Canberra T.4					
WJ877	Canberra T.4					
WJ879	Canberra T.4					
WJ880	Canberra T.4					8491M

The second production batch of Varsity T.1's totalled 50 aircraft (WJ886-WJ921, WJ937-WJ950) built by Vickers-Armstrongs Ltd at Hurn against Contract 6/Aircraft/5946/CB6(c). Deliveries took place between 11.52 and 3.53. Some aircraft were later modified for special trials.

serial	type	sqdn/unit	code	where&when seen		remarks
WJ893	Varsity T.1					

The only production batch of Canberra B.2's built by A.V.Roe & Co at Woodford totalled 75 aircraft (WJ971-WJ995, WK102-WK146, WK161-WK165) against Contract 5990. WJ971 f/f 25.11.52 and deliveries took place between 2.53 and 2.55. Several aircraft were later converted by BAC to T.4's, T.17's, TT.18's and T.11/19's, whilst others were modified for trials (eg WK163). Note that the original order placed with Avro called for 100 aircraft but the following 25 were cancelled: WK166-WK190.

serial	type	sqdn/unit	code	where&when seen		remarks
WJ975	Canberra T.19					
WJ977	Canberra T.17					
WJ981	Canberra T.17					
WJ986	Canberra T.17					
WJ992	Canberra T.4					
WK102	Canberra T.17					
WK111	Canberra T.17					
WK116	Canberra B.2					
WK118	Canberra TT.18					
WK122	Canberra TT.18					
WK123	Canberra TT.18					
WK124	Canberra TT.18					
WK126	Canberra TT.18					
WK127	Canberra TT.18					
WK128	Canberra B.2					
WK142	Canberra TT.18					
WK143	Canberra B.2					
WK144	Canberra B.2					
WK162	Canberra B.2					
WK163	Canberra B.2/6					

WK164-WL635

serial	type	sqdn/unit	code	where&when seen		remarks
WK164	Canberra B.2					

The fourth production batch of Chipmunk T.10's for the RAF totalled 100 aircraft (WK506-WK523, WK547-WK591, WK607-WK643). Deliveries took place between 1.52 and 6.52, some aircraft later being transferred to the Royal Navy and the Army Air Corps.

serial	type	sqdn/unit	code	where&when seen		remarks
WK511	Chipmunk T.10					
WK512	Chipmunk T.10					
WK517	Chipmunk T.10					
WK518	Chipmunk T.10					
WK550	Chipmunk T.10					
WK554	Chipmunk T.10					
WK559	Chipmunk T.10					
WK562	Chipmunk T.10					
WK572	Chipmunk T.10					
WK574	Chipmunk T.10					
WK585	Chipmunk T.10					
WK586	Chipmunk T.10					
WK589	Chipmunk T.10					
WK590	Chipmunk T.10					
WK608	Chipmunk T.10					
WK609	Chipmunk T.10					
WK613	Chipmunk T.10					
WK620	Chipmunk T.10					
WK624	Chipmunk T.10					
WK630	Chipmunk T.10					
WK633	Chipmunk T.10					
WK634	Chipmunk T.10					
WK635	Chipmunk T.10					
WK638	Chipmunk T.10					
WK639	Chipmunk T.10					
WK640	Chipmunk T.10					
WK642	Chipmunk T.10					
WK643	Chipmunk T.10					

The sixth and final production batch of Meteor F.8's totalled 343 aircraft (WK647-WK696, WK783-WK827, WK849-WK893, WK935-WK955, WK966-WK994, WL104-WL143, WL158-WL191 all built by Gloster Aircraft Co Ltd at Hucclecote during 1951/54 and WK707-WK756, WK906-WK934 all built by Sir W.G. Armstrong-Whitworth Aircraft Ltd at Coventry during 1951/53) ordered against Contract 6/Aircraft/6066 C.B.7(b). WL191 was the last Meteor F.8 built and first flew on 9.4.54. Several aircraft were later modified for trials purposes and to U.16/D.16 standard.

serial	type	sqdn/unit	code	where&when seen		remarks
WK800	Meteor D.16					

The sixth production batch of Meteor T.7's totalled 139 aircraft (WL332-WL381, WL397-WL436, WL453-WL488, WN309-WN321) built by Gloster Aircraft Co Ltd at Hucclecote during 1951/53 against Contract 6/Aircraft/6066/CB7(b). Deliveries took place between 3.52 and 8.53 and one was subsequently converted to Special standard for ejector-seat trials.

serial	type	sqdn/unit	code	where&when seen		remarks
WL419	Meteor T.7 Special					

The third production batch of Varsity T.1's totalled 50 aircraft (WL621-WL642, WL665-WL692) and was built at Hurn by Vickers-Armstrongs Ltd against Contract 6/Aircraft/6125/CB6(a). Deliveries took place between 4.53 and 2.54 and several aircraft were later modified for trials work. Note that the original order called for 67 aircraft but the following 17 were cancelled before construction:- WL693-WL709.

serial	type	sqdn/unit	code	where&when seen		remarks
WL635	Varsity T.1					

serial	type	sqdn/unit	code	where&when seen		remarks
WL679	Varsity T.1 (mod)					

The second production batch of Shackleton MR.2's totalled 40 aircraft (WL737-WL759, WL785-WL801) and was built at Woodford against Contract 6/Aircraft/6129. Deliveries took place between 1.53 and 11.53, with most being updated to phase 1, phase 2 and in many cases phase 3 standard from 1959 onwards. Beginning in 1971, nine aircraft of this batch were converted by HSA at Woodford and Bitteswell to AEW.2 standard by fitting radar equipment, taken from RN Gannet AEW.3's, under the forward fuselage.

serial	type	sqdn/unit	code	where&when seen		remarks
WL741	Shackleton AEW.2					
WL745	Shackleton AEW.2					
WL747	Shackleton AEW.2					
WL754	Shackleton AEW.2					
WL756	Shackleton AEW.2					
WL757	Shackleton AEW.2					
WL790	Shackleton AEW.2					
WL793	Shackleton AEW.2					
WL795	Shackleton AEW.2					
WL798	Shackleton MR.2/3					8114M
WL801	Shackleton MR.2/3					8629M

The second production batch of Sea Prince T.1's totalled 8 aircraft (WM735-WM742) and was built at Luton in 1952, deliveries being completed later that year.

serial	type	sqdn/unit	code	where&when seen		remarks
WM735	Sea Prince T.1					
WM739	Sea Prince T.1					To G-TACA

The third production batch of Sea Prince T.1's totalled 15 aircraft (WP307-WP321) and was built at Luton in 1952. Deliveries were completed in 1953.

serial	type	sqdn/unit	code	where&when seen		remarks
WP308	Sea Prince T.1					
WP313	Sea Prince T.1					
WP314	Sea Prince T.1					8634M
WP320	Sea Prince T.1					
WP321	Sea Prince T.1					

In 1951 English Electric built 2 Canberra B.2's to replace aircraft diverted off RAF Contract 3520 to overseas air arms. The replacement aircraft were WP514-WP515.

serial	type	sqdn/unit	code	where&when seen		remarks
WP515	Canberra B.2					

The fifth production batch of Chipmunk T.10's totalled 145 aircraft (WP772-WP811, WP828-WP872, WP898-WP930, WP962-WP988) against Contract 6449. Deliveries took place between 6.52 and 4.53, several aircraft later being transferred to the Royal Navy and Army Air Corps.

serial	type	sqdn/unit	code	where&when seen		remarks
WP772	Chipmunk T.10					
WP776	Chipmunk T.10					
WP786	Chipmunk T.10					
WP795	Chipmunk T.10					
WP801	Chipmunk T.10					
WP803	Chipmunk T.10					
WP805	Chipmunk T.10					
WP809	Chipmunk T.10					
WP833	Chipmunk T.10					
WP837	Chipmunk T.10					
WP839	Chipmunk T.10					
WP840	Chipmunk T.10					
WP844	Chipmunk T.10					
WP855	Chipmunk T.10					
WP856	Chipmunk T.10					
WP859	Chipmunk T.10					

WP860-WT308

serial	type	sqdn/unit	code	where&when seen		remarks
WP860	Chipmunk T.10					
WP871	Chipmunk T.10					
WP872	Chipmunk T.10					
WP896	Chipmunk T.10					
WP900	Chipmunk T.10					
WP901	Chipmunk T.10					
WP904	Chipmunk T.10					
WP906	Chipmunk T.10					
WP914	Chipmunk T.10					
WP920	Chipmunk T.10					
WP925	Chipmunk T.10					
WP928	Chipmunk T.10					
WP929	Chipmunk T.10					
WP930	Chipmunk T.10					
WP962	Chipmunk T.10					
WP964	Chipmunk T.10					
WP967	Chipmunk T.10					
WP970	Chipmunk T.10					
WP972	Chipmunk T.10					
WP974	Chipmunk T.10					
WP979	Chipmunk T.10					
WP980	Chipmunk T.10					
WP981	Chipmunk T.10					
WP983	Chipmunk T.10					
WP984	Chipmunk T.10					

The third production batch of Shackleton MR.2's totalled 19 aircraft (WR951-WR969) and was built at Woodford against Contract 6408, deliveries taking place between 11.53 and 9.54. From 1959 most were updated to phase 1, phase 2 and in many cases phase 3 standard. In early 1967 four aircraft of this batch were modified by Hawker Siddeley Aviation at Langar to flying classrooms as replacements for the Shackleton T.4's and have been variously quoted as T.2's and MR(T).2's. From 1971 onwards, 3 MR.2/3's of this batch were converted by HSA at Bitteswell to AEW.2's.

serial	type	sqdn/unit	code	where&when seen		remarks
WR960	Shackleton AEW.2					
WR963	Shackleton AEW.2					
WR965	Shackleton AEW.2					
WR967	Shackleton T.2					8398M (simulator)

The Shackleton MR.3 followed the MR.2 on the production line at Woodford and the first batch totalled 21 aircraft (WR970-WR999). WR970 f/f 2.9.55 and deliveries commenced in 8.57. From 1959 onwards most aircraft were updated to phase 1, phase 2 and phase 3 standard.

serial	type	sqdn/unit	code	where&when seen		remarks
WR971	Shackleton MR.3/3					8119M
WR974	Shackleton MR.3/3					8117M
WR982	Shackleton MR.3/3					8106M
WR985	Shackleton MR.3/3					8103M

The first production batch of Meteor NF.12's totalled 100 aircraft (WS590-WS639, WS658-WS700, WS715-WS721) and was built by AWA at Coventry during 1953/54 against Contract 6/Aircraft/6412 C.B.5(b). WS590 f/f 21.4.53 and deliveries began in 1953.

serial	type	sqdn/unit	code	where&when seen		remarks
WS692	Meteor NF.12					7605M

The second production batch of Canberra B.6's built by English Electric Co totalled 22 aircraft (WT301-WT303, WT307-WT325) against Contract 6445. WT307-WT325 were completed as B(I).6's while WT304-WT306 were transferred to Contract 5786. Deliveries took place between 10.54 and 11.54 (B.6's) and 4.55 and 2.56 (B(I).6's).

serial	type	sqdn/unit	code	where&when seen		remarks
WT308	Canberra B(I).6					

WT309-WT809

serial	type	sqdn/unit	code	where&when seen		remarks
WT309	Canberra B(I).6					

The first production batch of Canberra B(I).8's totalled 25 aircraft (WT326-WT348, WT362-WT368) and was built against Contract 6445 by English Electric at Preston. They had originally been ordered as B.6's and WT369-WT374 were completed as such. Deliveries of the B(I).8's took place between 12.54 and 3.57 with aircraft being diverted off contract to India (WT338) and Peru (WT343/348/367). A further 56 aircraft ordered against this Contract were cancelled: WT397-WT422, WT440-WT469.

serial	type	sqdn/unit	code	where&when seen		remarks
WT327	Canberra B(I).8					
WT333	Canberra B(I).8					
WT339	Canberra B(I).8					8198M

The fourth production batch of Canberra T.4's totalled 18 aircraft (WT475-WT492) and was built by English Electric at Preston in 1955 against Contract 6445. Deliveries took place between 2.55 and 10.55.

serial	type	sqdn/unit	code	where&when seen		remarks
WT478	Canberra T.4					
WT480	Canberra T.4					
WT483	Canberra T.4					
WT488	Canberra T.4					

The third production batch of Canberra PR.7's totalled 40 aircraft (WT503-WT542) and was built by English Electric at Preston against Contract 6445. Deliveries took place between 10.54 and 3.56. Some aircraft were later converted to T.22's by BAC.

serial	type	sqdn/unit	code	where&when seen		remarks
WT507	Canberra PR.7					8548M
WT509	Canberra PR.7					
WT510	Canberra T.22					
WT518	Canberra PR.7					
WT519	Canberra PR.7					
WT525	Canberra T.22					
WT530	Canberra PR.7					
WT532	Canberra PR.7					
WT534	Canberra PR.7					8549M
WT535	Canberra T.22					
WT536	Canberra PR.7					8063M
WT537	Canberra PR.7					
WT538	Canberra PR.7					

The first production batch of Hunter F.1's built by Hawker Aircraft Ltd at Kingston-upon-Thames totalled 113 aircraft against Contract 5910 (WT555-WT595, WT611-WT660, WT679-WT700). WT555 f/f 16.5.53 with deliveries commencing to the Central Fighter Establishment in 7.54.

serial	type	sqdn/unit	code	where&when seen		remarks
WT684	Hunter F.1					7422M

87 Hunter F.4's built by Hawker Aircraft Ltd at Kingston-upon-Thames continuing Contract 5910 (WT701-WT723, WT734-WT780, WT795-WT811). WT702 f/f 20.10.54 and deliveries began in 3.55. Several were later converted by Hawker's to T.8 and GA.11 standard.

serial	type	sqdn/unit	code	where&when seen		remarks
WT702	Hunter T.8C					
WT711	Hunter GA.11					
WT722	Hunter T.8C					
WT723	Hunter GA.11					
WT744	Hunter GA.11					
WT745	Hunter T.8					
WT746	Hunter F.4					7770M
WT799	Hunter T.8C					
WT804	Hunter GA.11					
WT806	Hunter GA.11					
WT809	Hunter GA.11					

WT867-WV746

serial	type	sqdn/unit	code	where&when seen	remarks

The first production batch of Cadet TX.3 gliders was built by Slingsby Sailplanes Ltd at Kirkbymoorside and totalled 40 aircraft (WT865-WT877, WT893-WT919) against Contract 6023. Deliveries took place between 6.51 and 3.52.

serial	type	sqdn/unit	code	where&when seen	remarks
WT867	Cadet TX.3				
WT868	Cadet TX.3				
WT869	Cadet TX.3				
WT870	Cadet TX.3				
WT871	Cadet TX.3				
WT872	Cadet TX.3				
WT873	Cadet TX.3				
WT877	Cadet TX.3				
WT895	Cadet TX.3				
WT898	Cadet TX.3				
WT899	Cadet TX.3				
WT900	Cadet TX.3				
WT901	Cadet TX.3				
WT902	Cadet TX.3				
WT903	Cadet TX.3				
WT904	Cadet TX.3				
WT905	Cadet TX.3				
WT906	Cadet TX.3				
WT908	Cadet TX.3				
WT909	Cadet TX.3				
WT910	Cadet TX.3				
WT911	Cadet TX.3				
WT913	Cadet TX.3				
WT914	Cadet TX.3				
WT915	Cadet TX.3				
WT917	Cadet TX.3				
WT918	Cadet TX.3				
WT919	Cadet TX.3				

The second production batch of Hunter F.4's totalled 100 aircraft (WV253-WV281, WV314-WV334, WV363-WV412) and was built by Hawker Aircraft Ltd at Kingston-upon-Thames against Contract 6867. Several aircraft were later converted to T.7 standard while others were converted to T.8, T.8C and GA.11 standard for the Royal Navy.

serial	type	sqdn/unit	code	where&when seen	remarks
WV256	Hunter GA.11				
WV267	Hunter GA.11				
WV276	Hunter F.4				7847M
WV318	Hunter T.7B				
WV322	Hunter T.8C				
WV363	Hunter T.8				
WV372	Hunter T.7				
WV382	Hunter GA.11				
WV383	Hunter T.7				
WV396	Hunter T.8C				

The first production batch of Pembroke C.1's totalled 42 aircraft (WV698-WV712, WV729-WV755) against Contract 6847, a further 11 aircraft (WV756-WV766) being cancelled. Production took place at Hunting Percival's at Luton during 1953/56, the last two aircraft being completed as C(PR).1's (later converted to C.1's).

serial	type	sqdn/unit	code	where&when seen	remarks
WV701	Pembroke C.1				
WV740	Pembroke C.1				
WV746	Pembroke C.1				

WV787-WZ791

serial	type	sqdn/unit	code	where&when seen	remarks

One Canberra B.2 was built by English Electric against Contract 3520 as a Sapphire powered experimental aircraft. It was delivered in 8.52 and has since been modified so many times that it is now flying with major components from marks B.2/B.6/B(I).8 and defies designation.

serial	type	sqdn/unit	code	where&when seen	remarks
WV787	Canberra (mod)				

The first production batch of Sea Hawk FGA.4's totalled 85 aircraft (WV792-WV807, WV824-WV871, WV902-WV922) and was built by Sir W.G. Armstrong-Whitworth Aircraft Ltd at Coventry. WV792 f/f 26.8.54 and deliveries commenced at the turn of the year and were completed in mid-1955. Subsequent conversions to FGA.6 standard.

serial	type	sqdn/unit	code	where&when seen	remarks
WV794	Sea Hawk FGA.6				A2634/8152M
WV797	Sea Hawk FGA.6				A2637/8155M
WV903	Sea Hawk FGA.6				A2632/8153M
WV908	Sea Hawk FGA.6				FAAHF ex A2660/8154M
WV911	Sea Hawk FGA.4				A2526

The first batch of Hunter F.4's built at Blackpool by Hawker Aircraft Ltd totalled 20 aircraft (WW646-WW665) against Contract 6/Aircraft/8435/CB7(a) dated 15.8.53. Several aircraft were later returned to Hawker Aircraft Ltd at Dunsfold for conversion to GA.11 standard for the FAA.

serial	type	sqdn/unit	code	where&when seen	remarks
WW654	Hunter GA.11				

The final production batch of Chipmunk T.10's for the RAF totalled 40 aircraft (WZ845-WZ884) against Contract 7541, deliveries taking place between 4.53 and 10.53. WZ882 was later transferred to the Army Air Corps.

serial	type	sqdn/unit	code	where&when seen	remarks
WZ753	Grasshopper TX.1				
WZ754	Grasshopper TX.1				
WZ755	Grasshopper TX.1				
WZ756	Grasshopper TX.1				
WZ757	Grasshopper TX.1				
WZ758	Grasshopper TX.1				
WZ760	Grasshopper TX.1				
WZ761	Grasshopper TX.1				
WZ762	Grasshopper TX.1				
WZ764	Grasshopper TX.1				
WZ765	Grasshopper TX.1				
WZ767	Grasshopper TX.1				
WZ768	Grasshopper TX.1				
WZ769	Grasshopper TX.1				
WZ771	Grasshopper TX.1				
WZ772	Grasshopper TX.1				
WZ773	Grasshopper TX.1				
WZ774	Grasshopper TX.1				
WZ777	Grasshopper TX.1				
WZ778	Grasshopper TX.1				
WZ779	Grasshopper TX.1				
WZ780	Grasshopper TX.1				
WZ781	Grasshopper TX.1				
WZ782	Grasshopper TX.1				
WZ783	Grasshopper TX.1				
WZ784	Grasshopper TX.1				
WZ785	Grasshopper TX.1				
WZ786	Grasshopper TX.1				
WZ787	Grasshopper TX.1				
WZ788	Grasshopper TX.1				
WZ789	Grasshopper TX.1				
WZ791	Grasshopper TX.1				

WZ792-WZ884

serial	type	sqdn/unit	code	where&when seen		remarks
WZ792	Grasshopper TX.1					
WZ793	Grasshopper TX.1					
WZ794	Grasshopper TX.1					
WZ795	Grasshopper TX.1					
WZ796	Grasshopper TX.1					
WZ797	Grasshopper TX.1					
WZ798	Grasshopper TX.1					
WZ816	Grasshopper TX.1					
WZ817	Grasshopper TX.1					
WZ818	Grasshopper TX.1					
WZ819	Grasshopper TX.1					
WZ820	Grasshopper TX.1					
WZ822	Grasshopper TX.1					
WZ824	Grasshopper TX.1					
WZ825	Grasshopper TX.1					
WZ826	Grasshopper TX.1					
WZ827	Grasshopper TX.1					
WZ828	Grasshopper TX.1					
WZ829	Grasshopper TX.1					
WZ830	Grasshopper TX.1					
WZ831	Grasshopper TX.1					

The first production batch of Grasshopper TX.1's totalled 65 aircraft (WZ753-WZ798, WZ814-WZ832) and was built by Slingsby Sailplanes Ltd at Kirkbymoorside against Contract 7419, deliveries taking place between 5.52 and 1.53.

serial	type	sqdn/unit	code	where&when seen		remarks
WZ845	Chipmunk T.10					
WZ847	Chipmunk T.10					
WZ856	Chipmunk T.10					
WZ862	Chipmunk T.10					
WZ872	Chipmunk T.10					
WZ877	Chipmunk T.10					
WZ878	Chipmunk T.10					
WZ879	Chipmunk T.10					
WZ882	Chipmunk T.10					
WZ884	Chipmunk T.10					

HISTORICAL AIRCRAFT PRESERVED IN THE U.K.

304-N2078

serial	type	sqdn/unit	code	where&when seen		remarks
304	Cody Biplane					Pr Science Museum
*2345	Gunbus Replica					Pr Hendon
2699	BE.2C					Pr IWM Lambeth
*3066	Caudron G III					Pr Hendon
*5964	DH.2 Replica					G-BFVH Aw
8359	Short 184					Pr Yeovilton
A301	Morane BB					Pr Hendon
B1807	Pup					Ex G-EAVX On rebuild
*B7270	Camel Replica					G-BFCZ Aw
*C1701	Camel Replica					G-AWYY Aw
D7560	Avro 504K					Pr Science Museum
D8096	Bristol F.2B					G-AEPH Aw Old Warden
E449	Avro 504K					Ex G-EBKN Pr Hendon
E2581	Bristol F.2B					Pr IWM Lambeth
*E3404	Avro 504K					H5199 Aw Old Warden
F904	SE.5A					G-EBIA Aw Old Warden
*F938	SE.5A					Ex G-EBIC Pr Hendon
F939	SE.5A					G-EBIB Pr Sc Museum
F1010	DH.9A					Pr Cardington
F3556	RE.8					Pr IWM Duxford
*F6314	Camel					Pr Hendon
*F8010	SE.5A Replica					G-BDWJ Aw
*F8614	Vimy Replica					Pr Hendon
H2311	Avro 504K					Pr Henlow
H5199	Avro 504K					See E3404
J8067	Pterodactyl					Pr Science Museum
*J9941	Hart					Ex G-ABMR Pr Hendon
K1786	Tomtit					G-AFTA Aw Old Warden
*K2050	Fury Replica					G-ASCM Aw
K2571	Tiger Moth					Under restoration
K3215	Tutor					G-AHSA Aw Old Warden
K4232	Rota I					Ex SE-AZB Pr Card'ton
K4235	Rota I					G-AMHJ Pr Old Warden
K4972	Hart Trainer					1746M Pr Hendon
K6038	Wallace					Pr Henlow (remains)
K8042	Gladiator II					8372M Pr Hendon
K9942	Spitfire IA					8383M Pr Hendon
L1592	Hurricane I					Pr Science Museum
*L2301	Walrus I					Ex G-AIZG Pr Yeovilton
L2940	Skua I					Pr Yeovilton (remains)
L5343	Battle I					Pr Cardington
L6938	Tiger Moth					G-ANZU Aw
L8032	Gladiator I					G-AMRK Aw Old Warden
*L8756	Blenheim IV					RCAF 10001 Pr Hendon
*N220	S.5 Replica					G-BDFF Aw
N248	S.6A					Pr Southampton
*N2078	Baby (composite)					Pr Yeovilton

N5180-W4041

serial	type	sqdn/unit	code	where&when seen		remarks
*N5180	Pup					G-EBKY Aw Old Warden
N5182	Pup					G-APUP Aw
*N5430	Triplane Replica					G-BHEW Aw
N5912	Triplane					8385M Pr Hendon
N6812	2F.1 Camel					Pr IWM Lambeth
N9899	Southampton					Pr Cardington
N1671	Defiant I					8370M Pr Hendon
N1854	Fulmar II					Ex G-AIBE Pr Yeovilton
N3788	Magister					G-AKPF Pr Bassingbourn
N4172	Albacore I					Pr Wroughton (remains)
N4877	Anson I					G-AMDA Pr Duxford
N5628	Gladiator II					Pr Hendon (remains)
N5903	Sea Gladiator II					Pr Yeovilton
N6848	Tiger Moth T.2					G-BALX Aw
N9191	Tiger Moth T.2					G-ALND Aw
N9238	Tiger Moth T.2					G-ANEL Aw
N9389	Tiger Moth T.2					G-ANJA Aw
P2183	Battle I					Pr Henlow
P2617	Hurricane I					Pr Hendon
*P3308	Hurricane II					G-AWLW Aw Strathallan
*P6382	Magister					G-AJDR Aw Old Warden
P9444	Spitfire IA					Pr Science Museum
R1914	Magister					G-AHUJ Aw Strathallan
R3950	Battle I					Pr Strathallan
R4907	Tiger Moth T.2					G-ANCS Aw
R4959	Tiger Moth T.2					G-ARAZ Aw
R5250	Tiger Moth T.2					G-AODT Aw
R5868	Lancaster I					7325M Pr Hendon
R6915	Spitfire I					Pr IWM Lambeth
R7524	Proctor I					G-AIWA Aw
R9125	Lysander III					8377M Pr Hendon
*S1287	Flycatcher Replica					G-BEYB Aw FAAM
S1595	S.6B					Pr Science Museum
T5424	Tiger Moth T.2					G-AJOA Aw
T5493	Tiger Moth T.2					G-ANEF Aw
T5717	Tiger Moth T.2					Dt Rochester
T5854	Tiger Moth T.2					G-ANKK Aw
T5879	Tiger Moth T.2					G-AXBW Aw
T6296	Tiger Moth T.2					Pr Hendon
T6553	Tiger Moth T.2					G-APIG Aw
T6818	Tiger Moth T.2					G-ANKT Aw Old Warden
T7187	Tiger Moth T.2					G-AOBX Aw
T7281	Tiger Moth T.2					G-ARTL Aw
T7404	Tiger Moth T.2					G-ANMV Aw
T7794	Tiger Moth T.2					Dt Rochester
*T9707	Magister					8378M Pr Hendon
T9738	Magister					G-AKAT Pr Winthorpe
V3388	Oxford I					G-AHTW Pr Duxford
*V9281	Lysander III					G-BCWL Aw
*V9441	Lysander IIIA					G-AZWT Aw Strathallan
W1048	Halifax II					8465M Pr Henlow
W4041	E.28/39					Pr Science Museum

W4050-KD431

serial	type	sqdn/unit	code	where&when seen		remarks
W4050	Mosquito I					Pr London Colney
W5856	Swordfish II					Pr Strathallan
*W5984	Swordfish II					HS618 Pr Yeovilton
X4590	Spitfire IA					8384M Pr Hendon
Z2033	Firefly I					G-ASTL Pr Duxford
Z7015	Sea Hurricane IB					Pr Old Warden
Z7197	Proctor C.3					8380M Pr St Athan
*Z7258	Rapide					G-AHGD Aw
AL246	Martlet I					Pr Yeovilton
AP507	Rota I					G-ACWP Pr Sc Museum
AR213	Spitfire IB					G-AIST Aw
AR501	Spitfire VC					G-AWII Aw
BB694	Tiger Moth T.2					G-ADGV Aw
BB731	Tiger Moth T.2					A2126 St Yeovilton
BL614	Spitfire VB					Pr Abingdon
BM597	Spitfire VB					5713M Pr Church Fenton
*BS676	Spitfire Replica					G-KUKU Aw
DE208	Tiger Moth T.2					G-AGYU Pr Southend
DE363	Tiger Moth T.2					G-ANFC Pr London Clny
DE373	Tiger Moth T.2					A2127 St Yeovilton
DE623	Tiger Moth T.2					G-ANFI Aw
DE992	Tiger Moth T.2					G-AXXV Aw
DF130	Tiger Moth T.2					G-BACK Aw
DF155	Tiger Moth T.2					G-ANFV Pr Strathallan
DF198	Tiger Moth T.2					G-BBRB Aw
DG202	F.9/40					5758M Pr Cosford
DG590	Hawk Major					8379M G-ADMW Pr Henlow
DP872	Barracuda II					Pr Yeovilton (remains)
DR613	Wicko GM.1					G-AFJB Pr Berkswell
EE531	Meteor F.4(mod)					7090M Pr Baginton
EE549	Meteor F.4					6372M Pr Hendon
EJ693	Tempest V					Pr Henlow (fuselage)
EM726	Tiger Moth T.2					G-ANDE Aw
EM903	Tiger Moth T.2					G-APBI Aw
EP120	Spitfire VB					5377M Pr Wattisham
*EV851	Argus II					G-AJPI Aw
EX976	Harvard T.3					To/Ex PAF1657 Pr FAAM
FT229	Harvard T.2					G-AZKI Aw
FT323	Harvard T.2					G-AZSC Aw
FT391	Harvard T.2					G-AZBN Aw
FX301	Harvard T.2					G-JUDI Aw
FX442	Harvard T.2					Pr Bournemouth
HB751	Argus III					G-BCBL Aw
*HD368	Mitchell					N9089Z Pr Southend
HJ711	Mosquito NF.II					Pr York (composite)
HM354	Proctor C.3					G-ANPP
HS503	Swordfish IV					Pr Henlow
HS618	Swordfish II					A2001 See W5984
KB976	Lancaster B.10					G-BCOH Pr Strathallan
KD431	Corsair IV					Pr Yeovilton

KE209-NX611

serial	type	sqdn/unit	code	where&when seen		remarks
KE209	Hellcat II					Pr Yeovilton
*KG374	Dakota C.4					KN645 Pr Cosford
KK995	Hoverfly I					Pr Hendon
KN645	Dakota C.4					8355M See KG374
KN751	Liberator VI					Pr Cosford
KP208	Dakota C.4					Pr Aldershot
KX829	Hurricane IV					Pr B'ham Mus of Sc & I
LA198	Spitfire F.21					7118M Pr Locking
LA226	Spitfire F.21					7119M Pr Sth Marston
LA255	Spitfire F.21					6490M Pr Wittering
LA564	Seafire F.46					Pr Redbourn
LA607	Tempest F.2					Pr Duxford
LB312	Auster I					G-AHXE Aw
LF738	Hurricane IIC					5405M Pr Biggin Hill
LF751	Hurricane IIC					5466M Pr Bentley Priory
LF858	Queen Bee					Pr Old Warden
LZ551	Sea Vampire F.1					Pr Yeovilton
LZ766	Proctor C.3					G-ALCK Pr Duxford
MF628	Wellington T.10					Pr Hendon
MH434	Spitfire IX					G-ASJV Aw
MJ627	Spitfire IX					G-BMSB Pr Coventry
MK356	Spitfire IX					5690M Pr St Athan
MK732	Spitfire IX					8633M Pr Abingdon
ML407	Spitfire IX Tnr					G-LFIX Under Rest'n
ML427	Spitfire IX					Pr B'ham Mus of Sc & I
ML796	Sunderland GR.5					Pr Duxford
ML824	Sunderland GR.5					Pr Hendon
MN235	Typhoon IB					Pr Hendon
MP425	Oxford I					Pr Henlow
MT360	Auster 5					G-AKWT Under Rest'n
MT847	Spitfire FR.XIV					6960M Pr Cosford
MV262	Spitfire XIV					Under Restoration
MV293	Spitfire XIV					G-SPIT Under Rest'n
MV370	Spitfire XIV					G-FXIV Under Rest'n
*MW100	York C.1					TS798 Pr Cosford
*MX457	Stampe SV.4C					G-AZSA Aw
NF370	Swordfish II					Pr IWM Lambeth
NF389	Swordfish III					Pr Lee-on-Solent
NF875	Dominie I					G-AGTM Aw
NH238	Spitfire IX					Under Restoration
NH749	Spitfire XIV					G-MXIV Under Rest'n
NH904	Spitfire XIV					G-FIRE Under Rest'n
NJ695	Auster 4					G-AJXV Aw
NJ703	Auster 5					G-AKPI Aw
NL750	Tiger Moth T.2					A2123 St Yeovilton
NM140	Tiger Moth T.2					G-APGL Aw
NM181	Proctor C.4					G-AZGZ Aw
NP181	Proctor C.4					G-AOAR
NP184	Proctor C.4					G-ANYP Pr H Blagdon
NP294	Proctor C.4					Pr Friskney (fuselage)
NP303	Proctor C.4					G-ANZJ Pr Southend
NP339	Proctor C.4					G-AOBW Pr Southend
NR747	Dominie					G-AJHO Pr Bassingbourn
NV778	Tempest TT.5					8386M Pr Hendon
NX611	Lancaster B.VII					8375M Pr Scampton

PG617-TG505

serial	type	sqdn/unit	code	where&when seen		remarks
PG617	Tiger Moth T.2					G-AYVY Aw
PG651	Tiger Moth T.2					G-AYUX Aw
PK624	Spitfire F.22					8072M Pr Abingdon
PK664	Spitfire F.22					7759M Pr Binbrook
PK683	Spitfire F.24					7150M Pr Southampton
PK724	Spitfire F.24					7288M Pr Hendon
PL983	Spitfire PR.XI					Pr Duxford
PM651	Spitfitr PR.19					7758M Pr Benson
PS915	Spitfire PR.19					7711M Pr Coningsby
PV202	Spitfire IX Tnr					Under Restoration
RA848	Cadet TX.1					Pr Harrogate
RA854	Cadet TX.1					Pr Wigan
RD253	Beaufighter TF.10					7931M Pr Hendon
RF398	Lincoln B.2					8376M Pr Cosford
*RG333	Messenger					G-AKEZ Pr H Blagdon
*RG333	Messenger					G-AIEK Aw
RH377	Messenger C.1					Ex G-ALAH Pr Henlow
RH378	Messenger C.1					G-AJOE Aw
RH746	Brigand TF.1					Dt Failsworth
RL962	Dominie II					Pr Henlow
RM221	Proctor C.4					G-ANXR Aw
*RM619	Spitfire XIV					G-ALGT/RM689 Aw
RM689	Spitfire XIV					See RM619
RR299	Mosquito T.3					G-ASKH Aw Hawarden
RS709	Mosquito TT.35					N9797/(G-ASKA) Aw
RS712	Mosquito TT.35					G-ASKB Aw Strathallan
RW382	Spitfire LF.16					7245M Pr Uxbridge
RW386	Spitfire LF.16					6944M Pr Halton
RW388	Spitfire LF.16					6947M Pr Stoke
RW393	Spitfire LF.16					7293M Pr Turnhouse
SL542	Spitfire LF.16					8390M Pr Coltishall
SL574	Spitfire LF.16					8391M Pr Bentley Priory
SL674	Spitfire LF.16					8392M Pr Biggin Hill
SM832	Spitfire XIV					G-WWII Under Rest'n
SM969	Spitfire F.18					G-BRAF Under Rest'n
SX137	Seafire F.17					Pr Yeovilton
SX300	Seafire F.17					Pr Leamington
SX336	Seafire F.17					A2055 Pr Winthorpe
TA122	Mosquito FB.VI					Pr London Colney
TA634	Mosquito TT.35					G-AWJV Pr London Clny
TA639	Mosquito TT.35					7806M Pr Cosford
TA719	Mosquito TT.35					G-ASKC Pr Duxford
TB252	Spitfire LF.16					7257M/7281M Pr Leuchars
TB382	Spitfire LF.16					7244M Pr Abingdon
TB752	Spitfire LF.16					7256M/7279M Pr Manston
TB863	Spitfire LF.16					Pr Southam
TD248	Spitfire LF.16					7246M Pr Sealand
TE184	Spitfire LF.16					6850M Pr Holywood (NI)
TE311	Spitfire LF.16					7241M Pr Abingdon
TE356	Spitfire LF.16					6709M/7001M Pr Leeming
TE392	Spitfire LF.16					7000M Pr Credenhill
TE462	Spitfire LF.16					7243M Pr East Fortune
TE476	Spitfire LF.16					7451M/8071M Pr Northolt
TE566	Spitfire IX					Under Restoration
TG263	SRA.1					Ex G-12-1 Pr Duxford
TG505	Hastings T.5					Dt Pontrilas

TG511-VX461

serial	type	sqdn/unit	code	where&when seen		remarks
TG511	Hastings T.5					8554M Pr Cosford
TG517	Hastings T.5					Pr Winthorpe
TG528	Hastings C.1A					Pr Duxford
TG536	Hastings C.1A					8405M Dt Catterick
TG553	Hastings T.5					Dt Fairford
TG568	Hastings C.1A					Dt Bedford
TJ118	Mosquito TT.35					Pr Lndn Clny (fwd fus)
TJ138	Mosquito B.35					7807M Pr Swinderby
TJ343	Auster 5					G-AJXC Aw
*TJ472	Auster 5					Dt East Fortune
TJ672	Auster 5					G-ANIJ Aw
TJ707	Auster AOP.6					GI Perth (frame)
TS423	Dakota C.3					G-DAKS Aw
TS798	York C.1					See MW100
TV959	Mosquito T.3					Pr IWM Lambeth
TW117	Mosquito T.3					7805M Pr Hendon
TW439	Auster 5					G-ANRP Pr Warnham
TX183	Anson C.19					Pr Duxford
TX192	Anson C.19					Dt Guernsey
TX214	Anson C.19					7817M Pr Cosford
TX226	Anson C.19					7865M Pr L Staughton
TX228	Anson C.19					Pr Norwich
TX235	Anson C.19					Pr Higher Blagdon
VF301	Vampire F.1					7060M Pr Baginton
VH127	Firefly TT.4					Pr Yeovilton
VL348	Anson C.19					G-AVVO Pr Winthorpe
VL349	Anson C.19					G-AWSA Pr Flixton
VM325	Anson C.19					Pr Halfpenny Green
VM360	Anson C.19					G-APHV Pr East Fortune
*VM791	Cadet TX.3					Pr Halton
VN148	Grunau Baby					Pr Duxford
VP293	Shackleton T.4					Pr Strathallan
VP953	Devon C.2					Dt Manston
VP956	Devon C.2					Dt Manston
VP960	Devon C.2					Dt Manston
VP973	Devon C.2					8512M Dt Manston
VP974	Devon C.2					Dt Catterick
VP978	Devon C.2					8553M Dt Brize Norton
VR137	Wyvern TF.1					Pr Yeovilton
VR249	Prentice T.1					G-APIY Pr Winthorpe
VR930	Sea Fury FB.11					8382M Pr Wroughton
VS356	Prentice T.1					G-AOLU Pr Strathallan
VS562	Anson T.21					8012M Pr Llanbedr
VS610	Prentice T.1					G-AOKL Aw
VS623	Prentice T.1					GI Shoreham
VT229	Meteor F.4					7151M Pr Duxford
VT260	Meteor F.4					Dt Winterbourne Gunner
VT812	Vampire F.3					7200M Pr Hendon
VT921	Grunau Baby					Pr Honington
VT935	B.P. 111A					Pr Baginton
VV106	S.510					7175M Pr Cosford
VV217	Vampire FB.5					7323M Pr Bury St Edmunds
VV901	Anson T.21					Pr Burtonwood
VW453	Meteor T.7					Dt Porton Down
VW837	Valetta C.1					Dt Aldergrove
VX272	P.1052					7174M Pr Cosford
VX302	Sea Fury T.20					G-BCOV Aw
VX461	Vampire FB.5					7646M Pr Henlow

VX573-WF387

serial	type	sqdn/unit	code	where&when seen		remarks
VX573	Valetta C.2					8389M Pr Cosford
VX577	Valetta C.2					Pr Usworth
VX580	Valetta C.2					Pr Norwich
VX595	Dragonfly HR.5					Pr Henlow
VX653	Sea Fury FB.11					Pr Hendon
VZ304	Vampire FB.5					7630M Pr Duxford
VZ462	Meteor F.8					Pr Lasham
VZ608	Meteor FR.9					Pr Winthorpe
VZ634	Meteor T.7					Pr Wattisham
VZ638	Meteor T.7					Pr Southend
VZ728	Desford					G-AGOS Aw Strathallan
VZ962	Dragonfly HR.5					GI BRNC Dartmouth
VZ965	Dragonfly HR.5					Pr Culdrose
WA473	Attacker F.1					Pr Yeovilton
WA577	Sycamore HR.3					7718M Pr Shirley
WA591	Meteor T.7					7917M Pr Woodvale
WA634	Meteor T.7 Special					MBA634 Pr St Athan
WA984	Meteor F.8					Pr Wimborne
WB188	Hunter F.3					7154M Pr St Athan
WB491	Ashton 2					Dt Dunsfold (fuselage)
WB535	Devon C.2					Dt Otterburn
WB588	Chipmunk T.10					G-AOTD ntu
WB670	Chipmunk T.10					Pr London Colney
WB685	Chipmunk T.10					Pr Harrogate
WB758	Chipmunk T.10					7729M Pr H Blagdon
WB763	Chipmunk T.10					GI Southall G-BBMR ntu
WB847	Shackleton T.4					8020M Dt Kinloss
WD356	Chipmunk T.10					7625M Pr Nostell
WD413	Anson T.21					G-BFIR Under Rest'n
WD480	Hastings C.2					Dt Farnborough
WD496	Hastings C.2					Dt Boscombe Down
WD499	Hastings C.2					Dt Honington
WD646	Meteor TT.20					8189M Pr Sheldon
WD686	Meteor NF.11					Pr Duxford
WD833	Firefly AS.6					Pr Strathallan
WD909	Firefly AS.6					Dt Failsworth
WD918	Firefly AS.6					Dt Failsworth
WD935	Canberra B.2					8440M Pr St Athan
WD948	Canberra B.2					8530M Dt Manston
WE139	Canberra PR.3					8369M Pr Hendon
WE145	Canberra PR.3					7843M/8597M Dt Wyton
WE146	Canberra PR.3					Dt Llanbedr
WE168	Canberra PR.3					8049M Pr Manston
WE600	Auster T.7					7602M Pr St Athan
*WE726	Sea Fury FB.11					WJ231 Pr Yeovilton
WE925	Meteor F.8					Pr Rhoose
WF125	Sea Prince T.1					A2674 Dt Predannack
WF137	Sea Prince C.1					Pr Lasham
WF219	Sea Hawk F.1					A2439 Pr Yeovilton
WF225	Sea Hawk F.1					A2645 Pr Culdrose
WF259	Sea Hawk F.2					A2483 Pr East Fortune
WF299	Sea Hawk FB.5					A2509 Pr St Agnes
WF328	Varsity T.1					Dt Waddington
WF369	Varsity T.1					Pr Winthorpe
WF371	Varsity T.1					Dt Manston
WF372	Varsity T.1					Pr Sibson
WF376	Varsity T.1					GI Lulsgate
WF387	Varsity T.1					Dt Predannack

WF408-WJ886

serial	type	sqdn/unit	code	where&when seen		remarks
WF408	Varsity T.1					8395M Pr Cosford
WF410	Varsity T.1					GI Lulsgate
WF413	Varsity T.1					Dt Manston
WF414	Varsity T.1					Dt Finningley
WF417	Varsity T.1					Dt Aberporth
WF425	Varsity T.1					Pr Duxford
WF427	Varsity T.1					Dt Shawbury
WF643	Meteor F.8					Pr Flixton
WF784	Meteor T.7					7895M Pr Quedgeley
WF825	Meteor T.7					8359M Pr Lyneham
WF877	Meteor T.7 Special					Pr Higher Blagdon
WF922	Canberra PR.3					Dt Teversham
WG316	Chipmunk T.10					G-BCAH Aw
WG348	Chipmunk T.10					G-BBMV Aw
WG422	Chipmunk T.10					G-BFAX Aw
WG465	Chipmunk T.10					G-BCEY Aw
WG475	Chipmunk T.10					7989M/G-BFDC St N'ards
WG670	Dragonfly HR.5					Pr Southend
WG718	Dragonfly HR.5					A2531 Pr Rhoose
WG719	Dragonfly HR.5					G-BRMA Pr Weston-s-M
WG724	Dragonfly HR.5					Pr Usworth
WG725	Dragonfly HR.3					7703M Pr M Wallop
WG752	Dragonfly HR.5					Pr Dulwich
WG760	P.1A					7755M Pr Henlow
WG763	P.1A					7816M Pr Henlow
WG768	SB.5					8005M Pr Cosford
WG774	BAC 221					Pr Yeovilton
WG777	FD.2					7986M Pr Cosford
WH132	Meteor T.7					7906M Pr Chelmsford
WH166	Meteor T.7					8052M Pr Digby
WH291	Meteor F.8					Pr Kemble (Aw/Cn)
WH301	Meteor F.8					7930M Pr Hendon
WH364	Meteor F.8					8169M Pr Kemble
*WH456	Meteor F.8					WL169 Pr St Athan
WH589	Sea Fury FB.11					G-AGHB Dt Elstree
WH657	Canberra B.2					Dt Godalming
WH723	Canberra B.2					Dt Foulness
WH725	Canberra B.2					Pr Duxford
WH791	Canberra PR.7					8187M Pr Cottesmore
WH793	Canberra PR.7/9					Ex Farnborough
WH840	Canberra T.4					8350M Pr Locking
WH903	Canberra T.19					Dt Marham
WH946	Canberra B.6					Dt Pontrilas
WH952	Canberra B.6					GI Bedford
WH991	Dragonfly HR.5					Pr Tattershall
WJ231	Sea Fury FB.11					See WE726
WJ244	Sea Fury FB.11					G-FURY Under Rest'n
WJ288	Sea Fury FB.11					Pr Southend
WJ338	Hastings C.2					Dt Salisbury Plain
WJ350	Sea Prince C.2					Dt Guernsey
WJ568	Canberra T.4					Dt Teversham
WJ573	Canberra B.2					7656M Pr Henlow
WJ620	Canberra B.2					Dt Manston
WJ627	Canberra B.2					Dt Bedford
WJ635	Canberra B.2					Dt St Mawgan
WJ638	Canberra B.2(mod)					Dt Predannack
WJ676	Canberra B.2					7796M Pr Wroughton
WJ728	Canberra B.2					GI Farnborough
WJ886	Varsity T.1					Dt Brize Norton

WJ896-WN310

serial	type	sqdn/unit	code	where&when seen		remarks
WJ896	Varsity T.1					Dt Catterick
WJ897	Varsity T.1					G-BDFT Aw
WJ898	Varsity T.1					Dt Aldergrove
WJ902	Varsity T.1					Dt Wittering
WJ903	Varsity T.1					Dt Glasgow
WJ907	Varsity T.1					Dt Norwich
WJ909	Varsity T.1					Pr Sibson
WJ916	Varsity T.1					Dt Lyneham
WJ919	Varsity T.1					Dt Finningley
WJ944	Varsity T.1					Pr Rhoose
WJ945	Varsity T.1					G-BEDV Aw
WK119	Canberra B.2					Dt St Mawgan
WK145	Canberra B.2					Dt Llanbedr
WK198	Swift F.4					7428M Dt Failsworth
WK214	Swift F.4					7427M Dt Failsworth
WK275	Swift F.4					Dt Upperhill
WK277	Swift FR.5					7719M Pr Winthorpe
WK281	Swift FR.5					7712M Pr St Athan
WK509	Chipmunk T.10					Dt Biggin Hill
WK515	Chipmunk T.10					Dt Middle Wallop
WK549	Chipmunk T.10					Dt Currock Hill
WK564	Chipmunk T.10					Dt Husbands Bosworth
WK575	Chipmunk T.10					Dt Bury St Edmunds
WK654	Meteor F.8					8092M Pr Neatishead
WK914	Meteor F.8					Under Restoration
WK935	Meteor Prone Pilot					7869M Pr Cosford
WK968	Meteor F.8					8053M Pr Odiham
WK991	Meteor F.8					7825M Pr Duxford
WL161	Meteor F.8					GI Brunel Tech Coll
WL169	Meteor F.8					7750M See WH456
WL181	Meteor F.8					Pr Usworth
WL332	Meteor T.7					Pr Rhoose
WL345	Meteor T.7					Pr Hastings
WL349	Meteor T.7					Pr Staverton
WL360	Meteor T.7					7920M Pr Locking
WL375	Meteor T.7					Pr Dumfries
WL405	Meteor T.7					GI Farnborough
WL505	Vampire FB.9					7705M Pr St Athan
WL626	Varsity T.1					G-BHDD Pr Castle Don
WL627	Varsity T.1					8488M Dt Newton
WL628	Varsity T.1					Dt Wattisham
WL629	Varsity T.1					Dt Catterick
WL678	Varsity T.1					Dt Leeds-Bradford
WL732	Sea Balliol T.21					Pr Cosford
WL738	Shackleton MR.2/3					8567M Pr Lossiemouth
WM167	Meteor TT.20					Pr Blackbushe
WM224	Meteor TT.20					8177M Pr North Weald
WM292	Meteor TT.20					Pr Yeovilton
WM367	Meteor NF.13					Dt Boscombe Down
WM571	Sea Venom FAW.21					Pr Innsworth
WM756	Sea Prince C.2					Dt Yeovilton
WM913	Sea Hawk FB.5					A2510 Pr Fleetwood
WM961	Sea Hawk FB.5					A2517 Pr H Blagdon
WM969	Sea Hawk FB.5					A2530 Pr Duxford
WM983	Sea Hawk FB.5					A2511 Pr Helston
WM993	Sea Hawk FB.5					A2522 Pr Royal Arthur
WM994	Sea Hawk FB.5					A2503 Pr Swansea
WN108	Sea Hawk FB.5					GI Sydenham
WN310	Meteor T.7					Dt Catterick

WN464-WV483

serial	type	sqdn/unit	code	where&when seen		remarks
WN464	Gannet AS.6					A2540 Pr Helston
WN493	Dragonfly HR.5					Pr Yeovilton
WN499	Dragonfly HR.5					Pr Higher Blagdon
WN904	Hunter F.2					7544M Pr Duxford
*WP180	Hunter F.5					WP190 Pr Stanbridge
WP185	Hunter F.5					7583M Pr Hendon
WP190	Hunter F.5					7582M/8473M See WP180
WP270	Eton TX.1					8598M Pr Hendon
WP309	Sea Prince T.1					Dt Yeovilton
WP497	Dragonfly HR.5					Pr Uttoxeter
WP503	Dragonfly HR.3					Pr Elsham
WP790	Chipmunk T.10					G-BBNC Pr London Clny
WP800	Chipmunk T.10					G-BCXN Aw
WP808	Chipmunk T.10					G-BDEU Aw
WP835	Chipmunk T.10					G-BDCB Aw
WP851	Chipmunk T.10					G-BDET Aw
WP857	Chipmunk T.10					G-BDRJ Aw
WP870	Chipmunk T.10					G-BCOI Aw
WP912	Chipmunk T.10					8467M Pr Cosford
WP913	Chipmunk T.10					Dt Biggin Hill
WP969	Chipmunk T.10					G-ATHC Dt Sherburn
WR977	Shackleton MR.3/3					8186M Pr Winthorpe
WR984	Shackleton MR.3/3					8115M Dt Topcliffe
WS103	Meteor T.7					Pr Wroughton
WS726	Meteor NF(T).14					7960M Pr Royton
WS739	Meteor NF(T).14					7961M Pr Misson
WS760	Meteor NF(T).14					7964M Pr Duxford
WS774	Meteor NF(T).14					7959M Pr Ely
WS776	Meteor NF(T).14					7716M Pr N Luffenham
WS788	Meteor NF(T).14					7967M Pr Leeming
WS792	Meteor NF(T).14					7965M Pr Carlisle
WS807	Meteor NF(T).14					7973M Pr Watton
WS832	Meteor NF.14					Pr Carlisle
WS838	Meteor NF.14					Pr Cosford
WS840	Meteor NF(T).14					7969M Dt Aldergrove
WS843	Meteor NF(T).14					7937M Pr St Athan
WT121	Skyraider AEW.1					Pr Yeovilton
WT301	Canberra B.6(mod)					GI Chattenden
WT305	Canberra B.6(mod)					8511M Pr Wyton
WT319	Canberra B(I).6					GI Filton
WT346	Canberra B(I).8					8197M Pr Cosford
WT486	Canberra T.4					8102M Dt Aldergrove
WT520	Canberra PR.7					8184M Pr Swinderby
WT555	Hunter F.1					7499M Pr Cosford
WT569	Hunter F.1					7491M Pr Kenfig Hill
WT612	Hunter F.1					7496M Pr Credenhill
WT616	Hunter F.1					Dt Weston-super-Mare
WT619	Hunter F.1					7525M Pr Henlow
WT651	Hunter F.1					7532M Pr Credenhill
WT660	Hunter F.1					7421M Pr Carlisle
WT680	Hunter F.1					7533M Pr Aberporth
WT683	Hunter F.1					7535M Dt Speke
WT694	Hunter F.1					7510M Pr Newton
WT933	Sycamore HR.14					7709M Pr Sutton in Afd
WV106	Skyraider AEW.1					Pr Helston
WV381	Hunter GA.11					GI Culham (fuselage)
WV395	Hunter F.4					8001M Dt Dunsfold
WV444	Provost T.1					7692M Dt M Wallop
WV483	Provost T.1					7693M Pr Southend

WV493-WZ584

serial	type	sqdn/unit	code	where&when seen		remarks
WV493	Provost T.1					G-BDYG/7696M Aw Stlln
WV494	Provost T.1					G-BGSB/7922M Aw Bgntn
WV495	Provost T.1					7697M Pr Sutton in Afd
WV499	Provost T.1					7698M Pr St Athan
WV505	Provost T.1					Dt Oxford
WV538	Provost T.1					Dt Failsworth
WV544	Provost T.1					7700M Dt Netheravon
WV562	Provost T.1					7606M Pr Cosford
WV605	Provost T.1					Pr Flixton
WV606	Provost T.1					7622M Pr Winthorpe
WV614	Provost T.1					GI St Albans
WV679	Provost T.1					7615M Pr H Blagdon
WV703	Pembroke C.1					8108M Dt Coningsby
WV704	Pembroke C.1					8109M Dt Benson
WV733	Pembroke C.1					Dt Otterburn
WV735	Pembroke C.1					Dt Binbrook
WV753	Pembroke C.1					8113M Pr Rhoose
WV754	Pembroke C.1					Dt Catterick
WV781	Sycamore HR.12					7839M Pr Odiham
WV783	Sycamore HR.12					7841M Pr Henlow
WV795	Sea Hawk FGA.6					8151M Pr Rhoose
WV798	Sea Hawk FGA.6					A2557 Pr Thorpe Wat Pk
WV826	Sea Hawk FGA.6					A2532 Pr Swansea
WV831	Sea Hawk FGA.6					A2558 GI Fareham
WV856	Sea Hawk FGA.6					Pr Yeovilton
WW138	Sea Venom ECM.22					Pr Yeovilton
WW145	Sea Venom FAW.22					Pr East Fortune
WW217	Sea Venom FAW.22					Pr Ottershaw
WW220	Sea Venom FAW.22					Dt Sydenham
WW388	Provost T.1					7616M Pr Thorpe Wat Pk
WW391	Provost T.1					Dt Failsworth
WW397	Provost T.1					8060M Pr Lyneham
WW421	Provost T.1					7688M Pr Lytham St Ann'
WW442	Provost T.1					7618M GI Kidlington
WW444	Provost T.1					GI Bitteswell
WW453	Provost T.1					GI Perth
WX788	Venom NF.3					Pr Rhoose
WX853	Venom NF.3					7443M Pr London Colney
WX905	Venom NF.3					7458M Pr Henlow
WZ415	Vampire T.11					Dt Keevil
WZ416	Vampire T.11					Pr Hatfield (town)
WZ425	Vampire T.11					Pr Rhoose
WZ450	Vampire T.11					Pr Tile Cross
WZ458	Vampire T.11					Dt Foulness
WZ464	Vampire T.11					Dt Duxford
WZ476	Vampire T.11					Pr London Colney
WZ505	Vampire T.11					(Ex Bramhall)
WZ507	Vampire T.11					G-VTII Aw
WZ511	Vampire T.11					Pr Duxford
WZ514	Vampire T.11					Pr Birkenhead
WZ515	Vampire T.11					Pr Duxford
WZ518	Vampire T.11					Pr Usworth
WZ549	Vampire T.11					8118M Pr Tattershall
WZ550	Vampire T.11					7902M Dt Pontrilas
WZ553	Vampire T.11					Pr Castle Donington
WZ557	Vampire T.11					Pr Huntingdon
WZ576	Vampire T.11					8174M Pr Appleby
WZ581	Vampire T.11					Dt Keevil
WZ584	Vampire T.11					GI St Albans

WZ589-WZ821

serial	type	sqdn/unit	code	where&when seen		remarks
WZ589	Vampire T.11					Pr Headcorn
WZ590	Vampire T.11					Pr Duxford
WZ608	Vampire T.11					Dt Bitteswell
WZ616	Vampire T.11					Dt Keevil
WZ620	Vampire T.11					Dt Keevil
WZ662	Auster AOP.9					Pr Rhoose
*WZ670	Auster AOP.9					WZ724 Pr Middle Wallop
WZ672	Auster AOP.9					G-BDER Aw
WZ679	Auster AOP.9					'7822M' GI Marlborough
WZ706	Auster AOP.9					GI Shrivenham
WZ711	Auster AOP.9					G-AVHT Aw
WZ721	Auster AOP.9					Pr Middle Wallop
WZ724	Auster AOP.9					See WZ670
WZ736	Avro 707A					7868M Pr Cosford
WZ744	Avro 707C					7932M Pr Cosford
WZ775	Grasshopper TX.1					
WZ821	Grasshopper TX.1					

LATE ADDITIONS

serial	type	sqdn/unit	code	where&when seen		remarks
K5457	Hind					Under Restoration
*L6906	Magister					Ex G-AKKY Under Rest'n
WA576	Sycamore HR.14					Pr Strathallan
WP778	Chipmunk T.10					G-BBNF Aw

STATIC REPLICAS

serial	type	sqdn/unit	code	where&when seen		remarks
6232	BE.2C					St Athan
8151	Baby					Thorpe Water Park
A1742	Scout D					St Athan
B4863	SE.5A					Thorpe Water Park
C4912	Bristol M.1C					Thorpe Water Park
D3419	Camel					St Athan
F344	Avro 504K					Henlow
F373	Avro 504K					Henlow
H1968	Avro 504K					St Athan
K7271	Fury II					Cosford
L1592	Hurricane I					Higher Blagdon
N5492	Triplane					Thorpe Water Park
XX162	Hawk T.1					RAF Exhibition Flt
XX732	Jaguar GR.1					RAF Exhibition Flt
XX824	Jaguar GR.1					RAF Exhibition Flt

HISTORICAL AIRCRAFT PRESERVED ABROAD

serial	type	sqdn/unit	code	where&when seen	remarks

AUSTRALIA

serial	type	sqdn/unit	code	where&when seen	remarks
*C9539	SE.5A				Ex A2-4 Pr Canberra
F1287	DH.9				Pr Canberra
P7973	Spitfire IIA				Pr Canberra
R9883	Anson I				Ex VH-AGA Pr Narellan
W4783	Lancaster I				Pr Canberra
Z7212	Proctor C.3				Ex VH-BXU Pr Narellan
BL628	Spitfire VB				Pr North Ryde
EE853	Spitfire VC				Pr Parafield
EZ999	Vengeance IA				Pr Narellan
HR621	Mosquito FB.VI				Pr Narellan
JN200	Sea Otter I				Pr Nowra (fwd fus)
LZ842	Spitfire IX				Pr Point Cook
MV154	Spitfire VIII				Ex A58-671 Pr Bankstown
MV239	Spitfire VIII				Pr Narellan (sections)
*NP336	Proctor C.4				Ex VH-BCM Pr Narellan
NX622	Lancaster B.7				Ex WU-16 Pr Perth
PK481	Spitfire F.22				Pr Jandakot
RM797	Spitfire F.XIV				Ex '16' RThAF Pr Darwin
TE384	Spitfire LF.16				Ex 7207M Pr Narellan
VW623	Sea Fury FB.11				Pr Nowra
VW647	Sea Fury FB.11				Pr Narellan
VX388	Firefly TT.6				Pr Narellan
VX730	Sea Fury FB.11				Pr Sydney
WB518	Firefly TT.6				Pr Griffith
WD280	Avro 707A				Pr Melbourne
WD647	Meteor TT.20				Pr Archerfield
WD767	Meteor TT.20				Pr Mildura
WD826	Firefly TT.6				Pr Nowra
WD827	Firefly AS.6				Pr Point Cook
WD828	Firefly TT.6				Pr Moorabbin
WD954	Canberra T.4				Pr Mildura
WG630	Sea Fury FB.11				TI CEBS Ryde, Sydney
WH700	Canberra U.10				Dt Edinburgh
WJ109	Firefly TT.6				Pr Nowra
WK165	Canberra U.10				Dt Edinburgh
WK507	Chipmunk T.10				VH-SSJ Aw
WP919	Chipmunk T.10				VH-AFL Aw
WZ895	Sea Venom FAW.53				GI Nowra
WZ898	Sea Venom FAW.53				GI Schofields
WZ903	Sea Venom FAW.53				Pr Mildura
WZ907	Sea Venom FAW.53				Pr Narellan
WZ910	Sea Venom FAW.53				GI Ultimo
WZ911	Sea Venom FAW.53				Pr Chewing Gum Field
WZ931	Sea Venom FAW.53				Pr Nowra
WZ937	Sea Venom FAW.53				GI Schofields
WZ943	Sea Venom FAW.53				Pr Nowra (town)
WZ944	Sea Venom TT.53				Pr Mildura
WZ945	Sea Venom FAW.53				Pr Narellan (fuselage)
WZ946	Sea Venom FAW.53				Pr Bankstown

BELGIUM

serial	type	sqdn/unit	code	where&when seen	remarks
B5747	F.1 Camel				Pr Brussels
T9800	Magister I				Ex OO-NIC Pr Brussels
*LF345	Hurricane IIC				LF658 Pr Brussels
LF658	Hurricane IIC				See LF345

serial	type	sqdn/unit	code	where&when seen		remarks
MJ360	Spitfire LF.IXC					Ex SM-15 Pr Brussels

CANADA

serial	type	sqdn/unit	code	where&when seen		remarks
4112	BE.2C					Pr Ottawa
*A1958	Avro 504K Replica					Pr Ottawa
*A4737	Nieuport 12					Pr Ottawa
*B1566	Nieuport17 Replica					C-FDDK Pr Ottawa
*B2167	Pup Replica					C-FRFC Aw Ottawa
*B9913	Spad S.7 Replica					Pr Ottawa French marks
E6938	7F.1 Snipe					Pr Ottawa
E8107	7F.1 Snipe					Pr Ottawa (fuselage)
L7180	Hind					Pr Ottawa
*N5492	Triplane Replica					C-FCBM Aw Ottawa
N8156	2F.1 Camel					Pr Ottawa
P8332	Spitfire IIB					Pr Ottawa
R7384	Battle I(T)					Pr Ottawa
*R9003	Lysander III					Pr Ottawa (composite)
*T9422	Hudson IIIA					BW769 Pr Gander
V9312	Lysander IIIT					Pr Saskatchewan
AR614	Spitfire VC					Ex 5378M Pr Kapuskasing
BW769	Hudson IIIA					See T9422
FM104	Lancaster B.10					Pr Toronto
FM136	Lancaster 10-MP					Pr Calgary
FM159	Lancaster 10-MP					Pr Nanton
FM212	Lancaster B.10					Pr Windsor
FM213	Lancaster 10-MR					Pr Hamilton
*HD372	B-25J					C-GCWM Aw Hamilton
*HR151	Mosquito B.35					VP189 Pr Edmonton
HS517	Swordfish II					Dt London
HS554	Swordfish II					Pr Muirkirk
KA114	Mosquito FB.26					Dt Surrey, Vancouver
KB336	Mosquito B.20					Pr Ottawa
KB882	Lancaster 10-AR					Pr St Jacques
KB889	Lancaster 10-MP					Pr Oshawa
KB944	Lancaster B.10					Pr Ottawa
KB994	Lancaster B.10					Pr St Albert (fuselage)
*KD658	FG-1D Corsair					C-GCWX Aw Malton
KN451	Dakota C.4					Pr Ottawa
NH188	Spitfire LF.IX					Ex CF-NUS Pr Ottawa
*NS122	Swordfish III					Pr Ottawa
PK286	Oxford I					Ex G-AIKR Pr Ottawa
PM627	Spitfire PR.19					Ex HS964 IAF Pr Hamilton
PR410	Seafire F.15					See PR451
*PR451	Seafire F.15					PR410 Pr Tecumseh
PR503	Seafire F.15					Pr Buttonville
RD867	Beaufighter TT.10					Pr Ottawa
TD135	Spitfire LF.16					Ex 6798M Pr
TE214	Spitfire LF.16					Pr Ottawa
TE308	Spitfire T.IX					C-FRAF Aw
TG119	Sea Fury FB.11					Pr Ottawa
TG372	Vampire F.1					Pr Ottawa
*VF582	Auster AOP.6					Ex CF-KBV Pr Ottawa
VP189	Mosquito B.35					See HR151
VR796	Mosquito B.35					Ex CF-HML Pr Kapuskasing
WD840	Firefly AS.6					C-FCBH Aw Carman
WG565	Sea Fury FB.11					Pr Tecumseh
WH632	Firefly AS.6					Pr Shearwater

serial	type	sqdn/unit	code	where&when seen	remarks

CYPRUS

serial	type	sqdn/unit	code	where&when seen	remarks
WJ768	Canberra B.6(mod)				Dt Akrotiri

CZECHOSLOVAKIA

serial	type	sqdn/unit	code	where&when seen	remarks
TE565	Spitfire LF.IX				Pr Prague

DENMARK

serial	type	sqdn/unit	code	where&when seen	remarks
LB381	Auster AOP.1				OY-DSH Aw Stauning

FINLAND

serial	type	sqdn/unit	code	where&when seen	remarks
K5271	Gauntlet II				Pr Halli (frame only)

FRANCE

serial	type	sqdn/unit	code	where&when seen	remarks
9969	BE.2C				Pr Paris
F1258	DH.9				Pr Paris
K2570	Tiger Moth T.2				Pr Villacoublay
AJ561	Harvard II				Dt Rochefort
BS464	Spitfire IX				Pr Le Bourget
FS614	Argus II				Pr Etampes
PP972	Seafire III				Under Restoration
RR263	Spitfire LF.16				See TB597
*TB597	Spitfire LF.16				RR263 Pr Le Bourget
VX950	Vampire FB.5				Pr Mas Pelegry

GREECE

serial	type	sqdn/unit	code	where&when seen	remarks
MJ755	Spitfire IX				Pr Athens

GREENLAND

serial	type	sqdn/unit	code	where&when seen	remarks
WD492	Hastings C.2				Dt on ice cap

HONG KONG

serial	type	sqdn/unit	code	where&when seen	remarks
T6645	Tiger Moth T.2				G-AIIZ Aw Sek Kong
VN485	Spitfire F.24				7326M Pr Kai Tak

INDIA

serial	type	sqdn/unit	code	where&when seen	remarks
V6846	Hurricane I				Pr Patna
AP832	Hurricane IIB				Pr Palam
FT105	Harvard IIB				Pr Dehradun
NH631	Spitfire LF.VIII				Pr Palam

IRELAND

serial	type	sqdn/unit	code	where&when seen	remarks
VM659	Cadet TX.2				Dt Castlebridge

ISRAEL

serial	type	sqdn/unit	code	where&when seen	remarks
	Hurricane				Dt Jaffa

serial	type	sqdn/unit	code	where&when seen	remarks

KENYA

serial	type	sqdn/unit	code	where&when seen	remarks
WR493	Venom FB.4				Dt Embakasi

LIBYA

serial	type	sqdn/unit	code	where&when seen	remarks
	Blenheim IV				Dt in desert

MALTA

serial	type	sqdn/unit	code	where&when seen	remarks
N5519	Sea Gladiator				Pr Valletta
BR108	Spitfire VC				Pr Valletta (fwd fus)
VX574	Valetta C.2				Dt Luqa
WT482	Canberra T.4				Pr Hal Far

NETHERLANDS

serial	type	sqdn/unit	code	where&when seen	remarks
FR193	Mitchell II				Pr Overloon
MZ236	Auster AOP.3				Ex PH-NGH Pr Gilze Rijen
PL965	Spitfire PR.XI				Pr Overloon
WZ868	Chipmunk T.10				G-BCIW Aw

NEW ZEALAND

serial	type	sqdn/unit	code	where&when seen	remarks
*B168	SE.5A Replica				ZK- Aw
*K1790	Fury II Replica				ZK-DMN Aw
L8353	Magister				Ex ZK-AYW Pr Auckland
AE503	Hudson III				Pr Christchurch
HM579	Moth Minor				ZK-BFP Aw Ardmore
*ND752	Lancaster B.7				NX665 Pr Auckland
NX665	Lancaster B.7				See ND752, PB457
*PB457	Lancaster B.7				NX665 Pr Auckland
TE288	Spitfire LF.16				Pr Christchurch
TE456	Spitfire LF.16				Pr Auckland
WR202	Vampire FB.9				Ex NZ1717 Pr Auckland

NIUGINI

serial	type	sqdn/unit	code	where&when seen	remarks
FL461	Fortress I				Dt

NORWAY

serial	type	sqdn/unit	code	where&when seen	remarks
N5579	Gladiator II				Pr Rygge
N6972	Tiger Moth T.2				Ex 6317M Pr Gardermoen
MH350	Spitfire LF.IXE				Pr Bodo
PL979	Spitfire PR.XI				Pr Rygge

OMAN

serial	type	sqdn/unit	code	where&when seen	remarks
WV501	Provost T.1				Dt Bait Al Falaj

POLAND

serial	type	sqdn/unit	code	where&when seen	remarks
B7280	F.1 Camel				Pr Krakow
SM411	Spitfire LF.16				Ex 7242M Pr Krakow

SAUDI ARABIA

serial	type	sqdn/unit	code	where&when seen		remarks
WW447	Provost T.1					GI

SINGAPORE

serial	type	sqdn/unit	code	where&when seen		remarks
WA880	Meteor TT.8					SAFTECH 2 GI Changi
WH410	Meteor T.7					SAFTECH 3 Dt Changi

SOUTH AFRICA

serial	type	sqdn/unit	code	where&when seen		remarks
KK537	Argus III					Ex ZS-BAH Pr Lanseria
LR480	Mosquito PR.IX					Pr Johannesburg
MA793	Spitfire IX					See PT672
*PT672	Spitfire IX					MA793 Aw Lanseria
PV260	Spitfire LF.IX					Pr Salt River
VS609	Prentice T.1					ZS-EUS Pr Lanseria
WV203	Whirlwind HAS.22					Ex ZS-HDO Pr Lanseria
WV224	Whirlwind HAS.22					St Johannesburg

SPAIN

serial	type	sqdn/unit	code	where&when seen		remarks
JV111	Hellcat I					Dt Rosas

SWEDEN

serial	type	sqdn/unit	code	where&when seen		remarks
NF920	Lancaster I					Dt Porjus
WP867	Chipmunk T.10					SE-FNP Aw

THAILAND

serial	type	sqdn/unit	code	where&when seen		remarks
PS836	Spitfire PR.19					Dt Chieng Mei

UNION OF SOVIET SOCIALIST REPUBLICS

serial	type	sqdn/unit	code	where&when seen		remarks
	Triplane					N5486 (?) Pr Monino

UNITED STATES OF AMERICA

serial	type	sqdn/unit	code	where&when seen		remarks
*2984	BE.2C Replica					N1914B Aw Bealeton VT
*A635	Pup Replica					Aw Meadowlark CA
A2169	DH.4					Ex NX3258 Pr Santee SC
B3182	Avro 504J					Aw Boise ID
*B6313	Camel Replica					Aw Rhinebeck NY
B7270	F.1 Camel					N86678 Pr Orlando FL
B9913	Spad S.7					Aw Livermore CA
*E2939	Avro 504 Replica					Aw Rhinebeck NY
E6949	7F.1 Snipe					See E8105
*E8105	7F.1 Snipe					E6949 Pr Rhinebeck NY
*F6034	Camel Replica					Pr Wright-Patterson OH
*N5139	Pup Replica					Aw Rhinebeck NY
*N6254	F.1 Camel					Pr Santee SC
*N6459	Pup Replica					Aw Flabob CA
P9306	Spitfire IA					Pr Chicago IL
*R8731	Tiger Moth T.2					N8731R Aw Rhinebeck NY
AJ311	Ventura II					Pr Minneapolis MN
AK987	Kittyhawk IB					Pr Wright-Patterson OH
EN474	Spitfire HF.VII					Pr Washington DC
FF860	Bermuda I					Pr Barstow-Daggett CA
LF686	Hurricane IIC					Pr Washington DC

serial	type	sqdn/unit	code	where&when seen		remarks
MK297	Spitfire IX					NX913L Aw Harlingen TX
MK923	Spitfire IX					N93081 Aw Chicago IL
PM630	Spitfire PR.19					Pr CA
PS890	Spitfire PR.19					Pr Chino CA
SL721	Spitfire LF.16					N8WK Aw Phoenix AZ
TE330	Spitfire LF.16					Pr Wright-Patterson OH
TH998	Mosquito TT.35					Pr Washington DC
TZ138	Spitfire F.14					Pr
VP441	Seafire F.47					Pr San Marcos
WG364	Chipmunk T.10					N68030 Aw Palm Cnty FL
WJ948	Varsity T.1					N65388 Pr Winder
WR539	Venom FB.4					Pr Miami FL
WZ873	Chipmunk T.10					St Fort Lauderdale FL

WEST GERMANY

serial	type	sqdn/unit	code	where&when seen		remarks
PG732	Tiger Moth T.2					Pr Tegel
TG503	Hastings T.5					8555M Pr Gatow
WF382	Varsity T.1					Dt Gatow
WH792	Canberra PR.7					8095M Dt Laarbruch
WH804	Canberra PR.7					8126M Dt Laarbruch
WJ491	Valetta C.1					Dt Gatow
WT332	Canberra B(I).8					8200M Dt Bruggen
WT336	Canberra B(I).8					Dt Gutersloh
WT345	Canberra B(I).8					8150M Dt Laarbruch
WT512	Canberra PR.7					8093M Dt Bruggen
WT513	Canberra PR.7					8065M Dt Laarbruch
WT516	Canberra PR.7					8068M Dt Laarbruch
WT524	Canberra PR.7					8136M Dt Laarbruch
WT527	Canberra PR.7					8137M Dt Laarbruch

ZIMBABWE

serial	type	sqdn/unit	code	where&when seen		remarks
PK350	Spitfire F.22					Aw Salisbury

INSTRUCTIONAL AIRFRAMES

Many aircraft, having reached the end of their operational flying life, are found new roles as instructional airframes for use by the many different trades within the armed forces. When this occurs aircraft are allotted new serial numbers within special sequences evolved by the RAF, FAA and AAC. This appendix explains the origins of these serials.

"M" SERIALS

A number followed by the letter 'M' was the initial serial system encompassing RAF, Navy and Army instructional airframes, prior to the latter two services initiating their own sequences. Besides aircraft used for instructional purposes, many of those allotted to RAF stations or fire schools for fire practice or crash rescue training are allocated 'M' serials. During recent years, this practice has also spread to gate guardians and even aircraft belonging to the RAF Museum, although this is not consistent.

The enthusiast is presented with a number of problems. For example, many aircraft do not actually carry their 'M' serials, and cases also occur where the same aircraft is given more than one allocation. The reasons for this are varied and are not always clear, but are frequently no more than clerical errors. In this appendix, and the remarks column of the main text where 'M' numbers are referred to, the abbreviation 'ntu' has frequently been used, the context of which requires the following clarification. The term 'ntu' has been applied where the 'M' serial has been allocated and subsequently cancelled, and for this reason is not taken up. Official records go back as far as 1940 (when 2001M was allotted) and it is not known exactly where allocations started, whether at 1M, or at some later number. To date the earliest allocation known is 540M, a Bristol Fighter. In this publication it has been decided to list from 7000M onwards, as this covers the period of the main text, ie XA100 onwards.

"A" SERIALS

When the Navy first started using aircraft for instructional use they were allotted 'M' serials due to the fact that all Naval aircraft at that time came under the jurisdiction of the Royal Air Force. Control passed to the Royal Navy on 24th May 1939 and it was decided that the Fleet Air Arm should have their own system of instructional airframe serials. This they achieved in early 1942 in the form of consecutive numbers prefixed by the letter 'A'. The initial allocations were issued by the Rear Admiral Reserve Aircraft (RARA) and ran in the range A1 - A750. In 1948 the RARA was replaced by the Flag Officer Reserve Aircraft (FORA) and the whole range A1 - A750 was renumbered in a sequence beginning at A2000. In this publication we have listed from A2400 onwards.

Further information on this subject can be found in another BARG publication, 'Royal Navy Instructional Airframes'.

"TAD" SERIALS

Like the Navy, the Army initially used 'M' serials for their instructional airframes. In the 1960's the Army elected to start their own numbering system. This differs from the other two services in that the service serial numbers are retained and the letters 'TAD' are added in front, but needless to say there has been the odd inexplicable exception.

The Army Air Corps is the only service in the British armed forces to have received purpose-built training aids known as CIM's or Classroom Instructional Models. These examples have to date been given a numerical sequence, but only time will tell whether this practice is to continue.

ROYAL AIR FORCE INSTRUCTIONAL AIRFRAMES

7000M-7119M

7000M	Spitfire LF.16	TE392	7060M	Vampire F.1	VF301
7001M	Spitfire LF.16	TE356	7061M	Vampire F.1	VF311
7002M	Tiger Moth T.2	N6854	7062M	Vampire F.1	VF272
7003M	Tiger Moth T.2 (ntu)	DE156	7063M	Vampire F.1	TG308
7004M	Vampire F.1	TG277	7064M	Vampire F.1	TG309
7005M	Meteor F.8	WH276	7065M	Vampire F.1	TG312
7006M	Vampire F.1	TG299	7066M	Vampire F.1	TG337
7007M	Varsity T.1	WF324	7067M	Vampire F.1	TG373
7008M	Meteor F.4	EE549	7068M	Vampire F.1	TG376
7009M	Tiger Moth T.2	DE156	7069M	Vampire F.1	TG385
7010M	Spitfire FR.18	TP378	7070M	Vampire F.1	TG387
7011M	Proctor C.4	NP234	7071M	Vampire F.1	TG420
7012M	Meteor F.4	VW790	7072M	Vampire F.1	TG432
7013M	Mosquito T.3	VA882	7073M	Vampire F.1	TG442
7014M	Tiger Moth T.2	N6720	7074M	Vampire F.1	VF304
7015M	Tiger Moth T.2	NL985	7075M	Vampire F.3	VV205
7016M	Anson T.22	VS600	7076M	Vampire F.3	VF316
7017M	Brigand B.1 (ntu)	RH810	7077M	Vampire F.3	VF319
7018M	Lincoln B.2	RE312	7078M	Vampire F.3	VT801
7019M	Lincoln B.2	RF387	7079M	Vampire F.3	VT821
7020M	Lincoln B.2	RF409	7080M	Vampire F.3	VT854
7021M	Lincoln B.2	RF498	7081M	Vampire F.3	VT859
7022M	Lincoln B.2	RF363	7082M	Vampire F.3	VT810
7023M	Lincoln B.2	RF397	7083M	Vampire F.3	VF321
7024M	Lincoln B.2	RF401	7084M	Vampire F.3	VF335
7025M	Lincoln B.2	RE377	7085M	Vampire F.3	VF342
7026M	Lincoln B.2	RF390	7086M	Vampire F.3	VG697
7027M	Lincoln B.2	RF482	7087M	Vampire F.3	VT796
7028M	Lincoln B.2	RF405	7088M	Vampire F.3	VT800
7029M	Mosquito NF.36	RK959	7089M	Vampire F.3	VF332
7030M	Mosquito NF.36	RL133	7090M	Meteor F.4 (ntu)	EE531
7031M	Proctor C.3	HM345	7091M	Tiger Moth T.2 (ntu)	DE658
7032M	Proctor C.3	HM480	7092M	Tiger Moth T.2 (ntu)	T7164
7033M	Proctor C.3	Z7237	7093M	Tiger Moth T.2 (ntu)	DE854
7034M	Tiger Moth T.2	DE219	7094M	Balliol T.2	VR591
7035M	Tiger Moth T.2	DE306	7095M	Balliol T.2	VW899
7036M	Tiger Moth T.2	DE739	7096M	Meteor F.8	VZ454
7037M	Tiger Moth T.2	DE779	7097M	Prentice T.1	VR191
7038M	Tiger Moth T.2	N9385	7098M	Venom NF.2	WP227
7039M	Tiger Moth T.2	DE889	7099M	Meteor F.4	EE597
7040M	Tiger Moth T.2	N6804	7100M	Mosquito NF.30	NT471
7041M	Tiger Moth T.2	N9374	7101M	Anson C.12	PH804
7042M	Tiger Moth T.2	R5019	7102M	Lancaster B.3	PB529
7043M	Tiger Moth T.2	R5114	7103M	Anson C.12	PH749
7044M	Tiger Moth T.2	W7950	7104M	Wellington B.10	RP322
7045M	Vampire F.1	VF274	7105M	Wellington T.10	NA845
7046M	Vampire F.1	VF307	7106M	Prentice T.1	TV168
7047M	Vampire F.1	TG382	7107M	Harvard T.2B	FT303
7048M	Vampire F.1	TG429	7108M	Hastings C.1	TG559
7049M	Vampire F.1	TG437	7109M	Meteor F.4	EE470
7050M	Vampire F.1	TG440	7110M	Anson C.12	PH834
7051M	Vampire F.1	TG447	7111M	Lincoln B.2	RE321
7052M	Vampire F.1	TG289	7112M	Meteor F.3	EE272
7053M	Vampire F.1	TG300	7113M	Harvard T.2B	KF513
7054M	Vampire F.1	TG304	7114M	Auster AOP.5	TW461
7055M	Vampire F.1	TG336	7115M	Venom FB.1 (ntu)	WE417
7056M	Vampire F.1	TG371	7116M	Harvard T.2B	KF209
7057M	Vampire F.1	TG381	7117M	Anson C.12	PH586
7058M	Vampire F.1	TG389	7118M	Spitfire F.21	LA198
7059M	Vampire F.1	TG445	7119M	Spitfire F.21	LA226

7120M-7239M

7120M	Spitfire F.21	LA228	7180M	Prentice T.1	VS268
7121M	Spitfire F.21	LA263	7181M	Prentice T.1	VR241
7122M	Mosquito NF.36	RK987	7182M	Prentice T.1	VS245
7123M	Mosquito NF.36	RK997	7183M	Prentice T.1	VS263
7124M	Mosquito NF.36	RK980	7184M	Meteor F.3	EE248
7125M	Mosquito NF.36	RK990	7185M	Meteor F.3	EE359
7126M	Mosquito TT.35	RS717	7186M	Meteor F.3	EE389
7127M	Meteor F.3	EE292	7187M	Venom FB.1	WE255
7128M	Meteor F.3	EE358	7188M	Balliol T.2	VR597
7129M	Auster AOP.5	TJ396	7189M	Venom NF.3	WV928
7130M	Meteor F.4	RA434	7190M	Venom FB.1	WE267
7131M	Meteor F.4	RA435	7191M	Prentice T.1	VS368
7132M	Vampire FB.5	VZ117	7192M	Prentice T.1	VR224
7133M	Venom FB.1	WE257	7193M	Lincoln B.2	SX986
7134M	Venom FB.1	WE262	7194M	Meteor F.8	WA788
7135M	Venom FB.1	WE278	7195M	Lincoln B.2	SX978
7136M	Venom FB.1	WE273	7196M	Lincoln B.2	RE415
7137M	Venom FB.1	WE270	7197M	Vampire F.3 (ntu)	VV199
7138M	Venom FB.1	WE276	7198M	Vampire F.3 (ntu)	VT871
7139M	Venom FB.1	WE263	7199M	Vampire F.3	VT856
7140M	Venom FB.1	WE274	7200M	Vampire F.3	VT812
7141M	Meteor F.8	WA820	7201M	Vampire F.3 (ntu)	VT861
7142M	Mosquito NF.38	VT697	7202M	Vampire F.3 (ntu)	VF344
7143M	Balliol T.2	VR605	7203M	Vampire F.1	TG349
7144M	Balliol T.2	VR592	7204M	Meteor F.4	VT128
7145M	Tiger Moth T.2	DE175	7205M	Meteor F.8	WF641
7146M	Sunderland GR.5	NJ180	7206M	Swift F.1	WK203
7147M	Mosquito PR.34 (ntu)	PF677	7207M	Spitfire LF.16	TE384
7148M	Buckmaster B.1	RP151	7208M	Prentice T.1	VS627
7149M	Meteor F.8	VZ472	7209M	Meteor F.8	VZ478
7150M	Spitfire F.24	PK683	7210M	Meteor F.8	WL125
7151M	Meteor F.4	VT229	7211M	Venom FB.1	WE266
7152M	Tiger Moth T.2	N6539	7212M	Hunter F.1	WW640
7153M	Lincoln B.2	SX933	7213M	Meteor F.8	VZ480
7154M	Hunter F.3	WB188	7214M	Meteor F.8	VZ464
7155M	Chipmunk T.10	WK580	7215M	Viking 1A	VX238
7156M	Lincoln B.2 (ntu)	RF565	7216M	Spitfire LF.16	RR263
7157M	Venom FB.1	WE259	7217M	Meteor F.8	WK888
7158M	Canberra B.2	WJ765	7218M	Meteor F.8	WE943
7159M	Provost T.1	WG503	7219M	Anson C.12	PH553
7160M	Lincoln B.2	RF336	7220M	Brigand B.1 (ntu)	RH798
7161M	Balliol T.2	VR590	7221M	Meteor F.4	RA449
7162M	Venom FB.1	WE264	7222M	Meteor F.4	RA456
7163M	Meteor T.7	VW454	7223M	Meteor F.4	VT125
7164M	Lincoln B.2	WD127	7224M	Meteor F.4	VT134
7165M	Meteor F.3	EE278	7225M	Meteor F.4	VT317
7166M	Meteor F.3	EE339	7226M	Meteor F.4	VT318
7167M	Meteor F.3	EE352	7227M	Provost T.1	WW435
7168M	Meteor F.3	EE397	7228M	Venom FB.1	WE256
7169M	Meteor F.4	EE478	7229M	Harvard T.2B (ntu)	KF126
7170M	Meteor F.4	EE479	7230M	Hornet F.3	WF967
7171M	Meteor F.4	EE481	7231M	Anson T.22	VV361
7172M	Sunderland MR.5	JM667	7232M	Anson T.22	VV367
7173M	Lincoln B.2	SX931	7233M	Prentice T.1	VS275
7174M	Hawker P.1052	VX272	7234M	Prentice T.1	VS260
7175M	Supermarine 510	VV106	7235M	Vampire F.1	TG329
7176M	Vampire FB.5	VZ216	7236M	Balliol T.2	WN165
7177M	Prentice T.1	VR230	7237M	Balliol T.2	WN535
7178M	Prentice T.1	VR307	7238M	Balliol T.2	WG138
7179M	Prentice T.1	VS261	7239M	Balliol T.2	WG142

7240M-7359M

7240M	Spitfire LF.16	TE400	7300M	Swift F.2	WK240
7241M	Spitfire LF.16	TE311	7301M	Swift F.2	WK241
7242M	Spitfire LF.16	SM411	7302M	Swift F.2	WK242
7243M	Spitfire LF.16	TE462	7303M	Swift F.2	WK245
7244M	Spitfire LF.16	TB382	7304M	Swift F.1	WK210
7245M	Spitfire LF.16	RW382	7305M	Swift F.1	WK211
7246M	Spitfire LF.16	TD248	7306M	Swift F.1	WK212
7247M	Meteor F.3	EE419	7307M	Swift F.2	WK219
7248M	Meteor F.3	EE424	7308M	Swift F.2	WK220
7249M	Anson T.21	VV912	7309M	Swift F.2	WK244
7250M	Anson T.21	VS581	7310M	Swift F.1	WK197
7251M	Anson T.21	VV329	7311M	Swift F.1	WK201
7252M	Anson T.21	VV320	7312M	Swift F.1	WK205
7253M	Prentice T.1	VS250	7313M	Swift F.1	WK206
7254M	Meteor F.8	WH357	7314M	Swift F.1	WK207
7255M	Spitfire LF.16	TB308	7315M	Swift F.3	WK249
7256M	Spitfire LF.16	TB752	7316M	Swift F.2	WK246
7257M	Spitfire LF.16	TB252	7317M	Meteor F.8	VZ544
7258M	Spitfire LF.16	RW394	7318M	Meteor F.8	WH366
7259M	Meteor F.8	WL112	7319M	Meteor F.8	WE949
7260M	Meteor F.8	VZ552	7320M	Meteor F.8	WF742
7261M	Meteor F.8	VZ568	7321M	Meteor F.8	WA963
7262M	Meteor F.8	WA841	7322M	Meteor F.8	VZ517
7263M	Meteor F.8	WA897	7323M	Vampire FB.5	VV217
7264M	Meteor F.8	WA765	7324M	Meteor F.8	WA885
7265M	Meteor F.8	WH382	7325M	Lancaster I	R5868
7266M	Meteor F.8	VZ561	7326M	Spitfire F.24	VN485
7267M	Prentice T.1	VR219	7327M	Swift F.3	WK255
7268M	Prentice T.1	VR223	7328M	Swift F.3	WK256
7269M	Prentice T.1	VR225	7329M	Swift F.3	WK257
7270M	Prentice T.1	VR237	7330M	Swift F.3	WK258
7271M	Prentice T.1	VR273	7331M	Swift F.3	WK259
7272M	Prentice T.1	VR275	7332M	Swift F.3	WK250
7273M	Prentice T.1	VR281	7333M	Swift F.3	WK251
7274M	Prentice T.1	VR283	7334M	Swift F.3	WK252
7275M	Prentice T.1	VR291	7335M	Swift F.3	WK254
7276M	Prentice T.1	VR293	7336M	Swift F.3	WK260
7277M	Tempest TT.5	SN331	7337M	Swift F.3	WK261
7278M	Oxford T.1	DF308	7338M	Swift F.3	WK247
7279M	Spitfire LF.16	TB752	7339M	Swift F.3	WK262
7280M	Spitfire LF.16	RW394	7340M	Swift F.3	WK263
7281M	Spitfire LF.16	TB252	7341M	Swift F.3	WK264
7282M	Oxford T.1	R6248	7342M	Swift F.3	WK265
7283M	Meteor F.8	VZ515	7343M	Swift F.3	WK266
7284M	Hunter F.1	WB195	7344M	Swift F.3	WK267
7285M	Supermarine 535	VV119	7345M	Swift F.3	WK268
7286M	Chipmunk T.10	WB706	7346M	Swift F.3	WK269
7287M	Spitfire LF.16	TE288	7347M	Swift F.3	WK270
7288M	Spitfire F.24	PK724	7348M	Swift F.3	WK271
7289M	Swift PR.6	XD143	7349M	Swift F.4	WK194
7290M	Hunter F.1	WW607	7350M	Swift F.1	WK202
7291M	Meteor F.8	WE966	7351M	Meteor F.8	WK652
7292M	Hunter F.5	WP143	7352M	Venom FB.1	WE455
7293M	Spitfire LF.16	RW393	7353M	Meteor NF.14	WS831
7294M	Meteor F.8	WF759	7354M	Meteor F.8	WE859
7295M	Meteor F.8	WE966	7355M	Anson T.21	VV990
7296M	Vampire T.11	XE989	7356M	Vampire FB.5	VV695
7297M	Meteor F.8	WK888	7357M	Vampire FB.5	VX953
7298M	Meteor F.8	WK943	7358M	Venom FB.1	WE272
7299M	Swift F.2	WK218	7359M	Meteor NF.11	WM185

7360M-7479M

7360M	Meteor NF.11	WM192	7420M	Vampire T.11	WZ419
7361M	Meteor F.4	RA476	7421M	Hunter F.1	WT660
7362M	Fi 156C-1 Storch	VP546	7422M	Hunter F.1	WT684
7363M	Venom FB.1	WE315	7423M	Vampire T.11	XD457
7364M	Prentice T.1	VS274	7424M	Hunter F.1	WW643
7365M	Vampire FR.9	WG849	7425M	Provost T.1 (ntu)	XF902
7366M	Meteor F.8	WH449	7426M	Hunter F.1	WT624
7367M	Meteor F.8	WH304	7427M	Swift F.2	WK214
7368M	Vampire T.11	WZ575	7428M	Swift F.1	WK198
7369M	Jet Provost T.1 (ntu)	XD692	7429M	Swift F.4 (ntu)	WK279
7370M	Vampire FB.5	WA275	7430M	Meteor F.8	WE901
7371M	Vampire FB.5	VV480	7431M	Auster AOP.9	WZ667
7372M	Vampire FB.5	VZ335	7432M	Auster AOP.9	WZ724
7373M	Vampire FB.9	WL498	7433M	Auster AOP.6	TW624
7374M	Hunter F.1	WT577	7434M	Auster AOP.6	TW575
7375M	Hunter F.1	WT637	7435M	Auster T.7	WE539
7376M	Meteor F.8	WK676	7436M	Auster AOP.9	WZ726
7377M	Lincoln B.2	RF510	7437M	Chipmunk T.10	WP773
7378M	Meteor F.8	WE855	7438M	Chipmunk T.10	WP905
7379M	Canberra B.2 (ntu)	WD999	7439M	Chipmunk T.10	WZ867
7380M	Canberra B.2 (ntu)	WF907	7440M	Hunter F.2	WN898
7381M	Provost T.1 (ntu)	XF611	7441M	Hunter F.2	WN948
7382M	Swift F.3	WK253	7442M	Hunter F.1	WT681
7383M	Meteor FR.9	VW364	7443M	Venom NF.3	WX853
7384M	Meteor FR.9	WB116	7444M	Venom NF.3	WX866
7385M	Varsity T.1	WF421	7445M	Swift F.4	WK279
7386M	Canberra B.2	WF907	7446M	Vampire T.11	XE923
7387M	Canberra B.2	WD999	7447M	Swift FR.5	XD951
7388M	Swift F.1	WK196	7448M	Venom NF.3 (ntu)	WX912
7389M	Meteor F.8 (ntu)	WH297	7449M	Spitfire LF.16 (ntu)	TE330
7390M	Meteor F.8 (ntu)	WA981	7450M	Vampire T.11	XD430
7391M	Meteor F.8 (ntu)	WA993	7451M	Spitfire LF.16 (ntu)	TE476
7392M	Venom FB.1	WE284	7452M	Venom NF.3	WX792
7393M	Venom FB.1	WE293	7453M	Venom NF.3	WX938
7394M	Venom FB.1	WE332	7454M	Venom NF.3	WX857
7395M	Venom FB.1	WE345	7455M	Venom NF.3	WZ318
7396M	Venom FB.1	WE349	7456M	Venom NF.3	WX922
7397M	Hunter F.5	WN958	7457M	Venom NF.3	WX847
7398M	Prentice T.1	VR247	7458M	Venom NF.3	WX905
7399M	Prentice T.1	VR262	7459M	Venom NF.3	WX801
7400M	Prentice T.1	VS264	7460M	Canberra B.2 (ntu)	WD958
7401M	Prentice T.1	VS279	7461M	Vampire T.11	XE828
7402M	Prentice T.1	VR282	7462M	Meteor F.8	WA824
7403M	Prentice T.1	VR290	7463M	Meteor F.8	WF657
7404M	Prentice T.1	VS331	7464M	Javelin FAW.1	XA564
7405M	Prentice T.1	VS369	7465M	Marathon T.1	XA255
7406M	Prentice T.1	VS624	7466M	Provost T.1 (ntu)	XF598
7407M	Hunter F.5	WN957	7467M	Chipmunk T.10	WP978
7408M	Swift FR.5	WK308	7468M	Valetta C.1	VL268
7409M	Vampire FB.5	VZ851	7469M	Valetta C.1	VL269
7410M	Hunter F.1	WT646	7470M	Javelin FAW.1	XA553
7411M	Hunter F.1 (ntu)	WT591	7471M	Hunter F.5	WP192
7412M	Hunter F.1 (ntu)	WT679	7472M	Vampire T.11	XE926
7413M	Hunter F.1 (ntu)	WW603	7473M	Vampire T.11	XE946
7414M	Hunter F.2 (ntu)	WN914	7474M	Valetta C.1	VL274
7415M	Whirlwind HAR.2	XK989	7475M	Valetta C.1	VL276
7416M	Hunter F.2 (ntu)	WN907	7476M	Valetta C.1	VL277
7417M	Meteor T.7	WG981	7477M	Meteor FR.9	WL256
7418M	Valetta C.1 (ntu)	VL279	7478M	Provost T.1 (ntu)	WW396
7419M	Vampire NF.10	WP244	7479M	Valetta C.1	WD168

7480M-7599M

7480M	Valetta C.1	VW838
7481M	Valetta C.1 (ntu)	VW850
7482M	Valetta C.1 (ntu)	VW163
7483M	Valetta C.1 (ntu)	VW190
7484M	Javelin FAW.1	XA550
7485M	Javelin FAW.1 (proto)	WT830
7486M	Hunter F.2	WN888
7487M	Hunter F.2	WN910
7488M	Hunter F.1	WT560
7489M	Hunter F.1	WT567
7490M	Hunter F.1	WT568
7491M	Hunter F.1	WT569
7492M	Hunter F.1	WT558
7493M	Hunter F.1	WT559
7494M	Hunter F.1	WT566
7495M	Hunter F.1	WT592
7496M	Hunter F.1	WT612
7497M	Hunter F.1	WT570
7498M	Hunter F.1	WT576
7499M	Hunter F.1	WT555
7500M	Hunter F.1	WT616
7501M	Hunter F.1	WT578
7502M	Hunter F.1	WT583
7503M	Hunter F.1	WT584
7504M	Hunter F.1	WT588
7505M	Hunter F.1	WT593
7506M	Hunter F.1	WT595
7507M	Hunter F.1	WT686
7508M	Hunter F.1	WT687
7509M	Hunter F.1	WT692
7510M	Hunter F.1	WT694
7511M	Hunter F.2	WN894
7512M	Hunter F.2	WN895
7513M	Hunter F.2	WN897
7514M	Hunter F.1	WT636
7515M	Hunter F.1	WT696
7516M	Hunter F.1	WW632
7517M	Hunter F.1	WW634
7518M	Hunter F.1	WW637
7519M	Hunter F.1	WW638
7520M	Hunter F.1	WW641
7521M	Hunter F.1	WW644
7522M	Hunter F.2	WN908
7523M	Hunter F.1	WT613
7524M	Hunter F.1	WT617
7525M	Hunter F.1	WT619
7526M	Hunter F.1	WT622
7527M	Hunter F.1	WT625
7528M	Hunter F.1	WT626
7529M	Hunter F.1	WT641
7530M	Hunter F.1	WT648
7531M	Hunter F.1	WT649
7532M	Hunter F.1	WT651
7533M	Hunter F.1	WT680
7534M	Hunter F.1	WT682
7535M	Hunter F.1	WT683
7536M	Hunter F.1	WT685
7537M	Hunter F.1	WT693
7538M	Hunter F.1	WW601
7539M	Hunter F.1	WW602
7540M	Hunter F.1	WW604
7541M	Hunter F.1	WW609
7542M	Hunter F.2 (ntu)	WN899
7543M	Hunter F.2	WN901
7544M	Hunter F.2	WN904
7545M	Hunter F.2	WN906
7546M	Canberra B.6	WJ769
7547M	Venom NF.3	WX932
7548M	Spitfire PR.19	PS915
7549M	Venom NF.3	WX843
7550M	Hunter F.5	WP110
7551M	Javelin FAW.1	XA567
7552M	Javelin FAW.1 (proto)	WT836
7553M	Vampire T.11	XK629
7554M	Harvard T.2B	FS890
7555M	Spitfire VC	AR614
7556M	Chipmunk T.10	WK584
7557M	Vampire T.11	WZ423
7558M	Javelin FAW.1	XA544
7559M	Spitfire LF.16	TB287
7560M	Vampire T.11	XK630
7561M	Shackleton MR.1A	WB846
7562M	Auster T.7	WE547
7563M	Hunter F.2	WN892
7564M	Vampire T.11	XE982
7565M	Venom NF.3	WX849
7566M	Meteor NF.12	WS687
7567M	Meteor NF.12	WS603
7568M	Meteor NF.12	WS666
7569M	Hunter F.5	WP126
7570M	Jet Provost T.1	XD674
7571M	Hunter F.5 (ntu)	WP146
7572M	Hunter F.5 (ntu)	WP122
7573M	Hunter F.5 (ntu)	WP150
7574M	Hunter F.5 (ntu)	WP179
7575M	Vampire FB.9	WL607
7576M	Meteor T.7	WL414
7577M	Vampire FB.5	VV542
7578M	Valetta C.1	VL278
7579M	Meteor T.7	WG940
7580M	Hunter F.5	WP147
7581M	Hunter F.5	WP184
7582M	Hunter F.5	WP190
7583M	Hunter F.5	WP185
7584M	Hunter F.5	WP191
7585M	Vampire T.11	XE822
7586M	Javelin FAW.1	XA551
7587M	Valetta C.1	VX546
7588M	Vampire FB.5	VZ183
7589M	Canberra B.2	WD936
7590M	Canberra B.2	WH668
7591M	Hunter F.5	WN978
7592M	Javelin FAW.2 (proto)	XD158
7593M	Meteor FR.9	WB115
7594M	Hastings C.1	TG573
7595M	Auster AOP.6	VF582
7596M	Hunter F.4	WT719
7597M	Chipmunk T.10	WD352
7598M	Vampire FB.5	WA215
7599M	Meteor NF.11	WD707

7600M-7719M

7600M	Lincoln B.2	RF564
7601M	Chipmunk T.10	WB709
7602M	Auster T.7 Antarctic	WE600
7603M	Meteor NF.12	WS591
7604M	Vampire T.11	XD542
7605M	Meteor NF.12	WS692
7606M	Provost T.1	WV562
7607M	Mosquito TT.35	TJ138
7608M	Mosquito TT.35	TA722
7609M	Meteor T.7	WA697
7610M	Comet 2X	G-ALYT
7611M	Canberra B.2 (ntu)	WD937
7612M	Chipmunk T.10	WP775
7613M	Provost T.1	WV512
7614M	Provost T.1	WV618
7615M	Provost T.1	WV679
7616M	Provost T.1	WW388
7617M	Provost T.1	WV573
7618M	Provost T.1	WW442
7619M	Javelin FAW.1	XA560
7620M	Canberra B.2	WD959
7621M	Provost T.1	WV686
7622M	Provost T.1	WV606
7623M	Canberra B.2	WH735
7624M	Chipmunk T.10	WZ870
7625M	Chipmunk T.10	WD356
7626M	Shackleton MR.2 (proto)	VW126
7627M	Javelin FAW.1	XA563
7628M	Canberra B.2	WH723
7629M	Vampire T.11	XD386
7630M	Vampire FB.5	VZ304
7631M	Canberra B(I).8 (proto)	VX185
7632M	Chipmunk T.10	WP918
7633M	Chipmunk T.10	WK614
7634M	Vampire FB.5	WA450
7635M	Meteor NF.12	WS667
7636M	Canberra T.4	WJ878
7637M	Canberra B.2	WF887
7638M	Venom FB.4	WR433
7639M	Venom FB.4	WR493
7640M	Venom FB.4 (ntu)	WR412
7641M	Javelin FAW.2	XA634
7642M	Valetta C.1	WD171
7643M	Chipmunk T.10 (ntu)	WD375
7644M	Chipmunk T.10	WD332
7645M	Chipmunk T.10	WD293
7646M	Vampire FB.5	VX461
7647M	Chipmunk T.10	WG473
7648M	Bristol 173	XF785
7649M	Javelin FAW.5	XA706
7650M	Chipmunk T.10	WP895
7651M	Vampire T.11	XD519
7652M	Vampire T.11	WZ544
7653M	Balliol T.2	WN158
7654M	Balliol T.2	XF931
7655M	Chipmunk T.10	WP836
7656M	Canberra B.2 (ntu)	WJ573
7657M	Canberra B.2	WH695
7658M	Canberra T.4	WH884
7659M	Canberra B.2	WH701
7660M	Vampire FB.5	WA236
7661M	Javelin FAW.1	XA627
7662M	Javelin FAW.1	XA554
7663M	Javelin FAW.1	XA571
7664M	Javelin FAW.1 (ntu)	XA624
7665M	Javelin FAW.1 (ntu)	XA628
7666M	Javelin FAW.1	XA626
7667M	Javelin FAW.1 (ntu)	XA620
7668M	Hunter F.4	WV324
7669M	Hunter F.4	WV326
7670M	Hunter F.4	WV327
7671M	Hunter F.4	WV329
7672M	Hunter F.4	WV330
7673M	Hunter F.4	WV332
7674M	Hunter F.4	WV364
7675M	Hunter F.4	WV369
7676M	Hunter F.4	WV316
7677M	Hunter F.4	WV367
7678M	Hunter F.4	WV371
7679M	Hunter F.4	WV375
7680M	Hunter F.4	WV376
7681M	Hunter F.4	WV377
7682M	Hunter F.4	WV378
7683M	Hunter F.4	WV379
7684M	Hunter F.4	WV265
7685M	Hunter F.4	WV320
7686M	Hunter F.4	WV323
7687M	Meteor F.8	WK952
7688M	Provost T.1	WW421
7689M	Provost T.1	WW450
7690M	Provost T.1	WV428
7691M	Provost T.1	WV438
7692M	Provost T.1	WV444
7693M	Provost T.1	WV483
7694M	Provost T.1	WV486
7695M	Provost T.1	WV492
7696M	Provost T.1	WV493
7697M	Provost T.1	WV495
7698M	Provost T.1	WV499
7699M	Provost T.1	WV541
7700M	Provost T.1	WV544
7701M	Hunter F.4	WV268
7702M	Alouette AH.2	XN133
7703M	Dragonfly HR.3	WG725
7704M	Auster AOP.6	TW536
7705M	Vampire FB.9	WL505
7706M	Chipmunk T.10	WB584
7707M	Valiant B.1	WP201
7708M	Britannia 101	G-ALBO
7709M	Sycamore 3	WT933
7710M	Cadet TX.3	WT897
7711M	Spitfire PR.19	PS915
7712M	Swift FR.5	WK281
7713M	Valiant B.1	WP203
7714M	Swift FR.5 (ntu)	WK307
7715M	Gnat F.1	XK724
7716M	Meteor NF(T).14	WS776
7717M	Javelin FAW.1	XA549
7718M	Sycamore 3	WA577
7719M	Swift FR.5	WK277

7720M-7839M

7720M	Javelin FAW.1	XA628	7780M	Hunter F.4	WV261
7721M	Javelin FAW.1 (ntu)	XA554	7781M	Hunter F.4	WV266
7722M	Javelin FAW.1 (ntu)	XA571	7782M	Hunter F.4	WV272
7723M	Javelin FAW.1	XA620	7783M	Hunter F.4	WV331
7724M	Victor B.1	XA919	7784M	Hunter F.4	WW653
7725M	Javelin FAW.4	XA755	7785M	Hunter F.4	XE659
7726M	Jet Provost T.3	XM373	7786M	Hunter F.4	XE678
7727M	Vampire T.11	WZ494	7787M	Hunter F.4	XE679
7728M	Vampire T.11	WZ458	7788M	Hunter F.4	XE704
7729M	Chipmunk T.10	WB758	7789M	Hunter F.4	WT801
7730M	Shackleton MR.1	VP289	7790M	Hunter F.4	WT716
7731M	Meteor FR.9	WH546	7791M	Hunter F.4	WT778
7732M	Vampire T.11	XD393	7792M	Hunter F.4	WT797
7733M	Chipmunk T.10	WP841	7793M	Sycamore HR.14	XG523
7734M	Vampire T.11	XD536	7794M	Hunter F.4	XE702
7735M	Beaver AL.1	XP812	7795M	Meteor F.8	WK712
7736M	Vampire T.11	WZ559	7796M	Canberra B.2	WJ676
7737M	Vampire T.11	XD602	7797M	Javelin FAW.7	XH782
7738M	Vulcan B.1A	XA904	7798M	Javelin FAW.7	XH783
7739M	Javelin FAW.2	XA801	7799M	Javelin FAW.7	XH784
7740M	Javelin FAW.9	XH840	7800M	Javelin FAW.7	XH901
7741M	Meteor F.8	VZ477	7801M	Javelin FAW.7	XH902
7742M	Meteor F.8	VZ511	7802M	Canberra B.2	WD996
7743M	Javelin FAW.6 (ntu)	XH698	7803M	Hunter F.6	XF385
7744M	Javelin FAW.4 (ntu)	XA727	7804M	Hunter F.4	XF946
7745M	Sycamore HR.14	XG509	7805M	Mosquito T.3	TW117
7746M	Vulcan B.1	XA892	7806M	Mosquito TT.35	TA639
7747M	Chipmunk T.10	WP854	7807M	Hunter F.4	XE715
7748M	Javelin FAW.7	XH710	7808M	Javelin FAW.7	XH790
7749M	Javelin FAW.6	XA821	7809M	Javelin FAW.5	XA699
7750M	Meteor F.8	WL168	7810M	Whirlwind HAR.10	XK991
7751M	Meteor F.8	WL131	7811M	Javelin FAW.7	XH900
7752M	Javelin FAW.6	XA820	7812M	Vulcan B.1	XA899
7753M	Valiant B.1	WP204	7813M	Meteor NF.14	WS777
7754M	Chipmunk T.10	WD303	7814M	Vampire T.11	XD511
7755M	E.E. P.1A	WG760	7815M	Vampire T.11	XD617
7756M	Meteor F.8	WK818	7816M	E.E. P.1A	WG763
7757M	Javelin FAW.7	XH795	7817M	Anson C.19	TX214
7758M	Spitfire PR.19	PM651	7818M	Meteor T.7	WH226
7759M	Spitfire F.22	PK664	7819M	Jet Provost T.4	XP661
7760M	Vampire T.11	XH298	7820M	Skeeter AOP.12	XM527
7761M	Vampire T.11	XH318	7821M	Whirlwind HAR.10	XJ428
7762M	Hunter F.4	XE670	7822M	Auster AOP.9	XP248
7763M	Vampire T.11	XH358	7823M	Auster AOP.9	XP250
7764M	Canberra B.2	WD990	7824M	Vampire T.11	XE887
7765M	Javelin FAW.5 (ntu)	XA701	7825M	Meteor F.8	WK991
7766M	Not issued	-	7826M	Auster AOP.9	WZ675
7767M	Hunter F.4	WV398	7827M	Victor B.1	XA917
7768M	Hunter F.4	WV404	7828M	Canberra B.2	WF908
7769M	Hunter F.4	WW590	7829M	Javelin FAW.8	XH992
7770M	Hunter F.4	WT746	7830M	Vampire T.11	XH273
7771M	Hunter F.4	XF309	7831M	Javelin FAW.8	XH991
7772M	Hunter F.4	XF370	7832M	Javelin FAW.8	XJ116
7773M	Hunter F.4	XF317	7833M	Javelin FAW.8	XJ117
7774M	Hunter F.4	XF302	7834M	Javelin FAW.8	XH972
7775M	Hunter F.4	WV386	7835M	Hastings C.1	TG610
7776M	Hunter F.4	XF306	7836M	Javelin FAW.8 (ntu)	XJ122
7777M	Hunter F.4	XF308	7837M	Javelin FAW.8 (ntu)	XJ126
7778M	Hunter F.4	XF316	7838M	Lightning F.1A	XM187
7779M	Hunter F.4	WV258	7839M	Sycamore HR.12	WV781

7840M-7959M

7840M	Skeeter AOP.10	XK482
7841M	Sycamore HR.12	WV783
7842M	Javelin FAW.8	XH986
7843M	Canberra PR.3	WE145
7844M	Victor B.1	XA924
7845M	Cadet TX.3	XN195
7846M	Valiant B.1	WP214
7847M	Hunter F.4	WV276
7848M	Hunter F.4	XF312
7849M	Hunter F.4	XF319
7850M	Victor B.1	XA923
7851M	Auster AOP.9	WZ706
7852M	Sycamore HR.14	XG506
7853M	Whirlwind HAR.4 (ntu)	XD164
7854M	Lightning F.1A	XM191
7855M	Auster AOP.9	XK416
7856M	Vulcan B.1	XA898
7857M	Vulcan B.1	XA905
7858M	Valetta C.1	WD159
7859M	Auster AOP.9	XP283
7860M	Skeeter AOP.12	XL738
7861M	Skeeter AOP.12	XM565
7862M	Auster AOP.9	XR246
7863M	Auster AOP.9	WZ679
7864M	Auster AOP.9	XP244
7865M	Anson C.19	TX226
7866M	Vampire T.11	XH278
7867M	Javelin FAW.8	XH980
7868M	Avro 707A	WZ736
7869M	Meteor F.8 (mod)	WK935
7870M	Skeeter AOP.12	XM556
7871M	Vampire T.11	XE890
7872M	Valiant BK.1	XD826
7873M	Valiant BK.1	WZ382
7874M	Gnat T.1	XR568
7875M	Valetta C.1	VW148
7876M	Valetta C.1	VX527
7877M	Lightning F.1A	XM170
7878M	Vampire T.11	XD601
7879M	Valetta C.1	VW837
7880M	Vampire T.11	WZ502
7881M	Anson T.21	WD413
7882M	Vampire T.11	XD525
7883M	Sioux AH.1	Airframe
7884M	Sioux AH.1	Airframe
7885M	Shackleton T.4	WB832
7886M	Gnat T.1	XR985
7887M	Vampire T.11	XD375
7888M	Valiant B(PR)K.1	WZ397
7889M	Vampire T.11	WZ577
7890M	Vampire T.11	XD453
7891M	Gnat T.1	XM693
7892M	Javelin FAW.9	XH760
7893M	Vampire T.11	WZ562
7894M	Valiant BK.1	XD818
7895M	Meteor T.7	WF784
7896M	Vulcan B.1A	XA900
7897M	Vulcan B.1A	XA901
7898M	Scout AH.1 (ntu)	XP854
7899M	Sycamore HR.14	XG540
7900M	Sycamore HR.3	WA576
7901M	Valetta T.3	WJ484
7902M	Vampire T.11	WZ550
7903M	Javelin FAW.9 (ntu)	XH757
7904M	Hunter F.4	XF933
7905M	Comet C.2	XK715
7906M	Meteor T.7	WH132
7907M	Hunter F.4	XF944
7908M	Hunter F.4	XF973
7909M	Sycamore HR.14 (ntu)	XL826
7910M	Sycamore HR.14 (ntu)	XJ915
7911M	Valetta C.2	VX578
7912M	Canberra B.2	WK131
7913M	Canberra B.2	WK132
7914M	Canberra B.2	WK134
7915M	Sycamore HR.14	XJ915
7916M	Sycamore HR.14	XL826
7917M	Meteor T.7	WA591
7918M	Vampire T.11	XD444
7919M	Valetta T.3	WJ476
7920M	Meteor T.7	WL360
7921M	Whirlwind HAR.10	XJ757
7922M	Provost T.1	WV494
7923M	Sioux AH.1	XT133
7924M	Chipmunk T.10	WB555
7925M	Provost T.1	WV666
7926M	Comet C.2	XK670
7927M	Comet C.2	XK671
7928M	Vampire T.11	XE849
7929M	Javelin FAW.9	XH768
7930M	Meteor F.8	WH301
7931M	Beaufighter TF.10	RD253
7932M	Avro 707C	WZ744
7933M	TSR.2	XR220
7934M	Vampire T.11	XE932
7935M	Hunter F.4	XF969
7936M	Hunter F.4	XF970
7937M	Meteor NF(T).14	WS843
7938M	Javelin FAW.9	XH903
7939M	Vampire T.11	XD596
7940M	Skeeter AOP.12	XL764
7941M	Hunter F.4	XF369
7942M	Hunter F.4	XF360
7943M	Hunter F.4	WW589
7944M	Hunter F.4	WV393
7945M	Hunter F.4	XF975
7946M	Hunter F.4	XF982
7947M	Hunter F.4	XF951
7948M	Hunter F.4	XF972
7949M	Hunter F.4	XF974
7950M	Hunter F.4	XF998
7951M	Vampire T.11	XD538
7952M	Provost T.1	WV471
7953M	Provost T.1	WV677
7954M	Provost T.1	XF608
7955M	Javelin FAW.9	XH767
7956M	Hunter F.4	XF950
7957M	Provost T.1	XF545
7958M	Comet C.2	XK716
7959M	Meteor NF(T).14	WS774

7960M-8077M

7960M	Meteor NF(T).14	WS726	8020M	Shackleton T.4	WB847
7961M	Meteor NF(T).14	WS739	8021M	Sycamore HR.14	XL824
7962M	Meteor NF(T).14	WS744	8022M	Skeeter AOP.12	XN341
7963M	Meteor NF.14 (ntu)	WS751	8023M	Vampire T.11	XD463
7964M	Meteor NF(T).14	WS760	8024M	Skeeter AOP.12	XN348
7965M	Meteor NF(T).14	WS792	8025M	Beverley C.1	XH124
7966M	Meteor NF(T).14	WS797	8026M	Shackleton T.4	WB849
7967M	Meteor NF(T).14	WS788	8027M	Skeeter AOP.12	XM555
7968M	Meteor NF(T).14	WS802	8028M	Shackleton T.4	WB844
7969M	Meteor NF(T).14	WS840	8029M	Varsity T.1	WF333
7970M	Chipmunk T.10	WP907	8030M	Whirlwind HAR.10	XS412
7971M	Comet C.2	XK699	8031M	Comet C.2	XK698
7972M	Javelin FAW.9	XH764	8032M	Javelin FAW.7	XH837
7973M	Meteor NF(T).14	WS807	8033M	Vampire T.11	XD382
7974M	Vulcan B.1A	XH479	8034M	Pioneer CC.1	XL703
7975M	Javelin FAW.9	XH849	8035M	Provost T.1	WV443
7976M	Auster AOP.9	XK418	8036M	Provost T.1	WV505
7977M	Auster AOP.9	XN443	8037M	Provost T.1	XF555
7978M	Twin Pioneer CC.1	XM961	8038M	Provost T.1	XF689
7979M	Skeeter AOP.12	XM529	8039M	Provost T.1	XF841
7980M	Skeeter AOP.12	XM561	8040M	Scout AH.1	XR493
7981M	Skeeter AOP.12	XL769	8041M	Provost T.1 (ntu)	XF690
7982M	Javelin FAW.9	XH892	8042M	Anson C.19	VM368
7983M	Vampire T.11	XD506	8043M	Provost T.1 (ntu)	XF836
7984M	Jet Provost T.3	XN597	8044M	Auster AOP.9	XP286
7985M	Hastings C.2	WD490	8045M	Beverley C.1	XH122
7986M	Fairey FD.2	WG777	8046M	Skeeter AOP.12	XL770
7987M	Hastings C.1	TG605	8047M	Vulcan B.1A	XH478
7988M	Beverley C.1	XL149	8048M	Vulcan B.2 (ntu)	XH533
7989M	Chipmunk T.10	WG475	8049M	Canberra PR.3	WE168
7990M	Vampire T.11 (ntu)	XD452	8050M	Lightning F.1	XG329
7991M	Varsity T.1	WL639	8051M	Buccaneer S.1	XN929
7992M	Gnat T.1	XM704	8052M	Meteor T.7	WH166
7993M	Vulcan B.1A	XH498	8053M	Meteor F.8	WK968
7994M	Vulcan B.1A	XH500	8054AM	Jet Provost T.3	XM410
7995M	Vulcan B.1A	XA910	8054BM	Jet Provost T.3	XM417
7996M	Vulcan B.1A	XH475	8055AM	Jet Provost T.3	XM402
7997M	Belvedere HC.1	XG452	8055BM	Jet Provost T.3	XM404
7998M	Vampire T.11	XD515	8056M	Lightning F.1	XG337
7999M	Valetta T.3 (ntu)	WG257	8057M	Auster AOP.9	XR243
8000M	Whirlwind HAR.10	XL111	8058M	Auster AOP.9	XK419
8001M	Hunter F.4	WV395	8059M	Buccaneer S.1	XN956
8002M	Hunter F.4	XF307	8060M	Provost T.1	WW397
8003M	Hunter F.4	XF323	8061M	Pembroke C.1	WV751
8004M	Hunter F.4	XF366	8062M	Jet Provost T.4	XR669
8005M	Short SB.5	WG768	8063M	Canberra PR.7	WT536
8006M	Hunter F.4	XF941	8064M	Pembroke C.1	WV706
8007M	Hunter F.4	XF990	8065M	Canberra PR.7	WT513
8008M	Sycamore HR.14	XG515	8066M	Canberra PR.7	WT533
8009M	Sycamore HR.14	XG518	8067M	Canberra PR.7	WH802
8010M	Sycamore HR.14	XG547	8068M	Canberra PR.7	WT516
8011M	Beaver AL.1	XV269	8069M	Canberra B(I).6	WT314
8012M	Anson T.21	VS562	8070M	Spitfire V	EP120
8013M	Varsity T.1	WF412	8071M	Spitfire LF.16	TE476
8014M	Valetta T.3	WJ462	8072M	Spitfire F.22	PK624
8015M	Canberra B.15	WH965	8073M	Spitfire LF.16	TB252
8016M	Wessex HC.2	XT677	8074M	Spitfire LF.16	TE392
8017M	Skeeter AOP.12	XL762	8075M	Spitfire LF.16	RW382
8018M	Skeeter AOP.12	XN344	8076M	Jet Provost T.3	XM386
8019M	Chipmunk T.10	WZ869	8077M	Jet Provost T.3	XN594

8078M-8197M

8078M	Jet Provost T.3	XM351
8079M	Jet Provost T.3	XN492
8080M	Jet Provost T.3	XM480
8081M	Jet Provost T.3	XM468
8082M	Jet Provost T.3	XM409
8083M	Jet Provost T.3	XM367
8084M	Jet Provost T.3	XM369
8085M	Jet Provost T.3	XM467
8086M	Spitfire LF.16	TB752
8087M	Buccaneer S.1	XN925
8088M	Jet Provost T.3	XN602
8089M	Shackleton MR.3/3	XF706
8090M	Gnat T.1	XM698
8091M	Lightning F.1	XG336
8092M	Meteor F.8	WK654
8093M	Canberra PR.7	WT512
8094M	Canberra PR.7 (ntu)	WT520
8095M	Canberra PR.7	WH792
8096M	Varsity T.1	WJ891
8097M	Jet Provost T.4	XS213
8098M	Varsity T.1 (ntu)	WL682
8099M	Chipmunk T.10	WD355
8100M	Chipmunk T.10	WZ861
8101M	Canberra B.15	WH984
8102M	Canberra T.4	WT486
8103M	Shackleton MR.3/3	WR985
8104M	Shackleton MR.3/3 (ntu)	WR979
8105M	Varsity T.1	WL637
8106M	Shackleton MR.3/3	WR982
8107M	Shackleton MR.3/3	WR990
8108M	Pembroke C.1	WV703
8109M	Pembroke C.1	WV704
8110M	Pembroke C.1	WV741
8111M	Pembroke C.1	WV742
8112M	Pembroke C.1	WV743
8113M	Pembroke C.1	WV753
8114M	Shackleton MR.2/3	WL798
8115M	Shackleton MR.3/3	WR984
8116M	Chipmunk T.10	WG460
8117M	Shackleton MR.3/3	WR974
8118M	Vampire T.11	WZ549
8119M	Shackleton MR.3/3	WR971
8120M	Shackleton MR.3/3	WR981
8121M	Jet Provost T.3	XM474
8122M	Vampire T.11	XD613
8123M	Vampire T.11 (ntu)	XJ774
8124M	Vampire T.11 (ntu)	XD614
8125M	Vampire T.11 (ntu)	XE857
8126M	Canberra PR.7	WH804
8127M	Canberra B.2 (ntu)	WJ724
8128M	Canberra PR.7	WH775
8129M	Canberra PR.7 (ntu)	WH779
8130M	Canberra PR.7 (ntu)	WH798
8131M	Canberra PR.7 (ntu)	WT507
8132M	Canberra PR.7	WT514
8133M	Canberra PR.7 (ntu)	WT518
8134M	Canberra PR.7	WT521
8135M	Canberra PR.7	WT523
8136M	Canberra PR.7	WT524
8137M	Canberra PR.7	WT527
8138M	Sea Vixen FAW.2	XN700
8139M	Sea Vixen FAW.2	XJ582
8140M	Sea Vixen FAW.2	XJ571
8141M	Sea Vixen FAW.2	XN688
8142M	Sea Vixen FAW.2	XJ560
8143M	Sea Vixen FAW.2	XN691
8144M	Sea Vixen FAW.2	XN707
8145M	Sea Vixen FAW.2	XJ526
8146M	Varsity T.1	WJ919
8147M	Wessex HC.2	XR526
8148M	Sea Vampire T.22	XA165
8149M	Meteor TT.20	WD702
8150M	Canberra B(I).8	WT345
8151M	Sea Hawk FGA.6	WV795
8152M	Sea Hawk FGA.6	WV794
8153M	Sea Hawk FGA.4	WV903
8154M	Sea Hawk FGA.4	WV908
8155M	Sea Hawk FGA.4	WV797
8156M	Sea Hawk FGA.6	XE339
8157M	Sea Hawk FGA.6	XE390
8158M	Sea Hawk FGA.6	XE369
8159M	Vampire T.11	XD528
8160M	Vampire T.11	XD622
8161M	Vampire T.11	XE993
8162M	Sea Hawk FB.3 (ntu)	WM913
8163M	Sea Vixen FAW.2	XP919
8164M	Sea Hawk FB.5	WF299
8165M	Canberra PR.7 (ntu)	WH791
8166M	Lightning F.3	XP752
8167M	Canberra B(I).8	XH208
8168M	Shackleton MR.3/3	XF703
8169M	Meteor F.8	WH364
8170M	Canberra B(I).8	XM274
8171M	Sea Vixen FAW.2	XJ607
8172M	Sea Vixen FAW.2	XJ609
8173M	Sea Vixen FAW.2	XN685
8174M	Vampire T.11	WZ576
8175M	Vampire T.11	XE950
8176M	Canberra PR.7 (ntu)	WH791
8177M	Meteor TT.20	WM224
8178M	Canberra B(I).8 (ntu)	XM276
8179M	Buccaneer S.1	XN928
8180M	Buccaneer S.1	XN930
8181M	Buccaneer S.1	XN972
8182M	Buccaneer S.1	XN953
8183M	Buccaneer S.1	XN962
8184M	Canberra PR.7	WT520
8185M	Canberra B.6	WH946
8186M	Shackleton MR.3/3	WR977
8187M	Canberra PR.7	WH791
8188M	Lightning F.1	XG327
8189M	Meteor TT.20	WD646
8190M	Sycamore HR.14	XJ918
8191M	Pembroke C.1 (ntu)	XK862
8192M	Jet Provost T.4	XR658
8193M	Jet Provost T.4	XR707
8194M	Pembroke C.1	XK862
8195M	Argosy C.1	XN848
8196M	Vampire T.11	XE920
8197M	Canberra B(I).8	WT346

8198M-8404M

8198M	Canberra B(I).8	WT339
8199M	Canberra B(I).8	XM265
8200M	Canberra B(I).8	WT332
8201M	Canberra B(I).8	XH209
8202M	Canberra B(I).8	XM244
8203M	Vampire T.11	XD377
8204M	Canberra B(I).8	XM271
8205M	Argosy C.1	XN819
8206M	Chipmunk T.10	WG419
8207M	Chipmunk T.10	WD318
8208M	Chipmunk T.10	WG303
8209M	Chipmunk T.10	WG418
8210M	Chipmunk T.10	WG471
8211M	Chipmunk T.10	WK570
8212M	Chipmunk T.10	WK587
8213M	Chipmunk T.10	WK626
8214M	Chipmunk T.10	WP864
8215M	Chipmunk T.10	WP869
8216M	Chipmunk T.10	WP927
8217M	Chipmunk T.10	WZ866
8218M	Chipmunk T.10 (ntu)	WB645
8219M	Whirlwind HAR.10	XR455
8220M	Argosy C.1	XN847
8221M	Argosy C.1	XP409
8222M	Sea Vixen FAW.2	XJ604
8223M	Sea Vixen FAW.2	XN658
8224M	Sea Vixen FAW.2	XN699
8225M	Sea Vixen FAW.2	XN705
8226M	Sea Vixen FAW.2	XP921
8227M	Canberra B(I).8	XM264
8228M	Whirlwind HAR.10	XP363
8229M	Jet Provost T.3	XM355
8230M	Jet Provost T.3	XM362
8231M	Jet Provost T.3	XM375
8232M	Jet Provost T.3	XM381
The following were carried but never issued.		
8233M	Jet Provost T.3	XM408
8234M	Jet Provost T.3	XN458
8235M	Jet Provost T.3	XN549
8236M	Jet Provost T.4	XP573
8237M	Jet Provost T.4	XS179
8238M	Jet Provost T.4	XS180
8239M	Jet Provost T.4	XS210
8233M to 8332M	Not issued	
The following were issued but never carried.		
8333M	Jet Provost T.3	XM408
8334M	Jet Provost T.3	XN458
8335M	Jet Provost T.3	XN549
8336M	Jet Provost T.4	XP573
8337M	Jet Provost T.4	XS179
8338M	Jet Provost T.4	XS180
8339M	Jet Provost T.4	XS210
8340M	Whirlwind HAR.10	XP341
8341M	Chipmunk T.10	WP963
8342M	Chipmunk T.10	WP848
8343M	Hastings C.1 (ntu)	TG500
8344M	Canberra B.15	WH960
8345M	Sycamore HR.14	XG540
8346M	Lightning F.2A	XN734
8347M	Lightning F.2	XN768
8348M	Lightning F.2	XN779
8349M	Lightning F.2	XN794
8350M	Canberra T.4	WH840
8351M	Comet 1XB	XM823
8352M	Jet Provost T.3	XN632
8353M	Jet Provost T.3	XN633
8354M	Meteor T.7 (ntu)	WF791
8355M	Dakota C.4	KN645
8356M	Whirlwind HAS.7 (ntu)	XL835
8357M	Chipmunk T.10	WK576
8358M	Varsity T.1 (ntu)	WF414
8359M	Meteor T.7	WF825
8360M	Chipmunk T.10	WP863
8361M	Chipmunk T.10	WB670
8362M	Chipmunk T.10	WG477
8363M	Chipmunk T.10	WG463
8364M	Chipmunk T.10	WG464
8365M	Auster AOP.9	XK421
8366M	Belvedere HC.1	XG454
8367M	Belvedere HC.1	XG474
8368M	Bristol 188	XF926
8369M	Canberra PR.3	WE139
8370M	Defiant I	N1671
8371M	E.E. P.1B	XA847
8372M	Gladiator II	K8042
8373M	Hurricane I	P2617
8374M	Jet Provost T.4	XR660
8375M	Lancaster I	NX611
8376M	Lincoln B.2	RF398
8377M	Lysander III	R9125
8378M	Magister	T9707
8379M	Hawk Major	DG590
8380M	Proctor C.2	Z7197
8381M	Rotachute	P.5
8382M	Sea Fury FB.11	VR930
8383M	Spitfire I	K9942
8384M	Spitfire I	X4590
8385M	Gladiator II	N5912
8386M	Tempest TT.5	NV778
8387M	Tiger Moth T.2	T6296
8388M	Twin Pioneer CC.1	XL993
8389M	Valetta C.2	VX573
8390M	Spitfire LF.16	SL542
8391M	Spitfire LF.16	SL574
8392M	Spitfire LF.16	SL674
8393M	Whirlwind HAR.10	XK987
8394M	Chipmunk T.10	WG422
8395M	Varsity T.1	WF408
8396M	Gnat F.1	XK740
8397M	Sea Vixen FAW.2 (ntu)	XS583
8398M	Shackleton MR.2/3	WR967
8399M	Venom FB.4	WR539
8400M	Jet Provost T.4	XP583
8401M	Jet Provost T.4 (ntu)	XP686
8402M	Lightning F.2	XN769
8403M	Buccaneer S.1	XK531
8404M	Jet Provost T.4 (ntu)	XP548

8405M-8521M

8405M	Hastings C.1 (ntu)	TG536
8406M	Hawker P.1127	XP831
8407M	Jet Provost T.4	XP585
Reportedly carried by XN554		
8408M	Jet Provost T.4	XS186
8409M	Jet Provost T.4	XS209
8410M	Jet Provost T.4	XR662
8411M	Lightning F.1	XM139
8412M	Lightning F.1	XM147
8413M	Lightning F.1A	XM192
8414M	Lightning F.1A	XM173
8415M	Lightning F.1A	XM181
8416M	Lightning F.1A	XM183
8417M	Lightning F.1	XM144
8418M	Lightning F.1A	XM178
8419M	Meteor T.7 (ntu)	WA658
8420M	Lightning F.1A (ntu)	XM214
8421M	Lightning F.1A (ntu)	XM215
8422M	Lightning F.1A	XM169
8423M	Lightning F.1A	XM189
8424M	Lightning F.1A	XM180
8425M	Lightning F.1A	XM182
8426M	Lightning F.1A	XM216
8427M	Lightning F.1A	XM172
8428M	Victor K.1A	XH593
8429M	Victor K.1A	XH592
8430M	Sioux HT.2	XV312
8431M	Jet Provost T.4	XR651
8432M	Whirlwind HAS.7 (ntu)	XK937
8433M	Lightning T.5	XM967
8434M	Jet Provost T.3	XM411
8435M	Jet Provost T.3	XN512
8436M	Jet Provost T.3	XN554
Reportedly carried by XP585		
8437M	Chipmunk T.10	WG362
8438M	Lightning F.3	XP761
8439M	Chipmunk T.10	WZ846
8440M	Canberra B.2	WD935
8441M	Argosy C.1	XR107
8442M	Argosy C.1	XP411
8443M	Whirlwind HAR.10	XP302
8444M	Whirlwind HAR.10	XP400
8445M	Whirlwind HAR.10	XK968
8446M	Lightning F.3	XP748
8447M	Whirlwind HAR.10	XP359
8448M	Lightning F.2A	XN775
8449M	Beagle 206	G-ASWJ
8450M	Canberra PR.3 (ntu)	WE145
8451M	Canberra B.2 (ntu)	WJ611
8452M	Pembroke C.1	XK885
8453M	Lightning F.3	XP745
8454M	Argosy T.2	XP442
8455M	Argosy C.1	XP444
8456M	Lightning T.4 (ntu)	XM991
8457M	Wessex HAS.1	XS871
8458M	Jet Provost T.4	XP672
8459M	Jet Provost T.4	XR650
8460M	Jet Provost T.4	XP680
Reportedly carried by XR667		
8461M	Pembroke C.1	XF796
8462M	Jetstream T.1	XX477
8463M	Whirlwind HAR.10	XP355
8464M	Whirlwind HAR.10	XJ758
8465M	Halifax II	W1048
8466M	Catalina	L-866
8467M	Chipmunk T.10	WP912
8468M	Fiat CR.42	BT474
8469M	Focke Achegelis Fa 330	-
8470M	Fw 190F-8/U.1	PN999
8471M	Heinkel He 111H-23	-
8472M	Heinkel He 162A-2	VH513
8473M	Hunter F.1	WP190
8474M	Junkers Ju 87G-2	-
8475M	Junkers Ju 88R-1	PJ876
8476M	Kawasaki Ki-100	-
8477M	Messerschmitt Bf 109E-3	DG200
8478M	Messerschmitt Bf 109G-6	RN228
8479M	M'schmitt Bf 110G-4d/R3	AX772
8480M	M'schmitt Me 163B-1a	-
8481M	M'schmitt Me 163B-1a	-
8482M	Messerschmitt Me 262A	VK893
8483M	Messerschmitt Me 410A-1	-
8484M	Mitsubishi Ki-46 III	-
8485M	Ohka	-
8486M	Ohka	-
8487M	Vampire FB.6	J1172
8488M	Varsity T.1	WL627
8489M	Argosy E.1	XN816
8490M	Canberra B.2	WH703
8491M	Canberra T.4	WJ880
8492M	Canberra T.4	WJ872
8493M	Gnat T.1	XR571
8494M	Jet Provost T.4	XP557
8495M	Jet Provost T.4	XR672
8496M	Lightning F.2A	XN730
8497M	Gnat T.1	XM698
8498M	Jet Provost T.4	XR670
8499M	Whirlwind HAR.10	XP357
8500M	Lightning F.2A	XN786
8501M	Jet Provost T.4	XP640
8502M	Jet Provost T.4	XP686
8503M	Lightning T.5	XS451
8504M	Canberra T.19 (ntu)	WK106
8505M	Vulcan B.2	XL384
8506M	Jet Provost T.4	XR704
8507M	Jet Provost T.4	XS215
8508M	Jet Provost T.4	XS218
8509M	Sioux AH.1	XT141
8510M	Jet Provost T.4	XP567
8511M	Canberra B.6	WT305
8512M	Devon C.2	VP973
8513M	Lightning F.2A	XN724
8514M	Jet Provost T.4	XS176
8515M	Canberra B.2	WH869
8516M	Jet Provost T.4	XR643
8517M	Victor K.1	XA932
8518M	Lightning F.2A	XN731
8519M	Lightning F.2A	XN732
8520M	Lightning F.2A	XN733
8521M	Lightning F.2A	XN773

8522M-8638M

8522M	Lightning F.2A	XN787
8523M	Lightning F.2A	XN790
8524M	Lightning F.2A	XN791
8525M	Lightning F.2A	XN792
8526M	Lightning F.2A	XN783
8527M	Lightning F.2A	XN789
8528M	Lightning T.4	XM973
8529M	Lightning T.4	XM970
8530M	Canberra B.2 (ntu)	WD948
8531M	Lightning T.5	XS418
8532M	Lightning T.5	XS423
8533M	Lightning T.5	XS449
8534M	Lightning T.5	XS450
8535M	Lightning T.5	XS454
8536M	Lightning F.2A	XN777
8537M	Lightning F.2A	XN778
8538M	Lightning F.2A	XN781
8539M	Lightning F.2A	XN782
8540M	Lightning F.2A	XN784
8541M	Lightning T.4 (ntu)	XM968
8542M	Lightning T.4	XM995
8543M	Lightning F.2A	XN788
8544M	Lightning F.2A	XN793
8545M	Lightning F.2A (ntu)	XN726
8546M	Lightning F.2A	XN728
8547M	Lightning F.2A (ntu)	XN727
8548M	Canberra PR.7	WT507
8549M	Canberra PR.7	WT534
8550M	Phantom FG.1	XT595
8551M	Lightning F.2A	XN774
8552M	Lightning F.2A	XN735
8553M	Devon C.2	VP978
8554M	Hastings T.5	TG511
8555M	Hastings T.5	TG503
8556M	Argosy E.1	XN855
8557M	Gnat T.1	XP500
8558M	Argosy E.1	XP439
8559M	Jet Provost T.4	XN467
8560M	Gnat T.1	XR569
8561M	Gnat T.1	XS100
8562M	Gnat T.1	XS110
8563M	Jaguar GR.1	XW563
8564M	Whirlwind HAR.10	XN387
8565M	Hunter F.51	G-9-436
8566M	Harrier GR.1	XV279
8567M	Shackleton MR.2/3	WL738
8568M	Gnat T.1	XP503
8569M	Gnat T.1	XR535
8570M	Gnat T.1	XR954
8571M	Gnat T.1	XR984
8572M	Gnat T.1	XM706
8573M	Gnat T.1	XM708
8574M	Gnat T.1	XM705
8575M	Gnat T.1	XP542
8576M	Gnat T.1	XP502
8577M	Gnat T.1 (ntu)	XP532
8578M	Gnat T.1	XR534
8579M	Argosy E.1	XR140
8580M	Gnat T.1	XP516
8581M	Canberra B.6(mod)	WJ775
8582M	Vampire T.11	XE874
8583M	Fi 103	-
8584M *	Canberra B.2	WH903
8585M *	Hunter F.4	XE670
8586M *	Hunter F.6	XE643
8587M *	Jet Provost T.4	XP677
8588M *	Jet Provost T.4	XR681
8589M *	Jet Provost T.4	XR700
8590M *	Lightning F.1A	XM191
8591M *	Vulcan B.1	XA893
8592M	Lightning T.4	XM969
8593M	Jet Provost T.3	XM418
8594M	Jet Provost T.4	XP661
8595M	Vampire T.11	XH278
8596M	Horsa (Composite)	-
8597M	Canberra PR.3	WE145
8598M	Eton TX.1	WP270
8599M	Cadet	?
8600M	Jaguar GR.1 (cockpit)	XX761
8601M	Gannet AEW.3	XL450
8602M	Gnat T.1	XR541
8603M	Gnat T.1	XR951
8604M	Gnat T.1	XS104
8605M	Canberra T.19	XA536
8606M	Gnat T.1	XP530
8607M	Gnat T.1	XP538
8608M	Gnat T.1	XP540
8609M	Gnat T.1	XR953
8610M	Gannet AEW.3	XL502
8611M	Sea Prince T.1	WF128
8612M	Whirlwind HAR.10	XD182
8613M	Whirlwind HAR.10	XJ724
8614M	Gnat T.1	XP515
8615M	Gnat T.1 (ntu)	XP532
8616M	Gnat T.1	XP541
8617M	Gnat T.1	XM709
8618M	Gnat T.1	XP504
8619M	Gnat T.1	XP511
8620M	Gnat T.1	XP534
8621M	Gnat T.1	XR538
8622M	Gnat T.1	XR980
8623M	Gnat T.1	XR998
8624M	Gnat T.1	XS102
8625M	Gnat T.1	XS105
8626M	Gnat T.1	XS109
8627M	Gnat T.1	XP558
8628M	Sycamore HR.14	XJ380
8629M	Shackleton MR.2/3	WL801
8630M	Chipmunk T.10	WG362
8631M	Gnat T.1	XR574
8632M	Gnat T.1	XP533
8633M	Spitfire IX	MK732
8634M	Sea Prince T.1	WP314
8635M	Gnat T.1	XP514
8636M	Gnat T.1	XR540
8637M	Gnat T.1	XR991
8638M	Gnat T.1	XS101

Those marked by * are cockpit sections used for display purposes only.

8639M-8758M

Number	Aircraft	Serial
8639M	Gnat T.1	XS107
8640M	Gnat T.1	XR977
8641M	Gnat T.1	XR987
8642M	Gnat T.1	XR537
8643M	Canberra T.4	WJ867
8644M	Whirlwind HAR.10	XR457
8645M	Whirlwind HAR.10	XD163
8646M	Whirlwind HAR.10	XK969
8647M	Whirlwind HAR.10	XP338
8648M	Buccaneer S.2	XK526
8649M	Whirlwind HAR.10	XP331
8650M	Whirlwind HAR.10	XP333
8651M	Shackleton MR.2/3	WG556
8652M	Canberra PR.7	WH794
8653M	Wessex HAS.1	XS120
8654M	Whirlwind HAR.9	XL898
8655M		
8656M		
8657M		
8658M		
8659M		
8660M		
8661M		
8662M		
8663M		
8664M		
8665M		
8666M		
8667M		
8668M		
8669M		
8670M		
8671M		
8672M		
8673M		
8674M		
8675M		
8676M		
8677M		
8678M		
8679M		
8680M		
8681M		
8682M		
8683M		
8684M		
8685M		
8686M		
8687M		
8688M		
8689M		
8690M		
8691M		
8692M		
8693M		
8694M		
8695M		
8696M		
8697M		
8698M		
8699M		
8700M		
8701M		
8702M		
8703M		
8704M		
8705M		
8706M		
8707M		
8708M		
8709M		
8710M		
8711M		
8712M		
8713M		
8714M		
8715M		
8716M		
8717M		
8718M		
8719M		
8720M		
8721M		
8722M		
8723M		
8724M		
8725M		
8726M		
8727M		
8728M		
8729M		
8730M		
8731M		
8732M		
8733M		
8734M		
8735M		
8736M		
8737M		
8738M		
8739M		
8740M		
8741M		
8742M		
8743M		
8744M		
8745M		
8746M		
8747M		
8748M		
8749M		
8750M		
8751M		
8752M		
8753M		
8754M		
8755M		
8756M		
8757M		
8758M		

8759M-8878M

8759M
8760M
8761M
8762M
8763M
8764M
8765M
8766M
8767M
8768M
8769M
8770M
8771M
8772M
8773M
8774M
8775M
8776M
8777M
8778M
8779M
8780M
8781M
8782M
8783M
8784M
8785M
8786M
8787M
8788M
8789M
8790M
8791M
8792M
8793M
8794M
8795M
8796M
8797M
8798M
8799M
8800M
8801M
8802M
8803M
8804M
8805M
8806M
8807M
8808M
8809M
8810M
8811M
8812M
8813M
8814M
8815M
8816M
8817M
8818M
8819M
8820M
8821M
8822M
8823M
8824M
8825M
8826M
8827M
8828M
8829M
8830M
8831M
8832M
8833M
8834M
8835M
8836M
8837M
8838M
8839M
8840M
8841M
8842M
8843M
8844M
8845M
8846M
8847M
8848M
8849M
8850M
8851M
8852M
8853M
8854M
8855M
8856M
8857M
8858M
8859M
8860M
8861M
8862M
8863M
8864M
8865M
8866M
8867M
8868M
8869M
8870M
8871M
8872M
8873M
8874M
8875M
8876M
8877M
8878M

ROYAL NAVY & ARMY INSTRUCTIONAL AIRFRAMES

A2400-A2519

A2400	Attacker FB.2	WZ279	A2460	Sea Hawk FB.3	WM981
A2401	Attacker FB.2	WZ289	A2461	Sea Venom FAW.21	WW146
A2402	Attacker F.1	WA520	A2462	Sea Hawk F.2	WF257
A2403	Blackburn YB.1	WB797	A2463	Dragonfly HR.5	WH990
A2404	Sea Hawk F.1	WF211	A2464	Sea Venom FAW.21	WW285
A2405	Sea Hawk F.1	WF165	A2465	Dragonfly HR.5	VX596
A2406	Sea Hawk F.1	WF201	A2466	Gannet AS.1	WN364
A2407	Attacker F.1	WA482	A2467	Gannet AS.1	WN454
A2408	Attacker F.1	WA506	A2468	Whirlwind HAR.1	XA871
A2409	Sea Hawk F.1	WF200	A2469	Whirlwind HAS.3	XG581
A2410	Sea Hawk F.1	WF146	A2470	Gannet AS.1	WN391
A2411	Sea Venom FAW.20	WM564	A2471	Gannet AS.1	XA342
A2412	Gannet AS.1	WN354	A2472	Gannet T.2	XA508
A2413	Firefly AS.6	WD910	A2473	Sea Hawk F.1	WF220
A2414	Gannet AS.1	WN341	A2474	Gannet T.2	XG871
A2415	Firefly T.2	DK531	A2475	Sea Venom FAW.20	WM557
A2416	Gannet AS.1	WN462	A2476	Sea Venom FAW.20	WM520
A2417	Sea Venom FAW.21	WM569	A2477	Sea Venom FAW.20	WM513
A2418	Attacker FB.2	WK320	A2478	Sea Venom FAW.20	WM512
A2419	Gannet AS.1	WN421	A2479	Sea Venom FAW.20	WM509
A2420	Sea Hawk F.1	WF159	A2480	Sea Venom FAW.20	WM553
A2421	Gannet AS.1	WN393	A2481	DH110 prototype	WG240
A2422	Gannet AS.1	WN373	A2482	Sea Hawk FB.5	WM939
A2423	Attacker F.1	WA491	A2483	Sea Hawk F.2	WF259
A2424	Sea Hawk F.1	WF182	A2484	Sea Hawk FB.5	WM907
A2425	Sea Hawk F.2	WF243	A2485	Whirlwind HAR.3	XJ397
A2426	Sea Hawk F.1	WF183	A2486	Sea Venom FAW.20	WM543
A2427	Sea Hawk F.1	WF172	A2487	Whirlwind HAR.3	XG584
A2428	Sea Hawk F.1	WF163	A2488	Sea Venom FAW.21	WW194
A2429	Venom NF.2	WL806	A2489	Sea Hawk FB.3	WM918
A2430	Meteor F.8	WF752	A2490	Sea Hawk FB.3	WM920
A2431	Sea Hawk F.1	WM901	A2491	Sea Venom FAW.21	WW275
A2432	Sea Hawk FB.3	WN118	A2492	Sea Venom FAW.21	XG616
A2433	Sea Hawk FB.3	WM924	A2493	Gannet AS.1	WN346
A2434	Wyvern S.4	WL881	A2494	Sea Hawk FB.5	WM937
A2435	Gannet AS.1	WN376	A2495	Sea Hawk FB.5	WM965
A2436	Gannet AS.1	WN453	A2496	Whirlwind HAS.7	XK933
A2437	Gannet AS.1	WN344	A2497	Sea Hawk FGA.4	WV904
A2438	Wyvern S.4	VW870	A2498	Sea Venom FAW.21	XG621
A2439	Sea Hawk F.1	WF219	A2499	Supermarine 544	WT859
A2440	Sea Hawk F.1	WF213	A2500	DH110 Mk.20X	XF828
A2441	Sea Hawk F.1	WF158	A2501	Whirlwind HAS.7	XN307
A2442	Whirlwind HAS.7	XK908	A2502	Sea Hawk FB.5	WM936
A2443	Sea Hawk FB.3	WF294	A2503	Sea Hawk FB.5	WM994
A2444	Wyvern S.4	VZ777	A2504	Sea Venom FAW.21	XG622
A2445	Attacker FB.2	WZ299	A2505	Sea Hawk FB.5	WM943
A2446	Attacker FB.2	WP286	A2506	Sea Venom FAW.21	XG655
A2447	Sea Venom FAW.20	WM503	A2507	Sea Vixen FAW.1	XJ583
A2448	Sea Venom FAW.21	WW148	A2508	Sea Venom FAW.21	WW218
A2449	Sea Venom FAW.21	WW219	A2509	Sea Hawk FB.5	WF299
A2450	Gannet AS.1	WN343	A2510	Sea Hawk FB.5	WM913
A2451	Sea Hawk F.1	WF196	A2511	Sea Hawk FB.5	WM983
A2452	Sea Hawk F.1	WF144	A2512	Sea Venom FAW.21	XG637
A2453	Sea Venom FAW.21	WW223	A2513	Sea Venom FAW.21	WW267
A2454	Sea Hawk F.2	WF277	A2514	Wessex prototype	XL722
A2455	Sea Venom FAW.20	WM514	A2515	Sea Hawk FGA.6	XE366
A2456	Sea Venom FAW.21	WW261	A2516	Wessex HAS.1	XM835
A2457	Sea Venom FAW.21	WW269	A2517	Sea Hawk FB.5	WM961
A2458	Sea Venom FAW.21	WM570	A2518	Sea Venom FAW.21	WW189
A2459	Gannet T.2	XA523	A2519	P.531-0/N	XN333

A2520-A2637

A2520	Sea Venom FAW.21	WW270
A2521	Sea Hawk FGA.6	WV841
A2522	Sea Hawk FB.5	WM993
A2523	Sea Hawk FB.3	WM915
A2524	Sea Hawk FB.5	WM998
A2525	P.531-0/N	XN334
A2526	Sea Hawk FGA.4	WV911
A2527	Wessex HAS.1	XP107
A2528	Gannet AS.1	XA363
A2529	Supermarine 508	VX133
A2530	Sea Hawk FB.5	WM969
A2531	Dragonfly HR.5	WG718
A2532	Sea Hawk FGA.6	WV826
A2533	Gannet AS.4	XA456
A2534	Sea Hawk FGA.6	XE368
A2535	Sea Vixen FAW.1	XJ484
A2536	Sea Hawk FGA.6	WV914
A2537	Whirlwind HAR.21	WV190
A2538	Whirlwind HAR.3	XJ393
A2539	Gannet ECM.6	XG831
A2540	Gannet ECM.6	WN464
A2541	Whirlwind HAR.1	XA869
A2542	Whirlwind HAR.1	XA862
A2543	Whirlwind HAR.1	XA870
A2544	Sea Vixen FAW.1	XJ487
A2545	Sea Hawk FGA.6	WV836
A2546	Sea Hawk FGA.6	WV870
A2547	Sea Hawk FGA.6	WV860
A2548	Sea Hawk FGA.6	WV861
A2549	Sea Hawk FGA.6	WV909
A2550	Whirlwind HAR.1	XA866
A2551	Whirlwind HAR.1	XA868
A2552	Buccaneer S.1	XN932
A2553	Buccaneer S.1	XN924
A2554	Sea Hawk FGA.6	WV865
A2555	Sea Hawk FGA.6	XE330
A2556	Sea Hawk FGA.6	XE327
A2557	Sea Hawk FGA.6	WV798
A2558	Sea Hawk FGA.6	WV831
A2559	Sea Hawk FGA.6	WV792
A2560	Hunter F.4	XF363
A2561	Hunter F.4	XF365
A2562	Scimitar F.1	XD226
A2563	Hunter F.4	WV405
A2564	Hunter F.4	WV411
A2565	Hunter F.4	XF303
A2566	Hunter F.4	XF311
A2567	Hunter F.4	XF318
A2568	Hunter F.4	XF947
A2569	Hunter F.4	XF976
A2570	Hunter F.4	XF984
A2571	Whirlwind HAR.3	XG577
A2572	Whirlwind HAR.3	XJ402
A2573	Scimitar F.1	XD215
A2574	Scimitar F.1	XD332
A2575	Whirlwind HAR.3	XG574
A2576	Whirlwind HAR.21	WV198
A2577	Hiller HT.1	XB480
A2578	Whirlwind HAR.3	XJ399
A2579	P.531-0/N	XN332
A2580	Sea Hawk FGA.6	XE369
A2581	Buccaneer S.1	XK532
A2582	Buccaneer S.1	XK534
A2583	Scimitar F.1	XD280
A2584	Scimitar F.1	XD274
A2585	Scimitar F.1	XD272
A2586	Scimitar F.1	XD278
A2587	Scimitar F.1	XD275
A2588	Scimitar F.1	XD243
A2589	Scimitar F.1	XD271
A2590	Scimitar F.1	XD324
A2591	Scimitar F.1	XD276
A2592	Sea Hawk FGA.6	WV828
A2593	Sea Hawk FGA.6	WV825
A2593	'FR Pod Mk. 20E'	E110
A2594	Wessex HAS.3	XM920
A2595	Whirlwind HAS.7	XL868
A2596	Wessex HU.5	XT448
A2597	Wessex HU.5	XS509
A2598	Sea Vixen FAW.1	XJ482
A2599	Sea Vixen FAW.1	XJ486
A2600	Buccaneer S.1	XN934
A2601	Sea Vixen FAW.1	XJ477
A2602	Buccaneer S.1	XN925
A2603	Whirlwind HAS.7	XK911
A2604	Whirlwind HAS.7	XN259
A2605	Whirlwind HAS.7	XN308
A2606	Whirlwind HAS.7	XN305
A2607	Whirlwind HAS.7	XK944
A2608	Gannet ECM.6	XA459
A2609	Wessex HAS.1	XM329
A2610	Sea Vixen FAW.2	XN647
A2611	Sea Vixen FAW.2	XJ575
A2612	Sea Vixen FAW.2	XN650
A2612	Sea Vixen FAW.2	XJ521
A2613	Sea Vixen FAW.2	XN706
A2614	Whirlwind HAS.7	XN314
A2615	Wessex HAS.3	XT256
A2616	Sea Vixen FAW.2	XN651
A2617	Buccaneer S.1	XN954
A2618	Wessex HAS.3	XP116
A2619	Kestrel	XS695
A2620	Sea Vixen FAW.2	XN650
A2621	Sea Vixen FAW.2	XJ584
A2622	Sea Vixen FAW.2	XJ602
A2623	Sea Vixen FAW.2	XN697
A2624	Sea Vixen FAW.2	XN692
A2625	Whirlwind HAS.7	XL846
A2626	Whirlwind HAS.7	XL847
A2627	Buccaneer S.1	XN967
A2628	Jet Provost T.4	XP558
A2629	Whirlwind HAS.7	XM667
A2630	Whirlwind HAS.7	XL853
A2631	Sioux HT.2	XV312
A2632	Sea Hawk FGA.6	WV903
A2633	Sea Hawk FGA.6	XE369
A2634	Sea Hawk FGA.6	WV794
A2635	Sea Hawk FGA.6	XE339
A2636	Sea Hawk FGA.6	XE390
A2637	Sea Hawk FGA.6	WV797

A2638-A2701

A2638	Sioux HT.2	XV317
A2639	Sea Vixen FAW.2	XN650
A2640	Wessex HAS.1	XP155
A2641	Wessex HAS.1	XL729
A2642	Whirlwind HAS.7	XL836
A2643	Whirlwind HAR.9	XN311
A2644	Whirlwind HAS.7	XN358
A2645	Sea Hawk F.1	WF225
A2646	Whirlwind HAR.10	XK988
A2647	Wasp HAS.1	XS463
A2648	Wessex HAS.1	XS125
A2649	Wessex HAS.1	XS869
A2650	Wessex HAS.1	XP160
A2651	Whirlwind HAS.7	XG596
A2652	Whirlwind HAS.7	XN261
A2653	Whirlwind HAS.7	XK943
A2654	Whirlwind HAS.7	XN302
A2655	Buccaneer S.1	XN953
A2656	Wasp HAS.1	XS476
A2657	Lynx	XX469
A2658	P.1127	XP984
A2659	Sea King HAS.1	XV669
A2660	Sea Hawk FGA.6	WV908
A2661	Sea Hawk FGA.6	WV795
A2662	Sea Hawk FB.5	WF299
A2663	Whirlwind HAR.9	XN309
A2664	Sea King HAS.1	XV644
A2665	Whirlwind HAR.9	XL839
A2666	Wessex HAS.1	XS872
A2667	Gannet AEW.3	XP226
A2668	Wessex HAS.1	XS885
A2669	Wessex HAS.1	XP149
A2670	Wessex HAS.1	XS128
A2671	Wessex HAS.1	XS867
A2672	Wasp HAS.1	XS537
A2673	Sea Prince T.1	WF122
A2674	Sea Prince T.1	WF125
A2675	Wessex HAS.1	XS881
A2676	Gnat T.1	XR572
A2677	Gnat T.1	XR993
A2678	Gnat T.1	XR955
A2679	Gnat T.1	XP535
A2680	Wessex HAS.1	XP157
A2681	Wessex HAS.1	XP117
A2682	Wessex HAS.1	XM845
A2683	Wessex HAS.1	XS878
A2684	Wessex HAS.1	XP151
A2685	Wessex HAS.1	XS886
A2686	Wessex HAS.1	XS873
A2687	Wessex HAS.1	XS877
A2688	Wessex HAS.1	XP158
A2689	Wessex HAS.1	XM874
A2690	Wessex HAS.1	XS887
A2691	Wessex HAS.1	XS868
A2692		
A2693		
A2694		
A2695		
A2696		
A2697		
A2698		
A2699		
A2700		
A2701		

TAD01-TAD900

TAD01	Gazelle CIM	-
TAD02	Gazelle CIM	-
TAD03	Gazelle CIM	-
TAD007	Lynx CIM	-
TAD009	Lynx CIM	-
TAD043	Scout AH.1	XP854
TAD175	Sioux AH.1	XT175
TA200	Auster AOP.9	XK378
TAD625	Scout AH.1	XT625
TAD900	Gazelle AH.1	XW900

WL419 Meteor T.7 Special, Martin-Baker Ltd, at Chalgrove 9.11.78. This is one of the many aircraft that have been used post war by the Company for ejection-seat trials. (M.H. Pettit)

WW654 '833' Hunter GA.11, FRADU, at Greenham Common 31.7.76. Part of the aerobatic team "Blue Herons", it also displays a 'Heron' emblem on the under-wing fuel tank. (I. MacFarlane)

WZ744 Avro 707C on display at Finningley 20.9.69. This was one of several 707 variants built to test the various features of the Avro 698 Vulcan during that aircraft's early development. It subsequently moved to Cosford for display. (R.A. Walker)

WZ827 Grasshopper TX.1, Central Gliding School, at Syerston 13.8.79. The very spartan nature of construction is plainly evident. In the background can be seen the fuselage of another example of the type, XP493. (R.A. Walker)

WZ943 'NW/876' Sea Venom FAW.53, on display in Nowra town 25.11.76 in the markings of 724 Sqdn, RAN. It was presented to the town by the nearby RANAS 1.3.73 and had retained its original serial throughout its RAN service. (T.E. Stone)

7436M (WZ726) Auster AOP.9, AETW, at Middle Wallop 7.7.62. Prior to the introduction of 'TAD' numbers the Army Air Corps instructional airframes were given standard 'M' serials. (L.G. Pain)

MC8054AM (XM410) Jet Provost T.3, No 1 SoTT, at Halton 1.8.70. As can be seen, this is a deviation from the standard method of 'M' serial allocation. (R.A. Walker)

8081/M/69 (XM468) Jet Provost T.3, No 1 SoTT, at Halton 1.8.70. Another example of non-standard 'M' serial application, this aircraft also displays the year that it became a training airframe. (R.A. Walker)

A2492/XG616 Sea Venom FAW.21, at Lee-on-Solent in the mid 1960's. Still resplendent in 766 Sqdn markings, this instructional airframe carries its 'A' serial just ahead of the unit motif on the forward fuselage. (L.G. Pain)

A2609/XM329 Wessex HAS.1, at Lee-on-Solent 21.7.79. Still retaining its 737 Sqdn markings, this instructional airframe wears its 'A' serial just beneath the 'RO' of ROYAL on the fuselage side. (R.A. Walker)

XA842 Sikorsky S-55, WHL. The serial was applied to this imported 'pattern' aircraft circa 24.6.52 for a demonstration to RAF Coastal Command. Following the demonstration it reverted to its RN evaluation serial of WW339. (RAF Museum)

XB453 – XB470 have been reported as allocations for 18 Bell HSL–1 anti-submarine helicopters that were reserved for the RN. The aircraft were not delivered but this photograph of a USN example at least illustrates the type. (via E. Myall)

XJ524 Sea Vixen FAW.2 modified by Flight Refuelling in 7.78 for target towing duties (cable just visible). It has light grey topsides; black/yellow TT striped undersides and day-glo bands on booms and wing upper surfaces. (Flight Refuelling)

'XS341' Scott Furlong Predator, at Biggin Hill in the early 1960's. This full size taxying model was made for the television series "The Plane Makers", the true XS341 being a Shelduck D.1 drone. (B. Stainer)

'XV196' CL-44 at Stansted in the early 1970's. In reality this aircraft was G-ATZH and had been hired for filming purposes during the making of "O Lucky Man". Along the fuselage cheat line can be seen 'Royal Air Force Air Support Command.' (via A.W. Hall)

XV474/F Phantom FGR.2, 56 Sqdn at Wattisham 16.4.80. This all-over grey low visibility colour scheme is gradually being introduced on the RAF Phantom force. The unit's red/white checks are apparent on the ECM fillet and flank the phoenix nose motif. (R.L. Ward)

XZ286 Nimrod AEW.3 prototype at Woodford 30.4.80 following its roll-out. Selected by the UK Government in 4.77, a total of eleven aircraft was required for service entry from early 1982 onwards as replacements for the Shackleton AEW.2 fleet. (R.L. Ward)

XZ457 'VL/104' Sea Harrier FRS.1, 899 Sqdn, at Yeovilton 23.4.80. 899 was born out of the IFTU, 700A Sqdn and is the shore-based, front-line and training squadron. 800 Sqdn is the first carrier based unit. (R.L. Ward)

XZ695 'BW/346' Lynx HAS.2, 702 Sqdn, HMS Broadsword Flight, at Yeovilton 23.4.80. The white broadsword marking painted on the fin is unique. No other RN small ships' flights(whether Wasp or Lynx) carry any fin markings. (R.L. Ward)

ZA500/G-LYNX Lynx (AH.1) is actually Westland's Lynx demonstrator. The serial was initially allocated for a live rocket firing demonstration in Spain during 6.79 and later at Middle Wallop. Unfortunately, the nose and tail are clipped on the original photo. (via Avia Press)

A92-274 Jindivik Mk 102BL being readied for flight at RAE Llanbedr in 11.65 (note "successful mission" marks on the fuselage). Though extensively used by RAE Llanbedr, these recoverable drones retain Australian serials. British serials have never been allocated. (Crown)

GLOSSARY

A

AAC	Army Air Corps
AAM	Air-to-Air Missile
A&AEE	Aeroplane and Armament Experimental Establishment
a/c	Aircraft
ADAF	Abu Dhabi Air Force
AEF	Air Experience Flight
Aero	Aerobatic
AETW	Aircraft Engineering Training Wing
AEW	Airborne Early Warning
AF	Air Force
AFB	Air Force Base
ANGK LAUT	Indonesian Navy
ANS	Air Navigation School
A&OASW	Aircrewman and Officer Anti-Submarine Warfare
A&OFT	Aircrewman and Officer Flying Training
ARW	Advanced Rotary Wing
ARWS	Advanced Rotary Wing Squadron
ASR	Air Sea Rescue/Air Staff Requirement
ASW	Anti-submarine Warfare
ATC	Air Training Corps
Avn	Aviation
Aw	Airworthy
AWA	Armstrong Whitworth Aircraft
Aw/cn	Awaiting Collection
AZ	Arizona

B

BAC	British Aircraft Corporation
BAe	British Aerospace
BAF	Belgian Air Force
BAFM	Belgian Air Force Museum
BAOR	British Army of the Rhine
BARG	British Aviation Research Group
BATUS	British Army Training Unit Suffield
BoBMF	Battle of Britain Memorial Flight
BEAH	British European Airways Helicopters
BFWF	Basic Fixed Wing Flight
BGA	British Gliding Association
Bgntn	Baginton
B'ham	Birmingham
B'ham Mus of Sc&I	Birmingham Museum of Science and Industry
BHC	British Hovercraft Corporation
BOAC	British Overseas Airways Corporation
BoB	Battle of Britain
B'tol	Bristol
BRM	British Rotorcraft Museum
BRNC	Britannia Royal Naval College
Bros	Brothers
BSE	Bristol-Siddeley Engines
Bu Aer	Bureau of Aeronautics
BzN	Brazilian Navy

C

c.	circa
CA	California
CAFU	Civil Aviation Flying Unit
canx	Cancelled
Card'ton	Cardington
CBAS	Commando Brigade Air Squadron

CCAS	*Civilian Craft Apprentice School*
CEBS	*Commonwealth Experimental Building Station*
CFS	*Central Flying School*
Ch	*Chile*
ChAF	*Chilean Air Force*
CIM	*Classroom Instruction Model*
C in C AFNE	*Commander in Chief Armed Forces, Northern Europe*
Cmdr	*Commander*
c/n	*construction number*
Co	*County*
Co Down	*County Down, Northern Ireland*
Col	*College*
Comms	*Communications*
Complet'n	*Completion*
Constrn	*Construction*
Conv	*Conversion*
Corp	*Corporation*
c/s	*colour scheme/callsign*

D

DC	*District of Columbia*
del, dels	*delivery/delivered/deliveries*
det	*detachment*
DFCS	*Day Fighter Combat School*
DH	*de Havilland*
Dk	*Dock*
Don	*Donington*
Dr	*Doctor*
Dt	*Derelict*
D&T	*Development and Trials*

E

E	*East*
ECM	*Electronic Counter Measures*
EE	*English Electric*
EFTS	*Elementary Flying Training School*
ETPS	*Empire Test Pilots School*

F

FAA	*Fleet Air Arm*
FAAHF	*Fleet Air Arm Historic Flight*
FAAM	*Fleet Air Arm Museum*
FEAF	*Far East Air Force*
Feb	*February*
F/F, f/f	*First Flight*
Fi AF	*Finnish Air Force*
FL	*Florida*
Flt	*Flight*
FMAF	*Federation of Malaya Air Force*
FN	*French Navy (Aéronavale)*
FORA	*Flag Officer Reserve Aircraft*
FR	*Flight Refuelling Limited*
Fr Govt	*French Government*
FRADU	*Fleet Requirements and Air Direction Unit*
FRU	*Fleet Requirements Unit*
FSS	*Flying Selection Squadron*
FTS	*Flying Training School*
fus, fuse	*fuselage*
FVRDE	*Fighting Vehicles Research Development Establishment*
FW	*Fixed Wing*
Fwd	*forward*

G

GAC	Gloster Aircraft Company/General Aircraft Company
Gdn	Garden
GI	Ground Instructional
G'land	Greenland
Govt	Government
Gt Yarmouth	Great Yarmouth

H

HAM	Historic Aircraft Museum
H Blagdon	Higher Blagdon
H de H	Hawker de Havilland
HDL	Hovercraft Development Limited
HK	Hong Kong
HMAS	His/Her Majesty's Australian Ship
HMS	His/Her Majesty's Ship
HP	Handley-Page
HQ	Headquarters
HRH	Her Royal Highness
HSA	Hawker Siddeley Aviation
HTS	Hovercraft Trials Squadron
Huddesf'l'd	Huddersfield

I

IAC	Irish Air Corps
IAF	Indian Air Force
IAM	Institute of Aviation Medicine
ID	Indiana
IFTU	Intensive Flying Trials Unit
IHTU	Interservices Hovercraft Trials Unit
IHU	Interservices Hovercraft Unit
IL	Illinois
In	Inclusive
Inc	Incorporated
Ind	Industrial
INS	Indian Naval Service
IoW	Isle of Wight
It AF	Italian Air Force
IWM	Imperial War Museum

J

JAF	Jugoslavian Air Force
JP's	Jet Provosts
JSPA	Joint Services Parachute Association

K

KAF	Kenyan Air Force
Klu	Koninkluke Luchtmacht (Royal Netherlands Air Force)
Ku AF	Kuwait Air Force

L

Le AF	Lebanese Air Force
London Lndn Clny	London Colney
L-o-O	Linton-on-Ouse
L-o-S	Lee-on-Solent
L Staughton	Little Staughton
Ltd	Limited

M

M	Museum
MATS	Military Aircraft Target System (see page 304)

MDAP	Mutual Defence Aid Programme
METS	Multi-Engine Training Squadron
Min	Ministry
Min Tech	Ministry of Technology
Mk	Mark
MLD	Marine Luchtvaart Dienst (Royal Netherlands Navy)
M Mowbray	Melton Mowbray
MN	Minnesota
mod	modified/modification
MoD	Ministry of Defence
MoD(PE)	Ministry of Defence (Procurement Executive)
MoS	Ministry of Supply
MRCA	Multi-Role Combat Aircraft
MU	Maintenance Unit
MVEE	Military Vehicle Engineering Establishment
MW	Middle Wallop

N

N	North
NACC	National Aeronautical Collection of Canada
N'ards	Newtonards
NARIU	Naval Aircraft Radio Installation Unit
NASA	National Aeronautics and Space Administration
NASU	Naval Aircraft Support Unit
NEAF	Near East Air Force
NI	Northern Ireland
NMI	National Maritime Institute
No	Number
Nostell Py	Nostell Priory
NPL	National Physics Laboratory
Nr, nr	near
NSFK	Nationale Sozialistische Flieger Korps
Nstl	Nostell Priory
NSW	New South Wales
ntu	not taken up
NY	New York
NZ	New Zealand

O

O	Old
Obs	Observer
OCU	Operational Conversion Unit
OFT	Officer Flying Training
OH	Ohio

P

PA	Pennsylvania
PAF	Portuguese Air Force
Pe AF	Peruvian Air Force
PFA	Popular Flying Association
Photo	Photograph
Pk	Park
Pr	Preserved
Proto	Prototype
PTA	Pilotless Target Aircraft
PTAS	Pilotless Target Aircraft Squadron

R

RACM	Royal Armoured Corps(Tank) Museum
RAE	Royal Aircraft Establishment
RAF	Royal Air Force

RAFGSA	Royal Air Force Gliding and Soaring Association
RAFM	Royal Air Force Museum
RAM	Royal Artillery Museum
RAN	Royal Australian Navy
RANAS	Royal Australian Naval Air Station
RANFAA	Royal Australian Navy Fleet Air Arm
RARA	Rear Admiral Reserve Aircraft
RCAF	Royal Canadian Air Force
RCT	Royal Corps of Transport
R&D	Research and Development
regn	registration
Regt	Regiment
Repl	Replica
resp	respectively
retd	retired
RFA	Royal Fleet Auxillary
RFC	Royal Flying Corps
Rh AF	Rhodesian Air Force
RJAF	Royal Jordanian Air Force
RN	Royal Navy
RNAS	Royal Naval Air Service
RNAS	Royal Naval Air Station
RNAY	Royal Naval Aircraft Yard
RNPT	Royal Navy Presentation Team
RNPTA	Royal Navy Pilotless Target Aircraft
RNPTAS	Royal Navy Pilotless Target Aircraft Squadron
RNR	Royal Naval Reserve
RNZAF	Royal New Zealand Air Force
R-R	Rolls Royce
RRAF	Royal Rhodesian Air Force
RRE	Royal Radar Establishment
RSAF	Royal Saudi Air Force
RS&RJAF	Royal Saudi and Royal Jordanian Air Force
R ThAF	Royal Thai Air Force
r/t	radio telegraphy
Rtnd	returned

S

S, Sth	South
SADC	Singapore Air Defence Command
SAM	Surface-to-Air Missile
SAR	Search and Rescue
SARTS	Search and Rescue Training Squadron
SBAC	Society of British Aerospace Companies
Sc	Science
SC	South Carolina
SEPECAT	Société Européenne de Production de l'avion Ecole de Combat et d'appui Tactique
SNIAS	Société Nationale Industrielle Aérospatiale
SOAF	Sultan of Oman's Air Force
SOC	Struck of charge
SoTT	School of Technical Training
Soton	Southampton
Spec	Specification
Sqdn	Squadron
SRAF	Southern Rhodesian Air Force
Srs	Series
St	Stored
St	Saint
Stn Flt	Station Flight
Strath'l'n, Stlln	Strathallan

Sut Coldfield	Sutton Coldfield
Sutton in Afd	Sutton in Ashfield
Swz	Swiss
SwAF	Swiss Air Force
SWAPS	South Wales Aircraft Preservation Society

T

Tech, Tech Coll	Technical College
TI	Trial Installation
Tnr	Trainer
Trng	Training
TT	Target Tower/Target Tug
TV	Television
TWU	Tactical Weapons Unit
TX	Texas

U

UAS	University Air Squadron
UK	United Kingdom
Un	University
UN	United Nations
Under Rest'n	Under Restoration
UNFICYP	United Nations Forces in Cyprus
US	United States
USA	United States of America
USAF	United States Air Force
USAFM	United States Air Force Museum
USMC	United States Marine Corps
USN	United States Navy
USSR	Union of Soviet Socialist Republics

V

VAF	Venezuelan Air Force
VIP	Very Important Person
V/STOL	Vertical/Short take-off and landing
VTOL	Vertical take-off and landing

W

W	West
WHL	Westland Helicopters Limited
WGN	West German Navy (Bundesmarine)
Wg Cdr	Wing Commander
W'hampton	Wolverhampton
Wroughtn	Wroughton
W-s-M, Weston-s-Mare	Weston-super-Mare
W'wind	Whirlwind

2

2TAF	2nd Tactical Air Force

late additions

VA	Virginia